# The Year 2000
# Computing Crisis

# The Year 2000 Computing Crisis

A Millennium Date Conversion Plan

Jerome T. Murray

Marilyn J. Murray

**McGraw-Hill**

New York  San Francisco  Washington, D.C.  Auckland  Bogotá
Caracas  Lisbon  London  Madrid  Mexico City  Milan
Montreal  New Delhi  San Juan  Singapore
Sydney  Tokyo  Toronto

# McGraw-Hill

*A Division of The McGraw-Hill Companies*

Library of Congress Cataloging-in-Publication Data

Murray, Jerome T.
    The year 2000 computing crisis : a millennium date conversion plan
/ by Jerome T. Murray & Marilyn J. Murray.
        p.    cm.
    Includes index.
    ISBN 0-07-912945-5 (p)
    1. Software maintenance.    2. Year 2000 date conversion (Computer
systems)    I. Murray, Marilyn J.    II. Title.
    QA76.76.S64M87  1996
    005.1'6—dc20                                             96-649
                                                             CIP

hc  1 2 3 4 5 6 7 8 9 0  DOC/DOC  9 0 0 9 8 7 6

ISBN 0-07-912945-5

*The sponsoring editor for this book was Jennifer Holt DiGiovanna, the book editor was Kellie Hagan, and the executive editor was Robert E. Ostrander. The production supervisor was Katherine G. Brown.*

*Printed and bound by R. R. Donnelley & Sons, Crawfordsville, Indiana.*

McGraw-Hill books are available at special quantity discounts to use as premiums and sales promotions, or for use in corporate training programs. For more information, please write to the Director of Special Sales, McGraw-Hill, 11 West 19th Street, New York, NY 10011. Or contact your local bookstore.

Product or brand names used in this book may be trade names or trademarks. Where we believe that there may be proprietary claims to such trade names or trademarks, the name has been used with an initial capital or it has been capitalized in the style used by the name claimant. Regardless of the capitalization used, all such names have been used in an editorial manner without any intent to convey endorsement of or other affiliation with the name claimant. Neither the author nor the publisher intends to express any judgment as to the validity or legal status of any such proprietary claims.

*In order to receive additional information on these or any other McGraw-Hill titles, in the United States please call 1-800-822-8158. In other countries, contact your local McGraw-Hill representative.*

MH96
9129455

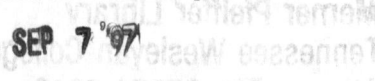

*To*
*Our Holy Father*
*John Paul II*
*and*
*the men and women*
*of*
*Opus Dei*

# Contents

# Acknowledgments

The world tends to become more complex over time rather than less so. If men and women were, at one time, able to accomplish their goals single-handedly, those days are past. We are indebted to many for their assistance, words of encouragement, and understanding.

This book might not have been undertaken were it not for a lengthy telephone discussion of the date problem with Ms. Roxe Murray, the president of Reppin Consulting and Software Ltd. of Ottawa, Ontario, Canada. Her interest and encouragement have been unflagging.

Dr. Margaret Murray, of the Virginia Polytechnic Institute and State University Mathematics Department, read early drafts of the manuscript and offered numerous suggestions. The mathematical elegance you find here we owe to Margaret (the mathematical shortcomings are entirely our own).

Mr. John Kaur, president of Digitgraph Computer Systems Company of Tucson, Arizona, provided file-conversion services not otherwise available.

Mr. Reginald E. Browning, field manager, and Mr. W. H. Brown, support specialist of IBM U.S. Marketing & Services of Tucson, Arizona, gave generously of their technical knowledge.

There were the many who gave unselfishly of their time in an effort to aid us by answering questions and by being brave enough to admit that their companies had done little or nothing to correct their date problem. We will never divulge their identities. They know who they are and we thank them.

Finally, when those difficult times came as they do in every task that's worthwhile, Rev. Robert Stulting, CSP, would explain that we live in perilous times but always urged us on by saying: "You can make it." We did! Thanks, Father Bob.

# Introduction

Imagine the following scenario, the technical explanation of which can be found in the epilogue: You open your mail and find a credit card billing notifying you that payment for the luncheon you charged two weeks ago is now 99 years overdue. The finance charges come to $6,243.00. "It's incredible!" you think, realizing that you'll have to write six or seven letters to get this one straightened out.

You flip on the radio to discover that trading on the big board is suspended today and that the Amex is closed down too. The NASDAQ hasn't even been heard from so far, and you're warned not to cash checks today . . . something about fund transfers not being made.

You finish your last cup of coffee and drive to the office. On the way, you pass two small chemical companies still smoldering from the explosions that rocked them over the weekend. "A hell of a way to start a new year," you say to yourself as you park the car and head into the building.

There on your desk sits your ever-friendly terminal with its screen as dark as a villain's heart. You grab the telephone and dial the computer center to learn: "We have a little problem down here. It might take a while to get it fixed. We'd suggest that you implement manual backup procedures in all departments immediately."

Yes, it is one hell of a way to start a new year. The date? Monday, January 3rd. The year? 2000! The crisis has begun. What has happened? The world's computers have become lost in the fourth dimension. They no longer have the ability to calculate time values.

You've just had a glimpse down the time tunnel at what will certainly come to pass unless a major portion of the world's mainframe application software is modified or rewritten. An exploratory discussion of the impending crisis was conducted with members of leading vendors' systems engineering and management staffs. The summary comments from this discussion were: "This is a user problem—a crisis for which computer users alone are responsible." Indeed, and rightly so, vendors cannot be held liable for the use or misuse of their computing equipment.

There are actually two problems that are so intimately intertwined that we often see neither the warp nor the woof: the problems of programming practice and the mathematics of time computation. Programming practice has brought us to a crisis in computation. Retracing the steps that have led us to the precipice is simple.

Widespread employment of computers began in the United States with the introduction of the IBM 1401 in 1959. Prior to this time, the majority of machine-based data processing was supported by electromechanical accounting machines. Calendar dates were introduced to these devices via punched date cards bearing the date appropriate to the particular processing job. Transaction files were moderate in size and consisted largely of card decks. The use of a six-digit date was adequate for the calculation of the tasks then at hand.

With the announcement of the IBM System/360 in the early 1960s, operating systems became a common part of the computing scene. The operating system served as the manager of the computer's resources, taking many of the arduous programming chores away from programmers, freeing them for the more creative effort of application problem-solving. Although System/360 introduced many innovative departures from the 1400 technology, 1400 programs were executable through the use of emulators. In the interest of compatibility, the operating system's system date was also six digits.

On November 1, 1968, the U.S. Department of Commerce, National Bureau of Standards, issued *Federal Information Processing Standards Publication 4* (FIPS PUB 4). It specified the use of six-digit dates for all information exchange among federal agencies. This standard became effective January 1, 1970. And so through the years, the generations of computing systems, and the bureaucracy of government, the six-digit date not only has survived but has been enshrined. Throughout the business and governmental communities there was little thought of the year 2000. Then as now, the major emphasis was placed on the creation of application software and the maintenance of existing programming.

Programming practice has brought us to this crisis by providing us with worldwide systems whose databases are permeated by six-digit dates and whose application programs' data definitions address six-digit fields. Consider Monday, January 3, 2000 as it appears in a six-digit format: 01/03/00. Which is the later date: 12/31/99 or 01/03/00? Common sense and context will tell you that 01/03/00 is the later date. Alas, the computer program isn't socially adept and is free to make its judgment solely on the basis of mathematical evaluations. The program finds 99 greater than 00 and so 12/31/99 is the later date. Thus you have the ingredients of a problem that affects accounts receivable aging, pension and trust fund accounting, asset depreciation, insurance premium calculations, interest rate determination, funds transfer, benefit eligibility, accounts payable issuance, inventory-carrying cost determination, process control, and so on.

Programming practice's contribution to this difficulty is but a portion of the anatomy of the crisis. The mathematics of time computation is tailored to the specifications of the inadequate data, and so it too is inadequate. Given a six-digit date environment, we're limited to a modular arithmetic whose number set is unable to adequately measure the intervals being presented.

The essence of the crisis is that the world's application software cannot continue to function by using six-digit dates. Without extensive modification or complete rewriting, this software won't function even if provided with adequate dating data. The absolute time to failure depends on the nature of the computing tasks for any given computer user. Those computing in more distant time horizons are already experiencing the pain. The certain deadline is Saturday, January 1, 2000.

The immediacy of this crisis will allow us to determine the extent to which it's also an emergency. Some data processing installations might be confronting task-versus-personnel time constraints of such severity that extraordinary measures will be required for them to survive. If even one organization, given the worst circumstance, is unable to respond in time, then we might conclude that we're all at risk. In this event none of us will be able to assume that sufficient time exists to allow an unhurried response to this crisis. If we're faced with such a threat, surely there must be no delay in determining the status of our own application software.

The need to rewrite an entire application program library certainly qualifies as the worst circumstance. Fortunately, the literature abounds with material necessary for a worst-circumstance analysis.

Lyons (1981: 337) cites a Chicago-based Fortune 500 company with a library of 50,000 mainframe COBOL programs. At an average of 750 lines of code per program, Lyons finds a total of 37,500,000 lines of code in this library. If you employ industry study results cited by Yourdon (1975: 28), which are today largely unchanged, you'll find mainframe programmer productivity levels at about 15 debugged lines of code per day. Thus you can calculate 37,500,000 / 15 = 2,500,000 work days. After allowing for vacation time (10 days), holidays (10 days), and sick days (10 days) only 230 work days per year remain. Consequently, 2,500,000 / 230 or 10,870 work years are required to rewrite this library. Thus you must employ the services of 500 programmers to complete this rewrite in 21.7 calendar years.

Clearly, the programmer productivity constant determines the results of the calculations. Further, ignoring the insurmountable shortage of professional personnel, there's reason to fear that, beyond some point, increasing the number of programmers will not proportionally reduce the time to task completion and might even be counterproductive.

It's unsettling to conclude that some organizations will fail under the worst circumstance because there are less than four years available for such a rewrite. Even more unsettling is the fact that Lyon's program count is probably obsolete, while the programmer productivity level hasn't changed over the years. At this writing, that 50,000-program library is probably much larger and more complex. The Fortune 500 company has probably incorporated in its configuration a number of client/server applications, and their software must be reviewed too. Any sense of security provided by the apparent temporal distance separating us from the year 2000 can be quickly shattered by simple arithmetic.

At best, the task of modifying programs is immense. At worst, for those of us facing a rewrite requirement, the task might be impossible.

Not only is the crisis immediate, its extent threatens our social stability. The danger to society presented by a sudden confrontation with a computer brown-out cannot be exaggerated. Recall the effect a failed air-controller system had on Chicago's O'Hare Airport operations during the summer of 1995. Woe to those unlucky travelers! How much worse the fate of those who find themselves rebuked on all sides by "Sorry, the computer is down." How long before social upheaval with citizens looting what they're unable to purchase?

During 1983, the late J. Peter Grace, Chairman of the President's Private Sector Survey on Cost Control, publicly addressed the status of federal computing resources. Mr. Grace's remarks were shocking.

He pointed out that there were 19,000 computers and a work force of over 250,000 in the federal government and that they were, by and large, twice the age, both hardware and software, as those in the private sector. He went on to explain that these computers were obsolete. In fact, he lamented, they were so obsolete that in some cases federal employees had to maintain the computers because the manufacturers had discontinued servicing them. No one at Chicago's O'Hare Airport should have been surprised when the air controller's computer systems crashed.

Our calculations indicate that, with staffing of about 13 people per government computer, the worst circumstance test reduces to an absurdity. In fact, and without further hesitation, the crisis must be considered a federal emergency. The air controllers' ancient systems are apparently just the tip of the iceberg.

Time constraints eliminate the total rewrite option in both public and private sectors. Still, be assured that some considerable rewriting of application programming will be necessary in many cases. The parameters of the task before each of us are well hidden. We are faced with a massive and unprecedented conversion problem.

The solution is multifaceted. We must examine the valid range of our calendar in order to determine the number of date digits reasonable in terms of social significance. New algorithms must be devised for the calculation of time values across the entire spectrum of such requirements. Pseudocode must be devised, enabling the conversion of these algorithms into source programming code. Finally, usable subroutines must be created, allowing their incorporation into application programming. And this undertaking would not be complete unless a conversion plan were provided.

Consequently, this book begins in chapter 1 by investigating the limits of the Gregorian calendar through a review of historical time measurement. For the sake of completeness, the role of relativistic time as a dimension is included.

Chapter 2 defines the algorithms and presents the mathematical notation and concepts involved in the time computations to follow. The leap-year algorithm, which will be used repeatedly throughout the text, is developed to illustrate using pseudocode as a bridge between the algorithms and the source program code.

Chapter 3 introduces an integrated system of time computation algorithms that we have developed during the past several years as the result of repeated encounters with the time problem in application software design. Beginning with chapter 3 and continuing through chapter 10, the following general format is employed:

1. The problem is defined.

2. The solution strategy is set forth.

3. The algorithm is described.

4. The algorithm is translated to a generalized pseudocode.

5. The documented source programming code is exhibited in an assembly post listing.

6. A sample of the test results is displayed.

7. Comments on the source code are presented.

8. A brief tutorial on applications is presented. Each chapter's source program code is in the form of a subroutine coded inline with a calling test program.

The language we've used is IBM's ALC (BAL). Thus, the subroutines can be used in other ALC programs or can be called by COBOL or PL/I under MVS, called by RPG or by COBOL, used under VSE either in batch environments, or used under CICS/VS in command-level programs. Example IBM VSE linkage conventions appear in the appendices. All source code was assembled and tested under VSE or MVS. For ease of use, the assembly post listings are presented in the book.

A 3.5-inch high-density diskette accompanies this text. The diskette contains three subdirectories. One subdirectory contains the book's ALC (BAL) source language, while the other two contain RPG and COBOL source language. The diskette's root directory contains a tour of the RPG subroutines that you can activate by making your 3.5-inch drive the default drive, inserting the diskette, typing 2000, and pressing Enter. The tour, however, will be meaningful only after you're familiar with the book and its algorithms.

The development of each algorithm is presented in an intuitive way that circumvents the need for lengthy mathematical preparation. Chapter 2 contains the necessary mathematical background. Hence, there are no specific prerequisites to understanding the algorithms. The generalized pseudocode allows non-IBM users to create other programming-language translations.

Chapter 3 explores the problem of storing and recording dates in their various forms: commercial (month, day, year), FIPS (year, month, day), and European (day, month, year). The six bytes currently used for zoned decimal storage and the four bytes reserved for packed decimal storage of the six-digit date amply accommodate the retention of an adequate date equivalent. The neo-Julian date is then introduced and the conversion algorithm allowing its development presented.

Chapter 4 addresses the problem of short-interval aging, which identifies periods in the 30-, 60-, 90-, or 120-day range popular in such processing as accounts receivable and inventory turnover. The mathematics of chapter 3 are augmented to provide the basis for the algorithm in chapter 4.

Chapter 5 again expands on the previous chapter's algorithm to allow the exposition of an aging algorithm that, although usable for short intervals, presents time-lapse results in years, months, and days.

Chapter 6 builds on the mathematics of previous chapters in order to develop the algorithm of translation. A given Gregorian date can be either incremented or decremented by a specified number of days. The algorithm translates the value to the resultant Gregorian date.

Chapter 7 uses the mathematics already presented to develop an algorithm that associates the day's name with an input Gregorian date, thus solving a problem popular in order entry, production scheduling, and other time-boundary situations.

Chapter 8 closes the circle by presenting two algorithms, based on the logic developed above, that allow the conversion of an already presented neo-Julian date to a Gregorian date. The algorithms are equivalent but distinct. Chapter 8 demonstrates that all Julian-format dates ($y.ddd$, where $y$ is the year and $ddd$ is a three-digit ordinal day) are of the Gregorian form 01/01/y + (ddd – 1). Hence, you can use the algorithm of chapter 6 to convert a stored neo-Julian date to Gregorian format for use in calculating dates. Therefore, current six-digit Gregorian dates can be replaced with packed neo-Julian equivalents. Existing storage layouts need not be disturbed.

Chapter 9 goes back to A.D. 1800 for the algorithm of Easter, from the hand of Karl Friedrich Gauss. Gauss's algorithm calculates the date of Easter for any given Gregorian year. Thus, the complete set of related Christian days of celebration and feast could be quickly calculated.

Building on the sum of algorithms developed in the preceding text, chapter 10 presents the status identifier for Gregorian dates. This algorithm returns the status of the input Gregorian date; the day of the week as well as holiday occurrence is calculated and returned to the calling program. The subroutine is developed for Canadian and American holidays.

Finally, chapter 11 outlines the conversion plan that will be needed by most data-processing departments.

Appendix A presents the collected subroutines in macro format for users who prefer this convenient way of preserving sensitive code from programming accidents, while appendix B presents IBM linkage conventions. Appendix C reviews the use of the subroutines in software vendor offerings.

In sum, you'll see that this crisis demands immediate attention. In each information system, the scheduling of the conversion implementation stage is a function of several variables. Among the important variables to be considered are the system's design, the complexity of date computation, involvement with distributed processing via satellite, personal computers, client/server configurations, telecommunications network structure, and available technical and managerial resources versus commitment to ongoing backlog and maintenance requirements. As a consequence, it's imperative that the preimplementation stages be addressed immediately. Current and future software programming efforts must abandon computation with six-digit dates. This book addresses not only the worldwide need for the greatest deadline conversion in the history of computing, but also the immediate worldwide need for a basic change in programming practice.

Perhaps even more important is the philosophical issue raised—beyond the scope of this work and hence not addressed here. In the presence of vast governmental resources for standardization (National Bureau of Standards, etc.), professional associations such as IEEE, and committees (CODASYL, etc.), we have placed our confidence, physical and economic well-being, and future hope in the development of a technology now seen to be fatally flawed through collective human oversight. What have we done? What will we do? What of the technological doomsday dates that lie yet hidden from our view?

Jerome T. Murray and Marilyn J. Murray
Tucson, Arizona

# Time Measurement: A Brief Review

Although computing with time values can be difficult, it's a natural continuation of history. Few of us are inclined to question such things as calendars and clocks. A closer look at the phenomena we so often take for granted usually reveals that we're coping with solutions today that our forebears wrought in the face of extremely meager resources. We see too that these solutions are often tainted by powerful egos as much as they're illuminated by brilliance and practicality. Perhaps a brief review of past encounters with the problem of time will make our present predicament more understandable . . . if not simpler.

## Primitive Time Measurement

As ancient people graduated from hunting and gathering to cultivating and domesticating, the ability to predict weather on the grand scale grew in importance. The rhythm of the seasons determined when to prepare and when to plant. These people took note of the behavior of the moon and determined that roughly 12 displays of the new-moon-to-new-moon cycle was the basis for recurring seasons. The division of daylight into 12 units is a natural consequence of this discovery. The earliest calendars and sundials, with their respect for the 12-unit measure, testify to a primeval desire for consistency.

Religious festivals and observances even today remain tied to the moon's cycles. The behavior of the moon became integrated with human activity at a very early point in social development, and rightly so. The sun's activity is far more subtle as it traverses the horizon, measuring the seasons. Early cultures were not completely without an appreciation of the importance of the sun in measuring time, but using the sun in this regard was clearly limited to segmenting the period of daylight into smaller units in order to allocate time to various activities. As a predictor of seasonality, the moon was apparently a near-unanimous choice, and moon-watchers were seemingly everywhere. The calendars of the Egyptians, Babylonians, and Greeks each bore the marks of the moon in respect to the 12 cycles, or *lunations*. You could safely say that life was quite in harmony with the lunar sphere.

Early on, however, it became apparent that something was seriously wrong. If you look at the moon's activity as the first computer and the calendar as the first effort in software development, as would be true to most current experience with these two, there were bugs in the design.

The seasons began to slip out of place, with the moon dictating that planting was at hand while the weather plainly demonstrated an unwillingness to cooperate. Our ancestors were searching for a way to determine the tropical year—the time required for the path of the sun to cross the equator from south to north. What they were counting was the frequencies of the lunations, the assumption being that 12 lunations were equal to 1 tropical year. The tropical year encompasses approximately 365.242199 days, so the number of lunations in a tropical year is approximately 12.368267. Any calendar designed on the assumption that 12 lunations institute a new seasonal cycle would run quite fast. Spring would come earlier every (lunar) year, while the actual appearance of the season would be quite tardy.

Having designed an almost usable calendar, it became clear that some adjustment was required. As a solution, a thirteenth lunation was added periodically to bring the lunar calendar more nearly in step with the (tropical) year of the seasons. Like so many advertised remedies, the practical benefits were far exceeded by the claims. The thirteenth lunation was inserted capriciously by officials seeking to profit from their ability to manipulate time-related affairs. Not unlike today's playwrights, Aristophanes exposed the procedures to public audiences in his play, *Clouds*, in 432 B.C.

Away from public clamor and dissent, another Greek spent sleepless nights in heavenly observation and hours of grueling calculation. Meton discovered in 432 B.C. that there was a relationship between lunations and the tropical year. Meton had discovered the 19-year cycle: if a tropical year begins simultaneously with a lunar cycle, 235 lunations later the tropical year and the lunar cycle will be synchronized to begin again. Meton found the length of the cycle to be 6,940 days, giving an average length of 365.2632 days to the tropical year. It was now possible to establish a rule for the insertion of the thirteenth lunation.

Later, in 383 B.C., the Chaldean astronomer Kidinnu created a system involving the 19-year cycle, allowing it to be used in the Babylonian calendar—which bears testimony to the proposition that if necessity is the mother of invention, then multiple births must be expected. It would seem that Kidinnu's discovery was independent. His calculations found the average length of the tropical year to be 365.2468 days—a bit more accurate than Meton.

Reconstructing the arithmetic is elementary. If there are 235 lunations every 19 years, then:

$$\text{Average length of year} = \frac{235 \times \text{average length of lunation}}{19}$$

Meton calculated that a lunation takes 29.5319 days on the average:

$$\text{Average length of year} = \frac{235 \times 29.5319}{19}$$

$$= \frac{6,939.9965}{19}$$

$$\cong \frac{6,940}{19}$$

$$\cong 365.2632$$

Kidinnu's average lunation was a more accurate 29.5306 days and he didn't round his numbers; his year was 365.2468 days. Because the time required for a lunation isn't constant (due to perturbations in the elliptical orbit of the moon as both it and the earth travel around the sun in an elliptical path), its average must be computed from a large number of observations. The average is currently 29.530598 days. Kidinnu was accurate to four decimal places. A century, from Meton's perspective, would require about 36,526.3 days, while Kidinnu's century would require about 36,524.7 days. The small difference of 1.6 days becomes significant as the centuries roll by.

Kidinnu's introduction of what is now known as the Metonic cycle resulted in a system of seven insertions of an additional lunation at fixed points in each 19-year cycle in the Babylonian calendar. The Babylonian calendar technology was adopted by the Jewish leaders and lives on today, reflecting Kidinnu's year length and his use of the 19-year cycle.

By 330 B.C., Callippus of Greece modified Meton's calculations and his 19-year cycle by combining four cycles into a 76-year cycle. He also reduced the number used as the length of a lunation, producing a year of 365 and ¼ days, a value commonly accepted in Egypt and Babylon.

And so the primeval problem of reconciling the moon's cycles with the cycles of the seasons was solved only after centuries of effort. The tropical year was assigned 365 and ¼ days, and general harmony was maintained through the periodic introduction of an extra lunation. The key to the solution was the discovery of the Metonic cycle.

## The Julian and Gregorian Calendars

Strangely enough, the Roman calendar was an almost complete mess. By 47 B.C., the month of January, the beginning of winter, fell in what was actually October. The following year Julius Caesar acted to remedy the situation in a way so drastic that it was possible only for one of his power and authority as head of the government and the then prevalent religion. With the aid of Sosigenes, an astronomer from Alexandria, 46 B.C. became 445 days in length, so setting the soon-to-be-implemented new calendar in step with the tropical year.

Sosigenes knew that the tropical year was commonly held to be 365 and ¼ days. It became clear that every four years the addition of one day would keep the tropical year and the calendar together. It's interesting to note the manner in which the extra day was added to the new calendar.

The Romans referred to their dates in a manner similar to our countdown to Christmas. The days of the month were counted backward from various named points. The first of each month was referred to as the *Kalends*. The middle of the month was referred to as the *Ides*, which fell on the 15th day of any 31-day month and on the 13th day of other months. Romans would cite a particular date, therefore, as "four days before the Ides of March." After a named point had passed, remaining dates were referred to the next named point, such as "six days before the Kalends of April," which would translate to March 27.

The Roman calendar in its antiquity saw the year begin on the first day of March (the Kalends of March), when they celebrated the feast of *Terminalia*—similar to our New Year's celebration. Subsequent reorganizations had by Caesar's time placed January as the first month of the year (named after Janus, the god with two faces, looking in two directions). Caesar chose to insert the extra day, every four years, on the sixth day before the Kalends of March, perhaps for sentimental reasons. Consequently, the "sixth" day before the Kalends of March occurred twice in those years. The extra day was referred to in Latin as *ante diem bis sextum Kalendas Martias*, which usage quickly reduced to *bissextum*. Today the year during which the extra day is inserted is called *bisextile*—loosely translated "having two sixes." That fourth year (now called a *leap year* in the United States) consisted of the months of January (31 days), February (30 days), March (31 days), April (30 days), May (31 days), June (30 days), Quintilis (31 days), Sextilis (30 days), September (30 days), October (31 days), November (30 days), and December (31 days).

Here you can see an almost perfect alternating of 31-day and 30-day months. If either Caesar or Sosigenes had been a programmer, certainly September, October, November, and December would have been modified to make the pattern perfect. Because they lacked the foresight to anticipate what the next 2,000 years and computers would bring, they not only omitted this elegant touch but they decided that during nonbisextile years, February would lose a day, making it a 29-day month. In honor of that accomplishment, the month of Quintilis was renamed July (Julius) after Caesar.

The Julian calendar was a triumph over earlier attempts to reconcile lunations with the tropical year. The periodic need to insert an extra lunation was avoided. In every respect the creation was innovative. Unfortunately, by 9 B.C. it was discovered that the Roman priests had erroneously added an extra day every three years. Plainly, further adjustment was needed. Augustus Caesar, now ruler of Rome, took advantage of the adjustment period and had the month of Sextilis named in his honor. August, a 30-day month, was appropriately lengthened to 31 days, with February becoming the donor once again. February was now reduced to 28 days during nonbisextile years.

The Julian calendar became the dominant calendar of the world. By the time of Constantine, Christianity was a strong influence and the months were subdivided into seven-day weeks—a measure common to the Jewish calendar from its inception. The days of the week, strangely enough, were named astrologically after the planets: Saturn, the Sun, Moon, Mars, Mercury, Jupiter, and Venus. This was the practice of the astrology-conscious Egyptians, although the Egyptian month was formally divided into 10-day periods called *Decans*. As the teutonic influence grew,

Mars, Mercury, Jupiter, and Venus were renamed for the teutonic divinities, Tiu, Woden, Thor, and Freya. Hence, Saturn, Sun, Moon, Tiu, Woden, Thor, and Freya are with us still.

And so, the Julian calendar, designed by astronomers and despots, bearing the names of pagan gods, dictators, and planets, became the calendar of popes, cardinals, bishops, and priests. Set in step with the tropical seasons from the time of Constantine, A.D. 325, it marked the Christian feast days.

But the Julian calendar was also found wanting. It was a small but significant error of 11 minutes 14 seconds in the average Julian year that made the Julian calendar longer than the tropical year. The actual length of the tropical year is approximately 365 days, 5 hours, 48 minutes, and 45.66 seconds. Consequently, every 128 years the Julian calendar was announcing the arrival of spring one additional day later than its actual occurrence. The seasons were now drifting backward relative to the calendar. While this small difference was not important to the planters and harvesters, it was considerably unsettling to the churchmen. Easter was being determined using tables that assumed that Spring began March 21 on the Julian calendar. Alas, spring was actually arriving 1 additional day earlier each 128 years and, hence, Easter was occurring later each spring on the Julian calendar.

The English scholar and monk, Roger Bacon, wrote to Pope Urban IV in A.D. 1263 urging a calendar adjustment. Astronomers were well aware of the problem and there were numerous possibilities for solution. Unfortunately, three centuries elapsed before the then Pope, Gregory XIII, acted on a solution proposed by a Neapolitan physician, Aloysius Lilius. In 1582, aided by the advice of the German astronomer Christopher Clavius, it was decreed that the 10 days that had accumulated since the time of Constantine would be dropped. October 5, 1582 would be followed by October 15, 1582, and the too-long calendar would be put back in synchronization with the tropical year. Following this adjustment, the calendar would be prohibited from again accumulating error days through an adjustment in the manner of calculating leap years. The Gregorian calendar would continue to allow every fourth year to be a leap year, but any centesimal year (a year ending in two zeros, e.g., 1600, 1700, 1800) not evenly divisible by 400 would not be considered a leap year. Hence, 1600, being divisible by 4 and by 400, qualified as a leap year. But 1700, although divisible by 4, is not divisible by 400 and, consequently, was disqualified from leap-year status.

While the solution was workable, the Protestant Reformation occurred prior to its announcement and created a climate quite inhospitable to papal decrees. The Gregorian calendar was adopted from time to time and from place to place. The Roman Catholic countries of Italy, Spain, Portugal, and France immediately adopted the Gregorian calendar, with Hungary and Catholic Germany agreeing shortly thereafter. Denmark, the Netherlands, and Protestant Germany waited until 1700 to adopt Pope Gregory's calendar. England, and so the Colonies (including America), did not adopt the Gregorian calendar until 1752.

Because 1700 was a Julian leap year but not so on the Gregorian calendar, England and the colonies were forced to drop not 10 but 11 days to get in step with the sun. A profusion of dates mark this period in history with documents bearing OS (old style) following their dates to signify the use of the Julian calendar, or NS (new style) to indicate a Gregorian date. A review of social commentary from this period in history proves that major conversions result in major problems. Unscrupulous landlords demanded a full month's rent even though the dropping of days obviously shortened the month, and citizens cried out that their lives were being shortened because they were prematurely aged by the dropped days.

Old calendars die slowly. Japan converted to Gregorian dating in 1873, China in 1912, Greece in 1924, and Turkey as late as 1927. Moslems in the Middle East still honor the Mohammedan calendar, which is purely lunar and does not relate to the tropical year. (A near catastrophe occurred when this calendar was misinterpreted by Canadians attempting to export several Americans from Iran under the authority of forged passports during the takeover of the American Embassy there.)

The average Gregorian year is approximately 365 days, 5 hours, 49 minutes, and 12 seconds—still about 25 seconds longer than the true tropical year. Fortunately this error is small enough to keep the seasons from slipping out of place by even one day until the year 3400 when, barring a correction, spring will arrive one day earlier than predicted by the calendar. Some extrapolations place this date as late as 4317.

The Soviet Union has adopted a slightly different method of appointing leap years, so the Russian year averages only two seconds longer than the tropical year. Hence the Russian calendar will not need a one-day adjustment for about 35,000 years.

All of this calendar turmoil had its effect on the computing community—those who calculated with time—even prior to the advent of electronic computers. The astronomers were much in need of a unit of measure that was free of the vagaries of cardinals and kings. During the Julian-to-Gregorian transition, Joseph Scaliger proposed that, while debates over months and years went on, no one questioned the length of a day nor the meaning of the concept. Why not make the day the unit of measurement among astronomers and thus free astronomy from the debates? The Metonic cycle was only one of a number of cycles known to astronomers by Scaliger's time. If a common starting point was found for all the known cycles back far enough in time, Scaliger reasoned, astronomers could study astronomical events without encountering negatively numbered days and they would be able to communicate in a shared frame of reference. A common starting point was determined as occurring every 7,980 Julian years. Scaliger counted backward to find the beginning of the last such Julian cycle. He arrived at January 1, 4713 B.C. and so suggested that this be taken as day number 1. For astronomical purposes each day is numbered beginning with that day on January 1, 4713 B.C. Unfortunately, Scaliger named the date the *Julian Day* after his father, Julius Scaliger. Consequently, the Julian Day 2,438,763 converts to January 2, 1965 on the Gregorian calendar. The uninitiated might confuse the Julian Day and the Julian calendar, but then such is the history of calendar-making.

## Replacing the Sundial

Time passed, whether measured well or not, and needs changed, stimulating creative minds. Nighttime or overcast days were ill-served by sundials. The profusion of innovations adopted over the years is enough material for whole libraries—far more than can be addressed in a brief review. Nighttime hours were measured by burning candles, dripping water that elevated floats, leaking water that emptied bowls, leaking bowls that sank, and the famous pendulum of Galileo. In its time the hourglass with its falling sand was a useful and graceful device. The need for accurate hourly time measurement was felt most keenly by the seafarer. From the practical need to measure the speed of the ship and the length of watches to the imperatives of navigation, time knowledge was vital. The hours of watch and rate of the ship's speed were determined with a small sandglass. To measure the watch, one bell was rung the first time the sandglass emptied, two bells the second time, and so on. Speed was determined by counting the number of knots on a rope pulled from the moving ship by a floating log astern during a fixed interval. The sounding bells, knot measure, and the ship's log survive today with modifications.

A far more fundamental need for exact time measurement related to navigation. While it was possible to determine latitude (north-south position) by stellar observation, longitude (east-west position) required an accurate time measure. In lieu of an accurate time measure, dead-reckoning was used—largely a system of deduction that often resulted in shipwreck and loss of life. It was not until 1761 that John Harrison built a clock that provided England with the time-keeping accuracy necessary to determine longitude at sea.

Today, longitude determines local time. An imaginary line connecting the north and south poles and passing through Greenwich, England, is chosen as 0° longitude. Fifteen degrees east of Greenwich, local time is 1 hour later than at Greenwich. Local time increases 1 hour each additional 15° east of Greenwich until we reach the opposite side of the globe (180° east of Greenwich) where we encounter the international date line. Once across the date line, the date jumps ahead by 24 hours. In opposite fashion, if we travel west across the date line, we lose 24 hours and the date is moved backward. For astronomical purposes, 12:00 noon is considered the start of a new day and the end of the old. In a practical sense this is sound, for when it's noon at Greenwich it's midnight at the international date line. Crossing the date line at midnight December 24 means that you lose December 25 and go to a new date: December 26. This system of time-keeping produces unusual conditions that fortunately aren't commonly experienced since the date line is almost entirely at sea. In order to avoid too much time confusion, many local governments manipulate time zones so they can approximate the longitudinal requirements, thus maintaining regional consistency in clock settings.

While astronomical observations at Greenwich, England formerly maintained the accuracy of time-keeping, atomic clocks are now used. Under computer control and by international agreement, the passage of measured time is periodically halted for one or two seconds to adjust for variations in planetary rotational velocities. Thus, a system of worldwide time-keeping is maintained to a high degree of accuracy.

## Time as a Dimension

If only for the sake of completeness, it's practical to review the contemporary role of time as a dimension. Obviously, our practical computing requirements won't lead us to consider such phenomena as time dilation, but it's good for understanding to transcend need.

Mathematicians from the time of Descartes have had no difficulty building models of three-dimensional objects, such as spheres and cones. After Newton and Leibnitz discovered calculus (independently and almost simultaneously), mathematicians were able to accurately calculate the volumes of three-dimensional objects of various shapes. But the universe was still viewed as Euclid had portrayed it in his geometry. Euclid's view implies that all clocks of equal quality keep the same time. The most distant star visible to us is at the end of a straight line drawn from our eye to it. Euclid's universe is like the 12-lunation year—not quite true.

By 1840, Nicholas Lobachevski challenged the assumption that the universe was as Euclid portrayed it. In his Theory of Parallels, he demonstrated that another interpretation was possible. Mathematicians Riemann and Bolyai likewise published geometries that were non-Euclidean and depicted universes of curved space. In 1905, Albert Einstein published a paper that gave birth to his theory of special relativity, and challenged the assumption that time was universally the same. An oversimplification of Einstein's reasoning is as follows:

> Imagine you're riding on a vehicle traveling at a uniform speed of 100 miles per hour, straight ahead. Now imagine that you throw a ball in the direction of the vehicle's motion. Assume that you can and always do throw a ball so it travels at a speed of 100 miles per hour. A stationary observer measuring the speed of the thrown ball would find it traveling at a speed of 200 miles per hour. This is what you'd expect, since the ball's in-flight velocity is the sum of the vehicle's speed and the speed imparted to it by the thrower.
>
> You'd also expect that light, which travels at approximately 186,000 miles per second, would travel faster if emitted from a high-speed vehicle, that the speed of the vehicle would be added to the speed of the light beam when measured by a stationary observer. Not so! The speed of light is constant. All observers will find the speed of light to be the same regardless of their frame of reference—whether observing from onboard the high-speed vehicle or from a stationary position.

This provable fact was contrary to what most scientists wanted to believe. More profound was its effect on the concepts of universal time. In order to more fully appreciate this, consider an experiment with light conducted on a vehicle moving at a uniformly high speed.

A top view of a high-speed vehicle is shown in Figure 1.1. A flash of light is emitted from point A to a mirror at point B, and is reflected back to point A. The experimental apparatus at point A consists of a clock and a light sensor necessary to measure the time required for the light flash to make the trip from A to B and back to A.

Because the distance from A to B is known, it's easy to compute the speed of the light beam. Where T is the elapsed time:

$$\frac{2\,\overline{AB}}{T} = 186,000 \text{ miles per second}$$

Now let's erect a stationary overhead platform to observe the same experiment as the speeding vehicle passes beneath it. Figure 1.2 displays what the light-sensitive equipment on the overhead platform measures.

Here you see that, due to the vehicle's motion, the mirror at B and the flash emitter/detector/timing device at A occupy different positions at successive instants in time for the duration of the experiment. Hence, the distance the light travels is greater as computed by the measuring equipment on the stationary platform. Also,

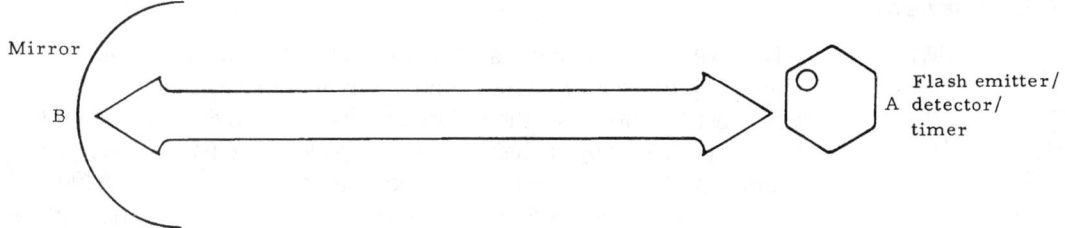

**Figure 1.1**  A top view of the light flash experiment as measured from within the high-speed vehicle.

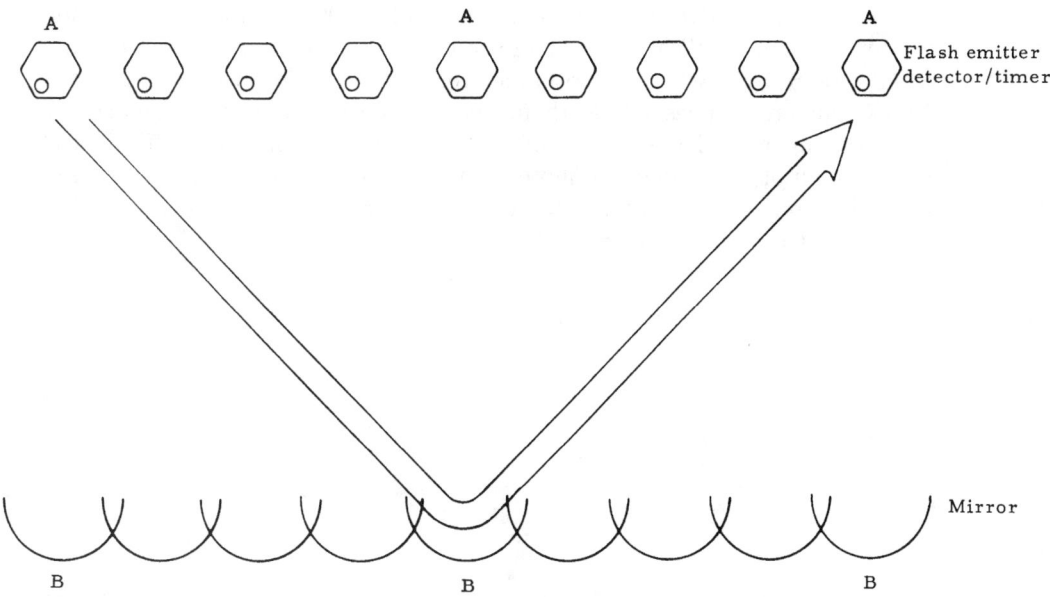

**Figure 1.2**  The light flash experiment as measured from a stationary overhead platform.

the time required for the flash of light to return to point A, as measured on the stationary overhead platform, is greater than the time lapse measured on the moving vehicle. Both experimental calculations result in finding the speed of the light flash to be 186,000 miles per second. This leads to the conclusion that clocks on uniformly moving, high-speed vehicles run slower than clocks at rest relative to those vehicles. Time is not universal, but is relative to the frame of reference in which it's measured.

Later, Einstein's general theory of relativity, which considered accelerated motion, interpreted gravity as a curvature of space. Further, the general theory finds that strong gravitational fields have a slowing impact on time. The mathematical view of the universe is now largely based on the non-Euclidean geometry of Riemann. In order to build a consistent mathematical interpretation of the physical universe, the Polish mathematician Hermann Minkowski created, with Einstein's theory, a four-dimensional space-time model.

## A Brief Review

Whether time is viewed on the grand scale for planting and harvesting or on the microscale for scientific purposes, progress in understanding time has been slow. From the discovery of the 12 lunations to the theory of general relativity, civilization has been exalted and confounded by each successive step along the path. Clearly, however, the valid range of the Gregorian calendar extends at least to the year 3400 and at most to 4317. In either event, a four-digit allowance for the year portion of the date structure is both necessary and sufficient to ensure accurate calculations of dates during this interval. Thus, it's plain that an eight-digit date is necessary for successful time calculations using the Gregorian calendar.

For the purpose of the algorithms, consider A.D. 3399 to be the upper limit for the Gregorian calendar. We've reviewed exercises appearing in the literature, such as Knuth (1968: 156), whose algorithm addresses the possibility of a Gregorian year 14,250. Such references are clearly for teaching purposes, however, and cannot be used for this book. The selection of a four-digit-year value would offer crisis-free computation of time values for more than 1,000 years. But major modifications in time measurement will certainly be required before then if we become involved in space travel and extraterrestrial colonization.

# 2

# Algorithms, Notation, Pseudocode, and Programming

During elementary school, most of us learned how to calculate solutions to whole classes of problems, for example, how to find linear volume. After being taught the calculation steps necessary, we were bombarded with problems that required us to apply our newly acquired method. Our intuitive grasp of the method was enriched by practice. Later we learned that the several mathematical methods we acquired in school were *algorithms*. And so we developed an intuitive notion of what an algorithm must be.

Intuitive grasp is important in any technical area, but it varies with the individual and ultimately has its limit. For instance, most of us would have to admit that while our understanding of volume is of the wordless, intuitive type, our understanding of the Pythagorean theorem—the length of the hypotenuse c of a right triangle ABC = $\sqrt{a^2 + b^2}$—is considerably more dependent on reason. In order to take advantage of intuition as well as reason, it would be good to discover when a method is truly an algorithm, what notation we'll use to represent our algorithms, and how we'll create programming for them.

## Algorithms

Early calculation methods were generally carried out with the abacus. They were brute-force techniques, long and inelegant. About the 9th century A.D. the Islamic mathematician al-Khowarizm wrote several works dealing with arithmetic and algebra. Three hundred years later a collection of these works were translated into then-popular Latin and called the *Algorismus*. The books described calculation procedures that differed considerably from the prevalent, complex, and lengthy abacus methods. Today a set of calculation steps is called an *algorithm*.

An *algorithm* is a procedure for solving a specific class of problems and is characterized by a clearly defined set of features. An algorithm transforms a set of specified inputs into a specified set of outputs with a system of transformation rules that must meet the following requirements:

- The application of the algorithm must result in a finite number of actions.
- The actions must have a unique first step.
- Each step must have a subsequent step.
- When the transformation is complete the sequence must end, producing the specified output or signifying that no solution can be found.

Using these criteria, all properly functioning computer-programs are to be considered algorithms.

Probably the single greatest cause for failure in translating a mathematical algorithm to computer algorithm (program) status is the fourth criterion. It's possible to create a sound mathematical algorithm that, because of inadequate coding, later becomes a nonalgorithm when converted to computer programming. It's often because the inputs don't conform with the specifications, and so the sequence either never ends (infinite loop) or a nonsense result is output. We'll attempt to guard against this possibility with our notational system.

## Notation

An algorithm describes the solution steps for a class of problems. Because of this, the inputs consist of a set or collection of definable elements. Consider the formula for linear volume:

$$V = L \times W \times H$$

The inputs L (length), W (width), and H (height) must be defined since zero or a negative number cannot be substituted for L, W, or H. You'll use definitions such as:

$$L, W, \text{ and } H \in \{x : x > 0\}$$

which means that L, W, and H belong to the set of numbers x such that x is a number greater than zero. The Greek epsilon ($\in$) stands for membership in the set, and the colon (:) means "such that." The definition notifies the programmer of the need to eliminate the possibility of either zero or a negative number entering the calculations to produce a nonsense result. It's evident, then, that you must exclude certain kinds of numbers from certain algorithms.

Mathematicians have a convenient system for classifying numbers in sets, but for the sake of practicality we'll simply describe the numbers we'll be using and marry meaning to notation more quickly.

## The integers

You'll be dealing with the set of integers, often represented by a capital Z. The integers are the set of whole numbers: negative, zero, and positive. If you specify a number to be an integer greater than zero, you're specifying that it belongs to the set of positive numbers. This is useful since you automatically exclude all the nonwhole values, zero, and negative numbers. For example, 1, 2, 3, . . ., 101 are all members of the set, but numbers such as 1.723 are excluded since they aren't whole numbers. Similarly, 0, –9, and –1.77 are excluded.

Using the definition notation and Z, you can rewrite the input specification for the linear-volume algorithm as:

$$L, W, \text{and } H \in \{x{:}x \text{ belongs to } Z \text{ and } x > 0\}$$

This is a more restricted definition since it rules out all dimensions that are not integral values (whole numbers). There are many algorithms valid for only integer input. If you consider the insurance questionnaire that asks for age as of nearest birthday, the valid input is clearly:

$$\text{Age} \in \{x{:}x \text{ belongs to } Z \text{ and } x > 0\}$$

Fractions are excluded.

## Integer truncation

Just as it's necessary to specify integer values as inputs, it's often necessary to specify integer values as outputs or as the intermediate results of calculations. For example, if you're managing an assembly line that constructs 9.2 refrigerators per day and you're asked how many completed units you can have ready for shipment in 8 days, you'll automatically perform integer truncation. The calculation $9.2 \times 8 = 73.6$ informs you that 73 is the number of completed refrigerators. You automatically truncated or cut off the noninteger portion of the result. The notation to indicate this activity is: $[9.2 \times 8]$. Brackets enclosing a calculation or numerical value indicate that the result is to be the whole-number portion only.

The placement of the brackets is important. Consider six assembly lines each capable of assembling 9.2 refrigerators per day, therefore $[9.2 \times 8 \times 6] = 441$, while $[9.2 \times 8] \times 6 = 438$. Clearly 438 is a valid eight-day measure of completed units for the six assembly lines; 441 is the result of accumulated fractional units and would produce a false picture of completed production.

## Modular arithmetic

In the course of performing division, you need to deal only with the remainder. Recall your first encounters with modular arithmetic in elementary or high school. Modular arithmetic deals only with the remainder after division of integers, for example, $25 \div 6 = 4$, R1. The remainder 1 is the value of 25, modulo 6. Mathematicians represent this with the notation $1 = 25_{(\text{Mod } 6)}$. Because we'll also use the left and right parentheses to delimit our calculations, we'll display modulo notation in reduced size. Note that modulo notation implies integer truncation in the quotient. That is, $Q = x \div y = [x \div y]$. Consequently, whether the brackets are displayed or not, the quotient that results from the division of two numbers in what follows is considered to be only the integer portion. Therefore, we can minimize the number of brackets. We should agree that $X_{(\text{Mod } 0)}$ makes no sense at all. Regardless of the value of X, division by zero is undefined. Assume that:

$$X > 0, X_{(\text{Mod } n)} = R, R \in \{r : r \text{ belongs to } Z \text{ and } 0 \leq r < n\}$$

which translates to this: For positive X, division by any value n results in a remainder R such that R is an integer equal to or greater than zero and less than n. In short, the remainder is always less than the divisor.

## Absolute value

Depending on the purpose of your calculations, negative values produced by subtraction can be important or you can disregard the sign. For example, when paying bills, most people are quite attentive to the possibility that a payment, when subtracted from their indebtedness, might result in a negative balance due. They rarely overpay. When calculating distances, however, you often want to ignore the negative sign that develops from a subtraction, since any attempt to find the sum of such calculated values would result in a distorted total distance. For instance, most distance calculations seek solutions to problems such as:

Given that A is 25 miles from B, and C is 80 miles from A, how many miles separate B from C, assuming all three points are in a straight line with B located between A and C?

The difference between 80 and 25 can immediately be calculated, and it's immaterial how you do it: 80 – 25 and 25 – 80 produce the same numbers but with opposite signs. And similar to the unconscious use of integer truncation, we usually just find the number 55 and treat it as a positive value, regardless of whether the subtrahend was larger than the minuend in the actual calculation.

The mathematical notation that specifies this treatment of negative value is:

$$|X| = \begin{cases} X, \text{ if } X \geq 0 \\ -X, \text{ if } X < 0 \end{cases}$$

which simply states that the absolute value of any number X is represented by enclosing that number within vertical bars. The value is then taken as positive regardless of sign.

## Sequence of operations

While notation provides a compact vehicle for communication, rules are necessary if you're to perform calculations in an unambiguous manner. The goal here is, after all, to create mathematical algorithms using notation to ultimately write a correctly functioning computer program. The bridge between the mathematical algorithm and the computer program is called *pseudocode*. In order to develop the pseudocode, there must be rules governing the sequence of calculations prompted by the notation.

We'll use parentheses to delimit the operations so we can calculate unambiguously. For example, the following expression resolves in two ways:

$$\left[\frac{6}{4}\right] + 9 \times 3 \quad or \quad \left[\frac{6}{4}\right] + 9 \times 3$$

$$\begin{array}{lll} 1 & +9 \times 3 & \quad 1 \quad +9 \times 3 \\ & 10 \times 3 & \quad 1 \quad +27 \\ & 30 & \quad 28 \end{array}$$

But parentheses eliminate the ambiguity:

$$\left(\left[\frac{6}{4}\right] + 9\right) \times 3$$

$$(1 + 9) \times 3$$

$$10 \times 3$$

$$30$$

Because of the parentheses, you can invoke the commutative law of multiplication and write:

$$3\left(\left[\frac{6}{4}\right] + 9\right) = 3(1 + 9) = 3(10) = 30$$

This eliminates the multiplication sign and establishes the convention that adjacent values with no intervening operation sign are to be multiplied.

When multiple parentheses are used, we'll impose the rule that the innermost quantity is calculated first, left to right. Hence, the following displays the effects of the sequence:

$$\begin{array}{l} 2(3([25_{(\text{Mod }6)} + 1.5]) + 4) \\ 2(3([\ 1 \quad\quad + 1.5]) + 4) \\ 2(3([\quad\quad\quad 2.5\ ]) + 4) \\ 2(3(\quad\quad\quad 2 \quad\ ) + 4) \\ 2(\quad\quad\quad 6 \quad\ + 4) \\ 2(\quad\quad\quad\quad 10 \quad\ ) = 20 \end{array}$$

The spacing in this equation highlights the manner in which the integer truncation brackets and parentheses are discarded as the calculations proceed. Within integer truncation brackets, decimal values are retained and integer truncation doesn't occur until the final bracket removal when all calculations have resulted in one numerical value.

## Pseudocode

Pseudocode is code written with human-readable words and sentences that approximates a programming language. It simplifies the final programming task because it sequences the operations to be performed and allows timely development of values that will be used frequently in the program. Creating a subroutine to test the leap-year status of a four-digit year will allow for a demonstration of notation in the development of an algorithm. Having created an algorithm, we'll then illustrate the way in which pseudocode bridges the gap between the algorithm and the final source programming code.

## The leap-year algorithm

Recall the Gregorian leap year: Every fourth year is a leap year, and any centesimal year not evenly divisible by 400 is not a leap year. First, consider the input values. The Gregorian calendar wasn't adopted until 1582 and then not everywhere. Obviously, an input year prior to 1582 would be valuable only if you're interested in finding date equivalents in antiquity. Because 1600 was both a centesimal year and a leap year, 1601 qualifies as the beginning of the cycle and as a valid lower limit. As you'll see in later chapters, this choice simplifies the calculations. Hence, the inputs are defined as such:

$$Y \in \{y : y \text{ belongs to } Z \text{ and } 1600 < y < 3400\}$$

In other words, Y is a member of a set such that each member of the set is an integer greater than 1600 and less than 3400. Thus, you have 1601, 1602, . . . 3399 as valid inputs. The limit $y < 3400$ reflects the fact that the Gregorian calendar becomes invalid during the year 3400.

Now you can translate Pope Gregory's rules to mathematical notation by allowing L to be the value of the calculations. If $L = 1$, the input year is a leap year. If $L = 0$, the input year is not a leap year. Translating:

$$L = \begin{cases} 0, \text{ if } Y_{(\text{Mod } 4)} \neq 0 \\ 1, \text{ if } Y_{(\text{Mod } 4)} = 0 \text{ and } Y_{(\text{Mod } 100)} \neq 0 \\ 0, \text{ if } Y_{(\text{Mod } 4)} = 0 \text{ and } Y_{(\text{Mod } 100)} = 0 \text{ and } Y_{(\text{Mod } 400)} \neq 0 \\ 1, \text{ if } Y_{(\text{Mod } 4)} = 0 \text{ and } Y_{(\text{Mod } 100)} = 0 \text{ and } Y_{(\text{Mod } 400)} = 0 \end{cases}$$

In other words, if Y is not divisible by 4 ($Y_{(\text{Mod } 4)} \neq 0$), then Y is not a leap year. If Y is divisible by 4 ($Y_{(\text{Mod } 4)} = 0$) and Y is not a centesimal ($Y_{(\text{Mod } 100)} \neq 0$), then Y is a leap year. If Y is divisible by 4 ($Y_{(\text{Mod } 4)} = 0$) and Y is a centesimal ($Y_{(\text{Mod } 100)} = 0$) but Y is not divisible by 400 ($Y_{(\text{Mod } 400)} \neq 0$), then Y is not a leap year. If Y is divisible by 4 ($Y_{(\text{Mod } 4)} = 0$), Y is a centesimal ($Y_{(\text{Mod } 100)} = 0$), and Y is divisible by 400 ($Y_{(\text{Mod } 400)} = 0$), then Y is a leap year.

A final but important step in developing the algorithm is specifying a return code to indicate either that the calculation was successful or that no solution was found. Allow CODE1 to act as your return code:

$$CODE1 = \begin{cases} 0, \text{ if } Y \in \{y : y \text{ belongs to } Z \text{ and } 1600 < y < 3400\} \\ 2, \text{ if } Y \in \{y : y \text{ does not belong to } Z \text{ or sign} \neq +\} \\ 4, \text{ if } Y \in \{y : y \text{ belongs to } Z \text{ but not } 1600 < y < 3400\} \end{cases}$$

Here, zero indicates a successful calculation predicated on the proper input data. Two indicates bad input data and four indicates good data that violates limits defined for the algorithm—a bad year. These are the three possibilities implied by the previous input definition. The pseudocode can be written directly as:

```
 1) Let CODE1 = 0
 2) Let L = 9
 3) If Y ∈ {y : y belongs to Z and sign = +}, go to 6
 4) Let CODE1 = 2
 5) Go to 14
 6) If Y ∈ {y : 1600 < y < 3400}, go to 9
 7) Let CODE1 = 4
 8) Go to 14
 9) Let L = 0
10) If Y (Mod 4) ≠ 0, go to 14
11) If Y (Mod 100) ≠ 0, go to 13
12) If Y (Mod 400) ≠ 0, go to 14
13) Let L = 114) Exit
```

## Comments on the pseudocode

Step 1 of the pseudocode assumes that the input value belongs to the set of valid inputs by initializing the return code CODE1 to zero. Step 2 assumes that the input value does not belong to the set of valid inputs and so initializes L to 9, an undefined value. Step 3 tests the input value to determine whether it belongs to the set of positive signed integers. If not, the branch to step 6 is not taken and step 4 resets the return code CODE1 to 2 (bad data). Step 5 branches to exit the subroutine, returning control to the calling program.

Step 6 executes only if the input value is a positive integer. Here the positive integer is tested to determine whether it's within the limits specified for members of the valid input set. If so, the branch to step 9 is taken. If not, step 7 resets the return code CODE1 to 4 (bad year). Step 8 branches to exit the subroutine, returning control to the calling program.

Step 9 resets L to zero. This step executes only if the input value belongs to the specified set of valid inputs for our algorithm. Step 9 assumes that the input year is not a leap year. Step 10 tests for the input value's divisibility by 4. If the remainder isn't zero, the branch is taken to exit the subroutine. The value of L is zero and CODE1 contains zero. The input is not a leap year.

Step 11 executes only if the input was divisible by 4. Step 11 tests for divisibility by 100 (determining whether or not the input is a centesimal). If the remainder isn't zero, the input is a noncentesimal divisible by 4. Hence, the input is a leap year, and the branch to 13 is taken to reset L to 1 and then 14 to exit.

Step 12 executes only if the input is a centesimal. Step 12 tests for divisibility by 400. If the centesimal is divisible by 400, the remainder is zero and the branch isn't taken. The input is a centesimal leap year, and so step 13 executes to reset L to 1 and then step 14 exits. The value of CODE1 is zero and L is 1. If the centesimal isn't divisible by 400, the branch to exit at step 14 is taken. The input is a centesimal non-leap year. The value of CODE1 is zero and L is zero.

The calling program must interrogate the return code CODE1 in order to ascertain the result of the subroutine's execution. If the return code isn't zero, the returned value identifies the cause of failure. Consequently, it's imperative that the source code for the subroutine be such that no input results in an abend. The method of achieving this is explained in the source code's editing conventions in the next section.

## Programming

We urge you to carefully review the subroutine's introductory documentation in Figure 2.1, which displays TEST01, the TIMESUB1 test program. The documentation is part of TIMESUB1 and contains necessary information if you're interested in incorporating this subroutine into a calling program.

### Comments on the source code's transparency

The labeling convention renders the subroutine's fields transparent to the calling program in that the #$1 prefix is used throughout. Uniqueness is achieved because the subroutine labeling in successive chapters will correspond to the subroutine's enumerative title; TIMESUB2 features prefixes such as #$2. Thus, more than one of the subroutines can be incorporated into inline code by a calling program. Obviously, anyone writing a calling program must refrain from using such prefixes if the subroutines are to be used in inline code.

### Comments on the source code's editing conventions

The input value must be passed to the subroutine in zoned decimal format. This is accomplished by the calling program (statement #233: "MVC YEAR,TSTYEAR"). The subroutine initially employs Translate and Test (TRT) to determine that a valid IBM positive sign and digit are in the low-order (right-most byte) position of the input field. The second execution of TRT ascertains that all other bytes of the input field are zoned decimal digits, i.e., X'F0', . . . X'F9'. ALC programmers are cautioned that *fabricating* a zoned decimal field could result in a bad data return code (CODE1 = 2) if they're not careful.

For example, Table 2.1 doesn't produce a zoned-decimal field in YEAR for the purposes of TRT as used here. Although the data is unpacked, the C zone embedded in YEAR's second byte will result in a bad data return code. TRT will find the byte containing X'C9' invalid, since X'F9' is expected. You can correct the situation via MVZ YEAR + 1(1), =C'0' prior to passing the field. Other than 'F', any of the following— 'C', 'A', or 'E'—can appear as a zone only in the low-order byte of a zoned decimal field passed to any subroutine in this text. These are valid IBM + signs that can occupy the low-order bytes of zoned decimal fields in worldwide databases.

**TABLE 2.1  Zoned Decimal Demonstration.**

| Label | Opcd. | Operand | Year contents | FIELDB contents |
|-------|-------|---------|---------------|-----------------|
|       | MVC   | YEAR,FIELDA | F0F0F0F0 | undetermined |
|       | ZAP   | FIELDB, = P'19' | F0F0F0F0 | 019C |
|       | MVC   | YEAR + 2(2), = C'79' | F0F0F7F9 | 019C |
|       | UNPK  | YEAR (2),FIELDB | F1C9F7F9 | 019C |
|       |       |         |               |      |
|       |       |         |               |      |
| FIELDA | DC   | C'0000' |               |      |
| FIELDB | DS   | PL2     |               |      |

```
                                    EXTERNAL SYMBOL DICTIONARY

SYMBOL      TYPE              ID  ADDR   LENGTH LD-ID

TEST01      SD (CSECT)        001 000000 000618
PRMOD       ER (EXTRN)        002
PRMOD       SD (CSECT)        003 000000 000088

                                    DUMMY SECTION DICTIONARY

SYMBOL      ID LENGTH

IJDPD002    1FF 000030
```

**Figure 2.1**   Assembly post listing of TEST01 with its called TIMESUB1 subroutine.

```
LOC     OBJECT CODE     ADDR1  ADDR2   STMT   SOURCE STATEMENT

000000

                                         1            PRINT NOGEN
                                         2   TESTO1   START
                                         3   *  LIST
                                         4   LIST     DTFPR  DEVADDR=SYSO1O.            X
                                                             IOAREA1=OUT.              X
                                                             BLKSIZE=132.              X
                                                             DEVICE=1403.              X
                                                             PRINTOV=YES,              X
                                                             MODNAME=PRMOD,            X
                                                             CONTROL=YES

                                        25   *
                                        26   PRMOD    PRMOD  CONTROL=YES.              X
                                                             PRINTOV=YES

                                       135   *
                                       136   TESTFIL  ACB    AM=VSAM,                  X
                                                             MACRF=(ADR,IN,SEQ).       X
                                                             EXLST=EXITLST

                                       168   *
                                       169   EXITLST  EXLST  AM=VSAM,                  X
                                                             EODAD=FINI

                                       180   *
                                       181   REQUEST  RPL    ACB=TESTFIL,              X
                                                             AREA=TESTFLE.             X
                                                             AREALEN=80,               X
                                                             OPTCD=(ADR,SEQ,NUP,MVE)

000B4  0550                   000B6      210   *
                              003AF       211   BEGIN    BALR   5,0
                                          212            USING  *,5
000B6  41D0 52F9              003AF       213            LA     13,SAVE
                                          214            OPEN   TESTFIL,LIST
000CE  9240 51C2       00278              223            MVI    OUT,X'40'
000D2  D282 51C3 51C2  00279 00278        224            MVC    OUT+1(131),OUT
                                          225   READ     GET    RPL=REQUEST
000EA  FA20 5273 5556  00329 0060C        232            AP     TOT,=P'1'
000F0  D203 5410 5172  004C6 00228        233            MVC    YEAR,TSTYEAR
000F6  41B0 5342       003F8              234            LA     11,TIMESUB1
000FA  056B                               235            BALR   6,11
000FC  9540 52F8       003AE              236            CLI    SWITCH,X'40'
000100 4770 508E       00144              237            BNE    TEST
000104 92F1 52F8       003AE              238            MVI    SWITCH,X'F1'
000108 D22D 51C2 52CA  00278 00380        239            MVC    OUT(46),HDG
                                          24C            CNTRL  LIST,SK,1
                                          246            CNTRL  LIST,SP,3
                                          252            PUT    LIST
                                          257            CNTRL  LIST,SP,1
000144 9240 51C2       00278              263   TEST     MVI    OUT,X'40'
000148 D282 51C3 51C2  00279 00278        264            MVC    OUT+1(131),OUT
00014E D203 51C2 5410  00278 004C6        265            MVC    OUT(4),YEAR
000154 F900 540F 5557  004C5 0060D        266            CP     CODE1,=P'2'
00015A 4780 50C0       00176              267            BE     INDATA
00015E 4720 50CA       00180              268            BH     INVALID
000162 F900 540E 5556  004C4 0060C        269            CP     L,=P'1'
000168 4780 50D4       0018A              270            BE     YES
00016C D211 51C7 52B8  0027D 0036E        271            MVC    OUT+5(18),NOTLEAP
000172 47F0 50DA       00190              272            B      NEXT
```

```
                                                    DOS/VSE ASSEMBLER 16.13 99-12-31

LOC    OBJECT CODE       ADDR1 ADDR2  STMT  SOURCE STATEMENT

000176 D20D 51C7 5276    0027D 0032C  273 INDATA  MVC   OUT+5(14),BADDATA
00017C 47F0 50DA               00190  274         B     NEXT
000180 D20D 51C7 5284    0027D 0033A  275 INVALID MVC   OUT+5(14),BADYEAR
000186 47F0 50DA               00190  276         B     NEXT
00018A D20D 51C7 5292    0027D 00348  277 YES     MVC   OUT+5(14),ISLEAP
000190 D20D 51DD 52AA    00293 00360  278 NEXT    MVC   OUT+27(14),RVALUE
000196 F300 51ED 540F    002A3 004C5  279         UNPK  OUT+43(1),CODE1
00019C D300 51ED 5558    002A3 0060E  280         MVC   OUT+43(1),=C'O'
0001A2 D209 51F2 52A0    002A8 00356  281         MVC   OUT+48(10),LVALUE
0001A8 F300 51FE 540E    002B4 004C4  282         UNPK  OUT+60(1),L
0001AE D300 51FE 5558    002B4 0060E  283         MVZ   OUT+60(1),=C'O'
                                      284         PRTOV LIST,12
                                      290         PUT   LIST
                                      295         B     READ
0001CE 47F0 5022               000D8  296 FINI    CLOSE TESTFIL
                                      304         MVI   OUT,X'40'
0001E2 9240 51C2               00278  305         MVC   OUT+1(131),OUT
0001E6 D282 51C3 51C2    00279 00278  306         MVC   OUT(39),TOTAL
0001EC D226 51C2 5246    00278 002FC  307         MVC   OUT+27(6),MASK
0001F2 D205 51DD 526D    00293 00323  308         ED    OUT+27(6),TOT
0001F8 DE05 51DD 5273    00293 00329  309         CNTRL LIST,SP,1
                                      315         PUT   LIST
                                      320         CLOSE LIST
                                      328         EOJ

000228                                331 TESTFLE DS    OCL80
000228                                332 TSTYEAR DS    ZL4
00022C                                333 VOID    DS    CL76
000278                                334 OUT     DS    CL132
0002FC E3C8C540E2E4C2D9               335 TOTAL   DC    C'THE SUBROUTINE WAS EXECUTED TIMES'
000323 402020202020                   336 MASK    DC    X'402020202020'
000329 0000C                          337 TOT     DC    PL3'O'
00032C 5C40C9D5E5C1D3C9               338 BADDATA DC    C'* INVALID DATA'
00033A 5C40C9D5E5C1D3C9               339 BADYEAR DC    C'* INVALID YEAR'
000348 C9E240C140D3C5C1               340 ISLEAP  DC    C'IS A LEAP YEAR'
000356 D340C3D6D5E3C5D5               341 LVALUE  DC    C'L CONTENTS'
000360 C3D6C4C5F140C3D6               342 RVALUE  DC    C'CODE1 CONTENTS'
00036E C9E240D5D6E340C1               343 NOTLEAP DC    C'IS NOT A LEAP YEAR'
000380 E3C5E2E340D6C640               344 HDG     DC    C'TEST OF TIMESUB1 TO DETERMINE LEAP YEAR STATUS'
0003AE 40                             345 SWITCH  DC    X'40'
0003AF                                346 SAVE    DS    CL72
                                      347 *
```

**Figure 2.1** *Continued*

```
LOC   OBJECT CODE   ADDR1 ADDR2   STMT   SOURCE STATEMENT                                                          DOS/VSE ASSEMBLER 16.13  99-12-31

                                  349  * ****************************************************************************   TS100010
                                  350  *                                                                              TS100020
                                  351  *                                                                              TS100030
                                  352  *    TTTTTTT   III   MM    MM   EEEEE   SSSSS   UU  UU   BBBBB   1             TS100040
                                  353  *       T       I    M M  M M   E       S       UU  UU   B   B   11            TS100050
                                  354  *       T       I    M  MM  M   EEEE    SSSS    UU  UU   BBB B   1             TS100060
                                  355  *       T       I    M      M   E           S   UU  UU   B   B   1             TS100070
                                  356  *       T      III   M      M   EEEEE   SSSS    UUUUU    BBBBB   111           TS100080
                                  357  *                                                                              TS100090
                                  358  * ****************************************************************************   TS100100
                                  359  * ********** L E A P  Y E A R   S U B R O U T I N E **********                  TS100110
                                  360  * ****************************************************************************   TS100120
                                  361  *                                                                              TS100130
                                  362  *                                                                              TS100140
                                  363  * ****************************************************************************   TS100150
                                  364  *                                                                              TS100160
                                  365  *    THIS SUBROUTINE IDENTIFIES GREGORIAN LEAP YEARS                           TS100170
                                  366  *                                                                              TS100180
                                  367  *  1.  VALID INPUT YEARS FOR THIS SUBROUTINE ARE THE YEARS                     TS100190
                                  368  *      1601 THROUGH 3399 A. D.                                                 TS100200
                                  369  *                                                                              TS100210
                                  370  *  2.  THE CALLING PROGRAM MUST PLACE A POSITIVE FOUR DIGIT                    TS100220
                                  371  *      YEAR, IN ZONED DECIMAL, IN A SUBROUTINE DEFINED FOUR                    TS100230
                                  372  *      BYTE FIELD, 'YEAR', BEFORE EXECUTION.  YEAR IS NOT                      TS100240
                                  373  *      ALTERED BY THE SUBROUTINE.                                              TS100250
                                  374  *                                                                              TS100260
                                  375  *  3.  A SUBROUTINE DEFINED ONE BYTE FIELD, 'CODE1,' IS                       TS100270
                                  376  *      RETURNED TO THE CALLING PROGRAM AS A RETURN CODE.                       TS100280
                                  377  *                                                                              TS100290
                                  378  *      A PACKED 0 INDICATES SUCCESSFUL EXECUTION OF THE SUB-                   TS100300
                                  379  *      ROUTINE.                                                                TS100310
                                  380  *                                                                              TS100320
                                  381  *      A PACKED 2 INDICATES UNSUCCESSFUL EXECUTION:  INVALID                   TS100330
                                  382  *      DATA IN YEAR.                                                           TS100340
                                  383  *                                                                              TS100350
                                  384  *      INVALID DATA ARE DETERMINED IF THE FIELD'S LOW ORDER                    TS100360
                                  385  *      BYTE'S ZONE CONTAINS AN INVALID SIGN, (NOT ONE OF                       TS100370
                                  386  *      X'C', X'A', X'E', OR X'F'), OR IF THE PRECEDING BYTES'                  TS100380
                                  387  *      ZONES ARE OTHER THAN X'F', OR IF ANY BYTE'S LOW ORDER                   TS100390
                                  388  *      NIBBLE CONTAINS A VALUE GREATER THAN X'9'.                              TS100400
                                  389  *                                                                              TS100410
                                  390  *      A PACKED 4 INDICATES UNSUCCESSFUL EXECUTION:  THE VALUE                 TS100420
                                  391  *      OF YEAR VIOLATES THE LIMITS SPECIFIED IN 1.. ABOVE.                     TS100430
                                  392  *                                                                              TS100440
                                  393  *  4.  A SUBROUTINE DEFINED, ONE BYTE FIELD, 'L', IS RETURNED                  TS100450
                                  394  *      TO THE CALLING PROGRAM AND CONTAINS A PACKED 1 IF THE                   TS100460
                                  395  *      YEAR IS A LEAP YEAR.  A PACKED 0 INDICATES NO LEAP YEAR.                TS100470
                                  396  *      IF THE EXECUTION WAS UNSUCCESSFUL, THAT IS IF THE RETURN                TS100480
                                  397  *      CODE FIELD, CODE1, CONTAINS A NON-ZERO VALUE, THEN L                    TS100490
                                  398  *      WILL CONTAIN A PACKED 9 AS PROTECTION AGAINST ILLEGAL                   TS100500
                                  399  *      USE OF A PRIOR EXECUTION'S LEAP YEAR INDICATION.                        TS100510
                                  400  *                                                                              TS100520
                                  401  *  5.  ALL OTHER SUBROUTINE DEFINED FIELDS AND LABELS ARE                     TS100530
                                  402  *      TRANSPARENT TO THE CALLING PROGRAM.                                     TS100540
                                  403  *  6.  THIS SUBROUTINE IS WRITTEN TO BE ASSEMBLED WITH THE                    TS100550
```

```
LOC    OBJECT CODE    ADDR1 ADDR2    STMT   SOURCE STATEMENT                                          DOS/VSE ASSEMBLER 16.13 99-12-31

                                     404 *          CALLING PROGRAM AND SHOULD BE INSERTED IN THE CALLING          *  TS100560
                                     405 *          PROGRAM IMMEDIATELY BEFORE THE 'END' OPCODE.                   *  TS100570
                                     406 *                                                                         *  TS100580
                                     407    7.  THIS SUBROUTINE USES REGISTER 6 AS THE LINK REGISTER.             *  TS100590
                                     408 *          IF REGISTER 6 IS ASSIGNED IN THE CALLING PROGRAM FOR           *  TS100600
                                     409 *          OTHER USES, IT MUST BE SAVED PRIOR TO EXECUTING THE            +  TS100610
                                     410 *          'BALR.'                                                        *  TS100620
                                     411 *                                                                         *  TS100630
                                     412 *                                                                         *  TS100640
                                     413 *                                            JEROME T. MURRAY            *  TS100650
                                     414 *                                            MARILYN J. MURRAY           *  TS100660
                                     415 * GLEN ELLYN, ILLINOIS                                                    *  TS100670
                                     416 *                                                                         *  TS100680
                                     417 * ***********************************************************************  *  TS100690
                                     418 * ***********************************************************************  *  TS100700
                                     419 *                                                                            TS100710
                                     420 *          +++ SECTION 1- GENERAL HOUSEKEEPING  +++                           TS100720
                                     421 *                                                                            TS100730
                                     422 *          INITIALIZE INDICATIVE FIELD, CODE1 AND                             TS100740
                                     423 *          OUTPUT FIELD, L                                                    TS100750
                                     424 *                                                                            TS100760

0003F7 00                            425 TIMESUB1 ZAP  CODE1,=P'0'                                                     TS100770
0003F8 F800 540F 5559   0060F        426          ZAP  L,=P'9'                                                         TS100780
0003FE F800 540E 555A   00610        427 *                                                                            TS100790
                                     428 *                                                                            TS100800
                                     429 *          SAVE REGISTERS 1 AND 2 IN SAVE FIELDS                              TS100810
000404 9012 5526        005DC        430          STM  1,2,#$1RSAVE                                                    TS100820
                                     431 *                                                                            TS100830
                                     432 *          MOVE YEAR TO WORK FIELD AND ISOLATE SIGN                          TS100840
                                     433 *                                                                            TS100850
000408 D203 551F 5410 005D5 004C6    434          MVC  #$1WORK4,YEAR                                                   TS100860
00040E D200 551E 5522 005D4 005D8    435          MVC  #$1SIGN,#$1WORK4+3                                              TS100870
                                     436 *                                                                            TS100880
                                     437 *          +++ SECTION 2- NUMERIC VALIDATION  +++                            TS100890
                                     438 *                                                                            TS100900
                                     439 *          AUGMENT TABLE FOR VALID '+' SIGNS OTHER THAN                      TS100910
                                     440 *          X'F' FOR WHICH TABLE IS DEFINED: X'A', X'C'                       TS100920
                                     441 *          X'E'- EDIT FOR VALID '+' SIGN USING TRT                           TS100930
                                     442 *                                                                            TS100940
000414 D209 54B4 5514 0056A 005CA    443          MVC  #$1TABL+160(10),#$1ZRO                                          TS100950
00041A D209 54D4 5514 0058A 005CA    444          MVC  #$1TABL+192(10),#$1ZRO                                          TS100960
000420 D209 54F4 5514 005AA 005CA    445          MVC  #$1TABL+224(10),#$1ZRO                                          TS100970
000426 DD00 551E 5414 005D4 004CA    446          TRT  #$1SIGN(1),#$1TABL                                              TS100980
00042C 4780 537E        00434        447          BC   8,#$1NUM                                                        TS100990
000430 47F0 538E        00444        448          B    #$1BDATA                                                        TS101000
                                     449 *                                                                            TS101010
                                     450 *          REINITIALIZE TABLE AND EDIT FOR VALID ZONE                        TS101020
                                     451 *          AND DIGIT CONFIGURATIONS IN REMAINING BYTES                       TS101030
                                     452 *                                                                            TS101040
000434 D2EE 5415 5414 004CB 004CA    453 #$1NUM   MVC  #$1TABL+1(239),#$1TABL                                          TS101050
00043A DD02 551F 5398 005D5          454          TRT  #$1WORK4(3),#$1TABL                                             TS101060
000440 4780 5398        0044E        455          BC   8,#$1PACK                                                       TS101070
                                     456 *                                                                            TS101080
                                     457 *          POST 'BAD DATA' RETURN CODE AND EXIT                              TS101090
```

**Figure 2.1** *Continued*

```
                                        DOS/VSE ASSEMBLER 16.13  99-12-31

LOC    OBJECT CODE       ADDR1 ADDR2  STMT  SOURCE STATEMENT

                                      458  *                                                                TS101100
000444 F800 540F 5557   004C5 0006D   459 #$1BDATA  ZAP   CODE1,=P'2'                                        TS101110
00044A 47F0 5534         005EA        460           B     #$1TERM                                            TS101120
                                      461  *                                                                TS101130
                                      462  *          +++   SECTION 3- EDIT YEAR FOR LIMIT VIOLATIONS  +++   TS101140
                                      463  *                                                                TS101150
                                      464  *          PACK YEAR IN WORK FIELD                               TS101160
                                      465  *                                                                TS101170
00044E F223 5523 5410   005D9 004C6   466 #$1PACK   PACK  #$1YR,YEAR                                         TS101180
                                      467  *                                                                TS101190
                                      468  *          EDIT YEAR VALUE FOR LOWER LIMIT VIOLATION             TS101200
                                      469  *                                                                TS101210
000454 F922 5523 555B   005D9 00611   470           CP    #$1YR,=P'1600'                                    TS101220
00045A 4720 53B2         00468        471           BH    #$1YRHI                                           TS101230
                                      472  *                                                                TS101240
                                      473  *          POST 'BAD YEAR' RETURN CODE AND EXIT                  TS101250
                                      474  *                                                                TS101260
00045E F800 540F 555E   004C5 00614   475 #$1BADYR  ZAP   CODE1,=P'4'                                        TS101270
000464 47F0 5534         005EA        476           B     #$1TERM                                            TS101280
                                      477  *                                                                TS101290
                                      478  *          EDIT YEAR VALUE FOR UPPER LIMIT VIOLATION             TS101300
                                      479  *                                                                TS101310
000468 F922 5523 555F   005D9 00615   480 #$1YRHI   CP    #$1YR,=P'3399'                                    TS101320
00046E 4720 53A8         0045E        481           BH    #$1BADYR                                           TS101330
                                      482  *                                                                TS101340
                                      483  *          +++   SECTION 4- DETERMINE LEAP YEAR STATUS  +++      TS101350
                                      484  *                                                                TS101360
                                      485  *          EXECUTE LEAP YEAR ALGORITHM                           TS101370
                                      486  *                                                                TS101380
000472 F800 540E 5559   004C4 0060F   487           ZAP   L,=P'0'                                            TS101390
000478 F842 5523 552E   005E4 005D9   488           ZAP   #$1WORK,#$1YR                                      TS101400
00047E FD40 552E 5532   005E4 00614   489           DP    #$1WORK,=P'4'                                      TS101410
000484 F900 5532 5559   005E8 0060F   490           CP    #$1WORK+4(1),=P'0'                                 TS101420
00048A 4720 5534         005EA        491           BH    #$1TERM                                            TS101430
00048E F842 5523 552E   005E4 005D9   492           ZAP   #$1WORK,#$1YR                                      TS101440
000494 FD41 5552 5531   005E4 00608   493           DP    #$1WORK,=P'100'                                    TS101450
00049A F910 5531 5559   005E7 0060F   494           CP    #$1WORK+3(2),=P'0'                                 TS101460
0004A0 4720 5404         004BA        495           BH    #$1LPYR                                            TS101470
0004A4 F842 5523 552E   005E4 005D9   496           ZAP   #$1WORK,#$1YR                                      TS101480
0004AA FD41 5552 5531   005E4 0060A   497           DP    #$1WORK,=P'400'                                    TS101490
0004B0 F910 5531 5559   005E7 0060F   498           CP    #$1WORK+3(2),=P'0'                                 TS101500
0004B6 4720 5534         005EA        499           BH    #$1TERM                                            TS101510
                                      500  *                                                                TS101520
                                      501  *          IF YEAR IS A LEAP YEAR, REINITIALIZE L TO 1           TS101530
                                      502  *          ELSE INITIALIZED O VALUE REMAINS                      TS101540
                                      503  *                                                                TS101550
0004BA F800 540E 5556   004C4 0060C   504 #$1LPYR   ZAP   L,=P'1'                                            TS101560
                                      505  *                                                                TS101570
                                      506  *          +++   SECTION 5- TO RESTORE REGISTERS AND EXIT  +++   TS101580
                                      507  *                                                                TS101590
0004C0 47F0 5534         005EA        508           B     #$1TERM                                            TS101600
                                      509  *                                                                TS101610
                                      510  *          +++   SECTION 6- DEFINE CONSTANTS AND STORAGE  +++    TS101620
                                      511  *                                                                TS101630
0004C4 9C                             512  L         DC    PL1'9'                                            TS101640
```

DOS/VSE ASSEMBLER 16.13 99-12-31

| LOC | OBJECT CODE | ADDR1 | ADDR2 | STMT | SOURCE STATEMENT | | | |
|---|---|---|---|---|---|---|---|---|
| 0004C5 | 4C | | | 513 | CODE1 | DC | PL1'4' | TS101650 |
| 0004C6 | F0F0F0C0 | | | 514 | YEAR | DC | ZL4'0' | TS101660 |
| | | | | 515 | * | | | TS101670 |
| | | | | 516 | * | | TRANSLATION TABLE DEFINED FOR X'F0' - X'F9' | TS101680 |
| | | | | 517 | * | | (ALL TABLE POSITIONS EXCEPT THOSE CORRESPONDING | TS101690 |
| | | | | 518 | * | | TO X'F0' THROUGH X'F9' ARE SET TO A VALUE OTHER | TS101700 |
| | | | | 519 | * | | THAN X'00') | TS101710 |
| | | | | 520 | * | | | TS101720 |
| 0004CA | 1C1C1C1C1C1C1C1C | | | 521 | #$1TABL | DC | 240X'1C' | TS101730 |
| 0005BA | 0000000000000000 | | | 522 | | DC | 10X'00' | TS101740 |
| 0005C4 | 1C1C1C1C1C | | | 523 | | DC | 6X'1C' | TS101750 |
| | | | | 524 | * | | | TS101760 |
| 0005CA | 0000000000000000 | | | 525 | #$1ZRO | DC | 10X'00' | TS101770 |
| 0005D4 | | | | 526 | #$1SIGN | DS | CL1 | TS101780 |
| 0005D5 | | | | 527 | #$1WORK4 | DS | ZL4 | TS101790 |
| 0005D9 | | | | 528 | #$1YR | DS | PL3 | TS101800 |
| 0005DC | | | | 529 | #$1RSAVE | DS | 2F | TS101810 |
| 0005E4 | | | | 530 | #$1WORK | DS | PL5 | TS101820 |
| 0005E9 | 00 | | | | | | | |
| 0005EA | 9812 5526 | | 005DC | 531 | #$1TERM | LM | 1,2,#$1RSAVE | TS101830 |
| 0005EE | 07F6 | | 000B4 | 532 | | BR | 6 | TS101840 |
| | | | | 533 | END | | BEGIN | |
| 0005F0 | 5B5BC2D6D7C5D540 | | | 534 | | | =C'$$BOPEN ' | |
| 0005F8 | 5B5BC2C3D3D6E2C5 | | | 535 | | | =C'$$BCLOSE' | |
| 000600 | 00000080 | | | 536 | | | =A(REQUEST) | |
| 000604 | 00000000 | | | 537 | | | =A(LIST) | |
| 000608 | 100C | | | 538 | | | =P'100' | |
| 00060A | 400C | | | 539 | | | =P'400' | |
| 00060C | 1C | | | 540 | | | =P'1' | |
| 00060D | 2C | | | 541 | | | =P'2' | |
| 00060E | F0 | | | 542 | | | =C'0' | |
| 00060F | 0C | | | 543 | | | =P'0' | |
| 000610 | 9C | | | 544 | | | =P'9' | |
| 000611 | 01600C | | | 545 | | | =P'1600' | |
| 000614 | 4C | | | 546 | | | =P'4' | |
| 000615 | 03399C | | | 547 | | | =P'3399' | |

Figure 2.1 *Continued*

RELOCATION DICTIONARY

99-12-31

| ESDID FOR ADDR CON | ESDID FOR REF SYMBOL | TYPE | LENGTH | ADDRESS |
|---|---|---|---|---|
| 001 | +001 | A | 4 | 000008 |
| 001 | +002 | V | 3 | 000011 |
| 001 | +001 | A | 4 | 000018 |
| 001 | +001 | CCW | 3 | 000029 |
| 001 | +001 | A | 4 | 000060 |
| 001 | +001 | A | 4 | 00007A |
| 001 | +001 | A | 4 | 00008C |
| 001 | +001 | A | 4 | 000098 |
| 001 | +001 | A | 4 | 0000C4 |
| 001 | +001 | A | 4 | 0000C8 |
| 001 | +001 | A | 4 | 0001DC |
| 001 | +001 | A | 4 | 000220 |
| 001 | +001 | A | 4 | 000600 |

DIAGNOSTICS AND STATISTICS

99-12-31

NO ERRORS FOUND

THE FOLLOWING MACRO NAMES HAVE BEEN FOUND IN MACRO INSTRUCTIONS
DTFPR    PRMOD    ACB      EXLST    RPL      OPEN     GET      CNTRL    PUT      PRTOV    CLOSE    EOJ      EXCP
WAIT     IKQERMAC IKQACB1  ISTACB1  IKQEXL1  ISTEXL1  IKQRPL1  ISTRPL1  BTWAIT   IKQACBG  IKQEXLG  IKQRPLG

OPTIONS FOR THIS ASSEMBLY - ALIGN, LIST, NOXREF, LINK, RLD, NODECK, NOEDECK

THE ASSEMBLER WAS RUN IN 524168 BYTES
END OF ASSEMBLY

Figure 2.1 *Continued*

```
TEST OF TIMESUB1 TO DETERMINE LEAP YEAR STATUS

1700 IS NOT A LEAP YEAR   CODE1 CONTENTS 0   L CONTENTS 0
1800 IS NOT A LEAP YEAR   CODE1 CONTENTS 0   L CONTENTS 0
1900 IS NOT A LEAP YEAR   CODE1 CONTENTS 0   L CONTENTS 1
2000 IS A LEAP YEAR       CODE1 CONTENTS 0   L CONTENTS 0
2100 IS NOT A LEAP YEAR   CODE1 CONTENTS 0   L CONTENTS 0
2200 IS NOT A LEAP YEAR   CODE1 CONTENTS 0   L CONTENTS 1
2300 IS NOT A LEAP YEAR   CODE1 CONTENTS 0   L CONTENTS 0
2400 IS A LEAP YEAR       CODE1 CONTENTS 0   L CONTENTS 0
2500 IS NOT A LEAP YEAR   CODE1 CONTENTS 0   L CONTENTS 0
2600 IS NOT A LEAP YEAR   CODE1 CONTENTS 0   L CONTENTS 1
2700 IS NOT A LEAP YEAR   CODE1 CONTENTS 0   L CONTENTS 0
2800 IS A LEAP YEAR       CODE1 CONTENTS 0   L CONTENTS 0
2900 IS NOT A LEAP YEAR   CODE1 CONTENTS 0   L CONTENTS 0
3000 IS NOT A LEAP YEAR   CODE1 CONTENTS 0   L CONTENTS 1
3100 IS NOT A LEAP YEAR   CODE1 CONTENTS 0   L CONTENTS 0
3200 IS A LEAP YEAR       CODE1 CONTENTS 0   L CONTENTS 0
3300 IS NOT A LEAP YEAR   CODE1 CONTENTS 0   L CONTENTS 1
3399 IS NOT A LEAP YEAR   CODE1 CONTENTS 0   L CONTENTS 0
1601 IS NOT A LEAP YEAR   CODE1 CONTENTS 0   L CONTENTS 0
1602 IS NOT A LEAP YEAR   CODE1 CONTENTS 0   L CONTENTS 0
1603 IS NOT A LEAP YEAR   CODE1 CONTENTS 0   L CONTENTS 0
1604 IS A LEAP YEAR       CODE1 CONTENTS 0   L CONTENTS 1
1605 IS NOT A LEAP YEAR   CODE1 CONTENTS 0   L CONTENTS 0
1606 IS NOT A LEAP YEAR   CODE1 CONTENTS 0   L CONTENTS 0
1607 IS NOT A LEAP YEAR   CODE1 CONTENTS 0   L CONTENTS 1
1608 IS A LEAP YEAR       CODE1 CONTENTS 0   L CONTENTS 0
1801 IS NOT A LEAP YEAR   CODE1 CONTENTS 0   L CONTENTS 0
1702 IS NOT A LEAP YEAR   CODE1 CONTENTS 0   L CONTENTS 1
1603 IS NOT A LEAP YEAR   CODE1 CONTENTS 0   L CONTENTS 0
1904 IS A LEAP YEAR       CODE1 CONTENTS 0   L CONTENTS 0
2105 IS NOT A LEAP YEAR   CODE1 CONTENTS 0   L CONTENTS 1
2706 IS NOT A LEAP YEAR   CODE1 CONTENTS 0   L CONTENTS 0
3117 IS NOT A LEAP YEAR   CODE1 CONTENTS 0   L CONTENTS 1
3308 IS A LEAP YEAR       CODE1 CONTENTS 0   L CONTENTS 0
1644 IS A LEAP YEAR       CODE1 CONTENTS 0   L CONTENTS 0
1789 IS NOT A LEAP YEAR   CODE1 CONTENTS 0   L CONTENTS 1
1984 IS A LEAP YEAR       CODE1 CONTENTS 0   L CONTENTS 1
2201 IS NOT A LEAP YEAR   CODE1 CONTENTS 0   L CONTENTS 0
2034 IS NOT A LEAP YEAR   CODE1 CONTENTS 0   L CONTENTS 0
1600 * INVALID YEAR       CODE1 CONTENTS 4   L CONTENTS 9
3400 * INVALID DATA       CODE1 CONTENTS 2   L CONTENTS 9
  19 * INVALID DATA       CODE1 CONTENTS 2   L CONTENTS 9
  95 * INVALID DATA       CODE1 CONTENTS 2   L CONTENTS 9

THE SUBROUTINE WAS EXECUTED    44 TIMES
```

**Figure 2.2** A subset of the test results produced during tests of the leap-year algorithm TIMESUB1.

Using TRT ensures the integrity of each subroutine. No input will result in a data check and abend.

Figure 2.2 shows the test results produced by the execution of TEST01. Although not shown in its entirety for the sake of space, the complete input set—1601 through 3399—was submitted during testing. TIMESUB1 is a valid algorithm.

# The Eight-Digit Date Puzzle

This chapter seeks to solve the problems associated with adequate database dates, storage reservation, date-structure limitations, reconciling diverse dating standards, and converting inadequate date data in existing databases.

## Defining the Central Problem

You've seen that continued computation with six-digit dates will ultimately lead to disastrous consequences. We must convert to using an eight-digit date in order to assure computational integrity. This raises questions regarding the adequacy of our existing peripheral and main-storage reservations. The minimum storage requirement for an eight-digit date in packed format is five bytes. Currently, dates occupy six bytes if stored in zoned decimal format. Even less storage is reserved for six-digit dates stored in packed decimal format—only four bytes. Clearly, a new date structure must be devised that can be accommodated in only four bytes of storage if our solution is to be universally applicable. Any less-stringent constraint won't offer a generally useful structure for eight digits of information without creating a need to reformat magnetic storage media. If it becomes necessary to reformat tape and disk storage, the main storage reserved in programs addressing these data sets will have to be modified as well. The programming task would be immense and costly.

The central problem is, then, how to go beyond the limitations of current date structures to create a new data form capable of conveying, through an equivalent, the needed eight digits of information but with a four-byte limitation.

## Defining the Secondary Problems

The problems of reconciling the currently existing diverse dating standards and converting the inadequate dating data in databases become quite tractable once the new data form exists. Whether in zoned decimal or packed format, three stored-date standards currently exist:

- Commercial, mm/dd/yy (most widely used in U.S. business)
- FIPS, yy/mm/dd (U.S. government standard)
- European, dd/mm/yy (common in Europe and Canada)

In all cases of six-digit date storage, the standard is known and the two-year digits represent a year of the 20th century. Where this is not true, you can perform record segregation in order to establish categorically pure data sets, i.e., data sets whose standard and century are known. The problem is then reduced to one of expanding the six-digit date to eight digits, converting it to the new four-byte form from its stored standard, and subsequently updating the element from which the six-digit image was accessed.

## A Two-Stage Solution Strategy

Having created a new form, the problem changes to one of creating algorithms to facilitate the solution of the secondary problems: reconciling diverse standards and converting existing data.

### Finding the new form

In seeking something new, we often simply remodel the past. The Julian date has long been popular in computer-operating system use. This familiar yy.ddd date was created from the two-digit year of the system's six-digit date with ddd, the three-digit ordinal day implied by the month and day values. The Julian date was used by operating systems in such activities as creation and data-set dating. Its chief virtue lies in the fact that it's in place value form and can be handily compared to other system-created Julian dates.

While the Julian date is rarely if ever retained in user database storage, it takes little imagination to visualize the five-digit date as it would appear in packed decimal format: YY DD DC. Because only three bytes are required, a modification offers our solution. A date two digits greater and of the form yyyy.ddd can be stored in packed decimal format in the four bytes to which we're limited: YY YY DD DC. Thus a new data form is created—a neo-Julian date we'll identify as Y.E in future references. Y is provided directly by the four-digit year; E is the ordinal day and is calculated from the eight-digit date's month and day values. Cumulative, monthly, day values can be obtained from a table. Hence the development of a neo-Julian date provides the data form needed to store the required additional information without disturbing existing storage layouts and so requiring extensive program modification.

### Designing the algorithms

It's clear that two algorithms are indicated. One algorithm must accept a six-digit date along with an indicator identifying the standard to which it conforms: Commercial,

FIPS, or European. Assuming that the input six-digit date is a date in the twentieth century, this algorithm must expand the date to eight digits, placed in commercial standard format. An eight-digit date is the output of the first algorithm. Because this algorithm is a utility, we'll name it TIMESUBF (F = format).

The other algorithm must accept an eight-digit date in commercial standard as its input. Using this input, the algorithm must compute as its output Y.E, the neo-Julian equivalent. Because little additional overhead is incurred by also creating a Julian date (yyddd) in this algorithm, it too can be an output for use in those instances where such a date is needed to interface with the operating system's Julian date. This algorithm will be called TIMESUB2.

Choosing the commercial standard for these algorithms establishes it as the standard for all eight-digit dates in this book. This is a practical choice since it conforms with business usage in the United States. If you want to continue to print or screen-display either FIPS or European standards, a facility to do so will be provided in a later chapter.

## Describing the Algorithm: TIMESUB2

To meet a primary requirement in algorithm development, you must first define the input values. You're now dealing with three different units of measurement: months, days, and years. Each must be defined individually. Because eight-digit Gregorian dates in commercial format are used frequently throughout this text, the following definition will hence be referred to as Commercial-8. Where M/D/Y is an eight-digit Gregorian date with M, D, and Y the month, day, and year respectively:

$$M \, \varepsilon \, \{m: m \text{ belongs to } Z \text{ and } 0 < m < 13\}$$

$$Y \, \varepsilon \, \{y: y \text{ belongs to } Z \text{ and } 1600 < y < 3400\}$$

Because Y implies a leap year status, you must also define L:

$$L = \begin{cases} 1, \text{ if Y is a leap year} \\ 0, \text{ if Y is a non-leap year} \end{cases}$$

and now D:

$$D \, \varepsilon \, \{d: d \text{ belongs to } Z \text{ and } 0 < d < 32\} \text{ and } \begin{cases} \text{If M = 4, 6, 9 or 11, } 0 < D < 31 \\ \text{If M = 2 and L = 1, } 0 < D < 30 \\ \text{If M = 2 and L = 0, } 0 < D < 29 \end{cases}$$

Here you can see double limits imposed on D. The secondary limits depend on M and L for their applicability.

Having defined Commercial-8, you can now define the neo-Julian output (Y.E) you're creating. Because the value of Y is output-unaltered, the previous definition of Y will suffice. E's value is then defined as such:

$$E \, \varepsilon \, \begin{cases} \text{If L = 1, } \{e: e \text{ belongs to } Z \text{ and } 0 < e < 367\} \\ \text{If L = 0, } \{e: e \text{ belongs to } Z \text{ and } 0 < e < 366\} \end{cases}$$

Because it's a truncated version of Y.E, the Julian date output by TIMESUB2 doesn't have to be defined. A return code designated as CODE2, however, must be defined:

$$CODE2 = \begin{cases} 0, \text{If M/D/Y is Commercial-8} \\ 2, \text{If M/D/Y is not valid numeric} \\ 4, \text{If Y } \varepsilon \text{ \{y: } 1600 < y < 3400\} \\ 6, \text{If M } \varepsilon \text{ \{m: } 0 < m < 13\} \\ 8, \text{If D } \varepsilon \text{ \{d\} as defined in Commercial-8} \end{cases}$$

Here you can see CODE2's information content:

$$CODE2 = \begin{cases} 0 = \text{Successful execution} \\ 2 = \text{Bad data} \\ 4 = \text{Bad year value} \\ 6 = \text{Bad month value} \\ 8 = \text{Bad day value} \end{cases}$$

## The Pseudocode for TIMESUB2

The pseudocode assumes that its input has been passed to it in the field DATEA. Access to each component M, D, and Y of the input is also assumed. In actual programming you might need to manipulate DATEA to gain such access. Further, the output fields JULIAN and NEOJUL are assumed to be three and four packed bytes, respectively. The input field DATEA is assumed to be eight zoned bytes. In order to identify the pseudocode's various tasks in data validation and computation, we'll interject comments. An asterisk (*) identifies a comment line.

```
     * Perform general housekeeping
 1) Let JULIAN = 0
 2) Let NEOJUL = 0
 3) Let CODE2 = 0
 4) Move DATEA to WORK8
     * Validate input data as numeric
 5) If WORK8 is numeric, go to 7
 6) Let CODE2 = 2, go to 19
     * Test Y for limit violation
 7) If Y is within limits per Commercial-8, go to 9
 8) Let CODE2 = 4, go to 19
     * Perform leap year algorithm for Y.
 9) Let L = 0
10) If Y is a leap year, let L = 1
     * Test M for limit violation
11) If M is within limits per Commercial-8, go to 13
12) Let CODE2 = 6, go to 19
     * Test D for limit violation
13) If D is within limits per Commercial-8, go to 15
14) Let CODE2 = 8, go to 19
     * Compute the ordinal day E, of Y.E
15) Let JULIAN = elapsed days through (M-1)
16) Let JULIAN = JULIAN + D
     * Construct output fields JULIAN and NEOJUL
17) Let JULIAN = JULIAN + 1000(Y(Mod 100))
18) Let NEOJUL = JULIAN(Mod 1000) + 1000Y
19) Exit
```

## The Source Programming Code for TIMESUB2

Figure 3.1 displays the TIMESUB2 portion of the assembly post listing of TEST02. The calling code, which is a variation of the code displayed for TEST01 in Figure 2.1 back in chapter 2, has been omitted to save space. Again, we encourage you to carefully review the introductory documentation. Non-assembly-language programmers will benefit from the in-code comments and the forthcoming discussion of the coding techniques. TIMESUB2 was tested using 1,096 consecutive dates: 01/01/1999 through 12/31/2001. Invalid dates and invalid data types covering the full spectrum of edit exceptions were added to this test data set. A subset of the test results is shown in Figure 3.2.

### Comments on the source code of TIMESUB2

The interjected comments of the pseudocode correspond to the numbered sections of the post listing's in-code comments. Beyond this, the actual implementation of each pseudocode instruction is language-dependent.

In order to fully exploit the facilities of ALC, three tables are employed. To enable the use of TRT in numeric validation and in editing M for limit violations, table #$2TABL is employed (see in-code sections 2 and 5). In editing D for maximum limit violations, table #$2DATAB is directly addressed with the binary equivalent of (M-1) as a displacement. Thus, for month 1, the displacement is zero and the first element of the table is addressed, and so on. The table elements are maximum day-values for months 1 through 12. Table #$2DAYS provides the elapsed day-counts as of the prior month's end. It's addressed directly, again using the displacement provided by binary (M-1). In this way you can compute the ordinal day by adding the table function to D. The value of L determines whether the leap-year or non-leap-year function is used.

Finally, the pseudocode instructions at steps 17 and 18 express the mathematical constructs of JULIAN and NEOJUL. ALC implementation via byte addressing allows for a literal translation of the mathematics involved. Other implementations of the pseudocode using other languages will be language-dependent and will reflect the strengths and weaknesses of the language chosen. In any event, the pseudocode leads to the desired result and allows for considerable latitude in the language chosen for implementation.

### Describing the Algorithm: TIMESUBF

Turning to TIMESUBF, the subroutine whose task it is to reconcile diverse dating standards and expand the six-digit input date to Commercial-8, you'll find a less than satisfying situation. Any attempt to define the input value of TIMESUBF will bring you face to face with the total inadequacy of the six-digit date. Because you can't adequately define the leap year status L, you can't define D. The six-digit date finds L = 1 for all centesimals, because 00 divided by 4 or 400 results in a zero remainder. Thus for M = 2, you can't determine an upper value for D. Consequently, you can define DATEF only as numeric.

DOS/VSE ASSEMBLER 16.15    99-12-31

```
LOC   OBJECT CODE   ADDR1 ADDR2   STMT   SOURCE STATEMENT

                                  374  *  ***************************************************
                                  375  *  *
                                  376  *  *
                                  377  *  *  TTTTTT  III  MM   MM  EEEEE  SSSSS  U   U  BBBBB   222
                                  378  *  *    T      I   M M M M  E      S      U   U  B   B      2
                                  379  *  *    T      I   M  M  M  EEEE   SSSS   U   U  BBB B      2
                                  380  *  *    T      I   M     M  E          S  U   U  B   B      2
                                  381  *  *    T     III  M     M  EEEEE  SSSSS  UUUUU  BBBB    2222
                                  382  *  *
                                  383  *  *
                                  384  *  *  G R E G O R I A N   T O   N E O - J U L I A N   S U B R O U T I N E
                                  385  *  *
                                  386  *  *
                                  387  *  *
                                  388  *  ***************************************************
                                  389  *     THIS SUBROUTINE CONVERTS GREGORIAN DATES TO NEO-JULIAN FORMAT
                                  390  *
                                  391  *     1.  VALID INPUT YEARS FOR THIS SUBROUTINE ARE THE YEARS
                                  392  *         1601 THROUGH 3399 A. D.
                                  393  *
                                  394  *     2.  VALID INPUT MONTH VALUES FOR THIS SUBROUTINE ARE 01
                                  395  *         THROUGH 12.
                                  396  *
                                  397  *     3.  VALID INPUT DAY VALUES FOR THIS SUBROUTINE ARE 01
                                  398  *         THROUGH 31 WITH EXCEPTIONS FOR THE MONTHS LISTED:
                                  399  *                  MONTH          MAXIMUM DAY VALUE
                                  400  *                   04              30
                                  401  *                   06              30
                                  402  *                   09              30
                                  403  *                   11              30
                                  404  *                   02              28
                                  405  *                   02 DURING LEAP YEAR   29
                                  406  *
                                  407  *     4.  THE DATE FORMAT MUST BE MMDDYYYY. WHERE MM = THE TWO
                                  408  *         DIGIT MONTH VALUE, DD = THE TWO DIGIT DAY VALUE AND
                                  409  *         YYYY = THE FOUR DIGIT YEAR.
                                  410  *
                                  411  *     5.  THE CALLING PROGRAM MUST PLACE THE EIGHT DIGIT DATE,
                                  412  *         IN ZONED DECIMAL, IN A SUBROUTINE DEFINED EIGHT BYTE
                                  413  *         FIELD, 'DATEA,' BEFORE EXECUTION OF THE SUBROUTINE.
                                  414  *         DATEA IS NOT ALTERED BY THE SUBROUTINE.
                                  415  *
                                  416  *     6.  A SUBROUTINE DEFINED ONE BYTE FIELD, 'CODE2,' IS RETURNED
                                  417  *         TO THE CALLING PROGRAM AND CONTAINS A PACKED 0 IF THE
                                  418  *         EXECUTION WAS SUCCESSFUL. NON-ZERO VALUES INDICATE
                                  419  *         THE FOLLOWING:
                                  420  *
                                  421  *         A PACKED 2 INDICATES UNSUCCESSFUL EXECUTION: INVALID DATA
                                  422  *         IN DATEA.
                                  423  *
                                  424  *         INVALID DATA ARE DETERMINED IF THE LOW ORDER BYTE'S ZONE
                                  425  *         CONTAINS AN INVALID SIGN, (AN INVALID SIGN IS OTHER THAN
                                  426  *         X'C', X'A', X'E', OR X'F'), OR IF THE PRECEDING BYTES'
                                  427  *         ZONES ARE OTHER THAN X'F', OR IF ANY BYTE'S LOW ORDER
                                  428  *         NIBBLE CONTAINS A VALUE GREATER THAN X'9'.
```

```
TS200010
TS200020
TS200030
TS200040
TS200050
TS200060
TS200070
TS200080
TS200090
TS200100
TS200110
TS200120
TS200130
TS200140
TS200150
TS200160
TS200170
TS200180
TS200190
TS200200
TS200210
TS200220
TS200230
TS200240
TS200250
TS200260
TS200270
TS200280
TS200290
TS200300
TS200310
TS200320
TS200330
TS200340
TS200350
TS200360
TS200370
TS200380
TS200390
TS200400
TS200410
TS200420
TS200430
TS200440
TS200450
TS200460
TS200470
TS200480
TS200490
TS200500
TS200510
TS200520
TS200530
TS200540
TS200550
```

```
LOC   OBJECT CODE   ADDR1 ADDR2   STMT   SOURCE STATEMENT                                        DOS/VSE ASSEMBLER 16.15  99-12-31

                                   429 * A PACKED 4 INDICATES UNSUCCESSFUL EXECUTION: INVALID YEAR                              * TS200560
                                   430 * VALUE IN DATEA- A VALUE THAT EXCEEDS THE LIMITS SPECIFIED                             * TS200570
                                   431 * IN 1.. ABOVE.                                                                        * TS200580
                                   432 *                                                                                      * TS200590
                                   433 *                                                                                      * TS200600
                                   434 * A PACKED 6 INDICATES UNSUCCESSFUL EXECUTION: INVALID                                  * TS200610
                                   435 * MONTH VALUE IN DATEA- A VALUE THAT EXCEEDS THE LIMITS                                 * TS200620
                                   436 * SPECIFIED IN 2.. ABOVE.                                                               * TS200630
                                   437 *                                                                                      * TS200640
                                   438 * A PACKED 8 INDICATES UNSUCCESSFUL EXECUTION: INVALID DAY                              * TS200650
                                   439 * VALUE IN DATEA- A VALUE THAT EXCEEDS THE LIMITS SPECIFIED                             * TS200660
                                   440 * IN 3.. ABOVE.                                                                        * TS200670
                                   441 *                                                                                      * TS200680
                                   442 * INSPECTION OF THE RETURN CODE IS IMPORTANT.  THE RETURN                               * TS200690
                                   443 * CODE, CODE2, REFLECTS THE LEVEL OF EDITING.  A RETURN                                 * TS200700
                                   444 * CODE OF 2, FOR EXAMPLE, NOT ONLY INDICATES INVALIDITY OF                              * TS200710
                                   445 * DATA, IT ALSO INDICATES THAT NO EDITING HAS BEEN DONE TO                              * TS200720
                                   446 * VALIDATE THE YEAR, MONTH OR DAY VALUES.  A RETURN CODE OF                             * TS200730
                                   447 * 4 INDICATES THAT THE DATA ARE VALID BUT THAT THE YEAR WAS                             * TS200740
                                   448 * FOUND INVALID- THE MONTH AND DAY VALUES HAVE NOT BEEN ED-                             * TS200750
                                   449 * ITED.  A RETURN CODE OF 6 INDICATES THAT THE DATA AND                                 * TS200760
                                   450 * YEAR ARE VALID BUT THAT THE MONTH IS INVALID- THE DAY                                 * TS200770
                                   451 * VALUE HAS NOT BEEN EDITED.  FINALLY, A RETURN CODE OF 8                               * TS200780
                                   452 * INDICATES THAT THE DATA, YEAR AND MONTH ARE VALID BUT                                 * TS200790
                                   453 * THAT THE DAY WAS FOUND INVALID FOR THE VALID MONTH GIVEN.                             * TS200800
                                   454 * IN SHORT, THE RETURN CODE INDICATES THE LEVEL OF EDITING.                             * TS200810
                                   455 * THE EDIT SEQUENCE IS DATA, YEAR, MONTH AND DAY.                                       * TS200820
                                   456 *                                                                                      * TS200830
                                   457 7. * A SUBROUTINE DEFINED THREE BYTE FIELD, 'JULIAN,' IS                                * TS200840
                                   458 * RETURNED TO THE CALLING PROGRAM.  THE JULIAN FORMAT DATE:                             * TS200850
                                   459 * YYDDD, IS CONTAINED IN THIS FIELD IN PACKED FORMAT.  HERE                             * TS200860
                                   460 * YY = THE LAST TWO DIGITS OF THE YEAR GIVEN IN THE GREG-                               * TS200870
                                   461 * ORIAN INPUT DATE.  DDD = THE THREE DIGIT NUMBER OF DAYS                               * TS200880
                                   462 * EXPIRED TO AND INCLUDING THE GREGORIAN INPUT DATE GIVEN.                              * TS200890
                                   463 * IF THE EXECUTION IS UNSUCCESSFUL, THAT IS, IF THE RETURN                              * TS200900
                                   464 * CODE FIELD, CODE2, CONTAINS A NON-ZERO VALUE, THEN                                    * TS200910
                                   465 * JULIAN WILL CONTAIN PACKED ZEROS.  THIS IS PROTECTION                                 * TS200920
                                   466 * AGAINST ILLEGAL USE OF A PRIOR EXECUTION'S RESULT.                                    * TS200930
                                   467 *                                                                                      * TS200940
                                   468 8. * A SUBROUTINE DEFINED FOUR BYTE FIELD, 'NEOJUL,' IS                                 * TS200950
                                   469 * RETURNED TO THE CALLING PROGRAM.  THE NEO-JULIAN DATE:                                * TS200960
                                   470 * YYYYDDD, IS CONTAINED IN THIS FIELD IN PACKED FORMAT.                                 * TS200970
                                   471 * HERE YYYY = THE FULL FOUR DIGITS OF THE YEAR GIVEN IN THE                             * TS200980
                                   472 * GREGORIAN INPUT DATE.  DDD = THE THREE DIGIT NUMBER OF                                * TS200990
                                   473 * DAYS EXPIRED TO AND INCLUDING THE GREGORIAN INPUT DATE                                * TS201000
                                   474 * GIVEN.  IF THE EXECUTION IS UNSUCCESSFUL, THAT IS, IF THE                             * TS201010
                                   475 * RETURN CODE FIELD, CODE2, CONTAINS A NON-ZERO VALUE, THEN                             * TS201020
                                   476 * NEOJUL WILL CONTAIN PACKED ZEROS.  THIS IS PROTECTION                                 * TS201030
                                   477 * AGAINST ILLEGAL USE OF A PRIOR EXECUTION'S RESULT.                                    * TS201040
                                   478 *                                                                                      * TS201050
                                   479 9. * ALL OTHER SUBROUTINE DEFINED FIELDS AND LABELS ARE                                 * TS201060
                                   480 * TRANSPARENT TO THE CALLING PROGRAM.                                                   * TS201070
                                   481 *                                                                                      * TS201080
                                   482 10. * THIS SUBROUTINE IS WRITTEN TO BE ASSEMBLED WITH THE                              * TS201090
                                   483 * CALLING PROGRAM AND SHOULD BE INSERTED IN THE CALLING                                 * TS201100
```

**Figure 3.1**  The TIMESUB2 portion of the assembly post listing of TEST02, displaying introductory documentation.

```
LOC    OBJECT CODE       ADDR1 ADDR2   STMT  SOURCE STATEMENT                                    DOS/VSE ASSEMBLER 16.15   99-12-31

                                        484  *                                                                                    * TS201110
                                        485  *      PROGRAM IMMEDIATELY BEFORE THE 'END' OPCODE.                                   * TS201120
                                        486  * 11.  THIS SUBROUTINE USES REGISTER 6 AS THE LINK REGISTER.                         * TS201130
                                        487  *      IF REGISTER 6 IS ASSIGNED IN THE CALLING PROGRAM FOR                          * TS201140
                                        488  *      OTHER USES, IT MUST BE SAVED PRIOR TO EXECUTING THE                           * TS201150
                                        489  *      'BALR.'                                                                       * TS201160
                                        490  *                                                                                    * TS201170
                                        491  *                                     JEROME T. MURRAY                               * TS201180
                                        492  *                                     MARILYN J. MURRAY                              * TS201190
                                        493  *  GLEN ELLYN, ILLINOIS                                                              * TS201200
                                        494  *  **************************************************                                 TS201210
                                        495  *  **************************************************                                 TS201220
                                        496  *  **************************************************                                 TS201230
                                        497  *  **************************************************                                 TS201240
                                        498  *  **************************************************                                 TS201250
                                        499  *                                                                                      TS201260
                                        500  *      +++  SECTION 1- GENERAL HOUSEKEEPING  +++                                       TS201270
                                        501  *                                                                                      TS201280
                                        502  *              INITIALIZE INDICATIVE FIELDS                                            TS201290
                                        503  *                                                                                      TS201300
000454 F820 753C 7760   005F2 00816     504  TIMESUB2 ZAP   JULIAN,=P'0'                                                           TS201310
00045A F830 753F 7760   005F5 00816     505           ZAP   NEQJUL,=P'0'                                                           TS201320
000460 F800 7543 7760   005F9 00816     506           ZAP   CODE2,=P'0'                                                            TS201330
                                        507  *                                                                                      TS201340
                                        508  *              SAVE REGISTERS 1 THROUGH 5 IN SAVE FIELDS                               TS201350
                                        509  *                                                                                      TS201360
000466 9015 76D2         00788          510           STM   1,5,#$2RSAVE                                                           TS201370
                                        511  *                                                                                      TS201380
                                        512  *              MOVE DATE TO WORK FIELD AND ISOLATE SIGN                                TS201390
                                        513  *                                                                                      TS201400
00046A D207 76BA 7544   00770 005FA     514           MVC   #$2WORK8,DATEA                                                         TS201410
000470 D200 76BB 76C1   0076E 00777     515           MVC   #$2SIGN,#$2WORK8+7                                                     TS201420
                                        516  *                                                                                      TS201430
                                        517  *      +++   SECTION 2- NUMERIC VALIDATION   +++                                       TS201440
                                        518  *                                                                                      TS201450
                                        519  *              AUGMENT TABLE FOR VALID '+' SIGNS OTHER THAN                            TS201460
                                        520  *              X'F' FOR WHICH TABLE IS DEFINED: X'A', X'C',                            TS201470
                                        521  *              X'E'- EDIT FOR VALID '+' SIGN USING TRT                                 TS201480
                                        522  *                                                                                      TS201490
000476 D209 764C 76AC   00762 00762     523           MVC   #$2TABL+160(10),#$2ZR0                                                 TS201500
00047C D209 766C 76AC   00722 00762     524           MVC   #$2TABL+192(10),#$2ZR0                                                 TS201510
000482 D209 768C 76AC   00742 00762     525           MVC   #$2TABL+224(10),#$2ZR0                                                 TS201520
000488 DD00 76B8 75AC   0076E 00662     526           TRT   #$2SIGN(1),#$2TABL                                                     TS201530
00048E 4780 73E0         004A6          527           BC    8,#$2NUM                                                               TS201540
000492 47F0 73F0         004B0          528           B     #$2BDATA                                                              TS201550
                                        529  *                                                                                      TS201560
                                        530  *              REINITIALIZE TABLE AND EDIT FOR VALID ZONE                             TS201570
                                        531  *              AND DIGIT CONFIGURATIONS IN REMAINING BYTES                            TS201580
                                        532  *                                                                                      TS201590
000496 D2EE 75AD 75AC   00663 00662     533  #$2NUM   MVC   #$2TABL+1(239),#$2TABL                                                 TS201600
00049C DD06 76BA 75AC   00662 00662     534           TRT   #$2WORK8(7),#$2TABL                                                    TS201610
0004A2 4780 73FA         004B0          535           BC    8,#$2PACK                                                              TS201620
                                        536  *                                                                                      TS201630
                                        537  *              POST 'BAD DATA' RETURN CODE AND EXIT                                    TS201640
                                        538  *                                                                                      TS201650
```

```
                                                                DOS/VSE ASSEMBLER 16.15  99-12-31

LOC    OBJECT CODE    ADDR1 ADDR2  STMT  SOURCE STATEMENT

0004A6 F800 7543 7761 005F9 00817  539  #$2BDATA ZAP   CODE2,=P'2'                                          TS201670
0004AC 47F0 76F2            007A8  540           B     #$2TERM                                              TS201680
                                   541  *                                                                   TS201690
                                   542  *                                                                   TS201700
                                   543  *     +++  SECTION 3- EDIT YEAR FOR LIMIT VIOLATIONS  +++           TS201710
                                   544  *                                                                   TS201720
                                   545  *     PACK MONTH, DAY AND YEAR IN WORK FIELDS                       TS201730
0004B0 F211 76C2 76BA 00778 00770  546  #$2PACK  PACK  #$2MO,#$2WORK8(2)                                    TS201740
0004B6 F211 76C4 76BC 0077A 00772  547           PACK  #$2DA,#$2WORK8+2(2)                                  TS201750
0004BC F223 76C6 76BE 0077C 00774  548           PACK  #$2YR,#$2WORK8+4(4)                                  TS201760
                                   549  *                                                                   TS201770
                                   550  *     EDIT YEAR VALUE FOR LOWER LIMIT VIOLATION                     TS201780
                                   551  *                                                                   TS201790
0004C2 F922 76C6 77B7 0077C 0086D  552           CP    #$2YR,=P'1600'                                       TS201800
0004C8 4720 7420            004D6  553           BH    #$2YRHI                                              TS201810
                                   554  *                                                                   TS201820
                                   555  *     POST 'BAD YEAR' RETURN CODE AND EXIT                          TS201830
                                   556  *                                                                   TS201840
0004CC F800 7543 7762 005F9 00818  557  #$2BADYR ZAP   CODE2,=P'4'                                          TS201850
0004D2 47F0 76F2            007A8  558           B     #$2TERM                                              TS201860
                                   559  *                                                                   TS201870
                                   560  *     EDIT YEAR VALUE FOR UPPER LIMIT VIOLATION                     TS201880
                                   561  *                                                                   TS201890
0004D6 F922 76C6 77BA 0077C 00870  562  #$2YRHI  CP    #$2YR,=P'3399'                                       TS201900
0004DC 4720 76CC            004CC  563           BH    #$2BADYR                                             TS201910
                                   564  *                                                                   TS201920
                                   565  *     +++  SECTION 4- DETERMINE LEAP YEAR STATUS  +++               TS201930
                                   566  *                                                                   TS201940
                                   567  *     EXECUTE LEAP YEAR ALGORITHM                                   TS201950
                                   568  *                                                                   TS201960
0004E0 F800 76B9      0076F 00816  569           ZAP   #$2L,=P'0'                                           TS201970
0004E6 F842 76C6      0077F 0077C  570           ZAP   #$2WORK,=#$2YR                                       TS201980
0004EC FD40 76C9 76C9 0077F 00818  571           DP    #$2WORK,=P'4'                                        TS201990
0004F2 F900 76CD 7783 00783 00816  572           CP    #$2WORK+4(1),=P'0'                                   TS202000
0004F8 4720 7478      0052E        573           BH    #$2MOEDT                                             TS202010
0004FC F842 76C9      0077F 0077C  574           ZAP   #$2WORK,=#$2YR                                       TS202020
000502 FD41 76C9 7758 0077F 0080E  575           DP    #$2WORK,=P'100'                                      TS202030
000508 F910 76CC 7760 00782 00816  576           CP    #$2WORK+3(2),=P'0'                                   TS202040
00050E 4720 7472      00528        577           BH    #$2LPYR                                              TS202050
000512 F842 76C9      0077F 0077C  578           ZAP   #$2WORK,=#$2YR                                       TS202060
000518 FD41 76C9 775A 0077F 00810  579           DP    #$2WORK,=P'400'                                      TS202070
00051E F910 76CC 7760 00782 00816  580           CP    #$2WORK+3(2),=P'0'                                   TS202080
000524 4720 7478      0052E        581           BH    #$2MOEDT                                             TS202090
                                   582  *                                                                   TS202100
                                   583  *     IF YEAR IS A LEAP YEAR, SET INCREMENT TO 1                    TS202110
                                   584  *     ELSE INITIALIZED VALUE WILL REMAIN: 0                         TS202120
                                   585  *                                                                   TS202130
000528 F800 76B9 775E 0076F 00814  586  #$2LPYR  ZAP   #$2L,=P'1'                                           TS202140
                                   587  *                                                                   TS202150
                                   588  *     +++  SECTION 5- EDIT MONTH FOR LIMIT VIOLATIONS  +++          TS202160
                                   589  *                                                                   TS202170
                                   590  *     VERIFY THAT MONTH IS WITHIN RANGE: 1 - 12                     TS202180
                                   591  *     A) CONVERT MONTH TO BINARY IN REGISTER 3                      TS202190
                                   592  *                                                                   TS202200
00052E F871 76EA 76C2 007A0 00778  593  #$2MOEDT ZAP   #$2CVB,#$2MO
```

**Figure 3.1** *Continued*

DOS/VSE ASSEMBLER 16.15  99-12-31

| LOC | OBJECT CODE | ADDR1 | ADDR2 | STMT | SOURCE STATEMENT | |
|---|---|---|---|---|---|---|
| 000534 | 4F30 76EA | | 007A0 | 594 | CVB | 3,#$2CVB | TS202210 |
| | | | | 595 | * | | TS202220 |
| | | | | 596 | * | B) STORE BINARY BYTE FROM REG 3 IN #$2FLD | TS202230 |
| | | | | 597 | * | | TS202240 |
| 000538 | 4230 76CE | | 00784 | 598 | STC | 3,#$2FLD | TS202250 |
| | | | | 599 | * | | TS202260 |
| | | | | 600 | * | C) INITIALIZE TABLE WITH X'00' FOR TRT | TS202270 |
| | | | | 601 | * | | TS202280 |
| 00053C | D20B 75AD 76AC | 00663 | 00762 | 602 | MVC | #$2TABL+1(12),#$2ZRO | TS202290 |
| | | | | 603 | * | | TS202300 |
| | | | | 604 | * | D) EXECUTE TRT USING #$2FLD | TS202310 |
| | | | | 605 | * | | TS202320 |
| 000542 | DD00 76CE 75AC | 00784 | 00662 | 606 | TRT | #$2FLD(1),#$2TABL | TS202330 |
| 000548 | 4780 74A6 | | 0055C | 607 | BC | 8,#$2DAEDT | TS202340 |
| | | | | 608 | * | | TS202350 |
| | | | | 609 | * | F) RESTORE TABLE - POST BAD MONTH RETURN CODE | TS202360 |
| | | | | 610 | * | | TS202370 |
| 00054C | D20B 75AC 00663 | | 00662 | 611 | MVC | #$2TABL+1(12),#$2TABL | TS202380 |
| 000552 | F800 7543 7763 | 005F9 | 00819 | 612 | ZAP | CODE2,=P'6' | TS202390 |
| 000558 | 47F0 76F2 | | 007A8 | 613 | B | #$2TERM | TS202400 |
| | | | | 614 | * | | TS202410 |
| | | | | 615 | * | +++ SECTION 6- EDIT DAY FOR LIMIT VIOLATIONS +++ | TS202420 |
| | | | | 616 | * | | TS202430 |
| | | | | 617 | * | RESTORE TABLE | TS202440 |
| | | | | 618 | * | | TS202450 |
| 00055C | D20B 75AD 76AC | 00663 | 00662 | 619 | #$2DAEDT MVC | #$2TABL+1(12),#$2TABL | TS202460 |
| | | | | 620 | * | | TS202470 |
| | | | | 621 | * | GET ADDRESS OF DAY TABLE IN REGISTER 4 | TS202480 |
| | | | | 622 | * | | TS202490 |
| 000562 | 4140 754C | | 00602 | 623 | LA | 4,#$2DATAB | TS202500 |
| | | | | 624 | * | | TS202510 |
| | | | | 625 | * | IF LEAP YEAR, INCREMENT TO LEAP YEAR FUNCTION | TS202520 |
| | | | | 626 | * | | TS202530 |
| 000566 | F900 76B9 7760 | 0076F | 00816 | 627 | CP | #$2L,=P'0' | TS202540 |
| 00056C | 4780 74BE | | 00574 | 628 | BE | #$2NOL | TS202550 |
| 000570 | 4144 0002 | | 00002 | 629 | LA | 4,2(4) | TS202560 |
| | | | | 630 | * | | TS202570 |
| | | | | 631 | * | DIRECTLY ADDRESS TABLE DAY LIMIT FOR THIS MONTH | TS202580 |
| | | | | 632 | * | A) SUBTRACT 1 FROM BINARY MONTH VALUE IN REG 3 | TS202590 |
| | | | | 633 | * | | TS202600 |
| 000574 | 0630 | | | 634 | #$2NOL BCTR | 3,0 | TS202610 |
| | | | | 635 | * | | TS202620 |
| | | | | 636 | * | B) MULTIPLY VALUE IN REG 3 BY 4 | TS202630 |
| | | | | 637 | * | | TS202640 |
| 000576 | 8930 0002 | | 00002 | 638 | SLL | 3,2 | TS202650 |
| | | | | 639 | * | | TS202660 |
| | | | | 640 | * | C) LOAD ADDRESS OF DAY TABLE ENTRY IN REG 4 | TS202670 |
| | | | | 641 | * | | TS202680 |
| 00057A | 4143 4000 | | 00000 | 642 | LA | 4,0(3,4) | TS202690 |
| | | | | 643 | * | | TS202700 |
| | | | | 644 | * | CONVERT SIGN OF PACKED DAY FROM X'F' TO X'C' | TS202710 |
| | | | | 645 | * | | TS202720 |
| 00057E | F811 76C4 76C4 | 0077A | 0077A | 646 | ZAP | #$2DA,#$2DA | TS202730 |
| | | | | 647 | * | | TS202740 |
| | | | | 648 | * | COMPARE DAY TABLE ENTRY (LIMIT) WITH INPUT DAY | TS202750 |

```
                                        DOS/VSE ASSEMBLER 16.15  99-12-31

LOC    OBJECT CODE      ADDR1 ADDR2  STMT  SOURCE STATEMENT

                                     649  *                                                          TS202760
000584 D501 76C4 4000   0077A 00000  650        CLC   #$2DA,O(4)                                     TS202770
                                     651  *                                                          TS202780
                                     652  *      IF INPUT IS WITHIN LIMIT, EDIT DAY FOR ZERO         TS202790
                                     653  *                                                          TS202800
00058A 47D0 74E2        00598        654        BNH   #$2DALO                                        TS202810
                                     655  *                                                          TS202820
                                     656  *      ELSE POST BAD DAY RETURN CODE AND EXIT              TS202830
                                     657  *                                                          TS202840
00058E F800 7543 7771   005F9 007A8  658  #$2BADA ZAP  CODE2,=P'8'                                   TS202850
000594 47F0 76F2        007A8        659        B     #$2TERM                                        TS202860
                                     660  *                                                          TS202870
                                     661  *      EDIT DAY VALUE FOR ZERO                             TS202880
                                     662  *                                                          TS202890
000598 F911 76C4 775C   0077A 00812  663  #$2DALO CP   #$2DA,=P'00'                                  TS202900
00059E 4780 74D8        0058E        664        BE    #$2BADA                                        TS202910
                                     665  *                                                          TS202920
                                     666  *      +++  SECTION 7- COMPUTE ORDINAL DAY  +++           TS202930
                                     667  *                                                          TS202940
                                     668  *      FIRST, COMPUTE ELAPSED DAYS THIS YEAR TO MONTH     TS202950
                                     669  *                                                          TS202960
                                     670  *      DIRECTLY ADDRESS ELAPSED DAY TABLE THIS MONTH      TS202970
                                     671  *      A) LOAD ADDRESS OF DAYS TABLE IN REGISTER 5        TS202980
                                     672  *                                                          TS202990
0005A2 4150 757C        00632        673        LA    5,#$2DAYS                                      TS203000
                                     674  *                                                          TS203010
                                     675  *      B) IF LEAP YEAR, INCREMENT TO LEAP YEAR            TS203020
                                     676  *         FUNCTION                                         TS203030
                                     677  *                                                          TS203040
0005A6 F900 76B9 7760   0076F 00816  678        CP    #$2L,=P'O'                                     TS203050
0005AC 4780 74FE        005B4        679        BE    #$2NOLL                                        TS203060
0005B0 4155 0002        00002        680        LA    5,2(5)                                         TS203070
                                     681  *                                                          TS203080
                                     682  *      C) LOAD ADDRESS OF TABLE ELEMENT IN REGISTER 5     TS203090
                                     683  *         (REG 3 CONTAINS CONVERTED MONTH VALUE)          TS203100
                                     684  *                                                          TS203110
0005B4 4153 5000        00000        685  #$2NOLL LA   5,O(3,5)                                      TS203120
                                     686  *                                                          TS203130
                                     687  *      ADD DIRECTLY ADDRESSED ELAPSED DAYS TO OUTPUT      TS203140
                                     688  *         FIELD                                            TS203150
                                     689  *                                                          TS203160
0005B8 F821 753C 5000   005F2 00000  690        ZAP   JULIAN,O(2,5)                                  TS203170
                                     691  *                                                          TS203180
                                     692  *      SECOND, ADD INPUT DAY TO OUTPUT FIELD              TS203190
                                     693  *                                                          TS203200
0005BE FA21 753C 76C4   005F2 0077A  694        AP    JULIAN,#$2DA                                   TS203210
                                     695  *                                                          TS203220
                                     696  *      +++  SECTION 8- CONSTRUCT OUTPUT DATES  +++        TS203230
                                     697  *                                                          TS203240
                                     698  *      CONSTRUCT YYDDD JULIAN FORMAT DATE                 TS203250
                                     699  *                                                          TS203260
                                     700  *                                                          TS203270
0005C4 F241 76C9 76C0   0077F 00776  701        PACK  #$2WORK,#$2WORK8+6(2)                          TS203280
0005CA FC42 76C9 77BD   0077F 00873  702        MP    #$2WORK,=P'1000'                               TS203290
0005D0 FA22 753C 76CB   005F2 00781  703        AP    JULIAN,#$2WORK+2(3)                            TS203300
```

Figure 3.1 *Continued*

DOS/VSE ASSEMBLER 16.15    99-12-31

```
LOC    OBJECT CODE       ADDR1 ADDR2  STMT  SOURCE STATEMENT

                                      704  *
                                      705  *                CONSTRUCT YYYYDDD NEO-JULIAN FORMAT DATE       TS203310
                                      706  *                                                               TS203320
0005D6 F273 76BA 76BE   00770 00774   707         PACK  #$2WORK8,#$2WORK8+4(4)                             TS203330
0005DC FC72 77BD        00770 00873   708         MP    #$2WORK8,=P'1000'                                  TS203340
0005E2 F833 753F 76BE   005F5 00774   709         ZAP   NEOJUL,#$2WORK8+4(4)                               TS203350
0005E8 FA31 753D        005F5 005F3   710         AP    NEOJUL,JULIAN+1(2)                                 TS203360
                                      711  *                                                               TS203370
                                      712  *       +++  SECTION 9- TO RESTORE REGISTERS AND EXIT  +++      TS203380
                                      713  *                                                               TS203390
0005EE 47F0 76F2         007A8        714         B     #$2TERM                                            TS203400
                                      715  *                                                               TS203410
                                      716  *       +++  SECTION 10- DEFINE CONSTANTS AND STORAGE  +++      TS203420
                                      717  *                                                               TS203430
0005F2 00000C                         718  JULIAN  DC    PL3'0'                                             TS203440
0005F5 0000000C                       719  NEOJUL  DC    PL4'0'                                             TS203450
0005F9 4C                             720  CODE2   DC    PL1'4'                                             TS203460
0005FA F0F0F0F0F0F0F0C0               721  DATEA   DC    ZL8'00000000'                                     TS203470
                                      722  *                                                               TS203480
                                      723  *       THE DAY TABLE IS DEFINED WITH A PAIR OF TWO BYTE        TS203490
                                      724  *       ENTRIES FOR EACH OF THE 12 MONTHS- AN ENTRY FOR         TS203500
                                      725  *       NON-LEAP YEAR AND AN ENTRY FOR LEAP YEAR                TS203510
                                      726  *                                                               TS203520
000602 031C031C                       727  #$2DATAB DC   PL2'31',PL2'31'       JAN                         TS203530
000606 028C029C                       728          DC    PL2'28',PL2'29'       FEB                         TS203540
00060A 031C031C                       729          DC    PL2'31',PL2'31'       MAR                         TS203550
00060E 030C030C                       730          DC    PL2'30',PL2'30'       APR                         TS203560
000612 031C031C                       731          DC    PL2'31',PL2'31'       MAY                         TS203570
000616 030C030C                       732          DC    PL2'30',PL2'30'       JUN                         TS203580
00061A 031C031C                       733          DC    PL2'31',PL2'31'       JUL                         TS203590
00061E 031C031C                       734          DC    PL2'31',PL2'31'       AUG                         TS203600
000622 030C030C                       735          DC    PL2'30',PL2'30'       SEP                         TS203610
000626 031C031C                       736          DC    PL2'31',PL2'31'       OCT                         TS203620
00062A 030C030C                       737          DC    PL2'30',PL2'30'       NOV                         TS203630
00062E 031C031C                       738          DC    PL2'31',PL2'31'       DEC                         TS203640
                                      739  *                                                               TS203650
                                      740  *       THE DAYS TABLE IS DEFINED WITH A PAIR OF TWO            TS203660
                                      741  *       BYTE ENTRIES FOR EACH OF THE 12 MONTHS CONTAIN-         TS203670
                                      742  *       ING THE CUMULATIVE NUMBER OF DAYS EXPIRED AT            TS203680
                                      743  *       THE END OF THE PRIOR MONTH- NON-LEAP YEAR AND           TS203690
                                      744  *       LEAP YEAR                                               TS203700
                                      745  *                                                               TS203710
000632 000C000C                       746  #$2DAYS DC    PL2'00',PL2'00'       JAN                         TS203720
000636 031C031C                       747          DC    PL2'31',PL2'31'       FEB                         TS203730
00063A 059C060C                       748          DC    PL2'59',PL2'60'       MAR                         TS203740
00063E 090C091C                       749          DC    PL2'90',PL2'91'       APR                         TS203750
000642 120C121C                       750          DC    PL2'120',PL2'121'     MAY                         TS203760
000646 151C152C                       751          DC    PL2'151',PL2'152'     JUN                         TS203770
00064A 181C182C                       752          DC    PL2'181',PL2'182'     JUL                         TS203780
00064E 212C213C                       753          DC    PL2'212',PL2'213'     AUG                         TS203790
000652 243C244C                       754          DC    PL2'243',PL2'244'     SEP                         TS203800
000656 273C274C                       755          DC    PL2'273',PL2'274'     OCT                         TS203810
00065A 304C305C                       756          DC    PL2'304',PL2'305'     NOV                         TS203820
00065E 334C335C                       757          DC    PL2'334',PL2'335'     DEC                         TS203830
                                      758  *                                                               TS203840
                                                                                                           TS203850
```

```
LOC     OBJECT CODE       ADDR1 ADDR2  STMT  SOURCE STATEMENT        DOS/VSE ASSEMBLER 16.15  99-12-31

                                        759  *                                                          TS203860
                                        760  *     TRANSLATION TABLE DEFINED FOR X'F0' - X'F9'          TS203870
                                        761  *     (ALL TABLE POSITIONS EXCEPT THOSE CORRESPONDING      TS203880
                                        762  *     TO X'F0' THROUGH X'F9' ARE SET TO A VALUE OTHER      TS203890
                                        763  *     THAN X'00')                                          TS203900
000662 1C1C1C1C1C1C1C1C                 764  #$2TABL  DC   240X'1C'                                     TS203910
000752 0000000000000000                 765           DC   10X'00'                                      TS203920
00075C 1C1C1C1C1C                       766           DC   6X'1C'                                        TS203930
                                        767  *                                                          TS203940
000762 0000000000000000                 768  #$2R0    DC   12X'00'                                      TS203950
00076E                                  769  #$2SIGN  DS   ZL1                                          TS203960
00076F                                  770  #$2L     DS   PL1                                          TS203970
000770                                  771  #$2WORK8 DS   CL8                                          TS203980
000778                                  772  #$2MO    DS   PL2                                          TS203990
00077A                                  773  #$2DA    DS   PL2                                          TS204000
00077C                                  774  #$2YR    DS   PL3                                          TS204010
00077F                                  775  #$2WORK  DS   PL5                                          TS204020
000784                                  776  #$2FLD   DS   CL1                                          TS204030
000788                                  777  #$2RSAVE DS   5F                                           TS204040
000788                                  778  #$2CVB   DS   1D                                           TS204050
0007A8 9815 76D2            00788       779  #$2TERM  LM   1,5,#$2RSAVE                                  TS204060
0007AC 07F6                             780           BR   6                                            TS204070
                                        781           END                                              
0007B0 5B5B8C2D6D7C5D540    000B4       782  BEGIN  =C'$$BDOPEN ,'
0007B8 E2E4C2D9D6E4E3C9                 783         =C'SUBROUTINE ERROR'
0007C8 C3D6D5E5C5D9E3E2                 784         =C'CONVERTS TO JULIAN DATE:'
0007E0 5B5B8C2C3D3D6D62C5               785         =C'$$BCLOSE'
0007E8 00000080                         786         =A(REQUEST)
0007EC 00000000                         787         =A(LIST)
0007F0 C9D5E5C1D3C9C440                 788         =C'INVALID DATA'
0007FC C9D5E5C1D3C9C440                 789         =C'INVALID YEAR'
000808 6B4C4C4C1E840                    790         =C', DAY ,'
00080E 100C                             791         =P'100'
000810 400C                             792         =P'400'
000812 000C                             793         =P'00'
000814 1C                               794         =P'1'
000815 61                               795         =C'/'
000816 0C                               796         =P'0'
000817 2C                               797         =P'2'
000818 4C                               798         =P'4'
000819 6C                               799         =P'6'
00081A C9D5E5C1D3C9C440                 800         =C'INVALID MONTH'
000827 8C                               801         =P'8'
000828 C9D5E5C1D3C9C440                 802         =C'INVALID DAY'
000833 F0                               803         =C'0'
000834 4B                               804         =C'.'
000835 D5C5D66D01E4D3C9                 805         =C'NEO-JULIAN DATE'
000844 6B                               806         =C','
000845 C3D6C4C5F24CC3D6                 807         =C'CODE2 CONTENTS:'
000854 C3D6D4D7D6D5C5D5                 808         =C'COMPONENT CONTENTS- YEAR '
00086D 0160OC                           809         =P'1600'
000870 03399C                           810         =P'3399'
000873 01000C                           811         =P'1000'
```

**Figure 3.1** *Continued*

```
TEST OF TIMESUB2  -  GREGORIAN  TO  NEO-JULIAN

AK/BI/JRQO   INVALID DATA                          CODE2 CONTENTS: 2                                   COMPONENT CONTENTS- YEAR 0000, DAY 000
)8/-%/$#@U   INVALID DATA                          CODE2 CONTENTS: 2                                   COMPONENT CONTENTS- YEAR 0000, DAY 000
01/01/1600   INVALID YEAR                          CODE2 CONTENTS: 4                                   COMPONENT CONTENTS- YEAR 0000, DAY 000
01/31/1601   CONVERTS TO JULIAN DATE:  01.031,     CODE2 CONTENTS: 0.   NEO-JULIAN DATE 1601.031,      COMPONENT CONTENTS- YEAR 1601, DAY 031
02/29/1602   INVALID DAY                           CODE2 CONTENTS: 8                                   COMPONENT CONTENTS- YEAR 0000, DAY 000
12/28/1603   CONVERTS TO JULIAN DATE:  03.362,     CODE2 CONTENTS: 0.   NEO-JULIAN DATE 1603.362,      COMPONENT CONTENTS- YEAR 1603, DAY 362
03/31/1604   CONVERTS TO JULIAN DATE:  04.091,     CODE2 CONTENTS: 0.   NEO-JULIAN DATE 1604.091,      COMPONENT CONTENTS- YEAR 1604, DAY 091
04/30/1605   CONVERTS TO JULIAN DATE:  05.120,     CODE2 CONTENTS: 0.   NEO-JULIAN DATE 1605.120,      COMPONENT CONTENTS- YEAR 1605, DAY 120
05/31/1606   CONVERTS TO JULIAN DATE:  06.151,     CODE2 CONTENTS: 0.   NEO-JULIAN DATE 1606.151,      COMPONENT CONTENTS- YEAR 1606, DAY 151
06/30/1607   CONVERTS TO JULIAN DATE:  07.181,     CODE2 CONTENTS: 0.   NEO-JULIAN DATE 1607.181,      COMPONENT CONTENTS- YEAR 1607, DAY 181
07/31/1608   CONVERTS TO JULIAN DATE:  08.213,     CODE2 CONTENTS: 0.   NEO-JULIAN DATE 1608.213,      COMPONENT CONTENTS- YEAR 1608, DAY 213
08/31/1609   CONVERTS TO JULIAN DATE:  09.243,     CODE2 CONTENTS: 0.   NEO-JULIAN DATE 1609.243,      COMPONENT CONTENTS- YEAR 1609, DAY 243
09/30/1603   CONVERTS TO JULIAN DATE:  03.273,     CODE2 CONTENTS: 0.   NEO-JULIAN DATE 1603.273,      COMPONENT CONTENTS- YEAR 1603, DAY 273
10/31/1604   CONVERTS TO JULIAN DATE:  04.305,     CODE2 CONTENTS: 0.   NEO-JULIAN DATE 1604.305,      COMPONENT CONTENTS- YEAR 1604, DAY 305
11/30/1605   CONVERTS TO JULIAN DATE:  05.334,     CODE2 CONTENTS: 0.   NEO-JULIAN DATE 1605.334,      COMPONENT CONTENTS- YEAR 1605, DAY 334
12/31/1606   CONVERTS TO JULIAN DATE:  06.365,     CODE2 CONTENTS: 0.   NEO-JULIAN DATE 1606.365,      COMPONENT CONTENTS- YEAR 1606, DAY 365
06/19/1883   CONVERTS TO JULIAN DATE:  83.170,     CODE2 CONTENTS: 0.   NEO-JULIAN DATE 1883.170,      COMPONENT CONTENTS- YEAR 1883, DAY 170
08/21/2001   CONVERTS TO JULIAN DATE:  01.233,     CODE2 CONTENTS: 0.   NEO-JULIAN DATE 2001.233,      COMPONENT CONTENTS- YEAR 2001, DAY 233
06/13/2000   CONVERTS TO JULIAN DATE:  00.165,     CODE2 CONTENTS: 0.   NEO-JULIAN DATE 2000.165,      COMPONENT CONTENTS- YEAR 2000, DAY 165
11/25/2401   CONVERTS TO JULIAN DATE:  01.329,     CODE2 CONTENTS: 0.   NEO-JULIAN DATE 2401.329,      COMPONENT CONTENTS- YEAR 2401, DAY 329
12/31/1999   CONVERTS TO JULIAN DATE:  99.365,     CODE2 CONTENTS: 0.   NEO-JULIAN DATE 1999.365,      COMPONENT CONTENTS- YEAR 1999, DAY 365
00/29/1601   INVALID MONTH                         CODE2 CONTENTS: 6                                   COMPONENT CONTENTS- YEAR 0000, DAY 000
13/29/1601   INVALID MONTH                         CODE2 CONTENTS: 6                                   COMPONENT CONTENTS- YEAR 0000, DAY 000
02/29/1601   INVALID DAY                           CODE2 CONTENTS: 8                                   COMPONENT CONTENTS- YEAR 0000, DAY 000
03/32/1601   INVALID DAY                           CODE2 CONTENTS: 8                                   COMPONENT CONTENTS- YEAR 0000, DAY 000
12/  /1601   INVALID DATA                          CODE2 CONTENTS: 2                                   COMPONENT CONTENTS- YEAR 0000, DAY 000
12/31/       INVALID DATA                          CODE2 CONTENTS: 2                                   COMPONENT CONTENTS- YEAR 0000, DAY 000
  /  /       INVALID DATA                          CODE2 CONTENTS: 2                                   COMPONENT CONTENTS- YEAR 0000, DAY 000
13/01/1999   INVALID MONTH                         CODE2 CONTENTS: 6                                   COMPONENT CONTENTS- YEAR 0000, DAY 000
00/01/1999   INVALID MONTH                         CODE2 CONTENTS: 6                                   COMPONENT CONTENTS- YEAR 0000, DAY 000
01/32/1999   INVALID DAY                           CODE2 CONTENTS: 8                                   COMPONENT CONTENTS- YEAR 0000, DAY 000
01/00/1999   INVALID DAY                           CODE2 CONTENTS: 8                                   COMPONENT CONTENTS- YEAR 0000, DAY 000
01/01/1600   INVALID YEAR                          CODE2 CONTENTS: 4                                   COMPONENT CONTENTS- YEAR 0000, DAY 000
01/01/3400   INVALID YEAR                          CODE2 CONTENTS: 8                                   COMPONENT CONTENTS- YEAR 0000, DAY 000
02/29/1601   INVALID DAY                           CODE2 CONTENTS: 8                                   COMPONENT CONTENTS- YEAR 0000, DAY 000
01/01/1999   CONVERTS TO JULIAN DATE:  99.001,     CODE2 CONTENTS: 0.   NEO-JULIAN DATE 1999.001,      COMPONENT CONTENTS- YEAR 1999, DAY 001
01/02/1999   CONVERTS TO JULIAN DATE:  99.002,     CODE2 CONTENTS: 0.   NEO-JULIAN DATE 1999.002,      COMPONENT CONTENTS- YEAR 1999, DAY 002
01/03/1999   CONVERTS TO JULIAN DATE:  99.003,     CODE2 CONTENTS: 0.   NEO-JULIAN DATE 1999.003,      COMPONENT CONTENTS- YEAR 1999, DAY 003
01/04/1999   CONVERTS TO JULIAN DATE:  99.004,     CODE2 CONTENTS: 0.   NEO-JULIAN DATE 1999.004,      COMPONENT CONTENTS- YEAR 1999, DAY 004
01/05/1999   CONVERTS TO JULIAN DATE:  99.005,     CODE2 CONTENTS: 0.   NEO-JULIAN DATE 1999.005,      COMPONENT CONTENTS- YEAR 1999, DAY 005
01/06/1999   CONVERTS TO JULIAN DATE:  99.006,     CODE2 CONTENTS: 0.   NEO-JULIAN DATE 1999.006,      COMPONENT CONTENTS- YEAR 1999, DAY 006
01/07/1999   CONVERTS TO JULIAN DATE:  99.007,     CODE2 CONTENTS: 0.   NEO-JULIAN DATE 1999.007,      COMPONENT CONTENTS- YEAR 1999, DAY 007
01/08/1999   CONVERTS TO JULIAN DATE:  99.008,     CODE2 CONTENTS: 0.   NEO-JULIAN DATE 1999.008,      COMPONENT CONTENTS- YEAR 1999, DAY 008

THE SUBROUTINE WAS EXECUTED   44 TIMES
```

**Figure 3.2**  A subset of the output resulting from testing the subroutine TIMESUB2.

You can, however, define the indicator SIGF, which indicates the standard to which the six-digit date DATEF conforms. Note that SIGF can be only X'F0', X'F1', or X'F2'; zones other than X'F' are invalid.

$$SIGF = \begin{cases} 0, \text{If DATEF is Commercial} \\ 1, \text{If DATEF is FIPS} \\ 2, \text{If DATEF is European} \end{cases}$$

Armed only with the definition of DATEF as numeric and with the assumption that it's a date in the 20th century, you can proceed to define the output FORMAT as Commercial-8.

It's pointless to edit the year value for limit violations since, if DATEF is numeric, the year value must be within limits given the assumption that it belongs to the 20th century. The pseudocode will reflect this situation, as will the return code. No provision will be made for a "bad year." Let's, therefore, define CODEF, the return code:

$$CODEF = \begin{cases} 0, \text{If SIGF} = 0, 1, \text{or } 2, \text{DATEF is numeric and} \\ \quad \text{FORMAT is Commercial-8} \\ 1, \text{IF SIGF} \neq 0, 1 \text{ or } 2 \\ 2, \text{IF DATEF is non-numeric} \\ 6, \text{IF M } \varepsilon \text{ \{m\} as defined in Commercial-8} \\ 8, \text{If D } \varepsilon \text{ \{d\} as defined in Commercial-8} \\ \quad \text{assuming Y} = 1900 + Y \end{cases}$$

## The Pseudocode for TIMESUBF

The pseudocode assumes that its input has been passed to it in a one-byte field SIGF and in a six-byte field DATEF. The output field FORMAT is assumed to be five packed bytes. We'll introduce the pseudocode symbol →, which will indicate that DATEF contents have been moved left to right to receiving fields in the order of the fields to which the arrow points.

```
 *  Perform general housekeeping
1) Let FORMAT = 0
2) Let CODEF = 0
 * Validate SIGF = 0, 1 or 2
3) If SIGF = 0, 1 or 2, go to 5
4) Let CODEF = 1, go to 21
 * Internal housekeeping
5) Move DATEF to WORK6
 * Validate DATEF as numeric
6) If WORK6 is numeric, go to 8
7) Let CODEF = 2, go to 21
 * Determine DATEF's standard—expand Y to 4 digits
8) If SIGF = 1, DATEF → Y, M, D, go to 11
9) If SIGF = 2, DATEF → D, M, Y, go to 11
10) DATEF → M, D, Y
11) Let Y = Y + 1900
 * Perform leap year algorithm for Y
12) Let L = 0
13) If Y is a leap year, let L = 1
 * Test M for limit violation
14) If M is within limits per Commercial-8, go to 16
```

```
15) Let CODEF = 6, go to 21
 * Test D for limit violation
16) If D is within limits per Commercial-8, go to 18
17) Let CODEF = 8, go to 21
  * Assemble output, FORMAT
18) Let FORMAT = 1000000M
19) Let FORMAT = FORMAT + 10000D
20) Let FORMAT = FORMAT + Y
21) Exit
```

## The Source Programming Code for TIMESUBF

Figure 3.3 shows the TIMESUBF portion of the assembly post listing of TEST0F, the test-calling program. Input data submitted to test TIMESUBF consists of six-digit dates belonging to the twentieth century and of the standards indicated by the accompanying indicator SIGF. Also submitted are a number of invalid SIGF codes as well as various nonnumeric DATEF contents and numeric but out-of-limits values for month and day components. The output of this testing appears in Figure 3.4. All test results were as expected.

### Comments on the source code of TIMESUBF

Once more you'll see a straightforward ALC translation of the pseudocode. SIGF is simultaneously validated for data and limits via the application of TRT. Clearly, SIGF must have a X'F' zone; unpacked X'0C', X'1C', or X'2C' bytes produce X'C0', X'C1', or X'C2' bytes and don't qualify. Immediately following DATEF's validation as numeric, SIGF is interrogated to determine the standard in which DATEF has been formatted. The year component is then expanded from two digits to a four-digit year of the 20th century. The ensuing editing is identical to that seen in TIMESUB2, with the exception that the limit violation check for the year is omitted for reasons explained earlier. As usual, L determines the table function. Again the pseudocode's mathematical construct for FORMAT is circumvented by ALC's byte-addressing capability.

## Applying TIMESUB2 and TIMESUBF

TIMESUBF and TIMESUB2 are used to convert six-digit database dates to stored neo-Julian dates. As we noted earlier, the stored six-digit date, whether in packed or in zoned decimal formats, can be replaced by a packed neo-Julian date. Regardless of the language being used (ALC, COBOL, or RPG), the stored six-digit date can be retrieved and presented to TIMESUBF in zoned decimal format for expansion to Commercial-8. (The linkage conventions for RPG and COBOL appear in the appendices.) Once the date is expanded to Commercial-8 and is returned to the calling program, packed in the field FORMAT, the calling program has but to make it available to TIMESUB2 in zoned decimal format, placed in the field DATEA.

TIMESUB2 computes the neo-Julian date and returns it to the calling program packed in the four-byte field NEOJUL. The calling program can then return NEOJUL to the four-byte or six-byte storage location formerly occupied by the six-digit date.

```
LOC    OBJECT CODE    ADDR1 ADDR2   STMT   SOURCE STATEMENT                                    DOS/VSE ASSEMBLER  16.09  99-12-31

                                    391  *                                                                          TSF00010
                                    392  *  *********************************************************************   TSF00020
                                    393  *                                                                          TSF00030
                                    394  *  TTTTTT  III   MM    MM   EEEEE   SSSSS   U   U   BBBBB   FFFFF       *   TSF00040
                                    395  *    T      I    M M   M M   E       S       U   U   B   B   F           *   TSF00050
                                    396  *    T      I    M  M M  M   EEEE    SSSSS   U   U   BBB B   FFF         *   TSF00060
                                    397  *    T      I    M   M   M   E           S   U   U   B   B   F           *   TSF00070
                                    398  *    T     III   M       M   EEEEE   SSSSS   UUUUU   BBBBB   F           *   TSF00080
                                    399  *                                                                     *   TSF00090
                                    400  *  *********************************************************************   TSF00100
                                    401  *  D A T E   F O R M A T   C O N V E R S I O N   S U B R O U T I N E   *   TSF00110
                                    402  *  *********************************************************************   TSF00120
                                    403  *                                                                     *   TSF00130
                                    404  *                                                                     *   TSF00140
                                    405  *  *********************************************************************   TSF00150
                                    406  *  THIS SUBROUTINE CONVERTS SIX DIGIT INPUT DATES WHOSE FORMATS ARE        TSF00160
                                    407  *            FIPS - COMMERCIAL - EUROPEAN                                  TSF00170
                                    408  *  TO PACKED STANDARD EIGHT DIGIT COMMERCIAL DATES                         TSF00180
                                    409  *                                                                          TSF00190
                                    410  *  1.  THE INPUT DATE FORMAT MAY BE:                                       TSF00200
                                    411  *                       FIPS       = YYMMDD                                TSF00210
                                    412  *                       COMMERCIAL = MMDDYY                                TSF00220
                                    413  *                       EUROPEAN   = DDMMYY                                TSF00230
                                    414  *                                                                          TSF00240
                                    415  *      IN ALL CASES: YY IS THE TWO DIGIT YEAR VALUE.                       TSF00250
                                    416  *                    MM IS THE TWO DIGIT MONTH VALUE.                      TSF00260
                                    417  *                    DD IS THE TWO DIGIT DAY VALUE.                        TSF00270
                                    418  *                                                                          TSF00280
                                    419  *  2.  VALID INPUT YEARS FOR THIS SUBROUTINE ARE ANY TWO DIGIT             TSF00290
                                    420  *      NUMERIC VALUES.                                                     TSF00300
                                    421  *                                                                          TSF00310
                                    422  *      NOTE:   THIS SUBROUTINE ASSUMES THAT ALL INPUT YEARS                TSF00320
                                    423  *              ARE YEARS OF THE TWENTIETH CENTURY, THAT IS,                TSF00330
                                    424  *              WHEN CONVERTED TO FOUR DIGITS, THEY WILL                    TSF00340
                                    425  *              REPRESENT THE YEARS 1900 TO 1999, INCLUSIVE.               TSF00350
                                    426  *              IF ANOTHER CENTURY IS DESIRED, IT IS NECESS-               TSF00360
                                    427  *              ARY TO MODIFY THE #$FCENT FIELD OF THIS                     TSF00370
                                    428  *              SUBROUTINE.                                                 TSF00380
                                    429  *                                                                          TSF00390
                                    430  *              AFTER EXPANSION OF THE INPUT DATE TO COMM-                  TSF00400
                                    431  *              ERCIAL-8, THE MONTH AND DAY VALUES EXPECTED                 TSF00410
                                    432  *              ARE DEFINED IN 3. AND 4.. BELOW.                            TSF00420
                                    433  *                                                                          TSF00430
                                    434  *  3.  VALID INPUT MONTH VALUES FOR THIS SUBROUTINE ARE 01                 TSF00440
                                    435  *      THROUGH 12.                                                         TSF00450
                                    436  *                                                                          TSF00460
                                    437  *  4.  VALID INPUT DAY VALUES FOR THIS SUBROUTINE ARE 01                   TSF00470
                                    438  *      THROUGH 31 WITH EXCEPTIONS FOR THE MONTHS LISTED:                   TSF00480
                                    439  *          MONTH             MAXIMUM DAY VALUE                             TSF00490
                                    440  *           04                     30                                      TSF00500
                                    441  *           06                     30                                      TSF00510
                                    442  *           09                     30                                      TSF00520
                                    443  *           11                     30                                      TSF00530
                                    444  *           02                     28                                      TSF00540
                                    445  *           02  DURING LEAP YEAR    29                                      TSF00550
```

**Figure 3.3**  The TIMESUBF portion of TESTOF's assembly post listing.

```
LOC   OBJECT CODE   ADDR1 ADDR2   STMT   SOURCE STATEMENT                                              DOS/VSE ASSEMBLER  16.09  99-12-31

                                  446  *                                                                           *  TSF00560
                                  447  *                                                                           *  TSF00570
                                  448  *    5.  THE CALLING PROGRAM MUST PLACE THE SIX DIGIT DATE,                 *  TSF00580
                                  449  *        IN ZONED DECIMAL, IN A SUBROUTINE DEFINED SIX BYTE                 *  TSF00590
                                  450  *        FIELD, 'DATEF,' BEFORE EXECUTION OF THE SUBROUTINE.               *  TSF00600
                                  451  *        DATEF IS NOT ALTERED BY THE SUBROUTINE.                            *  TSF00610
                                  452  *                                                                           *  TSF00620
                                  453  *    6.  THE CALLING PROGRAM MUST PLACE A ONE DIGIT INDICATOR,              *  TSF00630
                                  454  *        IN ZONED DECIMAL, IN A SUBROUTINE DEFINED ONE BYTE                 *  TSF00640
                                  455  *        FIELD, 'SIGF,' BEFORE EXECUTION OF THE SUBROUTINE.                *  TSF00650
                                  456  *        SIGF IS NOT ALTERED BY THE SUBROUTINE.                             *  TSF00660
                                  457  *                                                                           *  TSF00670
                                  458  *        THE ONE DIGIT INDICATOR MAY BE A 0, 1 OR 2 SIGNIFYING             *  TSF00680
                                  459  *        THE STANDARD OF THE INPUT DATE AND REQUESTED FUNCTION             *  TSF00690
                                  460  *        AS FOLLOWS:                                                        *  TSF00700
                                  461  *                                                                           *  TSF00710
                                  462  *        0.  CONVERT COMMERCIAL SIX DIGIT FORMAT TO COMMERCIAL-8           *  TSF00720
                                  463  *        1.  CONVERT FIPS SIX DIGIT FORMAT TO COMMERCIAL-8                 *  TSF00730
                                  464  *        2.  CONVERT EUROPEAN SIX DIGIT FORMAT TO COMMERCIAL-8             *  TSF00740
                                  465  *                                                                           *  TSF00750
                                  466  *                                                                           *  TSF00760
                                  467  *    7.  A SUBROUTINE DEFINED ONE BYTE FIELD, 'CODEF,' IS RETURNED         *  TSF00770
                                  468  *        TO THE CALLING PROGRAM AND CONTAINS A PACKED 0 IF THE             *  TSF00780
                                  469  *        EXECUTION WAS SUCCESSFUL.  NON-ZERO VALUES INDICATE               *  TSF00790
                                  470  *        THE FOLLOWING:                                                     *  TSF00800
                                  471  *                                                                           *  TSF00810
                                  472  *        A PACKED 1 INDICATES UNSUCCESSFUL EXECUTION: INVALID              *  TSF00820
                                  473  *        DATA IN SIGF- EITHER NONNUMERIC OR A VALUE THAT EXCEEDS           *  TSF00830
                                  474  *        THE LIMITS SPECIFIED IN 6., ABOVE.                                 *  TSF00840
                                  475  *                                                                           *  TSF00850
                                  476  *        A PACKED 2 INDICATES UNSUCCESSFUL EXECUTION: INVALID DATA         *  TSF00860
                                  477  *        IN DATEF.                                                          *  TSF00870
                                  478  *                                                                           *  TSF00880
                                  479  *        INVALID DATA ARE DETERMINED IF THE LOW ORDER BYTE'S ZONE          *  TSF00890
                                  480  *        CONTAINS AN INVALID SIGN, (AN INVALID SIGN IS OTHER THAN          *  TSF00900
                                  481  *        X'C', X'A', X'E', OR X'F'), OR IF THE PRECEDING BYTES'            *  TSF00910
                                  482  *        ZONES ARE OTHER THAN X'F', OR IF ANY BYTE'S LOW ORDER             *  TSF00920
                                  483  *        NIBBLE CONTAINS A VALUE GREATER THAN X'9'.                        *  TSF00930
                                  484  *                                                                           *  TSF00940
                                  485  *        A PACKED 6 INDICATES UNSUCCESSFUL EXECUTION: INVALID              *  TSF00950
                                  486  *        MONTH VALUE IN DATEF- A VALUE THAT EXCEEDS THE LIMITS             *  TSF00960
                                  487  *        SPECIFIED IN 2., ABOVE.                                            *  TSF00970
                                  488  *                                                                           *  TSF00980
                                  489  *        A PACKED 8 INDICATES UNSUCCESSFUL EXECUTION: INVALID DAY          *  TSF00990
                                  490  *        VALUE IN DATEF- A VALUE THAT EXCEEDS THE LIMITS SPECIFIED         *  TSF01000
                                  491  *        IN 3., ABOVE.                                                      *  TSF01010
                                  492  *                                                                           *  TSF01020
                                  493  *        INSPECTION OF THE RETURN CODE IS IMPORTANT.  THE RETURN           *  TSF01030
                                  494  *        CODE, CODEF, REFLECTS THE LEVEL OF EDITING.                       *  TSF01040
                                  495  *                                                                           *  TSF01050
                                  496  *        A RETURN CODE OF 1 INDICATES THAT SIGF WAS INVALID AND            *  TSF01060
                                  497  *        THAT NO FURTHER EDITING WAS POSSIBLE.                              *  TSF01070
                                  498  *                                                                           *  TSF01080
                                  499  *        A RETURN CODE OF 2, INDICATES INVALID DATA IN DATEF.              *  TSF01090
                                  500  *        IT ALSO INDICATES THAT NO EDITING HAS BEEN DONE TO                *  TSF01100
```

```
LOC   OBJECT CODE   ADDR1 ADDR2   STMT   SOURCE STATEMENT              DOS/VSE ASSEMBLER  16.09  99-12-31

                                  501 *   VALIDATE THE MONTH OR DAY VALUES.                               * TSF01110
                                  502 *                                                                   * TSF01120
                                  503 *   A RETURN CODE OF 6 INDICATES THAT THE DATA ARE VALID BUT        * TSF01130
                                  504 *   THAT THE MONTH IS INVALID- THE DAY VALUE HAS NOT BEEN           * TSF01140
                                  505 *   EDITED.                                                         * TSF01150
                                  506 *                                                                   * TSF01160
                                  507 *   A RETURN CODE OF 8 INDICATES THAT THE DATA AND MONTH            * TSF01170
                                  508 *   ARE VALID BUT THAT THE DAY WAS FOUND INVALID FOR THE            * TSF01180
                                  509 *   VALID MONTH GIVEN.                                              * TSF01190
                                  510 *                                                                   * TSF01200
                                  511 *   IN SHORT, THE RETURN CODE INDICATES THE LEVEL OF EDITING.       * TSF01210
                                  512 *   THE EDIT SEQUENCE IS SIGF. DATA, MONTH, AND DAY.                * TSF01220
                                  513 *                                                                   * TSF01230
                                  514 *   NOTE:                                                           * TSF01240
                                  515 *   A PACKED 4 IS OMITTED FROM THE CODEF RETURN CODE VALUES.        * TSF01250
                                  516 *   THE YEAR VALUE IS ASSUMED VALID WHEN THE INPUT'S TEST FOR       * TSF01260
                                  517 *   NUMERIC IS SUCCESSFULLY PASSED.  NO RETURN CODE MAY BE          * TSF01270
                                  518 *   LOGICALLY ASSIGNED FOR AN INVALID YEAR VALUE SINCE AT           * TSF01280
                                  519 *   INPUT THE YEAR MAY BE DEFINED ONLY AS TWO DIGIT NUMERIC         * TSF01290
                                  520 *   WITH ANY OF 00 THROUGH 99 CONSIDERED WITHIN LIMITS.             * TSF01300
                                  521 *                                                                   * TSF01310
                                  522 *  8.  A SUBROUTINE DEFINED FIVE BYTE FIELD, 'FORMAT,' IS           * TSF01320
                                  523 *   RETURNED TO THE CALLING PROGRAM.  FORMAT CONTAINS THE           * TSF01330
                                  524 *   REFORMATTED INPUT DATE.  THE FORM OF THE REFORMATTED            * TSF01340
                                  525 *   DATE IS PACKED EIGHT BYTE COMMERCIAL STANDARD.                  * TSF01350
                                  526 *                                                                   * TSF01360
                                  527 *   IF THE EXECUTION IS UNSUCCESSFUL, THAT IS, IF THE RETURN        * TSF01370
                                  528 *   CODE FIELD, CODEF, CONTAINS A NON-ZERO VALUE, THEN              * TSF01380
                                  529 *   FORMAT WILL CONTAIN PACKED ZEROS.  THIS IS PROTECTION           * TSF01390
                                  530 *   AGAINST ILLEGAL USE OF A PRIOR EXECUTION'S RESULT.              * TSF01400
                                  531 *                                                                   * TSF01410
                                  532 *                                                                   * TSF01420
                                  533 *  9.  ALL OTHER SUBROUTINE DEFINED FIELDS AND LABELS ARE           * TSF01430
                                  534 *   TRANSPARENT TO THE CALLING PROGRAM.                             * TSF01440
                                  535 *                                                                   * TSF01450
                                  536 * 10.  THIS SUBROUTINE IS WRITTEN TO BE ASSEMBLED WITH THE          * TSF01460
                                  537 *   CALLING PROGRAM AND SHOULD BE INSERTED IN THE CALLING           * TSF01470
                                  538 *   PROGRAM IMMEDIATELY BEFORE THE 'END' OPCODE.                    * TSF01480
                                  539 *                                                                   * TSF01490
                                  540 * 11.  THIS SUBROUTINE USES REGISTER 6 AS THE LINK REGISTER.        * TSF01500
                                  541 *   IF REGISTER 6 IS ASSIGNED IN THE CALLING PROGRAM FOR            * TSF01510
                                  542 *   OTHER USES, IT MUST BE SAVED PRIOR TO EXECUTING THE             * TSF01520
                                  543 *   'BALR.'                                                         * TSF01530
                                  544 *                                                                   * TSF01540
                                  545 *                                                                   * TSF01550
                                  546 *                              JEROME T. MURRAY                     * TSF01560
                                  547 *   GLEN ELLYN, ILLINOIS       MARILYN J. MURRAY                    * TSF01570
                                  548 *                                                                   * TSF01580
                                  549 * ***********************************************************        * TSF01590
                                  550 * ***********************************************************        * TSF01600
                                  551 * ***********************************************************        * TSF01610
                                  552 * ***********************************************************        * TSF01620
                                  553 *      +++   SECTION 1- GENERAL HOUSEKEEPING   +++                   * TSF01630
                                  554 *                                                                   * TSF01640
                                  555 *                                                                   * TSF01650
```

Figure 3.3  Continued

```
                                                    DOS/VSE ASSEMBLER 16.09  99-12-31

LOC    OBJECT CODE      ADDR1 ADDR2   STMT   SOURCE STATEMENT

                                      556  *
                                      557  *                 INITIALIZE INDICATIVE FIELDS          TSF01660
0004AC F840 77AF 0065E 00865          558  TIMESUBF ZAP   FORMAT,=P'0'                             TSF01670
0004B2 F800 77AF 00663 00865          559           ZAP   CODEF,=P'0'                              TSF01680
                                      560  *                                                       TSF01690
                                      561  *                 SAVE REGISTERS 1 THROUGH 4 IN SAVE FIELDS  TSF01700
                                      562  *                                                       TSF01710
0004B8 9014 7716        007CC         563           STM   1,4,#$FRSAVE                             TSF01720
                                      564  *                                                       TSF01730
                                      565  * +++ SECTION 2- EDIT SIGF CONTENTS   +++               TSF01740
                                      566  *                                                       TSF01750
                                      567  *                 INITIALIZE TABLE FOR 'F0' THROUGH 'F2' ONLY  TSF01760
                                      568  *                                                       TSF01770
0004BC D206 7802 078E 008B8           569           MVC   #$FTABL+243(7),=X'1C1C1C1C1C1C1C'        TSF01780
                                      570  *                                                       TSF01790
                                      571  *                 EDIT SIGF USING TRT                    TSF01800
                                      572  *                                                       TSF01810
0004C2 DD00 75B4 066A 0069B           573           TRT   SIGF(1),#$FTABL                          TSF01820
0004C8 4780 7426      004DC           574           BC    8,#$FHKEP                                TSF01830
                                      575  *                                                       TSF01840
                                      576  *                 IF TEST FAILS, RESTORE TABLE AND EXIT  TSF01850
                                      577  *                                                       TSF01860
0004CC D206 7809 078E 008BF           578           MVC   #$FTABL+243(7),=X'00000000000000'        TSF01870
0004D2 F800 77AE 00663 00864          579           ZAP   CODEF,=P'1'                              TSF01880
0004D8 47F0 7732      007E8           580           B     #$FTERM                                  TSF01890
                                      581  *                                                       TSF01900
                                      582  * +++ SECTION 3- INTERNAL HOUSEKEEPING  +++             TSF01910
                                      583  *                                                       TSF01920
                                      584  *                 RESTORE TABLE                          TSF01930
                                      585  *                                                       TSF01940
                                      586  *                                                       TSF01950
0004DC D206 7809 078E 008BF           587  #$FHKEP  MVC   #$FTABL+243(7),=X'00000000000000'        TSF01960
                                      588  *                                                       TSF01970
                                      589  *                 MOVE DATE TO WORK FIELD AND ISOLATE SIGN  TSF01980
                                      590  *                                                       TSF01990
0004E2 D207 75AE 07B4 00664           591           MVC   #$FWORK6,DATEF                           TSF02000
0004E8 D200 76F4 07AA 007B9           592           MVC   #$FSIGN,#$FWORK6+5                       TSF02010
                                      593  *                                                       TSF02020
                                      594  * +++ SECTION 4- NUMERIC VALIDATION  +++                TSF02030
                                      595  *                                                       TSF02040
                                      596  *                 AUGMENT TABLE FOR VALID '+' SIGNS OTHER THAN  TSF02050
                                      597  *                 X'F' FOR WHICH TABLE IS DEFINED: X'A', X'C',   TSF02060
                                      598  *                 X'E'- EDIT FOR VALID '+' SIGN USING TRT  TSF02070
                                      599  *                                                       TSF02080
0004EE D209 7685 76E5 0073B 0079B     600           MVC   #$FTABL+160(10),#$FZRO                   TSF02090
0004F4 D209 76A5 76E5 0075B 0079B     601           MVC   #$FTABL+192(10),#$FZRO                   TSF02100
0004FA D209 76C5 76E5 0077B 0079B     602           MVC   #$FTABL+224(10),#$FZRO                   TSF02110
000500 DD00 76F4 75E5 007AA 0069B     603           TRT   #$FSIGN(1),#$FTABL                       TSF02120
000506 4780 745E      00514           604           BC    8,#$FNUM                                 TSF02130
                                      605  *                                                       TSF02140
                                      606  *                 IF TEST FAILS, RESTORE TABLE AND EXIT  TSF02150
                                      607  *                                                       TSF02160
00050A D2EE 75E6 75E5 0069C 0069B     608           MVC   #$FTABL+1(239),#$FTABL                   TSF02170
000510 47F0 746E      00524           609           B     #$FBDATA                                 TSF02180
                                      610  *                                                       TSF02190
                                                                                                   TSF02200
```

```
                                                      DOS/VSE ASSEMBLER 16.09   99-12-31

LOC    OBJECT CODE      ADDR1 ADDR2  STMT   SOURCE STATEMENT

                                      611  *
                                      612  *        RESTORE TABLE AND EDIT FOR VALID ZONE
                                      613  *        AND DIGIT CONFIGURATIONS IN REMAINING BYTES
000514 D2EE 75E5        0069C 0069B   614  #$FNUM    MVC  #$FTABL+1(239),#$FTABL
00051A DDO4 76FE        0069B         615            TRT  #$FWORK6(5),#$FTABL
000520 4780 7478              0052E   616            BC   8,#$FPACK
                                      617  *
                                      618  *                         POST 'BAD DATA' RETURN CODE AND EXIT
                                      619  *
000524 F800 75AD 77B0   00663 00866   620  #$FBDATA  ZAP  CODEF,=P'2'
00052A 47F0 7732              007E8   621            B    #$FTERM
                                      622  *
                                      623  *   +++   SECTION 5- DETERMINE STANDARD- EXPAND YEAR  +++
                                      624  *
                                      625  *                         INTERROGATE SIGF-
                                      626  *
                                      627  *        IF 0, EXECUTE COMMERCIAL TO COMMERCIAL-8
                                      628  *        IF 1, BRANCH TO FC: FIPS TO COMMERCIAL-8
                                      629  *        IF 2, BRANCH TO EC: EUROPEAN TO COMMERCIAL-8
                                      630  *
00052E D500 75B4 77D8   0066A 0088E   631  #$FPACK   CLC  SIGF,=C'1'
000534 4780 74B2              00568   632            BE   #$FFC
000538 4720 749C              00552   633            BH   #$FEC
                                      634  *
                                      635  *                         PACK MONTH, DAY AND YEAR IN WORK FIELDS
                                      636  *
                                      637  *                         COMMERCIAL IN
                                      638  *
00053C F211 770B 76FE   007C1 007B4   639            PACK  #$FMO,#$FWORK6(2)
000542 F211 770D 7700   007C3 007B6   640            PACK  #$FDA,#$FWORK6+2(2)
000548 F221 770F 7702   007C5 007B8   641            PACK  #$FYR,#$FWORK6+4(2)
00054E 47F0 74C4              0057A   642            B     #$FMAT
                                      643  *
                                      644  *                         EUROPEAN IN
                                      645  *
000552 F211 770B 7700   007C1 007B6   646  #$FEC     PACK  #$FMO,#$FWORK6+2(2)
000558 F211 770D 76FE   007C3 007B4   647            PACK  #$FDA,#$FWORK6(2)
00055E F221 770F 7702   007C5 007B8   648            PACK  #$FYR,#$FWORK6+4(2)
000564 47F0 74C4              0057A   649            B     #$FMAT
                                      650  *
                                      651  *                         FIPS IN
                                      652  *
000568 F211 770B 7700   007C1 007B6   653  #$FFC     PACK  #$FMO,#$FWORK6+2(2)
00056E F211 770D 7702   007C3 007B8   654            PACK  #$FDA,#$FWORK6+4(2)
000574 F221 770F 76FE   007C5 007B4   655            PACK  #$FYR,#$FWORK6(2)
                                      656  *
                                      657  *                         EXPAND YEAR TO FOUR DIGITS
                                      658  *
00057A FA22 770F 76F1   007C5 007A7   659  #$FMAT    AP   #$FYR,#$FCENT
                                      660  *
                                      661  *   +++  SECTION 6- DETERMINE LEAP YEAR STATUS  +++
                                      662  *
                                      663  *                         EXECUTE LEAP YEAR ALGORITHM
                                      664  *
000580 F800 76F5 77AF   007AB 00865   665  #$LPYRT   ZAP  #$FL,=P'0'
```

Figure 3.3  *Continued*

```
                                              DOS/VSE ASSEMBLER  16.09  99-12-31

LOC    OBJECT CODE   ADDR1 ADDR2  STMT  SOURCE STATEMENT

000586 F842 7706 770F 007C5        666        ZAP  #$FWORK,#$FYR                                       TSF02760
00058C FD40 7706 7810 008C6        667        DP   #$FWORK,=P'4'                                       TSF02770
000592 F900 770A 77AF 00865        668        CP   #$FWORK+4(1),=P'O'                                  TSF02780
000598 4720 7518      005CE        669        BH   #$FMOEDT                                            TSF02790
00059C F842 7706 770F 007C5        670        ZAP  #$FWORK,#$FYR                                       TSF02800
0005A2 FD41 7706 77A8 0085E        671        DP   #$FWORK,=P'100'                                     TSF02810
0005A8 F910 7709 77AF 00865        672        CP   #$FWORK+3(2),=P'O'                                  TSF02820
0005AE 4720 7512      005C8        673        BH   #$FLPYR                                             TSF02830
0005B2 F842 7706 770F 007C5        674        ZAP  #$FWORK,#$FYR                                       TSF02840
0005B8 FD41 7706 77AA 00860        675        DP   #$FWORK,=P'400'                                     TSF02850
0005BE F910 7709 77AF 00865        676        CP   #$FWORK+3(2),=P'O'                                  TSF02860
0005C4 4720 7518      005CE        677        BH   #$FMOEDT                                            TSF02870
                                   678 *                                                              TSF02880
                                   679 *         IF YEAR IS A LEAP YEAR, SET INCREMENT TO 1           TSF02890
                                   680 *                                                              TSF02900
0005C8 F800 76F5 77AE 00864        681 #$FLPYR  ZAP  #$FL,=P'1'                                        TSF02910
                                   682 *                                                              TSF02920
                                   683 *     +++ SECTION 7- EDIT MONTH FOR LIMIT VIOLATIONS  +++      TSF02930
                                   684 *                                                              TSF02940
                                   685 *         VERIFY THAT MONTH IS WITHIN RANGE: 1 - 12            TSF02950
                                   686 *         A) CONVERT MONTH TO BINARY IN REGISTER 3             TSF02960
                                   687 *                                                              TSF02970
0005CE F871 772A 770B 007C1        688 #$FMOEDT ZAP  #$FCVB,#$FMO                                      TSF02980
0005D4 4F30 772A      007E0        689        CVB  3,#$FCVB                                            TSF02990
                                   690 *                                                              TSF03000
                                   691 *         B) STORE BINARY BYTE FROM REG 3 IN #$FFLD            TSF03010
                                   692 *                                                              TSF03020
0005D8 4230 7712      007C8        693        STC  3,#$FFLD                                            TSF03030
                                   694 *                                                              TSF03040
                                   695 *         C) INITIALIZE TABLE WITH X'OO' FOR TRT               TSF03050
                                   696 *                                                              TSF03060
0005DC D20B 75E6 76E5 0069C 0069B  697        MVC  #$FTABL+1(12),#$FZRO                                TSF03070
                                   698 *                                                              TSF03080
                                   699 *         D) EXECUTE TRT USING #$FFLD                          TSF03090
                                   700 *                                                              TSF03100
0005E2 DD00 7712 75E5 007C8 0069B  701        TRT  #$FFLD(1),#$FDAEDT                                  TSF03110
0005E8 4780 7546      005FC        702        BC   8,#$FTABL                                          TSF03120
                                   703 *                                                              TSF03130
                                   704 *         F) RESTORE TABLE - POST BAD MONTH RETURN CODE.       TSF03140
                                   705 *            ZERO FORMAT AND EXIT                              TSF03150
                                   706 *                                                              TSF03160
0005EC D20B 75E6 76E5 0069C 0069B  707        MVC  #$FTABL+1(12),#$FTABL                              TSF03170
0005F2 F800 75AD 77B1 00663 00867  708        ZAP  CODEF,=P'6'                                        TSF03180
0005F8 47F0 7732      007E8        709        B    #$FTERM                                            TSF03190
                                   710 *                                                              TSF03200
                                   711 *     +++ SECTION 8- EDIT DAY FOR LIMIT VIOLATIONS  +++        TSF03210
                                   712 *                                                              TSF03220
                                   713 *         RESTORE TABLE                                        TSF03230
                                   714 *                                                              TSF03240
0005FC D20B 75E6 76E5 0069C 0069B  715 #$FDAEDT MVC  #$FTABL+1(12),#$FTABL                            TSF03250
                                   716 *                                                              TSF03260
                                   717 *         GET ADDRESS OF DAY TABLE IN REGISTER 4               TSF03270
                                   718 *                                                              TSF03280
000602 4140 75B5      0066B        719        LA   4,#$FDATAB                                         TSF03290
                                   720 *                                                              TSF03300
```

```
LOC     OBJECT CODE          ADDR1 ADDR2   STMT   SOURCE STATEMENT                    DOS/VSE ASSEMBLER 16.09  99-12-31

                                            721  *
                                            722  *          IF LEAP YEAR, INCREMENT TO LEAP YEAR FUNCTION      TSF03310/20
000606 F900 76F5 77AF  007AB 00865          723          CP    #$FL,=P'O'                                      TSF03330
00060C 4780 755E       00614                724          BE    #$FNDL                                          TSF03340
000610 4144 0002       00002                725          LA    4,2(4)                                          TSF03350
                                            726  *
                                            727  *          DIRECTLY ADDRESS TABLE DAY LIMIT FOR THIS MONTH     TSF03370
                                            728  *          A) SUBTRACT 1 FROM BINARY MONTH VALUE IN REG 3      TSF03380
                                            729  *
000614 0630            #$FNDL               730          BCTR  3,0                                             TSF03400
                                            731  *
                                            732  *          B) MULTIPLY VALUE IN REG 3 BY 4                     TSF03420
                                            733  *
000616 8930 0002       00002                734          SLL   3,2                                             TSF03440
                                            735  *
                                            736  *          C) LOAD ADDRESS OF DAY TABLE ENTRY IN REG 4         TSF03460
                                            737  *
00061A 4143 4000       00000                738          LA    4,O(3,4)                                        TSF03480
                                            739  *
                                            740  *          CONVERT SIGN OF PACKED DAY FROM X'F' TO X'C'        TSF03500
                                            741  *
00061E F811 770D       007C3 007C3          742          ZAP   #$FDA,#$FDA                                     TSF03520
                                            743  *
                                            744  *          COMPARE DAY TABLE ENTRY (LIMIT) WITH INPUT DAY      TSF03540
                                            745  *
000624 D501 770D 4000  007C3 00000          746          CLC   #$FDA,O(4)                                      TSF03560
                                            747  *
                                            748  *          IF INPUT IS WITHIN LIMIT, EDIT DAY FOR ZERO         TSF03580
                                            749  *
00062A 47DO 7582       00638                750          BNH   #$FDALO                                         TSF03600
                                            751  *
                                            752  *          ELSE POST BAD DAY RETURN CODE, ZERO FORMAT          TSF03620
                                            753  *          AND EXIT                                            TSF03630
                                            754  *
00062E F800 75AD 77BF  00875   #$FBADA      755          ZAP   CODEF,=P'8'                                     TSF03650
000634 47FO 7732       007E8                756          B     #$FTERM                                         TSF03660
                                            757  *
                                            758  *          EDIT DAY VALUE FOR ZERO                             TSF03680
                                            759  *
000638 F911 770D 77AC  007C3 00862 #$FDALO  760          CP    #$FDA,=P'OO'                                    TSF03700
00063E 4780 7578       0062E                761          BE    #$FBADA                                         TSF03710
                                            762  *
                                            763  *          +++ SECTION 9- ASSEMBLE OUTPUT  +++                 TSF03730
                                            764  *
000642 F332 76FA 770F  007B0 007C5          765          UNPK  #$FWORK8+4(4),#$FYR                             TSF03750
000648 F311 76F8 76FC  007AE 007C3          766          UNPK  #$FWORK8+2(2),#$FDA                             TSF03760
00064E F311 76F6 770B  007AC 007C1          767          UNPK  #$FWORK8(2),#$FMO                               TSF03770
000654 F247 75A8 76F6  0065E 007AC          768          PACK  FORMAT,#$FWORK8                                TSF03780
                                            769  *
                                            770  *          +++ SECTION 10- TO RESTORE REGISTERS AND EXIT  +++  TSF03800
                                            771  *
00065A 47FO 7732       007E8                772          B     #$FTERM                                         TSF03820
                                            773  *
                                            774  *          +++ SECTION 11- DEFINE CONSTANTS AND STORAGE  +++   TSF03840
                                            775  *                                                             TSF03850
```

Figure 3.3 *Continued*

```
LOC    OBJECT CODE        ADDR1  ADDR2   STMT  SOURCE STATEMENT                        DOS/VSE ASSEMBLER 16.09  99-12-31

00065E 000000000C                          776  FORMAT    DC    PL5'0'                                                 TSF03860
000663 2C                                   777  CODEF     DC    PL1'2'                                                 TSF03870
000664 F0F0F0F0F0C0                         778  DATEF     DC    ZL6'000000'                                            TSF03880
00066A C0                                   779  SIGF      DC    ZL1'0'                                                 TSF03890
                                            780  *                                                                     TSF03900
                                            781  *               THE DAY TABLE IS DEFINED WITH A PAIR OF TWO BYTE       TSF03910
                                            782  *               ENTRIES FOR EACH OF THE 12 MONTHS- AN ENTRY FOR        TSF03920
                                            783  *               NON-LEAP YEAR AND AN ENTRY FOR LEAP YEAR               TSF03930
                                            784  *                                                                     TSF03940
00066B 031C031C                             785  #$FDATAB  DC    PL2'31',PL2'31'       JAN                             TSF03950
00066F 028C029C                             786            DC    PL2'28',PL2'29'       FEB                             TSF03960
000673 031C031C                             787            DC    PL2'31',PL2'31'       MAR                             TSF03970
000677 030C030C                             788            DC    PL2'30',PL2'30'       APR                             TSF03980
00067B 031C031C                             789            DC    PL2'31',PL2'31'       MAY                             TSF03990
00067F 030C030C                             790            DC    PL2'30',PL2'30'       JUN                             TSF04000
000683 031C031C                             791            DC    PL2'31',PL2'31'       JUL                             TSF04010
000687 031C031C                             792            DC    PL2'31',PL2'31'       AUG                             TSF04020
00068B 030C030C                             793            DC    PL2'30',PL2'30'       SEP                             TSF04030
00068F 031C031C                             794            DC    PL2'31',PL2'31'       OCT                             TSF04040
000693 030C030C                             795            DC    PL2'30',PL2'30'       NOV                             TSF04050
000697 031C031C                             796            DC    PL2'31',PL2'31'       DEC                             TSF04060
                                            797  *                                                                     TSF04070
                                            798  *               TRANSLATION TABLE DEFINED FOR X'F0' - X'F9'           TSF04080
                                            799  *               (ALL TABLE POSITIONS EXCEPT THOSE CORRESPONDING       TSF04090
                                            800  *               TO X'F0' THROUGH X'F9' ARE SET TO A VALUE OTHER       TSF04100
                                            801  *               THAN X'00')                                          TSF04110
                                            802  *                                                                     TSF04120
00069B 1C1C1C1C1C1C1C1C                     803  #$FTABL   DC    240X'1C'                                               TSF04130
00078B 0000000000000000                     804            DC    10X'00'                                                TSF04140
000795 1C1C1C1C1C1C                         805            DC    6X'1C'                                                 TSF04150
                                            806  *                                                                     TSF04160
00079B 000000000000000000                   807  #$FZRO    DC    12X'00'                                                TSF04170
0007A7 01900C                               808  #$FCENT   DC    PL3'1900'                                              TSF04180
0007AA                                      809  #$FSIGN   DS    ZL1                                                    TSF04190
0007AB                                      810  #$FL      DS    PL1                                                    TSF04200
0007AC                                      811  #$FWORK8  DS    CL8                                                    TSF04210
0007B4                                      812  #$FWORK6  DS    CL8                                                    TSF04220
0007BC                                      813  #$FWORK   DS    PL5                                                    TSF04230
0007C1                                      814  #$FMO     DS    PL2                                                    TSF04240
0007C3                                      815  #$FDA     DS    PL2                                                    TSF04250
0007C5                                      816  #$FYR     DS    PL3                                                    TSF04260
0007C8                                      817  #$FFLD    DS    CL1                                                    TSF04270
0007CC                                      818  #$FRSAVE  DS    4F                                                     TSF04280
0007E0                                      819  #$FCVB    DS    1D                                                     TSF04290
0007E8 9814 7716        007CC               820  #$FTERM   LM    1,4,#$FRSAVE                                           TSF04300
0007EC 07F6             000B4               821            BR    6                                                      TSF04310
                                            822            END   BEGIN
0007F0 5B5BC2D6D7C5D540                     823                  =C'$$BOPEN '
0007F8 E2E4C2D9D6E4E3C9                     824                  =C'SUBROUTINE ERROR'
000808 5B5BC2C3D3D6E2C5                     825                  =C'$$BCLOSE'
000810 00000080                             826                  =A(REQUEST)
000814 00000000                             827                  =A(LIST)
000818 C9D5E5C1D3C9C440                     828                  =C'INVALID DATA'
000824 C6C9D7E240E3D640                     829                  =C'FIPS TO COMMERCIAL '
00083A C5E4D9D6D7C5C1D5                     830                  =C'EUROPEAN TO COMMERCIAL'
```

**Figure 3.3** *Continued*

```
TEST OF TIMESUBF TO CONVERT AMONG DATE FORMATS

01/05/83   COMMERCIAL - COMMERCIAL  01/05/1983   CODEF CONTENTS: 0  SIGF CONTENTS: 0
05/01/83   EUROPEAN TO COMMERCIAL   01/05/1983   CODEF CONTENTS: 0  SIGF CONTENTS: 2
83/01/05   FIPS TO COMMERCIAL       01/05/1983   CODEF CONTENTS: 0  SIGF CONTENTS: 1
130583     INVALID MONTH                         CODEF CONTENTS: 6  SIGF CONTENTS: 0
050083     INVALID MONTH                         CODEF CONTENTS: 6  SIGF CONTENTS: 2
83  05     INVALID DATA                          CODEF CONTENTS: 2  SIGF CONTENTS: 1
010083     INVALID DAY                           CODEF CONTENTS: 8  SIGF CONTENTS: 0
320183     INVALID DAY                           CODEF CONTENTS: 8  SIGF CONTENTS: 2
830229     INVALID DAY                           CODEF CONTENTS: 8  SIGF CONTENTS: 0
8302       INVALID SIGF                          CODEF CONTENTS: 1  SIGF CONTENTS: 2
           INVALID SIGF                          CODEF CONTENTS: 1  SIGF CONTENTS: 1


THE SUBROUTINE WAS EXECUTED     11 TIMES
```

**Figure 3.4**  Output from a test of TIMESUBF, the date reformatting subroutine.

While TIMESUBF is clearly a utility that prepares a six-digit date for subsequent processing that requires Commercial-8 date input, TIMESUBF's input can originate at any number of sources in either online or batch environments. This leads to possible implementations where TIMESUBF interfaces with a six-digit system date or CPU networks whose nodes have not yet converted to eight-digit usage. Although this doesn't extend the conversion deadline, it facilitates planning.

TIMESUB2 obviously has a more limited scope of application when you consider that all date calculations in this book are defined for eight-digit date input and eight-digit date output, and the calculations result in the output of a date. Neo-Julian dates are limited to packed-decimal peripheral storage. Consequently, TIMESUB2 is a tool for converting Commercial-8 to neo-Julian for subsequent peripheral storage.

It's practical here to address the rationale that produced this partitioning of the environment into neo-Julian date storage and Commercial-8 date computation. The constraints of existing date-storage limitations lead to peripheral storage of neo-Julian dates. The fact that neither programmers nor users will find Julian dates meaningful leads directly to the decision to require Commercial-8 as input to all algorithms in this book (save the algorithm that acts as the inverse of TIMESUB2). Thus, each algorithm accepts its input as though it came from a terminal operator. The data is edited and, only when found valid, is involved in computation. Whenever date output results from an algorithm, it's packed Commercial-8.

Conversion to or from neo-Julian format occurs only at the storage interface. Should a memory printout be reviewed in conjunction with a calling program problem, the subroutines presented here will display meaningful Commercial-8 data. Each algorithm's input field is left unchanged by the actions of the algorithm. Chapter 8 presents algorithms allowing the conversion of the neo-Julian date to Commercial-8 when accessed for use in computation or display. You'll also find TIMESUBG in that chapter. TIMESUBG accepts a Commercial-8 date along with a request indicator signifying the desired format of the output date: FIPS or European. Designed for maximum flexibility, TIMESUBG will also accept FIPS-8 or European-8 as input and provide the requested format on output. Both FIPS-8 and European-8 are dates whose components are implicitly defined within the definition of Commercial-8 as format variations of Commercial-8 dates.

# 4

# Short-Interval Aging

Anyone familiar with the business world prior to using electromechanical tabulating equipment will testify to the oppressive nature of periodic tasks that required large numbers of people to pore over mountains of ledger cards. Aging the accounts receivable was brutal but necessary work if a firm's doors were to remain open. Everyone is someone else's customer and if payments weren't made in a timely manner, companies had to borrow and pay interest if their businesses were to survive. As credit-buying permeated society, the importance of aging vast numbers of transactions became paramount. Add to this the need to age inventory to determine turnover, employee service to determine seniority, assets to determine depreciation, and so forth. It's not difficult to conclude that time is in fact inextricably bound to our concept of money. Time truly is of the essence.

## Defining the Problem

Just as it's true that both clocks and calendars measure time but in different magnitudes, so aging deals with short and long intervals. It's the task of this chapter to solve the problem of short-interval aging—usually in the 30-, 60-, 90-, or 120-day range. The next chapter will approach this problem in its longer-range aspect.

Fundamental to aging is finding the difference between two given dates. Because the idea of difference conjures up images of simple subtraction, laypeople often dismisses the problem as trivial. Few programmers who have been required to create aging programs would be so hasty. At the heart of the problem is the task of converting three disparate units of measurement—months, days, and years—to a common unit so subtraction is possible. Beyond this, the problem-solver is usually faced with determining which date is the later of the two so a positive difference results from the subtraction. As always, you age from the end of the first date to the end of the last.

## Devising the Solution Strategy

The most thoroughly traveled avenue in problem-solving is research. It's always practical to make sure you aren't reinventing the wheel, as the saying goes. Unfortunately, reviewing the commonly employed aging algorithms highlights the fact that the eight-digit date introduces complexities not present in the more restricted modular arithmetic of the two-digit year. New solutions are required.

You must reduce the two given dates to two numbers representing elapsed days. The subtraction then produces the number of days by which the two dates differ. The question then arises, "Days elapsed since when?" You must find a point of origin. Unlike the number line of arithmetic, on the time line there's no zero year. A.D. 1 immediately follows 1 B.C.

You could follow Scaliger and the astronomers and convert each date to its Julian Day using 01/01/4713 B.C. as the origin. Indeed, an early solution of this nature was offered by Henry F. Fliegel of the Georgetown University Observatory and Thomas C. Van Flandern of the U.S. Naval Observatory (1968: 657). Neither Fliegel nor Van Flandern was anticipating a crisis in computation. They were simply attempting to lead the computing community to a mathematical solution of the aging problem within the context of Fortran. Being relatively complex, their solution gained only limited popularity even in the Fortran environment.

Let us attempt to simplify the situation and choose 01/01/1601 as the point of origin. This is the beginning of both the 4- and the 400-year Gregorian leap-year cycles. Given a Commercial-8 date M/D/Y, you can compute the elapsed days beginning 01/01/1601 through the year (Y – 1). When you add to this result the ordinal day in Y represented by M and D, you've calculated the total elapsed days for the given date. Having accomplished this calculation for each of any two given Commercial-8 dates, the absolute value of the difference of the two computed day counts will render the number of days by which the later date exceeds the earlier. This solution strategy provides greatly simplified calculations, with no need to determine the chronological order of the input dates.

## Creating the Algorithm

Chapter 3 gave you the algorithm necessary to compute the ordinal day E in Y for any given Commercial-8 date. Your task here is reduced to formulating an equation that will produce the elapsed days from 12/31/1600, through the end of the year (Y – 1), the year prior to the year of the input date. More simply expressed, you need to find the number of elapsed days for the years 1601, 1602, . . ., (Y – 1).

In order to accomplish this, you must first determine the number of years involved. Thus, (Y – 1) – 1600 produces this result quite simply. For example, for the input date 01/02/2223, substitute 2223 for Y as follows:

$$(2223 - 1) - 1600 = 622 \text{ years}$$

If you're algebraically inclined, you'll see that the expression can be simplified, since:

$$(Y - 1) - 1600 = Y - (1 + 1600) = Y - 1601$$

Hence, for the previous example you have:

$$2223 - 1601 = 622 \text{ years}$$

Because you're looking for the total number of days expired in 622 years and because the lower limit coincides with the start of both the 4- and the 400-year leap-year cycles, assume a leap year for *every* four years. Thus, term #1 in the equation is:

$$[365.25(Y - 1601)]$$

For the example:

$$[365.25(622)] = [227,185.50] = 227,185$$

Term #1 is a useful element, although it's in error because it has allowed the extra day for each non-leap-year centesimal. Because the lower limit is at the beginning of the 400-year cycle, it's to adjust for this error by subtracting the non-leap-year centesimals' contribution via the creation of appropriate additional terms. For each leap-year centesimal, there are three intervening non-leap-year centesimals. Hence, term #2 is:

$$3\left(\frac{Y - 1601}{400}\right)$$

For the example:

$$3\left(\frac{622}{400}\right) = 3(1) = 3$$

Subtract term #2 from term #1 to eliminate one day for each intervening non-leap-year centesimal. Finally, you have only to eliminate one additional day for each non-leap-year centesimal remaining after the division in term #2. Consequently, create term #3 as:

$$\frac{(Y - 1601)_{(\text{Mod } 400)}}{100}$$

For the example, 222/100 = 2. Here you can see that in the third term you simply divide the remainder produced in term #2 (222) by 100 to find the number of remaining non-leap-year centesimals, 2. Thus the equation that produces the number of elapsed days—1601, 1602, . . . (Y – 1)—is term #1 minus term #2 minus term #3. You can abbreviate this as: T1 – T2 – T3. For the example, this is 227,185 – 3 – 2 = 227,180. When you add to this the ordinal day E, you have the total elapsed days beginning 01/01/1601 to and including the given Commercial-8 date. The equation you set out to create, then, is: total elapsed days = T1 – T2 – T3 + E.

### Defining the algorithm's components

Let's proceed to define the inputs, return code, and output of the algorithm TIME-SUB3. Two inputs are required, DATE1 and DATE2. Both must be eight-digit dates conforming to the definition of Commercial-8. The return code CODE3 is defined as follows:

$$CODE3 = \begin{cases} 0, \text{If DATE1 and DATE2 are M/D/Y, Commercial-8} \\ 2, \text{If DATE1, M/D/Y is not valid numeric} \\ 3, \text{If DATE2, M/D/Y is not valid numeric} \\ 4, \text{If for DATE1, Y } \varepsilon \text{ \{y: 1600 < y < 3400\}} \\ 5, \text{If for DATE2, Y } \varepsilon \text{ \{y: 1600 < y < 3400\}} \\ 6, \text{If for DATE1, M } \varepsilon \text{ \{m: 0 < m < 13\}} \\ 7, \text{If for DATE2, M } \varepsilon \text{ \{m: 0 < m < 13\}} \\ 8, \text{If for DATE1, D } \varepsilon \text{ \{d\} as defined in Commercial-8} \\ 9, \text{If for DATE2, D } \varepsilon \text{ \{d\} as defined in Commercial-8} \end{cases}$$

Here again you find that the return code uses 0 to signal a successful execution. For DATE1 and DATE2, these are the following codes: 2 or 3 indicate bad data, 4 or 5 a bad year, 6 or 7 a bad month, and 8 or 9 a bad day.

The output is DCOUNT, the difference in days between DATE1 and DATE2. Note that DCOUNT's definition differs from previous output definitions in that it's doubly defined for a zero value. The output fields of previous subroutines were set to an undefined value when the return code was nonzero. This isn't possible for DCOUNT because DCOUNT has no upper limit. This is consistent with our previous remarks concerning the future of the Gregorian calendar in chapter 1.

$$DCOUNT = \begin{cases} 0, \text{If CODE3} \neq 0 \\ 0, \text{If CODE3} = 0 \text{ and DATE1} = \text{DATE2} \\ N, \text{If CODE3} = 0 \text{ and DATE1} \neq \text{DATE2, where} \\ \quad N \varepsilon \text{ \{n: n belongs to Z, 0 < n\}} \end{cases}$$

## The Pseudocode for TIMESUB3

The pseudocode assumes that its input has been received in two eight-byte zoned decimal fields, DATE1 and DATE2. The output field DCOUNT is a four-byte packed field. Again, you'll employ → to indicate the point in the pseudocode and the sequence in which a field's components are distributed to named work fields in order to provide access.

```
 *  Perform general housekeeping
1) Let DCOUNT = 0
2) Let CODE3 = 0
3) Let DAS1 = 0
 *  Input-related housekeeping: DATE1
4) Move DATE1 to WORK8
5) Let CONSTANT2 = 2
6) Let CONSTANT4 = 4
7) Let CONSTANT6 = 6
8) Let CONSTANT8 = 8
9) Go to 15
 *  Input-related housekeeping: DATE2
10) Move DATE2 to WORK8
```

```
11) Let CONSTANT2 = 3
12) Let CONSTANT4 = 5
13) Let CONSTANT6 = 7
14) Let CONSTANT8 = 9
 * Validate input data as numeric
15) If WORK8 is numeric, go to 17
16) Let CODE3 = CONSTANT2, go to 39
 * Test Y for limit violation
17) WORK8 → M,D,Y
18) If Y is within limits per Commercial-8, go to 20
19) Let CODE3 = CONSTANT4, go to 39
 * Perform leap-year algorithm for Y
20) Let L = 0
21) If Y is a leap year, let L = 1
 * Test M for limit violation
22) If M is within limits per Commercial-8, go to 24
23) Let CODE3 = CONSTANT6, go to 39
 * Test D for limit violation
24) If D is within limits per Commercial-8, go to 26
25) Let CODE3 = CONSTANT8, go to 39
 * Compute elapsed days, 01/01/1601 through input date
 * First, compute ordinal day, E, of input date
26) Let JLIAN = elapsed days through (M-1)
27) Let JLIAN = JLIAN + D
 * Second, compute elapsed days 01/01/1601 to input year
28) Compute T1 = [365.25(Y - 1601)]
29) Compute T2 = 3((Y - 1601) ÷ 400)
30) Compute T3 = ((Y - 1601)(Mod 400)) ÷ 100
 * Third, compute the sum
31) Let JLIAN = JLIAN + T1
32) Let JLIAN = JLIAN - T2
33) Let JLIAN = JLIAN - T3
 * Determine which date processed
34) If DAS1 ≠ 0, go to 37
35) Let DAS1 = JLIAN
36) Go to 10
37) Let DAS2 = JLIAN
 * Compute absolute difference of DAS1 and DAS2
38) Let DCOUNT = |DAS1 - DAS2|
39) Exit
```

## Comments on the pseudocode

Unlike prior algorithms, TIMESUB3 employs a loop. The loop control is based on the content of DAS1. You might inquire about the possibility of DAS1 never having a value greater than zero and thus producing an infinite loop. This isn't possible since the earliest date that will pass the editing is 01/01/1601, for which T1, T2, and T3 are all zero; however, E = 1. Hence, DAS1 will always be greater than zero after the first iteration. Thus, the algorithm is valid on its domain, 01/01/1601 to 12/31/3399 inclusive.

The pseudocode initializes the constants that serve CODE3 with values appropriate to the input being processed. The overriding assumption is that the calling program will be consistent in its submission of inputs. Therefore, if the calling program executes TIMESUB3 from multiple points, the programmer must distinguish DATE1 from DATE2 in interrogating CODE3's return values. Thus, a nonzero return code can be accurately related to the offending data.

## The Source Code for TIMESUB3

Figure 4.1 displays the TIMESUB3 portion of TEST03's assembly post listing. We invite you to closely review the documentation. TIMESUB3 was tested using a constant 12/31/1999 input for DATE1, while DATE2 was varied from 01/01/2000 by one day through 12/31/2000. Another series of inputs was added to the test data set, with DATE1 constant at 12/31/2000 and DATE2 varied by one day from 01/01/2001 through 12/31/2001. The test data set was further augmented by the insertion of invalid dates (such as 02/29/2001) and invalid date components, as well as dates violating the limits for all components. Finally, a random series of valid dates were added. The test produced the expected output. The subroutine represents a valid algorithm. A subset of the test results is shown in Figure 4.2.

### Comments on the source code of TIMESUB3

The source code's sequence of activities closely follows what's indicated in the pseudocode. Table usage is conditioned by the L value as each input is converted to a count of elapsed days, from 01/01/1601 through the input date. The inline comments highlight the various language-dependent facilities invoked to produce integer truncation and absolute value results. Once more, rather simple and straightforward programming results from careful algorithm design.

## Using TIMESUB3

Assuming a six-digit system date, you can use TIMESUBF to convert it to Commercial-8, initializing DATE1 with the input. Thereafter, move Commercial-8 dates to DATE2, execute TIMESUB3, and compare DCOUNT with 30-, 60-, 90-, and 120-day constants (or any desired constant) to determine the age of the DATE2 date relative to the system date.

If you're interested in aging database dates stored in neo-Julian format, a later chapter in this book provides algorithms that will allow you to convert neo-Julian dates to Commercial-8. Following this, you can use DATE2 as described previously in the aging processes.

Assuming a stepwise conversion to eight-digit date usage, you can also invoke TIMESUBF to expand stored six-digit dates to Commercial-8 prior to moving the stored date to DATE2 for aging. Thus, it's possible to convert programming to eight-digit computation prior to converting the database. Hence the conversion might be on a program-by-program basis until the final conversion of the database. Chapter 11 details the multiple conversion options available.

The central feature of TIMESUB3 is that it presents differences between dates in *day* counts. If you're looking for meaningful aging results that vary from zero to hundreds of days, you might find the next chapter's algorithm more rewarding.

```
LOC   OBJECT CODE   ADDR1  ADDR2   STMT   SOURCE STATEMENT                              DOS/VSE ASSEMBLER  16.17   99-12-31

                                   396  *                                                                            * TS300010
                                   397  *                                                                            * TS300020
                                   398  *                                                                            * TS300030
                                   399  * TTTTTTT  III  MM    MM  EEEEE  SSSSS  U   U  BBBBB  3333                    * TS300040
                                   400  *    T      I   M M  M M  E      S      U   U  B   B      3                   * TS300050
                                   401  *    T      I   M  MM  M  EEEE   SSSSS  U   U  BBB B     33                   * TS300060
                                   402  *    T      I   M      M  E          S  U   U  B   B      3                   * TS300070
                                   403  *    T     III  M      M  EEEEE  SSSSS  UUUUU  BBBBB  3333                    * TS300080
                                   404  *                                                                            * TS300090
                                   405  *                                                                            * TS300100
                                   406  * E L A P S E D   D A Y S   B E T W E E N   G R E G O R I A N   D A T E S     * TS300110
                                   407  * * * * * * * * * * * * * * * * * * * * * * * * * * * * * * * * * * * * * * * * TS300120
                                   408  * * * * * * * * * * * * * * * * * * * * * * * * * * * * * * * * * * * * * * * * TS300130
                                   409  * * * * * * * * * * * * * * * * * * * * * * * * * * * * * * * * * * * * * * * * TS300140
                                   410  *                                                                            * TS300150
                                   411  *         THIS SUBROUTINE CALCULATES ELAPSED DAYS BETWEEN TWO                 * TS300160
                                   412  *         GREGORIAN DATES                                                    * TS300170
                                   413  *                                                                            * TS300180
                                   414  *    1.   VALID INPUT YEARS FOR THIS SUBROUTINE ARE THE YEARS                * TS300190
                                   415  *         1601 THROUGH 3399 A. D.                                            * TS300200
                                   416  *                                                                            * TS300210
                                   417  *    2.   VALID INPUT MONTH VALUES FOR THIS SUBROUTINE ARE 01                * TS300220
                                   418  *         THROUGH 12.                                                        * TS300230
                                   419  *                                                                            * TS300240
                                   420  *    3.   VALID INPUT DAY VALUES FOR THIS SUBROUTINE ARE 01                  * TS300250
                                   421  *         THROUGH 31 WITH EXCEPTIONS FOR THE MONTHS LISTED:                  * TS300260
                                   422  *                  MONTH           MAXIMUM DAY VALUE                         * TS300270
                                   423  *                   04                  30                                   * TS300280
                                   424  *                   06                  30                                   * TS300290
                                   425  *                   09                  30                                   * TS300300
                                   426  *                   11                  30                                   * TS300310
                                   427  *                   02                  28                                   * TS300320
                                   428  *                   02 DURING LEAP YEAR 29                                   * TS300330
                                   429  *                                                                            * TS300340
                                   430  *    4.   THE DATE FORMAT MUST BE MMDDYYYY.  WHERE MM = THE TWO              * TS300350
                                   431  *         DIGIT MONTH VALUE, DD = THE TWO DIGIT DAY VALUE AND                * TS300360
                                   432  *         YYYY = THE FOUR DIGIT YEAR.                                        * TS300370
                                   433  *                                                                            * TS300380
                                   434  *    5.   THE CALLING PROGRAM MUST PLACE ONE EIGHT DIGIT DATE,               * TS300390
                                   435  *         IN ZONED FORMAT, IN A SUBROUTINE DEFINED EIGHT BYTE                * TS300400
                                   436  *         FIELD, 'DATE1,' THE CALLING PROGRAM MUST PLACE THE OTHER           * TS300410
                                   437  *         EIGHT DIGIT DATE, IN ZONED FORMAT, IN ANOTHER SUBROUTINE           * TS300420
                                   438  *         DEFINED EIGHT BYTE FIELD, 'DATE2,' PRIOR TO EXECUTION OF.          * TS300430
                                   439  *         THE SUBROUTINE.  NEITHER FIELD IS ALTERED BY THE SUB-              * TS300440
                                   440  *         ROUTINE.                                                           * TS300450
                                   441  *         NOTE:  ***  THE ORDER OF THE DATES IS IMMATERIAL.                  * TS300460
                                   442  *                                                                            * TS300470
                                   443  *    6.   A SUBROUTINE DEFINED ONE BYTE FIELD, 'CODE3,' IS RETURNED          * TS300480
                                   444  *         TO THE CALLING PROGRAM AND CONTAINS A PACKED 0 IF THE              * TS300490
                                   445  *         EXECUTION WAS SUCCESSFUL.  NON-ZERO VALUES INDICATE                * TS300500
                                   446  *         THE FOLLOWING:                                                     * TS300510
                                   447  *                                                                            * TS300520
                                   448  *         A PACKED 2 FOR DATE1 (3 FOR DATE2) INDICATES UNSUCCESS-            * TS300530
                                   449  *         FUL EXECUTION: INVALID DATA.                                       * TS300540
                                   450  *                                                                            * TS300550
```

**Figure 4.1** Introductory documentation and source code for the TIMESUB3 portion of TEST03's assembly post listing.

```
LOC   OBJECT CODE   ADDR1 ADDR2   STMT   SOURCE STATEMENT                                              DOS/VSE ASSEMBLER 16.17  99-12-31

                                  451 *   INVALID DATA ARE DETERMINED IF THE LOW ORDER BYTE'S ZONE                          TS300560
                                  452 *   CONTAINS AN INVALID SIGN. (AN INVALID SIGN IS OTHER THAN                          TS300570
                                  453 *   X'C', X'A', X'E', OR X'F') OR IF THE PRECEDING BYTES'                             TS300580
                                  454 *   ZONES ARE OTHER THAN X'F', OR IF THE LOW ORDER NIBBLE                             TS300590
                                  455 *   OF ANY BYTE CONTAINS A VALUE GREATER THAN X'9'.                                   TS300600
                                  456 *                                                                                     TS300610
                                  457 *   A PACKED 4 FOR DATE1 (5 FOR DATE2) INDICATES UNSUCCESS-                           TS300620
                                  458 *   FUL EXECUTION: INVALID YEAR- YEAR VALUE VIOLATES LIMITS                           TS300630
                                  459 *   SPECIFIED IN 1.. ABOVE.                                                           TS300640
                                  460 *                                                                                     TS300650
                                  461 *   A PACKED 6 FOR DATE1 (7 FOR DATE2) INDICATES UNSUCCESS-                           TS300660
                                  462 *   FUL EXECUTION: INVALID MONTH- MONTH VALUE VIOLATES LIMITS                         TS300670
                                  463 *   SPECIFIED IN 2.. ABOVE.                                                           TS300680
                                  464 *                                                                                     TS300690
                                  465 *   A PACKED 8 FOR DATE1 (9 FOR DATE2) INDICATES UNSUCCESS-                           TS300700
                                  466 *   FUL EXECUTION: INVALID DAY- DAY VALUE VIOLATES LIMITS                             TS300710
                                  467 *   SPECIFIED IN 3.. ABOVE.                                                           TS300720
                                  468 *                                                                                     TS300730
                                  469 *   INSPECTION OF THE RETURN CODE IS IMPORTANT.  THE RETURN                           TS300740
                                  470 *   CODE, CODE3, REFLECTS THE LEVEL OF EDITING.  A RETURN                             TS300750
                                  471 *   CODE OF 2, FOR EXAMPLE, NOT ONLY INDICATES INVALIDITY OF                         TS300760
                                  472 *   DATA, IT ALSO INDICATES THAT NO EDITING HAS BEEN DONE TO                         TS300770
                                  473 *   VALIDATE THE YEAR, MONTH OR DAY VALUES.  A RETURN CODE OF                        TS300780
                                  474 *   4 INDICATES THAT THE DATA ARE VALID BUT THAT THE YEAR WAS                        TS300790
                                  475 *   FOUND INVALID- THE MONTH AND DAY VALUES HAVE NOT BEEN ED-                        TS300800
                                  476 *   ITED.  A RETURN CODE OF 6 INDICATES THAT THE DATA AND                            TS300810
                                  477 *   YEAR ARE VALID BUT THAT THE MONTH IS INVALID- THE DAY                            TS300820
                                  478 *   VALUE HAS NOT BEEN EDITED.  FINALLY, A RETURN CODE OF 8                          TS300830
                                  479 *   INDICATES THAT THE DATA, YEAR AND MONTH ARE VALID BUT                           TS300840
                                  480 *   THAT THE DAY WAS FOUND INVALID FOR THE VALID MONTH GIVEN.                        TS300850
                                  481 *   IN SHORT, THE RETURN CODE INDICATES THE LEVEL OF EDITING.                        TS300860
                                  482 *   THE EDIT SEQUENCE IS DATE1: DATA, YEAR, MONTH AND DAY.                           TS300870
                                  483 *   THEN DATE2: DATA, YEAR, MONTH AND DAY.                                           TS300880
                                  484 *                                                                                     TS300890
                                  485 7. * A SUBROUTINE DEFINED, FOUR BYTE FIELD, 'DCOUNT' IS RE-                          TS300900
                                  486 *   TURNED TO THE CALLING PROGRAM.  THE NUMBER OF ELAPSED                            TS300910
                                  487 *   DAYS BETWEEN THE TWO INPUT DATES IS CONTAINED IN DCOUNT                          TS300920
                                  488 *   AS AN ABSOLUTE VALUE, IN PACKED FORMAT.  IF THE SUB-                             TS300930
                                  489 *   ROUTINE EXECUTION IS UNSUCCESSFUL, THAT IS IF THE RETURN                        TS300940
                                  490 *   CODE FIELD, CODE3, CONTAINS A NON-ZERO VALUE, THEN                              TS300950
                                  491 *   DCOUNT WILL CONTAIN PACKED ZEROS.  THIS IS PROTECTION                           TS300960
                                  492 *   AGAINST ILLEGAL USE OF A PRIOR EXECUTION'S RESULT.                              TS300970
                                  493 *   BE AWARE THAT PACKED ZEROS IN DCOUNT CONSTITUTE A VALID                         TS300980
                                  494 *   RESULT FOR INPUT DATES THAT ARE IDENTICAL, HOWEVER.                             TS300990
                                  495 *                                                                                     TS301000
                                  496 8. * ALL OTHER SUBROUTINE DEFINED FIELDS AND LABELS ARE                             TS301010
                                  497 *   TRANSPARENT TO THE CALLING PROGRAM.                                              TS301020
                                  498 *                                                                                     TS301030
                                  499 9. * THIS SUBROUTINE IS WRITTEN TO BE ASSEMBLED WITH THE                            TS301040
                                  500 *   CALLING PROGRAM AND SHOULD BE INSERTED IN THE CALLING                           TS301050
                                  501 *   PROGRAM IMMEDIATELY BEFORE THE 'END' OPCODE.                                     TS301060
                                  502 *                                                                                     TS301070
                                  503 10. * THIS SUBROUTINE USES REGISTER 6 AS THE LINK REGISTER.                         TS301080
                                  504 *   IF REGISTER 6 IS ASSIGNED IN THE CALLING PROGRAM FOR                            TS301090
                                  505 *   OTHER USES, IT MUST BE SAVED PRIOR TO EXECUTING THE                            TS301100
```

```
LOC    OBJECT CODE      ADDR1 ADDR2 STMT  SOURCE STATEMENT                                    DOS/VSE ASSEMBLER 16.17  99-12-31

                                    506  *                                                 *                          TS301110
                                    507  *                                                 *                          TS301120
                                    508  *        'BALR.'                                   *                          TS301130
                                    509  *                                                 *                          TS301140
                                    510  *                                      JEROME T. MURRAY  *                    TS301150
                                    511  *        GLEN ELLYN. ILLINOIS          MARILYN J. MURRAY *                    TS301160
                                    512  *                                                 *                          TS301170
                                    513  *        *************************************************                    TS301180
                                    514  *        *************************************************                    TS301190
                                    515  *        *************************************************                    TS301200
                                    516  *                                                                             TS301210
                                    517  *        +++ SECTION 1- GENERAL HOUSEKEEPING +++                              TS301220
                                    518  *                                                                             TS301230
                                    519  *        INITIALIZE INDICATIVE AND WORK FIELDS                                TS301240
                                    520  *                                                                             TS301250
0004BC F830 77B1 78B2  00867 00968  521  TIMESUB3 ZAP   DCOUNT,=P'0'                                                   TS301260
0004C2 F800 77B5 78B2  0086B 00968  522           ZAP   CODE3,=P'0'                                                    TS301270
0004C8 F840 77C6 78B2  0087C 00968  523           ZAP   #$3DAS1,=P'0'                                                  TS301280
                                    524  *                                                                             TS301290
                                    525  *        SAVE REGISTERS 1 THROUGH 5 IN SAVE FIELDS                            TS301300
                                    526  *                                                                             TS301310
0004CE 9015 7802       00BB8        527           STM   1,5,#$3RSAVE                                                   TS301320
                                    528  *                                                                             TS301330
                                    529  *        +++ SECTION 2- INPUT-RELATED HOUSEKEEPING +++                        TS301340
                                    530  *                                                                             TS301350
                                    531  *        (THIS SECTION BEGINS EACH OF TWO ITERATIONS                          TS301360
                                    532  *         THAT EXECUTE FOR EACH INPUT SET)                                    TS301370
                                    533  *                                                                             TS301380
                                    534  *        MOVE DATE1 TO WORK FIELD, ESTABLISH RETURN                           TS301390
                                    535  *        CODE VALUES FOR DATE1- BRANCH TO VALIDATE DATE1                      TS301400
                                    536  *                                                                             TS301410
0004D2 D207 77DC 77B6  00892 0086C  537           MVC   #$3WORK8,DATE1                                                 TS301420
0004D8 F800 77D0 78B3  00886 00969  538           ZAP   #$32,=P'2'                                                     TS301430
0004DE F800 77D1 78B5  00887 0096B  539           ZAP   #$34,=P'4'                                                     TS301440
0004E4 F800 77D2 78B7  00888 0096D  540           ZAP   #$36,=P'6'                                                     TS301450
0004EA F800 77D3 78E7  00889 0099D  541           ZAP   #$38,=P'8'                                                     TS301460
0004F0 47F0 745C       00512        542           B     #$31DATE                                                       TS301470
                                    543  *                                                                             TS301480
                                    544  *        MOVE DATE2 TO WORK FIELD, ESTABLISH RETURN                           TS301490
                                    545  *        CODE VALUES FOR DATE2- PROCEED TO VALIDATE DATE2                     TS301500
                                    546  *                                                                             TS301510
0004F4 D207 77DC 77BE  00892 00874  547  #$32DATE MVC   #$3WORK8,DATE2                                                 TS301520
0004FA F800 77D0 78B4  00886 0096A  548           ZAP   #$32,=P'3'                                                     TS301530
000500 F800 77D1 78B6  00887 0096C  549           ZAP   #$34,=P'5'                                                     TS301540
000506 F800 77D2 78CF  00888 00985  550           ZAP   #$36,=P'7'                                                     TS301550
00050C F800 77D3 78FD  00889 009B3  551           ZAP   #$38,=P'9'                                                     TS301560
                                    552  *                                                                             TS301570
                                    553  *        +++ SECTION 3- NUMERIC VALIDATION +++                                TS301580
                                    554  *                                                                             TS301590
                                    555  *        ISOLATE THE SIGN BYTE IN A WORK FIELD AND                            TS301600
                                    556  *        AUGMENT TABLE FOR VALID '+' SIGNS OTHER THAN                         TS301610
                                    557  *        X'F' FOR WHICH TABLE IS DEFINED: X'A', X'C'.                         TS301620
                                    558  *        X'E'- EDIT FOR VALID '+' SIGN USING TRT                              TS301630
                                    559  *                                                                             TS301640
000512 D200 77D5 77E3  00BBB 00899  560  #$31DATE MVC   #$3SIGN,#$3WORK8+7                                             TS301650
```

**Figure 4.1** *Continued*

```
                                                          DOS/VSE ASSEMBLER 16.17   99-12-31

LOC    OBJECT CODE     ADDR1 ADDR2  STMT  SOURCE STATEMENT

000518 D209 7745 77A5  007FB 0085B   561         MVC   #$3TABL+160(10),#$3ZRO              TS301660
00051E D209 7765 77A5  0081B 0085B   562         MVC   #$3TABL+192(10),#$3ZRO              TS301670
000524 D209 7785 77A5  0083B 0085B   563         MVC   #$3TABL+224(10),#$3ZRO              TS301680
00052A DD00 77D5 76A5  0088B 0075B   564         TRT   #$3SIGN(1),#$3TABL                  TS301690
000530 4780 7482             0548    565         BC    8,#$3NUM                            TS301700
000534 47F0 7492             0548    566         B     #$3BDATA                            TS301710
                                     567   *                                              TS301720
                                     568   *          REINITIALIZE TABLE AND EDIT FOR VALID ZONE  TS301730
                                     569   *          AND DIGIT CONFIGURATIONS IN REMAINING BYTES TS301740
                                     570   *                                              TS301750
000538 D2EE 76A6 76A5  0075C 0075B   571  #$3NUM MVC  #$3TABL+1(239),#$3TABL               TS301760
00053E DD06 77DC 749C        0075B   572         TRT   #$3WORK8(7),#$3TABL                 TS301770
000544 4780 749C             0552    573         BC    8,#$3PACK                           TS301780
                                     574   *                                              TS301790
                                     575   *          POST 'BAD DATA' RETURN CODE AND EXIT TS301800
                                     576   *                                              TS301810
000548 F800 77B5 77D0  0086B 00BD8   577 #$3BDATA ZAP  CODE3,#$32                          TS301820
00054E 47F0 7822             00BD8   578         B     #$3TERM                             TS301830
                                     579   *                                              TS301840
                                     580   *      +++  SECTION 4- EDIT YEAR FOR LIMIT VIOLATIONS +++ TS301850
                                     581   *                                              TS301860
                                     582   *          PACK MONTH, DAY AND YEAR IN WORK FIELDS TS301870
                                     583   *                                              TS301880
000552 F211 77DC 77ED  008A3 00892   584 #$3PACK PACK #$3MO,#$3WORK8(2)                    TS301890
000558 F211 77EF 77DE  008A5 00894   585         PACK  #$3DA,#$3WORK8+2(2)                 TS301900
00055E F223 77F1 77EO  008A7 00896   586         PACK  #$3YR,#$3WORK8+4(4)                 TS301910
                                     587   *                                              TS301920
                                     588   *          EDIT YEAR VALUE FOR LOWER LIMIT VIOLATION TS301930
                                     589   *                                              TS301940
000564 F922 77F1 74C2  008A7 00578   590         CP    #$3YR,=P'1600'                      TS301950
00056A 4720 7578             00578   591         BH    #$3YRHI                             TS301960
                                     592   *                                              TS301970
                                     593   *          POST 'BAD YEAR' RETURN CODE AND EXIT TS301980
                                     594   *                                              TS301990
00056E F800 77B5 77D1  0086B 00BD8   595 #$3BADYR ZAP  CODE3,#$34                          TS302000
000574 47F0 7822             00BD8   596         B     #$3TERM                             TS302010
                                     597   *                                              TS302020
                                     598   *          EDIT YEAR VALUE FOR UPPER LIMIT VIOLATION TS302030
                                     599   *                                              TS302040
000578 F922 77F1 74B8  008A7 0056E   600 #$3YRHI  CP   #$3YR,=P'3399'                      TS302050
00057E 4720 74C2             0056E   601         BH    #$3BADYR                            TS302060
                                     602   *                                              TS302070
                                     603   *      +++  SECTION 5- DETERMINE LEAP YEAR STATUS +++ TS302080
                                     604   *                                              TS302090
                                     605   *          EXECUTE LEAP YEAR ALGORITHM         TS302100
                                     606   *                                              TS302110
000582 F800 77D4 7882  0088A 00968   607         ZAP   #$3L,=P'O'                          TS302120
000588 F842 77FC 77F1  008B2 008A7   608         ZAP   #$3WORK,#$3YR                       TS302130
00058E FD40 77FC 7885  008B2 0096B   609         DP    #$3WORK,=P'4'                       TS302140
000594 F900 7800 7882  008B6 00968   610         CP    #$3WORK+4(1),=P'O'                  TS302150
00059A 4720 751A             005D0   611         BH    #$3MOEDT                            TS302160
00059E F842 77FC 77F1  008B2 008A7   612         ZAP   #$3WORK,#$3YR                       TS302170
0005A4 FD41 77FC 78AA  008B2 00960   613         DP    #$3WORK,=P'100'                     TS302180
0005AA F910 77FF 7882  008B5 00968   614         CP    #$3WORK+3(2),=P'O'                  TS302190
0005B0 4720 7514             005CA   615         BH    #$3LPYR                             TS302200
```

```
LOC     OBJECT CODE     ADDR1 ADDR2  STMT  SOURCE STATEMENT                       DOS/VSE ASSEMBLER 16.17   99-12-31

0005B4 F842 77FC 77F1   00BB2 00BA7   616            ZAP   #$3WORK,#$3YR                                       TS302210
0005BA FD41 77FC 78AC   00BB2 00962   617            DP    #$3WORK,=P'400'                                     TS302220
0005C0 F910 77FF 78B2   00BB5 00968   618            CP    #$3WORK+3(2),=P'0'                                  TS302230
0005C6 4720 751A              005D0   619            BH    #$3MOEDT                                            TS302240
                                      620    *                                                                TS302250
                                      621    *         IF YEAR IS A LEAP YEAR, SET INCREMENT TO 1              TS302260
                                      622    *                                                                TS302270
0005CA F800 77D4 78B0   00BBA 00966   623 #$3LPYR    ZAP   #$3L,=P'1'                                          TS302280
                                      624    *                                                                TS302290
                                      625    *  +++   SECTION 6- EDIT MONTH FOR LIMIT VIOLATIONS   +++         TS302300
                                      626    *                                                                TS302310
                                      627    *         VERIFY THAT MONTH IS WITHIN RANGE: 1 - 12               TS302320
                                      628    *         A) CONVERT MONTH TO BINARY IN REGISTER 3                TS302330
                                      629    *                                                                TS302340
0005D0 F871 781A 77ED   00BD0 00BA3   630 #$3MOEDT   ZAP   #$3CVB,#$3MO                                        TS302350
0005D6 4F30 781A              00BD0   631            CVB   3,#$3CVB                                            TS302360
                                      632    *                                                                TS302370
                                      633    *         B) STORE BINARY BYTE FROM REG 3 IN #$3FLD              TS302380
                                      634    *                                                                TS302390
0005DA 4230 7801              00BB7   635            STC   3,#$3FLD                                            TS302400
                                      636    *                                                                TS302410
                                      637    *         C) INITIALIZE TABLE WITH X'00' FOR TRT                 TS302420
                                      638    *                                                                TS302430
0005DE D20B 76A6 77A5   0075C 0085B   639            MVC   #$3TABL+1(12),#$32R0                               TS302440
                                      640    *                                                                TS302450
                                      641    *         D) EXECUTE TRT USING #$3FLD                            TS302460
                                      642    *                                                                TS302470
0005E4 DD00 7801 76A5   00BB7 0075B   643            TRT   #$3FLD(1),#$3TABL                                  TS302480
0005EA 4780 7548              005FE   644            BC    8,#$3DAEDT                                          TS302490
                                      645    *                                                                TS302500
                                      646    *         F) RESTORE TABLE - POST BAD MONTH RETURN CODE          TS302510
                                      647    *                            AND EXIT                            TS302520
                                      648    *                                                                TS302530
0005EE D20B 76A6 76A5   0075C 0075B   649            MVC   #$3TABL+1(12),#$3TABL                              TS302540
0005F4 F800 77B5 77D2   00868 00888   650            ZAP   CODE3,#$36                                         TS302550
0005FA 47F0 7822              008D8   651            B     #$3TERM                                            TS302560
                                      652    *                                                                TS302570
                                      653    *  +++   SECTION 7- EDIT DAY FOR LIMIT VIOLATIONS   +++           TS302580
                                      654    *                                                                TS302590
                                      655    *         RESTORE TABLE                                          TS302600
                                      656    *                                                                TS302610
0005FE D20B 76A6 76A5   0075C 0075B   657 #$3DAEDT   MVC   #$3TABL+1(12),#$3TABL                              TS302620
                                      658    *                                                                TS302630
                                      659    *         GET ADDRESS OF DAY TABLE IN REGISTER 4                 TS302640
                                      660    *                                                                TS302650
000604 4140 7645              006FB   661            LA    4,#$3DATAB                                          TS302660
                                      662    *                                                                TS302670
                                      663    *         IF LEAP YEAR, INCREMENT TO LEAP YEAR FUNCTION          TS302680
                                      664    *                                                                TS302690
000608 F900 77D4 78B2   00BBA 00968   665            CP    #$3L,=P'0'                                          TS302700
00060E 4780 7560              00616   666            BE    #$3NOL                                             TS302710
000612 4144 0002              00002   667            LA    4,2(4)                                             TS302720
                                      668    *                                                                TS302730
                                      669    *         DIRECTLY ADDRESS TABLE DAY LIMIT FOR THIS MONTH        TS302740
                                      670    *         A) SUBTRACT 1 FROM BINARY MONTH VALUE IN REG 3         TS302750
```

**Figure 4.1** *Continued*

```
                                                      DOS/VSE ASSEMBLER 16.17  99-12-31

LOC     OBJECT CODE     ADDR1 ADDR2   STMT   SOURCE STATEMENT

                                       671 *
000616  0630                           672 #$3NOL  BCTR  3,0
                                       673 *
                                       674 *
                                       675 *       B) MULTIPLY VALUE IN REG 3 BY 4              TS302760
000618  8930  0002            00002    676         SLL   3,2                                    TS302810
                                       677 *
                                       678 *       C) LOAD ADDRESS OF DAY TABLE ENTRY IN REG 4
                                       679 *
00061C  4143  4000            00000    680         LA    4,0(3,4)
                                       681 *
                                       682 *       CONVERT SIGN OF PACKED DAY FROM X'F' TO X'C'
                                       683 *
000620  F811  77EF 77EF 008A5 008A5    684         ZAP   #$3DA,#$3DA
                                       685 *
                                       686 *       COMPARE DAY TABLE ENTRY (LIMIT) WITH INPUT DAY
                                       687 *
000626  D501  77EF 4000 008A5 00000    688         CLC   #$3DA,0(4)
                                       689 *
                                       690 *       IF INPUT IS WITHIN LIMIT, EDIT DAY FOR ZERO
                                       691 *
00062C  47D0  7584         0063A       692         BNH   #$3DALO
                                       693 *
                                       694 *       ELSE POST BAD DAY RETURN CODE AND EXIT
                                       695 *
000630  F800  77B5 77D3 0086B 00889    696 #$3BADA ZAP   CODE3,#$38
000636  47F0  7822         00BD8       697         B     #$3TERM
                                       698 *
                                       699 *       EDIT DAY VALUE FOR ZERO
                                       700 *
00063A  F911  77EF 78AE 008A5 00964    701 #$3DALO CP    #$3DA,=P'00'
000640  4780  757A         00630       702         BE    #$3BADA
                                       703 *
                                       704 *       +++ SECTION 8- COMPUTE ELAPSED DAYS PER DATE  +++
                                       705 *
                                       706 *       FIRST, COMPUTE ELAPSED DAYS THIS YEAR TO MONTH
                                       707 *
                                       708 *       DIRECTLY ADDRESS ELAPSED DAY TABLE THIS MONTH
                                       709 *       A) LOAD ADDRESS OF DAYS TABLE IN REGISTER 5
                                       710 *
000644  4150  7675         0072B       711         LA    5,#$3DAYS
                                       712 *
                                       713 *       B) IF LEAP YEAR, INCREMENT TO LEAP YEAR
                                       714 *          FUNCTION
                                       715 *
000648  F900  77D4 78B2 0088A 00968    716         CP    #$3L,=P'0'
00064E  4780  75A0         00656       717         BE    #$3NOLL
000652  4155  0002            00002    718         LA    5,2(5)
                                       719 *
                                       720 *       C) LOAD ADDRESS OF TABLE ELEMENT IN REGISTER 5
                                       721 *          (REG 3 CONTAINS CONVERTED MONTH VALUE)
                                       722 *
000656  4153  5000            00000    723 #$3NOLL LA    5,0(3,5)
                                       724 *
                                       725 *       ADD DIRECTLY ADDRESSED ELAPSED DAYS TO WORK
```

```
LOC    OBJECT CODE         ADDR1 ADDR2  STMT  SOURCE STATEMENT                    DOS/VSE ASSEMBLER 16.17  99-12-31

                                         726 *                                                                      TS303310
                                         727 *                    FIELD                                            TS303320
00065A F841 7640 5000  006F6 00000       728     ZAP   #$3JLIAN,O(2,5)                                              TS303330
                                         729 *                                                                      TS303340
                                         730 *                    ADD INPUT DAY TO WORK FIELD                       TS303350
                                         731 *                                                                      TS303360
000660 FA41 7640 77EF  006F6 008A5       732     AP    #$3JLIAN,#$3DA                                               TS303370
                                         733 *                                                                      TS303380
                                         734 *           SECOND, COMPUTE ELAPSED DAYS 1601 TO INPUT YEAR            TS303390
                                         735 *                                                                      TS303400
                                         736 *                                                                      TS303410
                                         737 *                    COMPUTE #$3T1                                     TS303420
000666 F852 77D6 77F1  0088C 008A7       738     ZAP   #$3WORK6,#$3YR                                               TS303430
00066C F852 77D6 7958  0088C 00A0E       739     SP    #$3WORK6,=P'1601'                                            TS303440
000672 FC52 77D6 795B  0088C 00A11       740     MP    #$3WORK6,=P'36525'                                           TS303450
                                         741 *                                                                      TS303460
                                         742 *           INTEGER TRUNCATION EFFECTED BY UNPK - PACK                 TS303470
                                         743 *                                                                      TS303480
000678 F384 77E4 77D7  0089A 0088D       744     UNPK  #$3WORK9,#$3WORK6+1(5)                                       TS303490
00067E F246 77F4 77E4  008AA 0089A       745     PACK  #$3T1,#$3WORK9(7)                                            TS303500
                                         746 *                                                                      TS303510
                                         747 *           COMPUTE NUMBER OF NON-LEAP YEAR CENTESSIMALS               TS803520
                                         748 *                                                                      TS303530
                                         749 *                    COMPUTE #$3T2                                     TS303540
                                         750 *                                                                      TS303550
000684 F842 77FC 77F1  008B2 008A7       751     ZAP   #$3WORK,#$3YR                                                TS303560
00068A F842 77FC 7958  008B2 00A0E       752     SP    #$3WORK,=P'1601'                                             TS303570
000690 FD41 77FC 78AC  008B2 00962       753     DP    #$3WORK,=P'400'                                              TS303580
000696 F811 77F9 77FD  008AF 008B3       754     ZAP   #$3T2,#$3WORK+1(2)                                           TS303590
00069C FC10 77F9 78B4  008AF 0096A       755     MP    #$3T2,=P'3'                                                  TS303600
                                         756 *                                                                      TS303610
                                         757 *                    COMPUTE #$3T3                                     TS303620
                                         758 *                                                                      TS303630
0006A2 F841 77FC 77FF  008B2 008B5       759     ZAP   #$3WORK,#$3WORK+3(2)                                         TS303640
0006A8 FD41 77FC 78AA  008B2 00960       760     DP    #$3WORK,=P'100'                                              TS303650
0006AE F800 77FE 77FB  008B1 008B4       761     ZAP   #$3T3,#$3WORK+2(1)                                           TS303660
                                         762 *                                                                      TS303670
                                         763 *           COMPUTE THE SUM OF ELAPSED DAYS                            TS303680
                                         764 *                                                                      TS303690
0006B4 FA44 7640 77F4  006F6 008AA       765     AP    #$3JLIAN,#$3T1                                               TS303700
0006BA FB41 7640 77F9  006F6 008AF       766     SP    #$3JLIAN,#$3T2                                               TS303710
0006C0 FB40 7640 77FB  006F6 008B1       767     SP    #$3JLIAN,#$3T3                                               TS303720
                                         768 *                                                                      TS303730
                                         769 *  +++  SECTION 9- DETERMINE WHICH DATE PROCESSED  +++                TS303740
                                         770 *                                                                      TS303750
                                         771 *           IF FIRST DATE JUST PROCESSED, FIRST DATE WORK             TS303760
                                         772 *           FIELD IS ZERO, ADD ELAPSED DAYS TO WORK FIELD             TS303770
                                         773 *           AND BRANCH TO SECTION 2 TO PROCESS SECOND DATE            TS303780
                                         774 *                                                                      TS303790
0006C6 F940 77C6 78B2  0087C 00968       775     CP    #$3DAS1,=P'0'                                                TS303800
0006CC 4720 7624       006DA             776     BH    #$3DAY2                                                      TS303810
0006D0 F844 77C6 7640  0087C 006F6       777     ZAP   #$3DAS1,#$3JLIAN                                             TS303820
0006D6 47F0 743E       004F4             778     B     #$32DATE                                                     TS303830
                                         779 *                                                                      TS303840
                                         780 *           ELSE SECOND DATE HAS JUST PROCESSED- ADD                  TS303850
```

**Figure 4.1** *Continued*

```
LOC    OBJECT CODE  ADDR1 ADDR2  STMT   SOURCE STATEMENT                          DOS/VSE ASSEMBLER 16.17  99-12-31

                                 781   *        ELAPSED DAYS TO SECOND DATE WORK FIELD              TS303860
                                 782   *                                                           TS303870
0006DA F844 77CB 7640 00881 006F6 783 #$3DAY2 ZAP  #$3DAS2,#$3JLIAN                                 TS303880
                                 784   *                                                           TS303900
                                 785   *        +++ SECTION 10- COMPUTE ABSOLUTE DIFFERENCE +++    TS303910
                                 786   *                                                           TS303920
0006E0 FB44 77C6 00881 0087C     787          SP   #$3DAS2,#$3DAS1                                  TS303930
                                 788   *                                                           TS303940
                                 789   *        ABSOLUTE VALUE ASSURED VIA MVN TRANSFER OF         TS303950
                                 790   *        POSITIVE SIGN TO PACKED WORK FIELD                 TS303960
                                 791   *                                                           TS303970
0006E6 D100 77CF 78B0 00885 00966 792         MVN  #$3DAS2+4(1),=P'1'                               TS303980
0006EC F833 77B1 77CC 00867 00882 793         ZAP  DCOUNT,#$3DAS2+1(4)                              TS303990
                                 794   *                                                           TS304000
                                 795   *        +++ SECTION 11- TO RESTORE REGISTERS AND EXIT +++  TS304010
                                 796   *                                                           TS304020
0006F2 47F0 7822 008D8           797          B    #$3TERM                                          TS304030
                                 798   *                                                           TS304040
                                 799   *        +++ SECTION 12- DEFINE CONSTANTS AND STORAGE +++   TS304050
                                 800   *                                                           TS304060
0006F6 0000000C                  801 #$3JLIAN DC   PL5'0'                                           TS304070
                                 802   *                                                           TS304080
                                 803   *        THE DAY TABLE IS DEFINED WITH A PAIR OF TWO BYTE   TS304090
                                 804   *        ENTRIES FOR EACH OF THE 12 MONTHS- AN ENTRY FOR    TS304100
                                 805   *        NON-LEAP YEAR AND AN ENTRY FOR LEAP YEAR           TS304110
                                 806   *                                                           TS304120
0006FB 031C031C                  807 #$3DATAB DC   PL2'31',PL2'31'    JAN                          TS304130
0006FF 028C029C                  808          DC   PL2'28',PL2'29'    FEB                          TS304140
000703 031C031C                  809          DC   PL2'31',PL2'31'    MAR                          TS304150
000707 030C030C                  810          DC   PL2'30',PL2'30'    APR                          TS304160
00070B 031C031C                  811          DC   PL2'31',PL2'31'    MAY                          TS304170
00070F 030C030C                  812          DC   PL2'30',PL2'30'    JUN                          TS304180
000713 031C031C                  813          DC   PL2'31',PL2'31'    JUL                          TS304190
000717 031C031C                  814          DC   PL2'31',PL2'31'    AUG                          TS304200
00071B 030C030C                  815          DC   PL2'30',PL2'30'    SEP                          TS304210
00071F 031C031C                  816          DC   PL2'31',PL2'31'    OCT                          TS304220
000723 030C030C                  817          DC   PL2'30',PL2'30'    NOV                          TS304230
000727 031C031C                  818          DC   PL2'31',PL2'31'    DEC                          TS304240
                                 819   *                                                           TS304250
                                 820   *        THE DAYS TABLE IS DEFINED WITH A PAIR OF TWO       TS304260
                                 821   *        BYTE ENTRIES FOR EACH OF THE 12 MONTHS CONTAIN-    TS304270
                                 822   *        ING THE CUMULATIVE NUMBER OF DAYS EXPIRED AT       TS304280
                                 823   *        THE END OF THE PRIOR MONTH- NON-LEAP YEAR AND      TS304290
                                 824   *        LEAP YEAR                                          TS304300
                                 825   *                                                           TS304310
00072B 000C000C                  826 #$3DAYS  DC   PL2'00',PL2'00'    JAN                          TS304320
00072F 031C031C                  827          DC   PL2'31',PL2'31'    FEB                          TS304330
000733 059C060C                  828          DC   PL2'59',PL2'60'    MAR                          TS304340
000737 090C091C                  829          DC   PL2'90',PL2'91'    APR                          TS304350
00073B 120C121C                  830          DC   PL2'120',PL2'121'  MAY                          TS304360
00073F 151C152C                  831          DC   PL2'151',PL2'152'  JUN                          TS304370
000743 181C182C                  832          DC   PL2'181',PL2'182'  JUL                          TS304380
000747 212C213C                  833          DC   PL2'212',PL2'213'  AUG                          TS304390
00074B 243C244C                  834          DC   PL2'243',PL2'244'  SEP                          TS304400
00074F 273C274C                  835          DC   PL2'273',PL2'274'  OCT
```

```
 LOC    OBJECT CODE      ADDR1 ADDR2  STMT  SOURCE STATEMENT                    DOS/VSE ASSEMBLER 16.17  99-12-31

000753  304C305C                       836           DC   PL2'304',PL2'305'     NOV                              TS304410
000757  334C335C                       837           DC   PL2'334',PL2'335'     DEC                              TS304420
                                       838  *                                                                    TS304430
                                       839  *        TRANSLATION TABLE DEFINED FOR X'F0' - X'F9'                 TS304440
                                       840  *        (ALL TABLE POSITIONS EXCEPT THOSE CORRESPONDING            TS304450
                                       841  *        TO X'F0' THROUGH X'F9' ARE SET TO A VALUE OTHER            TS304460
                                       842  *        THAN X'00')                                                 TS304470
                                       843  *                                                                    TS304480
00075B  1C1C1C1C1C1C1C1C               844  #$3TABL  DC   240X'1C'                                               TS304490
00084B  0000000000000000               845           DC   10X'00'                                               TS304500
000855  1C1C1C1C1C                     846           DC   6X'1C'                                                 TS304510
                                       847  *                                                                    TS304520
00085B  0000000000000000               848  #$3ZRO   DC   12X'00'                                               TS304530
000867  0000000C                       849  DCOUNT   DC   PL4'0'                                                 TS304540
00086B  4C                             850  CODE3    DC   PL1'4'                                                 TS304550
00086C  FOFOFOFOFOFOFOCO               851  DATE1    DC   ZL8'00000000'                                          TS304560
000874  FOFOFOFOFOFOFOCO               852  DATE2    DC   ZL8'00000000'                                          TS304570
00087C                                 853  #$3DAS1  DS   PL5                                                    TS304580
000881                                 854  #$3DAS2  DS   PL5                                                    TS304590
000886                                 855  #$32     DS   PL1                                                    TS304600
000887                                 856  #$34     DS   PL1                                                    TS304610
000888                                 857  #$36     DS   PL1                                                    TS304620
000889                                 858  #$38     DS   PL1                                                    TS304630
00088A                                 859  #$3L     DS   PL1                                                    TS304640
00088B                                 860  #$3SIGN  DS   ZL1                                                    TS304650
00088C                                 861  #$3WORK6 DS   PL6                                                    TS304660
000892                                 862  #$3WORK8 DS   ZL8                                                    TS304670
00089A                                 863  #$3WORK9 DS   ZL9                                                    TS304680
00089A                                 864  #$3MO    DS   PL2                                                    TS304690
0008A3                                 865  #$3DA    DS   PL2                                                    TS304700
0008A5                                 866  #$3YR    DS   PL3                                                    TS304710
0008A7                                 867  #$3T1    DS   PL5                                                    TS304720
0008AA                                 868  #$3T2    DS   PL2                                                    TS304730
0008AF                                 869  #$3T3    DS   PL1                                                    TS304740
0008B1                                 870  #$3WORK  DS   PL5                                                    TS304750
0008B2                                 871  #$3FLD   DS   CL1                                                    TS304760
0008B7                                 872  #$3RSAVE DS   5F                                                     TS304770
0008B8                                 873  #$3CVB   DS   1D                                                     TS304780
0008D8  9815 7802        008B8         874  #$3TERM  LM   1,5,#$3RSAVE                                           TS304790
0008DC  07F6             008B4         875           BR   6                                                      TS304800
                                       876           END  BEGIN
0008E0  5B5BC2D6D7C5D540               877           =C'$$BOPEN '
0008E8  E2E4C2D9D6E4E3C9               878           =C'SUBROUTINE ERROR'
0008F8  5B5BC2C3D3D6E2C5               879           =C'$$BCLOSE'
000900  00000080                       880           =A(REQUEST)
000904  00000000                       881           =A(LIST)
000908  C9D5E5C1D3C9C440               882           =C'INVALID DATA *** DATE1'
00091E  C9D5E5C1D3C9C440               883           =C'INVALID DATA *** DATE2'
000934  C9D5E5C1D3C9C440               884           =C'INVALID YEAR *** DATE1'
00094A  C9D5E5C1D3C9C440               885           =C'INVALID YEAR *** DATE2'
000960  100C                           886           =P'100'
000962  400C                           887           =P'400'
000964  000C                           888           =P'00'
000966  1C                             889           =P'1'
000967  61                             890           =C'/'
```

**Figure 4.1** *Continued*

```
TEST OF TIMESUB3 TO CALCULATE ELAPSED DAYS

DATE1      DATE2
12/31/1999 01/01/2000 ELAPSED DAYS BETWEEN DATES:       1 CODE3 CONTENTS: 0.  DCOUNT CONTENTS: 000001
12/31/1999 01/02/2000 ELAPSED DAYS BETWEEN DATES:       2 CODE3 CONTENTS: 0.  DCOUNT CONTENTS: 000002
12/31/1999 01/03/2000 ELAPSED DAYS BETWEEN DATES:       3 CODE3 CONTENTS: 0.  DCOUNT CONTENTS: 000003
12/31/1999 01/04/2000 ELAPSED DAYS BETWEEN DATES:       4 CODE3 CONTENTS: 0.  DCOUNT CONTENTS: 000004
12/31/1999 01/05/2000 ELAPSED DAYS BETWEEN DATES:       5 CODE3 CONTENTS: 0.  DCOUNT CONTENTS: 000005
12/31/1999 01/06/2000 ELAPSED DAYS BETWEEN DATES:       6 CODE3 CONTENTS: 0.  DCOUNT CONTENTS: 000006
12/31/1999 01/07/2000 ELAPSED DAYS BETWEEN DATES:       7 CODE3 CONTENTS: 0.  DCOUNT CONTENTS: 000007
12/31/1999 01/08/2000 ELAPSED DAYS BETWEEN DATES:       8 CODE3 CONTENTS: 0.  DCOUNT CONTENTS: 000008
12/31/1999 01/09/2000 ELAPSED DAYS BETWEEN DATES:       9 CODE3 CONTENTS: 0.  DCOUNT CONTENTS: 000009
12/31/1999 01/10/2000 ELAPSED DAYS BETWEEN DATES:      10 CODE3 CONTENTS: 0.  DCOUNT CONTENTS: 000010
12/31/1999 01/11/2000 ELAPSED DAYS BETWEEN DATES:      11 CODE3 CONTENTS: 0.  DCOUNT CONTENTS: 000011
12/31/1999 01/12/2000 ELAPSED DAYS BETWEEN DATES:      12 CODE3 CONTENTS: 0.  DCOUNT CONTENTS: 000012
12/31/1999 01/13/2000 ELAPSED DAYS BETWEEN DATES:      13 CODE3 CONTENTS: 0.  DCOUNT CONTENTS: 000013
12/31/1999 01/14/2000 ELAPSED DAYS BETWEEN DATES:      14 CODE3 CONTENTS: 0.  DCOUNT CONTENTS: 000014
12/31/1999 01/15/2000 ELAPSED DAYS BETWEEN DATES:      15 CODE3 CONTENTS: 0.  DCOUNT CONTENTS: 000015
12/31/1999 01/16/2000 ELAPSED DAYS BETWEEN DATES:      16 CODE3 CONTENTS: 0.  DCOUNT CONTENTS: 000016
12/31/1999 01/17/2000 ELAPSED DAYS BETWEEN DATES:      17 CODE3 CONTENTS: 0.  DCOUNT CONTENTS: 000017
12/31/1999 01/18/2000 ELAPSED DAYS BETWEEN DATES:      18 CODE3 CONTENTS: 0.  DCOUNT CONTENTS: 000018
12/31/1999 01/19/2000 ELAPSED DAYS BETWEEN DATES:      19 CODE3 CONTENTS: 0.  DCOUNT CONTENTS: 000019
02/28/1999 02/29/2000 ELAPSED DAYS BETWEEN DATES:     366 CODE3 CONTENTS: 0.  DCOUNT CONTENTS: 000366
03/30/2000 02/29/2001 INVALID DAY *** DATE2              CODE3 CONTENTS: 9.  DCOUNT CONTENTS: 000000
02/29/2000 03/31/2000 ELAPSED DAYS BETWEEN DATES:      31 CODE3 CONTENTS: 0.  DCOUNT CONTENTS: 000031
08/22/2000 08/06/2001 ELAPSED DAYS BETWEEN DATES:     349 CODE3 CONTENTS: 0.  DCOUNT CONTENTS: 000349
05/30/2000 12/07/2001 ELAPSED DAYS BETWEEN DATES:     556 CODE3 CONTENTS: 0.  DCOUNT CONTENTS: 000556
02/28/2000 06/08/2001 ELAPSED DAYS BETWEEN DATES:     466 CODE3 CONTENTS: 0.  DCOUNT CONTENTS: 000466
07/31/2000 12/09/2001 ELAPSED DAYS BETWEEN DATES:     496 CODE3 CONTENTS: 0.  DCOUNT CONTENTS: 000496
11/17/2000 03/10/2001 ELAPSED DAYS BETWEEN DATES:     113 CODE3 CONTENTS: 0.  DCOUNT CONTENTS: 000113
02/29/2000 02/29/2001 INVALID DAY *** DATE2              CODE3 CONTENTS: 9.  DCOUNT CONTENTS: 000000
01/31/2000 06/14/2001 ELAPSED DAYS BETWEEN DATES:     500 CODE3 CONTENTS: 0.  DCOUNT CONTENTS: 000500
09/29/2000 09/29/2001 ELAPSED DAYS BETWEEN DATES:     396 CODE3 CONTENTS: 0.  DCOUNT CONTENTS: 000396
07/01/2000 07/01/2001 ELAPSED DAYS BETWEEN DATES:     335 CODE3 CONTENTS: 0.  DCOUNT CONTENTS: 000335
03/31/2000 01/20/2001 ELAPSED DAYS BETWEEN DATES:     295 CODE3 CONTENTS: 0.  DCOUNT CONTENTS: 000295
04/30/2000 04/21/2001 ELAPSED DAYS BETWEEN DATES:     356 CODE3 CONTENTS: 0.  DCOUNT CONTENTS: 000356
09/15/2000 01/22/2001 ELAPSED DAYS BETWEEN DATES:     129 CODE3 CONTENTS: 0.  DCOUNT CONTENTS: 000129
00/31/2000 12/31/2001 INVALID DATA *** DATE1             CODE3 CONTENTS: 2.  DCOUNT CONTENTS: 000000
12/32/2000 12/31/2001 INVALID MONTH *** DATE1            CODE3 CONTENTS: 6.  DCOUNT CONTENTS: 000000
12/00/2000 12/31/2001 INVALID DAY *** DATE1              CODE3 CONTENTS: 8.  DCOUNT CONTENTS: 000000
12/31/1600 12/31/2001 INVALID YEAR *** DATE1             CODE3 CONTENTS: 8.  DCOUNT CONTENTS: 000000
12/31/3400 12/31/2001 INVALID YEAR *** DATE1             CODE3 CONTENTS: 4.  DCOUNT CONTENTS: 000000
12/31/0000 12/31/2001 INVALID YEAR *** DATE1             CODE3 CONTENTS: 4.  DCOUNT CONTENTS: 000000
12/31/1999 12/31/2100 ELAPSED DAYS BETWEEN DATES:   36890 CODE3 CONTENTS: 0.  DCOUNT CONTENTS: 036890
12/31/2099 12/31/2100 ELAPSED DAYS BETWEEN DATES:     365 CODE3 CONTENTS: 0.  DCOUNT CONTENTS: 000365
12/31/2099 01/01/2100 ELAPSED DAYS BETWEEN DATES:       1 CODE3 CONTENTS: 0.  DCOUNT CONTENTS: 000001

THE SUBROUTINE WAS EXECUTED    44 TIMES
```

**Figure 4.2**  A subset of test results produced by TEST03's execution of TIMESUB3 in calculating elapsed days between dates.

# 5

# Extended-Interval Aging

Short-interval aging produces a single parameter, say 45, 60, or even 120 days. The parameter is meaningful but relevant only as long as its range doesn't exceed the scope of comprehension. A result such as 10,220 days old would convey little information to an inquirer seeking to determine the age of an employee.

The more you become involved in activity bearing on distant dates, the more you need to age in the area of extended intervals. Extended-interval aging addresses worker's ages, unexpired time on contracts, remaining time to maturity of financial instruments such as bonds, remaining life for leases, royalty agreements, and copyrights, and the like.

Clearly, there's a need for meaningful aging of extended intervals—intervals in the range of years, months, and days. This chapter, then, will produce a subroutine that can be used to age such extended intervals.

## The Problem of Extended Intervals

In searching for a set of parameters that measure the age difference between two Commercial-8 dates, you're essentially asking "How many years, months, and days have elapsed between the earlier and the later date?" Implicit in the problem is the need to determine at some point the chronology of the input dates.

More important, however, is the need for a functional definition of *month*. You must deal with three units of measurement in calendar form, and of these the month is by far the most variable. Rarely do two units have equal magnitudes. Moreover, *month* is commonly referred to in one of two ways, either of which can lead to undesired consequences.

One definition of a month is the time elapsed when the relative displacement of a date to the next consecutive month has occurred. For instance, the period of time from July 18 through August 18 would count as one month. Few would fault this definition until asked "Is February 28, 1999 to March 31, 1999 one month or one month and three days?" Obviously, the argument can be settled by tearing one page from the calendar, thus demonstrating that the period is exactly one month. Of course, with such a demonstration the relative-displacement definition is often torn up also. It need not be. It simply isn't functional on month-end boundaries.

This leads to the second definition. Traditionally, one month is the period of time that allows one calendar page to be torn from the calendar, in other words, the period from the last day of a month to the last day of the next month. Attempts to use this definition will find you counting the days from a given date to the end of that date's month-boundary. You then count calendar pages and finally add the surplus days to those initially counted to determine the time lapse between the two dates. In practice, however, this definition, which finds the time lapse between 02/15/1999 and 04/10/1999 by adding the days elapsed between 02/15 and 02/28 to the 10 days from 04/01 to 04/10 for a total of 23 days, simply counts whole months to arrive at a solution: in this example, 1 month and 23 days. Unhappily, when given two dates such as 02/02/1999 and 04/25/1999, a distorted result is obtained: one month and 51 days. Because 51 days is certainly more than one month by any measure, relative displacement gives a more acceptable solution in this case.

Members of the business community often date contracts, leases, and the like as of the first day of the following month, with costs prorated if the agreement is to take effect a number of days prior to the first of the month. In this way, the aging debate is avoided and the calendar page becomes the unit of measurement. Unfortunately, businessmen have begun to throw caution to the wind in the belief that computers can count. Often, their enthusiasm springs from a conviction that you can subtract dates to find elapsed time. Insurance professionals have long subtracted the earlier date from the later to find time lapse—perhaps without realizing the false assumption inherent in this. The algorithm produces errors that might go undetected. While you can subtract in decimal arithmetic without concern, the Gregorian calendar features multiple modular arithmetics. You cannot subtract dates because the modulus in these arithmetics varies with the month and is 28, 29, 30, or 31 depending upon the month's number and whether it's a leap year.

Extended interval aging is indeed a problem. Consider Joseph Scaliger's claim that no one disputes the concept of the day. Beyond the day, all is variable and contentious in human affairs.

## A Solution Strategy

In forging the solution strategy we'll proceed from the obvious to the more subtle. Clearly, if you're given two dates A and B, with A the earlier of the two, you must count calendar months (pages) if A is on its month-end boundary. For example, given 12/31/1999 (A) and 03/28/2000 (B), simply count January and February as two full months and then count 28 days to provide time-lapse parameters: PYEAR = 0, PMONTH = 2, and PDAY = 28.

You'll consistently count calendar months. Even when A is not on a month-end boundary, count the days until the next month-end boundary, count the intervening calendar months, and finally take the sum of counted days and days remaining to find your time-lapse parameters. For example, given 12/25/1999 (A) and 04/05/2001 (B), you'll find six days (31 – 25) until A's next month-end boundary. Calendar months separating the two dates is 15 and remaining days is 5. The parameters are then PYEAR = 1, PMONTH = 3, and PDAY = (6 + 5) = 11.

As you've seen, this procedure might result in a distorted PDAY value. In the last example, had B been 04/29/2001, the parameters would have been PYEAR = 1, PMONTH = 3, and PDAY = 35—hence the case for switching to relative date displacement. This strategy would displace A (12/25/1999) forward one year and four months to 04/25/2001 to produce these parameters: PYEAR = 1, PMONTH = 4, and PDAY = 4. Few would disagree with that result.

This introduces the need to define the smallest PDAY value to be considered *distorted*. The minimum PDAY value that allows a switch in strategy is the value of the maximum day limit of A's initial month (IMAX). But this criterion leads to difficulty. Given 06/29/1998 (A) and 07/30/1999 (B), witness the following logical anomaly. You first use the preferred calendar-month strategy to find PYEAR = 1, PMONTH = 0, and PDAY = 31. Since IMAX is 30 (less than PDAY), you switch to relative displacement and obtain PYEAR = 1, PMONTH = 1, and PDAY = 1. Implicit in the relative displacement is the displacement from 01/29 to 02/29, which we've counted as one month—there is in fact no 29-day February in the given interval. Obviously this criterion by itself is inadequate to assure logical consistency and freedom from error in the extended interval.

Consequently, another criterion must be invoked to determine the validity of a switch to relative date-displacement aging. Not only must PDAY be greater than IMAX, but A's initial day (ID) must be less than 29 to assure that an invalid displacement doesn't occur in a nonleap year. These restrictions to your ability to switch to relative date-displacement aging result in the possible development of a maximum PDAY parameter of 32. Consider 12/29/1997 (A) and 03/30/1998 (B). By calendar-month counting, you'll find that PYEAR = 0, PMONTH = 2, and PDAY = 32. You can't switch to relative date displacement in order to reduce PDAY, since the criterion ID < 29 cannot be met. Further, this particular interval can't be aged logically in any other manner. Relative date-displacement aging is logically impossible. Hence, by the only remaining valid definition of the month, you must accept a PDAY value as great as 32.

Your first emotional response to a PDAY value of 32 might be that some logical possibility has been overlooked. It has! If you could develop a universally acceptable numerical definition of the month for use in instances prohibiting the logical application of relative date-displacement to reduce PDAY values, you'd have a totally satisfying solution strategy. Sadly, universal acceptance is elusive. The average month's length, taken over a four-year leap-year cycle, is 30.4375 days. Hence there's a case for postulating in these instances that 31 days do constitute one month. However, many bankers will argue that 30 days constitute one month. Labor unions might insist on another value—say, 31 if PDAY = 32 and 30 if PDAY = 31. A good deal of importance might be attached to the differences.

To be sure, the occurrence of PDAY parameters of 31 or 32 in the extended interval is a function of the dates delimiting the aging interval. The A dates whose day values are less than 29 automatically switch to relative date displacement aging in the presence of PDAY ≥ IMAX, assuring a reduced PDAY value. Similarly, B dates on day 27 of the month or earlier assure an agreeable PDAY value, even if it's as large as 30—regardless of the A date's value. Hence, the solution strategy we've developed will produce an algorithm whose results meet with effortless agreement in all but a minority of cases.

The decision to convert 31-day or 32-day PDAY values to equivalent PMONTH increments can be left to the installation employing this algorithm. It might be practical to allow the programmer, acting in accord with user standards or industry fiat, to interrogate the returned PDAY parameter. If its value exceeds the convention, you can subtract to reduce PDAY, with the PMONTH parameter subsequently incremented. Alternatively, a solution that's described later in the chapter can be adopted.

## Designing the Algorithm

Anticipating a straightforward and relatively simple algorithm, let's identify the several elements that will be involved. You can distinguish the two input dates, allowing M, D, and Y to represent the components of the earlier date and TM, TD, and TY representing the later date's components. Here the T indicates that in the aging activities the later date's components actually become target values that, when reached in the incrementation of the earlier date, signal termination of the procedure.

Let (Max D of M) be the maximum number of days that can occur in month M. Implicit in this definition is the dependence of (Max D of M) on the leap-year status of Y at the time of its determination. Let IMAX be the (Max D of M) for the initial M of the earliest date A, that is, M prior to the start of the aging process. Further, allow ID to be the value of the initial day of the earliest date, the D of A. Similar to IMAX, ID is the value of D prior to the start of the aging process. Allow C to be a counter.

The outputs are the three parameters PYEAR, PMONTH, and PDAY, which specify the number of years, months, and days that have elapsed between the earlier date M-D-Y and the later date TM-TD-TY. Finally, initially assume that C = 0. The calculation, then, consists of the observance of rules 1, 2, and 3:

```
Rule 1

If M = TM and Y = TY,
    1.1 PDAY = TD - D
    1.2 PYEAR = 0
    1.3 PMONTH = 0
    1.4 Exit

Rule 2

If M ≠ TM or Y ≠ TY,
    2.1 Let M = M + 1
    2.2 Let C = C + 1
    2.3 Let Y = Y + (M ÷ 13)
    2.4 Let M = M(Mod 13) + (M ÷ 13)
    2.5 Do Rule 2 until the antecedent is false

Rule 3
```

```
Let X = TD - (Max D of M),
   3.1 If X ≥ 0,
       3.1.1 PYEAR = C ÷ 12
       3.1.2 PMONTH = C(Mod 12)
       3.1.3 PDAY = IMAX - ID + X
       3.1.4 Exit
   3.2 X < 0
       3.2.1 Let C = C - 1
       3.2.2 Let PDAY = IMAX - ID + TD
             a) If PDAY ≥ IMAX and if ID < 29,
                Let C = C + 1
                PYEAR = C ÷ 12
                PMONTH = C(Mod 12)
                PDAY = TD - ID
                Exit
             b) If PDAY < IMAX or if ID ≥ 29,
                PYEAR = C ÷ 12
                PMONTH = C(Mod 12)
                PDAY = IMAX - ID + TD
                Exit
```

Rule 1 produces the parameters sought for equal dates or those dates differing only in their day values. If rule 1 fails to apply, rule 2 increments the unequal Y and M values until they reach the values of TY and TM, respectively. Rules 2.3 and 2.4 increment Y and set M = 1 whenever M reaches 13. Otherwise, M continues to grow with each increment and Y isn't affected. When the components are equal, the iterations cease. Note that rule 2 employs the usual inclusive OR.

Rule 3 determines whether M has been excessively incremented. In Rule 3.1, the parameters are calculated directly. In Rule 3.2, X < 0, overshoot has occurred in that M has been incremented to equality with TM, but TD is less than the (Max D of M) for the incremented M. Recall that you're counting calendar pages and this implies that each increment places D on its month-end boundary—that is, D after each increment becomes equal to (Max D of M) for the newly created M.

If overshoot has occurred, you must reduce the counter by one and add the days from the initial D to the end of the month to TD, the surplus days. This is accomplished with 3.2.1 and 3.2.2.

Your final task is to adjust the PDAY value by switching to relative date displacement if the criteria permit. The adjustment is made with 3.2.2(a). Here you see that the counter is incremented. The parameters are calculated directly, with PDAY becoming the difference between TD and ID. Thus, when the criteria are met, you switch from counting calendar months to aging the relative date displacement. In place of adding beginning and ending days, calculate PDAY as a difference—the difference between the beginning-day value that was displaced to the month TM and TD, a day in TM. Thus you can avoid date subtraction, which involves *intermonth* computation and the false assumption of a constant modulus, because you restrict your final days calculation to an *intramonth* computation.

Rule 3.2.2(b) proceeds to calculate the parameters when the criteria fail either in whole or in part. The parameters here are the product of calendar-month counting. Note that the development of 31-day and 32-day PDAY values is directly attributable to the inconstancy of the modulus in Gregorian-calendar arithmetic. Finding it impossible to logically engage in relative date displacement, Rule

3.2.2(b) calculates the PDAY parameter as the sum of days from *two* different months. Hence, in the absence of a constant modulus, only an arbitrarily imposed standard or an authoritarian fiat can be invoked to find equivalents for values as large as 31 or 32 days.

With close inspection, it becomes clear that the 29-day criterion for the A date guarantees accuracy in an interval containing a non-leap-year February—a certainty in all intervals of 24 months or more. You can conclude that intervals of less than two years are liable to produce a debatable PDAY = 30; for instance, 04/29/1999 to 01/29/2001 renders PYEAR = 1, PMONTH = 8, and PDAY = 30. Relative date displacement aging here produces PYEAR = 1, PMONTH = 9, and PDAY = 0. Given the interval, it's the method of choice. Hence, while the example intervals were short and were chosen for illustrative purposes, an interval can be extended only at two years or more.

### Defining the algorithm's components

Now you must define the inputs, return code, and outputs of the algorithm TIME-SUB4. Two inputs are required, DATEX and DATEY. Each must be Commercial-8. CODE4, the return code, is defined as follows:

$$
CODE4 = \begin{cases}
0, \text{If DATEX and DATEY are M/D/Y, Commercial-8} \\
2, \text{If DATEX, M/D/Y is not valid numeric} \\
3, \text{If DATEY, M/D/Y is not valid numeric} \\
4, \text{If for DATEX, Y } \varepsilon \text{ \{y: } 1600 < y < 3400\} \\
5, \text{If for DATEY, Y } \varepsilon \text{ \{y: } 1600 < y < 3400\} \\
6, \text{If for DATEX, M } \varepsilon \text{ \{m: } 0 < m < 13\} \\
7, \text{If for DATEY, M } \varepsilon \text{ \{m: } 0 < m < 13\} \\
8, \text{If for DATEX, D } \varepsilon \text{ \{d\} as defined in Commercial-8} \\
9, \text{If for DATEY, D } \varepsilon \text{ \{d\} as defined in Commercial-8}
\end{cases}
$$

In CODE4, 0 means that execution was successful, 2 or 3 identify bad data, 4 or 5 indicate a bad year, 6 or 7 identify a bad month, and 8 or 9 result from a bad day for DATEX or DATEY, respectively.

The outputs consist of PDAY, PMONTH, and PYEAR, representing the days, months, and years that, elapsed since the earlier DATEX and DATEY, will produce the later date. Hence, in keeping with our comments in chapter 1, PYEAR is defined as:

$$
PYEAR = \begin{cases}
0, \text{If CODE4} \neq 0 \\
0, \text{If CODE4} = 0, \text{ and DATEX} = DATEY \\
N, \text{If CODE4} = 0, \text{ and DATEX} \neq DATEY, \text{ where} \\
\quad N \varepsilon \text{ \{n: n belongs to Z, } 0 \leq n\}
\end{cases}
$$

PMONTH, however, is limited:

$$PMONTH = \begin{cases} 0, \text{If CODE4} \neq 0 \\ 0, \text{If CODE4} = 0, \text{and DATEX} = \text{DATEY} \\ N, \text{If CODE4} = 0, \text{and DATEX} \neq \text{DATEY, where} \\ \quad N \, \varepsilon \, \{n: n \text{ belongs to } Z, 0 \leq n < 12\} \end{cases}$$

PDAY too is limited:

$$PDAY = \begin{cases} 0, \text{If CODE4} \neq 0 \\ 0, \text{If CODE4} = 0, \text{and DATEX} = \text{DATEY} \\ N, \text{If CODE4} = 0, \text{and DATEX} \neq \text{DATEY, where} \\ \quad N \, \varepsilon \, \{n: n \text{ belongs to } Z, 0 \leq n < 33\} \end{cases}$$

In no case where DATEX $\neq$ DATEY, can PYEAR, PMONTH, and PDAY = 0.

## The Pseudocode for TIMESUB4

The pseudocode assumes that its input has been passed to it in two eight-byte zoned decimal fields, DATEX and DATEY. The output fields PYEAR, PMONTH, and PDAY are three-bytes packed, two-bytes packed, and two-bytes packed, respectively. A counter, constants, and work fields are self-evident.

```
     * Perform general housekeeping.
 1) Let CODE4 = 0
 2) Let YRSAVX = 0
 3) Let PDAY = 0
 4) Let PMONTH = 0
 5) Let PYEAR = 0
 6) Let COUNTER = 0
     * Input-related housekeeping: DATEX.
 7) Move DATEX to WORK8
 8) Move DATEX to WORK8X in FIPS-8 format
 9) Let CONSTANT2 = 2
10) Let CONSTANT4 = 4
11) Let CONSTANT6 = 6
12) Let CONSTANT8 = 8
13) Go to 20
     * Input-related housekeeping: DATEY.
14) Move DATEY to WORK8
15) Move DATEY to WORK8Y in FIPS-8 format
16) Let CONSTANT2 = 3
17) Let CONSTANT4 = 5
18) Let CONSTANT6 = 7
19) Let CONSTANT8 = 9
     * Validate input date as numeric.
20) If WORK8 is numeric, go to 22
21) Let CODE4 = CONSTANT2, go to 88
     * Save components of WORK8 and edit Y for limit violation.
22) WORK8 → M,D,Y
23) If YRSAVX ≠ 0, go to 28
24) Move M to MOSAVX
25) Move D to DASAVX
26) Move Y to YRSAVX
27) Go to 31
28) Move M to MOSAVY
29) MOVE D to DASAVY
30) Move Y to YRSAVY
31) If Y is within limits per Commercial-8, go to 33
32) Let CODE4 = CONSTANT4, go to 88
```

```
       * Execute leap-year algorithm for Y.
33) Let L = 0
34) If Y is a leap year, let L = 1
       * Edit M for limit violation.
35) If M is within limits per Commercial-8, go to 37
36) Let CODE4 = CONSTANT6, go to 88
       * Edit D for limit violation.
37) If D is within limits per Commercial-8, go to 39
38) Let CODE4 = CONSTANT8, go to 88
       * Determine which date has processed.
39) If CONSTANT8 = 9, go to 41
40) Go to 14
       * Compute elapsed time.
       * First, determine date chronology and move earliest date
       * to Y, M, and D. Then move latest date to TY, TM, and TD.
41) If WORK8X > WORK8Y, go to 49
42) Move YRSAVX to Y
43) Move YRSAVY to TY
44) Move MOSAVX to M
45) Move MOSAVY to TM
46) Move DASAVX to D
47) Move DASAVY to TD
48) Go to 55
49) Move YRSAVY to Y
50) Move YRSAVX to TY
51) Move MOSAVY to M
52) Move MOSAVX to TM
53) Move DASAVY to D
54) Move DASAVX to TD
       * Second, find parameters for all M = TM, Y = TY.
55) If M ≠ TM or Y ≠ TY, go to 58
56) Let PDAY = TD - D
57) Go to 88
       * Third, store (Max D of M) in IMAX, D in ID.
58) Let L = 0
59) If Y is a leap year, Let L = 1
60) Let IMAX = (Max D of M)
61) Let ID = D
       * Fourth, begin incrementing M.
62) If Y < TY, go to 65
63) If M < TM, go to 65
64) Go to 70
65) Let M = M + 1
66) Let COUNTER = COUNTER + 1
67) Let Y = Y + (M ÷ 13)
68) Let M = M(Mod 13) + (M ÷ 13)
69) Go to 62
       * Fifth, Let D = (Max D of M) for incremented Y and M.
70) Let L = 0
71) If Y is a leap year, let L = 1
72) Let D = (Max D of M)
       * Sixth, test for overshoot.
73) Let X = TD
74) Let X = X - D
75) If X < 0, go to 79
       * If no overshoot, calculate PDAY value in TD.
76) Let TD = X
77) Let TD = TD + (IMAX - ID)
78) Go to 85
       * Seventh, correct overshoot.
79) Let COUNTER = COUNTER - 1
80) Let TD = TD + (IMAX - ID)
81) If TD < IMAX, go to 85
```

```
82) If ID ≥ 29, go to 85
   * Switch to date displacement:
   * TD ≥ IMAX and ID < 29 . . . let TD = TD - ID
83) Let TD = TD - IMAX
   * Note: see Step 80, above . TD - IMAX renders TD - ID
84) Let COUNTER = COUNTER + 1
   * Build parameters.
85) Let PYEAR = COUNTER ÷ 12
86) Let PMONTH = COUNTER(Mod 12)
87) Let PDAY = TD
88) Exit
```

## The Source Code for TIMESUB4

Figure 5.1 shows the TIMESUB4 portion of the post listing of TEST04's assembly. TIMESUB4 was extensively tested using both short-interval and extended-interval inputs. All results were as predicted. Figure 5.2 displays a subset of the test data. TIMESUB4 was judged to be a valid algorithm.

### Comments on the source code of TIMESUB4

TIMESUB4, like TIMESUB3, features a loop that's executed once for each input date. The loop in TIMESUB4, however, is an edit-and-save loop; no problem-solving calculations are performed until both inputs are edited and their FIPS-8 images stored in #$4WRK8X and #$4WRK8Y, respectively. In order to facilitate later manipulation, components #$4MOSVX, #$4DASVX, and #$4YRSVX (related to #$4WRK8X and DATEX) become recipients of month, day, and year values. A similar set of save fields is assigned to DATEY.

Within the edit loop, section 2 of the source code initializes the CODE4 constants and reformats each date to its #$4WRK8X or #$4WRK8Y FIPS-8 save field. In section 4, the content or absence of content in #$4YRSVX indicates the set of component save fields to be used for the input currently in process. Finally, section 8 determines which date has just completed processing by interrogating the constant, #$48. Immediately following the edit loop, section 9 computes elapsed-time parameters and creates the output fields. The source code follows the pseudocode and earlier-discussed algorithm's rules rather closely. Exceptions are purely language-dependent features.

TIMESUB4 features two embedded subroutines that facilitate executing, from multiple points in the program, the leap-year algorithm and the algorithm that accesses the address of M's day-limit for a given M. TIMESUB4 saves and restores registers 5 and 6 prior to returning control to the calling program in order to make them available for the execution of these subroutines.

## The Application of TIMESUB4

It's clear from the test data displayed in Figure 5.2 that PDAY values of 31 and 32 can develop in the extended interval. A debatable PDAY of 30 can also appear in the shorter interval (less than two years). These unusual values are the result of the dates delimiting the interval.

```
                                        DOS/VSE ASSEMBLER 16.19  99-12-31

LOC   OBJECT CODE  ADDR1 ADDR2  STMT  SOURCE STATEMENT

                                407  *
                                408  ******************************************************  TS400010
                                409  *                                                    *  TS400020
                                410  * TTTTTTT  III   MM     MM  EEEEE  SSSSS        BBBBB    4  *  TS400030
                                411  *    T      I    M M   M M   E     S            B   B     4  *  TS400040
                                412  *    T      I    M  M M  M   EEEE   SSSSS  U  U BBB B  44444 *  TS400050
                                413  *    T      I    M   M   M   E          S  U  U B   B     4  *  TS400060
                                414  *    T     III   M       M   EEEEE  SSSSS UUUUU BBBBB     4  *  TS400070
                                415  *                                                    *  TS400080
                                416  ******************************************************  TS400090
                                417  *                                                    *  TS400100
                                418  * E L A P S E D  D A Y S ,  M O N T H S ,  Y E A R S  B E T W E E N  TS400110
                                419  *           G R E G O R I A N   D A T E S            *  TS400120
                                420  *                                                    *  TS400130
                                421  ******************************************************  TS400140
                                422  *                                                    *  TS400150
                                423  *  THIS SUBROUTINE CALCULATES ELAPSED DAYS, MONTHS AND *  TS400160
                                424  *             YEARS BETWEEN TWO GREGORIAN DATES       *  TS400170
                                425  *                                                    *  TS400180
                                426  *  1.  VALID INPUT YEARS FOR THIS SUBROUTINE ARE THE YEARS  TS400190
                                427  *      1601 THROUGH 3399 A. D.                        *  TS400200
                                428  *                                                    *  TS400210
                                429  *  2.  VALID INPUT MONTH VALUES FOR THIS SUBROUTINE ARE 01  TS400220
                                430  *      THROUGH 12.                                    *  TS400230
                                431  *                                                    *  TS400240
                                432  *  3.  VALID INPUT DAY VALUES FOR THIS SUBROUTINE ARE 01   TS400250
                                433  *      THROUGH 31 WITH EXCEPTIONS FOR THE MONTHS LISTED:   TS400260
                                434  *          MONTH              MAXIMUM DAY VALUE        *  TS400270
                                435  *           04                     30                 *  TS400280
                                436  *           06                     30                 *  TS400290
                                437  *           09                     30                 *  TS400300
                                438  *           11                     30                 *  TS400310
                                439  *           02                     28                 *  TS400320
                                440  *           02  DURING LEAP YEAR   29                 *  TS400330
                                441  *                                                    *  TS400340
                                442  *  4.  THE DATE FORMAT MUST BE MMDDYYYY, WHERE MM = THE TWO  TS400350
                                443  *      DIGIT MONTH VALUE, DD = THE TWO DIGIT DAY VALUE AND  TS400360
                                444  *      YYYY = THE FOUR DIGIT YEAR.                    *  TS400370
                                445  *                                                    *  TS400380
                                446  *  5.  THE CALLING PROGRAM MUST PLACE ONE EIGHT DIGIT DATE.  TS400390
                                447  *      IN ZONED FORMAT, IN A SUBROUTINE DEFINED EIGHT BYTE  TS400400
                                448  *      FIELD, 'DATEX.'  THE CALLING PROGRAM MUST PLACE THE OTHER  TS400410
                                449  *      EIGHT DIGIT DATE, IN ZONED FORMAT, IN ANOTHER SUBROUTINE  TS400420
                                450  *      DEFINED EIGHT BYTE FIELD, 'DATEY.'  PRIOR TO EXECUTION OF  TS400430
                                451  *      THE SUBROUTINE.  NEITHER FIELD IS ALTERED BY THE SUB-  TS400440
                                452  *      ROUTINE.                                       *  TS400450
                                453  *      NOTE:  ***  THE ORDER OF THE DATES IS IMMATERIAL.  TS400460
                                454  *                                                    *  TS400470
                                455  *  6.  A SUBROUTINE DEFINED ONE BYTE FIELD, 'CODE4,' IS RETURNED  TS400480
                                456  *      TO THE CALLING PROGRAM AND CONTAINS A PACKED 0 IF THE  TS400490
                                457  *      EXECUTION WAS SUCCESSFUL.  NON-ZERO VALUES INDICATE  TS400500
                                458  *      THE FOLLOWING:                                 *  TS400510
                                459  *                                                    *  TS400520
                                460  *      A PACKED 2 FOR DATEX (3 FOR DATEY) INDICATES UNSUCCESS-  TS400530
                                461  *      FUL EXECUTION: INVALID DATA.                   *  TS400540
                                                                                             TS400550
```

```
LOC   OBJECT CODE   ADDR1 ADDR2   STMT   SOURCE STATEMENT                                             DOS/VSE ASSEMBLER 16.19  99-12-31

                                   462 *  INVALID DATA ARE DETERMINED IF THE LOW ORDER BYTE'S ZONE                          * TS400560
                                   463 *  CONTAINS AN INVALID SIGN, (AN INVALID SIGN IS OTHER THAN                          * TS400570
                                   464 *  X'C', X'A', X'E', OR X'F') OR IF THE PRECEDING BYTES'                             * TS400580
                                   465 *  ZONES ARE OTHER THAN X'F', OR IF THE LOW ORDER NIBBLE                             * TS400590
                                   466 *  OF ANY BYTE CONTAINS A VALUE GREATER THAN X'9'.                                   * TS400600
                                   467 *                                                                                    * TS400610
                                   468 *                                                                                    * TS400620
                                   469 *  A PACKED 4 FOR DATEX (5 FOR DATEY) INDICATES UNSUCCESS-                           * TS400630
                                   470 *  FUL EXECUTION: INVALID YEAR- YEAR VALUE VIOLATES LIMITS                           * TS400640
                                   471 *  SPECIFIED IN 1.. ABOVE.                                                           * TS400650
                                   472 *                                                                                    * TS400660
                                   473 *  A PACKED 6 FOR DATEX (7 FOR DATEY) INDICATES UNSUCCESS-                           * TS400670
                                   474 *  FUL EXECUTION: INVALID MONTH- MONTH VALUE VIOLATES LIMITS                         * TS400680
                                   475 *  SPECIFIED IN 2., ABOVE.                                                           * TS400690
                                   476 *                                                                                    * TS400700
                                   477 *  A PACKED 8 FOR DATEX (9 FOR DATEY) INDICATES UNSUCCESS-                           * TS400710
                                   478 *  FUL EXECUTION: INVALID DAY- DAY VALUE VIOLATES LIMITS                             * TS400720
                                   479 *  SPECIFIED IN 3., ABOVE.                                                           * TS400730
                                   480 *                                                                                    * TS400740
                                   481 *  INSPECTION OF THE RETURN CODE IS IMPORTANT.   THE RETURN                          * TS400750
                                   482 *  CODE, CODE4, REFLECTS THE LEVEL OF EDITING.    A RETURN                           * TS400760
                                   483 *  CODE OF 2, FOR EXAMPLE, NOT ONLY INDICATES INVALIDITY OF                          * TS400770
                                   484 *  DATA, IT ALSO INDICATES THAT NO EDITING HAS BEEN DONE TO                          * TS400780
                                   485 *  VALIDATE THE YEAR, MONTH OR DAY VALUES.   A RETURN CODE OF                        * TS400790
                                   486 *  4 INDICATES THAT THE DATA ARE VALID BUT THAT THE YEAR WAS                         * TS400800
                                   487 *  FOUND INVALID- THE MONTH AND DAY VALUES HAVE NOT BEEN ED-                         * TS400810
                                   488 *  ITED. A RETURN CODE OF 6 INDICATES THAT THE DATA AND                             * TS400820
                                   489 *  YEAR ARE VALID BUT THAT THE MONTH IS INVALID- THE DAY                            * TS400830
                                   490 *  VALUE HAS NOT BEEN EDITED.  FINALLY, A RETURN CODE OF 8                          * TS400840
                                   491 *  INDICATES THAT THE DATA, YEAR AND MONTH ARE VALID BUT                            * TS400850
                                   492 *  THAT THE DAY WAS FOUND INVALID FOR THE VALID MONTH GIVEN.                         * TS400860
                                   493 *  IN SHORT, THE RETURN CODE INDICATES THE LEVEL OF EDITING.                         * TS400870
                                   494 *  THE EDIT SEQUENCE IS DATEX: DATA, YEAR, MONTH AND DAY                             * TS400880
                                   495 *  THEN DATEY: DATA, YEAR, MONTH AND DAY.                                            * TS400890
                                   496 *                                                                                    * TS400900
                                   497 7. A SET OF SUBROUTINE DEFINED FIELDS ARE RETURNED TO THE                           * TS400910
                                   498 *  CALLING PROGRAM:                                                                  * TS400920
                                   499 *                                                                                    * TS400930
                                   500 *                                                                                    * TS400940
                                   501 *        FIELD NAME       PACKED BYTES                                              * TS400950
                                   502 *        PDAY                  2                                                     * TS400960
                                   503 *        PMONTH                2                                                     * TS400970
                                   504 *        PYEAR                 3                                                     * TS400980
                                   505 *                                                                                    * TS400990
                                   506 *  IF CODE4 CONTAINS A PACKED 0, SOME OF THESE FIELDS MAY                            * TS401000
                                   507 *  CONTAIN POSITIVE INTEGERS.  THE INTEGERS REPRESENT THE                           * TS401010
                                   508 *  ABSOLUTE VALUE OF YEARS, MONTHS AND DAYS THAT, WHEN ADDED                         * TS401020
                                   509 *  TO THE EARLIER OF THE TWO INPUT DATES, WILL PRODUCE THE                           * TS401030
                                   510 *  LATER INPUT DATE.  IF THE TWO INPUT DATES ARE EQUAL OR IF                         * TS401040
                                   511 *  CODE4 CONTAINS A NON-ZERO RETURN CODE, THEN ALL THREE                            * TS401050
                                   512 *  PARAMETER FIELDS; PDAY, PMONTH AND PYEAR WILL CONTAIN                             * TS401060
                                   513 *  PACKED ZEROS.  THE PACKED ZEROS, IN THE PRESENCE OF A                            * TS401070
                                   514 *  NON-ZERO RETURN CODE, PROTECT AGAINST THE ILLEGAL USE OF                          * TS401080
                                   515 *  A PRIOR EXECUTION'S RESULT.  THE PACKED ZEROS, IN THE                            * TS401090
                                   516 *  PRESENCE OF A ZERO RETURN CODE, CONSTITUTE A VALID                               * TS401100
                                       *  PARAMETER SET FOR EQUAL INPUT DATES.
```

**Figure 5.1** The TIMESUB4 portion of TEST04's assembly post listing.

```
LOC    OBJECT CODE        ADDR1 ADDR2   STMT  SOURCE STATEMENT                    DOS/VSE ASSEMBLER  16.19  99-12-31

                                         517  *                                                                        * TS401110
                                         518  *        8.  ALL OTHER SUBROUTINE DEFINED FIELDS AND LABELS ARE           * TS401120
                                         519  *            TRANSPARENT TO THE CALLING PROGRAM.                          * TS401130
                                         520  *                                                                        * TS401140
                                         521  *        9.  THIS SUBROUTINE IS WRITTEN TO BE ASSEMBLED WITH THE          * TS401150
                                         522  *            CALLING PROGRAM AND SHOULD BE INSERTED IN THE CALLING        * TS401160
                                         523  *            PROGRAM IMMEDIATELY BEFORE THE 'END' OPCODE.                 * TS401170
                                         524  *                                                                        * TS401180
                                         525  *       10.  THIS SUBROUTINE USES REGISTER 6 AS THE LINK REGISTER.       * TS401190
                                         526  *            IF REGISTER 6 IS ASSIGNED IN THE CALLING PROGRAM FOR        * TS401200
                                         527  *            OTHER USES, IT MUST BE SAVED PRIOR TO EXECUTING THE         * TS401210
                                         528  *            'BALR.'                                                     * TS401220
                                         529  *                                                                        * TS401230
                                         530  *                                                                        * TS401240
                                         531  *                                             JEROME T. MURRAY           * TS401250
                                         532  *                                             MARILYN J. MURRAY          * TS401260
                                         533            GLEN ELLYN, ILLINOIS                                           * TS401270
                                         534  *                                                                        * TS401280
                                         535  ***********************************************************************  * TS401290
                                         536  ***********************************************************************  * TS401300
                                         537  ***********************************************************************  * TS401310
                                         538  *         +++  SECTION 1- GENERAL HOUSEKEEPING  +++                      * TS401320
                                         539  *                                                                        * TS401330
                                         540  *             INITIALIZE INDICATIVE AND WORK FIELDS                      * TS401340
                                         541  *                                                                        * TS401350
                                         542  *                                                                        * TS401360
000520 F800 77EE 7A48  008A4 00AFE       543  TIMESUB4  ZAP   CODE4,=P'0'                                              * TS401370
000526 F820 7984 7A48  00A3A 00AFE       544            ZAP   #$4YRSVX,=P'0'                                           * TS401380
00052C F810 793D 7A48  009F3 00AFE       545            ZAP   PDAY,=P'0'                                               * TS401390
000532 F810 793B 7A48  009F1 00AFE       546            ZAP   PMONTH,=P'0'                                             * TS401400
000538 F820 793F 7A48  009F5 00AFE       547            ZAP   PYEAR,=P'0'                                              * TS401410
00053E F820 7965 7A48  00A1B 00AFE       548            ZAP   #$4COUNT,=P'0'                                           * TS401420
                                         549  *                                                                        * TS401430
                                         550  *                 SAVE REGISTERS 1 THROUGH 6 IN SAVE FIELDS              * TS401440
                                         551  *                                                                        * TS401450
000544 9016 7992       00A48             552            STM   1,6,#$4RSAVE                                             * TS401460
                                         553  *                                                                        * TS401470
                                         554  *         +++  SECTION 2- INPUT-RELATED HOUSEKEEPING  +++                * TS401480
                                         555  *                                                                        * TS401490
                                         556  *             (THIS SECTION INITIALIZES FOR TWO ITERATIONS-             * TS401500
                                         557  *              ONE FOR EACH INPUT DATE)                                 * TS401510
                                         558  *                                                                        * TS401520
                                         559  *             MOVE DATEX TO WORK FIELDS, CONVERT TO FIPS-8             * TS401530
                                         560  *             FORMAT IN #$4WRK8X, ESTABLISH RETURN                      * TS401540
                                         561  *             CODE VALUES- BRANCH TO VALIDATE DATEX                     * TS401550
000548 D207 794D 792B  00A03 009E1       562            MVC   #$4WORK8,DATEX                                           * TS401560
00054E D203 7955 792F  00A0B 009E5       563            MVC   #$4WRK8X(4),DATEX+4                                      * TS401570
000554 D300 7958 7ACD  00A0E 00B83       564            MVZ   #$4WRK8X+3(1),=C'0'                                      * TS401580
00055A D203 7959 792B  00A0F 009E1       565            MVC   #$4WRK8X+4(4),DATEX                                      * TS401590
000560 F800 7942 7A49  009F8 00AFF       566            ZAP   #$42,=P'2'                                               * TS401600
000566 F800 7943 7A4C  009F9 00B02       567            ZAP   #$44,=P'4'                                               * TS401610
00056C F800 7944 7A4E  009FA 00B04       568            ZAP   #$46,=P'6'                                               * TS401620
000572 F800 7945 7A7E  009FB 00B34       569            ZAP   #$48,=P'8'                                               * TS401630
000578 47F0 74F6       005AC             570            B     #$41DATE                                                 * TS401640
                                         571                                                                           * TS401650
```

```
LOC    OBJECT CODE      ADDR1 ADDR2  STMT  SOURCE STATEMENT                          DOS/VSE ASSEMBLER 16.19  99-12-31

                                     572  *                                                                           TS401660
                                     573  *        MOVE DATEY TO WORK FIELDS, CONVERT TO FIPS-8                        TS401670
                                     574  *        FORMAT IN #$4WRK8Y. ESTABLISH RETURN                               TS401680
                                     575  *        CODE VALUES- PROCEED TO VALIDATE DATEY                             TS401690
                                     576  *                                                                           TS401700
00057C  D207 794D 7933  00A03 009E9  577  #$42DATE MVC  #$4WORK8,DATEY                                                TS401710
000582  D203 795D 7937  00A13 009ED  578           MVC  #$4WRK8Y(4),DATEY+4                                          TS401720
000588  D300 7960 7ACD  00A16 00883  579           MVZ  #$4WRK8Y+3(1),=C'O'                                          TS401730
00058E  D203 7961 7933  00A17 009E9  580           MVC  #$4WRK8Y+4(4),DATEY                                          TS401740
000594  F800 7942 7A4B  009F8 00B01  581           ZAP  #$42,=P'3'                                                   TS401750
00059A  F800 7943 7A4D  009F9 00B03  582           ZAP  #$44,=P'5'                                                   TS401760
0005A0  F800 7944 7A66  009FA 00B1C  583           ZAP  #$46,=P'7'                                                   TS401770
0005A6  F800 7945 7A94  009FB 00B4A  584           ZAP  #$48,=P'9'                                                   TS401780
                                     585  *                                                                           TS401790
                                     586  *        +++  SECTION 3- NUMERIC VALIDATION  +++                            TS401800
                                     587  *                                                                           TS401810
                                     588  *        ISOLATE THE SIGN BYTE IN A WORK FIELD AND                          TS401820
                                     589  *        AUGMENT TABLE FOR VALID '+' SIGNS OTHER THAN                       TS401830
                                     590  *        X'F' FOR WHICH TABLE IS DEFINED: X'A', X'C',                      TS401840
                                     591  *        X'E'- EDIT FOR VALID '+' SIGN USING TRT                           TS401850
                                     592  *                                                                           TS401860
0005AC  D200 7947 7954  009FD 00A0A  593  #$41DATE MVC  #$4SIGN,#$4WORK8+7                                            TS401870
0005B2  D209 78BF 791F  00975 009D5  594           MVC  #$4TABL+160(10),#$4ZRO                                       TS401880
0005B8  D209 78DF 791F  00995 009D5  595           MVC  #$4TABL+192(10),#$4ZRO                                       TS401890
0005BE  D209 78FF 791F  009B5 009D5  596           MVC  #$4TABL+224(10),#$4ZRO                                       TS401900
0005C4  DD00 7947 781F  009FD 009D5  597           TRT  #$4SIGN(1),#$4TABL                                           TS401910
0005CA  4780 751C                    598           BC   8,#$4NUM                                                      TS401920
0005CE  47F0 7530        005E6        599           B    #$4BDATA                                                     TS401930
                                     600  *                                                                           TS401940
                                     601  *        REINITIALIZE TABLE AND EDIT FOR VALID ZONE                        TS401950
                                     602  *        AND DIGIT CONFIGURATIONS IN REMAINING BYTES                       TS401960
                                     603  *                                                                           TS401970
0005D2  921C 781F        008D5        604  #$4NUM   MVI  #$4TABL,X'1C'                                                TS401980
0005D6  D2EE 7820 781F   008D6 008D5  605           MVC  #$4TABL+1(239),#$4TABL                                      TS401990
0005DC  DD06 794D 781F   00A03 008D5  606           TRT  #$4WORK8(7),#$4TABL                                         TS402000
0005E2  4780 753A        005F0        607           BC   8,#$4PACK                                                   TS402010
                                     608  *                                                                           TS402020
                                     609  *        POST 'BAD DATA' RETURN CODE AND EXIT                              TS402030
                                     610  *                                                                           TS402040
0005E6  F800 77EE 7942  008A4 009F8  611  #$4BDATA ZAP  CODE4,#$42                                                   TS402050
0005EC  47F0 79B2        00A68        612           B    #$4TERM                                                     TS402060
                                     613  *                                                                           TS402070
                                     614  *        +++  SECTION 4- EDIT YEAR FOR LIMIT VIOLATIONS  +++               TS402080
                                     615  *                                                                           TS402090
                                     616  *        PACK MONTH, DAY AND YEAR IN WORK FIELDS                           TS402100
                                     617  *                                                                           TS402110
0005F0  F211 7968 794D  00A1E 00A03  618  #$4PACK  PACK #$4M,#$4WORK8(2)                                             TS402120
0005F6  F211 796E 794F  00A24 00A05  619           PACK #$4D,#$4WORK8+2(2)                                           TS402130
0005FC  F223 797E 7951  00A34 00A07  620           PACK #$4Y,#$4WORK8+4(4)                                           TS402140
                                     621  *                                                                           TS402150
                                     622  *        MOVE MONTH, DAY AND YEAR TO SAVE FIELDS FOR                       TS402160
                                     623  *        USE IN SECTION 9 WHERE THE TIME DIFFERENCE                        TS402170
                                     624  *        BETWEEN THE TWO DATES WILL BE ACCUMULATED                         TS402180
                                     625  *        AS PYEAR, PMONTH, AND PDAY-                                        TS402190
                                     626  *                                                                           TS402200
```

Figure 5.1  Continued

```
                                                    DOS/VSE ASSEMBLER 16.19  99-12-31

LOC    OBJECT CODE    ADDR1 ADDR2   STMT  SOURCE STATEMENT

                                     627  *         IF #$4YRSVX IS EMPTY, SAVE THE DATA IN            TS402210
                                     628  *         #$4MOSVX, #$4DASVX AND #$4YRSVX                    TS402220
                                     629  *                                                          TS402230
000602 F920 7984 7A48  00A3A 00AFE   630         CP   #$4YRSVX,=P'0'                                 TS402240
000608 4720 756C       00622         631         BH   #$4SECND                                       TS402250
00060C F811 796A 7968  00A20 00A1E   632         ZAP  #$4MOSVX,#$4M                                  TS402260
000612 F811 7972 796E  00A28 00A24   633         ZAP  #$4DASVX,#$4D                                  TS402270
000618 F822 7984 797E  00A3A 00A34   634         ZAP  #$4YRSVX,#$4Y                                  TS402280
00061E 47F0 757E       0634          635         B    #$4YRX                                         TS402290
                                     636  *                                                          TS402300
                                     637  *         IF #$4YRSVX IS NOT EMPTY, THIS IS THE SECOND       TS402310
                                     638  *         ITERATION AND THE SECOND DATE IS BEING             TS402320
                                     639  *         PROCESSED- SAVE DATA IN #$4MOSVY, #$4DASVY         TS402330
                                     640  *         AND #$4YRSVY                                       TS402340
                                     641  *                                                          TS402350
000622 F811 796C 7922  00A22 00A1E   642 #$4SECND  ZAP  #$4MOSVY,#$4M                                 TS402360
000628 F811 7974 792A  00A2A 00A24   643         ZAP  #$4DASVY,#$4D                                  TS402370
00062E F822 7987 793D  00A3D 00A34   644         ZAP  #$4YRSVY,#$4Y                                  TS402380
                                     645  *                                                          TS402390
                                     646  *         EDIT YEAR VALUE FOR LOWER LIMIT VIOLATION          TS402400
                                     647  *                                                          TS402410
000634 F922 797E 7ADD  00A34 00B93   648 #$4YRX    CP   #$4Y,=P'1600'                                 TS402420
00063A 4720 7592       0648          649         BH   #$4YRHI                                        TS402430
                                     650  *                                                          TS402440
                                     651  *         POST 'BAD YEAR' RETURN CODE AND EXIT              TS402450
                                     652  *                                                          TS402460
00063E F800 77EE 7943  00A44 009F9   653 #$4BADYR  ZAP  CODE4,#$44                                    TS402470
000644 47F0 79B2       0A68          654         B    #$4TERM                                        TS402480
                                     655  *                                                          TS402490
                                     656  *         EDIT YEAR VALUE FOR UPPER LIMIT VIOLATION          TS402500
                                     657  *                                                          TS402510
000648 F922 797E 7AE0  00A34 00B96   658 #$4YRHI   CP   #$4Y,=P'3399'                                 TS402520
00064E 4720 7588       063E          659         BH   #$4BADYR                                       TS402530
                                     660  *                                                          TS402540
                                     661  *+++ SECTION 5- DETERMINE LEAP YEAR STATUS   +++            TS402550
                                     662  *                                                          TS402560
                                     663  *         EXECUTE LEAP YEAR ALGORITHM                        TS402570
                                     664  *                                                          TS402580
000652 4150 7780       00836         665         LA   5,#$4LEAPY                                     TS402590
000656 05B5            0565          666         BALR 6,5                                            TS402600
                                     667  *                                                          TS402610
                                     668  *+++ SECTION 6- EDIT MONTH FOR LIMIT VIOLATIONS   +++       TS402620
                                     669  *                                                          TS402630
                                     670  *         VERIFY THAT MONTH IS WITHIN RANGE: 1 - 12         TS402640
                                     671  *         A) CONVERT MONTH TO BINARY IN REGISTER 3          TS402650
                                     672  *                                                          TS402660
000658 F871 79AA 7968  00A60 00A1E   673         ZAP  #$4CVB,#$4M                                    TS402670
00065E 4F30 79AA       00A60         674         CVB  3,#$4CVB                                       TS402680
                                     675  *                                                          TS402690
                                     676  *         B) STORE BINARY BYTE FROM REG 3 IN #$4FLD         TS402700
                                     677  *                                                          TS402710
000662 4230 798F       00A45         678         STC  3,#$4FLD                                       TS402720
                                     679  *                                                          TS402730
                                     680  *         C) INITIALIZE TABLE WITH X'00' FOR TRT            TS402740
                                     681  *                                                          TS402750
```

```
LOC     OBJECT CODE       ADDR1 ADDR2   STMT   SOURCE STATEMENT                                          DOS/VSE ASSEMBLER 16.19  99-12-31

000666  D20B 7820 791F    008D6 009D5    682          MVC   #$4TABL+1(12),#$4ZRO                                                  TS402760
                                         683   *                                                                                   TS402770
                                         684   *             D) EXECUTE TRT USING #$4FLD                                           TS402780
                                         685   *                                                                                   TS402790
00066C  DD00 798F 781F    00A45 008D5    686          TRT   #$4FLD(1),#$4TABL                                                     TS402800
000672  4780 75D0               00686    687          BC    8,#$4DAEDT                                                             TS402810
                                         688   *                                                                                   TS402820
                                         689   *             F) RESTORE TABLE - POST BAD MONTH RETURN CODE                        TS402830
                                         690   *                                                                                   TS402840
000676  D20B 7820 781F    008D6 008D5    691          MVC   #$4TABL+1(12),#$4TABL                                                 TS402850
00067C  F800 77EE 7944    008A4 009FA    692          ZAP   CODE4,#$46                                                            TS402860
000682  47F0 79B2               00A68    693          B     #$4TERM                                                               TS402870
                                         694   *                                                                                   TS402880
                                         695   *      +++   SECTION 7- EDIT DAY FOR LIMIT VIOLATIONS   +++                         TS402890
                                         696   *                                                                                   TS402900
                                         697   *             RESTORE TABLE                                                         TS402910
                                         698   *                                                                                   TS402920
000686  D20B 7820 781F    008D6 008D5    699 #$4DAEDT MVC   #$4TABL+1(12),#$4TABL                                                 TS402930
                                         700   *                                                                                   TS402940
                                         701   *             EXECUTE ADDRESS OF MONTH'S DAY LIMIT ALGORITHM                       TS402950
                                         702   *                                                                                   TS402960
00068C  4150 77D0               00886    703          LA    5,#$4GETAB                                                            TS402970
000690  0565                             704          BALR  6,5                                                                   TS402980
                                         705   *                                                                                   TS402990
                                         706   *             CONVERT SIGN OF PACKED DAY FROM X'F' TO X'C'                         TS403000
                                         707   *                                                                                   TS403010
000692  F811 796E 796E    00A24 00A24    708          ZAP   #$4D,#$4D                                                             TS403020
                                         709   *                                                                                   TS403030
                                         710   *             COMPARE DAY TABLE ENTRY (LIMIT) WITH INPUT DAY                       TS403040
                                         711   *                                                                                   TS403050
000698  D501 796E 4000    00A24 00000    712          CLC   #$4D,0(4)                                                             TS403060
                                         713   *                                                                                   TS403070
                                         714   *             IF INPUT IS WITHIN LIMIT, EDIT DAY FOR ZERO                          TS403080
                                         715   *                                                                                   TS403090
00069E  47D0 75F6               006AC    716          BNH   #$4DALD                                                               TS403100
                                         717   *                                                                                   TS403110
                                         718   *             ELSE POST BAD DAY RETURN CODE AND EXIT                               TS403120
                                         719   *                                                                                   TS403130
0006A2  F800 77EE 7945    008A4 009FB    720 #$4BADA  ZAP   CODE4,#$48                                                            TS403140
0006A8  47F0 79B2               00A68    721          B     #$4TERM                                                               TS403150
                                         722   *                                                                                   TS403160
                                         723   *             EDIT DAY VALUE FOR ZERO                                              TS403170
                                         724   *                                                                                   TS403180
0006AC  F911 796E 7A3A    00A24 00AF0    725 #$4DALD  CP    #$4D,=P'00'                                                           TS403190
0006B2  4780 75EC               006A2    726          BE    #$4BADA                                                               TS403200
                                         727   *                                                                                   TS403210
                                         728   *      +++   SECTION 8- DETERMINE WHICH DATE PROCESSED   +++                        TS403220
                                         729   *                                                                                   TS403230
                                         730   *             #$48 = 9 IF SECOND DATE HAS ALREADY PROCESSED.                       TS403240
                                         731   *             GO TO SECTION 9 ELSE GO TO PROCESS SECOND DATE                       TS403250
                                         732   *                                                                                   TS403260
0006B6  F900 7945 7A94    009FB 00B4A    733          CP    #$48,=P'9'                                                            TS403270
0006BC  4770 74C6               0057C    734          BNE   #$2DATE                                                               TS403280
                                         735   *                                                                                   TS403290
                                         736   *      +++   SECTION 9- COMPUTE ELAPSED TIME   +++                                  TS403300
```

**Figure 5.1** *Continued*

DOS/VSE ASSEMBLER 16.19  99-12-31

```
LOC    OBJECT CODE      ADDR1 ADDR2  STMT   SOURCE STATEMENT

                                     737  *
                                     738  *           DETERMINE WHICH INPUT DATE IS THE EARLIEST
                                     739  *           (USING FIPS-8 FORMATS) AND INITIALIZE WORK
                                     740  *           FIELDS ACCORDINGLY
                                     741  *
0006C0 D507 7955 795D  00A0B 00A13   742          CLC  #$4WRK8X,#$4WRK8Y
0006C6 4720 763C              00716? 743          BH   #$4YR2
0006CA F822 797E 7984  00A34 00A3A   744          ZAP  #$4Y,#$4YRSVX
0006D0 F822 7981 7987  00A37 00A3D   745          ZAP  #$4TY,#$4YRSVY
0006D6 F811 7968 796A  00A1E 00A20   746          ZAP  #$4M,#$4MOSVX
0006DC F811 797C 796C  00A32 00A22   747          ZAP  #$4TM,#$4MOSVY
0006E2 F811 796E 7972  00A24 00A28   748          ZAP  #$4D,#$4DASVX
0006E8 F811 7976 7974  00A2C 00A2A   749          ZAP  #$4TD,#$4DASVY
0006EE 47F0 7660       00716         750          B    #$4YRMO
0006F2 F822 797E 7987  00A34 00A3D   751  #$4YR2  ZAP  #$4Y,#$4YRSVY
0006F8 F822 7981 7984  00A37 00A3A   752          ZAP  #$4TY,#$4YRSVX
0006FE F811 7968 796C  00A1E 00A22   753          ZAP  #$4M,#$4MOSVY
000704 F811 797C 796A  00A32 00A20   754          ZAP  #$4TM,#$4MOSVX
00070A F811 796E 7974  00A24 00A2A   755          ZAP  #$4D,#$4DASVY
000710 F811 7976 7972  00A2C 00A28   756          ZAP  #$4TD,#$4DASVX
                                     757  *
                                     758  *           IF M = TM AND Y = TY, LET PDAY = TD - D. EXIT
                                     759  *
000716 F922 797E 7981  00A34 00A37   760  #$4YRMO CP   #$4Y,#$4TY
00071C 4770 7684       0073A         761          BNE  #$4DALIM
000720 F911 7968 797C  00A1E 00A32   762          CP   #$4M,#$4TM
000726 4770 7684       0073A         763          BNE  #$4DALIM
00072A F811 793D 7976  009F3 00A2C   764          ZAP  PDAY,#$4TD
000730 F811 793D 796E  009F3 00A24   765          SP   PDAY,#$4D
000736 47F0 79B2       00A68         766          B    #$4TERM
                                     767  *
                                     768  *           FIND MONTH'S MAXIMUM DAY VALUE (MAX D OF M)
                                     769  *           A)  EXECUTE LEAP YEAR ALGORITHM
                                     770  *
00073A 4150 7780       00836         771  #$4DALIM LA  5,#$4LEAPY
00073E 0565                          772          BALR 6,5
                                     773  *
                                     774  *           B)  INITIALIZE REGISTER 3 WITH BINARY MONTH
                                     775  *
000740 F871 79AA 7968  00A60 00A1E   776          ZAP  #$4CVB,#$4M
000746 4F30 79AA       00A60         777          CVB  3,#$4CVB
                                     778  *
                                     779  *           c)  EXECUTE ADDRESS OF MONTH'S DAY LIMIT
                                     780  *               ALGORITHM
                                     781  *
00074A 4150 77D0       00886         782          LA   5,#$4GETAB
00074E 0565                          783          BALR 6,5
                                     784  *
                                     785  *           LET IMAX = (MAX D OF M)
                                     786  *           (SAVE (MAX D OF M) FOR INITIAL M)
                                     787  *
000750 F811 797A 4000  00A30 00000   788          ZAP  #$4IMAX,0(2,4)
                                     789  *
                                     790  *           LET ID = D
                                     791  *           (SAVE INITIAL VALUE OF D)
```

TS403310
TS403320
TS403330
TS403340
TS403350
TS403360
TS403370
TS403380
TS403390
TS403400
TS403410
TS403420
TS403430
TS403440
TS403450
TS403460
TS403470
TS403480
TS403490
TS403500
TS403510
TS403520
TS403530
TS403540
TS403550
TS403560
TS403570
TS403580
TS403590
TS403600
TS403610
TS403620
TS403630
TS403640
TS403650
TS403660
TS403670
TS403680
TS403690
TS403700
TS403710
TS403720
TS403730
TS403740
TS403750
TS403760
TS403770
TS403780
TS403790
TS403800
TS403810
TS403820
TS403830
TS403840
TS403850

```
                                                                    DOS/VSE ASSEMBLER 16.19  99-12-31

LOC     OBJECT CODE        ADDR1 ADDR2  STMT   SOURCE STATEMENT

                                        792 *                                                                          TS403860
                                        793 *         ZAP    #$41D,#$4D    INCREMENT EARLIEST YEAR AND MONTH UNTIL EQUAL TS403870
000756  F811 7970 796E  00A26 00A24                                                                                    TS403880
                                        794 *                                                                          TS403890
                                        795 *                        TO LATEST YEAR AND MONTH WHILE COUNTING           TS403900
                                        796 *                        CALENDAR MONTHS                                   TS403910
                                        797 *                                                                          TS403920
                                        798 *                                                                          TS403930
00075C  F922 797E 7981  00A34 00A37     799 #$4AGE    CP     #$4Y,#$4TY                                                 TS403940
000762  4740 76BE       00774           800           BL     #$UNDER                                                   TS403950
000766  F911 7968 797C  00A1E 00A32     801           CP     #$4M,#$4TM                                                TS403960
00076C  4740 76BE       00774           802           BL     #$UNDER                                                   TS403970
000770  47F0 76E4       0079A           803           B      #$4EVEN                                                   TS403980
000774  FA10 7968 7A46  00A1E 00AFC     804 #$UNDER   AP     #$4M,=P'1'                                                TS403990
00077A  FA20 7965 7A46  00A1B 00AFC     805           AP     #$4COUNT,=P'1'                                            TS404000
000780  F911 7968 7A3C  00A1E 00AF2     806           CP     #$4M,=P'13'                                               TS404010
000786  4740 76A6       0075C           807           BL     #$4AGE                                                    TS404020
00078A  FB11 7968 7A3E  00A1E 00AFE     808           SP     #$4M,=P'12'                                               TS404030
000790  FA20 797E 7A46  00A34 00AFC     809           AP     #$4Y,=P'1'                                                TS404040
000796  47F0 76A6       0075C           810           B      #$4AGE                                                    TS404050
                                        811 *                                                                          TS404060
                                        812 *              FIND MONTH'S MAXIMUM DAY VALUE (MAX D OF M)                 TS404070
                                        813 *              FOR NEWLY CALCULATED M                                      TS404080
                                        814 *              A) EXECUTE LEAP YEAR ALGORITHM                              TS404090
                                        815 *                                                                          TS404100
00079A  4150 7780       00836           816 #$4EVEN   LA     5,#$4LEAPY                                                 TS404110
00079E  0565                            817           BALR   6,5                                                       TS404120
                                        818 *                                                                          TS404130
                                        819 *              B) INITIALIZE REGISTER 3 WITH BINARY MONTH                 TS404140
                                        820 *                                                                          TS404150
0007A0  F871 79AA 7968  00A60 00A1E     821           ZAP    #$4CVB,#$4M                                               TS404160
0007A6  4F30 79AA       00A60           822           CVB    3,#$4CVB                                                  TS404170
                                        823 *                                                                          TS404180
                                        824 *              C) EXECUTE ADDRESS OF MONTH'S DAY LIMIT                    TS404190
                                        825 *                 ALGORITHM                                                TS404200
                                        826 *                                                                          TS404210
0007AA  4150 77D0       00886           827           LA     5,#$4GETAB                                                TS404220
0007AE  0565                            828           BALR   6,5                                                       TS404230
                                        829 *                                                                          TS404240
                                        830 *              LET D = (MAX D OF M)                                        TS404250
                                        831 *              (NEWLY CALCULATED M MAY HAVE DIFFERENT DAY LIMIT            TS404260
                                        832 *              THAN EARLIEST M DID AT START OF CALCULATIONS)               TS404270
                                        833 *                                                                          TS404280
0007B0  F811 796E 4000  00A24 00000     834           ZAP    #$4D,0(2,4)                                              TS404290
                                        835 *                                                                          TS404300
                                        836 *              LET X = TD                                                  TS404310
                                        837 *              (PLACE TARGET DAY IN WORK FIELD)                            TS404320
                                        838 *                                                                          TS404330
0007B6  F811 7978 7976  00A2E 00A2C     839           ZAP    #$4X,#$4TD                                               TS404340
                                        840 *                                                                          TS404350
                                        841 *              LET X = X - D                                               TS404360
                                        842 *              (SUBTRACT NEWLY INITIALIZED D TO FIND REMAINING             TS404370
                                        843 *              DIFFERENCE DAYS- TO BE ADDED TO (IMAX - ID)                 TS404380
                                        844 *              TO PRODUCE THE DAYS PARAMETER)                              TS404390
                                        845 *                                                                          TS404400
0007BC  FB11 7978 796E  00A2E 00A24     846           SP     #$4X,#$4D
```

**Figure 5.1** *Continued*

```
                                                      DOS/VSE ASSEMBLER 16.19  99-12-31

LOC    OBJECT CODE    ADDR1 ADDR2  STMT  SOURCE STATEMENT

                                   847  *                                                    TS404410
                                   848  *          IF X < O. OVERSHOOT HAS OCCURRED- BRANCH TO  TS404420
                                   849  *          CORRECT                                    TS404430
                                   850  *                                                    TS404440
0007C2 F910 7978 7A48 OOA2E OOAFE  851        CP    #$4X,=P'O'                                TS404450
0007C8 4740 772C            007E2  852        BL    #$4OSHOT                                  TS404460
                                   853  *                                                    TS404470
                                   854  *          IF NOT X < O. NO OVERSHOOT HAS OCCURRED-    TS404480
                                   855  *          LET TD = X + (IMAX - ID) AND BRANCH TO OUTPUT TS404490
                                   856  *          (TD NOW CONTAINS THE SUM OF THE DAYS COUNTED TO TS404500
                                   857  *          THE END OF THE EARLIEST MONTH, PLUS THE DAYS TS404510
                                   858  *          COUNTED TO THE TARGET DAY FROM THE END OF THE TS404520
                                   859  *          NEWLY CALCULATED MONTH- THIS SUM IS THE PDAY TS404530
                                   860  *          PARAMETER'S VALUE)                         TS404540
                                   861  *                                                    TS404550
0007CC F811 7976 7978 OOA2C OOA2E  862        ZAP   #$4TD.#$4X                                TS404560
0007D2 FA11 7976 797A OOA2C OOA30  863        AP    #$4TD.#$4IMAX                             TS404570
0007D8 FB11 7976 7970 OOA2C OOA26  864        SP    #$4TD.#$4ID                               TS404580
0007DE 47FO 775E            00814  865        B     #$4PARAM                                  TS404590
                                   866  *                                                    TS404600
                                   867  *          THIS IS THE OVERSHOOT CORRECTION           TS404610
                                   868  *          LET COUNT = COUNT - 1                      TS404620
                                   869  *                                                    TS404630
0007E2 FB20 7965 7A46 OOA1B OOAFC  870 #$4OSHOT SP  #$4COUNT.=P'1'                            TS404640
                                   871  *                                                    TS404650
                                   872  *          LET TD = TD + (IMAX - ID)                  TS404660
                                   873  *          (OVERSHOOT IMPLIES THAT TD, PLUS THE DAYS  TS404670
                                   874  *          COUNTED FROM THE EARLIEST DAY TO THE END OF TS404680
                                   875  *          THE EARLIEST MONTH CONSTITUTE THE VALUE OF TS404690
                                   876  *          THE PARAMETER, PDAY)                       TS404700
                                   877  *                                                    TS404710
0007E8 FA11 7976 797A OOA2C OOA30  878        AP    #$4TD.#$4IMAX                             TS404720
0007EE FB11 7976 7970 OOA2C OOA26  879        SP    #$4TD.#$4ID                               TS404730
                                   880  *                                                    TS404740
                                   881  *          IF TD NOT < IMAX AND INITIAL D < 29. SWITCH TO TS404750
                                   882  *          RELATIVE DATE DISPLACEMENT AGEING ELSE OUTPUT TS404760
                                   883  *                                                    TS404770
0007F4 F911 7976 797A OOA2C OOA30  884        CP    #$4TD.#$4IMAX                             TS404780
0007FA 4740 775E            00814  885        BL    #$4PARAM                                  TS404790
0007FE F911 7970 7A40 OOA26 OOAF6  886        CP    #$4ID.=P'29'                              TS404800
000804 47BO 775E            00814  887        BNL   #$4PARAM                                  TS404810
                                   888  *                                                    TS404820
                                   889  *          TD NOT < IMAX AND INITIAL D < 29.          TS404830
                                   890  *          SWITCH TO RELATIVE DATE DISPLACEMENT AGEING- TS404840
                                   891  *          (SUBTRACT IMAX FROM THE CURRENT VALUE OF TD) TS404850
                                   892  *          PDAY PARAMETER WILL BE:                    TS404860
                                   893  *                -1 < PDAY < 33                       TS404870
                                   894  *                                                    TS404880
000808 FB11 7976 797A OOA2C OOA30  895        SP    #$4TD.#$4IMAX                             TS404890
00080E FA20 7965 7A46 OOA1B OOAFC  896        AP    #$4COUNT.=P'1'                            TS404900
                                   897  *                                                    TS404910
                                   898  *          BUILD PARAMETER FIELDS                     TS404920
                                   899  *                                                    TS404930
000814 F842 7948 7965 OO9FE OOA1B  900 #$4PARAM ZAP #$4WORK5.#$4COUNT                         TS404940
00081A FD41 7948 7A3E OO9FE OOAF4  901        DP  #$4WORK5.=P'12'                             TS404950
```

```
                                                          DOS/VSE ASSEMBLER 16.19  99-12-31

LOC    OBJECT CODE       ADDR1 ADDR2  STMT  SOURCE STATEMENT

000820 FA22 793F 7948    009FE        902        AP    PYEAR,#$4WORK5(3)            TS404960
000826 FA11 793B 794B    009F1 00A01  903        AP    PMONTH,#$4WORK5+3(2)         TS404970
00082C FA11 793D 7976    009F3 00A2C  904        AP    PDAY,#$4TD                   TS404980
                                      905  *                                        TS404990
                                      906  *  +++  SECTION 10- TO RESTORE REGISTERS AND EXIT  +++   TS405000
                                      907  *                                        TS405010
000832 47F0 79B2         00A68        908        B     #$4TERM                      TS405020
                                      909  *                                        TS405030
                                      910  *  +++  SECTION 11- SUBROUTINES  +++      TS405040
                                      911  *                                        TS405050
                                      912  *  *******************************       TS405060
                                      913  *  * LEAP YEAR ALGORITHM SUBROUTINE *    TS405070
                                      914  *  *******************************       TS405080
                                      915  *                                        TS405090
000836 F800 7946 7A48    009FC 00AFE  916  #$4LEAPY  ZAP  #$4L,=P'0'                 TS405100
00083C F842 798A 797E    00A40 00A34  917            ZAP  #$4WORK,#$4Y              TS405110
000842 FD40 798A 7A4C    00A40 00B02  918            DP   #$4WORK,=P'4'             TS405120
000848 F900 798E 7A48    00A44 00AFE  919            CP   #$4WORK+4(1),=P'0'        TS405130
00084E 4720 77CE         00884        920            BH   #$4NOLPY                  TS405140
000852 F842 798A 797E    00A40 00A34  921            ZAP  #$4WORK,#$4Y              TS405150
000858 FD41 798A 7A42    00A40 00AF8  922            DP   #$4WORK,=P'100'           TS405160
00085E F910 798D 7A43    00A43 00AF9  923            CP   #$4WORK+3(2),=P'0'        TS405170
000864 4720 77C8         00B7E        924            BH   #$4LPYR                   TS405180
000868 F842 798A 797E    00A40 00A34  925            ZAP  #$4WORK,#$4Y              TS405190
00086E FD41 798A 7A44    00A40 00AFA  926            DP   #$4WORK,=P'400'           TS405200
000874 F910 798D 7A48    00A43 00AFE  927            CP   #$4WORK+3(2),=P'0'        TS405210
00087A 4720 77CE         00884        928            BH   #$4NOLPY                  TS405220
                                      929  *                                        TS405230
                                      930  *      IF YEAR IS A LEAP YEAR, REINITIALIZE TO 1   TS405240
                                      931  *      ELSE INITIALIZED O REMAINS- EXIT   TS405250
                                      932  *                                        TS405260
00087E F800 7946 7A46    009FC 00AFC  933  #$4LPYR   ZAP  #$4L,=P'1'                 TS405270
000884 07F6                           934  #$4NOLPY  BR   6                         TS405280
                                      935  *                                        TS405290
                                      936  *  *******************************       TS405300
                                      937  *  * MONTH'S DAY LIMIT ADDRESS SUBROUTINE *   TS405310
                                      938  *  *******************************       TS405320
                                      939  *                                        TS405330
000886 4140 77EF         008A5        940  #$4GETAB  LA   4,#$4DATAB                 TS405340
                                      941  *                                        TS405350
                                      942  *      AFTER LOADING ADDRESS OF DAY TABLE IN REGISTER   TS405360
                                      943  *      4. IF LEAP YEAR, INCREMENT TO LEAP YEAR FUNCTION  TS405370
                                      944  *                                        TS405380
00088A F900 7946 7A48    009FC 00AFE  945            CP   #$4L,=P'0'                 TS405390
000890 4780 77E2         00898        946            BE   #$4NOL                    TS405400
000894 4144 0002         0002         947            LA   4,2(4)                    TS405410
                                      948  *                                        TS405420
                                      949  *      DIRECTLY ADDRESS TABLE DAY LIMIT FOR THIS MONTH   TS405430
                                      950  *         A) SUBTRACT 1 FROM BINARY MONTH VALUE IN REG 3 TS405440
                                      951  *                                        TS405450
000898 0630                           952  #$4NOL    BCTR 3,0                       TS405460
                                      953  *                                        TS405470
                                      954  *         B) MULTIPLY VALUE IN REG 3 BY 4 TS405480
                                      955  *                                        TS405490
00089A 8930 0002         0002         956            SLL  3,2                       TS405500
```

Figure 5.1 Continued

DOS/VSE ASSEMBLER 16.19   99-12-31

| LOC | OBJECT CODE | ADDR1 | ADDR2 | STMT | SOURCE STATEMENT | | | |
|---|---|---|---|---|---|---|---|---|
| | | | | 957 | * | | | TS405510 |
| | | | | 958 | * | | | TS405520 |
| | | | | 959 | *   C) LOAD ADDRESS OF DAY TABLE ENTRY IN REG 4 | | | TS405530 |
| 0008A9E | 4143 4000 | | 00000 | 960 | LA | 4,0(3,4) | | TS405540 |
| | | | | 961 | * | | | TS405550 |
| | | | | 962 | * | | | TS405560 |
| | | | | 963 | *   EXIT | | | TS405570 |
| 0008A2 | 07F6 | | | 964 | BR | 6 | | TS405580 |
| | | | | 965 | * | | | TS405590 |
| | | | | 966 | *   +++  SECTION 12- DEFINE CONSTANTS AND STORAGE  +++ | | | TS405600 |
| | | | | 967 | * | | | TS405610 |
| 0008A4 | 2C | | | 968 | CODE4 | DC | PL1'2' | TS405620 |
| | | | | 969 | * | | | TS405630 |
| | | | | 970 | *   THE DAY TABLE IS DEFINED WITH A PAIR OF TWO BYTE | | | TS405640 |
| | | | | 971 | *   ENTRIES FOR EACH OF THE 12 MONTHS- AN ENTRY FOR | | | TS405650 |
| | | | | 972 | *   NON-LEAP YEAR AND AN ENTRY FOR LEAP YEAR | | | TS405660 |
| | | | | 973 | * | | | TS405670 |
| 0008A5 | 031C031C | | | 974 | #$4DATAB | DC | PL2'31',PL2'31'   JAN | TS405680 |
| 0008A9 | 028C029C | | | 975 | | DC | PL2'28',PL2'29'   FEB | TS405690 |
| 0008AD | 031C031C | | | 976 | | DC | PL2'31',PL2'31'   MAR | TS405700 |
| 0008B1 | 030C030C | | | 977 | | DC | PL2'30',PL2'30'   APR | TS405710 |
| 0008B5 | 031C031C | | | 978 | | DC | PL2'31',PL2'31'   MAY | TS405720 |
| 0008B9 | 030C030C | | | 979 | | DC | PL2'30',PL2'30'   JUN | TS405730 |
| 0008BD | 031C031C | | | 980 | | DC | PL2'31',PL2'31'   JUL | TS405740 |
| 0008C1 | 031C031C | | | 981 | | DC | PL2'31',PL2'31'   AUG | TS405750 |
| 0008C5 | 030C030C | | | 982 | | DC | PL2'30',PL2'30'   SEP | TS405760 |
| 0008C9 | 031C031C | | | 983 | | DC | PL2'31',PL2'31'   OCT | TS405770 |
| 0008CD | 030C030C | | | 984 | | DC | PL2'30',PL2'30'   NOV | TS405780 |
| 0008D1 | 031C031C | | | 985 | | DC | PL2'31',PL2'31'   DEC | TS405790 |
| | | | | 986 | * | | | TS405800 |
| | | | | 987 | *   TRANSLATION TABLE DEFINED FOR X'F0' - X'F9' | | | TS405810 |
| | | | | 988 | *   (ALL TABLE POSITIONS EXCEPT THOSE CORRESPONDING | | | TS405820 |
| | | | | 989 | *   TO X'F0' THROUGH X'F9' ARE SET TO A VALUE OTHER | | | TS405830 |
| | | | | 990 | *   THAN X'00') | | | TS405840 |
| | | | | 991 | * | | | TS405850 |
| 0008D5 | 1C1C1C1C1C1C1C1C | | | 992 | #$4TABL | DC | 240X'1C' | TS405860 |
| 0009C5 | 0000000000000000 | | | 993 | | DC | 10X'00' | TS405870 |
| 0009CF | 1C1C1C1C1C1C | | | 994 | | DC | 6X'1C' | TS405880 |
| | | | | 995 | * | | | TS405890 |
| 0009D5 | 000000000000000000 | | | 996 | #$4ZRD | DC | 12X'00' | TS405900 |
| 0009E1 | F0F0F0F0F0F0F0F0 | | | 997 | DATEX | DC | ZL8'00000000' | TS405910 |
| 0009E9 | F0F0F0F0F0F0F0F0 | | | 998 | DATEY | DC | ZL8'00000000' | TS405920 |
| 0009F1 | 000C | | | 999 | PMONTH | DC | PL2'0' | TS405930 |
| 0009F3 | 000C | | | 1000 | PDAY | DC | PL2'0' | TS405940 |
| 0009F5 | 00000C | | | 1001 | PYEAR | DC | PL3'0' | TS405950 |
| 0009F8 | | | | 1002 | #$42 | DS | PL1 | TS405960 |
| 0009F9 | | | | 1003 | #$44 | DS | PL1 | TS405970 |
| 0009FA | | | | 1004 | #$46 | DS | PL1 | TS405980 |
| 0009FB | | | | 1005 | #$48 | DS | PL1 | TS405990 |
| 0009FC | | | | 1006 | #$4L | DS | PL1 | TS406000 |
| 0009FD | | | | 1007 | #$4SIGN | DS | ZL1 | TS406010 |
| 0009FE | | | | 1008 | #$4WORK5 | DS | PL5 | TS406020 |
| 000A03 | | | | 1009 | #$4WORK8 | DS | ZL8 | TS406030 |
| 000A0B | | | | 1010 | #$4WRK8X | DS | ZL8 | TS406040 |
| 000A13 | | | | 1011 | #$4WRK8Y | DS | ZL8 | TS406050 |

```
                                                              DOS/VSE ASSEMBLER 16.19 99-12-31

LOC    OBJECT CODE         ADDR1 ADDR2  STMT  SOURCE STATEMENT

000A1B                                  1012  #$4COUNT  DS    PL3                        TS406060
000A1E                                  1013  #$4M      DS    PL2                        TS406070
000A20                                  1014  #$4MOSVX  DS    PL2                        TS406080
000A22                                  1015  #$4MOSVY  DS    PL2                        TS406090
000A24                                  1016  #$4D      DS    PL2                        TS406100
000A26                                  1017  #$4ID     DS    PL2                        TS406110
000A28                                  1018  #$4DASVX  DS    PL2                        TS406120
000A2A                                  1019  #$4DASVY  DS    PL2                        TS406130
000A2C                                  1020  #$4TD     DS    PL2                        TS406140
000A2E                                  1021  #$4X      DS    PL2                        TS406150
000A30                                  1022  #$4IMAX   DS    PL2                        TS406160
000A32                                  1023  #$4TM     DS    PL2                        TS406170
000A34                                  1024  #$4Y      DS    PL3                        TS406180
000A37                                  1025  #$4TY     DS    PL3                        TS406190
000A3A                                  1026  #$4YRSVX  DS    PL3                        TS406200
000A3D                                  1027  #$4YRSVY  DS    PL3                        TS406210
000A40                                  1028  #$4WORK   DS    PL5                        TS406220
000A45                                  1029  #$4FLD    DS    CL1                        TS406230
000A48                                  1030  #$4RSAVE  DS    6F                         TS406240
000A60                                  1031  #$4CVB    DS    1D                         TS406250
000A68  9816 7992           00A48       1032  #$4TERM   LM    1,6,#$4RSAVE               TS406260
000A6C  07F6                000B4       1033            BR    6                          TS406270
                                        1034            END

000A70  5B5BC2D6D7C5D540               1035  =C'$$BOPEN '
000A78  E2E4C2D9D6E4E3C9               1036  =C'SUBROUTINE ERROR'
000A88  5B5BC2C3D3D6E2C5               1037  =C'$BCLOSE'
000A90  00000080                       1038  =A(LIST)
000A94  00000000                       1039  =A(REQUEST)
000A98  C9D5E5C1D3C9C440               1040  =C'INVALID DATA *** DATEX'
000AAE  C9D5E5C1D3C9C440               1041  =C'INVALID DATA *** DATEY'
000AC4  C9D5E5C1D3C9C440               1042  =C'INVALID YEAR *** DATEX'
000ADA  C9D5E5C1D3C9C440               1043  =C'INVALID YEAR *** DATEY'
000AF0  000C                           1044  =P'00'
000AF2  013C                           1045  =P'13'
000AF4  012C                           1046  =P'12'
000AF6  029C                           1047  =P'29'
000AF8  100C                           1048  =P'100'
000AFA  400C                           1049  =P'400'
000AFC  1C                             1050  =P'1'
000AFD  61                             1051  =C'/'
000AFE  0C                             1052  =P'0'
000AFF  2C                             1053  =P'2'
000B00  6B                             1054  =C','
000B01  3C                             1055  =P'3'
000B02  4C                             1056  =P'4'
000B03  5C                             1057  =P'5'
000B04  6C                             1058  =P'6'
000B05  C9D5E5C1D3C9C440               1059  =C'INVALID MONTH *** DATEX'
000B1C  7C                             1060  =P'7'
000B1D  C9D5E5C1D3C9C440               1061  =C'INVALID MONTH *** DATEY'
000B34  8C                             1062  =P'8'
000B35  C9D5E5C1D3C9C440               1063  =C'INVALID DAY *** DATEX'
000B4A  9C                             1064  =P'9'
000B4B  C9D5E5C1D3C9C440               1065  =C'INVALID DAY *** DATEY'
000B60  D7E8C5C1D97A40E8               1066  =C'PYEAR: YYYY, PMONTH: MM, PDAY: DD, '
```

**Figure 5.1** *Continued*

TEST OF TIMESUB4 TO CALCULATE ELAPSED YEAR, MONTH AND DAY PARAMETERS BETWEEN DATES

| DATEX | DATEY | PYEAR | PMONTH | PDAY | CODE4 CONTENTS | |
|---|---|---|---|---|---|---|
| 08/29/1997 | 03/30/2000 | 0002, | 06, | 32, | 0 | |
| 06/29/1998 | 08/30/2203 | 0205, | 01, | 31, | 0 | |
| 04/29/1999 | 01/29/2001 | 0001, | 08, | 30, | 0 | |
| 06/15/1999 | 08/15/2121 | 0122, | 02, | 22, | 0 | |
| 12/31/1999 | 08/22/2408 | 0408, | 07, | 22, | 0 | |
| 12/31/1999 | 03/01/2711 | 0711, | 02, | 01, | 0 | |
| 12/30/2001 | 02/28/2009 | 0007, | 01, | 01, | 0 | |
| 03/05/2100 | 05/08/2483 | 0383, | 02, | 03, | 0 | |
| 03/31/2000 | 12/23/2004 | 0003, | 11, | 23, | 0 | |
| 12/31/1998 | 05/23/2085 | 0085, | 01, | 23, | 0 | |
| 12/30/1998 | 02/28/2003 | 0004, | 02, | 01, | 0 | |
| 12/31/1999 | 02/28/2115 | 0116, | 02, | 03, | 0 | |
| 11/12/1999 | 01/04/2057 | 0057, | 00, | 22, | 0 | |
| 08/29/1999 | 01/05/2091 | 0091, | 04, | 07, | 9 | . INVALID DAY *** DATEY |
| 04/29/1999 | 02/29/2051 | 0051, | 00, | 00, | 0 | |
| 09/18/1996 | 10/02/2561 | 0565, | 00, | 14, | 0 | |
| 12/31/1999 | 03/04/2016 | 0016, | 02, | 04, | 0 | |
| 03/31/2002 | 02/28/2031 | 0028, | 11, | 00, | 9 | . INVALID DAY *** DATEY |
| 06/29/2001 | 02/29/2059 | 0059, | 00, | 00, | 9 | . INVALID DAY *** DATEY |
| 06/29/2006 | 02/29/2041 | 0041, | 00, | 00, | 0 | |
| 08/15/2003 | 08/15/2053 | 0050, | 00, | 00, | 0 | |
| 03/03/1988 | 03/03/2019 | 0031, | 00, | 00, | 0 | |
| 02/28/2000 | 02/28/2066 | 0066, | 00, | 01, | 0 | |
| 08/31/2003 | 04/09/2021 | 0017, | 07, | 09, | 0 | |
| 12/31/2001 | 12/23/2011 | 0009, | 11, | 23, | 0 | |
| 12/31/2009 | 12/27/2091 | 0081, | 11, | 27, | 2 | . INVALID DATA *** DATEX |
| 00/31/2000 | 12/31/2000 | 0000, | 00, | 00, | 8 | . INVALID MONTH *** DATEX |
| 12/00/2006 | 12/31/2001 | 0000, | 00, | 00, | 4 | . INVALID DAY *** DATEX |
| 12/31/1600 | 12/31/2007 | 0000, | 00, | 00, | 4 | . INVALID YEAR *** DATEX |
| 12/15/3400 | 12/31/1600 | 0000, | 00, | 00, | 4 | . INVALID YEAR *** DATEX |
| 12/12/2100 | 13/31/2006 | 0000, | 00, | 00, | 7 | . INVALID MONTH *** DATEY |
| 11/30/2006 | 12/32/2020 | 0000, | 00, | 00, | 9 | . INVALID DAY *** DATEY |
| 10/31/2004 | 12/00/2001 | 0000, | 00, | 00, | 5 | . INVALID DAY *** DATEY |
| 12/21/2001 | 12/31/1600 | 0000, | 00, | 00, | 5 | . INVALID YEAR *** DATEY |
| 12/20/0000 | 12/31/3400 | 0000, | 00, | 00, | 5 | . INVALID YEAR *** DATEY |
| 01/01/1601 | 12/31/3399 | 1798, | 11, | 30, | 0 | |
| 05/24/2134 | 05/24/2134 | 0000, | 00, | 00, | 0 | |
| 07/01/2100 | 09/01/2118 | 0018, | 02, | 00, | 0 | |
| 11/15/1999 | 01/02/2022 | 0022, | 01, | 17, | 0 | |
| 11/25/1799 | 12/02/1999 | 0200, | 00, | 07, | 0 | |

THE SUBROUTINE WAS EXECUTED    44 TIMES

**Figure 5.2**  A subset of test results from TEST04's execution of TIMESUB4, the extended-interval aging subroutine.

Assume the subroutine is being used to determine the age of workers whose birth-dates are retained in an employee master file. The calculations are based on the birthdate A and the current date B. If the current date is less than day 28 of the month on which the aging is being executed, nothing unusual will appear in the PDAY value, regardless of the input birthdate's values.

This is true for any aging using an interval shorter than two years. Consequently, the subroutine is invulnerable 89% of the time during any year when one of the dates delimiting the aging interval is the current date. The inconstant modulus of Gregorian arithmetic is neutralized.

This leads to an alternative solution that can be invoked to avoid these unusual PDAY values. It isn't necessary to interrogate the PDAY value returned in order to adjust the value using an invoked standard or fiat if you first establish a simple protocol. If the aging is being executed when the current date is later than day 27 of the month, you can write the calling program to substitute the first day of the next consecutive month. In those instances, the output results need to be identified only with the terminal date—the B date—to avoid unwarranted assumptions that the actual current date was the effective date of the aging.

# 6

# The Translation Algorithm

The lexicon of date manipulations wouldn't be complete without a way to translate or move a given Gregorian date forward or backward within the defined interval 1601–3399. A common requirement in the business environment is the ability to initiate activity at some future time or to determine that time-dependent requirements were met during a past period.

Given the mathematical ability to add a number of days to a given date, you could stamp records for follow-up any number of days into the future merely by generating a date displacing the current date by a constant. You could similarly gauge past activity by displacing current or stored dates by adding a negative constant. And alternative methods of aging would also be available. You could generate a standard date from the current date for use in processing, and all transaction dates less than the standard would identify overage transactions. Optionally, you could calculate due dates from the transaction date and store them in the receivable record.

While earlier chapters developed algorithms whose objectives were met in determining the time-lapse between two Commercial-8 dates, it's the goal of this chapter to create an algorithm that can accept a Commercial-8 date and a negative or positive time-lapse parameter in days. From these, it must produce a new date.

## The Nature of the Problem

Our investigations thus far have amply established that we can neither add to nor subtract from a Gregorian date if there is a danger of developing an intermonth calculation. The inconstant nature of the Gregorian calendar's modulus threatens the accuracy of any such computation. The requirements of our problem are simple. We would like to add a given number of days to a Commercial-8 date and in so doing arrive at the Commercial-8 date an equivalent number of days in the future. Similarly, we would like to subtract a given number of days from a Commercial-8 date and thus translate it to a Commercial-8 date an equivalent number of days earlier.

## The Solution Strategy

Because you can neither add nor subtract directly, the solution must be indirect—in that a Commercial-8 date equivalent must be employed. Recall your first encounter with aging in chapter 4, where you converted each input date to an equivalent day count relative to the beginning of 1601. You found the absolute difference of the two counts and thus solved the aging problem.

You can meet the present objectives by converting a Commercial-8 input date to a similar day count. First add the given parameter, which will result in the date's equivalent number of days from the beginning of 1601. The remaining task is clear, if not simple. You must devise the algorithmic rules to convert the resultant day count back to a Commercial-8 date.

Because you can use much of the logic of TIMESUB3 in the initial conversion of the input date to a net day count, we'll begin discussing the strategy with the gross day count—that value resulting from the application of the given parameter. We'll refer to this value as J.

Given J with the objective of finding the Gregorian equivalent, you're at once faced with the need to find the number of years involved. From the remaining days, you can determine the number of months simply by performing the inverse of the operation that allowed you to convert the month of the given date to its day equivalent. Thus, the remaining days constitute the day portion of the Gregorian date you're searching for.

## Designing the Algorithm

You can quickly find a candidate year C by dividing J by 365. The remainder, R, will obviously constitute an inflated value, since the division made no allowance for the extra day during leap years. Consequently, you can reduce the remainder by the number of four-year cycles in C as follows: $R = R - (C \div 4)$. (Note that division by 365.25 introduces a scaling and rounding problem in R. It's avoided with this method.)

This has excessively reduced R in that a day has been subtracted for each non-leap-year centesimal. You must calculate the number of such centesimals and credit R with one day for each. Essentially, you must compute T2 and T3, which were introduced in TIMESUB3:

$$T2 = 3 \ (C \div 400) \text{ and } T3 = C_{(Mod\ 400)} \div 100$$

Hence, in crediting the non-leap-year centesimal days, you have:

$$R = R + T2 + T3$$

We'd like to believe that R is now fully adjusted for the candidate year that was calculated. Unfortunately, R might now suffer from overshoot, and be either negative or zero. This possibility is due to the fact that, over the interval you're addressing, 1601–3399, the occurrence of leap-year days might produce a number sufficiently great to allow the overstatement of the quotient C from dividing J by 365. The subsequent removal of net leap-year days from the remainder could result in a zero or negative value. You must now test for overshoot. This results in rule I, continuing the algorithm:

```
Rule I

If R ≤ 0,
    1) Let C = C - 1
    2) Let Y = C + 1601
    3) Let L = 0
    4) Perform the leap year algorithm for Y
    5) Let R = R + 365 + L
    6) Perform Rule I until the antecedent is false
```

Having corrected for overshoot, the value of the Commercial-8 year is NEWY = C + 1601. It's possible, however, that the increment/decrement effect of the applied parameter has created a year in violation of interval limits: 1600 < NEWY < 3400. Accordingly, you must test for a limit violation in NEWY and exit the subroutine if a violation is found. Otherwise rule II, the inverse operation of which we spoke earlier, is invoked (assume COUNTER = 0).

```
Rule II

To find Gregorian month and day equivalents of R:
    1) Let Y = NEWY
    2) Let L = 0
    3) Perform the leap year algorithm for Y
    4) Perform table lookup:
        A) If L = 1, address the table's leap year function
        B) Address the second table ENTRY
        C) Let COUNTER = COUNTER + 1
        D) If R > ENTRY
            1. Address next ENTRY
            2. Perform C) and D) until D) is false
    5) Let NEWM = COUNTER
    6) Let Z = ENTRY previous to last addressed
    7) Let NEWD = R - Z
```

Rule II simply determines from a table of cumulative elapsed days per month the number of months that can be counted until and including the month whose cumulative elapsed days are no longer exceeded by R. When such an entry is found, the count is ended. The counter then contains the equivalent month. All that remains is to subtract the cumulative elapsed days of the prior month from R to find the day value of the Gregorian date. Thus, the gross days have been converted to an equivalent Gregorian date.

### Defining the algorithm's components

Assume that the inputs are passed to the subroutine in two fields, DATEI and MODIFY. DATEI is an eight-digit date conforming to the definition of Commercial-8. MODIFY is a six-digit parameter that can be positive or negative. Because the parameter will translate the DATEI date via addition only, the sign of MODIFY's contents determines the chronological direction in which the translation will occur. MODIFY's limits are:

$$\text{MODIFY } \varepsilon \ \{n: n \text{ belongs to } Z, |n| \leq 657{,}070\}$$

The output NUDATE is an eight-digit date conforming to the definition of Commercial-8 if execution of the algorithm is successful. Otherwise, NUDATE will contain zero.

As usual, the status of the execution for any set of inputs is indicated by the contents of a return code. CODE5, the return code, is defined as follows:

$$
CODE5 = \begin{cases}
0, \text{ If execution is successful} \\
2, \text{ If DATEI, M/D/Y is not numeric} \\
4, \text{ If } Y \, \varepsilon \, \{y: 1600 < y < 3400\} \\
6, \text{ If } M \, \varepsilon \, \{m: 0 < m < 13\} \\
8, \text{ If } D \, \varepsilon \, \{d\} \text{ as defined in Commercial-8} \\
3, \text{ If MODIFY is not numeric} \\
5, \text{ If MODIFY } \varepsilon \, \{n: n \text{ belongs to } Z, |n| \leq 657{,}070\} \\
7, \text{ If NUDATE will violate Commercial-8 limits}
\end{cases}
$$

Note that the limit 657,070 imposed on MODIFY is the total number of days from the end of 01/01/1601 to the end of 12/31/3399. It thus constitutes the maximum parameter value that can be applied to DATEI. However, NUDATE can exceed Commercial-8 limits if ±657,070 is applied indiscriminately. Consequently, CODE5 provides a return value of 7 if a final violation be detected in the year value of NUDATE. Finally, it's clear that MODIFY = 0 is valid and will produce NUDATE = DATEI.

## The Pseudocode for TIMESUB5

The pseudocode assumes that its input has been received in two fields: an eight-byte zoned decimal field DATEI, and a six-byte zoned decimal field MODIFY. The output fields are a five-byte packed field NUDATE and the usual one-byte packed return code field, in this case CODE5.

```
 * Perform general housekeeping.
1) Let NUDATE = 0
2) Let CODE5 = 0
3) Let COUNTER = 0
 * Validate DATEI as numeric.
4) Move DATEI to WORK8
5) If WORK8 is numeric, go to 7
6) Let CODE5 = 2, go to 60
 * Test Y for limit violation.
7) WORK8 → M,D,Y
8) If Y is within limits per Commercial-8, go to 10
9) Let CODE5 = 4, go to 60
 * Perform leap-year algorithm for Y.
10) Let L = 0
11) If Y is a leap year, let L = 1
 * Test M for limit violation.
12) If M is within limits per Commercial-8, go to 14
13) Let CODE5 = 6, go to 60
 * Test D for limit violation.
14) If D is within limits per Commercial-8, go to 16
15) Let CODE5 = 8, go to 60
 * Validate MODIFY for numeric.
16) If MODIFY is numeric, go to 18
17) Let CODE5 = 3, go to 60
 * Test MODIFY for limit violation.
18) If MODIFY = 0, let NUDATE = DATEI and go to 60
```

```
19) If |MODIFY| ≤ 657070, go to 21
20) Let CODE5 = 5, go to 60
  * Compute gross day equivalent.
  * First, compute ordinal day E of input date.
21) Let JLIAN = elapsed days through (M - 1)
22) Let JLIAN = JLIAN + D
  * Second, compute elapsed days 01/01/1601 to input year.
23) Compute T1 = [365.25(Y - 1601)]
24) Compute T2 = 3((Y - 1601) ÷ 400)
25) Compute T3 = ((Y - 1601) (Mod 400)) ÷ 100
  * Third, compute the sum.
26) Let JLIAN = JLIAN + T1
27) Let JLIAN = JLIAN - T2
28) Let JLIAN = JLIAN - T3
  * Finally, add MODIFY parameter to produce gross day value in JLIAN.
29) Let JLIAN = JLIAN + MODIFY
  * Convert gross days to Gregorian, Commercial-8.
  * Find candidate year C and remainder days R.
30) Let C = JLIAN ÷ 365
31) Let R = JLIAN (Mod 365)
  * Reduce R by the actual number of leap days implied by C.
32) Let R = R - (C ÷ 4)
33) Compute T2 = 3(C ÷ 400)
34) Compute T3 = C (Mod 400) ÷ 100
35) Let R = R + T2 + T3
  * Test for overshoot—if no overshoot, or upon correction, accept C.
36) If R > 0, go to 42
37) Let C = C - 1
38) Let Y = C + 1601
39) Execute leap-year algorithm for Y
40) Let R = R + 365 + L
41) Go to 36
  * Acceptance of C establishes new year: NEWY = C + 1601.
42) Let NEWY = C + 1601
  * Validate NEWY for Commercial-8 limits.
43) If 1600 < NEWY < 3400, go to 45
44) Let CODE5 = 7, go to 60
  * Find new month via table lookup.
45) Let Y = NEWY
46) Execute leap-year algorithm for Y
47) Address second ENTRY of cumulative-days table
48) If L = 1, address leap year ENTRY
49) Let COUNTER = COUNTER + 1
50) If R ⊅ ENTRY, go to 53
51) Address next ENTRY
52) Go to 49
53) Let NEWM = COUNTER
  * Find day value of NUDATE.
54) Address ENTRY prior to last addressed
55) Let Z = ENTRY
56) Let NEWD = R - Z
  * Build output field, NUDATE.
57) Let NUDATE = 1000000(NEWM)
58) Let NUDATE = NUDATE + 10000(NEWD)
59) Let NUDATE = NUDATE + NEWY
60) Exit
```

## The Source Code for TIMESUB5

Figure 6.1 shows the TIMESUB5 portion of TEST05's assembly post listing. The result displayed in Figure 6.2 is a subset of the test output from TIMESUB5's test-data set. All outputs were as predicted. Thus, you can conclude that TIMESUB5 is a valid algorithm.

```
LOC  OBJECT CODE   ADDR1 ADDR2  STMT  SOURCE STATEMENT                                    DOS/VSE ASSEMBLER 16.22  99-12-31

                                402 *****************************************************************************   TS500010
                                403 *                                                                         *   TS500020
                                404 *                                                                         *   TS500030
                                405 *   TTTTTT  III   MM   MM  EEEEE  SSSS   BBBBB   5555                     *   TS500040
                                406 *     T      I    M M M M  E      S      B   B   5                        *   TS500050
                                407 *     T      I    M  M  M  EEEE   SSSS   BBB B   5555                     *   TS500060
                                408 *     T      I    M     M  EEEE      S   B   B       5                    *   TS500070
                                409 *     T     III   M     M  EEEEE  SSSS   BBBBB   5555                     *   TS500080
                                410 *                                                                         *   TS500090
                                411 *****************************************************************************   TS500100
                                412 *  I N C R E M E N T / D E C R E M E N T  -  G R E G O R I A N  D A T E  *   TS500110
                                413 *****************************************************************************   TS500120
                                414 *                                                                         *   TS500130
                                415 *                                                                         *   TS500140
                                416 *                                                                         *   TS500150
                                417 *       THIS SUBROUTINE INCREMENTS/DECREMENTS A GIVEN                     *   TS500160
                                418 *       GREGORIAN DATE                                                    *   TS500170
                                419 *                                                                         *   TS500180
                                420 *  1.   VALID INPUT YEARS FOR THIS SUBROUTINE ARE THE YEARS              *   TS500190
                                421 *       1601 THROUGH 3399 A. D.                                           *   TS500200
                                422 *                                                                         *   TS500210
                                423 *  2.   VALID INPUT MONTH VALUES FOR THIS SUBROUTINE ARE 01              *   TS500220
                                424 *       THROUGH 12.                                                       *   TS500230
                                425 *                                                                         *   TS500240
                                426 *  3.   VALID INPUT DAY VALUES FOR THIS SUBROUTINE ARE 01                *   TS500250
                                427 *       THROUGH 31 WITH EXCEPTIONS FOR THE MONTHS LISTED:                *   TS500260
                                428 *                 MONTH          MAXIMUM DAY VALUE                        *   TS500270
                                429 *                  04                   30                                *   TS500280
                                430 *                  06                   30                                *   TS500290
                                431 *                  09                   30                                *   TS500300
                                432 *                  11                   30                                *   TS500310
                                433 *                  02                   28                                *   TS500320
                                434 *                  02 DURING LEAP YEAR  29                                *   TS500330
                                435 *                                                                         *   TS500340
                                436 *  4.   THE DATE FORMAT MUST BE MMDDYYYY.  WHERE MM = THE TWO            *   TS500350
                                437 *       DIGIT MONTH VALUE, DD = THE TWO DIGIT DAY VALUE AND              *   TS500360
                                438 *       YYYY = THE FOUR DIGIT YEAR.                                       *   TS500370
                                439 *                                                                         *   TS500380
                                440 *  5.   THE CALLING PROGRAM MUST PLACE THE EIGHT DIGIT DATE,             *   TS500390
                                441 *       IN ZONED DECIMAL, IN A SUBROUTINE DEFINED EIGHT BYTE             *   TS500400
                                442 *       FIELD, 'DATEI.' DATEI IS NOT ALTERED BY THE SUBROUTINE.          *   TS500410
                                443 *                                                                         *   TS500420
                                444 *  6.   THE CALLING PROGRAM MUST PLACE THE INCREMENTAL VALUE             *   TS500430
                                445 *       (NEGATIVE OR POSITIVE) IN ZONED DECIMAL, IN ANOTHER              *   TS500440
                                446 *       SUBROUTINE DEFINED SIX BYTE FIELD, 'MODIFY.'  THE               *   TS500450
                                447 *       SIX BYTES ARE DESIGNATED TO CONTAIN THE NUMBER OF DAYS           *   TS500460
                                448 *       BY WHICH DATEI IS TO BE INCREMENTED/DECREMENTED.                 *   TS500470
                                449 *                                                                         *   TS500480
                                450 *       THE LOW ORDER BYTE IS ASSUMED TO BEAR THE SIGN, NEGATIVE         *   TS500490
                                451 *       OR POSITIVE.  BECAUSE MODIFY'S CONTENTS ARE USED IN ADD-         *   TS500500
                                452 *       ITION ONLY, INCREMENTATION/DECREMENTATION OCCURS VIA THE         *   TS500510
                                453 *       FUNCTION OF THE SIGN.  THAT IS, A POSITIVE SIGN WILL             *   TS500520
                                454 *       INCREMENT DATEI BY THE GIVEN NUMBER OF DAYS WHILE A              *   TS500530
                                455 *       NEGATIVE SIGN WILL DECREMENT DATEI BY THE GIVEN NUMBER           *   TS500540
                                456 *       OF DAYS.  MODIFY IS NOT ALTERED BY THE SUBROUTINE.               *   TS500550
```

```
LOC   OBJECT CODE   ADDR1 ADDR2   STMT   SOURCE STATEMENT                                      DOS/VSE ASSEMBLER 16.22  99-12-31

                                   457 *   7. MODIFY HAS A LIMIT VALUE OF   657070 .  THAT IS, IT MAY          * TS500560
                                   458 *      NOT BE LESS THAN -657070 OR GREATER THAN +657070.                * TS500570
                                   459 *                                                                        * TS500580
                                   460 *                                                                        * TS500590
                                   461 *      EXAMPLES OF VALID USES OF MODIFY ARE AS FOLLOWS:                  * TS500600
                                   462 *                                                                        * TS500610
                                   463 *         A)   002136                                                    * TS500620
                                   464 *              DATEI WILL BE INCREMENTED BY 2,136 DAYS.                  * TS500630
                                   465 *                                                                        * TS500640
                                   466 *                                                                        * TS500650
                                   467 *         B)   002130                                                    * TS500660
                                   468 *             -DATEI WILL BE DECRFMENTED BY 2,136 DAYS.                  * TS500670
                                   469 *                                                                        * TS500680
                                   470 *   8. A SUBROUTINE DEFINED ONE BYTE FIELD, 'CODE5,' IS RETURNED        * TS500690
                                   471 *      TO THE CALLING PROGRAM AS A RETURN CODE.  IT CONTAINS             * TS500700
                                   472 *      A PACKED 0 IF THE EXECUTION WAS SUCCESSFUL.  NON-ZERO            * TS500710
                                   473 *      VALUES INDICATE THE FOLLOWING:                                    * TS500720
                                   474 *                                                                        * TS500730
                                   475 *      A PACKED 2 INDICATES UNSUCCESSFUL EXECUTION:  INVALID            * TS500740
                                   476 *      DATA IN DATEI.                                                    * TS500750
                                   477 *                                                                        * TS500760
                                   478 *      INVALID DATA ARE DETERMINED IF THE LOW ORDER BYTE'S ZONE         * TS500770
                                   479 *      CONTAINS AN INVALID SIGN, (AN INVALID SIGN IS OTHER THAN         * TS500780
                                   480 *      X'C', X'A', X'E', OR X'F') OR IF THE PRECEDING BYTES'            * TS500790
                                   481 *      ZONES ARE OTHER THAN X'F', OR IF THE LOW ORDER NIBBLE           * TS500800
                                   482 *      OF ANY BYTE CONTAINS A VALUE GREATER THAN X'9'.                  * TS500810
                                   483 *                                                                        * TS500820
                                   484 *      A PACKED 4 INDICATES UNSUCCESSFUL EXECUTION: INVALID            * TS500830
                                   485 *      YEAR IN DATEI- YEAR VALUE VIOLATES THE LIMITS SPECIFIED          * TS500840
                                   486 *      IN 1., ABOVE.                                                     * TS500850
                                   487 *                                                                        * TS500860
                                   488 *      A PACKED 6 INDICATES UNSUCCESSFUL EXECUTION: INVALID            * TS500870
                                   489 *      MONTH IN DATEI- MONTH VALUE VIOLATES LIMITS SPECIFIED            * TS500880
                                   490 *      IN 2., ABOVE.                                                     * TS500890
                                   491 *                                                                        * TS500900
                                   492 *      A PACKED 8 INDICATES UNSUCCESSFUL EXECUTION: INVALID DAY        * TS500910
                                   493 *      IN DATEI- DAY VALUE VIOLATES THE LIMITS SPECIFIED IN 3.,         * TS500920
                                   494 *      ABOVE.                                                            * TS500930
                                   495 *                                                                        * TS500940
                                   496 *      A PACKED 3 INDICATES UNSUCCESSFUL EXECUTION: INVALID            * TS500950
                                   497 *      DATA IN MODIFY.                                                   * TS500960
                                   498 *                                                                        * TS500970
                                   499 *      INVALID DATA ARE DETERMINED IF THE LOW ORDER BYTE'S ZONE         * TS500980
                                   500 *      CONTAINS AN INVALID SIGN, (AN INVALID SIGN IS OTHER THAN         * TS500990
                                   501 *      X'C', X'A', X'E', X'F', X'D' OR X'B') OR IF THE PRECEDING        * TS501000
                                   502 *      BYTES' ZONES ARE OTHER THAN X'F', OR IF THE LOW ORDER           * TS501010
                                   503 *      NIBBLE OF ANY BYTE CONTAINS A VALUE GREATER THAN X'9'.          * TS501020
                                   504 *                                                                        * TS501030
                                   505 *      A PACKED 5 INDICATES UNSUCCESSFUL EXECUTION: INVALID            * TS501040
                                   506 *      VALUE IN MODIFY- DAY VALUE VIOLATES LIMITS SPECIFIED IN          * TS501050
                                   507 *      7., ABOVE                                                         * TS501060
                                   508 *                                                                        * TS501070
                                   509 *      A PACKED 7 INDICATES UNSUCCESSFUL EXECUTION: INVALID            * TS501080
                                   510 *      DATE WILL BE DEVELOPED UPON OUTPUT- THE MODIFICATION            * TS501090
                                   511 *      WILL DEVELOP A NEW DATE PRIOR TO 01/01/1601 OR LATER            * TS501100
                                       *      THAN 12/31/3399.
```

**Figure 6.1**  Introductory documentation and source code for TIMESUB5, the date translation subroutine.

DOS/VSE ASSEMBLER 16.22    99-12-31

| LOC | OBJECT CODE | ADDR1 | ADDR2 | STMT | SOURCE STATEMENT |
|---|---|---|---|---|---|

```
512 *    INSPECTION OF THE RETURN CODE IS IMPORTANT.    THE RETURN        *  TS501110
513 *    CODE, CODE5, REFLECTS THE LEVEL OF EDITING.    A RETURN          *  TS501120
514 *    CODE OF 2, FOR EXAMPLE, NOT ONLY INDICATES INVALIDITY OF         *  TS501130
515 *    DATA, IT ALSO INDICATES THAT NO EDITING HAS BEEN DONE TO         *  TS501140
516 *    VALIDATE THE YEAR, MONTH OR DAY VALUES.   A RETURN CODE OF       *  TS501150
517 *    4 INDICATES THAT THE DATA ARE VALID BUT THAT THE YEAR WAS        *  TS501160
518 *    FOUND INVALID- THE MONTH AND DAY VALUES HAVE NOT BEEN ED-        *  TS501170
519 *    ITED.   A RETURN CODE OF 6 INDICATES THAT THE DATA AND           *  TS501180
520 *    YEAR ARE VALID BUT THAT THE MONTH IS INVALID- THE DAY            *  TS501190
521 *    VALUE HAS NOT BEEN EDITED.   FINALLY, A RETURN CODE OF 8         *  TS501200
522 *    INDICATES THAT THE DATA, YEAR AND MONTH ARE VALID BUT            *  TS501210
523 *    THAT THE DAY WAS FOUND INVALID FOR THE VALID MONTH GIVEN.        *  TS501220
524 *                                                                     *  TS501230
525 *                                                                     *  TS501240
526 *    AFTER DATEI IS EDITED, MODIFY IS EDITED.   A RETURN CODE         *  TS501250
527 *    OF 3 INDICATES THAT DATEI HAS BEEN ACCEPTED BUT THAT             *  TS501260
528 *    MODIFY CONTAINS NON-NUMERIC DATA.   A RETURN CODE OF 5           *  TS501270
529 *    INDICATES THAT DATEI HAS BEEN ACCEPTED BUT THAT MODIFY'S         *  TS501280
530 *    NUMERIC CONTENTS VIOLATE PARAMETER LIMITS.   FINALLY, A          *  TS501290
531 *    RETURN CODE OF 7 INDICATES THAT BOTH DATEI AND MODIFY            *  TS501300
532 *    ARE ACCEPTABLE BUT THAT DUE TO THE COMBINATION OF ELE-           *  TS501310
533 *    MENTS, A NEW DATE WILL FALL OUTSIDE OF THE DEFINED LIMITS        *  TS501320
534 *    OF DATE CALCULATIONS FOR THIS SUBROUTINE.                        *  TS501330
535 *                                                                     *  TS501340
536 *    IN SHORT, THE RETURN CODE INDICATES THE LEVEL OF EDITING.        *  TS501350
537 *    THE EDIT SEQUENCE IS DATEI; DATA, YEAR, MONTH AND DAY.           *  TS501360
538 *    THEN MODIFY; DATA, PARAMETER, AND FINALLY, THE RELATION-         *  TS501370
539 *    SHIP OF THE TWO INPUTS- THE VALIDITY OF THE CALCULATED           *  TS501380
540 *    RESULT.                                                          *  TS501390
541 *                                                                     *  TS501400
542 *  9.  A SUBROUTINE DEFINED FIVE BYTE FIELD, 'NUDATE,' IS RE-         *  TS501410
543 *    TURNED TO THE CALLING PROGRAM.   THE NEW DATE IS CONTAINED       *  TS501420
544 *    IN THIS FIELD IN PACKED FORMAT. IF EXECUTION HAS BEEN SUC-       *  TS501430
545 *    CESSFUL.   IF EXECUTION IS UNSUCCESSFUL, THAT IS IF CODE5        *  TS501440
546 *    CONTAINS A NON-ZERO VALUE, THEN NUDATE WILL CONTAIN              *  TS501450
547 *    PACKED ZEROS.   THIS IS PROTECTION AGAINST ILLEGAL USE OF        *  TS501460
548 *    A PRIOR EXECUTION'S RESULT.                                      *  TS501470
549 *                                                                     *  TS501480
550 * 10.  ALL OTHER SUBROUTINE DEFINED FIELDS AND LABELS ARE            *  TS501490
551 *    TRANSPARENT TO THE CALLING PROGRAM.                              *  TS501500
552 *                                                                     *  TS501510
553 * 11.  THIS SUBROUTINE IS WRITTEN TO BE ASSEMBLED WITH THE           *  TS501520
554 *    CALLING PROGRAM AND SHOULD BE INSERTED IN THE CALLING            *  TS501530
555 *    PROGRAM IMMEDIATELY BEFORE THE 'END' OPCODE.                     *  TS501540
556 *                                                                     *  TS501550
557 * 12.  THIS SUBROUTINE USES REGISTER 6 AS THE LINK REGISTER.         *  TS501560
558 *    IF REGISTER 6 IS ASSIGNED IN THE CALLING PROGRAM FOR             *  TS501570
559 *    OTHER USES, IT MUST BE SAVED PRIOR TO EXECUTING THE              *  TS501580
560 *    'BALR.'                                                          *  TS501590
561 *                                                                     *  TS501600
562 *                                                                     *  TS501610
563 *                                    JEROME T. MURRAY                 *  TS501620
564 *                                    MARILYN J. MURRAY                *  TS501630
565 *  GLEN ELLYN, ILLINOIS                                               *  TS501640
566 *                                                                     *  TS501650
```

```
LOC    OBJECT CODE       ADDR1 ADDR2  STMT                 SOURCE STATEMENT                            DOS/VSE ASSEMBLER 16.22  99-12-31

                                      567  *  ********************************************************  TS501660
                                      568  *  ********************************************************  TS501670
                                      569  *  ********************************************************  TS501680
                                      570  *                                                            TS501690
                                      571  *      +++ SECTION 1- GENERAL HOUSEKEEPING  +++              TS501700
                                      572  *                                                            TS501710
                                      573  *          INITIALIZE INDICATIVE AND WORK FIELDS             TS501720
                                      574  *                                                            TS501730
0004EB 00
0004EC F840 77E6 7A23  0089C 00AD9    575  TIMESUB5 ZAP   NUDATE,=P'0'                                  TS501740
0004F2 F800 795B 7A23  00A11 00AD9    576           ZAP   CODE5,=P'0'                                   TS501750
0004F8 F810 79A0 7A23  00A56 00AD9    577           ZAP   #$5MOCTR,=P'0'                                TS501760
                                      578  *                                                            TS501770
                                      579  *          SAVE REGISTERS 1 THROUGH 6 IN SAVE FIELDS         TS501780
                                      580  *                                                            TS501790
0004FE 9016 79C2       00A78          581           STM   1,6,#$5RSAVE                                  TS501800
                                      582  *                                                            TS501810
                                      583  *          MOVE DATE TO WORK FIELD AND ISOLATE SIGN BYTE     TS501820
                                      584  *                                                            TS501830
000502 D207 797B 795C  00A31 00A12    585           MVC   #$5WORK8,DATEI                                TS501840
000508 D200 7974 7982  00A2A 00A38    586           MVC   #$5SIGN,#$5WORK8+7                            TS501850
                                      587  *                                                            TS501860
                                      588  *      +++ SECTION 2- NUMERIC VALIDATION  +++                TS501870
                                      589  *                                                            TS501880
                                      590  *          AUGMENT TABLE FOR VALID '+' SIGNS OTHER THAN      TS501890
                                      591  *          X'F' FOR WHICH TABLE IS DEFINED: X'A', X'C'.      TS501900
                                      592  *          X'E'- EDIT FOR VALID '+' SIGN USING TRT           TS501910
                                      593  *                                                            TS501920
00050E D209 78EF 794F  009A5 00A05    594           MVC   #$5TABL+160(10),#$5ZRO                        TS501930
000514 D209 790F 794F  009C5 00A05    595           MVC   #$5TABL+192(10),#$5ZRO                        TS501940
00051A D209 792F 794F  009E5 00A05    596           MVC   #$5TABL+224(10),#$5ZRO                        TS501950
000520 DD00 7974 784F  00A2A 00905    597           TRT   #$5SIGN(1),#$5TABL                            TS501960
000526 4780 7478       0052E          598           BC    8,#$5NUM                                      TS501970
00052A 47F0 748C       00542          599           B     #$5BDATA                                      TS501980
                                      600  *                                                            TS501990
                                      601  *          REINITIALIZE TABLE AND EDIT FOR VALID ZONE        TS502000
                                      602  *          AND DIGIT CONFIGURATIONS IN REMAINING BYTES       TS502010
                                      603  *                                                            TS502020
00052E 921C 784F       00905          604  #$5NUM   MVI   #$5TABL,X'1C'                                 TS502030
000532 D2EE 7850 784F  00906 00905    605           MVC   #$5TABL+1(239),#$5TABL                        TS502040
000538 DD06 797B 7496  00A31 0054C    606           TRT   #$5WORK8(7),#$5PACK                           TS502050
00053E 4780 7496       0054C          607           BC    8,#$5PACK                                     TS502060
                                      608  *                                                            TS502070
                                      609  *          POST 'BAD DATA' RETURN CODE AND EXIT              TS502080
                                      610  *                                                            TS502090
000542 F800 795B 7A24  00A11 00A90    611  #$5BDATA ZAP   CODE5,=P'2'                                   TS502100
000548 47F0 79DA       00ADA          612           B     #$5TERM                                       TS502110
                                      613  *                                                            TS502120
                                      614  *      +++ SECTION 3- EDIT YEAR FOR LIMIT VIOLATIONS  +++    TS502130
                                      615  *                                                            TS502140
                                      616  *          PACK MONTH, DAY AND YEAR IN WORK FIELDS           TS502150
                                      617  *                                                            TS502160
00054C F211 7999 797B  00A4F 00A31    618  #$5PACK  PACK  #$5MO,#$5WORK8(2)                             TS502170
000552 F211 799B 797D  00A51 00A33    619           PACK  #$5DA,#$5WORK8+2(2)                           TS502180
000558 F223 799D 797F  00A53 00A35    620           PACK  #$5YR,#$5WORK8+4(4)                           TS502190
```

Figure 6.1  *Continued*

```
                                                       DOS/VSE ASSEMBLER  16.22  99-12-31

LOC    OBJECT CODE      ADDR1 ADDR2  STMT  SOURCE STATEMENT

                                     621  *                                                        TS502200
                                     622  *                                                        TS502210
                                     623  *            EDIT YEAR VALUE FOR LOWER LIMIT VIOLATION    TS502220
                                     624  *                                                        TS502230
00055E F922 799D 7AEC  00A53 00BA2   625        CP    #$5YR,=P'1600'                               TS502240
000564 4720 74BC       00572         626        BH    #$5YRHI                                      TS502250
                                     627  *            POST 'BAD YEAR' RETURN CODE AND EXIT         TS502260
                                     628  *                                                        TS502270
000568 F800 795B 7A3C  00A11 00AF2   629 #$5BADYR ZAP  CODE5,=P'4'                                 TS502280
00056E 47F0 79DA       00A90         630        B     #$5TERM                                      TS502290
                                     631  *                                                        TS502300
                                     632  *            EDIT YEAR VALUE FOR UPPER LIMIT VIOLATION    TS502310
                                     633  *                                                        TS502320
000572 F922 799D 7AEF  00A53 00BA5   634 #$5YRHI  CP   #$5YR,=P'3399'                              TS502330
000578 4720 74B2       00568         635        BH    #$5BADYR                                     TS502340
                                     636  *                                                        TS50236C
                                     637  *      +++ SECTION 4- DETERMINE LEAP YEAR STATUS  +++     TS502370
                                     638  *                                                        TS502380
                                     639  *            EXECUTE LEAP YEAR ALGORITHM                  TS502390
                                     640  *                                                        TS502400
00057C 4150 7772       00828         641        LA    5,#$5LEAPY                                    TS502410
000580 0565                          642        BALR  6,5                                           TS502420
                                     643  *                                                        TS502430
                                     644  *      +++ SECTION 5- EDIT MONTH FOR LIMIT VIOLATIONS  +++ TS502440
                                     645  *                                                        TS502450
                                     646  *            VERIFY THAT MONTH IS WITHIN RANGE: 1 - 12    TS502460
                                     647  *            A) CONVERT MONTH TO BINARY IN REGISTER 3     TS502470
                                     648  *                                                        TS502480
000582 F871 79BA 7999  00A70 00A4F   649        ZAP   #$5CVB,#$5MO                                 TS502490
000588 4F30 79BA       00A70         650        CVB   3,#$5CVB                                     TS502500
                                     651  *            B) STORE BINARY BYTE FROM REG 3 IN #$5FLD    TS502510
                                     652  *                                                        TS502520
                                     653  *                                                        TS502530
00058C 4230 79B3       00A69         654        STC   3,#$5FLD                                     TS502540
                                     655  *            C) INITIALIZE TABLE WITH X'00' FOR TRT       TS502550
                                     656  *                                                        TS502560
                                     657  *                                                        TS502570
000590 D20B 7850 794F  00906 00A05   658        MVC   #$5TABL+1(12),#$5ZRO                         TS502580
                                     659  *                                                        TS502590
                                     660  *            D) EXECUTE TRT USING #$5FLD                  TS502600
                                     661  *                                                        TS502610
000596 DD00 79B3 784F  00A69 005B0   662        TRT   #$5FLD(1),#$5DAEDT                           TS502620
00059C 4780 74FA       00620         663        BC    8,#$5TABL                                    TS502630
                                     664  *                                                        TS502640
                                     665  *      +++  F) RESTORE TABLE - POST BAD MONTH RETURN CODE TS502650
                                     666  *                                                        TS502660
0005A0 D20B 7850 784F  00906 00905   667        MVC   #$5TABL+1(12),#$5TABL                        TS502670
0005A6 F800 795B 7A54  00A11 00B0A   668        ZAP   CODE5,=P'6'                                  TS502680
0005AC 47F0 79DA       00A90         669        B     #$5TERM                                      TS502690
                                     670  *                                                        TS502700
                                     671  *      +++ SECTION 6- EDIT DAY FOR LIMIT VIOLATIONS  +++  TS502710
                                     672  *                                                        TS502720
                                     673  *            RESTORE TABLE                                TS502730
                                     674  *                                                        TS502740
0005B0 D20B 7850 784F  00906 00905   675 #$5DAEDT MVC  #$5TABL+1(12),#$5TABL
```

```
 LOC    OBJECT CODE   ADDR1 ADDR2  STMT  SOURCE STATEMENT                              DOS/VSE ASSEMBLER  16.22  99-12-31

                                   676  *
                                   677  *              EXECUTE ADDRESS OF MONTH'S DAY LIMIT ALGORITHM      TS502750
                                   678  *                                                                 TS502760
0005B6  4150 77C2         00878    679           LA    5,#$5GETAB                                         TS502770
0005BA  0565                       680           BALR  6,5                                                TS502780
                                   681  *                                                                 TS502790
                                   682  *              CONVERT SIGN OF PACKED DAY FROM X'F' TO X'C'        TS502800
                                   683  *                                                                 TS502810
0005BC  F811 799B 799B  00A51 00A51  684         ZAP   #$5DA,#$5DA                                        TS502820
                                   685  *                                                                 TS502830
                                   686  *              COMPARE DAY TABLE ENTRY (LIMIT) WITH INPUT DAY      TS502840
                                   687  *                                                                 TS502850
0005C2  D501 799B 4000  00A51 00C00  688         CLC   #$5DA,0(4)                                         TS502860
                                   689  *                                                                 TS502870
                                   690  *              IF INPUT IS WITHIN LIMIT, EDIT DAY FOR ZERO         TS502880
                                   691  *                                                                 TS502890
0005C8  47D0 7520         005D6    692           BNH   #$5DALO                                            TS502900
                                   693  *                                                                 TS502910
                                   694  *              ELSE POST BAD DAY RETURN CODE AND EXIT             TS502920
                                   695  *                                                                 TS502930
0005CC  F800 795B 7A6C  00A11 00B22  696  #$5BADA  ZAP   CODE5,=P'8'                                      TS502940
0005D2  47F0 79DA         00A90    697           B     #$5TERM                                            TS502950
                                   698  *                                                                 TS502960
                                   699  *              EDIT DAY VALUE FOR ZERO                             TS502970
                                   700  *                                                                 TS502980
0005D6  F911 799B 7A14  00A51 00ACA  701  #$5DALO  CP    #$5DA,=P'00'                                     TS502990
0005DC  4780 7516         005CC    702           BE    #$5BADA                                            TS503000
                                   703  *                                                                 TS503010
                                   704  *+++   SECTION 7- VALIDATE MODIFY FOR NUMERIC   +++               TS503020
                                   705  *                                                                 TS503030
                                   706  *              MOVE MODIFY DATA TO WORK FIELD AND ISOLATE          TS503040
                                   707  *              SIGN BYTE FOR EDIT                                  TS503050
                                   708  *                                                                 TS503060
0005E0  D205 798C 77E0  00A42 00896  709         MVC   #$5WORKX,MODIFY                                    TS503070
0005E6  D200 7974 7991  00A2A 00A47  710         MVC   #$5SIGN,#$5WORKX+5                                 TS503080
                                   711  *                                                                 TS503090
                                   712  *              INITIALIZE TABLE FOR VALID '+' AND '-' SIGNS        TS503100
                                   713  *              OTHER THAN X'F' FOR WHICH TABLE IS ALREADY          TS503110
                                   714  *              DEFINED: X'A', X'B', X'C', X'D', X'E'- EDIT         TS503120
                                   715  *              USING TRT                                          TS503130
                                   716  *                                                                 TS503140
0005EC  D209 78EF 794F  009A5 00A05  717         MVC   #$5TABL+160(10),#$5ZRO                             TS503150
0005F2  D209 78FF 794F  009B5 00A05  718         MVC   #$5TABL+176(10),#$5ZRO                             TS503160
0005F8  D209 790F 794F  009C5 00A05  719         MVC   #$5TABL+192(10),#$5ZRO                             TS503170
0005FE  D209 791F 794F  009D5 00A05  720         MVC   #$5TABL+208(10),#$5ZRO                             TS503180
000604  D209 792F 794F  009E5 00A05  721         MVC   #$5TABL+224(10),#$5ZRO                             TS503190
00060A  DD00 7974 784F  00A2A 00905  722         TRT   #$5SIGN(1),#$5TABL                                 TS503200
000610  4780 7562         00618    723           BC    8,#$5ZONE                                          TS503210
000614  47F0 7576         0062C    724           B     #$5BADMD                                           TS503220
                                   725  *                                                                 TS503230
                                   726  *              REINITIALIZE TABLE AND EDIT FOR VALID ZONE          TS503240
                                   727  *              AND DIGIT CONFIGURATIONS IN REMAINING BYTES         TS503250
                                   728  *                                                                 TS503260
000618  921C 784F         00905    729  #$5ZONE  MVI   #$5TABL,X'1C'                                      TS503270
00061C  D2EE 7850 784F  00906 00905  730         MVC   #$5TABL+1(239),#$5TABL                             TS503290
```

Figure 6.1 *Continued*

```
                                                                    DOS/VSE ASSEMBLER 16.22  99-12-31

LOC    OBJECT CODE   ADDR1 ADDR2  STMT  SOURCE STATEMENT

000622 DD04 798C 784F 00A42 00905  731       TRT   #$WORKX(5),#$TABL              TS503300
000628 4780 7580      00636        732       BC    8,#$5SIZE                      TS503310
                                   733  *                                         TS503320
                                   734  *           POST 'BAD MODIFY DATA' RETURN CODE AND EXIT   TS503330
                                   735  *                                         TS503340
00062C F800 795B 7A84 00A11 00B3A  736 #$5BADMD ZAP  CODE5,=P'3'                  TS503350
000632 47F0 79DA      00A90        737       B     #$5TERM                        TS503360
                                   738  *                                         TS503370
                                   739  *      +++  SECTION 8- EDIT MODIFY DATA FOR VIOLATIONS  +++   TS503380
                                   740  *                                         TS503390
                                   741  *           PACK MODIFY CONTENTS INTO WORK FIELD-      TS503400
                                   742  *           TAKE ABSOLUTE VALUE OF PARAMETER IN        TS503410
                                   743  *           PREPARATION FOR EDIT OF MODIFY VALUE       TS503420
                                   744  *                                         TS503430
000636 F235 79A2 798C 00A58 00A42  745 #$5SIZE PACK #$5MDA,#$WORKX                TS503440
00063C D103 79A5 7A1E 00A5B 00AD4  746       MVN  #$5MDA+3,=P'1'                  TS503450
                                   747  *                                         TS503460
                                   748  *           EDIT MODIFY VALUE FOR ZERO CONTENT OR      TS503470
                                   749  *           UPPER/LOWER LIMIT VIOLATION- IF ZERO, OUTPUT   TS503480
                                   750  *           INPUT DATE; IF VIOLATION, POST CODE AND EXIT   TS503490
                                   751  *                                         TS503500
000642 F930 79A2 75AC 00A58 00AD9  752       CP   #$5MDA,=P'O'                    TS503510
000648 4770 75AC      00662        753       BNE  #$5LIMIT                        TS503520
00064C F811 7995 7999 00A4B 00A4F  754       ZAP  #$5NEWM,#$5MO                   TS503530
000652 F811 7997 799B 00A4D 00A51  755       ZAP  #$5NEWD,#$5DA                   TS503540
000658 F822 7992 799D 00A48 00A53  756       ZAP  #$5NEWY,#$5YR                   TS503550
00065E 47F0 7756      00B0C        757       B    #$5BUILD                        TS503560
000662 F933 79A2 7A58 00A58 00AB0  758 #$5LIMIT CP #$5MDA,=P'657070'              TS503570
000668 47D0 75C0      00676        759       BNH  #$5SGN                          TS503580
                                   760  *                                         TS503590
                                   761  *           POST 'BAD PARAMETER' RETURN CODE AND EXIT   TS503600
                                   762  *                                         TS503610
00066C F800 795B 7A9C 00A11 00B52  763       ZAP  CODE5,=P'5'                     TS503620
000672 47F0 79DA      00A90        764       B    #$5TERM                         TS503630
                                   765  *                                         TS503640
                                   766  *           RESTORE SIGN TO PACKED MODIFY VALUE        TS503650
                                   767  *                                         TS503660
000676 F235 79A2 798C 00A58 00A42  768 #$5SGN PACK #$5MDA,#$WORKX                 TS503670
                                   769  *                                         TS503680
                                   770  *      +++  SECTION 9- COMPUTE GROSS DAY EQUIVALENT  +++   TS503690
                                   771  *                                         TS503700
                                   772  *           FIRST, COMPUTE ELAPSED DAYS- INPUT YEAR TO INPUT   TS503710
                                   773  *           MONTH (THIS BEGINS THE COMPUTATION OF E)   TS503720
                                   774  *                                         TS503730
                                   775  *           DIRECTLY ADDRESS ELAPSED DAY TABLE THIS MONTH   TS503740
                                   776  *           A) LOAD ADDRESS OF DAYS TABLE IN REGISTER 5   TS503750
                                   777  *                                         TS503760
00067C 4150 781B      008D1        778       LA   5,#$5DAYS                       TS503770
                                   779  *                                         TS503780
                                   780  *           B) IF LEAP YEAR, INCREMENT TO LEAP YEAR    TS503790
                                   781  *                             FUNCTION                 TS503800
                                   782  *                                         TS503810
000680 F900 7973 7A23 00A29 00AD9  783       CP   #$5L,=P'O'                      TS503820
000686 4780 75D8      0068E        784       BE   #$5NOLL                         TS503830
00068A 4155 0002      00002        785       LA   5,2(5)                          TS503840
```

```
                                            DOS/VSE ASSEMBLER 16.22  99-12-31

LOC    OBJECT CODE      ADDR1 ADDR2  STMT   SOURCE STATEMENT

                                     786  *
                                     787  *          C) LOAD ADDRESS OF TABLE ELEMENT IN REGISTER 5      TS503860
                                     788  *             (REGISTER 3 STILL CONTAINS THE ADJUSTED          TS503870
                                     789  *             BINARY VALUE OF THE CURRENT MONTH AS DEV-        TS503880
                                     790  *             ELOPED IN SECTION 5)                             TS503890
                                     791  *                                                             TS503900
00068E 4153 5000        00000        792  #$5NOLL LA    5,0(3,5)                                         TS503910
                                     793  *                                                             TS503920
                                     794  *          ADD DIRECTLY ADDRESSED ELAPSED DAYS TO WORK         TS503930
                                     795  *          FIELD                                              TS503940
                                     796  *                                                             TS503950
000692 F841 7964 5000   00A1A 00000  797          ZAP   #$5JLIAN,O(2,5)                                  TS503960
                                     798  *                                                             TS503970
                                     799  *          ADD INPUT DATE'S DAY FIELD TO WORK FIELD            TS503980
                                     800  *                                                             TS503990
000698 FA41 7964 799B   00A1A 00A51  801          AP    #$5JLIAN,#$5DA                                   TS504000
                                     802  *                                                             TS504010
                                     803  *          SECOND, COMPUTE ELAPSED DAYS 1601 TO INPUT YEAR     TS504020
                                     804  *                                                             TS504030
                                     805  *          COMPUTE #$5T1                                       TS504040
                                     806  *                                                             TS504050
00069E F852 7975 799D   00A2B 00A53  807          ZAP   #$5WORK6,#$5YR                                   TS504060
0006A4 FB52 7975 7AF2   00A2B 0BAB8  808          SP    #$5WORK6,=P'1601'                                TS504070
0006AA FC52 7975 7AF5   00A2B 0BAB   809          MP    #$5WORK6,=P'36525'                               TS504080
                                     810  *                                                             TS504090
                                     811  *          INTEGER TRUNCATION EFFECTED BY UNPK - PACK          TS504100
                                     812  *                                                             TS504110
0006B0 F384 7983 7976   00A39 00A2C  813          UNPK  #$5WORK9,#$5WORK6+1(5)                           TS504120
0006B6 F246 79A6 7983   00A5C 00A39  814          PACK  #$5T1,#$5WORK9(7)                                TS504130
                                     815  *                                                             TS504140
                                     816  *          COMPUTE NUMBER OF NON-LEAP YEAR CENTESSIMALS        TS504150
                                     817  *                                                             TS504160
                                     818  *          COMPUTE #$5T2                                       TS504170
                                     819  *                                                             TS504180
0006BC F842 79AE 799D   00A64 00A53  820          ZAP   #$5WORK,#$5YR                                    TS504190
0006C2 FB42 79AE 7AF2   00A64 0BAB8  821          SP    #$5WORK,=P'1601'                                 TS504200
0006C8 FD41 79AE 7A16   00A64 00ACC  822          DP    #$5WORK,=P'400'                                  TS504210
0006CE F811 79AB 79AF   00A61 00A65  823          ZAP   #$5T2,#$5WORK+1(2)                               TS504220
0006D4 FC10 79AB 7A84   00A61 0B3A   824          MP    #$5T2,=P'3'                                      TS504230
                                     825  *                                                             TS504240
                                     826  *          COMPUTE #$5T3                                       TS504250
                                     827  *                                                             TS504260
0006DA F841 79AE 79B1   00A64 00A67  828          ZAP   #$5WORK,#$5WORK+3(2)                             TS504270
0006E0 FD41 79AE 7A18   00A64 00ACE  829          DP    #$5WORK,=P'100'                                  TS504280
0006E6 F800 79AD 79B0   00A63 00A66  830          ZAP   #$5T3,#$5WORK+2(1)                               TS504290
                                     831  *                                                             TS504300
                                     832  *          COMPUTE THE SUM OF ELAPSED DAYS                     TS504310
                                     833  *                                                             TS504320
0006EC FA44 7964 79A6   00A1A 00A5C  834          AP    #$5JLIAN,#$5T1                                   TS504330
0006F2 FB41 7964 79AB   00A1A 00A61  835          SP    #$5JLIAN,#$5T2                                   TS504340
0006F8 FB40 7964 79AD   00A1A 00A63  836          SP    #$5JLIAN,#$5T3                                   TS504350
                                     837  *                                                             TS504360
                                     838  *          FINALLY, ADD DAYS PARAMETER OF MODIFY               TS504370
                                     839  *          TO PRODUCE GROSS DAY VALUE IN #$5JLIAN              TS504380
                                     840  *                                                             TS504390
```

**Figure 6.1** *Continued*

```
LOC    OBJECT CODE       ADDR1 ADDR2  STMT  SOURCE STATEMENT                                  DOS/VSE ASSEMBLER 16.22  99-12-31

0006FE FA43 7964 79A2    00A1A 00A58  841          AP   #$5JLIAN,#$5MDA                                                TS504400
                                      842   *                                                                         TS504410
                                      843   *        +++ SECTION 10- CONVERT GROSS DAYS TO GREGORIAN +++              TS504420
                                      844   *                                                                         TS504430
                                      845   *                                                                         TS504440
                                      846   *             FIRST, FIND CANDIDATE YEAR- #$5C                            TS504450
                                      847   *                                                                         TS504460
                                      848   *        REDUCE GROSS DAYS TO YEARS AND REMAINDER DAYS:                   TS504470
                                      849   *             A) #$5C = #$5JLIAN/365  AND REMAINDER DAYS;                 TS504480
                                      850   *                #$5R = #$5JLIAN(MOD 365)                                 TS504490
                                      851   *                                                                         TS504500
000704 F844 7964 79AE    00A64 00A1A  852          ZAP  #$5WORK,#$5JLIAN                                              TS504510
00070A FD41 79AE 7A1A    00A64 00AD0  853          DP   #$5WORK,=P'365'                                               TS504520
000710 F842 796E 79AE    00A64 00A64  854          ZAP  #$5C,#$5WORK(3)                                               TS504530
000716 F841 7969 79B1    00A1F 00A67  855          ZAP  #$5R,#$5WORK+3(2)                                             TS504540
                                      856   *                                                                         TS504550
                                      857   *        REDUCE REMAINING DAYS BY MAXIMUM NUMBER OF LEAP                  TS504560
                                      858   *        DAYS:                                                            TS504570
                                      859   *             B) #$5R = #$5R - #$5C/4                                     TS504580
                                      860   *                                                                         TS504590
00071C F844 796E 79AE    00A64 00A24  861          ZAP  #$5WORK,#$5C                                                  TS504600
000722 FD40 79AE 7A3C    00A64 00AF2  862          DP   #$5WORK,=P'4'                                                 TS504610
000728 FB41 7969 79B0    00A1F 00A66  863          SP   #$5R,#$5WORK+2(2)                                             TS504620
                                      864   *                                                                         TS504630
                                      865   *        COMPUTE NUMBER OF NON-LEAP YEAR CENTESSIMALS                     TS504640
                                      866   *        IN ORDER TO CREDIT #$5R                                          TS504650
                                      867   *             C) COMPUTE #$5T2                                            TS504660
                                      868   *                                                                         TS504670
00072E F844 796E 79AE    00A64 00A24  869          ZAP  #$5WORK,#$5C                                                  TS504680
000734 FD41 79AE 7A16    00A64 00ACC  870          DP   #$5WORK,=P'400'                                               TS504690
00073A F811 79AB 79AF    00A61 00A65  871          ZAP  #$5T2,#$5WORK+1(2)                                            TS504700
000740 FC10 79AB 7A84    00A61 00B3A  872          MP   #$5T2,=P'3'                                                   TS504710
                                      873   *                                                                         TS504720
                                      874   *             D) COMPUTE #$5T3                                            TS504730
                                      875   *                                                                         TS504740
000746 F841 79B1 79AE    00A67 00A64  876          ZAP  #$5WORK,#$5WORK+3(2)                                          TS504750
00074C FD41 79AE 7A18    00A64 00ACE  877          DP   #$5WORK,=P'100'                                               TS504760
000752 F800 79AD 79B0    00A63 00A66  878          ZAP  #$5T3,#$5WORK+2(1)                                            TS504770
                                      879   *                                                                         TS504780
                                      880   *             E) CREDIT EXCESS LEAP DAYS TO #$5R                          TS504790
                                      881   *                                                                         TS504800
000758 FA41 7969 79AB    00A1F 00A61  882          AP   #$5R,#$5T2                                                    TS504810
00075E FA40 7969 79AD    00A1F 00A63  883          AP   #$5R,#$5T3                                                    TS504820
                                      884   *                                                                         TS504830
                                      885   *             F) TEST REMAINDER, #$5R, FOR ZERO OR                        TS504840
                                      886   *                NEGATIVE- IF POSITIVE, ACCEPT #$5C                       TS504850
                                      887   *                AS MAXIMUM YEAR ELEMENT                                  TS504860
                                      888   *                                                                         TS504870
000764 F940 7969 7A23    00A1F 00796  889   #$5RETRY CP   #$5R,=P'0'                                                  TS504880
00076A 4720 76E0               00796  890          BH   #$5REMOK                                                      TS504890
                                      891   *                                                                         TS504900
                                      892   *             G) IF ZERO OR NEGATIVE, OVERSHOOT OCCURRED-                 TS504910
                                      893   *                DECREMENT #$5C IN PREPARATION FOR REVERSING             TS504920
                                      894   *                THE DEPLETION OF DAYS FROM #$5R                          TS504930
                                      895   *                                                                         TS504940
```

```
                                                      DOS/VSE ASSEMBLER 16.22  99-12-31

LOC     OBJECT CODE        ADDR1 ADDR2  STMT   SOURCE STATEMENT

00076E  FB40 796E 7A1E     00A24 00AD4   896          SP    #$5C,=P'1'      H) INITIALIZE #$5YR WITH NEW YEAR VALUE
                                         897   *
                                         898   *
                                         899   *
000774  F824 799D 796E     00A24         900          ZAP   #$5YR,#$5C
00077A  FA22 799D 7AF2     00A53 00BA8   901          AP    #$5YR,=P'1601'
                                         902   *
                                         903   *                            I) EXECUTE LEAP YEAR ALGORITHM
                                         904   *
000780  4150 7772          00828         905          LA    5,#$5LEAPY
000784  0565                             906          BALR  6,5
                                         907   *
                                         908   *                            J) INCREMENT REMAINDER DAYS BY 365 + #$5C'S
                                         909   *                               LEAP YEAR INCREMENT, #$5L- BRANCH TO
                                         910   *                               #$5RETRY. LOOPING UNTIL OVERSHOOT IS COR-
                                         911   *                               RECTED AS EVIDENCED BY POSITIVE VALUE IN
                                         912   *                               #$5R
                                         913   *
000786  FA41 7969 7A1A     00A1F 00AD0   914          AP    #$5R,=P'365'
00078C  FA40 7969 7973     00A1F 00A29   915          AP    #$5R,#$5L
000792  47F0 76AE          00764         916          B     #$5RETRY
                                         917   *
                                         918   *                            K) THE NEW YEAR: #$5NEWY = #$5C + 1601
                                         919   *
000796  F824 7992 796E     00A48 00A24   920  #$5REMOK ZAP  #$5NEWY,#$5C
00079C  FA22 7992 7AF2     00A48 00BA8   921          AP    #$5NEWY,=P'1601'
                                         922   *
                                         923   *                            L) VERIFY THAT NEW YEAR IS WITHIN LIMITS
                                         924   *                               (1600 < #$5NEWY < 3400) IF NOT, INSTALL
                                         925   *                               INVALID RESULT RETURN CODE AND EXIT
                                         926   *
0007A2  F922 7992 7AEC     00A48 00BA2   927          CP    #$5NEWY,=P'1600'
0007A8  4720 7700          007B6         928          BH    #$53399
0007AC  F800 795B 7AB4     00A11 00B6A   929  #$5OUT  ZAP   CODE5,=P'7'
0007B2  47F0 79DA          00A90         930          B     #$5TERM
0007B6  F922 7992 7AEF     00A48 00BA5   931  #$53399 CP    #$5NEWY,=P'3399'
0007BC  4720 76F6          007AC         932          BH    #$5OUT
                                         933   *
                                         934   *      SECOND, FIND NEW MONTH
                                         935   *
                                         936   *                            REDUCE REMAINDER DAYS TO MONTHS AND NET DAYS
                                         937   *                            A) INITIALIZE #$5YR WITH NEW YEAR VALUE
                                         938   *
0007C0  F822 799D 7992     00A53 00A48   939          ZAP   #$5YR,#$5NEWY
                                         940   *
                                         941   *                            B) EXECUTE LEAP YEAR ALGORITHM
                                         942   *
0007C6  4150 7772          00828         943          LA    5,#$5LEAPY
0007CA  0565                             944          BALR  6,5
                                         945   *
                                         946   *                            C) LOAD ADDRESS OF SECOND ENTRY OF DAYS TABLE
                                         947   *                               INTO REGISTER 5
                                         948   *
0007CC  4150 781F          008D5         949          LA    5,#$5DAYS+4
                                         950   *
```

**Figure 6.1** *Continued*

```
                                                              DOS/VSE ASSEMBLER 16.22  99-12-31

LOC    OBJECT CODE       ADDR1 ADDR2   STMT   SOURCE STATEMENT

                                        951  *
                                        952  *
                                        953  *        D) IF LEAP YEAR, INCREMENT TO LEAP YEAR
                                                      *           FUNCTION
0007D0 F900 7973 7A23    00A29 00AD9    954  *           CP   #$5L,=P'0'
0007D6 4780 7728               007DE    955  *           BE   #$5COUNT
0007DA 4155 0002               00002    956  *           LA   5,2(5)
                                        957  *
                                        958  *        E) COUNT AND COMPARE- IF #$5R IS NOT GREATER
                                        959  *           THAN TABLE ENTRY, EXIT LOOP...
                                        960  *
0007DE FA10 79A0 7A1E    00A56 00A1E    961  #$5COUNT  AP   #$5MOCTR,=P'1'
0007E4 F941 7969 5000    00A1F 00000    962  *           CP   #$5R,0(2,5)
0007EA 47D0 7740               007F6    963  *           BNH  #$5GOTNU
                                        964  *
                                        965  *        F) ELSE, LOAD ADDRESS OF NEXT TABLE ENTRY
                                        966  *           INTO REGSTER 5 AND DO LOOP
                                        967  *
0007EE 4155 0004               00004    968  *           LA   5,4(5)
0007F2 47F0 7728               007DE    969  *           B    #$5COUNT
                                        970  *
                                        971  *        G) COUNTER CONTAINS THE NEW MONTH, TRANSFER
                                        972  *           TO #$5NEWM
                                        973  *
0007F6 F811 7995 79A0    00A4B 00A56    974  #$5GOTNU  ZAP  #$5NEWM,#$5MOCTR
                                        975  *
                                        976  *        H) DECREMENT REGISTER 5 ADDRESS TO PRIOR
                                        977  *           TABLE ENTRY
                                        978  *
0007FC 4B50 7A1C               00AD2    979  *           SH   5,=H'4'
                                        980  *
                                        981  *        I) SUBTRACT THIS TABLE ENTRY FROM REMAINDER
                                        982  *           DAYS IN #$5R TO FIND NET DAYS
                                        983  *
000800 FB41 7969 5000    00A1F 00000    984  *           SP   #$5R,0(2,5)
                                        985  *
                                        986  *     THIRD, ASSEMBLE NEW DATE
                                        987  *
                                        988  *        CREATE OUTPUT FIELD- NUDATE
                                        989  *        A) MOVE NET DAYS TO #$5NEWD
                                        990  *
000806 F814 7997 7969    00A4D 00A1F    991  *           ZAP  #$5NEWD,#$5R
                                        992  *
                                        993  *        B) PACK DATE ELEMENTS INTO NUDATE
                                        994  *
00080C F372 797B 7992    00A48 00A31    995  #$5BUILD  UNPK #$5WORK8,#$5NEWY
000812 F311 797D 7997    00A4D 00A33    996  *           UNPK #$5WORK8+2(2),#$5NEWD
000818 F311 797B 7995    00A4B 00A31    997  *           UNPK #$5WORK8+2(2),#$5NEWM
00081E F247 77E6 797B    0089C 00A31    998  *           PACK NUDATE,#$5WORK8
                                        999  *
                                       1000  *     +++ SECTION 11- TO RESTORE REGISTERS AND EXIT +++
                                       1001  *
000824 47F0 79DA               00A90   1002  *           B    #$5TERM
                                       1003  *
                                       1004  *     +++ SECTION 12- SUBROUTINES +++
                                       1005  *
```

TS505500
TS505510
TS505520
TS505530
TS505540
TS505550
TS505560
TS505570
TS505580
TS505590
TS505600
TS505610
TS505620
TS505630
TS505640
TS505650
TS505660
TS505670
TS505680
TS505690
TS505700
TS505710
TS505720
TS505730
TS505740
TS505750
TS505760
TS505770
TS505780
TS505790
TS505800
TS505810
TS505820
TS505830
TS505840
TS505850
TS505860
TS505870
TS505880
TS505890
TS505900
TS505910
TS505920
TS505930
TS505940
TS505950
TS505960
TS505970
TS505980
TS505990
TS506000
TS506010
TS506020
TS506030
TS506040

```
LOC    OBJECT CODE      ADDR1  ADDR2  STMT  SOURCE STATEMENT                                            DOS/VSE ASSEMBLER 16.22  99-12-31

                                      1006  *****************************************                                            TS506050
                                      1007  * LEAP YEAR ALGORITHM SUBROUTINE *                                                   TS506060
                                      1008  *****************************************                                            TS506070
                                      1009  *                                                                                    TS506080
000828 F800 7973 7A23  00A29  00AD9   1010  #$5LEAPY ZAP  #$5L,=P'0'                                                             TS506090
00082E F842 79AE 799D  00A64  00A53   1011           ZAP  #$5WORK,#$5YR                                                          TS506100
000834 FD40 79AE 7A3C  00A64  00AF2   1012           DP   #$5WORK,=P'4'                                                          TS506110
00083A F900 79B2 7A23  00A68  00AD9   1013           CP   #$5WORK+4(1),=P'0'                                                     TS506120
000840 4720 77C0       00876          1014           BH   #$5NOLPY                                                               TS506130
000844 F842 79AE 799D  00A64  00A53   1015           ZAP  #$5WORK,#$5YR                                                          TS506140
00084A FD41 79AE 7A18  00A64  00ACE   1016           DP   #$5WORK,=P'100'                                                        TS506150
000850 F910 79B1 7A23  00A67  00AD9   1017           CP   #$5WORK+3(2),=P'0'                                                     TS506160
000856 4720 77BA       00870          1018           BH   #$5LPYR                                                                TS506170
00085A F842 79AE 799D  00A64  00A53   1019           ZAP  #$5WORK,#$5YR                                                          TS506180
000860 FD41 79AE 7A16  00A64  00ACC   1020           DP   #$5WORK,=P'400'                                                        TS506190
000866 F910 79B1 7A23  00A67  00AD9   1021           CP   #$5WORK+3(2),=P'0'                                                     TS506200
00086C 4720 77C0       00876          1022           BH   #$5NOLPY                                                               TS506210
                                      1023  *                                                                                    TS506220
                                      1024  *     IF YEAR IS A LEAP YEAR, REINITIALIZE TO 1                                      TS506230
                                      1025  *     ELSE INITIALIZED 0 REMAINS- EXIT                                              TS506240
                                      1026  *                                                                                    TS506250
000870 F800 7973 7A1E  00A29  00AD4   1027  #$5LPYR  ZAP  #$5L,=P'1'                                                             TS506260
000876 07F6                           1028  #$5NOLPY BR   6                                                                      TS506270
                                      1029  *                                                                                    TS506280
                                      1030  *                                                                                    TS506290
                                      1031  *****************************************                                            TS506300
                                      1032  * MONTH'S DAY LIMIT ADDRESS SUBROUTINE *                                             TS506310
                                      1033  *****************************************                                            TS506320
                                      1034  *                                                                                    TS506330
                                      1035  *     AFTER LOADING ADDRESS OF DAY TABLE IN REGISTER                                 TS506340
                                      1036  *     4, IF LEAP YEAR, INCREMENT TO LEAP YEAR FUNCTION                               TS506350
                                      1037  *                                                                                    TS506360
000878 4140 77EB       008A1          1038  #$5GETAB LA   4,#$5DATAB                                                             TS506370
00087C F900 7973 77D4  00A29  00AD9   1039           CP   #$5L,=P'0'                                                             TS506380
000882 4780 77D4       008BA          1040           BE   #$5NOL                                                                 TS506390
000886 4144 0002       00002          1041           LA   4,2(4)                                                                 TS506400
                                      1042  *                                                                                    TS506410
                                      1043  *     DIRECTLY ADDRESS TABLE DAY LIMIT FOR THIS MONTH                                TS506420
                                      1044  *        A) SUBTRACT 1 FROM BINARY MONTH VALUE IN REG 3                              TS506430
                                      1045  *                                                                                    TS506440
00088A 0630                           1046  #$5NOL   BCTR 3,0                                                                    TS506450
                                      1047  *                                                                                    TS506460
                                      1048  *        B) MULTIPLY VALUE IN REG 3 BY 4                                             TS506470
                                      1049  *                                                                                    TS506480
00088C 8930 0002       00002          1050           SLL  3,2                                                                    TS506490
                                      1051  *                                                                                    TS506500
                                      1052  *        C) LOAD ADDRESS OF DAY TABLE ENTRY IN REG 4                                 TS506510
                                      1053  *                                                                                    TS506520
000890 4143 4000       00000          1054           LA   4,0(3,4)                                                              TS506530
                                      1055  *                                                                                    TS506540
                                      1056  *     EXIT                                                                           TS506550
                                      1057  *                                                                                    TS506560
000894 07F6                           1058           BR   6                                                                      TS506570
                                      1059  *                                                                                    TS506580
                                      1060  *     +++ SECTION 15- DEFINE CONSTANTS AND STORAGE  +++                              TS506590
```

Figure 6.1 *Continued*

```
  LOC    OBJECT CODE    ADDR1  ADDR2  STMT   SOURCE STATEMENT                                              DOS/VSE ASSEMBLER 16.22   99-12-31

                                      1061   *                                                                                          TS506600
000896 FOFOFOFOFOCO                   1062   MODIFY   DC    ZL6'000000'                                                                 TS506610
00089C 000000000C                     1063   NUDATE   DC    PL5'0'                                                                      TS506620
                                      1064   *                                                                                          TS506630
                                      1065   *              THE DAY TABLE IS DEFINED WITH A PAIR OF TWO BYTE                            TS506640
                                      1066   *              ENTRIES FOR EACH OF THE 12 MONTHS- AN ENTRY FOR                             TS506650
                                      1067   *              NON-LEAP YEAR AND AN ENTRY FOR LEAP YEAR                                    TS506660
                                      1068   *                                                                                          TS506670
0008A1 031C031C                       1069   #$5DATAB DC    PL2'31',PL2'31'        JAN                                                 TS506680
0008A5 028C029C                       1070            DC    PL2'28',PL2'29'        FEB                                                 TS506690
0008A9 031C031C                       1071            DC    PL2'31',PL2'31'        MAR                                                 TS506700
0008AD 030C030C                       1072            DC    PL2'30',PL2'30'        APR                                                 TS506710
0008B1 031C031C                       1073            DC    PL2'31',PL2'31'        MAY                                                 TS506720
0008B5 030C030C                       1074            DC    PL2'30',PL2'30'        JUN                                                 TS506730
0008B9 031C031C                       1075            DC    PL2'31',PL2'31'        JUL                                                 TS506740
0008BD 031C031C                       1076            DC    PL2'31',PL2'31'        AUG                                                 TS506750
0008C1 030C030C                       1077            DC    PL2'30',PL2'30'        SEP                                                 TS506760
0008C5 031C031C                       1078            DC    PL2'31',PL2'31'        OCT                                                 TS506770
0008C9 030C030C                       1079            DC    PL2'30',PL2'30'        NOV                                                 TS506780
0008CD 031C031C                       1080            DC    PL2'31',PL2'31'        DEC                                                 TS506790
                                      1081   *                                                                                          TS506800
                                      1082   *              THE DAYS TABLE IS DEFINED WITH A PAIR OF TWO                               TS506810
                                      1083   *              BYTE ENTRIES FOR EACH OF THE 12 MONTHS CONTAIN-                            TS506820
                                      1084   *              ING THE CUMULATIVE NUMBER OF DAYS EXPIRED AT                              TS506830
                                      1085   *              THE END OF THE PRIOR MONTH- NON-LEAP YEAR AND                             TS506840
                                      1086   *              LEAP YEAR                                                                   TS506850
                                      1087   *                                                                                          TS506860
0008D1 000C000C                       1088   #$5DAYS  DC    PL2'00',PL2'00'        JAN                                                 TS506870
0008D5 031C031C                       1089            DC    PL2'31',PL2'31'        FEB                                                 TS506880
0008D9 059C060C                       1090            DC    PL2'59',PL2'60'        MAR                                                 TS506890
0008DD 090C091C                       1091            DC    PL2'90',PL2'91'        APR                                                 TS506900
0008E1 120C121C                       1092            DC    PL2'120',PL2'121'      MAY                                                 TS506910
0008E5 151C152C                       1093            DC    PL2'151',PL2'152'      JUN                                                 TS506920
0008E9 181C182C                       1094            DC    PL2'181',PL2'182'      JUL                                                 TS506930
0008ED 212C213C                       1095            DC    PL2'212',PL2'213'      AUG                                                 TS506940
0008F1 243C244C                       1096            DC    PL2'243',PL2'244'      SEP                                                 TS506950
0008F5 273C274C                       1097            DC    PL2'273',PL2'274'      OCT                                                 TS506960
0008F9 304C305C                       1098            DC    PL2'304',PL2'305'      NOV                                                 TS506970
0008FD 334C335C                       1099            DC    PL2'334',PL2'335'      DEC                                                 TS506980
000901 999C999C                       1100            DC    PL2'999',PL2'999'      END                                                 TS506990
                                      1101   *                                                                                          TS507000
                                      1102   *              TRANSLATION TABLE DEFINED FOR X'F0' - X'F9'                                TS507010
                                      1103   *              (ALL TABLE POSITIONS EXCEPT THOSE CORRESPONDING                           TS507020
                                      1104   *              TO X'F0' THROUGH X'F9' ARE SET TO A VALUE OTHER                           TS507030
                                      1105   *              THAN X'00')                                                                TS507040
                                      1106   *                                                                                          TS507050
000905 1C1C1C1C1C1C1C1C               1107   #$5TABL  DC    240X'1C'                                                                   TS507060
0009F5 0000000000000000               1108            DC    10X'00'                                                                    TS507070
0009FF 1C1C1C1C1C1C                   1109            DC    6X'1C'                                                                      TS507080
                                      1110   *                                                                                          TS507090
000A05 000000000000000000            1111   #$5ZRO   DC    12X'00'                                                                    TS507100
000A11 4C                             1112   CODE5    DC    PL1'4'                                                                     TS507110
000A12 FOFOFOFOFOCO                   1113   DATE1    DC    ZL8'00000000'                                                              TS507120
000A1A                                1114   #$5JLIAN DS    PL5                                                                        TS507130
000A1F                                1115   #$5R     DS    PL5                                                                        TS507140
```

DOS/VSE ASSEMBLER 16.22 99-12-31

| LOC | OBJECT CODE | ADDR1 | ADDR2 | STMT | SOURCE | STATEMENT | |
|---|---|---|---|---|---|---|---|
| 000A24 | | | | 1116 | #$5C | DS PL5 | TS507150 |
| 000A29 | | | | 1117 | #$5L | DS PL1 | TS507160 |
| 000A2A | | | | 1118 | #$5SIGN | DS ZL1 | TS507170 |
| 000A2B | | | | 1119 | #$5WORK6 | DS PL6 | TS507180 |
| 000A31 | | | | 1120 | #$5WORK8 | DS ZL8 | TS507190 |
| 000A39 | | | | 1121 | #$5WORK9 | DS ZL9 | TS507200 |
| 000A42 | | | | 1122 | #$5WORKX | DS ZL6 | TS507210 |
| 000A48 | | | | 1123 | #$5NEWY | DS PL3 | TS507220 |
| 000A4B | | | | 1124 | #$5NEWM | DS PL2 | TS507230 |
| 000A4D | | | | 1125 | #$5NEWD | DS PL2 | TS507240 |
| 000A4F | | | | 1126 | #$5MO | DS PL2 | TS507250 |
| 000A51 | | | | 1127 | #$5DA | DS PL2 | TS507260 |
| 000A53 | | | | 1128 | #$5YR | DS PL3 | TS507270 |
| 000A56 | | | | 1129 | #$5MOCTR | DS PL2 | TS507280 |
| 000A58 | | | | 1130 | #$5MDA | DS PL4 | TS507290 |
| 000A5C | | | | 1131 | #$5T1 | DS PL5 | TS507300 |
| 000A61 | | | | 1132 | #$5T2 | DS PL2 | TS507310 |
| 000A63 | | | | 1133 | #$5T3 | DS PL1 | TS507320 |
| 000A64 | | | | 1134 | #$5WORK | DS PL5 | TS507330 |
| 000A69 | | | | 1135 | #$5FLD | DS CL1 | TS507340 |
| 000A70 | | | | 1136 | #$5CVB | DS 1D | TS507350 |
| 000A78 | | | | 1137 | #$5RSAVE | DS 6F | TS507360 |
| 000A90 | 9816 79C2 | | 00A78 | 1138 | #$5TERM | LM 1,6,#$5RSAVE | TS507370 |
| 000A94 | 07F6 | | 00B4 | 1139 | | BR 6 | TS507380 |
| | | | | 1140 | BEGIN | END | |
| 000A98 | 5B5BC2D6D7C5D540 | | | 1141 | | =C'$$BOPEN ' | |
| 000AA0 | 5B5BC2C3D3D6E2C5 | | | 1142 | | =C'$$BCLOSE' | |
| 000AA8 | 00000080 | | | 1143 | | =A(REQUEST) | |
| 000AAC | 00000000 | | | 1144 | | =A(LIST) | |
| 000AB0 | 0657070C | | | 1145 | | =P'657070' | |
| 000AB4 | D5E4C4C1E3C540C5 | | | 1146 | | =C'NUDATE EXCEEDS LIMITS ' | |
| 000ACA | 000C | | | 1147 | | =P'00' | |
| 000ACC | 400C | | | 1148 | | =P'400' | |
| 000ACE | 100C | | | 1149 | | =P'100' | |
| 000AD0 | 365C | | | 1150 | | =P'365' | |
| 000AD2 | 0004 | | | 1151 | | =H'4' | |
| 000AD4 | 1C | | | 1152 | | =P'1' | |
| 000AD5 | 61 | | | 1153 | | =C'/' | |
| 000AD6 | 6B | | | 1154 | | =C',' | |
| 000AD7 | 60 | | | 1155 | | =C'-' | |
| 000AD8 | F0 | | | 1156 | | =C'0' | |
| 000AD9 | 0C | | | 1157 | | =P'0' | |
| 000ADA | 2C | | | 1158 | | =P'2' | |
| 000ADB | C9D5E5C1D3C9C440 | | | 1159 | | =C'INVALID DATE DATA *****' | |
| 000AF2 | 4C | | | 1160 | | =P'4' | |
| 000AF3 | C9D5E5C1D3C9C440 | | | 1161 | | =C'INVALID YEAR **********' | |
| 000B0A | 6C | | | 1162 | | =P'6' | |
| 000B0B | C9D5E5C1D3C9C440 | | | 1163 | | =C'INVALID MONTH *********' | |
| 000B22 | 8C | | | 1164 | | =P'8' | |
| 000B23 | C9D5E5C1D3C9C440 | | | 1165 | | =C'INVALID DAY ***********' | |
| 000B3A | 3C | | | 1166 | | =P'3' | |
| 000B3B | C9D5E5C1D3C9C440 | | | 1167 | | =C'INVALID INCR/DECR DATA ' | |
| 000B52 | 5C | | | 1168 | | =P'5' | |
| 000B53 | C9D5E5C1D3C9C440 | | | 1169 | | =C'INVALID INCR/DECR VALUE' | |
| 000B6A | 7C | | | 1170 | | =P'7' | |

**Figure 6.1** *Continued*

```
TEST OF TIMESUB5 TO INCREMENT/DECREMENT A GREGORIAN DATE

INPUT DATE + INCR/DECR VALUE = NUDATE

12/30/3399   000.001    12/31/3399                      CODE5 CONTENTS 0.   NUDATE CONTENTS: 12313399
12/31/3399   657.070-    1/01/1601                      CODE5 CONTENTS 0.   NUDATE CONTENTS: 01011601
01/01/1601   657.070    12/31/3399                      CODE5 CONTENTS 0.   NUDATE CONTENTS: 12313399
12/31/1999   000.000    12/31/1999                      CODE5 CONTENTS 0.   NUDATE CONTENTS: 12311999
12/31/1999   000.234     8/21/2000                      CODE5 CONTENTS 0.   NUDATE CONTENTS: 08212000
12/31/1999   000.060     2/29/2000                      CODE5 CONTENTS 0.   NUDATE CONTENTS: 02292000
01/01/2000   000.001-   12/31/1999                      CODE5 CONTENTS 0.   NUDATE CONTENTS: 12311999
01/01/1999   000.001-   12/31/1998                      CODE5 CONTENTS 0.   NUDATE CONTENTS: 12311998
03/01/1999   000.001-    2/28/1999                      CODE5 CONTENTS 0.   NUDATE CONTENTS: 02281999
03/01/2000   000.001-    2/29/2000                      CODE5 CONTENTS 0.   NUDATE CONTENTS: 02292000
11/30/1999   000.035-   10/26/1999                      CODE5 CONTENTS 0.   NUDATE CONTENTS: 10261999
01/01/160A   000.001-   NUDATE EXCEEDS LIMITS           CODE5 CONTENTS 7.   NUDATE CONTENTS: 00000000
01/01/160A   000.060-   NUDATE EXCEEDS LIMITS           CODE5 CONTENTS 7.   NUDATE CONTENTS: 00000000
01/01/1601   000.054-   NUDATE EXCEEDS LIMITS           CODE5 CONTENTS 7.   NUDATE CONTENTS: 00000000
01/01/1601   000.023-   INVALID DATE DATA *****         CODE5 CONTENTS 2.   NUDATE CONTENTS: 00000000
NE/GA/TIVE   END,       NUDATE EXCEEDS LIMITS           CODE5 CONTENTS 7.   NUDATE CONTENTS: 00000000
01/01/1601   000.365     1/01/1602                      CODE5 CONTENTS 0.   NUDATE CONTENTS: 01011602
12/31/3399   657.071    INVALID INCR/DECR VALUE         CODE5 CONTENTS 5.   NUDATE CONTENTS: 00000000
01/01/1601   657.071    NUDATE EXCEEDS LIMITS           CODE5 CONTENTS 7.   NUDATE CONTENTS: 00000000
01/01/1601   657.071-   INVALID INCR/DECR VALUE         CODE5 CONTENTS 5.   NUDATE CONTENTS: 00000000
01/01/1600   657.070    INVALID YEAR **********         CODE5 CONTENTS 4.   NUDATE CONTENTS: 00000000
13/01/1601   657.070    INVALID MONTH **********        CODE5 CONTENTS 6.   NUDATE CONTENTS: 00000000
01/32/1601   657.070    INVALID DAY ************         CODE5 CONTENTS 8.   NUDATE CONTENTS: 00000000
02/29/1601   657.070    INVALID DAY ************         CODE5 CONTENTS 8.   NUDATE CONTENTS: 00000000
01/31/1999   000.001     2/01/1999                      CODE5 CONTENTS 0.   NUDATE CONTENTS: 02011999
02/28/1999   000.001     3/01/1999                      CODE5 CONTENTS 0.   NUDATE CONTENTS: 03011999
03/31/1999   000.001     4/01/1999                      CODE5 CONTENTS 0.   NUDATE CONTENTS: 04011999
04/30/1999   000.031     5/31/1999                      CODE5 CONTENTS 0.   NUDATE CONTENTS: 05311999
05/31/1999   000.030     6/30/1999                      CODE5 CONTENTS 0.   NUDATE CONTENTS: 06301999
06/30/1999   000.031     7/31/1999                      CODE5 CONTENTS 0.   NUDATE CONTENTS: 07311999
07/31/1999   000.031     8/31/1999                      CODE5 CONTENTS 0.   NUDATE CONTENTS: 08311999
08/31/1999   000.030     9/30/1999                      CODE5 CONTENTS 0.   NUDATE CONTENTS: 09301999
09/30/1999   000.031    10/31/1999                      CODE5 CONTENTS 0.   NUDATE CONTENTS: 10311999
10/31/1999   000.030    11/30/1999                      CODE5 CONTENTS 0.   NUDATE CONTENTS: 11301999
11/30/1999   000.031    12/31/1999                      CODE5 CONTENTS 0.   NUDATE CONTENTS: 12311999
12/31/1999   000.001     1/01/2000                      CODE5 CONTENTS 0.   NUDATE CONTENTS: 01012000
01/31/2000   000.001     2/01/2000                      CODE5 CONTENTS 0.   NUDATE CONTENTS: 02012000
02/29/2000   000.001     3/01/2000                      CODE5 CONTENTS 0.   NUDATE CONTENTS: 03012000
03/31/2000   000.001     4/01/2000                      CODE5 CONTENTS 0.   NUDATE CONTENTS: 04012000
04/30/2000   000.001     5/01/2000                      CODE5 CONTENTS 0.   NUDATE CONTENTS: 05012000
05/31/2000   000.001     6/01/2000                      CODE5 CONTENTS 0.   NUDATE CONTENTS: 06012000
06/30/2000   000.001     7/01/2000                      CODE5 CONTENTS 0.   NUDATE CONTENTS: 07012000

THE SUBROUTINE WAS EXECUTED    44 TIMES
```

Figure 6.2   A subset of the translation algorithm test results produced by TIMESUB5 when employed by TEST05.

## Comments on the source code of TIMESUB5

The source code and pseudocode closely approximate each other, with the exception of the several language-dependent features related to ALC byte addressing and to binary-address conversions for table access. TIMESUB5, like its predecessors, uses embedded subroutines to facilitate execution of frequently used segments of code from multiple points within the program.

## Applying TIMESUB5

We've already discussed using TIMESUB5 in aging and due-date stamping of transaction records. TIMESUB5 can also be used to calculate time-dependent rates, for example, special travel rates that stipulate the number of elapsed days prior to the return trip in order to qualify for the rate. It's practical for the computing system to add the minimum-delay parameter to the departure date to determine that the planned return date is within qualifying limits before issuing passage at the given rate level.

TIMESUB5 can also be used in time-dependent scheduling of maintenance and production systems. Applications can be related to medical or dental appointments, reactor shutdown or gestation, and incubation and fermentation either in the laboratory or in the industrial process control environment. An adequate list would be lengthy. Any application of TIMESUB5 could produce a NUDATE coincident with a weekend or nonfunctional weekday. The following chapter addresses this problem.

# Date Versus Name of Day

Knowing today's date or the date exactly 26 days from now is important. However, in a society ostensibly governed by the Christian ethic, knowing the *name* of the day takes on an equal if not greater importance. Our lives are governed by the cycle of the Sabbath. We work, relax, and play according to the rhythm of the seven-day cycle. Products are marketed, foods and beverages consumed, and work performed or neglected in conformity with the name of the day.

We pay homage to this reality each time we respond to the question "What day is this?" Unfailingly, our response is a day name. On the other hand "What date is this?" produces a month name followed by numbers identifying that month's ordinal day and the year. The need for both date and name information is intensified in an environment controlled by overtime payment agreements, work rules, and day-related customs.

Work on Sunday normally pays more than work performed on Saturday, which in turn pays more than work performed on days having other names. Government agencies and bureaus are often closed on both Saturday and Sunday, physicians might not maintain office hours on Wednesdays, barber shops might be closed on Mondays, and airline fare restrictions often specify days to which travel is limited. Accuracy in using day names is economically, socially, and morally important.

## The Nature of the Problem

Numerous methods are available to determine the day name of any given date within limits usually specified in the formula's documentation. Often the formula requires century-specific constants or other adjustment calculations to accommodate the occurrence of centesimal leap years. Fortunately, choosing 01/01/1601 as the first day of our computational interval allows the calculation of a day name for any given date, 01/01/1601 or beyond.

## The Solution Strategy

Because you can reduce any given date within the interval 1601–3399 to a count of elapsed days from the end of 12/31/1600 to the given date, the problem of finding a day name is reduced to the level of the trivial. The day name for 01/01/1601 is Monday, and so the formula is both simple and self-evident. Where N is the count of elapsed days from the end of 12/31/1600 to the given date, you can simply divide N by 7. The remainder will be 0, 1, 2, 3, 4, 5, or 6 and will correspond to the days of the week beginning with Sunday. For example, given the date 01/01/1601, you can convert this to a day count of elapsed days. The result is 1. If divided by 7, the remainder is 1. Since 1 corresponds to Monday, you have the day name of 01/01/1601.

## The Design of the Algorithm

The logic and mathematics required to convert a Commercial-8 date to a day count was introduced in TIMESUB3 in chapter 4. TIMESUB6 presents this same logic and mathematics, except it divides the count by 7. TIMESUB6 then returns the remainder to the calling program in the packed one-byte field OUTDAY. If the return code CODE6 is nonzero, OUTDAY contains a packed nine. Otherwise, the packed value will be 0 through 6, corresponding to the seven day names Sunday through Saturday.

To avoid redundancy, we aren't going to present pseudocode for TIMESUB6. Figure 7.1 constitutes the TIMESUB6 portion of TEST06's assembly post listing. The associated documentation amply defines the inputs, outputs, and limits.

Figure 7.2 exhibits a subset of the test results. The calling program simply interrogates the return code to determine a successful execution and then equates the appropriate day name with the OUTDAY contents. The post listing of the rest of the calling test program is omitted in the interest of economy.

## On the Application of TIMESUB6

Beyond the obvious application of TIMESUB6 in determining that a requested delivery date coincides with a valid delivery day, the facilities of TIMESUB6 can be broadly applied. Situations that require you to compute a date for days such as the third Monday of March, 1999 or the second Tuesday of April, 2001 can be solved by this subroutine. You can generalize the requirements and develop a useful algorithm.

What is sought here is the $n$th occurrence of an X day during a given month of a given year. Here, $n$ can be any integer from 1 to 5, since five occurrences of a named week day are the most you can expect even during the longest months. X of X day stands for Sunday, Monday, Tuesday, Wednesday, Thursday, Friday, or Saturday. Be aware that INDATE is the input field of TIMESUB6 and that it's defined as Commercial-8. Now proceed to define the algorithm that will produce the date G of the $n$th X day in month M of year Y:

```
1) Let M be the given month and let Y be the given year.
   Then let INDATE = MDY where D = 01.

2) Where Mon = 1, Tues = 2, Wednes 3, Thurs = 4, Fri = 5, Satur = 6,
   and Sun = 0, let C = the value of the given X of X day.
```

3) Upon executing TIMESUB6, the input specified in Step 1 will result
   in an OUTDAY value:

   A) If OUTDAY = C,
      1. Let DATEI = INDATE
      2. Let MODIFY = 7(N - 1)
      3. Upon execution of TIMESUB5, NUDATE = G

   B) If OUTDAY < C,
      1. Let DATEI = INDATE
      2. Let MODIFY = C - OUTDAY + 7(N - 1)
      3. Upon execution of TIMESUB5, NUDATE = G

   C) If OUTDAY > C,
      1. Let DATEI = INDATE
      2. Let MODIFY = 7 - (OUTDAY - C) + 7(N - 1)
      3. Upon execution of TIMESUB5, NUDATE = G

Essentially, TIMESUB6 determines the day name of the first day of the given month in the given year. Having determined the day name, steps 3A2, 3B2, and 3C2 provide the number of days the date must be displaced in order to arrive at the $n$th occurrence of the specified day of the week.

The execution of TIMESUB5 merely assures that a valid Gregorian date will be found—perhaps there is no fifth Sunday in the given month. The date returned by TIMESUB5 will be a valid date, but in the following month if there's no $n$th occurrence of the X day in the given month. Without the execution of TIMESUB5, such an event would produce an invalid date when the displacement is added directly to the date value of INDATE. If N ≤ 4, TIMESUB5 need not be executed; the displacement can be added directly to the day value of the input date to find the date of the day sought.

```
LOC   OBJECT CODE   ADDR1 ADDR2   STMT   SOURCE STATEMENT                                    DOS/VSE ASSEMBLER 16.24  99-12-31

                                   382 *                                                                                    TS600010
                                   383 *                                                                                    TS600020
                                   384 *                                                                                    TS600030
                                   385 * TTTTTT  III  MM     MM  EEEEE  SSSSS  U   U  BBBBB    66                           TS600040
                                   386 *   T      I   M M   M M  E      S      U   U  B   B   6                             TS600050
                                   387 *   T      I   M  M M  M  EEEE   SSSSS  U   U  BBB B   G6666                         TS600060
                                   388 *   T      I   M   M   M  EEEE       S  U   U  B   B   6   6                         TS600070
                                   389 *   T     III  M       M  EEEEE  SSSSS  UUUUU  BBBBB    6666                         TS600080
                                   390 * ***********************************************                                    TS600090
                                   391 * D A Y   N A M E   O F   A   G I V E N   G R E G O R I A N   D A T E                TS600100
                                   392 * ***********************************************                                    TS600110
                                   393 * **********************************************                                    TS600120
                                   394 * **********************************************                                    TS600130
                                   395 * **********************************************                                    TS600140
                                   396 * **********************************************                                    TS600150
                                   397 *         THIS SUBROUTINE CALCULATES THE DAY NAME OF A GIVEN                         TS600160
                                   398 *         GREGORIAN DATE                                                            TS600170
                                   399 *                                                                                    TS600180
                                   400 *   1.  VALID INPUT YEARS FOR THIS SUBROUTINE ARE THE YEARS                         TS600190
                                   401 *       1601 THROUGH 3399 A. D.                                                     TS600200
                                   402 *                                                                                    TS600210
                                   403 *   2.  VALID INPUT MONTH VALUES FOR THIS SUBROUTINE ARE 01                         TS600220
                                   404 *       THROUGH 12.                                                                  TS600230
                                   405 *                                                                                    TS600240
                                   406 *   3.  VALID INPUT DAY VALUES FOR THIS SUBROUTINE ARE 01                           TS600250
                                   407 *       THROUGH 31 WITH EXCEPTIONS FOR THE MONTHS LISTED:                           TS600260
                                   408 *            MONTH              MAXIMUM DAY VALUE                                    TS600270
                                   409 *             04                       30                                           TS600280
                                   410 *             06                       30                                           TS600290
                                   411 *             09                       30                                           TS600300
                                   412 *             11                       30                                           TS600310
                                   413 *             02                       28                                           TS600320
                                   414 *             02 DURING LEAP YEAR      29                                           TS600330
                                   415 *                                                                                    TS600340
                                   416 *   4.  THE DATE FORMAT MUST BE MMDDYYYY.  WHERE MM = THE TWO                       TS600350
                                   417 *       DIGIT MONTH VALUE, DD = THE TWO DIGIT DAY VALUE AND                         TS600360
                                   418 *       YYYY = THE FOUR DIGIT YEAR.                                                  TS600370
                                   419 *                                                                                    TS600380
                                   420 *   5.  THE CALLING PROGRAM MUST PLACE AN EIGHT DIGIT DATE,                         TS600390
                                   421 *       IN ZONED DECIMAL, IN A SUBROUTINE DEFINED EIGHT BYTE                        TS600400
                                   422 *       FIELD, 'INDATE.'  INDATE IS NOT ALTERED BY THE                             TS600410
                                   423 *       SUBROUTINE.                                                                  TS600420
                                   424 *                                                                                    TS600430
                                   425 *   6.  A SUBROUTINE DEFINED ONE BYTE FIELD, 'CODE6,' IS RETURNED                   TS600440
                                   426 *       TO THE CALLING PROGRAM AS A RETURN CODE.  CODE6 CONTAINS                    TS600450
                                   427 *       A PACKED 0 IF EXECUTION IS SUCCESSFUL.  NON-ZERO VALUES                     TS600460
                                   428 *       INDICATE THE FOLLOWING:                                                      TS600470
                                   429 *                                                                                    TS600480
                                   430 *       A PACKED 2 INDICATES UNSUCCESSFUL EXECUTION:  INVALID                       TS600490
                                   431 *       DATA.                                                                        TS600500
                                   432 *                                                                                    TS600510
                                   433 *       INVALID DATA ARE DETERMINED IF THE LOW ORDER BYTE'S ZONE                    TS600520
                                   434 *       CONTAINS AN INVALID SIGN.  (AN INVALID SIGN IS OTHER THAN                   TS600530
                                   435 *       X'C', X'A', X'E', OR X'F')  OR IF THE PRECEDING BYTES'                      TS600540
                                   436 *       ZONES ARE OTHER THAN X'F', OR IF THE LOW ORDER NIBBLE                       TS600550
```

```
LOC   OBJECT CODE   ADDR1 ADDR2   STMT   SOURCE STATEMENT                                    DOS/VSE ASSEMBLER 16.24  99-12-31

                                  437 *        OF ANY BYTE CONTAINS A VALUE GREATER THAN '9'.                            * TS600560
                                  438 *                                                                                 * TS600570
                                  439 *        A PACKED 4 INDICATES UNSUCCESSFUL EXECUTION:  INVALID                    * TS600580
                                  440 *        YEAR- YEAR VALUE VIOLATES LIMITS SPECIFIED IN 1., ABOVE.                 * TS600590
                                  441 *                                                                                 * TS600600
                                  442 *        A PACKED 6 INDICATES UNSUCCESSFUL EXECUTION:  INVALID                    * TS600610
                                  443 *        MONTH- MONTH VALUE VIOLATES LIMITS SPECIFIED IN 2.,                      * TS600620
                                  444 *        ABOVE.                                                                   * TS600630
                                  445 *                                                                                 * TS600640
                                  446 *        A PACKED 8 INDICATES UNSUCCESSFUL EXECUTION:  INVALID                    * TS600650
                                  447 *        DAY- DAY VALUE VIOLATES LIMITS SPECIFIED IN 3., ABOVE.                   * TS600660
                                  448 *                                                                                 * TS600670
                                  449 *        INSPECTION OF THE RETURN CODE IS IMPORTANT.   THE RETURN                 * TS600680
                                  450 *        CODE, CODE6, REFLECTS THE LEVEL OF EDITING.   A RETURN                   * TS600690
                                  451 *        CODE OF 2, FOR EXAMPLE, NOT ONLY INDICATES INVALIDITY OF                 * TS600700
                                  452 *        DATA, IT ALSO INDICATES THAT NO EDITING HAS BEEN DONE TO                 * TS600710
                                  453 *        VALIDATE THE YEAR, MONTH OR DAY VALUES.   A RETURN CODE OF               * TS600720
                                  454 *        4 INDICATES THAT THE DATA ARE VALID BUT THAT THE YEAR WAS                * TS600730
                                  455 *        FOUND INVALID- THE MONTH AND DAY VALUES HAVE NOT BEEN ED-                * TS600740
                                  456 *        ITED.  A RETURN CODE OF 6 INDICATES THAT THE DATA AND                    * TS600750
                                  457 *        YEAR ARE VALID BUT THAT THE MONTH IS INVALID- THE DAY                    * TS600760
                                  458 *        VALUE HAS NOT BEEN EDITED.  FINALLY, A RETURN CODE OF 8                  * TS600770
                                  459 *        INDICATES THAT THE DATA, YEAR AND MONTH ARE VALID BUT                    * TS600780
                                  460 *        THAT THE DAY WAS FOUND INVALID FOR THE VALID MONTH GIVEN.                * TS600790
                                  461 *        IN SHORT, THE RETURN CODE INDICATES THE LEVEL OF EDITING.                * TS600800
                                  462 *        THE EDIT SEQUENCE IS:   DATA, YEAR, MONTH AND DAY.                       * TS600810
                                  463 *                                                                                 * TS600820
                                  464 *     7. A SUBROUTINE DEFINED ONE BYTE FIELD, 'OUTDAY,' IS                        * TS600830
                                  465 *        RETURNED TO THE CALLING PROGRAM.  OUTDAY CONTAINS                        * TS600840
                                  466 *        A PACKED VALUE LESS THAN 7 IF EXECUTION HAS BEEN SUC-                     * TS600850
                                  467 *        CESSFUL.  IF EXECUTION IS UNSUCCESSFUL, THAT IS, IF CODE6                * TS600860
                                  468 *        CONTAINS A NON-ZERO VALUE, THEN OUTDAY WILL CONTAIN                      * TS600870
                                  469 *        A PACKED 9.  THIS IS PROTECTION AGAINST ILLEGAL USE OF                   * TS600880
                                  470 *        A PRIOR EXECUTION'S RESULT.                                              * TS600890
                                  471 *                                                                                 * TS600900
                                  472 *        THE PACKED VALUES CONTAINED IN OUTDAY UPON SUCCESSFUL                    * TS600910
                                  473 *        EXECUTION CORRESPOND TO NAMES OF DAYS OF THE WEEK ON THE                 * TS600920
                                  474 *        GREGORIAN CALENDAR.  THE CORRESPONDENCES ARE AS FOLLOWS:                 * TS600930
                                  475 *                                                                                 * TS600940
                                  476 *          PACKED NUMERAL        DAY NAME REPRESENTED                             * TS600950
                                  477 *                                                                                 * TS600960
                                  478 *                0                    SUNDAY                                      * TS600970
                                  479 *                1                    MONDAY                                      * TS600980
                                  480 *                2                    TUESDAY                                     * TS600990
                                  481 *                3                    WEDNESDAY                                   * TS601000
                                  482 *                4                    THURSDAY                                    * TS601010
                                  483 *                5                    FRIDAY                                      * TS601020
                                  484 *                6                    SATURDAY                                    * TS601030
                                  485 *                                                                                 * TS601040
                                  486 *     8. ALL OTHER SUBROUTINE DEFINED FIELDS AND LABELS ARE                      * TS601050
                                  487 *        TRANSPARENT TO THE CALLING PROGRAM.                                      * TS601060
                                  488 *                                                                                 * TS601070
                                  489 *     9. THIS SUBROUTINE IS WRITTEN TO BE ASSEMBLED WITH THE                      * TS601080
                                  490 *        CALLING PROGRAM AND SHOULD BE INSERTED IN THE CALLING                    * TS601090
                                  491 *        PROGRAM IMMEDIATELY BEFORE THE 'END' OPCODE.                             * TS601100
```

**Figure 7.1** The introductory documentation and source code for TIMESUB6.

```
                                                     DOS/VSE ASSEMBLER 16.24  99-12-31

LOC    OBJECT CODE    ADDR1 ADDR2  STMT  SOURCE STATEMENT

                                   492  *         10.   THIS SUBROUTINE USES REGISTER 6 AS THE LINK REGISTER.    *  TS601110
                                   493  *               IF REGISTER 6 IS ASSIGNED IN THE CALLING PROGRAM FOR     *  TS601120
                                   494  *               OTHER USES, IT MUST BE SAVED PRIOR TO EXECUTING THE      *  TS601130
                                   495  *               'BALR.'                                                 *  TS601140
                                   496  *                                                                       *  TS601150
                                   497  *                                                                       *  TS601160
                                   498  *                                             JEROME T. MURRAY          *  TS601170
                                   499  *                                             MARILYN J. MURRAY         *  TS601180
                                   500  *  GLEN ELLYN, ILLINOIS                                                 *  TS601190
                                   501  *************************************************************************  TS601200
                                   502  *************************************************************************  TS601210
                                   503  *************************************************************************  TS601220
                                   504  *************************************************************************  TS601230
                                   505  *************************************************************************  TS601240
                                   506  *      +++    SECTION 1- GENERAL HOUSEKEEPING    +++                        TS601250
                                   507  *                                                                          TS601260
                                   508  *             INITIALIZE INDICATIVE AND WORK FIELDS                         TS601270
                                   509  *                                                                          TS601280
00048B  00                         510  TIMESUB6 ZAP   OUTDAY,=P'9'                                                 TS601290
00048C  F800 7734 7849  007EA 008FF 511          ZAP   CODE6,=P'0'                                                  TS601300
000492  F800 772B 77EE  007E1 008A4 512  *                                                                          TS601310
                                   513  *             SAVE REGISTERS 1 THROUGH 5 IN SAVE FIELDS                      TS601320
                                   514  *                                                                          TS601330
000498  9015 7766        0081C     515          STM   1,5,#$6RSAVE                                                  TS601340
                                   516  *                                                                          TS601350
                                   517  *      +++    SECTION 2- NUMERIC VALIDATION    +++                           TS601360
                                   518  *                                                                          TS601370
                                   519  *             MOVE DATE TO WORK FIELD AND ISOLATE SIGN BYTE                 TS601380
                                   520  *                                                                          TS601390
00049C  D207 773D 772C  007F3 007E2 521          MVC   #$6WORK8,INDATE                                              TS601400
0004A2  D200 7736 7744  007EC 007FA 522          MVC   #$6SIGN,#$6WORK8+7                                           TS601410
                                   523  *                                                                          TS601420
                                   524  *             AUGMENT TABLE FOR VALID '+' SIGNS OTHER THAN                  TS601430
                                   525  *             X'F' FOR WHICH TABLE IS DEFINED: X'A', X'C'.                  TS601440
                                   526  *             X'E'- EDIT FOR VALID '+' SIGN USING TRT                       TS601450
                                   527  *                                                                          TS601460
0004A8  D209 76BF 771F  007D5       528          MVC   #$6TABL+160(10),#$6ZRO                                       TS601470
0004AE  D209 76DF 771F  007D5       529          MVC   #$6TABL+192(10),#$6ZRO                                       TS601480
0004B4  D209 76FF 771F  007D5       530          MVC   #$6TABL+224(10),#$6ZRO                                       TS601490
0004BA  DD00 7736 761F  007EC 006D5 531          TRT   #$6SIGN(1),#$6TABL                                           TS601500
0004C0  4780 7412        004C8     532          BC    8,#$6NUM                                                      TS601510
0004C4  47F0 7426        004DC     533          B     #$6BDATA                                                      TS601520
                                   534  *                                                                          TS601530
                                   535  *             REINITIALIZE TABLE AND EDIT FOR VALID ZONE                   TS601540
                                   536  *             AND DIGIT CONFIGURATIONS IN REMAINING BYTES                  TS601550
                                   537  *                                                                          TS601560
0004C8  921C 761F        006D5     538  #$6NUM   MVI   #$6TABL,X'1C'                                                TS601570
0004CC  D2EE 7620 761F   006D6 006D5 539          MVC   #$6TABL+1(239),#$6TABL                                      TS601580
0004D2  DD06 773D 761F   007F3 006D5 540          TRT   #$6WORK8(7),#$6TABL                                         TS601590
0004D8  4780 7430        004E6     541          BC    8,#$6PACK                                                     TS601600
                                   542  *                                                                          TS601610
                                   543  *             POST 'BAD DATA' RETURN CODE AND EXIT                         TS601620
                                   544  *                                                                          TS601630
0004DC  F800 772B 77EF  007E1 008A5 545  #$6BDATA ZAP   CODE6,=P'2'                                                 TS601640
```

```
LOC    OBJECT CODE      ADDR1 ADDR2  STMT  SOURCE STATEMENT                              DOS/VSE ASSEMBLER 16.24  99-12-31

0004E2 47F0 7782         00838        546         B     #$6TERM                                                          TS601650
                                      547  *                                                                             TS601660
                                      548  *+++  SECTION 3- EDIT YEAR FOR LIMIT VIOLATIONS  +++                          TS601670
                                      549  *                                                                             TS601680
                                      550  *     PACK MONTH, DAY AND YEAR IN WORK FIELDS                                 TS601690
                                      551  *                                                                             TS601700
0004E6 F211 774E 773D   00804 007F3   552  #$6PACK PACK  #$6MO,#$6WORK8(2)                                               TS601710
0004EC F211 7750 773F   00806 007F5   553          PACK  #$6DA,#$6WORK8+2(2)                                             TS601720
0004F2 F223 7752 7741   00808 007F7   554          PACK  #$6YR,#$6WORK8+4(4)                                            TS601730
                                      555  *                                                                             TS601740
                                      556  *     EDIT YEAR VALUE FOR LOWER LIMIT VIOLATION                               TS601750
                                      557  *                                                                             TS601760
0004F8 F922 7752 784A   00808 00900   558          CP    #$6YR,=P'1600'                                                  TS601770
0004FE 4720 7456        0050C         559          BH    #$6YRHI                                                         TS601780
                                      560  *                                                                             TS601790
                                      561  *     INSTALL 'BAD YEAR' RETURN CODE AND EXIT                                 TS601800
                                      562  *                                                                             TS601810
000502 F800 772B 7809   007E1 008BF   563  #$6BADYR ZAP  CODE6,=P'4'                                                     TS601820
000508 47F0 7782        00838         564          B     #$6TERM                                                         TS601830
                                      565  *                                                                             TS601840
                                      566  *     EDIT YEAR VALUE FOR UPPER LIMIT VIOLATION                               TS601850
                                      567  *                                                                             TS601860
00050C F922 7752 784D   00808 00903   568  #$6YRHI CP    #$6YR,=P'3399'                                                  TS601870
000512 4720 744C        00502         569          BH    #$6BADYR                                                        TS601880
                                      570  *                                                                             TS601890
                                      571  *+++  SECTION 4- DETERMINE LEAP YEAR STATUS  +++                              TS601900
                                      572  *                                                                             TS601910
                                      573  *     EXECUTE LEAP YEAR ALGORITHM                                             TS601920
                                      574  *                                                                             TS601930
000516 F800 7735 77EE   007EB 008A4   575          ZAP   #$6L,=P'0'                                                      TS601940
00051C F842 775D 7752   00813 00808   576          ZAP   #$6WORK,#$6YR                                                   TS601950
000522 FD40 775D 7809   00813 008BF   577          DP    #$6WORK,=P'4'                                                   TS601960
000528 F900 7761 74AE   00817 00564   578          CP    #$6WORK+4(1),=P'0'                                             TS601970
00052E 4720 74AE        00564         579          BH    #$6MOEDT                                                        TS601980
000532 F842 775D 7752   00813 00808   580          ZAP   #$6WORK,#$6YR                                                   TS601990
000538 FD41 775D 77E6   00813 0089C   581          DP    #$6WORK,=P'100'                                                TS602000
00053E F910 7760 77EE   00816 008A4   582          CP    #$6WORK+3(2),=P'0'                                             TS602010
000544 4720 74A8        0055E         583          BH    #$6LPYR                                                         TS602020
000548 F842 775D 7752   00813 00808   584          ZAP   #$6WORK,#$6YR                                                   TS602030
00054E FD41 775D 77E8   00813 0089E   585          DP    #$6WORK,=P'400'                                                TS602040
000554 F910 7760 77EE   00816 008A4   586          CP    #$6WORK+3(2),=P'0'                                             TS602050
00055A 4720 74AE        00564         587          BH    #$6MOEDT                                                        TS602060
                                      588  *                                                                             TS602070
                                      589  *     IF YEAR IS A LEAP YEAR, REINITIALIZE TO 1                               TS602080
                                      590  *     ELSE INITIALIZED O REMAINS                                              TS602090
                                      591  *                                                                             TS602100
00055E F800 7735 77EC   007EB 008A2   592  #$6LPYR ZAP   #$6L,=P'1'                                                      TS602110
                                      593  *                                                                             TS602120
                                      594  *+++  SECTION 5- EDIT MONTH FOR LIMIT VIOLATIONS  +++                         TS602130
                                      595  *                                                                             TS602140
                                      596  *     VERIFY THAT MONTH IS WITHIN RANGE: 1 - 12                               TS602150
                                      597  *       A) CONVERT MONTH TO BINARY IN REGISTER 3                              TS602160
                                      598  *                                                                             TS602170
000564 F871 777A 774E   00830 00804   599  #$6MOEDT ZAP  #$6CVB,#$6MO                                                    TS602180
00056A 4F30 777A        00830         600          CVB   3,#$6CVB                                                        TS602190
```

Figure 7.1 *Continued*

```
                                                        DOS/VSE ASSEMBLER 16.24  99-12-31

LOC    OBJECT CODE     ADDR1 ADDR2  STMT  SOURCE STATEMENT

                                    601  *
                                    602  *                   B) STORE BINARY BYTE FROM REG 3 IN #$6FLD
                                    603  *
00056E 4230 7762        00818       604        STC    3,#$6FLD
                                    605  *
                                    606  *                   C) INITIALIZE TABLE WITH X'00' FOR TRT
                                    607  *
000572 D20B 7620 771F   006D6 007D5 608        MVC    #$6TABL+1(12),#$6ZRO
                                    609  *
                                    610  *                   D) EXECUTE TRT USING #$6FLD
                                    611  *
000578 DD00 7762 761F   00818 006D5 612        TRT    #$6FLD(1),#$6TABL
00057E 4780 740C        00592       613        BC     8,#$6DAEDT
                                    614  *
                                    615  *                   F) RESTORE TABLE - POST BAD MONTH RETURN CODE
                                    616  *
000582 D20B 7620 761F   006D6 006D5 617        MVC    #$6TABL+1(12),#$6TABL
000588 F800 772B 7823   007E1 008D9 618        ZAP    CDE6,=P'6'
00058E 47F0 7782        00838       619        B      #$6TERM
                                    620  *
                                    621  *             +++  SECTION 6- EDIT DAY FOR LIMIT VIOLATIONS  +++
                                    622  *
                                    623  *                   RESTORE TABLE
                                    624  *
000592 D20B 7620 761F   006D6 006D5 625 #$6DAEDT MVC   #$6TABL+1(12),#$6TABL
                                    626  *
                                    627  *                   GET ADDRESS OF DAY TABLE IN REGISTER 4
                                    628  *
000598 4140 75BF        00675       629        LA     4,#$6DATAB
                                    630  *
                                    631  *                   IF LEAP YEAR, INCREMENT TO LEAP YEAR FUNCTION
                                    632  *
00059C F900 7735 77EE   007EB 008A4 633        CP     #$6L,=P'0'
0005A2 4780 74F4        005AA       634        BE     #$6NOL
0005A6 4144 0002        00002       635        LA     4,2(4)
                                    636  *
                                    637  *                   DIRECTLY ADDRESS TABLE DAY LIMIT FOR THIS MONTH
                                    638  *                   A) SUBTRACT 1 FROM BINARY MONTH VALUE IN REG 3
                                    639  *
0005AA 0630             00002       640 #$6NOL  BCTR   3,0
                                    641  *
                                    642  *                   B) MULTIPLY VALUE IN REG 3 BY 4
                                    643  *
0005AC 8930 0002        00002       644        SLL    3,2
                                    645  *
                                    646  *                   C) LOAD ADDRESS OF DAY TABLE ENTRY IN REG 4
                                    647  *
0005B0 4143 4000        00000       648        LA     4,0(3,4)
                                    649  *
                                    650  *                   CONVERT SIGN OF PACKED DAY FROM X'F' TO X'C'
                                    651  *
0005B4 F811 7750 7750   00806 00806 652        ZAP    #$6DA,#$6DA
                                    653  *
                                    654  *                   COMPARE DAY TABLE ENTRY (LIMIT) WITH INPUT DAY
                                    655  *
```

```
LOC    OBJECT CODE       ADDR1 ADDR2  STMT  SOURCE STATEMENT                                                    DOS/VSE ASSEMBLER 16.24  99-12-31

0005BA D501 7750 4000    00806 00000   656       CLC   #$6DA,O(4)                                                                        TS602750
                                       657  *                                                                                           TS602760
                                       658  *           IF INPUT IS WITHIN LIMIT. EDIT DAY FOR ZERO                                       TS602770
                                       659  *                                                                                           TS602780
0005C0 47D0 7518         005CE          660       BNH   #$6DALO                                                                          TS602790
                                       661  *                                                                                           TS602800
                                       662  *           ELSE POST BAD DAY RETURN CODE AND EXIT                                           TS602810
                                       663  *                                                                                           TS602820
0005C4 F800 772B 7824    007E1 008DA   664 #$6BADA  ZAP   CODE6,=P'8'                                                                    TS602830
0005CA 47F0 7782         00838          665       B     #$6TERM                                                                          TS602840
                                       666  *                                                                                           TS602850
                                       667  *           EDIT DAY VALUE FOR ZERO                                                          TS602860
                                       668  *                                                                                           TS602870
0005CE F911 7750 77EA    00806 008A0   669 #$6DALO  CP    #$6DA,=P'OO'                                                                   TS602880
0005D4 4780 750E         005C4          670       BE    #$6BADA                                                                          TS602890
                                       671  *                                                                                           TS602900
                                       672  *       +++  SECTION 7- COMPUTE ELAPSED DAYS THIS DATE  +++                                  TS602910
                                       673  *                                                                                           TS602920
                                       674  *           FIRST, COMPUTE ELAPSED DAYS THIS YEAR TO MONTH                                   TS602930
                                       675  *                                                                                           TS602940
                                       676  *           DIRECTLY ADDRESS ELAPSED DAY TABLE THIS MONTH                                    TS602950
                                       677  *           A) LOAD ADDRESS OF DAYS TABLE IN REGISTER 5                                      TS602960
                                       678  *                                                                                           TS602970
0005D8 4150 75EF         006A5          679       LA    5,#$6DAYS                                                                        TS602980
                                       680  *                                                                                           TS602990
                                       681  *           B) IF LEAP YEAR, INCREMENT TO LEAP YEAR                                          TS603000
                                       682  *              FUNCTION                                                                      TS603010
                                       683  *                                                                                           TS603020
0005DC F900 7735 77EE    007EB 008A4   684       CP    #$6L,=P'O'                                                                        TS603030
0005E2 4780 7534         005EA          685       BE    #$6NOLL                                                                          TS603040
0005E6 4155 0002         00002          686       LA    5.2(5)                                                                           TS603050
                                       687  *                                                                                           TS603060
                                       688  *           C) LOAD ADDRESS OF TABLE ELEMENT IN REGISTER 5                                   TS603070
                                       689  *              (REG 3 CONTAINS CONVERTED MONTH VALUE)                                        TS603080
                                       690  *                                                                                           TS603090
0005EA 4153 5000         00000         691 #$6NOLL  LA    5.O(3.5)                                                                       TS603100
                                       692  *                                                                                           TS603110
                                       693  *           ADD DIRECTLY ADDRESSED ELAPSED DAYS TO WORK                                      TS603120
                                       694  *              FIELD                                                                         TS603130
                                       695  *                                                                                           TS603140
0005EE F841 75BA 5000    00670 00000   696       ZAP   #$6JULIAN,O(2,5)                                                                  TS603150
                                       697  *                                                                                           TS603160
                                       698  *           ADD INPUT DAY TO WORK FIELD                                                      TS603170
                                       699  *                                                                                           TS603180
0005F4 FA41 75BA 7750    00670 00806   700       AP    #$6JULIAN,#$6DA                                                                   TS603190
                                       701  *                                                                                           TS603200
                                       702  *           SECOND. COMPUTE ELAPSED DAYS 1601 TO INPUT YEAR                                  TS603210
                                       703  *                                                                                           TS603220
                                       704  *                                                                                           TS603230
                                       705  *           COMPUTE #$6P1                                                                    TS603240
0005FA F852 7737 7752    007ED 00808   706       ZAP   #$6WORK6,#$6YR                                                                    TS603250
000600 F852 7737 7850    007ED 00906   707       SP    #$6WORK6,=P'1601'                                                                TS603260
000606 FC52 7737 7853    007ED 00909   708       MP    #$6WORK6,=P'36525'                                                               TS603270
                                       709  *                                                                                           TS603280
                                       710  *           INTEGER TRUNCATION EFFECTED BY UNPK - PACK                                       TS603290
```

**Figure 7.1** *Continued*

```
                                                    DOS/VSE ASSEMBLER 16.24  99-12-31

LOC     OBJECT CODE   ADDR1 ADDR2  STMT  SOURCE STATEMENT

                                    711  *                                                        TS603300
00060C  F384 7745 7738  007FB 007EE 712        UNPK  #$6WORK9,#$6WORK6+1(5)                        TS603310
000612  F246 7755 7745  0080B 007FB 713        PACK  #$6P1,#$6WORK9(7)                            TS603320
                                    714  *                                                        TS803330
                                    715  *        COMPUTE NUMBER OF NON-LEAP YEAR CENTESSIMALS      TS803340
                                    716  *                                                        TS603350
                                    717  *        COMPUTE #$6P2                                     TS603360
                                    718  *                                                        TS603370
000618  F842 775D 7752  00813 00808 719        ZAP   #$6WORK,#$6YR                                TS603380
00061E  FB42 775D 7850  00813 00906 720        SP    #$6WORK,=P'1601'                             TS603390
000624  FD41 775D 77E8  00813 0089E 721        DP    #$6WORK,=P'400'                              TS603400
00062A  F811 775A 775E  00810 00814 722        ZAP   #$6P2,#$6WORK+1(2)                           TS603410
000630  FC10 775A 7856  00810 0090C 723        MP    #$6P2,=P'3'                                  TS603420
                                    724  *                                                        TS603430
                                    725  *        COMPUTE #$6Q1                                     TS603440
                                    726  *                                                        TS603450
000636  F841 775D 7760  00813 00816 727        ZAP   #$6WORK,#$6WORK+3(2)                         TS603460
00063C  FD41 775D 77E6  00813 0089C 728        DP    #$6WORK,=P'100'                              TS603470
000642  F800 775C 775F  00812 00815 729        ZAP   #$6Q1,#$6WORK+2(1)                           TS603480
                                    730  *                                                        TS603490
                                    731  *        COMPUTE THE SUM OF ELAPSED DAYS                   TS603500
                                    732  *                                                        TS603510
000648  FA44 75BA 7755  00670 0080B 733        AP    #$6JLIAN,#$6P1                               TS603520
00064E  FB41 75BA 775A  00670 00810 734        SP    #$6JLIAN,#$6P2                               TS603530
000654  FB40 75BA 775C  00670 00812 735        SP    #$6JLIAN,#$6Q1                               TS603540
                                    736  *                                                        TS603550
                                    737  *        +++  SECTION 8- COMPUTE NAME OF DAY CODE  +++    TS603560
                                    738  *                                                        TS603570
00065A  F844 775D 75BA  00813 00670 739        ZAP   #$6WORK,#$6JLIAN                             TS603580
000660  FD40 775D 7857  00813 0090D 740        DP    #$6WORK,=P'7'                                TS603590
000666  F800 7734 7761  007EA 00817 741        ZAP   OUTDAY,#$6WORK+4(1)                          TS603600
                                    742  *                                                        TS603610
                                    743  *        +++  SECTION 9- TO RESTORE REGISTERS AND EXIT +++ TS603620
                                    744  *                                                        TS603630
00066C  47F0 7782       00838       745        B     #$6TERM                                      TS603640
                                    746  *                                                        TS603650
                                    747  *        +++  SECTION 10- DEFINE CONSTANTS AND STORAGE +++ TS603660
                                    748  *                                                        TS603670
000670  000000000C                  749  #$6JLIAN DC   PL5'0'                                      TS603680
                                    750  *                                                        TS603690
                                    751  *        THE DAY TABLE IS DEFINED WITH A PAIR OF TWO BYTE  TS603700
                                    752  *        ENTRIES FOR EACH OF THE 12 MONTHS- AN ENTRY FOR   TS603710
                                    753  *        NON-LEAP YEAR AND AN ENTRY FOR LEAP YEAR          TS603720
                                    754  *                                                        TS603730
000675  031C031C                    755  #$6DATAB DC   PL2'31',PL2'31'    JAN                      TS603740
000679  028C029C                    756        DC    PL2'28',PL2'29'    FEB                        TS603750
00067D  031C031C                    757        DC    PL2'31',PL2'31'    MAR                        TS603760
000681  030C030C                    758        DC    PL2'30',PL2'30'    APR                        TS603770
000685  031C031C                    759        DC    PL2'31',PL2'31'    MAY                        TS603780
000689  030C030C                    760        DC    PL2'30',PL2'30'    JUN                        TS603790
00068D  031C031C                    761        DC    PL2'31',PL2'31'    JUL                        TS603800
000691  031C031C                    762        DC    PL2'31',PL2'31'    AUG                        TS603810
000695  030C030C                    763        DC    PL2'30',PL2'30'    SEP                        TS603820
000699  031C031C                    764        DC    PL2'31',PL2'31'    OCT                        TS603830
00069D  030C030C                    765        DC    PL2'30',PL2'30'    NOV                        TS603840
```

```
LOC      OBJECT CODE        ADDR1 ADDR2  STMT  SOURCE STATEMENT                           DOS/VSE ASSEMBLER 16.24  99-12-31

0006A1   031C031C                        766          DC    PL2'31',PL2'31'        DEC                                      TS603850
                                         767   *                                                                            TS603860
                                         768   *      THE DAYS TABLE IS DEFINED WITH A PAIR OF TWO                           TS603870
                                         769   *      BYTE ENTRIES FOR EACH OF THE 12 MONTHS CONTAIN-                        TS603880
                                         770   *      ING THE CUMULATIVE NUMBER OF DAYS EXPIRED AT                          TS603890
                                         771   *      THE END OF THE PRIOR MONTH- NON-LEAP YEAR AND                         TS603900
                                         772   *      LEAP YEAR                                                             TS603910
                                         773   *                                                                            TS603920
0006A5   000C000C                        774   #$6DAYS  DC  PL2'00',PL2'00'        JAN                                      TS603930
0006A9   031C031C                        775          DC    PL2'31',PL2'31'        FEB                                      TS603940
0006AD   059C060C                        776          DC    PL2'59',PL2'60'        MAR                                      TS603950
0006B1   090C091C                        777          DC    PL2'90',PL2'91'        APR                                      TS603960
0006B5   120C121C                        778          DC    PL2'120',PL2'121'      MAY                                      TS603970
0006B9   151C152C                        779          DC    PL2'151',PL2'152'      JUN                                      TS603980
0006BD   181C182C                        780          DC    PL2'181',PL2'182'      JUL                                      TS603990
0006C1   212C213C                        781          DC    PL2'212',PL2'213'      AUG                                      TS604000
0006C5   243C244C                        782          DC    PL2'243',PL2'244'      SEP                                      TS604010
0006C9   273C274C                        783          DC    PL2'273',PL2'274'      OCT                                      TS604020
0006CD   304C305C                        784          DC    PL2'304',PL2'305'      NOV                                      TS604030
0006D1   334C335C                        785          DC    PL2'334',PL2'335'      DEC                                      TS604040
                                         786   *                                                                            TS604050
                                         787   *      TRANSLATION TABLE DEFINED FOR X'F0' - X'F9'                           TS604060
                                         788   *      (ALL TABLE POSITIONS EXCEPT THOSE CORRESPONDING                      TS604070
                                         789   *      TO X'F0' THROUGH X'F9' ARE SET TO A VALUE OTHER                      TS604080
                                         790   *      THAN X'00')                                                           TS604090
                                         791   *                                                                            TS604100
0006D5   1C1C1C1C1C1C1C1C               792   #$6TABL  DC  240X'1C'                                                         TS604110
0007C5   0000000000000000               793          DC    10X'00'                                                          TS604120
0007CF   1C1C1C1C1C                     794          DC    6X'1C'                                                           TS604130
                                         795   *                                                                            TS604140
0007D5   000000000000000000            796   #$62RO   DC  12X'00'                                                           TS604150
0007E1   4C                            797   CODE6    DC  PL1'4'                                                            TS604160
0007E2   F0F0F0F0F0F0F0C0              798   INDATE   DC  ZL8'00000000'                                                     TS604170
0007EA   9C                            799   OUTDAY   DC  PL1'9'                                                            TS604180
0007EB                                  800   #$6L     DS  PL1                                                              TS604190
0007EC                                  801   #$6SIGN  DS  ZL1                                                              TS604200
0007ED                                  802   #$6WORK6 DS  PL6                                                              TS604210
0007F3                                  803   #$6WORK8 DS  ZL8                                                              TS604220
0007FB                                  804   #$6WORK9 DS  ZL9                                                              TS604230
000804                                  805   #$6MO    DS  PL2                                                              TS604240
000806                                  806   #$6DA    DS  PL2                                                              TS604250
000808                                  807   #$6YR    DS  PL3                                                              TS604260
000808                                  808   #$6P1    DS  PL5                                                              TS604270
000810                                  809   #$6P2    DS  PL2                                                              TS604280
000812                                  810   #$6Q1    DS  PL1                                                              TS604290
000813                                  811   #$6WORK  DS  PL5                                                              TS604300
000818                                  812   #$6FLD   DS  CL1                                                              TS604310
00081C                                  813   #$6RSAVE DS  5F                                                               TS604320
000830                                  814   #$6CVB   DS  1D                                                               TS604330
000838   9815 7766         0081C        815   #$6TERM  LM  1,5,#$6RSAVE                                                     TS604340
00083C   07F6              00084        816          BR    6                                                                TS604350
                                         817          END   BEGIN
000840   5B5BC2D6D7C5D540               818          =C'$BOPEN ,
000848   C9D5E5C1D3C9C440               819          =C'INVALID DAY *************'
000860   E2E4C2D9D6E4E3C9               820          =C'SUBROUTINE ERROR'
```

Figure 7.1 *Continued*

```
TEST OF TIMESUB6 TO CALCULATE DAY NAMES

DATE        NAME
12/31/1999  FRIDAY      CODE6 CONTENTS: 0.  OUTDAY CONTENTS...5
01/03/2000  MONDAY      CODE6 CONTENTS: 0.  OUTDAY CONTENTS...1
01/02/1989  MONDAY      CODE6 CONTENTS: 0.  OUTDAY CONTENTS...1
01/03/1987  SATURDAY    CODE6 CONTENTS: 0.  OUTDAY CONTENTS...6
01/04/1993  MONDAY      CODE6 CONTENTS: 0.  OUTDAY CONTENTS...1
01/05/1994  WEDNESDAY   CODE6 CONTENTS: 0.  OUTDAY CONTENTS...3
12/25/1998  FRIDAY      CODE6 CONTENTS: 0.  OUTDAY CONTENTS...5
01/01/1607  MONDAY      CODE6 CONTENTS: 0.  OUTDAY CONTENTS...1
12/31/2000  SUNDAY      CODE6 CONTENTS: 0.  OUTDAY CONTENTS...0
12/31/1984  MONDAY      CODE6 CONTENTS: 0.  OUTDAY CONTENTS...1
12/31/1985  TUESDAY     CODE6 CONTENTS: 0.  OUTDAY CONTENTS...2
12/31/1986  WEDNESDAY   CODE6 CONTENTS: 0.  OUTDAY CONTENTS...3
11/13/1985  WEDNESDAY   CODE6 CONTENTS: 0.  OUTDAY CONTENTS...3
09/02/1985  MONDAY      CODE6 CONTENTS: 0.  OUTDAY CONTENTS...1
01/01/1607  MONDAY      CODE6 CONTENTS: 0.  OUTDAY CONTENTS...1
01/01/1990  MONDAY      CODE6 CONTENTS: 0.  OUTDAY CONTENTS...1
01/02/1990  TUESDAY     CODE6 CONTENTS: 0.  OUTDAY CONTENTS...2
01/03/1990  WEDNESDAY   CODE6 CONTENTS: 0.  OUTDAY CONTENTS...3
01/04/1990  THURSDAY    CODE6 CONTENTS: 0.  OUTDAY CONTENTS...4
01/05/1990  FRIDAY      CODE6 CONTENTS: 0.  OUTDAY CONTENTS...5
01/06/1990  SATURDAY    CODE6 CONTENTS: 0.  OUTDAY CONTENTS...6
01/07/1990  SUNDAY      CODE6 CONTENTS: 0.  OUTDAY CONTENTS...0
01/01/1985  TUESDAY     CODE6 CONTENTS: 0.  OUTDAY CONTENTS...2
01/02/1985  WEDNESDAY   CODE6 CONTENTS: 0.  OUTDAY CONTENTS...3
01/03/1985  THURSDAY    CODE6 CONTENTS: 0.  OUTDAY CONTENTS...4
01/04/1985  FRIDAY      CODE6 CONTENTS: 0.  OUTDAY CONTENTS...5
01/05/1985  SATURDAY    CODE6 CONTENTS: 0.  OUTDAY CONTENTS...6
01/06/1985  SUNDAY      CODE6 CONTENTS: 0.  OUTDAY CONTENTS...0
01/07/1985  MONDAY      CODE6 CONTENTS: 0.  OUTDAY CONTENTS...1
01/08/1985  TUESDAY     CODE6 CONTENTS: 0.  OUTDAY CONTENTS...2
01/09/1985  WEDNESDAY   CODE6 CONTENTS: 0.  OUTDAY CONTENTS...3
01/10/1985  THURSDAY    CODE6 CONTENTS: 0.  OUTDAY CONTENTS...4
01/11/1985  FRIDAY      CODE6 CONTENTS: 0.  OUTDAY CONTENTS...5
01/12/1985  SATURDAY    CODE6 CONTENTS: 0.  OUTDAY CONTENTS...6
01/13/1985  SUNDAY      CODE6 CONTENTS: 0.  OUTDAY CONTENTS...0
01/14/1985  MONDAY      CODE6 CONTENTS: 0.  OUTDAY CONTENTS...1
01/15/1985  TUESDAY     CODE6 CONTENTS: 0.  OUTDAY CONTENTS...2
01/16/1985  WEDNESDAY   CODE6 CONTENTS: 0.  OUTDAY CONTENTS...3
01/17/1985  THURSDAY    CODE6 CONTENTS: 0.  OUTDAY CONTENTS...4
01/18/1985  FRIDAY      CODE6 CONTENTS: 0.  OUTDAY CONTENTS...5
01/19/1985  SATURDAY    CODE6 CONTENTS: 0.  OUTDAY CONTENTS...6
01/20/1985  SUNDAY      CODE6 CONTENTS: 0.  OUTDAY CONTENTS...0
01/21/1985  MONDAY      CODE6 CONTENTS: 0.  OUTDAY CONTENTS...1
01/22/1985  TUESDAY     CODE6 CONTENTS: 0.  OUTDAY CONTENTS...2

THE SUBROUTINE WAS EXECUTED   44 TIMES
```

**Figure 7.2**  A subset of TEST06 output produced in testing TIMESUB6.

# Converting the Neo-Julian Date

As explained back in chapter 3, the neo-Julian system was created to solve the problem of inadequate dating, caused by the storage and use of six-digit dates. When you create a new data form, however, you also need to provide a means of reconverting data to allow its unrestricted use in computation. We've delayed addressing this issue until now because much of the logical and mathematical equipment to effect such a conversion was explained, created, and demonstrated in prior chapters.

This chapter, however, does bear a number of burdens. Our goal is to present alternative methods of converting the neo-Julian date to Commercial-8 format for input to the subroutines we've presented. Also, you need to be able to reformat Commercial-8 to either of FIPS-8 or European-8 to allow continued display of dates in familiar formats.

## Defining the Problems

The initial problem is essentially one of converting the ordinal day E to its month/day equivalent. This problem was solved in TIMESUB5, which showed that the inverse of the operations that produced E from month and day values would reproduce month and day values from a given E. This logic was used to convert a gross day count to a new Gregorian date. While you'll develop an algorithm that specifically accepts Y.E as input and from it creates a Gregorian date, there should be an alternative and perhaps more useful tool for accomplishing this.

It would be practical to have an algorithm that will accept a Commercial-8 input date along with a request indicator and from these output either FIPS-8 or European-8 dates. Even more practical would be an algorithm to accept any of the Commercial-8, FIPS-8, or European-8 dates along with an indicator that would identify the input format and request a specific format on output. There are, then, a number of problems to be solved, however simple.

## Designing the Algorithms

Turning to the most obvious solution, you can use TIMESUB5 to accomplish the reconversion of E to a month/day value and thus effect the complete reconversion of the neo-Julian date. Perhaps a few well-chosen statements will uncover the underlying logic.

The neo-Julian date Y.E is composed of four year-digits and three day-digits, which represent the ordinal day. By definition of the Gregorian date, Y, E, M, and D, the following is true: $01/01/y = y.001$. Respecting the defined limit for E, you can add an appropriate number of days, $nnn$, to each side without affecting the validity of the equation, the sole requirement being that the definition of E not be violated on the right side:

$$01/01/y + nnn = y.001 + nnn$$

But if you allow that $ddd = 001 + nnn$, it follows that $nnn = ddd - 1$. Hence, substituting for $nnn$ on the left and for $001 + nnn$ on the right, you have:

$$01/01/y + ddd - 1 = y.ddd \tag{8.1}$$

But since TIMESUB5 will produce a valid Commercial-8 date for the values on the left of equation 8.1 and because the value on its right is a valid neo-Julian date, it follows that any neo-Julian date Y.E = $y.ddd$ can be transformed and thus submitted to TIMESUB5 for reconversion to Gregorian Commercial-8 format.

The benefits of equation 8.1 are sizable. Aging programs that read records containing neo-Julian dates can convert those dates to Commercial-8 and age the records, all within the same limited set of code. A demonstration of this equation is shown in Figure 8.1, which displays an example test program's post listing. Records containing packed neo-Julian dates are read, the dates transformed, and the equivalent Gregorian Commercial-8 date created by TIMESUB5.

The test program EXMP05 features the TIME5 macro that, combined with PRINT NOGEN, suppresses the superfluous printing of TIMESUB5's instructions. Figure 8.2 exhibits the program's output.

In pursuing the concept of multiple TIMESUB5 use, you'll be confronted with the practical need to design an algorithm that converts formats among the three Gregorian standards: Commercial-8, FIPS-8, and European-8. This algorithm must be capable of accepting any of these inputs and, for each, producing as output either of the other two. Hence, an indicator similar to SIGF of TIMESUBF must be submitted with the input date. In all, you must allow for three different inputs and six outputs, plus a null or identity output that merely outputs the input date with no format change. This reduces to a straightforward programming task. We'll call this algorithm TIMESUBG.

Finally, you need an algorithm that simply converts neo-Julian dates to Gregorian Commercial-8 dates. Such an algorithm relieves the application programmer of the task of transforming the neo-Julian date to $01/01/y + ddd - 1$ when TIMESUB5 might not have a secondary application—no small benefit in view of the conversion requirement the impending crisis presents. We'll call our pure neo-Julian-to-Commercial-8 conversion algorithm TIMESUB7.

Because no new algorithmic ground is broken by either algorithm, let's proceed directly to definitions and a presentation of the pseudocode.

```
                                                EXTERNAL SYMBOL DICTIONARY

SYMBOL      TYPE            ID  ADDR    LENGTH  LD-ID

EXMPO5      SD (CSECT)      001 000000 000B61
PRMOD       ER (EXTRN)      002
PRMOD       SD (CSECT)      003 000000 000088

                                                DUMMY SECTION DICTIONARY

SYMBOL      ID LENGTH

IJDPDO02    1FF 000030
```

**Figure 8.1** The entire assembly post listing of EXMP05, featuring the TIME5 macro equivalent of TIMESUB5.

```
LOC   OBJECT CODE   ADDR1 ADDR2   STMT   SOURCE STATEMENT                                              DOS/VSE ASSEMBLER 16.59 99-12-31

                                    1            PRINT NOGEN
                                    2  EXMPO5    START
                                    3  *
                                    4  *         THIS EXAMPLE PROGRAM IS DESIGNED TO READ A PACKED
                                    5  *         NEO-JULIAN DATE FROM A FILE, UNPACK IT AND.
                                    6  *         THROUGH THE USE OF THE FOLLOWING FORMULA:
                                    7  *
                                    8  *              YYYYDDD = O1O1YYYY + (DDD - 1)
                                    9  *
                                   10  *         EMPLOY TIMESUB5 IN THE CONVERSION OF THE
                                   11  *         NEO-JULIAN DATE TO ITS GREGORIAN EQUIVALENT.
                                   12  *
                                   13  *         THIS IS ACCOMPLISHED BY MOVING NEOJUL'S YEAR
                                   14  *         TO A FIELD CALLED TSTDATE1- TSTDATE1 IS A DEFINED
                                   15  *         CONSTANT 'O1O1OOOO'. THE LOW ORDER ZEROS ARE
                                   16  *         REPLACED BY THE NEOJUL YEAR UPON READING EACH
                                   17  *         INPUT DATE. TSTDATE1 IS THEN MOVED TO THE
                                   18  *         DATEI FIELD OF TIMESUB5.
                                   19  *
                                   20  *         NEOJUL'S THREE DIGIT DAY VALUE IS DECREMENTED BY
                                   21  *         ONE: (DDD - 1), AND MOVED TO THE MODIFY FIELD OF
                                   22  *         TIMESUB5. THUS, THE FORMULA IS IMPLEMENTED:
                                   23  *
                                   24  *              DATEI = O1O1YYYY         MODIFY = DDD - 1
                                   25  *
                                   26  *         THE EXECUTION OF TIMESUB5 PRODUCES THE GREGORIAN
                                   27  *         EQUIVALENT OF THE NEO-JULIAN DATE.
                                   28  *
                                   29  *                            JEROME T. MURRAY
                                   30  *                            MARILYN J. MURRAY
                                   31  *         GLEN ELLYN, ILLINOIS
                                   32  *
                                   33  LIST      DTFPR DEVADDR=SYSO1O,                                 X
                                                      IOAREA1=OUT,                                     X
                                                      BLKSIZE=132,                                     X
                                                      DEVICE=1403,                                     X
                                                      PRINTOV=YES,                                     X
                                                      MODNAME=PRMOD,                                   X
                                                      CONTROL=YES
                                   54  *
                                   55  PRMOD     PRMOD CONTROL=YES,                                    X
                                                      PRINTOV=YES
                                  164  *
                                  165  TESTFIL   ACB AM=VSAM,                                          X
                                                      MACRF=(ADR,IN,SEQ).                              X
                                                      EXLST=EXITLST
                                  197  *
                                  198  EXITLST   EXLST AM=VSAM,                                        X
                                                      EDDAD=FINI
                                  209  *
                                  210  REQUEST   RPL ACB=TESTFIL,                                      X
                                                      AREA=TESTFLE,                                    X
                                                      AREALEN=BO,                                      X
                                                      OPTCD=(ADR,SEQ,NUP,MVE)
                                  239  *

000000
```

```
                                                        DOS/VSE ASSEMBLER  16.59  99-12-31

LOC     OBJECT CODE       ADDR1  ADDR2    STMT   SOURCE STATEMENT

0000B4  0570                              240    BEGIN  BALR  7,0
                                          241           USING *,7
0000B6  41D0 7988         000B6  00A3E    242           LA    13,SAVE
                                          243           OPEN  TESTFIL,LIST
0000CE  9240 783C                008F2    252           MVI   OUT,X'40'
0000D2  D282 783D 783C    008F3  008F2    253           MVC   OUT+1(131),OUT
                                          254    READ   GET   RPL=REQUEST
0000EA  FA20 7901 7A0E    009B7  00AC4    261           AP    TOT,=P'1'
                                          262    *
                                          263    *      UNPACK NEOJUL FOR INPUT TO TIMESUB5
                                          264    *
0000F0  F363 782C 77DA    008E2  00890    265           UNPK  WORK7,NEOJUL
                                          266    *
                                          267    *      INITIALIZE TSTDATE1'S YEAR: TSTDATE1 = 0101YYYY
                                          268    *
0000F6  D203 78FD 782C    009B3  008E2    269           MVC   TSTDATE1+4(4),WORK7
                                          270    *
                                          271    *      INITIALIZE INCREMNT: INCREMNT = DDD - 1
                                          272    *
0000FC  F212 782A 7830    008E0  008E6    273           PACK  INCREMNT,WORK7+4(3)
000102  FB10 782A 7A0E    008E0  00AC4    274           SP    INCREMNT,=P'1'
                                          275    *
                                          276    *      TRANSFER TSTDATE1 TO DATEI FIELD AND INCREMNT
                                          277    *      TO MODIFY FIELD IN PREPARATION FOR EXECUTION
                                          278    *      OF TIMESUB5 MACRO. TIME5
                                          279    *
000108  D207 7584 78F9    0063A  009AF    280           MVC   DATEI,TSTDATE1
00010E  F351 7408 782A    004BE  008E0    281           UNPK  MODIFY,INCREMNT
                                          282    *
                                          283    *      EXECUTE TIMESUB5 IN ITS MACRO FORM- TIME5
                                          284    *
                                          285    TIME5
                                          523    *
                                          524    *      DISPLAY RESULTS
                                          525    *
0006BC  9540 7987                00A3D    526           CLI   SWITCH,X'40'
0006C0  4770 766A                00720    527           BNE   TEST
0006C4  92F1 7987                00A3D    528           MVI   SWITCH,X'F1'
0006C8  D23E 783C 7904    008F2  009BA    529           MVC   OUT(63),HDG
                                          530           CNTRL LIST,SK,1
                                          536           CNTRL LIST,SP,3
                                          542           PUT   LIST
0006F6  9240 783C                008F2    547           MVI   OUT,X'40'
0006FA  D282 783D 783C    008F3  008F2    548           MVC   OUT+1(131),OUT
000700  D243 783C 7943    008F2  009F9    549           MVC   OUT(68),HDG1
                                          550           CNTRL LIST,SP,1
                                          556           PUT   LIST
000720  9240 783C                008F2    561    TEST   MVI   OUT,X'40'
000724  D282 783D 783C    008F3  008F2    562           MVC   OUT+1(131),OUT
00072A  D203 783C 782C    008F2  008E2    563           MVC   OUT(4),WORK7
000730  D200 7840 7A23    008F6  00AD9    564           MVC   OUT+4(1),=C','
000736  D202 7841 7830    008F7  008E6    565           MVC   OUT+5(3),WORK7+4
00073C  D300 7843 7A24    008F9  00ADA    566           MVZ   OUT+7(1),=C'1'
000742  D200 7847 7A25    008FD  00ADB    567           MVC   OUT+11(1),=C','
000748  D201 7849 7584    008FF  0063A    568           MVC   OUT+13(2),DATEI
```

**Figure 8.1** *Continued*

```
LOC     OBJECT CODE      ADDR1 ADDR2   STMT         SOURCE STATEMENT

00074E  D200 784B 7A26   00901 00ADC   569          MVC   OUT+15(1),=C'/'
000754  D201 784C 7586   00902 0063C   570          MVC   OUT+16(2),DATEI+2
00075A  D200 784E 7A26   00904 00ADC   571          MVC   OUT+18(1),=C'/'
000760  D203 784F 7588   00905 0063E   572          MVC   OUT+19(4),DATEI+4
000766  D200 7854 7A27   0090A 00ADD   573          MVC   OUT+24(1),=C'+'
00076C  D202 7856 740B   0090C 004C1   574          MVC   OUT+26(3),MODIFY+3
000772  D300 7858 7A24   0090E 00ADA   575          MVZ   OUT+28(1),=C'1'
000778  D20B 77DE 78ED   00894 009A3   576          MVC   VOID(12),DATEMASK
00077E  DE0B 77DE 740E   00894 004C4   577          ED    VOID(12),NUDATE
000784  D209 7875 77E0   0092B 00896   578          MVC   OUT+57(10),VOID+2
00078A  F900 7583 7A0F   00639 00AC5   579          CP    CODE5,=P'0'
000790  4780 774E        00804         580          BE    NEXT
000794  F900 7583 7A10   00639 00AC6   581          CP    CODE5,=P'2'
00079A  4770 76F2        007A8         582          BNE   CK4
00079E  D216 7880 7A28   00936 00ADE   583          MVC   OUT+68(23),=C'INVALID DATE DATA ****'
0007A4  47F0 774E        00804         584          B     NEXT
0007A8  F900 7583 7A14   00639 00ACA   585 CK4      CP    CODE5,=P'4'
0007AE  4770 7706        007BC         586          BNE   CK8
0007B2  D216 7880 7A3F   00936 00AF5   587          MVC   OUT+68(23),=C'INVALID YEAR *********'
0007B8  47F0 774E        00804         588          B     NEXT
0007BC  F900 7583 7A19   00639 00ACF   589 CK8      CP    CODE5,=P'8'
0007C2  4770 771A        007D0         590          BNE   CK3
0007C6  D216 7880 7A56   00936 00B0C   591          MVC   OUT+68(23),=C'INVALID DAY **********'
0007CC  47F0 774E        00804         592          B     NEXT
0007D0  F900 7583 7A1A   00639 00AD0   593 CK3      CP    CODE5,=P'3'
0007D6  4770 772E        007E4         594          BNE   CK5
0007DA  D216 7880 7A6D   00936 00B23   595          MVC   OUT+68(23),=C'INVALID INCR/DECR DATA '
0007E0  47F0 774E        00804         596          B     NEXT
0007E4  F900 7583 7A1B   00639 00AD1   597 CK5      CP    CODE5,=P'5'
0007EA  4770 7742        007F8         598          BNE   CK7
0007EE  D216 7880 7A84   00936 00B3A   599          MVC   OUT+68(23),=C'INVALID INCR/DECR VALUE'
0007F4  47F0 774E        00804         600          B     NEXT
0007F8  F900 7583 7A22   00639 00AD8   601 CK7      CP    CODE5,=P'7'
0007FE  D215 7880 79F8   00936 00AAE   602          MVC   OUT+68(22),=C'NUDATE EXCEEDS LIMITS '
000804  D20E 7897 7A9B   0094D 00B51   603 NEXT     MVC   OUT+91(15),=C'CODE5 CONTENTS '
00080A  F300 77DE 7583   00894 00639   604          UNPK  VOID(1),CODE5
000810  D300 77DE 7AAA   00894 00B60   605          MVZ   VOID(1),=C'0'
000816  D200 78A6 77DE   0095C 00894   606          MVC   OUT+106(1),VOID
                                       607          PRTOV LIST,12
                                       613          PUT   LIST
                                       618          B     READ
000836  47F0 7022        000D8         619 FINI     CLOSE TESTFIL

00084A  9240 783C        008F2         627          MVI   OUT,X'40'
00084E  D282 783D 783C   008F3 008F2   628          MVC   OUT+1(131),OUT
000854  D226 783C 78C0   008F2 00976   629          MVC   OUT(39),TOTAL
00085A  D205 7857 78E7   0090D 0099D   630          MVC   OUT+27(6),MASK
000860  DE05 7857 7901   0090D 009B7   631          ED    OUT+27(6),TOT
                                       632          CNTRL LIST,SP,1
                                       638          PUT   LIST
                                       643          CLOSE LIST
                                       651          EOJ

000890                                 654 TESTFLE  DS    OCL80
000890                                 655 NEOJUL   DS    PL4
000894                                 656 VOID     DS    CL76
0008E0                                 657 INCREMNT DS    PL2
```

```
LOC      OBJECT CODE        ADDR1 ADDR2   STMT   SOURCE STATEMENT                                                   DOS/VSE ASSEMBLER 16.59 99-12-31

0008E2                                     658   WORK7     DS    ZL7
0008E9                                     659   WORK      DS    PL5
0008EE                                     660   YR        DS    PL3
0008F1                                     661   L         DS    PL1
0008F2                                     662   OUT       DS    CL132
000976   E3C8C540E2E4C2D9                  663   TOTAL     DC    C'THE SUBROUTINE WAS EXECUTED        TIMES'
00099D   402020202020                      664   MASK      DC    X'402020202020'
0009A3   F0F1F0F1F0F0F0F0                  665   DATEMASK  DC    X'40202020612020206120202020'
0009AF                                     666   TSTDATE1  DC    C'01010000'
0009B7   00000C                            667   TOT       DC    PL3'0'
0009BA   E3C5E2E34006C640                  668             DC    C'TEST OF TIMESUB5 EMPLOYED TO CONVERT NEO-JULIAN TO '
0009ED   C7D9C5C7D6D9C9C1                  669             DC    C'GREGORIAN '
0009F9   D5C5D66QD1E4D3C9                  670   HDG1      DC    C'NEO-JULIAN = 01/01/YYYY + DDD - 1 CONVERTED TO '
000A28   C7D9C5C7D6D9C9C1                  671             DC    C'GREGORIAN: MM/DD/YYYY'
000A3D   40                                672   SWITCH    DC    X'40'
000A3E                                     673   SAVE      DS    CL72
                                           674             END   BEGIN
000A88   5B5BC2D6D7C5D540         000B4    675             =C'$$BOPEN '
000A90   5B5BC2C3D3D6E2C5                  676             =C'$$BCLOSE'
000A98   00000080                          677             =A(REQUEST)
000A9C   0657070C                          678             =P'657070'
000AA0   00000000                          679             =A(LIST)
000AA4   000C                              680             =P'00'
000AA6   400C                              681             =P'400'
000AA8   100C                              682             =P'100'
000AAA   365C                              683             =P'365'
000AAC   0004                              684             =H'4'
000AAE   D5E4C4C1E3C540C5                  685             =C'NJDATE EXCEEDS LIMITS '
000AC4   1C                                686             =P'1'
000AC5   0C                                687             =P'0'
000AC6   2C                                688             =P'2'
000AC7   01600C                            689             =P'1600'
000ACA   4C                                690             =P'4'
000ACB   03399C                            691             =P'3399'
000ACE   6C                                692             =P'6'
000ACF   8C                                693             =P'8'
000AD0   3C                                694             =P'3'
000AD1   5C                                695             =P'5'
000AD2   01601C                            696             =P'1601'
000AD5   36525C                            697             =P'36525'
000AD8   7C                                698             =P'7'
000AD9   4B                                699             =C'.'
000ADA   F1                                700             =C'1'
000ADB   7E                                701             =C'='
000ADC   61                                702             =C'/'
000ADD   4E                                703             =C'+'
000ADE   C9D5E5C1D3C9C440                  704             =C'INVALID DATE DATA ****'
000AF5   C9D5E5C1D3C9C440                  705             =C'INVALID YEAR ********'
000B0C   C9D5E5C1D3C9C440                  706             =C'INVALID DAY *********'
000B23   C9D5E5C1D3C9C440                  707             =C'INVALID INCR/DECR DATA'
000B3A   C9D5E5C1D3C9C440                  708             =C'INVALID INCR/DECR VALUE'
000B51   C3D6C4C5F540C3D6                  709             =C'CODE5 CONTENTS '
000B60   F0                                710             =C'O'
```

**Figure 8.1** *Continued*

RELOCATION DICTIONARY                                    99-12-31

| ESDID FOR ADDR CON | ESDID FOR REF SYMBOL | TYPE | LENGTH | ADDRESS |
|---|---|---|---|---|
| 001 | +001 | A | 4 | 000008 |
| 001 | +002 | V | 3 | 000011 |
| 001 | +001 | A | 4 | 000018 |
| 001 | +001 | CCW | 3 | 000029 |
| 001 | +001 | A | 4 | 000060 |
| 001 | +001 | A | 4 | 00007A |
| 001 | +001 | A | 4 | 00008C |
| 001 | +001 | A | 4 | 000098 |
| 001 | +001 | A | 4 | 0000C4 |
| 001 | +001 | A | 4 | 0000C8 |
| 001 | +001 | A | 4 | 000844 |
| 001 | +001 | A | 4 | 000888 |
| 001 | +001 | A | 4 | 000A98 |
| 001 | +001 | A | 4 | 000AA0 |

DIAGNOSTICS AND STATISTICS                              99-12-31

NO ERRORS FOUND

THE FOLLOWING MACRO NAMES HAVE BEEN FOUND IN MACRO INSTRUCTIONS
DTFPR    PRMOD    ACB       EXLST     RPL       OPEN      GET       TIME5     CNTRL     PUT       PRTOV     CLOSE     EOJ
EXCP     WAIT     IKQERMAC  IKQACB1   ISTACB1   IKQEXL1   ISTEXL1   IKQRPL1   ISTRPL1   BTWAIT    IKQACBG   IKQEXLG   IKQRPLG

OPTIONS FOR THIS ASSEMBLY - ALIGN, LIST. NOXREF. LINK. RLD, NODECK. NODECK.

THE ASSEMBLER WAS RUN IN 524168 BYTES
END OF ASSEMBLY

**Figure 8.1** *Continued*

```
TEST OF TIMESUB5 EMPLOYED TO CONVERT NEO-JULIAN TO GREGORIAN

NEO-JULIAN = 01/01/YYYY + DDD - 1 CONVERTED TO GREGORIAN: MM/DD/YYYY
1999.001 = 01/01/1999 + 000             1/01/1999     CODE5 CONTENTS 0
1999.006 = 01/01/1999 + 005             1/06/1999     CODE5 CONTENTS 0
1999.001 = 01/01/1999 + 000             1/01/1999     CODE5 CONTENTS 0
1999.031 = 01/01/1999 + 030             1/31/1999     CODE5 CONTENTS 0
1999.059 = 01/01/1999 + 058             2/28/1999     CODE5 CONTENTS 0
1999.060 = 01/01/1999 + 059             3/01/1999     CODE5 CONTENTS 0
1999.090 = 01/01/1999 + 089             3/31/1999     CODE5 CONTENTS 0
1999.120 = 01/01/1999 + 119             4/30/1999     CODE5 CONTENTS 0
1999.151 = 01/01/1999 + 150             5/31/1999     CODE5 CONTENTS 0
1999.181 = 01/01/1999 + 180             6/30/1999     CODE5 CONTENTS 0
1999.212 = 01/01/1999 + 211             7/31/1999     CODE5 CONTENTS 0
1999.243 = 01/01/1999 + 242             8/31/1999     CODE5 CONTENTS 0
1999.273 = 01/01/1999 + 272             9/30/1999     CODE5 CONTENTS 0
1999.304 = 01/01/1999 + 303            10/31/1999     CODE5 CONTENTS 0
1999.365 = 01/01/1999 + 364            12/31/1999     CODE5 CONTENTS 0
1996.366 = 01/01/1996 + 365            12/31/1996     CODE5 CONTENTS 0
2000.060 = 01/01/2000 + 059             2/29/2000     CODE5 CONTENTS 0
2000.091 = 01/01/2000 + 090             3/31/2000     CODE5 CONTENTS 0
2000.121 = 01/01/2000 + 120             4/30/2000     CODE5 CONTENTS 0
2000.152 = 01/01/2000 + 151             5/31/2000     CODE5 CONTENTS 0
2000.182 = 01/01/2000 + 181             6/30/2000     CODE5 CONTENTS 0
2000.213 = 01/01/2000 + 212             7/31/2000     CODE5 CONTENTS 0
2000.244 = 01/01/2000 + 243             8/31/2000     CODE5 CONTENTS 0
2000.274 = 01/01/2000 + 273             9/30/2000     CODE5 CONTENTS 0
2000.305 = 01/01/2000 + 304            10/31/2000     CODE5 CONTENTS 0
2000.325 = 01/01/2000 + 324            11/20/2000     CODE5 CONTENTS 0
2001.115 = 01/01/2001 + 114             4/25/2001     CODE5 CONTENTS 0
2002.225 = 01/01/2002 + 224             8/13/2002     CODE5 CONTENTS 0
2003.145 = 01/01/2003 + 144             5/25/2003     CODE5 CONTENTS 0
2004.035 = 01/01/2004 + 034             2/04/2004     CODE5 CONTENTS 0
2005.305 = 01/01/2005 + 304            11/01/2005     CODE5 CONTENTS 0
2006.315 = 01/01/2006 + 314            11/11/2006     CODE5 CONTENTS 0
2007.325 = 01/01/2007 + 324            11/21/2007     CODE5 CONTENTS 0
2008.035 = 01/01/2008 + 034             2/04/2008     CODE5 CONTENTS 0
2009.005 = 01/01/2009 + 004             1/05/2009     CODE5 CONTENTS 0
2022.235 = 01/01/2022 + 234             8/23/2022     CODE5 CONTENTS 0
2022.031 = 01/01/2022 + 030             1/31/2022     CODE5 CONTENTS 0
2024.300 = 01/01/2024 + 299            10/26/2024     CODE5 CONTENTS 0
2399.325 = 01/01/2399 + 324            11/21/2399     CODE5 CONTENTS 0
1999.020 = 01/01/1999 + 019             1/20/1999     CODE5 CONTENTS 0
1604.001 = 01/01/1604 + 000             1/01/1604     CODE5 CONTENTS 0
1601.365 = 01/01/1601 + 364            12/31/1601     CODE5 CONTENTS 0
1601.065 = 01/01/1601 + 064             3/06/1601     CODE5 CONTENTS 0
3399.365 = 01/01/3399 + 364            12/31/3399     CODE5 CONTENTS 0

THE SUBROUTINE WAS EXECUTED    44 TIMES
```

**Figure 8.2** Test output from EXMP05, which demonstrates the validity of using the equation earlier in the chapter in conjunction with TIMESUB5 to convert neo-Julian to Gregorian dates.

## The Pseudocode for TIMESUBG

TIMESUBG assumes that its input date has been passed to it in an eight-byte zoned field, DATEG. The input date's components must conform to the definitions and limits of the components of the Commercial-8 date with which you're so familiar. However, the input date can be in either Commercial-8, FIPS-8, or European-8 format.

The input indicator SIGG is passed to the subroutine in a one-byte, one-digit, zoned field. SIGG's contents are determined by the format of the input date and/or the desired format of the output according to the following scheme:

$$SIGG = \begin{cases} 0, \text{If undefined input—no format change} \\ 1, \text{If Commercial-8 input—output European-8} \\ 2, \text{If Commercial-8 input—output FIPS-8} \\ 3, \text{If European-8 input—output Commercial-8} \\ 4, \text{If European-8 input—output FIPS-8} \\ 5, \text{If FIPS-8 input—output Commercial-8} \\ 6, \text{If FIPS-8 input—output European-8} \end{cases}$$

SIGG = 0 is provided as an identity element and will result in validation of the input for numeric content and its direct transfer to the output field, if validation succeeds. The return code CODEG is defined as a one-byte field, packed with content as follows:

$$CODEG = \begin{cases} 0, \text{If } 0 \leq SIGG < 7 \text{ and DATEG's components} \\ \quad \text{conform to Commercial-8 component definitions} \\ 1, \text{If not } 0 \leq SIGG < 7 \\ 2, \text{If DATEG is non-numeric} \\ 4, \text{If Y } \varepsilon \text{ \{y\} as defined in Commercial-8} \\ 6, \text{If M } \varepsilon \text{ \{m\} as defined in Commercial-8} \\ 8, \text{If D } \varepsilon \text{ \{d\} as defined in Commercial-8} \end{cases}$$

The output field FORMT8 is five packed bytes. In the presence of a zero return code, FORMT8 will contain the desired output if and only if SIGG's content accurately portrays both the input date's format and the desired format of the output. However, it's quite likely that if SIGG misidentifies the format of the input, the edits will fail and a nonzero return code will result. In that case, FORMT8 will contain zero. In any event, CODEG = 0 doesn't necessarily imply successful execution since there's no logical possibility of verifying that SIGG's content is properly correlated with that of DATEG and the desires of the user. It's up to the user applications designer and depends in part on the acquisition of categorically pure data sets. The pseudocode is as follows:

```
 * Perform general housekeeping.
1) Let FORMT8 = 0
2) Let CODEG = 0
 * Validate 0 ≤ SIGG < 7.
3) If 0 ≤ SIGG < 7, go to 5
4) Let CODEG = 1, go to 39
 * Internal housekeeping.
```

```
 5) Move DATEG to WORK8
  * Validate DATEG as numeric.
 6) If DATEG is numeric, go to 8
 7) Let CODEG = 2, go to 39
  * Determine DATEG's format.
 8) If SIGG > 4, go to 14
 9) If SIGG > 2, go to 13
10) If SIGG > 0, go to 12
  * SIGG = 0, no format change.
11) Let FORMT8 = DATEG, go to 39
  * Input is Commercial-8.
12) DATEG → M,D,Y, go to 15
  * Input is European-8.
13) DATEG → D,M,Y, go to 15
  * Input is FIPS-8.
14) DATEG → Y, M, D
  * Test Y for limit violations.
15) If Y is within limits per Commercial-8, go to 17
16) Let CODEG = 4, go to 39
  * Perform leap year algorithm for Y.
17) Let L = 0
18) If Y is a leap year, let L = 1
  * Test M for limit violation.
19) If M is within limits per Commercial-8, go to 21
20) Let CODEG = 6, go to 39
  * Test D for limit violation.
21) If D is within limits per Commercial-8, go to 23
22) Let CODEG = 8, go to 39.
  * Determine output format.
23) If SIGG > 5, go to 28
24) If SIGG > 4, go to 36
25) If SIGG > 3, go to 32
26) If SIGG > 2, go to 36
27) If SIGG > 1, go to 32
  * Output European-8.
28) Let FORMT8 = 1000000D
29) Let FORMT8 = FORMT8 + 10000M
30) Let FORMT8 = FORMT8 + Y
31) Go to 39
  * Output FIPS-8.
32) Let FORMT8 = 10000Y
33) Let FORMT8 = FORMT8 + 100M
34) Let FORMT8 = FORMT8 + D
35) Go to 39
  * Output Commercial-8.
36) Let FORMT8 = 1000000M
37) Let FORMT8 = FORMT8 + 10000D
38) Let FORMT8 = FORMT8 + Y
39) Exit
```

## The Source Code for TIMESUBG

Figure 8.3 shows the TIMESUBG portion of TEST0G's assembly post listing, and Figure 8.4 displays a subset of the test results. All results were as predicted, with the conclusion that TIMESUBG is a valid algorithm. The source code closely follows the pseudocode in producing a program devoid of algorithmic novelty. Once more you see that variations are language-dependent. The pseudocode can be translated to any language with no further requirement than a knowledge of that language's syntax.

```
LOC   OBJECT CODE   ADDR1 ADDR2   STMT   SOURCE STATEMENT                              DOS/VSE ASSEMBLER 16.12   99-12-31

                             455 *                                                                               TSG00010
                             456 *                                                                               TSG00020
                             457 *                                                                               TSG00030
                             458 * TTTTTT  III  MM   MM  EEEEE  SSSSS   U U   BBBBB  GGGG                         TSG00040
                             459 *   T      I   M M M M  E      S       U U   B   B  G                            TSG00050
                             460 *   T      I   M  M  M  EEEE   SSSSS   U U   BBB B  G  GG                        TSG00060
                             461 *   T      I   M     M  EEEEE      S   U U   B   B  G   G                        TSG00070
                             462 *   T     III  M     M  EEEEE  SSSSS  UUUUU  BBBBB  GGGG                         TSG00080
                             463 * *****************************************************                         TSG00090
                             464 * *D A T E   F O R M A T   C O N V E R S I O N   S U B R O U T I N E*           TSG00100
                             465 * *****************************************************                         TSG00110
                             466 * *                                                                             TSG00120
                             467 * *                                                                             TSG00130
                             468 * *                                                                             TSG00140
                             469 * THIS SUBROUTINE CONVERTS INPUT DATES FROM ONE FORMAT TO ANOTHER               TSG00150
                             470 *       FIPS   COMMERCIAL   EUROPEAN                                            TSG00160
                             471 *                                                                               TSG00170
                             472 *  1.  VALID INPUT YEARS FOR THIS SUBROUTINE ARE THE YEARS                      TSG00180
                             473 *      1601 THROUGH 3399 A. D.                                                  TSG00190
                             474 *                                                                               TSG00200
                             475 *  2.  VALID INPUT MONTH VALUES FOR THIS SUBROUTINE ARE 01                      TSG00210
                             476 *      THROUGH 12.                                                              TSG00220
                             477 *                                                                               TSG00230
                             478 *  3.  VALID INPUT DAY VALUES FOR THIS SUBROUTINE ARE 01                        TSG00240
                             479 *      THROUGH 31 WITH EXCEPTIONS FOR THE MONTHS LISTED:                        TSG00250
                             480 *        MONTH        MAXIMUM DAY VALUE                                         TSG00260
                             481 *         04              30                                                   TSG00270
                             482 *         06              30                                                   TSG00280
                             483 *         09              30                                                   TSG00290
                             484 *         11              30                                                   TSG00300
                             485 *         02              28                                                   TSG00310
                             486 *         02 DURING LEAP YEAR    29                                            TSG00320
                             487 *                                                                               TSG00330
                             488 *  4.  THE INPUT DATE FORMAT MAY BE:                                            TSG00340
                             489 *             FIPS       = YYYYMMDD                                             TSG00350
                             490 *             COMMERCIAL = MMDDYYYY                                             TSG00360
                             491 *             EUROPEAN   = DDMMYYYY                                             TSG00370
                             492 *                                                                               TSG00380
                             493 *      IN ALL CASES: YYYY IS THE FOUR DIGIT YEAR VALUE.                         TSG00390
                             494 *                    MM IS THE TWO DIGIT MONTH VALUE.                           TSG00400
                             495 *                    DD IS THE TWO DIGIT DAY VALUE.                             TSG00410
                             496 *                                                                               TSG00420
                             497 *  5.  THE CALLING PROGRAM MUST PLACE THE EIGHT DIGIT DATE,                     TSG00430
                             498 *      IN ZONED DECIMAL, IN A SUBROUTINE DEFINED EIGHT BYTE                     TSG00440
                             499 *      FIELD, 'DATEG,' BEFORE EXECUTION OF THE SUBROUTINE.                      TSG00450
                             500 *      DATEG IS NOT ALTERED BY THE SUBROUTINE.                                  TSG00460
                             501 *                                                                               TSG00470
                             502 *  6.  THE CALLING PROGRAM MUST PLACE A ONE DIGIT INDICATOR,                    TSG00480
                             503 *      IN ZONED DECIMAL, IN A SUBROUTINE DEFINED ONE BYTE                       TSG00490
                             504 *      FIELD, 'SIGG,' BEFORE EXECUTION OF THE SUBROUTINE.                       TSG00500
                             505 *      SIGG IS NOT ALTERED BY THE SUBROUTINE.                                   TSG00510
                             506 *                                                                               TSG00520
                             507 *      THE ONE DIGIT INDICATOR MAY BE ANY OF THE DIGITS 0 - 6.                  TSG00530
                             508 *      WITH THE EXCEPTION OF 0, THE IDENTITY ELEMENT, THE DIGIT                 TSG00540
                             509 *                                                                               TSG00550
```

```
LOC   OBJECT CODE   ADDR1   ADDR2   STMT   SOURCE STATEMENT                                              DOS/VSE ASSEMBLER 16.12   99-12-31

                                    510 *      IMPLIES THE NATURE OF THE INPUT AND SPECIFIES THE CON-     * TSG00560
                                    511 *      VERSION TO BE PERFORMED:                                   * TSG00570
                                    512 *                                                                 * TSG00580
                                    513 *      0, EDIT FOR NUMERIC, PACK AND PLACE IN OUTPUT FIELD        * TSG00590
                                    514 *      1, CONVERT COMMERCIAL-8 INPUT TO EUROPEAN-8 OUTPUT         * TSG00600
                                    515 *      2, CONVERT COMMERCIAL-8 INPUT TO FIPS-8 OUTPUT             * TSG00610
                                    516 *      3, CONVERT EUROPEAN-8 INPUT TO COMMERCIAL-8 OUTPUT         * TSG00620
                                    517 *      4, CONVERT EUROPEAN-8 INPUT TO FIPS-8 OUTPUT               * TSG00630
                                    518 *      5, CONVERT FIPS-8 INPUT TO COMMERCIAL-8 OUTPUT             * TSG00640
                                    519 *      6, CONVERT FIPS-8 INPUT TO EUROPEAN-8 OUTPUT               * TSG00650
                                    520 *                                                                 * TSG00660
                                    521 *   7. A SUBROUTINE DEFINED ONE BYTE FIELD, 'CODEG,' IS RETURNED  * TSG00670
                                    522 *      TO THE CALLING PROGRAM AND CONTAINS A PACKED O IF THE      * TSG00680
                                    523 *      EXECUTION WAS SUCCESSFUL.  NON-ZERO VALUES INDICATE        * TSG00690
                                    524 *      THE FOLLOWING:                                             * TSG00700
                                    525 *                                                                 * TSG00710
                                    526 *      A PACKED 1 INDICATES UNSUCCESSFUL EXECUTION: INVALID       * TSG00720
                                    527 *      DATA IN SIGG- EITHER NON-NUMERIC OR A VALUE THAT EXCEEDS   * TSG00730
                                    528 *      THE LIMITS SPECIFIED IN 6., ABOVE.                         * TSG00740
                                    529 *                                                                 * TSG00750
                                    530 *      A PACKED 2 INDICATES UNSUCCESSFUL EXECUTION: INVALID DATA  * TSG00760
                                    531 *      IN DATEG.                                                  * TSG00770
                                    532 *                                                                 * TSG00780
                                    533 *      INVALID DATA ARE DETERMINED IF THE LOW ORDER BYTE'S ZONE   * TSG00790
                                    534 *      CONTAINS AN INVALID SIGN, (AN INVALID SIGN IS OTHER THAN   * TSG00800
                                    535 *      X'C', X'A', X'E', OR X'F'), OR IF THE PRECEDING BYTES'     * TSG00810
                                    536 *      ZONES ARE OTHER THAN X'F', OR IF ANY BYTE'S LOW ORDER      * TSG00820
                                    537 *      NIBBLE CONTAINS A VALUE GREATER THAN X'9'.                 * TSG00830
                                    538 *                                                                 * TSG00840
                                    539 *      A PACKED 4 INDICATES UNSUCCESSFUL EXECUTION: INVALID YEAR  * TSG00850
                                    540 *      VALUE IN DATEG- A VALUE THAT EXCEEDS THE LIMITS SPECIFIED  * TSG00860
                                    541 *      IN 1., ABOVE.                                              * TSG00870
                                    542 *                                                                 * TSG00880
                                    543 *      A PACKED 6 INDICATES UNSUCCESSFUL EXECUTION: INVALID       * TSG00890
                                    544 *      MONTH VALUE IN DATEG- A VALUE THAT EXCEEDS THE LIMITS      * TSG00900
                                    545 *      SPECIFIED IN 2., ABOVE.                                    * TSG00910
                                    546 *                                                                 * TSG00920
                                    547 *      A PACKED 8 INDICATES UNSUCCESSFUL EXECUTION: INVALID DAY   * TSG00930
                                    548 *      VALUE IN DATEG- A VALUE THAT EXCEEDS THE LIMITS SPECIFIED  * TSG00940
                                    549 *      IN 3., ABOVE.                                              * TSG00950
                                    550 *                                                                 * TSG00960
                                    551 *      INSPECTION OF THE RETURN CODE IS IMPORTANT.  THE RETURN    * TSG00970
                                    552 *      CODE, CODEG, REFLECTS THE LEVEL OF EDITING.                * TSG00980
                                    553 *                                                                 * TSG00990
                                    554 *      A RETURN CODE OF 1 INDICATES THAT SIGG WAS INVALID AND     * TSG01000
                                    555 *      THAT NO FURTHER EDITING WAS POSSIBLE.                      * TSG01010
                                    556 *                                                                 * TSG01020
                                    557 *      A RETURN CODE OF 2, INDICATES INVALID DATA IN DATEG.       * TSG01030
                                    558 *      IT ALSO INDICATES THAT NO EDITING HAS BEEN DONE TO         * TSG01040
                                    559 *      VALIDATE THE YEAR, MONTH OR DAY VALUES.  A RETURN CODE OF  * TSG01050
                                    560 *      4 INDICATES THAT THE DATA ARE VALID BUT THAT THE YEAR WAS  * TSG01060
                                    561 *      FOUND INVALID- THE MONTH AND DAY VALUES HAVE NOT BEEN ED-  * TSG01070
                                    562 *      ITED.  A RETURN CODE OF 6 INDICATES THAT THE DATA AND      * TSG01080
                                    563 *      YEAR ARE VALID BUT THAT THE MONTH IS INVALID- THE DAY      * TSG01090
                                    564 *      VALUE HAS NOT BEEN EDITED.  A RETURN CODE OF 8 INDICATES   * TSG01100
```

**Figure 8.3**  The TIMESUBG portion of TEST0G's assembly post listing.

```
LOC    OBJECT CODE       ADDR1 ADDR2   STMT  SOURCE STATEMENT                                              DOS/VSE ASSEMBLER 16.12   99-12-31

                                       565  *         THAT THE DATA, YEAR AND MONTH ARE VALID BUT THAT THE DAY         * TSG01110
                                       566  *         WAS FOUND INVALID FOR THE VALID MONTH GIVEN.                      * TSG01120
                                       567  *                                                                          * TSG01130
                                       568  *         IN SHORT, THE RETURN CODE INDICATES THE LEVEL OF EDITING.        * TSG01140
                                       569  *         THE EDIT SEQUENCE IS SIGG, DATA, YEAR, MONTH, AND DAY.           * TSG01150
                                       570  *                                                                          * TSG01160
                                       571  *    8.   A SUBROUTINE DEFINED FIVE BYTE PACKED FIELD, 'FORMT8,' IS       * TSG01170
                                       572  *         RETURNED TO THE CALLING PROGRAM.  FORMT8 CONTAINS THE           * TSG01180
                                       573  *         REFORMATTED INPUT DATE.  THE FORM OF THE REFORMATTED            * TSG01190
                                       574  *         DATE IS DETERMINED BY THE CONTENTS OF SIGG AS INDICATED         * TSG01200
                                       575  *         IN 6. ABOVE.  IF SIGG CONTAINS O. THE IDENTITY ELEMENT.         * TSG01210
                                       576  *         FORMT8 WILL CONTAIN THE INPUT DATE IN PACKED FORMAT.            * TSG01220
                                       577  *                                                                          * TSG01230
                                       578  *         IF SIGG CONTAINS O, THE INPUT DATE WILL BE EDITED TO            * TSG01240
                                       579  *         ASSURE THAT FORMT8 CONTAINS A VALID PACKED NUMERIC             * TSG01250
                                       580  *         VALUE.  LIMIT VALUE EDITING IS NOT POSSIBLE, HOWEVER.          * TSG01260
                                       581  *         SIGG = O DOES NOT IDENTIFY THE INPUT DATE'S FORMAT.             * TSG01270
                                       582  *                                                                          * TSG01280
                                       583  *         IF THE EXECUTION IS UNSUCCESSFUL, THAT IS, IF THE RETURN        * TSG01290
                                       584  *         CODE FIELD, CODEG, CONTAINS A NON-ZERO VALUE, THEN             * TSG01300
                                       585  *         FORMT8 WILL CONTAIN PACKED ZEROS.  THIS IS PROTECTION          * TSG01310
                                       586  *         AGAINST ILLEGAL USE OF A PRIOR EXECUTION'S RESULT.             * TSG01320
                                       587  *                                                                          * TSG01330
                                       588  *    9.   ALL OTHER SUBROUTINE DEFINED FIELDS AND LABELS ARE            * TSG01340
                                       589  *         TRANSPARENT TO THE CALLING PROGRAM.                            * TSG01350
                                       590  *                                                                          * TSG01360
                                       591  *   10.   THIS SUBROUTINE IS WRITTEN TO BE ASSEMBLED WITH THE           * TSG01370
                                       592  *         CALLING PROGRAM AND SHOULD BE INSERTED IN THE CALLING         * TSG01380
                                       593  *         PROGRAM IMMEDIATELY BEFORE THE 'END' OPCODE.                   * TSG01390
                                       594  *                                                                          * TSG01400
                                       595  *   11.   THIS SUBROUTINE USES REGISTER 6 AS THE LINK REGISTER.          * TSG01410
                                       596  *         IF REGISTER 6 IS ASSIGNED IN THE CALLING PROGRAM FOR           * TSG01420
                                       597  *         OTHER USES, IT MUST BE SAVED PRIOR TO EXECUTING THE            * TSG01430
                                       598  *         'BALR.'                                                          * TSG01440
                                       599  *                                                                          * TSG01450
                                       600  *                                                                          * TSG01460
                                       601  *                                               JEROME T. MURRAY          * TSG01470
                                       602  *                                               MARILYN J. MURRAY         * TSG01480
                                       603  *         GLEN ELLYN, ILLINOIS                                            * TSG01490
                                       604  *                                                                          * TSG01500
                                       605  * ****************************************************************** TSG01510
                                       606  * ****************************************************************** TSG01520
                                       607  * ****************************************************************** TSG01530
                                       608  *         +++  SECTION 1- GENERAL HOUSEKEEPING  +++                      TSG01540
                                       609  * ****************************************************************** TSG01550
                                       610  *                                                                          TSG01560
                                       611  *              INITIALIZE INDICATIVE FIELDS                               TSG01570
                                       612  *                                                                          TSG01580
000618 F840 77B0 7A13  00866 00AC9     613  TIMESUBG ZAP    FORMT8,=P'O'                                               TSG01590
00061E F800 77B5 7A13  0086B 00AC9     614           ZAP    CODEG.,=P'O'                                               TSG01600
                                       615  *                                                                          TSG01610
                                       616  *         SAVE REGISTERS 1 THROUGH 4 IN SAVE FIELDS                        TSG01620
                                       617  *                                                                          TSG01630
000624 9014 791A       009D0           618           STM    1,4,#$GRSAVE                                               TSG01640
                                       619  *                                                                          TSG01650
```

```
LOC     OBJECT CODE         ADDR1 ADDR2  STMT  SOURCE STATEMENT                                              DOS/VSE ASSEMBLER 16.12 99-12-31

                                          620  *          +++   SECTION 2- EDIT SIGG CONTENTS   +++          TSG01660
                                          621  *                                                            TSG01670
                                          622  *          INITIALIZE TABLE FOR 'FO' THROUGH 'F6' ONLY       TSG01680
                                          623  *                                                            TSG01690
000628  D202 78E6 7A61      0099C 00B17   624        MVC   #$GTABL+247(3),=X'1C1C1C'                         TSG01700
                                          625  *                                                            TSG01710
                                          626  *          EDIT SIGG USING TRT                                TSG01720
                                          627  *                                                            TSG01730
00062E  DD00 77BE 77EF      00874 7592    628        TRT   SIGG(1),#$GTABL                                   TSG01740
000634  4780 7592                         629        BC    8,#$GHKEP                                         TSG01750
                                          630  *                                                            TSG01760
                                          631  *          IF TEST FAILS, RESTORE TABLE AND EXIT              TSG01770
                                          632  *                                                            TSG01780
000638  D202 78E6 7A64      0099C 00B1A   633        MVC   #$GTABL+247(3),=X'000000'                         TSG01790
00063E  F800 77B5 7A12      0086B 009E8   634        ZAP   CODEG,=P'1'                                       TSG01800
000644  47F0 7932                         635        B     #$GTERM                                           TSG01810
                                          636  *                                                            TSG01820
                                          637  *          +++   SECTION 3- INTERNAL HOUSEKEEPING   +++       TSG01830
                                          638  *                                                            TSG01840
                                          639  *                                                            TSG01850
                                          640  *          RESTORE TABLE                                      TSG01860
                                          641  *                                                            TSG01870
000648  D202 78E6 7A64      0099C 00B1A   642  #$GHKEP MVC #$GTABL+247(3),=X'000000'                         TSG01880
                                          643  *                                                            TSG01890
                                          644  *          MOVE DATE TO WORK FIELD AND ISOLATE SIGN           TSG01900
                                          645  *                                                            TSG01910
00064E  D207 78FD 77B6      009B3 0086C   646        MVC   #$GWORK8,DATEG                                    TSG01920
000654  D200 78FB 7904      009B1 009BA   647        MVC   #$GSIGN,#$GWORK8+7                                TSG01930
                                          648  *                                                            TSG01940
                                          649  *          +++   SECTION 4- NUMERIC VALIDATION   +++          TSG01950
                                          650  *                                                            TSG01960
                                          651  *          AUGMENT TABLE FOR VALID '+' SIGNS OTHER THAN       TSG01970
                                          652  *          X'F' FOR WHICH TABLE IS DEFINED: X'A', X'C',       TSG01980
                                          653  *          X'E'- EDIT FOR VALID '+' SIGN USING TRT            TSG01990
                                          654  *                                                            TSG02000
00065A  D209 788F 78EF      00945 009A5   655        MVC   #$GTABL+160(10),#$GZRO                            TSG02010
000660  D209 78AF 78EF      00965 009A5   656        MVC   #$GTABL+192(10),#$GZRO                            TSG02020
000666  D209 78CF 78EF      00985 009A5   657        MVC   #$GTABL+224(10),#$GZRO                            TSG02030
00066C  DD00 77FB 77EF      009B1 00680   658        TRT   #$GSIGN(1),#$GTABL                                TSG02040
000672  4780 75CA                         659        BC    8,#$GNUM                                          TSG02050
                                          660  *                                                            TSG02060
                                          661  *          IF TEST FAILS, RESTORE TABLE AND EXIT              TSG02070
                                          662  *                                                            TSG02080
000676  D2EE 77F0 77F0      008A6 008A5   663        MVC   #$GTABL+1(239),#$GTABL                            TSG02090
00067C  47F0 75DA           00690         664        B     #$GBDATA                                          TSG02100
                                          665  *                                                            TSG02110
                                          666  *          RESTORE TABLE AND EDIT FOR VALID ZONE              TSG02120
                                          667  *          AND DIGIT CONFIGURATIONS IN REMAINING BYTES        TSG02130
                                          668  *                                                            TSG02140
000680  D2EE 77F0 77F0      008A6 008A5   669  #$GNUM  MVC #$GTABL+1(239),#$GTABL                            TSG02150
000686  DD06 78FD 77EF      009B3 0069A   670        TRT   #$GWORK8(7),#$GTABL                               TSG02160
00068C  4780 75E4                         671        BC    8,#$GPACK                                         TSG02170
                                          672  *                                                            TSG02180
                                          673  *          POST 'BAD DATA' RETURN CODE AND EXIT               TSG02190
                                          674  *                                                            TSG02200
```

**Figure 8.3** *Continued*

DDS/VSE ASSEMBLER 16.12   99-12-31

```
LOC    OBJECT CODE      ADDR1 ADDR2  STMT  SOURCE STATEMENT

000690 F800 77B5 7A14   0086B 00ACA   675  #$GBDATA ZAP  CODEG,=P'2'                                        TSGO2210
000696 47F0 7932        009E8         676           B    #$GTERM                                            TSGO2220
                                      677  *                                                                TSGO2230
                                      678  *    +++ SECTION 5- INTERROGATE SIGG FOR STANDARD   +++          TSGO2240
                                      679  *                                                                TSGO2250
                                      680  *         IF 5 OR 6, BRANCH TO #$GFED: FIPS INPUT                TSGO2260
                                      681  *                                                                TSGO2270
00069A D500 77BE 7A40   00874 00AF6   682  #$GPACK  CLC  SIGG,=C'4'                                         TSGO2280
0006A0 4720 7638        006EE         683           BH   #$GFED                                             TSGO2290
                                      684  *                                                                TSGO2300
                                      685  *         IF 3 OR 4, BRANCH TO #$GEUR: EUROPEAN INPUT            TSGO2310
                                      686  *                                                                TSGO2320
0006A4 D500 77BE 7A3E   00874 00AF4   687           CLC  SIGG,=C'2'                                         TSGO2330
0006AA 4720 7622        006D8         688           BH   #$GEUR                                             TSGO2340
                                      689  *                                                                TSGO2350
                                      690  *         IF 1 OR 2, BRANCH TO #$GCOM: COMMERCIAL INPUT          TSGO2360
                                      691  *                                                                TSGO2370
0006AE D500 77BE 7A50   00874 00B06   692           CLC  SIGG,=C'O'                                         TSGO2380
0006B4 4720 760C        006C2         693           BH   #$GCOM                                             TSGO2390
                                      694  *                                                                TSGO2400
                                      695  *         IF O, NO FORMAT CHANGE- PACK INPUT IN FORMT8           TSGO2410
                                      696  *         AND EXIT NO FURTHER EDITING IS POSSIBLE                TSGO2420
                                      697  *                                                                TSGO2430
0006B8 F247 77B0 77B6   00866 0086C   698           PACK FORMT8,DATEG                                       TSGO2440
0006BE 47F0 7932        009E8         699           B    #$GTERM                                            TSGO2450
                                      700  *                                                                TSGO2460
                                      701  *    +++ SECTION 6- DISTRIBUTE INPUT COMPONENTS   +++            TSGO2470
                                      702  *                                                                TSGO2480
                                      703  *         PACK MONTH, DAY AND YEAR IN WORK FIELDS                TSGO2490
                                      704  *                                                                TSGO2500
                                      705  *                   COMMERCIAL INPUT                             TSGO2510
                                      706  *                                                                TSGO2520
0006C2 F211 7912 78FD   009C8 009B3   707  #$GCOM   PACK #$GMO,#$GWORK8(2)                                  TSGO2530
0006C8 F211 7914 78FF   009CA 009B5   708           PACK #$GDA,#$GWORK8+2(2)                                TSGO2540
0006CE F223 7916 7901   009CC 009B7   709           PACK #$GYR,#$GWORK8+4(4)                                TSGO2550
0006D4 47F0 764A        00700         710           B    #$GYEDT                                            TSGO2560
                                      711  *                                                                TSGO2570
                                      712  *                   EUROPEAN INPUT                               TSGO2580
                                      713  *                                                                TSGO2590
0006D8 F211 7914 78FD   009CA 009B3   714  #$GEUR   PACK #$GDA,#$GWORK8(2)                                  TSGO2600
0006DE F211 7912 78FF   009C8 009B5   715           PACK #$GMO,#$GWORK8+2(2)                                TSGO2610
0006E4 F223 7916 7901   009CC 009B7   716           PACK #$GYR,#$GWORK8+4(4)                                TSGO2620
0006EA 47F0 764A        00700         717           B    #$GYEDT                                            TSGO2630
                                      718  *                                                                TSGO2640
                                      719  *                   FIPS INPUT                                   TSGO2650
                                      720  *                                                                TSGO2660
0006EE F223 7916 78FD   009CC 009B3   721  #$GFED   PACK #$GYR,#$GWORK8(4)                                  TSGO2670
0006F4 F211 7912 7901   009C8 009B7   722           PACK #$GMO,#$GWORK8+4(2)                                TSGO2680
0006FA F211 7914 7903   009CA 009B9   723           PACK #$GDA,#$GWORK8+6(2)                                TSGO2690
                                      724  *                                                                TSGO2700
                                      725  *    +++ SECTION 7- EDIT YEAR FOR LIMIT VIOLATIONS   +++         TSGO2710
                                      726  *                                                                TSGO2720
                                      727  *         EDIT YEAR VALUE FOR LOWER LIMIT VIOLATION              TSGO2730
                                      728  *                                                                TSGO2740
000700 F922 7916 7A67   009CC 00B1D   729  #$GYEDT  CP   #$GYR,=P'1600'                                     TSGO2750
```

```
                                                      DOS/VSE ASSEMBLER 16.12  99-12-31

LOC     OBJECT CODE      ADDR1 ADDR2  STMT  SOURCE STATEMENT

000706  4720 765E              00714  730        BH    #$GYRHI                                    TSG02760
                                      731  *                                                      TSG02770
                                      732  *      POST 'BAD YEAR' RETURN CODE AND EXIT            TSG02780
                                      733  *                                                      TSG02790
00070A  F800 77B5 7A15   0086B 00ACB  734  #$GBADYR ZAP  CODEG,=P'4'                               TSG02800
000710  47F0 7932              09E8   735        B     #$GTERM                                    TSG02810
                                      736  *                                                      TSG02820
                                      737  *      EDIT YEAR VALUE FOR UPPER LIMIT VIOLATION       TSG02830
                                      738  *                                                      TSG02840
000714  F922 7916 7A6A   009CC 00B20  739  #$GYRHI  CP   #$GYR,=P'3399'                            TSG02850
00071A  4720 7654              0070A  740        BH    #$GBADYR                                   TSG02860
                                      741  *                                                      TSG02870
                                      742  *      +++ SECTION 8- DETERMINE LEAP YEAR STATUS  +++  TSG02880
                                      743  *                                                      TSG02890
                                      744  *      EXECUTE LEAP YEAR ALGORITHM                     TSG02900
                                      745  *                                                      TSG02910
00071E  F800 78FC 7A13   009B2 00AC9  746        ZAP   #$GL,=P'0'                                 TSG02920
000724  F842 7905 7916   009BB 009CC  747        ZAP   #$GWORK,#$GYR                              TSG02930
00072A  FD40 7905 7A15   009BB 00ACB  748        DP    #$GWORK,=P'4'                              TSG02940
000730  F903 7909 7A13   009BF 0076C  749        CP    #$GWORK+4(1),=P'0'                         TSG02950
000736  4720 76B6              0076C  750        BH    #$GMOEDT                                   TSG02960
00073A  F842 7905 7916   009BB 009CC  751        ZAP   #$GWORK,#$GYR                              TSG02970
000740  FD41 7905 7A0C   009BB 00AC2  752        DP    #$GWORK,=P'100'                            TSG02980
000746  F910 7908 7A13   009BE 00766  753        CP    #$GWORK+3(2),=P'0'                         TSG02990
00074C  4720 76B0              00766  754        BH    #$GLPYR                                    TSG03000
000750  F842 7905 7916   009BB 009CC  755        ZAP   #$GWORK,#$GYR                              TSG03010
000756  FD41 7905 7A0E   009BB 00AC4  756        DP    #$GWORK,=P'400'                            TSG03020
00075C  F910 7908 7A13   009BE 0076C  757        CP    #$GWORK+3(2),=P'0'                         TSG03030
000762  4720 76B6              0076C  758        BH    #$GMOEDT                                   TSG03040
                                      759  *                                                      TSG03050
                                      760  *      IF YEAR IS A LEAP YEAR, SET INCREMENT TO 1      TSG03060
                                      761  *                                                      TSG03070
000766  F800 78FC 7A12   009B2 00AC8  762  #$GLPYR  ZAP  #$GL,=P'1'                                TSG03080
                                      763  *                                                      TSG03090
                                      764  *      +++ SECTION 9- EDIT MONTH FOR LIMIT VIOLATIONS +++  TSG03100
                                      765  *                                                      TSG03110
                                      766  *      VERIFY THAT MONTH IS WITHIN RANGE: 1 - 12       TSG03120
                                      767  *      A) CONVERT MONTH TO BINARY IN REGISTER 3        TSG03130
                                      768  *                                                      TSG03140
00076C  F871 792A 7912   009E0 009C8  769  #$GMOEDT ZAP  #$GCVB,#$GMO                              TSG03150
000772  4F30 792A              009E0  770        CVB   3,#$GCVB                                   TSG03160
                                      771  *                                                      TSG03170
                                      772  *      B)  STORE BINARY BYTE FROM REG 3 IN #$GFLD      TSG03180
                                      773  *                                                      TSG03190
000776  4230 7919              009CF  774        STC   3,#$GFLD                                   TSG03200
                                      775  *                                                      TSG03210
                                      776  *      C) INITIALIZE TABLE WITH X'00' FOR TRT          TSG03220
                                      777  *                                                      TSG03230
00077A  D20B 77F0 78EF   008A6 009A5  778        MVC   #$GTABL+1(12),#$GZRD                       TSG03240
                                      779  *                                                      TSG03250
                                      780  *      D) EXECUTE TRT USING #$GFLD                     TSG03260
                                      781  *                                                      TSG03270
000780  DD00 7919 77EF   009CF 008A5  782        TRT   #$GFLD(1),#$GTABL                          TSG03280
000786  4780 76E4              0079A  783        BC    8,#$GDAEDT                                 TSG03290
                                      784  *                                                      TSG03300
```

**Figure 8.3** *Continued*

```
LOC    OBJECT CODE        ADDR1 ADDR2  STMT   SOURCE STATEMENT                                    DOS/VSE ASSEMBLER 16.12  99-12-31

                                        785 *         F) RESTORE TABLE - POST BAD MONTH RETURN CODE                        TSG03310
                                        786 *            AND EXIT                                                          TSG03320
                                        787 *                                                                              TSG03330
00078A D20B 77F0 77EF   008A6 008A5     788        MVC   #$GTABL+1(12),#$GTABL                                             TSG03340
000790 F800 77B5 7A16   0086B 00ACC     789        ZAP   CODEG,=P'6'                                                       TSG03350
000796 47F0 7932        009E8           790        B     #$GTERM                                                           TSG03360
                                        791 *                                                                              TSG03370
                                        792 *    +++  SECTION 1O- EDIT DAY FOR LIMIT VIOLATIONS  +++                       TSG03380
                                        793 *                                                                              TSG03390
                                        794 *         RESTORE TABLE                                                        TSG03400
                                        795 *                                                                              TSG03410
00079A D20B 77F0 77EF   008A6 008A5     796 #$GDAEDT MVC   #$GTABL+1(12),#$GTABL                                            TSG03420
                                        797 *                                                                              TSG03430
                                        798 *         GET ADDRESS OF DAY TABLE IN REGISTER 4                               TSG03440
                                        799 *                                                                              TSG03450
0007A0 4140 77BF        00875           800        LA    4,#$GDATAB                                                        TSG03460
                                        801 *                                                                              TSG03470
                                        802 *         IF LEAP YEAR, INCREMENT TO LEAP YEAR FUNCTION                        TSG03480
                                        803 *                                                                              TSG03490
0007A4 F900 78FC 7A13   009B2 00AC9     804        CP    #$GL,=P'O'                                                        TSG03500
0007AA 4780 76FC        007B2           805        BE    #$GNOL                                                            TSG03510
0007AE 4144 0002        00002           806        LA    4,2(4)                                                            TSG03520
                                        807 *                                                                              TSG03530
                                        808 *         DIRECTLY ADDRESS TABLE DAY LIMIT FOR THIS MONTH                      TSG03540
                                        809 *         A) SUBTRACT 1 FROM BINARY MONTH VALUE IN REG 3                       TSG03550
                                        810 *                                                                              TSG03560
0007B2 0630             011 #$GNOL BCTR 3,0                                                                                TSG03570
                                        812 *                                                                              TSG03580
                                        813 *         B) MULTIPLY VALUE IN REG 3 BY 4                                      TSG03590
                                        814 *                                                                              TSG03600
0007B4 8930 0002        00002           815        SLL   3,2                                                               TSG03610
                                        816 *                                                                              TSG03620
                                        817 *}        C) LOAD ADDRESS OF DAY TABLE ENTRY IN REG 4                          TSG03630
                                        818 *                                                                              TSG03640
0007B8 4143 4000        00000           819        LA    4,0(3,4)                                                          TSG03650
                                        820 *                                                                              TSG03660
                                        821 *         CONVERT SIGN OF PACKED DAY FROM X'F' TO X'C'                         TSG03670
                                        822 *                                                                              TSG03680
0007BC F811 7914 7914   009CA 009CA     823        ZAP   #$GDA,#$GDA                                                       TSG03690
                                        824 *                                                                              TSG03700
                                        825 *         COMPARE DAY TABLE ENTRY (LIMIT) WITH INPUT DAY                       TSG03710
                                        826 *                                                                              TSG03720
0007C2 D501 7914 4000   009CA 00000     827        CLC   #$GDA,0(4)                                                        TSG03730
                                        828 *                                                                              TSG03740
                                        829 *         IF INPUT IS WITHIN LIMIT, EDIT DAY FOR ZERO                          TSG03750
                                        830 *                                                                              TSG03760
0007C8 47D0 7720        007D6           831        BNH   #$GDALO                                                           TSG03770
                                        832 *                                                                              TSG03780
                                        833 *         ELSE POST BAD DAY RETURN CODE AND EXIT                               TSG03790
                                        834 *                                                                              TSG03800
0007CC F800 77B5 7A24   0086B 00ADA     835 #$GBADA ZAP   CODEG,=P'8'                                                      TSG03810
0007D2 47F0 7932        009E8           836        B     #$GTERM                                                           TSG03820
                                        837 *                                                                              TSG03830
                                        838 *         EDIT DAY VALUE FOR ZERO                                              TSG03840
                                        839 *                                                                              TSG03850
```

```
                                                    DOS/VSE ASSEMBLER  16.12  99-12-31

LOC     OBJECT CODE       ADDR1  ADDR2   STMT  SOURCE STATEMENT

0007D6  F911 7914 7A10    009CA  00AC6    840  #$GDALD  CP    #$GDA,=P'00'                          TSG03860
0007DC  4780 7716                007CC    841           BE    #$GBADA                               TSG03870
                                          842  *                                                    TSG03880
                                          843  *        +++  SECTION 11- CONSTRUCT OUTPUT FIELD +++ TSG03890
                                          844  *                                                    TSG03900
0007E0  D500 77BE 7A41    00874  00AF7    845           CLC   SIGG,=C'5'                            TSG03910
0007E6  4720 775C                00812    846           BH    #$GXE                                 TSG03920
0007EA  D500 77BE 7A40    00874  00AF6    847           CLC   SIGG,=C'4'                            TSG03930
0007F0  4720 7794                0084A    848           BH    #$GXC                                 TSG03940
0007F4  D500 77BE 7A3F    00874  00AF5    849           CLC   SIGG,=C'3'                            TSG03950
0007FA  4720 7778                0082E    850           BH    #$GXF                                 TSG03960
0007FE  D500 77BE 7A3E    00874  0084A    851           CLC   SIGG,=C'2'                            TSG03970
000804  4720 7794                0084A    852           BH    #$GXC                                 TSG03980
000808  D500 77BE 7A3D    00874  0082E    853           CLC   SIGG,=C'1'                            TSG03990
00080E  4720 7778                0082E    854           BH    #$GXF                                 TSG04000
                                          855  *                                                    TSG04010
                                          856  *                     EUROPEAN-8 OUTPUT             TSG04020
                                          857  *                                                    TSG04030
000812  F311 790A 7914    009C0  009CA    858  #$GXE    UNPK  #$GWRK(2),#$GDA                       TSG04040
000818  F311 790C 7912    009C2  009C8    859           UNPK  #$GWRK+2(2),#$GMO                     TSG04050
00081E  F332 790E 7916    009C4  009CC    860           UNPK  #$GWRK+4(4),#$GYR                     TSG04060
000824  F247 77B0 790A    00866  009C0    861           PACK  FORMT8,#$GWRK                         TSG04070
00082A  47F0 7932                009E8    862           B     #$GTERM                               TSG04080
                                          863  *                                                    TSG04090
                                          864  *                     FIPS-8 OUTPUT                 TSG04100
                                          865  *                                                    TSG04110
00082E  F332 790A 7916    009C0  009CC    866  #$GXF    UNPK  #$GWRK(4),#$GYR                       TSG04120
000834  F311 790E 7912    009C4  009C8    867           UNPK  #$GWRK+4(2),#$GMO                     TSG04130
00083A  F311 7910 7914    009C6  009CA    868           UNPK  #$GWRK+6(2),#$GDA                     TSG04140
000840  F247 77B0 790A    00866  009C0    869           PACK  FORMT8,#$GWRK                         TSG04150
000846  47F0 7932                009E8    870           B     #$GTERM                               TSG04160
                                          871  *                                                    TSG04170
                                          872  *                     COMMERCIAL-8 OUTPUT           TSG04180
                                          873  *                                                    TSG04190
00084A  F311 790A 7912    009C0  009C8    874  #$GXC    UNPK  #$GWRK(2),#$GMO                       TSG04200
000850  F311 790C 7914    009C2  009CA    875           UNPK  #$GWRK+2(2),#$GDA                     TSG04210
000856  F332 790E 7916    009C4  009CC    876           UNPK  #$GWRK+4(4),#$GYR                     TSG04220
00085C  F247 77B0 790A    00866  009C0    877           PACK  FORMT8,#$GWRK                         TSG04230
                                          878  *                                                    TSG04240
                                          879  *        +++  SECTION 12- TO RESTORE REGISTERS AND EXIT  +++  TSG04250
                                          880  *                                                    TSG04260
000862  47F0 7932         009E8           881  #$GTERM  B                                           TSG04270
                                          882  *                                                    TSG04280
                                          883  *        +++  SECTION 13- DEFINE CONSTANTS AND STORAGE  +++   TSG04290
                                          884  *                                                    TSG04300
000866  000000000C                        885  FORMT8   DC    PL5'0'                                TSG04310
00086B  2C                                886  CODEG    DC    PL1'2'                                TSG04320
00086C  F0F0F0F0F0F0C0                    887  DATEG    DC    ZL8'00000000'                         TSG04330
000874  C0                                888  SIGG     DC    ZL1'0'                                TSG04340
                                          889  *                                                    TSG04350
                                          890  *        THE DAY TABLE IS DEFINED WITH A PAIR OF TWO BYTE     TSG04360
                                          891  *        ENTRIES FOR EACH OF THE 12 MONTHS- AN ENTRY FOR      TSG04370
                                          892  *        NON-LEAP YEAR AND AN ENTRY FOR LEAP YEAR             TSG04380
                                          893  *                                                    TSG04390
000875  031C031C                          894  #$GDATAB DC    PL2'31',PL2'31'        JAN            TSG04400
```

**Figure 8.3** *Continued*

```
                                                      DOS/VSE ASSEMBLER  16.12  99-12-31

LOC     OBJECT CODE       ADDR1  ADDR2   STMT  SOURCE STATEMENT

000879  028C029C                          895         DC    PL2'28',PL2'29'          FEB        TSG04410
00087D  031C031C                          896         DC    PL2'31',PL2'31'          MAR        TSG04420
000881  030C030C                          897         DC    PL2'30',PL2'30'          APR        TSG04430
000885  031C031C                          898         DC    PL2'31',PL2'31'          MAY        TSG04440
000889  030C030C                          899         DC    PL2'30',PL2'30'          JUN        TSG04450
00088D  031C031C                          900         DC    PL2'31',PL2'31'          JUL        TSG04460
000891  031C031C                          901         DC    PL2'31',PL2'31'          AUG        TSG04470
000895  030C030C                          902         DC    PL2'30',PL2'30'          SEP        TSG04480
000899  031C031C                          903         DC    PL2'31',PL2'31'          OCT        TSG04490
00089D  030C030C                          904         DC    PL2'30',PL2'30'          NOV        TSG04500
0008A1  031C031C                          905         DC    PL2'31',PL2'31'          DEC        TSG04510
                                          906  *                                                TSG04520
                                          907  *              TRANSLATION TABLE DEFINED FOR X'F0' - X'F9'      TSG04530
                                          908  *              (ALL TABLE POSITIONS EXCEPT THOSE CORRESPONDING  TSG04540
                                          909  *              TO X'F0' THROUGH X'F9' ARE SET TO A VALUE OTHER  TSG04550
                                          910  *              THAN X'00')                        TSG04560
                                          911  *                                                TSG04570
0008A5  1C1C1C1C1C1C1C1C           912  #$GTABL   DC    240X'1C'                    TSG04580
000995  0000000000000000           913            DC    10X'00'                     TSG04590
00099F  1C1C1C1C1C1C               914            DC    6X'1C'                      TSG04600
                                          915  *                                                TSG04610
0009A5  000000000000000000000000   916  #$GZRO    DC    12X'00'                     TSG04620
0009B1                             917  #$GSIGN   DS    ZL1                         TSG04630
0009B2                             918  #$GL      DS    PL1                         TSG04640
0009B3                             919  #$GWORK8  DS    CL8                         TSG04650
0009BB                             920  #$GWORK   DS    PL5                         TSG04660
0009C0                             921  #$GWRK    DS    CL8                         TSG04670
0009C8                             922  #$GMO     DS    PL2                         TSG04680
0009CA                             923  #$GDA     DS    PL2                         TSG04690
0009CC                             924  #$GYR     DS    PL3                         TSG04700
0009CF                             925  #$GFLD    DS    CL1                         TSG04710
0009D0                             926  #$GRSAVE  DS    4F                          TSG04720
0009E0                             927  #$GCVB    DS    1D                          TSG04730
0009E8  9814 791A        009D0     928  #$GTERM   LM    1,4,#$GRSAVE                TSG04740
0009EC  07F6                00B4   929            BR    6                           TSG04750
                                          930            END   BEGIN
0009F0  5B5BC2D6D7C5D540           931            =C'$$BDOPEN '
0009F8  E2E4C2D9D6E4E3C9           932            =C'SUBROUTINE ERROR'
000A08  5B5BC2C3D3D6E2C5           933            =C'$$BCLOSE'
000A10  00000080                   934            =A(REQUEST)
000A14  00000000                   935            =A(LIST)
000A18  C9D5E5C1D3C9C440           936            =C'INVALID DATA'
000A24  C9D5E5C1D3C9C440           937            =C'INVALID YEAR'
000A30  C5E4D9D6D7C5C1D5           938            =C'EUROPEAN TO FIPS       '
000A46  C6C9D7E240E3D640           939            =C'FIPS TO COMMERCIAL     '
000A5C  C6C9D7E240E3D640           940            =C'FIPS TO EUROPEAN       '
000A72  C3D6D4D4C5D9C3C9           941            =C'COMMERCIAL TO EUROPEAN'
000A88  E2C9C7C740C3D6D5           942            =C'SIGG CONTENTS:'
000A96  C3D6D4D4C5D9C3C9           943            =C'COMMERCIAL TO FIPS     '
000AAC  C5E4D9D6D7C5C1D5           944            =C'EUROPEAN TO COMMERCIAL '
000AC2  100C                       945            =P'100'
000AC4  400C                       946            =P'400'
000AC6  000C                       947            =P'00'
000AC8  1C                         948            =P'1'
000AC9  0C                         949            =P'0'
```

Figure 8.3 Continued

```
TEST OF TIMESUBG TO CONVERT AMONG DATE FORMATS

02/14/2003  COMMERCIAL TO EUROPEAN    14/02/2003   CODEG CONTENTS: 0   SIGG CONTENTS: 1
02/14/1989  COMMERCIAL TO FIPS        1989/02/14   CODEG CONTENTS: 0   SIGG CONTENTS: 2
14/02/2100  EUROPEAN TO COMMERCIAL    02/14/2100   CODEG CONTENTS: 0   SIGG CONTENTS: 3
14/02/3399  EUROPEAN TO FIPS          3399/02/14   CODEG CONTENTS: 0   SIGG CONTENTS: 4
2316/02/14  FIPS TO COMMERCIAL        02/14/2316   CODEG CONTENTS: 0   SIGG CONTENTS: 5
2613/02/14  FIPS TO EUROPEAN          14/02/2613   CODEG CONTENTS: 0   SIGG CONTENTS: 6
02141999    NO FORMATTING             02141999     CODEG CONTENTS: 6   SIGG CONTENTS: 0
19831314    INVALID MONTH                          CODEG CONTENTS: 8   SIGG CONTENTS: 6
19830229    INVALID DAY                            CODEG CONTENTS: 4   SIGG CONTENTS: 6
34000214    INVALID YEAR                           CODEG CONTENTS: 6   SIGG CONTENTS: 6
19830014    INVALID MONTH                          CODEG CONTENTS: 4   SIGG CONTENTS: 5
19830200    INVALID DAY                            CODEG CONTENTS: 8   SIGG CONTENTS: 5
16000214    INVALID YEAR                           CODEG CONTENTS: 4   SIGG CONTENTS: 5
14131983    INVALID MONTH                          CODEG CONTENTS: 6   SIGG CONTENTS: 4
29021983    INVALID DAY                            CODEG CONTENTS: 8   SIGG CONTENTS: 4
14023400    INVALID YEAR                           CODEG CONTENTS: 4   SIGG CONTENTS: 4
14001983    INVALID MONTH                          CODEG CONTENTS: 6   SIGG CONTENTS: 3
00021983    INVALID DAY                            CODEG CONTENTS: 8   SIGG CONTENTS: 3
14021600    INVALID YEAR                           CODEG CONTENTS: 4   SIGG CONTENTS: 3
13141983    INVALID MONTH                          CODEG CONTENTS: 6   SIGG CONTENTS: 2
02291983    INVALID DAY                            CODEG CONTENTS: 8   SIGG CONTENTS: 2
02143400    INVALID YEAR                           CODEG CONTENTS: 4   SIGG CONTENTS: 2
00141983    INVALID MONTH                          CODEG CONTENTS: 6   SIGG CONTENTS: 1
02001983    INVALID DAY                            CODEG CONTENTS: 8   SIGG CONTENTS: 1
02141600    INVALID YEAR                           CODEG CONTENTS: 2   SIGG CONTENTS: 1
            INVALID DATA
02141983    INVALID SIGG                           CODEG CONTENTS: 1   SIGG CONTENTS: M
02141983    INVALID SIGG                           CODEG CONTENTS: 1   SIGG CONTENTS: 7
02141983    INVALID SIGG

THE SUBROUTINE WAS EXECUTED     29 TIMES
```

**Figure 8.4**  Subset of TESTOG output that illustrates TIMESUBG's usefulness in converting formats among eight-digit dates.

## The Pseudocode for TIMESUB7

Here the subroutine assumes the receipt of a neo-Julian date in a seven-byte zoned field, NEOJIN. The components of NEOJIN, Y,E, must conform to the definitions for Y and for E as presented in chapter 3. The return code CODE7 is defined as one packed byte. Its contents indicate the following:

$$CODE7 = \begin{cases} 0, \text{ successful execution} \\ 2, \text{ invalid data in NEOJIN} \\ 4, \text{ invalid year in NEOJIN} \\ 6, \text{ invalid ordinal day, E, in NEOJIN} \end{cases}$$

The output field EXJULI is five packed bytes and contains zero in the presence of a nonzero return code. Otherwise, EXJULI contains the Commercial-8 equivalent of the neo-Julian date input via NEOJIN. Let's turn directly to the pseudocode:

```
 * Perform general housekeeping.
1) Let EXJULI = 0
2) Let CODE7 = 0
3) Let COUNTER = 0
 * Internal housekeeping.
4) Move NEOJIN to WORK7
 * Validate NEOJIN as numeric.
5) If NEOJIN is numeric, go to 7
6) Let CODE7 = 2, go to 27
 * Test Y for limit violation.
7) NEOJIN → Y, D
8) If Y is within limits per Commercial-8, go to 10
9) Let CODE7 = 4, go to 27
 * Perform leap year algorithm for Y.
10) Let L = 0
11) If Y is a leap year, let L = 1
 * Test E for limit violation.
12) If D is within limits per definition, go to 14
13) Let CODE7 = 6, go to 27
 * Convert neo-Julian to Gregorian.
 * First, find Gregorian month via table lookup.
14) Address second ENTRY of cumulative days table
15) If L = 1, address leap year ENTRY
16) Let COUNTER = COUNTER + 1
17) If D ⊁ ENTRY, go to 20
18) Address next ENTRY
19) Go to 16
20) Let M = COUNTER
 * Second, calculate Gregorian D value.
21) Address ENTRY prior to last addressed
22) Let Z = ENTRY
23) Let D = D - Z
 * Construct EXJULI for Output.
24) Let EXJULI = 1000000M
25) Let EXJULI = EXJULI + 10000D
26) Let EXJULI = EXJULI + Y
27) Exit
```

## The Source Code for TIMESUB7

Figure 8.5 displays the TIMESUB7 portion of TEST07's assembly post listing, and Figure 8.6 is a subset of the test results. All results were as predicted. Consequently, consider TIMESUB7 a valid algorithm. Because TIMESUB7 is a subset of TIMESUB5, we'll forego comments on the source code.

```
LOC   OBJECT CODE   ADDR1 ADDR2   STMT   SOURCE STATEMENT                                    DOS/VSE ASSEMBLER  16.25  99-12-31

                                  367  *  **********************************************************************  TS700010
                                  368  *                                                                         TS700020
                                  369  *                                                                         TS700030
                                  370  *  TTTTTT   III   MM    MM   EEEEE   SSSSS   U   U   BBBBB   77777  *      TS700040
                                  371  *    T       I    M M  M M   E       S       U   U   B   B       7  *      TS700050
                                  372  *    T       I    M  MM  M   EEEE    SSSSS   U   U   BBB B       7  *      TS700060
                                  373  *    T       I    M      M   E           S   U   U   B   B       7  *      TS700070
                                  374  *    T      III   M      M   EEEEE   SSSSS   UUUUU   BBBBB       7  *      TS700080
                                  375  *                                                                         TS700090
                                  376  *  **********************************************************************  TS700100
                                  377  *    N E O - J U L I A N  T O  G R E G O R I A N  C O N V E R S I O N  *   TS700110
                                  378  *                                                                         TS700120
                                  379  *  **********************************************************************  TS700130
                                  380  *  **********************************************************************  TS700140
                                  381  *                                                                         TS700150
                                  382  *        THIS SUBROUTINE CONVERTS A NEO-JULIAN DATE TO                *    TS700160
                                  383  *                    A GREGORIAN DATE                                *    TS700170
                                  384  *                                                                         TS700180
                                  385  *   1.  VALID INPUT YEARS FOR THIS SUBROUTINE ARE THE YEARS          *    TS700190
                                  386  *       1601 THROUGH 3399 A. D.                                      *    TS700200
                                  387  *                                                                         TS700210
                                  388  *   2.  VALID INPUT DAY VALUES FOR THIS SUBROUTINE ARE 001           *    TS700220
                                  389  *       THROUGH 365 EXCEPT FOR LEAP YEAR WHEN THE UPPER LIMIT        *    TS700230
                                  390  *       IS 366.                                                      *    TS700240
                                  391  *                                                                         TS700250
                                  392  *   3.  THE DATE FORMAT MUST BE YYYYDDD. WHERE YYYY = THE FOUR       *    TS700260
                                  393  *       DIGIT YEAR AND DDD = THE THREE DIGIT DAY VALUE.              *    TS700270
                                  394  *                                                                         TS700280
                                  395  *   4.  THE CALLING PROGRAM MUST PLACE THE SEVEN DIGIT NEO-JULIAN    *    TS700290
                                  396  *       DATE, IN ZONED DECIMAL, IN A SUBROUTINE DEFINED SEVEN        *    TS700300
                                  397  *       BYTE FIELD, 'NEOJIN.' NEOJIN IS NOT ALTERED BY THE           *    TS700310
                                  398  *       SUBROUTINE.                                                  *    TS700320
                                  399  *                                                                         TS700330
                                  400  *   5.  A SUBROUTINE DEFINED ONE BYTE FIELD, 'CODE7,' IS RETURNED    *    TS700340
                                  401  *       TO THE CALLING PROGRAM AS A RETURN CODE. IT CONTAINS         *    TS700350
                                  402  *       A PACKED 0 IF THE EXECUTION WAS SUCCESSFUL. NON-ZERO         *    TS700360
                                  403  *       VALUES INDICATE THE FOLLOWING:                               *    TS700370
                                  404  *                                                                         TS700380
                                  405  *       A PACKED 2 INDICATES UNSUCCESSFUL EXECUTION:  INVALID        *    TS700390
                                  406  *       DATA IN NEOJIN.                                              *    TS700400
                                  407  *                                                                         TS700410
                                  408  *       INVALID DATA ARE DETERMINED IF THE LOW ORDER BYTE'S ZONE     *    TS700420
                                  409  *       CONTAINS AN INVALID SIGN, (AN INVALID SIGN IS OTHER THAN     *    TS700430
                                  410  *       X'C', X'A', X'E', OR X'F',) OR IF THE PRECEDING BYTES'       *    TS700440
                                  411  *       ZONES ARE OTHER THAN X'F', OR IF THE LOW ORDER NIBBLE        *    TS700450
                                  412  *       OF ANY BYTE CONTAINS A VALUE GREATER THAN X'9'.              *    TS700460
                                  413  *                                                                         TS700470
                                  414  *       A PACKED 4 INDICATES UNSUCCESSFUL EXECUTION: INVALID         *    TS700480
                                  415  *       YEAR IN NEOJIN. YEAR VALUE VIOLATES THE LIMITS               *    TS700490
                                  416  *       SPECIFIED IN 1.. ABOVE.                                      *    TS700500
                                  417  *                                                                         TS700510
                                  418  *       A PACKED 6 INDICATES UNSUCCESSFUL EXECUTION: INVALID         *    TS700520
                                  419  *       DAY IN NEOJIN. DAY VALUE VIOLATES LIMITS SPECIFIED           *    TS700530
                                  420  *       IN 2.. ABOVE.                                                *    TS700540
                                  421  *                                                                         TS700550
```

**Figure 8.5**  The introductory documentation and source code of TIMESUB7 from the post listing of TEST07.

```
LOC    OBJECT CODE    ADDR1 ADDR2    STMT    SOURCE STATEMENT                                    DOS/VSE ASSEMBLER 16.25  99-12-31
```

```
                                      422 *      INSPECTION OF THE RETURN CODE IS IMPORTANT.  THE RETURN          * TS700560
                                      423 *      CODE, CODE7, REFLECTS THE LEVEL OF EDITING.  A RETURN           * TS700570
                                      424 *      CODE OF 2, FOR EXAMPLE, NOT ONLY INDICATES INVALIDITY OF       * TS700580
                                      425 *      DATA, IT ALSO INDICATES THAT NO EDITING HAS BEEN DONE TO       * TS700590
                                      426 *      VALIDATE THE YEAR, OR DAY VALUES.  A RETURN CODE OF 4          * TS700600
                                      427 *      INDICATES THAT THE DATA ARE VALID BUT THAT THE YEAR WAS       * TS700610
                                      428 *      FOUND INVALID- THE DAY VALUE HAS NOT BEEN EDITED.  A          * TS700620
                                      429 *      RETURN CODE OF 6 INDICATES THAT THE DATA AND YEAR ARE         * TS700630
                                      430 *      VALID BUT THAT THE DAY IS INVALID.                            * TS700640
                                      431 *                                                                    * TS700650
                                      432 *  6.  A SUBROUTINE DEFINED FIVE BYTE FIELD, 'EXJULI,' IS RE-       * TS700660
                                      433 *      TURNED TO THE CALLING PROGRAM.  THE CONVERTED DATE IS         * TS700670
                                      434 *      IN THIS FIELD IN PACKED FORMAT IF EXECUTION HAS BEEN SUC-     * TS700680
                                      435 *      CESSFUL.  IF EXECUTION IS UNSUCCESSFUL, THAT IS IF CODE7      * TS700690
                                      436 *      CONTAINS A NON-ZERO VALUE, THEN EXJULI WILL CONTAIN           * TS700700
                                      437 *      PACKED ZEROS.  THIS IS PROTECTION AGAINST ILLEGAL USE OF      * TS700710
                                      438 *      A PRIOR EXECUTION'S RESULT.                                   * TS700720
                                      439 *                                                                    * TS700730
                                      440 *  7.  ALL OTHER SUBROUTINE DEFINED FIELDS AND LABELS ARE           * TS700740
                                      441 *      TRANSPARENT TO THE CALLING PROGRAM.                           * TS700750
                                      442 *                                                                    * TS700760
                                      443 *  8.  THIS SUBROUTINE IS WRITTEN TO BE ASSEMBLED WITH THE          * TS700770
                                      444 *      CALLING PROGRAM AND SHOULD BE INSERTED IN THE CALLING         * TS700780
                                      445 *      PROGRAM IMMEDIATELY BEFORE THE 'END' OPCODE.                  * TS700790
                                      446 *                                                                    * TS700800
                                      447 *  9.  THIS SUBROUTINE USES REGISTER 6 AS THE LINK REGISTER.        * TS700810
                                      448 *      IF REGISTER 6 IS ASSIGNED IN THE CALLING PROGRAM FOR          * TS700820
                                      449 *      OTHER USES. IT MUST BE SAVED PRIOR TO EXECUTING THE          * TS700830
                                      450 *      'BALR.'                                                       * TS700840
                                      451 *                                                                    * TS700850
                                      452 *                                    JEROME T. MURRAY               * TS700860
                                      453 *                                    MARILYN J. MURRAY              * TS700870
                                      454 *  GLEN ELLYN, ILLINOIS                                              * TS700880
                                      455 *                                                                    * TS700890
                                      456 *********************************************************************  TS700900
                                      457 *                                                                       TS700910
                                      458 *                                                                       TS700920
                                      459 *********************************************************************  TS700930
                                      460 *      +++  SECTION 1- GENERAL HOUSEKEEPING  +++                       TS700940
                                      461 *                                                                       TS700950
                                      462 *                                                                       TS700960
                                      463 *      INITIALIZE INDICATIVE AND WORK FIELDS                            TS700970
                                      464 *                                                                       TS700980
000455 00
000456 F840 7500 76F0  005B6 007A6   465 TIMESUB7 ZAP    EXJULI,=P'0'                                              TS700990
00045C F800 750C 76F0  005C2 007A6   466          ZAP    CODE7,=P'0'                                               TS701000
000462 F810 765E 76F0  00714 007A6   467          ZAP    #$7MOCTR,=P'0'                                            TS701010
                                      468 *                                                                       TS701020
                                      469 *                                                                       TS701030
                                      470 *      SAVE REGISTERS 1 THROUGH 3 IN SAVE FIELDS                         TS701040
000468 9013 766E        00724        471          STM    1,3,#$7RSAVE                                              TS701050
                                      472 *                                                                       TS701060
                                      473 *      +++  SECTION 2- NUMERIC VALIDATION  +++                           TS701070
                                      474 *                                                                       TS701080
                                      475 *      MOVE NEO-JULIAN DATE TO WORK FIELD AND ISOLATE                    TS701090
```

```
LOC     OBJECT CODE      ADDR1  ADDR2  STMT  SOURCE STATEMENT                                          DOS/VSE ASSEMBLER 16.25  99-12-31

                                       476  *                          SIGN BYTE                                                          TS701100
                                       477  *                                                                                             TS701110
00046C  D206 7660 7505   00716  005BB  478          MVC   #$7WORK7,NEOJIN                                                                 TS701120
000472  D200 764E 7666   00704  0071C  479          MVC   #$7SIGN,#$7WORK7+6                                                              TS701130
                                       480  *                                                                                             TS701140
                                       481  *             AUGMENT TABLE FOR VALID '+' SIGNS OTHER THAN                                     TS701150
                                       482  *             X'F' FOR WHICH TABLE IS DEFINED: X'A', X'C'.                                     TS701160
                                       483  *             X'E'- EDIT FOR VALID '+' SIGN USING TRT                                          TS701170
                                       484  *                                                                                             TS701180
000478  D209 75E1 7641   00697  006F7  485          MVC   #$7TABL+160(10),#$7ZRD                                                          TS701190
00047E  D209 7601 7641   006B7  006F7  486          MVC   #$7TABL+192(10),#$7ZRD                                                          TS701200
000484  D209 7621 7641   006D7  006F7  487          MVC   #$7TABL+224(10),#$7ZRO                                                          TS701210
00048A  DD00 764E 7541   00704  005F7  488          TRT   #$7SIGN(1),#$7TABL                                                              TS701230
000490  4780 73E2        00498         489          BC    8,#$7NUM                                                                        TS701240
000494  47F0 73F6        004AC         490          B     #$7BDATA                                                                        TS701250
                                       491  *                                                                                             TS701260
                                       492  *             REINITIALIZE TABLE AND EDIT FOR VALID ZONE                                      TS701270
                                       493  *             AND DIGIT CONFIGURATIONS IN REMAINING BYTES                                     TS701280
                                       494  *                                                                                             TS701290
000498  921C 7541        005F7         495  #$7NUM   MVI   #$7TABL,X'1C'                                                                   TS701300
00049C  D2EE 7542 7541   005F8  005F7  496          MVC   #$7TABL+1(239),#$7TABL                                                          TS701310
0004A2  DD05 7660 7541   00716  005F7  497          TRT   #$7WORK7(6),#$7TABL                                                             TS701320
0004A8  4780 7400        004B6         498          BC    8,#$7PACK                                                                       TS701330
                                       499  *                                                                                             TS701340
                                       500  *             POST 'BAD DATA' RETURN CODE AND EXIT                                            TS701350
                                       501  *                                                                                             TS701360
0004AC  F800 750C 76F1   005C2  007A7  502  #$7BDATA ZAP   CODE7,=P'2'                                                                     TS701370
0004B2  47F0 767A        00730         503          B     #$7TERM                                                                         TS701380
                                       504  *                                                                                             TS701390
                                       505  *       +++ SECTION 3- EDIT YEAR FOR LIMIT VIOLATIONS +++                                      TS701400
                                       506  *                                                                                             TS701410
                                       507  *             PACK YEAR AND JULIAN DAYS IN WORK FIELDS                                         TS701420
                                       508  *                                                                                             TS701430
0004B6  F223 765B 7660   00711  00716  509  #$7PACK  PACK  #$7YR,#$7WORK7(4)                                                               TS701440
0004BC  F212 7659 7664   0070F  0071A  510          PACK  #$7DA,#$7WORK7+4(3)                                                             TS701450
                                       511  *                                                                                             TS701460
                                       512  *             EDIT YEAR VALUE FOR LOWER LIMIT VIOLATION                                        TS701470
                                       513  *                                                                                             TS701480
0004C2  F922 765B 772F   00711  007E5  514          CP    #$7YR,=P'1600'                                                                  TS701490
0004C8  4720 7420        004D6         515          BH    #$7YRHI                                                                         TS701500
                                       516  *                                                                                             TS701510
                                       517  *             INSTALL 'BAD YEAR' RETURN CODE AND EXIT                                         TS701520
                                       518  *                                                                                             TS701530
0004CC  F800 750C 76F2   005C2  007A8  519  #$7BADYR ZAP   CODE7,=P'4'                                                                     TS701540
0004D2  47F0 767A        00730         520          B     #$7TERM                                                                         TS701550
                                       521  *                                                                                             TS701560
                                       522  *             EDIT YEAR VALUE FOR UPPER LIMIT VIOLATION                                        TS701570
                                       523  *                                                                                             TS701580
0004D6  F922 765B 7732   00711  007E8  524  #$7YRHI  CP    #$7YR,=P'3399'                                                                  TS701590
0004DC  4720 7416        004CC         525          BH    #$7BADYR                                                                        TS701600
                                       526  *                                                                                             TS701610
                                       527  *       +++ SECTION 4- DETERMINE LEAP YEAR STATUS +++                                         TS701620
                                       528  *                                                                                             TS701630
                                       529  *             EXECUTE LEAP YEAR ALGORITHM                                                      TS701640
                                       530  *
```

**Figure 8.5** *Continued*

```
LOC    OBJECT CODE     ADDR1 ADDR2  STMT  SOURCE STATEMENT

0004E0 F800 764D 76F0 00703 007A6   531           ZAP   #$7L,=P'0'                                              TS701650
0004E6 F842 7667 765B 0071D 00711   532           ZAP   #$7WORK,#$7YR                                           TS701660
0004EC FD40 7667 76F2 0071D 007A8   533           DP    #$7WORK,=P'4'                                           TS701670
0004F2 F900 766B 76F0 00721 007A6   534           CP    #$7WORK+4(1),=P'0'                                      TS701680
0004F8 4720 7478       0052E        535           BH    #$7DAEDT                                                TS701690
0004FC F842 7667 765B 0071D 00711   536           ZAP   #$7WORK,#$7YR                                           TS701700
000502 FD41 7667 76E2 0071D 00798   537           DP    #$7WORK,=P'100'                                         TS701710
000508 F910 766A 76F0 00720 007A6   538           CP    #$7WORK+3(2),=P'0'                                      TS701720
00050E 4720 7472       00528        539           BH    #$7LPYR                                                 TS701730
000512 F842 7667 765B 0071D 00711   540           ZAP   #$7WORK,#$7YR                                           TS701740
000518 FD41 7667 76E4 0071D 0079A   541           DP    #$7WORK,=P'400'                                         TS701750
00051E F910 766A 76F0 00720 007A6   542           CP    #$7WORK+3(2),=P'0'                                      TS701760
000524 4720 7478       0052E        543           BH    #$7DAEDT                                                TS701770
                                    544   *                                                                     TS701780
                                    545   *          IF YEAR IS A LEAP YEAR, REINITIALIZE TO 1                  TS701790
                                    546   *          ELSE INITIALIZED O REMAINS                                 TS701800
                                    547   *                                                                     TS701810
000528 F800 764D 76EE 00703 007A4   548   #$7LPYR  ZAP   #$7L,=P'1'                                             TS701820
                                    549   *                                                                     TS701830
                                    550   *     +++ SECTION 5- EDIT DAY FOR LIMIT VIOLATIONS  +++               TS701840
                                    551   *                                                                     TS701850
                                    552   *          EDIT DAY VALUE FOR LOWER LIMIT VIOLATION                   TS701860
                                    553   *                                                                     TS701870
00052E F911 7659 76E6 0070F 0079C   554   #$7DAEDT CP    #$7DA,=P'000'                                          TS701880
000534 4720 748C       00542        555           BH    #$7HIVAL                                               TS701890
                                    556   *                                                                     TS701900
                                    557   *          POST BAD DAY RETURN CODE AND EXIT                          TS701910
                                    558   *                                                                     TS701920
000538 F800 750C 76F3 005C2 007A9   559   #$7BADA  ZAP   CODE7,=P'6'                                            TS701930
00053E 47F0 767A       00730        560           B     #$7TERM                                                TS701940
                                    561   *                                                                     TS701950
                                    562   *          EDIT DAY VALUE FOR UPPER LIMIT VIOLATION                   TS701960
                                    563   *                                                                     TS701970
000542 F900 764D 76F0 00703 007A6   564   #$7HIVAL CP    #$7L,=P'0'                                             TS701980
000548 4720 74A0       00556        565           BH    #$7DAHI                                                TS701990
00054C F911 7659 76E8 0070F 0079E   566           CP    #$7DA,=P'365'                                          TS702000
000552 4720 7482       00538        567           BH    #$7BADA                                                TS702010
000556 F911 7659 76EA 0070F 007A0   568   #$7DAHI  CP    #$7DA,=P'366'                                          TS702020
00055C 4720 7482       00538        569           BH    #$7BADA                                                TS702030
                                    570   *                                                                     TS702040
                                    571   *     +++ SECTION 6- CONVERT NEO-JULIAN TO GREGORIAN  +++             TS702050
                                    572   *                                                                     TS702060
                                    573   *          FIND GREGORIAN MONTH                                       TS702070
                                    574   *                                                                     TS702080
                                    575   *          A) LOAD ADDRESS OF SECOND ENTRY OF DAYS TABLE              TS702090
                                    576   *             INTO REGISTER 3                                         TS702100
                                    577   *                                                                     TS702110
000560 4130 7511       005C7        578           LA    3,#$7DAYS+4                                            TS702120
                                    579   *                                                                     TS702130
                                    580   *          B) IF LEAP YEAR, INCREMENT TO LEAP YEAR                    TS702140
                                    581   *             FUNCTION                                                TS702150
                                    582   *                                                                     TS702160
000564 F900 764D 76F0 00703 007A6   583           CP    #$7L,=P'0'                                             TS702170
00056A 4780 74BC       00572        584           BE    #$7COUNT                                               TS702180
00056E 4133 0002       00002        585           LA    3,2(3)                                                 TS702190
```

```
LOC     OBJECT CODE          ADDR1 ADDR2  STMT  SOURCE STATEMENT                          DOS/VSE ASSEMBLER 16.25  99-12-31

                                           586  *                                                                            TS702200
                                           587  *          C) COUNT AND COMPARE- IF #$7DA IS NOT LARGER,                     TS702210
                                           588  *             EXIT LOOP                                                      TS702220
                                           589  *                                                                            TS702230
000572 FA10 765E 76EE  00714 007A4         590  #$7COUNT  AP  #$7MOCTR,=P'1'                                                 TS702240
000578 F911 7659 3000  0070F 00000         591            CP  #$7DA,O(2,3)                                                   TS702250
00057E 47D0 74D4       0058A               592            BNH #$7GOTNU                                                       TS702260
                                           593  *                                                                            TS702270
                                           594  *          D) ELSE, LOAD ADDRESS OF NEXT TABLE ENTRY                        TS702280
                                           595  *             INTO REGSTER 3 AND DO LOOP                                     TS702290
                                           596  *                                                                            TS702300
000582 4133 0004                           597            LA  3,4(3)                                                         TS702310
000586 47F0 74BC       00572               598            B   #$7COUNT                                                       TS702320
                                           599  *                                                                            TS702330
                                           600  *          F) COUNTER CONTAINS THE NEW MONTH, TRANSFER                      TS702340
                                           601  *             TO #$7MO                                                       TS702350
                                           602  *                                                                            TS702360
00058A FB11 7657 765E  0070D 00714         603  #$7GOTNU  ZAP #$7MO,#$7MOCTR                                                 TS702370
                                           604  *                                                                            TS702380
                                           605  *          G) DECREMENT REGISTER 3 ADDRESS TO PRIOR                         TS702390
                                           606  *             TABLE ENTRY                                                    TS702400
                                           607  *                                                                            TS702410
000590 4B30 76EC       007A2               608            SH  3,=H'4'                                                        TS702420
                                           609  *                                                                            TS702430
                                           610  *          H) SUBTRACT THIS TABLE ENTRY FROM JULIAN                         TS702440
                                           611  *             DAYS IN #$7DA TO FIND GREGORIAN DAYS                          TS702450
                                           612  *                                                                            TS702460
000594 FB11 7659 3000  0070F 00000         613            SP  #$7DA,O(2.3)                                                   TS702470
                                           614  *                                                                            TS702480
                                           615  *          CREATE OUTPUT FIELD- EXJULI                                       TS702490
                                           616  *                                                                            TS702500
00059A F372 764F 765B  00705 00711         617  #$7BUILD  UNPK #$7WORK8,#$7YR                                               TS702510
0005A0 F311 7651 7659  00707 0070F         618            UNPK #$7WORK8+2(2),#$7DA                                          TS702520
0005A6 F311 764F 7657  00705 0070D         619            UNPK #$7WORK8(2),#$7MO                                            TS702530
0005AC F247 7500 764F  005B6 00705         620            PACK EXJULI,#$7WORK8                                              TS702540
                                           621  *                                                                            TS702550
                                           622  *          +++ SECTION 7- TO RESTORE REGISTERS AND EXIT  +++               TS702560
                                           623  *                                                                            TS702570
0005B2 47F0 767A       00730               624            B   #$7TERM                                                       TS702580
                                           625  *                                                                            TS702590
                                           626  *          +++ SECTION 8- DEFINE CONSTANTS AND STORAGE  +++                TS702600
                                           627  *                                                                            TS702610
0005B6 000000000C                          628  EXJULI    DC  PL5'0'                                                         TS702620
0005BB FOFOFOFOFOFOCO                       629  NEDJIN    DC  ZL7'0000000'                                                   TS702630
0005C2 2C                                  630  CODE7     DC  PL1'2'                                                          TS702640
                                           631  *                                                                            TS702650
                                           632  *          THE DAYS TABLE IS DEFINED WITH A PAIR OF TWO                     TS702660
                                           633  *          BYTE ENTRIES FOR EACH OF THE 12 MONTHS CONTAIN-                  TS702670
                                           634  *          ING THE CUMULATIVE NUMBER OF DAYS EXPIRED AT                     TS702680
                                           635  *          THE END OF THE PRIOR MONTH- NON-LEAP YEAR AND                    TS702690
                                           636  *          LEAP YEAR                                                         TS702700
                                           637  *                                                                            TS702710
0005C3 000C000C                            638  #$7DAYS   DC  PL2'00',PL2'00'          JAN                                   TS702720
0005C7 031C031C                            639            DC  PL2'31',PL2'31'          FEB                                   TS702730
0005CB 059C060C                            640            DC  PL2'59',PL2'60'          MAR                                   TS702740
```

**Figure 8.5** *Continued*

```
LOC    OBJECT CODE         ADDR1  ADDR2   STMT  SOURCE STATEMENT                      DOS/VSE ASSEMBLER 16.25 99-12-31

0005CF 090C091C                            641        DC    PL2'90',PL2'91'           APR                  TS702750
0005D3 120C121C                            642        DC    PL2'120',PL2'121'         MAY                  TS702760
0005D7 151C152C                            643        DC    PL2'151',PL2'152'         JUN                  TS702770
0005DB 181C182C                            644        DC    PL2'181',PL2'182'         JUL                  TS702780
0005DF 212C213C                            645        DC    PL2'212',PL2'213'         AUG                  TS702790
0005E3 243C244C                            646        DC    PL2'243',PL2'244'         SEP                  TS702800
0005E7 273C274C                            647        DC    PL2'273',PL2'274'         OCT                  TS702810
0005EB 304C305C                            648        DC    PL2'304',PL2'305'         NOV                  TS702820
0005EF 334C335C                            649        DC    PL2'334',PL2'335'         DEC                  TS702830
0005F3 999C999C                            650        DC    PL2'999',PL2'999'         END                  TS702840
                                           651 *                                                           TS702850
                                           652 *            TRANSLATION TABLE DEFINED FOR X'F0' - X'F9'     TS702860
                                           653 *            (ALL TABLE POSITIONS EXCEPT THOSE CORRESPONDING TS702870
                                           654 *            TO X'F0' THROUGH X'F9' ARE SET TO A VALUE OTHER TS702880
                                           655 *            THAN X'00')                                     TS702890
                                           656 *                                                           TS702900
0005F7 1C1C1C1C1C1C1C1C              657 #$7TABL  DC    240X'1C'                                            TS702910
0006E7 0000000000000000             658        DC    10X'00'                                               TS702920
0006F1 1C1C1C1C1C1C                 659        DC    6X'1C'                                                 TS702930
                                           660 *                                                           TS702940
0006F7 000000000000000000           661 #$7ZRO   DC    12X'00'                                             TS702950
000703                                     662 #$7L     DS    PL1                                          TS702960
000704                                     663 #$7SIGN  DS    ZL1                                          TS702970
000705                                     664 #$7WORK8 DS    ZL8                                          TS702980
00070D                                     665 #$7MO    DS    PL2                                          TS702990
00070F                                     666 #$7DA    DS    PL2                                          TS703000
000711                                     667 #$7YR    DS    PL3                                          TS703010
000714                                     668 #$7MOCTR DS    PL2                                          TS703020
000716                                     669 #$7WORK7 DS    PL7                                          TS703030
00071D                                     670 #$7WORK  DS    PL5                                          TS703040
000724                                     671 #$7RSAVE DS    3F                                           TS703050
000730 9813 766E          00724            672 #$7TERM  LM    1,3,#$7RSAVE                                 TS703060
000734 07F6               000B4            673        BR    6                                              TS703070
                                           674        END
                                           675        BEGIN
000738 5B5BC2D6D7C5D540                    676        =C'$$BOPEN '
000740 C9D5E5C1D3C9C440                    677        =C'INVALID DATA **********'
000758 C9D5E5C1D3C9C440                    678        =C'INVALID YEAR **********'
000770 C9D5E5C1D3C9C440                    679        =C'INVALID DAY ***********'
000788 5B5BC2C3D3D6E2C5                    680        =C'$$BCLOSE'
000790 00000080                           681        =A(REQUEST)
000794 00000000                           682        =A(LIST)
000798 100C                               683        =P'100'
00079A 400C                               684        =P'400'
00079C 000C                               685        =P'000'
00079E 365C                               686        =P'365'
0007A0 366C                               687        =P'366'
0007A2 0004                               688        =H'4'
0007A4 1C                                 689        =P'1'
0007A5 4B                                 690        =C'.'
0007A6 0C                                 691        =P'0'
0007A7 2C                                 692        =P'2'
0007A8 4C                                 693        =P'4'
0007A9 6C                                 694        =P'6'
0007AA E2E4C2D9D6E4E3C9                   694        =C'SUBROUTINE ERROR ******'
0007C1 C3D6C4C5F740C3D6                   695        =C'CODE7 CONTENTS '
```

**Figure 8.5** *Continued*

```
TEST OF TIMESUB7 TO CONVERT A NEO-JULIAN DATE TO GREGORIAN DATE

NEO-JULIAN   GREGORIAN-VALIDATION COMMENTS                 CODE7 CONTENTS 0.   EXJULI CONTENTS..01041999
1999.004     1/04/1999                                     CODE7 CONTENTS 0.   EXJULI CONTENTS..01041999
1999.006     1/06/1999                                     CODE7 CONTENTS 0.   EXJULI CONTENTS..01061999
1999.001     1/01/1999                                     CODE7 CONTENTS 0.   EXJULI CONTENTS..01011999
1999.031     1/31/1999                                     CODE7 CONTENTS 0.   EXJULI CONTENTS..01311999
1999.059     2/28/1999                                     CODE7 CONTENTS 0.   EXJULI CONTENTS..02281999
1999.060     3/01/1999                                     CODE7 CONTENTS 0.   EXJULI CONTENTS..03011999
1999.090     3/31/1999                                     CODE7 CONTENTS 0.   EXJULI CONTENTS..03311999
1999.120     4/30/1999                                     CODE7 CONTENTS 0.   EXJULI CONTENTS..04301999
1999.151     5/31/1999                                     CODE7 CONTENTS 0.   EXJULI CONTENTS..05311999
1999.181     6/30/1999                                     CODE7 CONTENTS 0.   EXJULI CONTENTS..06301999
1999.212     7/31/1999                                     CODE7 CONTENTS 0.   EXJULI CONTENTS..07311999
1999.243     8/31/1999                                     CODE7 CONTENTS 0.   EXJULI CONTENTS..08311999
1999.273     9/30/1999                                     CODE7 CONTENTS 0.   EXJULI CONTENTS..09301999
1999.304     10/31/1999                                    CODE7 CONTENTS 0.   EXJULI CONTENTS..10311999
1999.334     11/30/1999                                    CODE7 CONTENTS 0.   EXJULI CONTENTS..11301999
1996.366     12/31/1996                                    CODE7 CONTENTS 0.   EXJULI CONTENTS..12311996
2000.060     2/29/2000                                     CODE7 CONTENTS 0.   EXJULI CONTENTS..02292000
2000.091     3/31/2000                                     CODE7 CONTENTS 0.   EXJULI CONTENTS..03312000
2000.121     4/30/2000                                     CODE7 CONTENTS 0.   EXJULI CONTENTS..04302000
2000.152     5/31/2000                                     CODE7 CONTENTS 0.   EXJULI CONTENTS..05312000
2000.182     6/30/2000                                     CODE7 CONTENTS 0.   EXJULI CONTENTS..06302000
2000.213     7/31/2000                                     CODE7 CONTENTS 0.   EXJULI CONTENTS..07312000
2000.244     8/31/2000                                     CODE7 CONTENTS 0.   EXJULI CONTENTS..08312000
2000.274     9/30/2000                                     CODE7 CONTENTS 0.   EXJULI CONTENTS..09302000
2000.305     10/31/2000                                    CODE7 CONTENTS 0.   EXJULI CONTENTS..10312000
2000.325     11/20/2000                                    CODE7 CONTENTS 0.   EXJULI CONTENTS..11202000
2001.115     4/25/2001                                     CODE7 CONTENTS 0.   EXJULI CONTENTS..04252001
2002.225     8/13/2002                                     CODE7 CONTENTS 0.   EXJULI CONTENTS..08132002
2003.145     5/25/2003                                     CODE7 CONTENTS 0.   EXJULI CONTENTS..05252003
2004.035     2/04/2004                                     CODE7 CONTENTS 0.   EXJULI CONTENTS..02042004
2005.305     11/01/2005                                    CODE7 CONTENTS 0.   EXJULI CONTENTS..11012005
2006.315     11/11/2006                                    CODE7 CONTENTS 0.   EXJULI CONTENTS..11112006
2007.325     11/21/2007                                    CODE7 CONTENTS 0.   EXJULI CONTENTS..11212007
2008.035     2/04/2008                                     CODE7 CONTENTS 0.   EXJULI CONTENTS..02042008
2009.005     1/05/2009                                     CODE7 CONTENTS 0.   EXJULI CONTENTS..01052009
2022.235     8/23/2022                                     CODE7 CONTENTS 0.   EXJULI CONTENTS..08232022
2022.031     1/31/2022                                     CODE7 CONTENTS 0.   EXJULI CONTENTS..01312022
2024.300     10/26/2024                                    CODE7 CONTENTS 0.   EXJULI CONTENTS..10262024
2399.325     11/21/2399                                    CODE7 CONTENTS 0.   EXJULI CONTENTS..11212399
1999.000     INVALID DAY ***********                       CODE7 CONTENTS 6.   EXJULI CONTENTS..00000000
1600.001     INVALID YEAR **********                       CODE7 CONTENTS 4.   EXJULI CONTENTS..00000000
1601.366     INVALID DAY ***********                       CODE7 CONTENTS 6.   EXJULI CONTENTS..00000000
1601.365     12/31/1601                                    CODE7 CONTENTS 0.   EXJULI CONTENTS..12311601
3400.001     INVALID YEAR **********                       CODE7 CONTENTS 4.   EXJULI CONTENTS..00000000

THE SUBROUTINE WAS EXECUTED    44 TIMES
```

**Figure 8.6** A subset of test results from TEST07's execution that uses TIMESUB7 to convert neo-Julian to Gregorian dates.

## Application of TIMESUBG, TIMESUB7, and TIMESUB5

There are multiple possible ways to use TIMESUBG. A sequence could include:

1. The calling program accesses the system date.
2. If the system date is a six-digit date, TIMESUBF is called.
3. The now eight-digit system date is provided with a negative 30-day parameter.
4. TIMESUB5 is called and the 30-day-old standard date is calculated from the system date and the parameter.
5. TIMESUBG is called to reformat the 30-day-old standard date from Commercial-8 to FIPS-8.
6. The calling program reads neo-Julian date-bearing records for aging.
7. The input date is transformed to $01/01/y + ddd - 1$.
8. TIMESUB5 is called to convert the transformed date to Commercial-8.
9. TIMESUBG is called to reformat to FIPS-8.
10. If the FIPS-8 input date is less than the standard, the record is overage.
11. TIMESUBG is called to reformat the input date's FIPS-8 image to European-8 for output to the statement.

You could create a similar sequence involving aging via TIMESUB3 to use TIMESUB7 instead of TIMESUB5. Just omit step 7 from the programming requirements. The subroutines and their macro counterparts are intended to be highly flexible time-savers. Like extended mnemonics, they're at your disposal.

# The Algorithm of Easter

The date of Easter determines the dates for Good Friday and Easter Monday, both of which are internationally recognized and celebrated holidays. The importance of Easter to the designer of the Easter algorithm, however, was of an entirely different nature.

In his Karl Friedrich Gauss: Titan of Science (1955:69), Guy Waldo Dunnington tells of Gauss's mathematical search for his birthday. Karl's mother was unable to recall the exact date of his birth. However, like most Christians of the time, she knew its precise relationship to the nearest Christian feast. Gauss had been born exactly eight days prior to Easter. The key to finding his birthday was in first finding the date of Easter that year.

During 1800 Gauss formulated an algorithm to allow him to calculate the date of Easter for any given year. Thus, he determined the date of his birth as it related to Easter in the year he was born. Like most of Gauss's accomplishments, the Easter algorithm required the reconciliation of diverse and seemingly unrelated facts from astronomy, church practice in the use of the *computus* (an ecclesiastical method of calculating the date of Easter), and an intimate knowledge of Gregorian-calendar architecture.

Moyer (1982:142), however, stated that even Gauss didn't succeed in developing a complete algorithm for the Easter calculation. His research had apparently led him to believe that the sheer difficulty of formulating an algorithm for Easter would exceed the grasp of even one of mathematics' most fertile minds. Not so!

It's pure conjecture to think that it was Gauss's preoccupation with the Gregorian calendar and its inconstant moduli that gave birth to the concept of residue classes. But if it truly was this that planted the seeds in his mind, then we've certainly been adequately compensated for the difficulties in contending with the unpleasant irregularities of our calendar. For Gauss is the father of modular arithmetic.

## The Design of the Gaussian Easter Algorithm

The calculations for the occurrence of Easter in any given year require a number of findings preliminary to the final calculation of the exact date. The golden number or position of the given year in the metonic cycle must first be computed. The golden number is subsequently used to calculate the position of the calendar moon. The number of non-leap-year centesimals must also be calculated.

Two additional calculations involve finding the Clavian correction for the metonic cycle—approximately eight days for every 2,500 years—and finally the *epact*, or age of the moon as of the first day of the given year. From the epact, the value of D is calculated. If D ≤ 31, the date of Easter is March D, YYYY. If D > 31, the date of Easter is April (D − 31), YYYY.

As is usually the case, constants in an algorithm are the key to its acuity. A detailed explanation of the constants in the Easter algorithm would take us far afield and offer little reward in regard to the current problem. Instead, we'll proceed directly to definitions of the algorithm's elements and the pseudocode.

## The Pseudocode for TIMESUB8, the Easter Algorithm

The subroutine assumes that its input were provided in a four-byte zoned field, EYEAR. EYEAR must contain the year for which the date of Easter is sought: EYEAR ε {y: y belongs to Z and 1600 < y < 3400}. A return code field, one-byte packed, is returned to the calling program. The return code CODE8 can contain any of the following values:

$$CODE8 = \begin{cases} 0, \text{If the execution is successful} \\ 2, \text{If EYEAR is non-numeric} \\ 4, \text{If EYEAR is not within the specified limits} \end{cases}$$

The result field EASTER is a five-byte packed field and contains zero in the presence of a nonzero return code. Otherwise, EASTER contains the date of Easter Sunday for the input year. EASTER is in Commercial-8 format. The pseudocode performs as follows:

```
   * General housekeeping.
  1) Let CODE8 = 0
  2) Let EASTER = 0
   * Internal housekeeping.
  3) Move EYEAR to WORK4
   * Validate EYEAR as numeric.
  4) If EYEAR is numeric, go to 6
  5) Let CODE8 = 2, go to 34
   * Test EYEAR for limit violation.
  6) EYEAR → Y
  7) If Y is within limits per Commercial-8, go to 9
  8) Let CODE8 = 4, go to 34
   * Compute century of EYEAR, CENT.
  9) Let CENT = (Y ÷ 100) + 1
   * Compute non-leap-year centesimals, NONL.
 10) Let T2 = 3((Y - 1600) ÷ 400)
 11) Let T3 = ((Y - 1600)(Mod 400)) ÷ 100
 12) Let NONL = T2 + T3
```

```
    * Compute EYEAR's position in metonic cycle, MET.
13) Let MET = Y(Mod 19) + 1
    * Compute correction for metonic cycle, METC.
14) Let METC = [(8CENT + 5) ÷ 25 - (5 + NONL)]
    * Compute day-count modifier, DMOD.
15) Let DMOD = [5Y ÷ 4 - (NONL + 10)]
    * Compute the EPACT.
16) Let EPACT = (11MET + 20 + METC)(Mod 30)
    * Determine EPACT value.
17) If EPACT ≠ 25, go to 20
    * Determine metonic cycle position for EPACT adjustment.
18) If MET ≯ 11, go to 20
19) Let EPACT = EPACT + 1
    * Determine EPACT value for adjustment.
20) If EPACT ≠ 24, go to 22
21) Let EPACT = EPACT + 1
    * Compute value of DAY.
22) Let DAY = 44 - EPACT
    * Determine DAY value for adjustment.
23) If DAY ≮ 21, go to 25
24) Let DAY = DAY + 30
    * Compute EASTER.
    * Find modified DAY value.
25) Let DAY = DAY + 7 - (DAY + DMOD)(Mod 7)
    * Find exact date.
26) If DAY ≯ 31, go to 31
27) Let EASTER = 4000000
28) Let EASTER = EASTER + 10000(DAY - 31)
29) Let EASTER = EASTER + Y
30) Go to 34
31) Let EASTER = 3000000
32) Let EASTER = EASTER + 10000(DAY)
33) Let EASTER = EASTER + Y
34) Exit
```

## The Source Code for TIMESUB8

Figure 9.1 displays the TIMESUB8 portion of TEST08's assembly post listing, and Figure 9.2 shows a subset of the test results from the test of TIMESUB8. All years 1601 through 3399 were submitted to TIMESUB8. Results were compared with published Easter dates in various almanacs and, insofar as these dates were available (1900 through 2100), all results agreed. Therefore, we deem TIMESUB8 a valid algorithm. The source code closely follows the pseudocode in a rather straightforward translation to ALC.

## Application of TIMESUB8

TIMESUB8 clearly provides a basis for the location of movable Christian feast days. Beyond this, there are commercial applications that are discussed in the following chapter.

In lieu of the availability of TIMESUB8, calendar files have been popular for providing holiday date information. These files, beyond their maintenance requirements, have the added overhead of increased I/O activity—an unwelcome element in online applications. Chapter 10 demonstrates an alternative.

```
LOC   OBJECT CODE   ADDR1 ADDR2   STMT   SOURCE STATEMENT                              DOS/VSE ASSEMBLER 16.27 99-12-31

                                  364  *******************************************************************  TS800010
                                  365  *******************************************************************  TS800020
                                  366  *                                                                 *  TS800030
                                  367  *  TTTTTT  III  MM    MM  EEEE  SSSS  BBBBB  88                    *  TS800040
                                  368  *    T      I   M M  M M  E     S     B   B  8 8                   *  TS800050
                                  369  *    T      I   M  M M M  EEE   SSSS  BBB B  88                    *  TS800060
                                  370  *    T      I   M   M  M  E        S  B   B  8 8                   *  TS800070
                                  371  *    T     III  M      M  EEEE  SSSS  BBBB   88                    *  TS800080
                                  372  *                                                                 *  TS800090
                                  373  *******************************************************************  TS800100
                                  374  *                  E A S T E R   S U B R O U T I N E              *  TS800110
                                  375  *******************************************************************  TS800120
                                  376  *                                                                 *  TS800130
                                  377  *                                                                 *  TS800140
                                  378  *******************************************************************  TS800150
                                  379  *                                                                 *  TS800160
                                  380  *     THIS SUBROUTINE CALCULATES THE DATE OF EASTER               *  TS800170
                                  381  *                                                                 *  TS800180
                                  382  *  1.  VALID INPUT YEARS FOR THIS SUBROUTINE ARE THE YEARS        *  TS800190
                                  383  *      1601 THROUGH 3399 A.D.                                     *  TS800200
                                  384  *                                                                 *  TS800210
                                  385  *  2.  THE CALLING PROGRAM MUST PLACE A POSITIVE FOUR DIGIT       *  TS800220
                                  386  *      YEAR, IN ZONED DECIMAL, IN A SUBROUTINE DEFINED FOUR       *  TS800230
                                  387  *      BYTE FIELD, 'EYEAR,' BEFORE EXECUTION.  EYEAR IS NOT       *  TS800240
                                  388  *      ALTERED BY THE SUBROUTINE.                                 *  TS800250
                                  389  *                                                                 *  TS800260
                                  390  *  3.  A SUBROUTINE DEFINED ONE BYTE FIELD, 'CODE8,' IS           *  TS800270
                                  391  *      RETURNED TO THE CALLING PROGRAM AS A RETURN CODE.          *  TS800280
                                  392  *                                                                 *  TS800290
                                  393  *      A PACKED 0 INDICATES SUCCESSFUL EXECUTION OF THE SUB-      *  TS800300
                                  394  *      ROUTINE.                                                   *  TS800310
                                  395  *                                                                 *  TS800320
                                  396  *      A PACKED 2 INDICATES UNSUCCESSFUL EXECUTION: INVALID       *  TS800330
                                  397  *      DATA IN EYEAR.                                             *  TS800340
                                  398  *                                                                 *  TS800350
                                  399  *      INVALID DATA ARE DETERMINED IF THE FIELD'S LOW ORDER       *  TS800360
                                  400  *      BYTE'S ZONE CONTAINS AN INVALID SIGN, (NOT ONE OF          *  TS800370
                                  401  *      X'C', X'A', X'E', OR X'F'), OR IF THE PRECEDING BYTES'     *  TS800380
                                  402  *      ZONES ARE OTHER THAN X'F', OR IF ANY BYTE'S LOW ORDER      *  TS800390
                                  403  *      NIBBLE CONTAINS A VALUE GREATER THAN X'9'.                 *  TS800400
                                  404  *                                                                 *  TS800410
                                  405  *      A PACKED 4 INDICATES UNSUCCESSFUL EXECUTION: THE VALUE     *  TS800420
                                  406  *      OF EYEAR VIOLATES THE LIMITS SPECIFIED IN 1.. ABOVE.       *  TS800430
                                  407  *                                                                 *  TS800440
                                  408  *  4.  A SUBROUTINE DEFINED, FIVE BYTE FIELD, 'EASTER,' IS        *  TS800450
                                  409  *      RETURNED TO THE CALLING PROGRAM AND CONTAINS THE PACKED    *  TS800460
                                  410  *      DATE OF EASTER FOR THE INPUT YEAR IN MMDDYYYY FORMAT.      *  TS800470
                                  411  *      IF THE EXECUTION WAS UNSUCCESSFUL, THAT IS IF THE RETURN   *  TS800480
                                  412  *      CODE FIELQ, CODE8, CONTAINS A NON-ZERO VALUE, THEN EASTER  *  TS800490
                                  413  *      WILL CONTAIN PACKED ZEROS AS PROTECTION AGAINST ILLEGAL    *  TS800500
                                  414  *      USE OF A PRIOR EXECUTION'S RESULT.                         *  TS800510
                                  415  *                                                                 *  TS800520
                                  416  *  5.  ALL OTHER SUBROUTINE DEFINED FIELDS AND LABELS ARE         *  TS800530
                                  417  *      TRANSPARENT TO THE CALLING PROGRAM.                        *  TS800540
                                  418  *  6.  THIS SUBROUTINE IS WRITTEN TO BE ASSEMBLED WITH THE        *  TS800550
```

```
LOC     OBJECT CODE      ADDR1 ADDR2  STMT   SOURCE STATEMENT                                    DOS/VSE ASSEMBLER  16.27  99-12-31

                                      419  *            CALLING PROGRAM AND SHOULD BE INSERTED IN THE CALLING      TS800560
                                      420  *            PROGRAM IMMEDIATELY BEFORE THE 'END' OPCODE.               TS800570
                                      421  *                                                                      TS800580
                                      422  *      7.    THIS SUBROUTINE USES REGISTER 6 AS THE LINK REGISTER.      TS800590
                                      423  *            IF REGISTER 6 IS ASSIGNED IN THE CALLING PROGRAM FOR       TS800600
                                      424  *            OTHER USES. IT MUST BE SAVED PRIOR TO EXECUTING THE        TS800610
                                      425  *            'BALR.'                                                    TS800620
                                      426  *                                                                      TS800630
                                      427  *                                                     JEROME T. MURRAY  TS800640
                                      428  *                                                    MARILYN J. MURRAY  TS800650
                                      429  *                                                                      TS800660
                                      430  *  GLEN ELLYN, ILLINOIS                                                 TS800670
                                      431  *                                                                      TS800680
                                      432  * ****************************************************************      TS800690
                                      433  * ****************************************************************      TS800700
                                      434  *                                                                      TS800710
                                      435  *          +++  SECTION 1- GENERAL HOUSEKEEPING  +++                   TS800720
                                      436  *                                                                      TS800730
                                      437  *            INITIALIZE INDICATIVE AND OUTPUT FIELDS                   TS800740
                                      438  *                                                                      TS800750
000440 F800 76BA  772F  00770 007E5   439  TIMESUB8 ZAP   CODE8,=P'0'                                             TS800760
000446 F840 76B5  772F  0076B 007E5   440           ZAP   EASTER,=P'0'                                            TS800770
                                      441  *                                                                      TS800780
                                      442  *            SAVE REGISTERS 1 AND 2 IN SAVE FIELDS                     TS800790
                                      443  *                                                                      TS800800
00044C 9012 76DA        00790         444           STM   1,2,#$BRSAVE                                            TS800810
                                      445  *                                                                      TS800820
                                      446  *            MOVE DATE TO A WORK FIELD AND ISOLATE                     TS800830
                                      447  *            SIGN FOR EDIT                                              TS800840
                                      448  *                                                                      TS800850
000450 D203 759F 76BB   00655 00771   449           MVC   #$WORK4,EYEAR                                           TS800860
000456 D200 759E 75A2   00654 00658   450           MVC   #$BSIGN,#$BWORK4+3                                      TS800870
                                      451  *                                                                      TS800880
                                      452  *          +++  SECTION 2- NUMERIC VALIDATION  +++                     TS800890
                                      453  *                                                                      TS800900
                                      454  *            AUGMENT TABLE FOR VALID '+' SIGNS OTHER THAN              TS800910
                                      455  *            X'F' FOR WHICH TABLE IS DEFINED: X'A', X'C'               TS800920
                                      456  *            X'E'- EDIT FOR VALID '+' SIGN USING TRT                   TS800930
                                      457  *                                                                      TS800940
00045C D209 764B 76AB   00701 00761   458           MVC   #$8TABL+160(10),#$8ZRO                                  TS800950
000462 D209 766B 76AB   00721 00761   459           MVC   #$8TABL+192(10),#$8ZRO                                  TS800960
000468 D209 768B 76AB   00741 00761   460           MVC   #$8TABL+224(10),#$8ZRO                                  TS800970
00046E DD00 759E 75AB   00654 00661   461           TRT   #$8SIGN(1),#$8TABL                                      TS800980
000474 4780 73C6        0047C         462           BC    8,#$8NUM                                                TS800990
000478 47F0 73DA        00490         463           B     #$8BDATA                                                TS801000
                                      464  *                                                                      TS801010
                                      465  *            REINITIALIZE TABLE AND EDIT FOR VALID ZONE               TS801020
                                      466  *            AND DIGIT CONFIGURATIONS IN REMAINING BYTES              TS801030
                                      467  *                                                                      TS801040
00047C 921C 75AB        00661         468  #$8NUM    MVI   #$8TABL,X'1C'                                           TS801050
000480 D2EE 75AC 75AB   00662 00661   469           MVC   #$8TABL+1(239),#$8TABL                                  TS801060
000486 DD02 759F 75AB   00655 00661   470           TRT   #$8WORK4(3),#$8TABL                                     TS801070
00048C 4780 73E4        0049A         471           BC    8,#$8PACK                                                TS801080
                                      472  *                                                                      TS801090
                                      473  *            POST 'BAD DATA' RETURN CODE AND EXIT                      TS801100
```

Figure 9.1   The TIMESUB8 documentation and source code from TEST08's assembly post listing.

```
                                                              DOS/VSE ASSEMBLER 16.27  99-12-31

LOC    OBJECT CODE      ADDR1 ADDR2  STMT  SOURCE STATEMENT

                                     474  *
000490 F800 76BA 7721   007D7        475  #$BBDATA DATA ZAP  CODE8,=P'2'
000496 47FO 76E2        00798        476            B    #$BTERM
                                     477  *
                                     478  *      +++ SECTION 3- EDIT YEAR FOR LIMIT VIOLATIONS   +++
                                     479  *
                                     480  *               PACK YEAR IN WORK FIELD
                                     481  *
00049A F223 75A3 76BB   00771        482  #$PACK   PACK #$YR,EYEAR
                                     483  *
                                     484  *               EDIT YEAR VALUE FOR LOWER LIMIT VIOLATION
                                     485  *
0004A0 F922 75A3 7730   00659 007E6  486            CP   #$YR,=P'1600'
0004A6 4720 73FE        004B4        487            BH   #$YRHI
                                     488  *
                                     489  *               POST 'BAD YEAR' RETURN CODE AND EXIT
                                     490  *
0004AA F800 76BA 7733   00770 007E9  491  #$BADYR  ZAP  CODE8,=P'4'
0004B0 47FO 76E2        00798        492            B    #$BTERM
                                     493  *
                                     494  *               EDIT YEAR VALUE FOR UPPER LIMIT VIOLATION
                                     495  *
0004B4 F922 75A3 7734   00659 007EA  496  #$YRHI   CP   #$YR,=P'3399'
0004BA 4720 73F4        004AA        497            BH   #$BADYR
                                     498  *
                                     499  *      +++ SECTION 4- COMPUTE CENTURY NUMBER   +++
                                     500  *
                                     501  *               #$CENT
0004BE F211 76C2 759F   00778 00655  502            PACK #$CENT,#$8WORK4(2)
0004C4 FA10 76C2 7720   00778 007D6  503            AP   #$CENT,=P'1'
                                     504  *
                                     505  *      +++ SECTION 5- FIND NON-LEAP YEAR CENTESSIMALS   +++
                                     506  *
                                     507  *               #$NONL
                                     508  *
                                     509  *               COMPUTE #$8T2
0004CA F842 75A6 75A3   0065C 00659  510            ZAP  #$8WORK,#$YR
0004D0 FB42 75A6 75A6   0065C 007E6  511            SP   #$8WORK,=P'1600'
0004D6 FD41 75A6 7704   0065C 007BA  512            DP   #$8WORK,=P'400'
0004DC FB11 76BF 75A7   00775 0065D  513            ZAP  #$8T2,#$8WORK+1(2)
0004E2 FC10 76BF 7737   00775 007ED  514            MP   #$8T2,=P'3'
                                     515  *
                                     516  *               COMPUTE #$8T3
                                     517  *
0004E8 F841 75A9 75A6   0065C 0065F  518            ZAP  #$8WORK,#$8WORK+3(2)
0004EE FD41 75A6 7706   0065C 007BC  519            DP   #$8WORK,=P'100'
0004F4 F800 76C1 75A8   00777 0065E  520            ZAP  #$8T3,#$8WORK+2(1)
                                     521  *
                                     522  *               COMPUTE #$NONL
                                     523  *
0004FA F811 76C4 76BF   0077A 00775  524            ZAP  #$NONL,#$8T2
000500 FA10 76C4 76C1   0077A 00777  525            AP   #$NONL,#$8T3
                                     526  *
                                     527  *      +++ SECTION 6- YEAR'S POSITION IN METONIC CYCLE   +++
                                     528  *               #$MET
```

```
TS801110
TS801120
TS801130
TS801140
TS801150
TS801160
TS801170
TS801180
TS801190
TS801200
TS801210
TS801220
TS801230
TS801240
TS801250
TS801260
TS801270
TS801280
TS801290
TS801300
TS801310
TS801320
TS801330
TS801350
TS801360
TS801370
TS801380
TS801390
TS801400
TS801410
TS801430
TS801440
TS801450
TS801460
TS801470
TS801480
TS801490
TS801500
TS801510
TS801520
TS801530
TS801540
TS801550
TS801560
TS801570
TS801580
TS801590
TS801600
TS801620
TS801630
TS801640
TS801650
```

```
LOC    OBJECT CODE      ADDR1 ADDR2  STMT  SOURCE STATEMENT                          DOS/VSE ASSEMBLER 16.27 99-12-31

000506 F842 75A6 75A3   0065C 00659   529  ZAP   ##$WORK,##$YR                                          TS01660
00050C FD41 75A6 7708   0065C 007BE   530  DP    ##$WORK,=P'19'                                         TS01670
000512 FA10 75A9 7720   0065F 007D6   531  AP    ##$WORK+3(2),=P'1'                                     TS01680
000518 F811 76C6 75A9   0077C 0065F   532  ZAP   ##$MET,##$WORK+3(2)                                    TS01690
                                      533  *                                                            TS01700
                                      534  *       +++ SECTION 7- CORRECTION FOR METONIC CYCLE +++      TS01710
                                      535  *            ##$METC                                         TS01720
                                      536  *                                                            TS01730
                                      537  *                                                            TS01740
00051E F841 75A6 76C2   0065C 00778   538  ZAP   ##$WORK,##$CENT                                        TS01750
000524 FC40 75A6 7738   0065C 007EE   539  MP    ##$WORK,=P'8'                                          TS01760
00052A FA40 75A6 7739   0065C 007EF   540  AP    ##$WORK,=P'5'                                          TS01770
000530 FD41 75A6 770A   0065C 007C0   541  DP    ##$WORK,=P'25'                                         TS01780
000536 FB20 75A6 7739   0065C 007EF   542  SP    ##$WORK(3),=P'5'                                       TS01790
00053C FB21 75A6 76C4   0065C 0077A   543  SP    ##$WORK(3),##$NONL                                     TS01800
000542 F811 76C8 75A7   0077E 0065D   544  ZAP   ##$METC,##$WORK+1(2)                                   TS01810
                                      545  *                                                            TS01820
                                      546  *       +++ SECTION 8- DAY COUNT MODIFIER +++                TS01830
                                      547  *            ##$DMOD                                          TS01840
                                      548  *                                                            TS01850
000548 F842 75A6 75A3   0065C 00659   549  ZAP   ##$WORK,##$YR                                          TS01860
00054E FC40 75A6 7739   0065C 007EF   550  MP    ##$WORK,=P'5'                                          TS01870
000554 FD40 75A6 7733   0065C 007E9   551  DP    ##$WORK,=P'4'                                          TS01880
00055A FB31 75A6 76C4   0065C 007C2   552  SP    ##$WORK(4),##$NONL                                     TS01890
000560 FB31 75A6 770C   0065C 007C2   553  SP    ##$WORK(4),=P'10'                                      TS01900
000566 F822 76CA 75A7   0780 0065D    554  ZAP   ##$DMOD,##$WORK+1(3)                                   TS01910
                                      555  *                                                            TS01920
                                      556  *       +++ SECTION 9- COMPUTE THE EPACT +++                 TS01930
                                      557  *            ##$EPACT                                         TS01940
                                      558  *                                                            TS01950
00056C F841 75A6 76C6   0065C 0077C   559  ZAP   ##$WORK,##$MET                                         TS01960
000572 FC41 75A6 770E   0065C 007C4   560  MP    ##$WORK,=P'11'                                         TS01970
000578 FA41 75A6 7710   0065C 007C6   561  AP    ##$WORK,=P'20'                                         TS01980
00057E F841 75A6 76C8   0065C 0077E   562  AP    ##$WORK,##$METC                                        TS01990
000584 FD41 75A6 7712   0065C 007C8   563  DP    ##$WORK,=P'30'                                         TS02000
00058A F811 76CD 75A9   0783 0065F    564  ZAP   ##$EPACT,##$WORK+3(2)                                  TS02010
                                      565  *                                                            TS02020
                                      566  *       +++ SECTION 10- DETERMINE EPACT VALUE +++            TS02030
                                      567  *            ##$EADJ                                          TS02040
000590 F911 76CD 770A   00783 007C0   568  CP    ##$EPACT,=P'25'                                        TS02050
000596 4770 74F4        005AA         569  BNE   ##$EADJ                                                TS02060
                                      570  *                                                            TS02070
                                      571  *       DETERMINE METONIC CYCLE POSITION FOR EPACT           TS02080
                                      572  *       ADJUSTMENT                                            TS02090
                                      573  *                                                            TS02100
00059A F911 76C6 770E   0077C 007C4   574  CP    ##$MET,=P'11'                                          TS02110
0005A0 47D0 74F4        005AA         575  BNH   ##$EADJ                                                TS02120
0005A4 FA10 76CD 7720   00783 007D6   576  AP    ##$EPACT,=P'1'                                         TS02130
                                      577  *                                                            TS02140
                                      578  *       DETERMINE EPACT VALUE FOR ADJUSTMENT                 TS02150
                                      579  *                                                            TS02160
0005AA F911 76CD 7714   00783 007CA   580  ##$EADJ CP   ##$EPACT,=P'24'                                 TS02170
0005B0 4770 7504        005BA         581  BNE   ##$DAYV                                                TS02180
0005B4 FA10 76CD 7720   00783 007D6   582  AP    ##$EPACT,=P'1'                                         TS02190
                                      583  *                                                            TS02200
```

**Figure 9.1** Continued

```
                                                    DOS/VSE ASSEMBLER 16.27  99-12-31

LOC    OBJECT CODE      ADDR1 ADDR2  STMT  SOURCE STATEMENT

                                      584  *
                                      585  *     +++  SECTION 11- COMPUTE DAY VALUE  +++      TS802220
                                      586  *          #$8DAY                                  TS802230
0005BA F811 76CF 7716   00785 007CC   587  #$8DAYV  ZAP   #$8DAY,=P'44'                        TS802240
0005C0 FB11 76CF 76CD   00785 00783   588           SP    #$8DAY,#$8EPACT                     TS802250
                                      589  *                                                  TS802260
                                      590  *            DETERMINE DAY VALUE FOR ADJUSTMENT     TS802270
                                      591  *                                                  TS802280
0005C6 F911 76CF 7718   00785 007CE   592           CP    #$8DAY,=P'21'                        TS802290
0005CC 47B0 05D6              005D6    593           BNL   #$8CANDA                            TS802300
0005D0 FA11 76CF 7712   00785 007C8   594           AP    #$8DAY,=P'30'                        TS802310
                                      595  *                                                  TS802320
                                      596  *     +++  SECTION 12- COMPUTE DATE OF EASTER  +++  TS802330
                                      597  *                                                  TS802340
0005D6 F831 759F 76CF   00655 00785   598  #$8CANDA ZAP   #$8WORK4,#$8DAY                      TS802350
0005DC FA30 759F 757C   00655 00632   599           AP    #$8WORK4,=P'7'                       TS802360
0005E2 F841 75A6 76CF   0065C 00785   600           ZAP   #$8WORK,#$8DAY                       TS802370
0005E8 FA42 75A6 76CA   0065C 00780   601           AP    #$8WORK,#$8DMOD                      TS802380
0005EE FD40 75A6 773A   0065C 007F0   602           DP    #$8WORK,=P'7'                        TS802390
0005F4 FB30 759F 75A3   00655 00659   603           SP    #$8WORK4,#$8WORK4+4(1)               TS802400
0005FA F811 759F 75A1   00655 00657   604           ZAP   #$8WORK4,#$8WORK4+2(2)               TS802410
                                      605  *                                                  TS802420
                                      606  *       IF #$8DAY < OR = 31, EASTER IS 03/#$8DAY/#$8YR   TS802430
                                      607  *       ELSE, EASTER IS 04/(#$8DAY - 31)/#$8YR     TS802440
                                      608  *                                                  TS802450
000600 F911 76CF 771A   00785 007D0   609           CP    #$8DAY,=P'31'                        TS802460
000606 47D0 0632              00632    610           BNH   #$8ESTER                            TS802470
00060A FB11 76CF 771A   00785 007D0   611           SP    #$8DAY,=P'31'                        TS802480
000610 F341 75A6 76CF   0065C 00785   612           UNPK  #$8WORK,#$8DAY                       TS802490
000616 D300 75AA 7722   00660 007D8   613           MVZ   #$8WORK+4(1),=C'1'                   TS802500
00061C D203 76D5 76BB   0078B 00771   614           MVC   #$8ZDATE+4(4),EYEAR                  TS802510
000622 D201 76D3 75A9   00789 0065F   615           MVC   #$8ZDATE+2(2),#$8WORK+3              TS802520
000628 D201 76D1 771C   00787 007D2   616           MVC   #$8ZDATE(2),=C'04'                   TS802530
00062E 47F0 7594              0064A    617           B     #$8PK                               TS802540
                                      618  *                                                  TS802550
                                      619  *     +++  SECTION 13- FABRICATE EASTER DATE  +++   TS802560
                                      620  *                                                  TS802570
000632 F341 75A6 76CF   0065C 00785   621  #$8ESTER UNPK  #$8WORK,#$8DAY                       TS802580
000638 D203 76D5 76BB   0078B 00771   622           MVC   #$8ZDATE+4(4),EYEAR                  TS802590
00063E D201 76D3 75A9   00789 0065F   623           MVC   #$8ZDATE+2(2),#$8WORK+3              TS802600
000644 D201 76D1 771E   00787 007D4   624           MVC   #$8ZDATE(2),=C'03'                   TS802610
00064A F247 76B5 76D1   0076B 00787   625  #$8PK    PACK  EASTER,#$8ZDATE                      TS802620
                                      626  *                                                  TS802630
                                      627  *     +++  SECTION 14- TO RESTORE REGISTERS AND EXIT  +++   TS802640
                                      628  *                                                  TS802650
000650 47F0 76E2              00798    629           B     #$8TERM                             TS802660
                                      630  *                                                  TS802670
                                      631  *     +++  SECTION 15- DEFINE CONSTANTS AND STORAGE  +++    TS802680
                                      632  *                                                  TS802690
000654                                633  #$8SIGN  DS    CL1                                  TS802700
000655                                634  #$8WORK4 DS    ZL4                                  TS802710
000659                                635  #$8YR    DS    PL3                                  TS802720
00065C                                636  #$8WORK  DS    PL5                                  TS802730
                                      637  *                                                  TS802740
                                      638  *            TRANSLATION TABLE DEFINED FOR X'F0' - X'F9'    TS802750
```

DOS/VSE ASSEMBLER 16.27    99-12-31

```
LOC     OBJECT CODE        ADDR1 ADDR2  STMT  SOURCE STATEMENT

                                        639   *                                           TS802760
                                        640   *   (ALL TABLE POSITIONS EXCEPT THOSE CORRESPONDING   TS802770
                                        641   *    TO X'F0' THROUGH X'F9' ARE SET TO A VALUE OTHER  TS802780
                                        642   *    THAN X'00')                            TS802790
000661  1C1C1C1C1C1C1C1C             643   #$8TABL  DC  240X'1C'                        TS802800
000751  0000000000000000             644            DC  10X'00'                          TS802810
00075B  1C1C1C1C1C1C                 645            DC  6X'1C'                            TS802820
                                        646   *                                           TS802830
000761  0000000000000000             647   #$8ZRO   DC  10X'00'                          TS802840
00076B  000000000C                   648   EASTER   DC  PL5'0'                           TS802850
000770  9C                           649   CODE8    DC  PL1'9'                           TS802860
000771  F0F0F0C0                     650   EYEAR    DC  ZL4'0'                           TS802870
000775                                 651   #$8T2    DS  PL2                             TS802880
000777                                 652   #$8T3    DS  PL1                             TS802890
000778                                 653   #$8CENT  DS  PL2                             TS802900
00077A                                 654   #$8NONL  DS  PL2                             TS802910
00077C                                 655   #$8MET   DS  PL2                             TS802920
00077E                                 656   #$8METC  DS  PL2                             TS802930
000780                                 657   #$8DMOD  DS  PL3                             TS802940
000783                                 658   #$8EPACT DS  PL2                             TS802950
000785                                 659   #$8DAY   DS  ZL8                             TS802960
000787                                 660   #$8ZDATE DS  2F                              TS802970
000790                                 661   #$8RSAVE DS  2F                              TS802980
000798  9812 76DA          00790     662   #$8TERM  LM  1,2,#$8RSAVE                     TS802990
00079C  07F6               000B4     663            BR  6                                 TS803000
                                        664            END BEGIN
0007A0  5B5BC2D6D7C5D540             665            =C'$$BOPEN '
0007A8  5B5BC2C3D3D6E2C5             666            =C'$$BCLOSE'
0007B0  00000080                     667            =A(REQUEST)
0007B4  00000000                     668            =A(LIST)
0007B8  003C                         669            =P'03'
0007BA  400C                         670            =P'400'
0007BC  100C                         671            =P'100'
0007C0  019C                         672            =P'19'
0007C2  025C                         673            =P'25'
0007C4  010C                         674            =P'10'
0007C6  011C                         675            =P'11'
0007C8  020C                         676            =P'20'
0007CA  030C                         677            =P'30'
0007CC  044C                         678            =P'44'
0007CE  021C                         679            =P'21'
0007D0  031C                         680            =P'31'
0007D2  F0F4                         681            =C'04'
0007D4  F0F3                         682            =C'03'
0007D6  1C                           683            =P'1'
0007D7  2C                           684            =P'2'
0007D8  F1                           685            =C'1'
0007D9  D4C1D9C3C8                   686            =C'MARCH'
0007DE  6B                           687            =C','
0007DF  C1D7D9C9D3                   688            =C'APRIL'
0007E4  F0                           689            =C'0'
0007E5  0C                           690            =P'0'
0007E6  01600C                       691            =P'1600'
0007E9  4C                           692            =P'4'
```

**Figure 9.1** *Continued*

```
TEST OF TIMESUB8 TO CALCULATE DATE OF EASTER

1901 EASTER OCCURS: APRIL 07, CODE8 CONTENTS: 1901, EASTER CONTENTS: 0. EASTER CONTENTS: 04071901
1902 EASTER OCCURS: MARCH 30, CODE8 CONTENTS: 1902, EASTER CONTENTS: 0. EASTER CONTENTS: 03301902
1903 EASTER OCCURS: APRIL 12, CODE8 CONTENTS: 1903, EASTER CONTENTS: 0. EASTER CONTENTS: 04121903
1904 EASTER OCCURS: APRIL 03, CODE8 CONTENTS: 1904, EASTER CONTENTS: 0. EASTER CONTENTS: 04031904
1905 EASTER OCCURS: APRIL 23, CODE8 CONTENTS: 1905, EASTER CONTENTS: 0. EASTER CONTENTS: 04231905
1906 EASTER OCCURS: APRIL 15, CODE8 CONTENTS: 1906, EASTER CONTENTS: 0. EASTER CONTENTS: 04151906
1907 EASTER OCCURS: MARCH 31, CODE8 CONTENTS: 1907, EASTER CONTENTS: 0. EASTER CONTENTS: 03311907
1908 EASTER OCCURS: APRIL 19, CODE8 CONTENTS: 1908, EASTER CONTENTS: 0. EASTER CONTENTS: 04191908
1909 EASTER OCCURS: APRIL 11, CODE8 CONTENTS: 1909, EASTER CONTENTS: 0. EASTER CONTENTS: 04111909
1910 EASTER OCCURS: MARCH 27, CODE8 CONTENTS: 1910, EASTER CONTENTS: 0. EASTER CONTENTS: 03271910
1980 EASTER OCCURS: APRIL 06, CODE8 CONTENTS: 1980, EASTER CONTENTS: 0. EASTER CONTENTS: 04061980
1981 EASTER OCCURS: APRIL 19, CODE8 CONTENTS: 1981, EASTER CONTENTS: 0. EASTER CONTENTS: 04191981
1982 EASTER OCCURS: APRIL 11, CODE8 CONTENTS: 1982, EASTER CONTENTS: 0. EASTER CONTENTS: 04111982
1983 EASTER OCCURS: APRIL 03, CODE8 CONTENTS: 1983, EASTER CONTENTS: 0. EASTER CONTENTS: 04031983
1984 EASTER OCCURS: APRIL 22, CODE8 CONTENTS: 1984, EASTER CONTENTS: 0. EASTER CONTENTS: 04221984
1985 EASTER OCCURS: APRIL 07, CODE8 CONTENTS: 1985, EASTER CONTENTS: 0. EASTER CONTENTS: 04071985
1986 EASTER OCCURS: MARCH 30, CODE8 CONTENTS: 1986, EASTER CONTENTS: 0. EASTER CONTENTS: 03301986
1987 EASTER OCCURS: APRIL 19, CODE8 CONTENTS: 1987, EASTER CONTENTS: 0. EASTER CONTENTS: 04191987
1988 EASTER OCCURS: APRIL 03, CODE8 CONTENTS: 1988, EASTER CONTENTS: 0. EASTER CONTENTS: 04031988
1989 EASTER OCCURS: MARCH 26, CODE8 CONTENTS: 1989, EASTER CONTENTS: 0. EASTER CONTENTS: 03261989
1990 EASTER OCCURS: APRIL 15, CODE8 CONTENTS: 1990, EASTER CONTENTS: 0. EASTER CONTENTS: 04151990
1991 EASTER OCCURS: MARCH 31, CODE8 CONTENTS: 1991, EASTER CONTENTS: 0. EASTER CONTENTS: 03311991
1999 EASTER OCCURS: APRIL 04, CODE8 CONTENTS: 1999, EASTER CONTENTS: 0. EASTER CONTENTS: 04041999
2000 EASTER OCCURS: APRIL 23, CODE8 CONTENTS: 2000, EASTER CONTENTS: 0. EASTER CONTENTS: 04232000
2001 EASTER OCCURS: APRIL 15, CODE8 CONTENTS: 2001, EASTER CONTENTS: 0. EASTER CONTENTS: 04152001
2002 EASTER OCCURS: MARCH 31, CODE8 CONTENTS: 2002, EASTER CONTENTS: 0. EASTER CONTENTS: 03312002
2003 EASTER OCCURS: APRIL 20, CODE8 CONTENTS: 2003, EASTER CONTENTS: 0. EASTER CONTENTS: 04202003
2004 EASTER OCCURS: APRIL 11, CODE8 CONTENTS: 2004, EASTER CONTENTS: 0. EASTER CONTENTS: 04112004
2005 EASTER OCCURS: MARCH 27, CODE8 CONTENTS: 2005, EASTER CONTENTS: 0. EASTER CONTENTS: 03272005
2006 EASTER OCCURS: APRIL 16, CODE8 CONTENTS: 2006, EASTER CONTENTS: 0. EASTER CONTENTS: 04162006
2007 EASTER OCCURS: APRIL 08, CODE8 CONTENTS: 2007, EASTER CONTENTS: 0. EASTER CONTENTS: 04082007
2008 EASTER OCCURS: MARCH 23, CODE8 CONTENTS: 2008, EASTER CONTENTS: 0. EASTER CONTENTS: 03232008
2009 EASTER OCCURS: APRIL 12, CODE8 CONTENTS: 2009, EASTER CONTENTS: 0. EASTER CONTENTS: 04122009
2029 EASTER OCCURS: APRIL 01, CODE8 CONTENTS: 2029, EASTER CONTENTS: 0. EASTER CONTENTS: 04012029
2030 EASTER OCCURS: APRIL 21, CODE8 CONTENTS: 2030, EASTER CONTENTS: 0. EASTER CONTENTS: 04212030
2041 EASTER OCCURS: APRIL 21, CODE8 CONTENTS: 2041, EASTER CONTENTS: 0. EASTER CONTENTS: 04212041
2055 EASTER OCCURS: APRIL 18, CODE8 CONTENTS: 2055, EASTER CONTENTS: 0. EASTER CONTENTS: 04182055
2063 EASTER OCCURS: APRIL 15, CODE8 CONTENTS: 2063, EASTER CONTENTS: 0. EASTER CONTENTS: 04152063
2088 EASTER OCCURS: APRIL 11, CODE8 CONTENTS: 2088, EASTER CONTENTS: 0. EASTER CONTENTS: 04112088
2090 EASTER OCCURS: APRIL 16, CODE8 CONTENTS: 2090, EASTER CONTENTS: 0. EASTER CONTENTS: 04162090
2096 EASTER OCCURS: APRIL 15, CODE8 CONTENTS: 2096, EASTER CONTENTS: 0. EASTER CONTENTS: 04152096
2098 EASTER OCCURS: APRIL 20, CODE8 CONTENTS: 2098, EASTER CONTENTS: 0. EASTER CONTENTS: 04202098
2099 EASTER OCCURS: APRIL 12, CODE8 CONTENTS: 2099, EASTER CONTENTS: 0. EASTER CONTENTS: 04122099
2100 EASTER OCCURS: MARCH 28, CODE8 CONTENTS: 2100, EASTER CONTENTS: 0. EASTER CONTENTS: 03282100

THE SUBROUTINE WAS EXECUTED    44 TIMES
```

**Figure 9.2**  A subset of Easter dates computed in tests of the TIMESUB8 subroutine.

# The Gregorian Status Indicator

Knowing the name of the day, as mentioned in chapter 7, is significant for much of our economic, academic, and social behavior. Certainly, as we relinquish more and more control of our destiny to computers, we must humanize them. Programs that "understand" some of our failings have been dubbed *user-friendly*. Now it's time to develop *user-sympathetic* software that can recognize our holidays and celebrations.

## The Holiday Problem

Beyond editing input dates to determine that they're valid elements of our calendar, the vast majority of user applications are unable to further identify the status of a given date without a calendar data set. While CPU MIPS (millions of instructions processed per second) rates have continued to increase, I/O activities still face mechanical limitations that present huge time-lapse factors by comparison.

This chapter addresses this problem and seeks to demonstrate that you can invoke the algorithms of earlier chapters to eliminate having to use a calendar data set, with its associated overhead. Thus, you can reduce online response time and free batch processing of potential dating errors as they relate to holidays.

A secondary objective is tutorial, in that this chapter's algorithm will illustrate how to combine tools from the macro library to arrive at novel solutions to unusual date-processing problems.

## The Solution Strategy

You must create an algorithm to accept a Commercial-8 input date, find its day-name code, calculate its neo-Julian equivalent Y.E, and place the three-digit ordinal day E as the last argument entry of a holiday table. The algorithm then must find the three-digit ordinal day E of each holiday in the input date's year, thus filling the remaining argument entries of the holiday table. The holiday table's function entries will consist of two-digit codes, each representing a described holiday. The last function, whose argument is the ordinal day of the input date, will be the code for no holiday.

Finally, after building this holiday table, the algorithm must perform an ascending table look-up, using the ordinal day of the input date as a search argument. When an equal condition is encountered, that entry's table function will be accessed. It will represent either "holiday" or "no holiday" since you're certain to find an equal condition in the last entry. The holiday indicator thus obtained along with the input date's day-name code, it will then be returned to the calling program.

## Describing the Algorithm

Assuming that the complete description of any given Gregorian date consists of the date's day name and its holiday status as it relates to the Gregorian calendar, you're faced with two objectives:

- Associating the day name with the date
- Associating the holiday's description with the date

Chapter 7 presented TIMESUB6 to attain the first objective. With the additional aid of TIMESUB1, TIMESUB2, and TIMESUB8, you can reach the second objective as well.

### Classifying the holidays

Note that all holidays fall into one of three primary classes:

**Class A.**  Designated by date

**Class B.**  Positional by day in month

**Class C.**  Movable—designated by calculated date

Clearly, class A contains holidays whose dates don't vary from year to year; examples that quickly come to mind are Christmas (December 25) and New Year's Day (January 1). Class B contains holidays whose occurrence is determined by day position within the month cited. Examples are Labor Day (the first Monday in September), Memorial Day (the last Monday in May), and Election Day (the first Tuesday after the first Monday in November). Class C is reserved for Easter, Good Friday, Easter Monday, and other Easter-related holidays.

Returning to Class A holidays, when one of these falls on a Saturday or Sunday, another "working day" is designated as a holiday. The rule is that a Class A holiday falling on Saturday is celebrated on the previous Friday. If the Class A holiday falls on Sunday, the celebration is transferred to the following Monday.

### Selecting the holidays

No one can deny that there are a variety of holidays. We chose a collection of almanacs as our guide in isolating those days that are recognized commercial holidays in Canada or the United States. There are days not on the list due to their limited geographical area of interest or because they're days imported from other calendars.

**TABLE 10.1  Holidays**

| Holiday | Class | Designation |
|---|---|---|
| New Year's Day (U.S., Canada) | A | January 1 |
| Martin Luther King's Birthday (U.S.) | A | January 15 |
| Abraham Lincoln's Birthday (U.S.) | A | February 12 |
| George Washington, Presidents Day (U.S.) | B | Third Monday in February |
| Good Friday (U.S., Canada) | C | Calculated |
| Easter Sunday (U.S., Canada) | C | Calculated |
| Easter Monday (Canada) | C | Calculated |
| Victoria Day (Canada) | B | Monday preceding May 25 |
| Memorial Day (U.S.) | B | Last Monday in May |
| St. Jean, Baptiste Day (Canada) | A | June 24 |
| Canada Day (Canada) | A | July 1 |
| Independence Day (U.S.) | A | July 4 |
| Civic Holiday (Canada) | B | First Monday in August |
| Labor Day (U.S., Canada) | B | First Monday in September |
| Thanksgiving Day (Canada) | B | Second Monday in October |
| Columbus Day (U.S.) | B | Second Monday in October |
| Election Day (U.S.) | B | First Tuesday after first Monday in November |
| Remembrance Day (Canada) | A | November 11 |
| Veterans Day (U.S.) | A | November 11 |
| Thanksgiving Day (U.S.) | B | Fourth Thursday in November |
| Christmas Day (U.S., Canada) | A | December 25 |
| Boxing Day (Canada) | A | December 26 |

Among the imported holidays are the Jewish high holidays. The Jewish calendar, as we noted in chapter 1, is Babylonian in origin. Thus, we've omitted the Jewish holidays from our list. Including them would require algorithms for the Jewish calendar with additional algorithm development to convert the calculated Jewish calendar dates to the Gregorian calendar. These algorithms either exist or can be developed, but the limited scope of this book prohibits their inclusion here. Similarly, there are numerous ethnic holidays that are recognized and celebrated widely, but because they're noncommercial they too have been omitted. The chosen holidays are shown in Table 10.1.

## Organizing the algorithm's data

The final step in the solution requires that we relate the results of the algorithm's calculations to the described holidays—thus, a table. In creating the coding scheme and table, however, you must consider the transfer possibility of Class A holidays. So in some years New Year's Day might in fact be celebrated during the previous year. This occurs when January 1 falls on a Saturday and hence the New Year's celebration transfers to December 31 of the current year. Consequently, New Year's Day requires two transfer entries.

While transferring Class A holidays is a clearly defined function in the United States, Canada is less systematic in this. In order to algorithmically address the holidays in both countries, we've imposed the same transfer standards on the Canadian Class A holidays.

Further, the occurrence of Boxing Day on the day immediately following Christmas requires an exception in the transfer procedure for Boxing Day. If Boxing Day occurs on Saturday or Sunday, it is transferred to the following Monday. However, if Boxing Day falls on Monday, it's transferred to Tuesday to permit Christmas's transfer to Monday.

These considerations give rise to table functions, each of which will be a two-digit code representing a holiday or a holiday's possible transfer day. The table's argument entries will be addressable, three-digit ordinal days E. The algorithm will be required to calculate the ordinal days and update the table arguments for all non-class-A holidays and all detected Class A transfer occurrences. The ordinal days of Class A holidays can be precalculated and stored in the table as constants since these dates don't change.

Finally, the table entries for Christmas and Boxing Day must be in chronological order, with the Christmas entry followed by its transfer entry and Boxing Day followed by its transfer entry, in that sequence. This is required in order to assure that the ascending table look-up will encounter the Christmas transfer entry before the Boxing Day entry. Their table arguments will be equal in years when Christmas occurs on Sunday, and you want to be certain that Christmas's transfer takes precedence over the Class A Boxing Day entry.

## The calculations

The algorithm's calculations depend on the macro equivalents of the subroutines TIME1, TIME2, TIME6, and TIME8. Beyond these, the $n$th-occurrence-of-an-$x$-day equations from chapter 7 are used to calculate the ordinal day of a given Class B holiday from the ordinal day of the given month's first or last day. Because any given month's first or last day is a neo-Julian constant, plus a leap year adjustment, only the displacement is calculated. The pseudocode will display this, as will the source code.

## The Pseudocode for TIMESUB9

The pseudocode assumes that its input was submitted as a Commercial-8 date in zoned decimal format in an eight-byte field, DATEH. Two outputs and a return code are generated. The output field WEEKDA contains the day of the week or day-name code and is identical to OUTDAY of TIMESUB6. The output HOLIDA is a two-byte packed field and contains a two-digit value, 00 through 99, representing the holiday status of the input date if execution was successful. The value 99 indicates no holiday. The meanings of values other than 99 are documented in the source code displayed in the next section of this chapter. The return code CODE9 is identical to CODE6 of TIMESUB6. If CODE9 contains a nonzero value, both WEEKDA and HOLIDA will contain nines. The pseudocode is as follows (all #$9 elements are table arguments):

```
     * General housekeeping.
  1) Let HOLIDA = 99
  2) Let WEEKDA = 9
  3) Let CODE9 = 0
  4) Let #$901, #$902, #$904, #$906, #$914 = 0
  5) Let #$916, #$918, #$924, #$927, #$929 = 0
  6) DATEH → M, D, Y
     * Find name of input day.
  7) Let INDATE = DATEH
  8) Execute TIME6
  9) Let CODE9 = CODE6
 10) If CODE9 > 0, go to 114
 11) Let WEEKDA = OUTDAY
     * Calculate ordinal day for DATEH.
 12) Let DATEA = DATEH
 13) Execute TIME2
 14) NEOJUL → Y,E, let ORD = E
     * Plug last table argument with E.
 15) Let #$9END = ORD
     * Find leap-year status of Y, L.
 16) Let YEAR = Y
 17) Execute TIME1
     * Find New Year transfer arguments.
 18) Let INDATE = 0101Y
 19) Execute TIME6
 20) If OUTDAY = 0, let #$901 = 002
 21) Let INDATE = INDATE + 1
 22) Execute TIME6
 23) If OUTDAY = 6, let #$902 = 365 + L
     * Find Martin Luther King transfer argument.
 24) Let INDATE = 0115Y
 25) Execute TIME6
 26) If OUTDAY = 6, let #$904 = 014
 27) If OUTDAY = 0, let #$904 = 016
     * Find Lincoln transfer argument.
 28) Let INDATE = 0212Y
 29) Execute TIME6
 30) If OUTDAY = 6, let #$906 = 042
 31) If OUTDAY = 0, let #$906 = 044
     * Find Washington/Presidents Day argument.
 32) Let INDATE = 0201Y
 33) Execute TIME6
 34) If OUTDAY = 1, let #$907 = 046
 35) If OUTDAY < 1, let #$907 = 047
 36) If OUTDAY > 1, let #$907 = 054 - OUTDAY
     * Compute Easter and related-day arguments.
 37) Let EYEAR = Y
 38) Execute TIME8
     * Calculate ordinal day for Easter.
 39) Let DATEA = EASTER
 40) Execute TIME2
 41) NEOJUL → Y,E
     * Good Friday.
 42) Let #$908 = E - 2
     * Easter.
 43) Let #$909 = E
     * Easter Monday.
 44) Let #$910 = #$909 + 1
     * Find Victoria Day argument.
```

```
45) Let INDATE = 0525Y
46) Execute TIME6
47) If OUTDAY = 1, let #$911 = 138 + L
48) If OUTDAY < 1, let #$911 = 139 + L
49) If OUTDAY > 1, let #$911 = 145 - (OUTDAY - 1) + L
  * Find Memorial Day argument.
50) Let INDATE = 0531Y
51) Execute TIME6
52) If OUTDAY = 1, let #$912 = 151 + L
53) If OUTDAY < 1, let #$912 = 145 + L
54) If OUTDAY > 1, let #$912 = 151 - (OUTDAY - 1) + L
  * Find St. Jean, Baptiste Day transfer argument.
55) Let #$913 = #$913 + L
56) Let INDATE = 0624Y
57) Execute TIME6
58) If OUTDAY = 6, let #$914 = #$913 - 1
59) If OUTDAY = 0, let #$914 = #$913 + 1
  * Find Canada Day transfer date argument.
60) Let #$915 = #$915 + L
61) Let INDATE = 0701Y
62) Execute TIME6
63) If OUTDAY = 6, let #$916 = #$915 - 1
64) If OUTDAY = 0, let #$916 = #$915 + 1
  * Find Independence Day transfer date argument.
65) Let #$917 = #$917 + L
66) Let INDATE = 0704Y
67) Execute TIME6
68) If OUTDAY = 6, let #$918 = #$917 - 1
69) If OUTDAY = 0, let #$918 = #$917 + 1
  * Find Civic Holiday date argument.
70) Let INDATE = 0801Y
71) Execute TIME6
72) If OUTDAY = 1, let #$919 = 213 + L
73) If OUTDAY < 1, let #$919 = 214 + L
74) If OUTDAY > 1, let #$919 = 221 - OUTDAY + L
  * Find Labor Day date argument.
75) Let INDATE = 0901Y
76) Execute TIME6
77) If OUTDAY = 1, let #$920 = 244 + L
78) If OUTDAY < 1, let #$920 = 245 + L
79) If OUTDAY > 1, let #$920 = 252 - OUTDAY + L
  * Find Canadian Thanksgiving/Columbus Day argument.
80) Let INDATE = 1001Y
81) Execute TIME6
82) If OUTDAY = 1, let #$921 = 281 + L
83) If OUTDAY < 1, let #$921 = 282 + L
84) If OUTDAY > 1, let #$921 = 289 - OUTDAY + L
  * Find Election Day argument.
85) Let INDATE = 1101Y
86) Execute TIME6
87) If OUTDAY = 1, let #$922 = 306 + L
88) If OUTDAY < 1, let #$922 = 307 + L
89) If OUTDAY > 1, let #$922 = 314 - OUTDAY + L
  * Find Remembrance/Veterans Day transfer argument.
90) Let #$923 = #$923 + L
91) Let INDATE = 1111Y
92) Execute TIME6
93) If OUTDAY = 6, let #$924 = #$923 - 1
94) If OUTDAY = 0, let #$924 = #$923 + 1
  * Find Thanksgiving argument.
95) Let INDATE = 1101Y
96) Execute TIME6
97) If OUTDAY = 4, let #$925 = 326 + L
98) If OUTDAY < 4, let #$925 = 330 - OUTDAY + L
```

```
 99) If OUTDAY > 4, let #$925 = 337 - OUTDAY + L
   * Find Christmas and Boxing Day transfer arguments.
100) Let #$926 = #$926 + L
101) Let #$928 = #$928 + L
102) Let INDATE = 1225Y
103) Execute TIME6
104) If OUTDAY = 5, let #$929 = #$926 + 3
105) If OUTDAY = 6, let #$927 = #$926 - 1, let #$929 = #$926 + 2
106) If OUTDAY = 0, let #$927 = #$926 + 1, let #$929 = #$926 + 2
   * Determine input holiday status via table look-up.
107) Address first table argument ENTRY
108) If ORD = ENTRY, go to 111
109) Address next table argument ENTRY
110) Go to 108
111) Let HOLIDA = table function of ENTRY
   * Remove L from constant arguments.
112) Subtract L from: #$913, #$915, #$917, #$923
113) Subtract L from: #$926, #$928
114) Exit
```

## The Source Code for TIMESUB9

Figure 10.1 shows the complete TEST09 program post listing including a subset of the test results. TIMESUB9 was tested using holiday and nonholiday dates from the period 1981–1991, inclusive. All results were as predicted, so TIMESUB9 is deemed a valid algorithm.

Reviewing the pseudocode as it relates to the source code displays the relationship between the table arguments' labels and the corresponding table functions. The last two digits of the label of any table argument indicate the content of the corresponding table function. This is a programming convenience.

The source code's inline documentation displays several equations for computing the constants that were used to conditionally update the table's arguments. Although it doesn't display these equations, you can translate the pseudocode to a language other than ALC with no loss of functionality.

The sole constraint on the table's design is that the Christmas and Boxing Day entries be sequenced as shown and that the input date's ordinal day occupy the last argument in the holiday table. Finally, the sole constraint on the table look-up is that it proceed from the first table argument to the last—ascending from the lowest storage address in the table arguments to the highest.

Note that the first execution of a TIME macro, TIME6, edits the input date. Although every TIME macro incorporates editing logic, subsequent return code contents are ignored because all macros, like their subroutine counterparts, adhere to a uniform set of editing conventions. Thus, it's necessary to be certain only that the complete input is subjected to an edit.

Had the first executed macro been TIME1, only the year component of the input date would have been edited. The later execution of a macro involving the whole input date would require that the corresponding return code be interrogated. TIME1 and TIME8, like their corresponding subroutines, edit the four-digit year only, while all other macros and subroutines edit the complete Commercial-8 date. Modular independence is usually obtainable at the minimum cost of redundant editing.

EXTERNAL SYMBOL DICTIONARY

| SYMBOL | TYPE | ID | ADDR | LENGTH | LD-ID |
|---|---|---|---|---|---|
| TEST09 | SD (CSECT) | 001 | 000000 | 001DC6 | |
| PRMOD | ER (EXTRN) | 002 | | | |
| PRMOD | SD (CSECT) | 003 | 000000 | 000088 | |

DUMMY SECTION DICTIONARY

| SYMBOL | ID | LENGTH |
|---|---|---|
| IJDPD002 | 1FF | 000030 |

```
                                                          DOS/VSE ASSEMBLER 08.14 99-12-31

LOC    OBJECT CODE   ADDR1 ADDR2  STMT  SOURCE STATEMENT

000000
                                    1        PRINT NOGEN
                                    2 TESTO9 START
                                    3 *
                                    4 LIST   DTFPR DEVADDR=SYSO10,          X
                                                  IOAREA1=OUT,             X
                                                  BLKSIZE=132,             X
                                                  DEVICE=1403,             X
                                                  PRINTOV=YES,             X
                                                  MODNAME=PRMOD,           X
                                                  CONTROL=YES

                                   25 *
                                   26 PRMOD  PRMOD CONTROL=YES,             X
                                                  PRINTOV=YES

                                  135 *
                                  136 TESTFIL ACB  AM=VSAM,                 X
                                                  MACRF=(ADR,IN,SEQ),      X
                                                  EXLST=EXITLST

                                  168 *
                                  169 EXITLST EXLST AM=VSAM,                X
                                                  EODAD=FINI

                                  180 *
                                  181 REQUEST RPL  ACB=TESTFIL,             X
                                                  AREA=TESTFLE,            X
                                                  AREALEN=80,              X
                                                  OPTCD=(ADR,SEQ,NUP,MVE ) X

000084 0580
                                  210 *
                                  211 BEGIN  BALR  8,0
                                  212        USING *,8,9
000086 5890 82DA      000B6       213 GO     L     9,ADDR
0000BA 41D0 88D2      00988       214        LA    13,SAVE
                                  215        OPEN  TESTFIL,LIST
0000D2 9240 8256      0030C       224        MVI   OUT,X'40'
0000D6 D282 8257 8256 0030D 0030C 225        MVC   OUT+1(131),OUT
                                  226 READ   GET   RPL=REQUEST
0000EE FA20 8890 9CBC 00946 01D72 233        AP    TOT,=P'1'
0000F4 D207 9B0C 8206 01BC2 002BC 234        MVC   DATEH,TSTDATE
0000FA 41A0 891A            009D0 235        LA    10,TIMESUB9
0000FE 056A                       236        BALR  6,10
000100 9540 88C2      00978       237        CLI   SWITCH,X'40'
000104 4770 809C      00152       238        BNE   TEST
000108 92F1 88C2      00978       239        MVI   SWITCH,X'F1'
00010C D22E 8256 8893 0030C 00949 240        MVC   OUT(47),HDG
                                  241        CNTRL LIST,SK,1
                                  247        CNTRL LIST,SP,3
                                  253        PUT   LIST
                                  258        CNTRL LIST,SP,1
000148 9240 8256      0030C       264 TEST   MVI   OUT,X'40'
00014C D282 8257 8256 0030D 0030C 265        MVC   OUT+1(131),OUT
000152 D201 8256 9B0C 0030C 01BC2 266        MVC   OUT(2),DATEH
000158 D200 8258 9CBD 0030E 01D73 267        MVC   OUT+2(1),=C'/'
00015E D201 8259 9B0E 0030F 01BC4 268        MVC   OUT+3(2),DATEH+2
000164 D200 825B 9CBD 00311 01D73 269        MVC   OUT+5(1),=C'/'
00016A D203 825C 9B10 00312 01BC6 270        MVC   OUT+6(4),DATEH+4
000170 F900 9B0B 9CBE 01BC1 01D74 271        CP    CODE9,=P'0'
000176 4780 811E      001D4       272        BE    OUTPUT
```

**Figure 10.1** The complete assembly post listing of TESTO9, including a subset of the results obtained in testing TIMESUB9.

DOS/VSE ASSEMBLER 08.14 99-12-31

| LOC | OBJECT CODE | ADDR1 | ADDR2 | STMT | SOURCE STATEMENT |
|---|---|---|---|---|---|
| 00017A | F900 9B0B 9CBF | 01BC1 | 01D75 | 273 | CP   CODE9,=P'2' |
| 000180 | 4770 80D8 | | 0018E | 274 | BNE  CK4 |
| 000184 | D20B 8263 9BEA | 00319 | 01CA0 | 275 | MVC  OUT+13(12),=C'INVALID DATA' |
| 00018A | 47F0 8172 | | 00228 | 276 | B    NEXT |
| 00018E | F900 9B0B 9CC0 | 01BC1 | 01D76 | 277 | CK4  CP   CODE9,=P'4' |
| 000194 | 4770 80EC | | 001A2 | 278 | BNE  CK6 |
| 000198 | D20B 8263 9BF6 | 00319 | 01CAC | 279 | MVC  OUT+13(12),=C'INVALID YEAR' |
| 00019E | 47F0 8172 | | 00228 | 280 | B    NEXT |
| 0001A2 | F900 9B0B 9CC1 | 01BC1 | 01D77 | 281 | CK6  CP   CODE9,=P'6' |
| 0001A8 | 4770 8100 | | 001B6 | 282 | BNE  CK8 |
| 0001AC | D20C 8263 9CC2 | 00319 | 01D78 | 283 | MVC  OUT+13(13),=C'INVALID MONTH' |
| 0001B2 | 47F0 8172 | | 00228 | 284 | B    NEXT |
| 0001B6 | F900 9B0B 9CCF | 01BC1 | 01D85 | 285 | CK8  CP   CODE9,=P'8' |
| 0001BC | 4770 8114 | | 001CA | 286 | BNE  SUBFAIL |
| 0001C0 | D20A 8263 9CD0 | 00319 | 01D86 | 287 | MVC  OUT+13(11),=C'INVALID DAY' |
| 0001C6 | 47F0 8172 | | 00228 | 288 | B    NEXT |
| 0001CA | D20F 8263 9BCA | 00319 | 01C80 | 289 | SUBFAIL  MVC  OUT+13(16),=C'SUBROUTINE ERROR' |
| 0001D0 | 47F0 8172 | | 00228 | 290 | B    NEXT |
| 0001D4 | D20D 8263 9C52 | 00319 | 01D08 | 291 | OUTPUT  ZAP  FLWD,WEEKDA |
| 0001DA | F870 88CA 88CA | 00980 | 00980 | 292 | CVB  3,FLWD |
| 0001E0 | 4F30 88CA | | 00980 | 293 | MH   3,=H'9' |
| 0001E4 | 4C30 9C60 | | 01D16 | 294 | LA   5,NAMTAB |
| 0001E8 | 4150 8824 | | 008DA | 295 | AR   5,3 |
| 0001EC | 1A53 | | | 296 | MVC  OUT+18(9),0(5) |
| 0001EE | D208 8268 5000 | 0031E | 00000 | 297 | CP   HOLIDA,=P'099' |
| 0001F4 | F911 8B09 9C62 | 01BBF | 01D18 | 298 | BE   NOHOL |
| 0001FA | 4780 816C | | 00222 | 299 | MVC  OUT+28(17),=C'HOLIDAY STATUS...' |
| 0001FE | D210 8272 9CDB | 00328 | 01D91 | 300 | ZAP  FLWD,HOLIDA |
| 000204 | F871 88CA 88BF | 00980 | 00980 | 301 | CVB  3,FLWD |
| 00020A | 4F30 88CA | | 00980 | 302 | MH   3,=H'45' |
| 000210 | 4C30 9C64 | | 01D1A | 303 | LA   5,NAMTABH |
| 000216 | 1A53 | | | 304 | AR   5,3 |
| 000218 | D22C 8284 5000 | 0033A | 00000 | 305 | MVC  OUT+46(45),0(5) |
| 00021E | 47F0 8172 | | 00228 | 306 | B    NEXT |
| 000222 | D213 82B2 9CC2 | 00328 | 01CB8 | 308 | NOHOL  MVC  OUT+28(20),=C'AND IS NOT A HOLIDAY' |
| 000228 | D20E 82B2 9CEC | 00328 | 01DA2 | 309 | NEXT   MVC  OUT+92(15),=C'CODE9 CONTENTS:' |
| 00022E | F300 820E 9B0B | 002C4 | 01BC1 | 310 | UNPK VOID(1),CODE9 |
| 000234 | D300 820E 9CFB | 002C4 | 01DB1 | 311 | MVZ  VOID(1),=C'0' |
| 00023A | D200 82C2 820E | 00378 | 002C4 | 312 | MVC  OUT+108(1),VOID |
| | | | | 313 | PRTOV LIST,12 |
| | | | | 319 | PUT  LIST |
| | | | | 319 | LIST |
| 00025A | 9240 8256 | 0030C | | 324 | MVI  OUT,X'40' |
| 00025E | D282 8257 8256 | 0030D | 0030C | 325 | MVC  OUT+1(131),OUT |
| 000264 | 47F0 8026 | | 000DC | 326 | B    READ |
| | | | | 327 | FINI  CLOSE TESTFIL |
| 000276 | 9240 8256 | 0030C | | 335 | MVI  OUT,X'40' |
| 00027A | D282 8257 8256 | 0030D | 0030C | 336 | MVC  OUT+1(131),OUT |
| 000280 | D226 8256 8863 | 0030C | 00919 | 337 | MVC  OUT(39),TOTAL |
| 000286 | D205 8271 888A | 00327 | 00940 | 338 | MVC  OUT+27(6),MASK |
| 00028C | DE05 8271 8890 | 00327 | 00946 | 339 | ED   OUT+27(6),TOT |
| | | | | 340 | CNTRL LIST,SP,1 |
| | | | | 346 | PUT  LIST |
| | | | | 351 | CLOSE LIST |
| | | | | 359 | EOJ |

```
                                                      DOS/VSE ASSEMBLER 08.14 99-12-31

LOC      OBJECT CODE       ADDR1 ADDR2  STMT  SOURCE STATEMENT

0002BC                                   362  TESTFLE  DS  OCLB0
0002BC                                   363  TSTDATE  DS  ZL8
0002C4                                   364  VOID     DS  CL72
00030C                                   365  OUT      DS  CL132
000390   00000106                        366  ADDR     DC  A(GO+4096)
                                         367  NAMTABH  DC  OCL1305
000394   E3D6C4C1E840C9E2                368           DC  CL45'TODAY IS NEW YEAR''S DAY '
0003C1   D5C5E640E8C5C1D9                369           DC  CL45'NEW YEAR FALLS ON SUNDAY- TRANSFERRED -->'
0003EE   D5C5E7E340D5C5E6                370           DC  CL45'NEXT NEW YEAR IS ON SATURDAY- TRANSFERRED <--'
00041B   E3D6C4C1E840C9E2                371           DC  CL45'TODAY IS MARTIN LUTHER KING''S BIRTHDAY '
000448   D4C1D9E3C9D540D3                372           DC  CL45'MARTIN LUTHER KING''S BIRTHDAY IS TRANSFERRED '
000475   E3D6C4C1E840C9E2                373           DC  CL45'TODAY IS LINCOLN''S BIRTHDAY '
0004A2   D3C9D5C3D6D3D57D                374           DC  CL45'LINCOLN''S BIRTHDAY IS TRANSFERRED '
0004CF   E3D6C4C1E840C9E2                375           DC  CL45'TODAY IS WASHINGTON - PRESIDENTS DAY '
0004FC   E3D6C4C1E840C9E2                376           DC  CL45'TODAY IS GOOD FRIDAY '
000529   E3D6C4C1E840C9E2                377           DC  CL45'TODAY IS EASTER SUNDAY '
000556   E3D6C4C1E840C9E2                378           DC  CL45'TODAY IS EASTER MONDAY IN CANADA '
000583   E3D6C4C1E840C9E2                379           DC  CL45'TODAY IS VICTORIA DAY IN CANADA '
0005B0   E3D6C4C1E840C9E2                380           DC  CL45'TODAY IS MEMORIAL DAY '
0005DD   E3D6C4C1E840C9E2                381           DC  CL45'TODAY IS ST. JOHN THE BAPTIST DAY IN CANADA '
00060A   E2E34B40D1D6C8D5                382           DC  CL45'ST. JOHN THE BAPTIST DAY IS TRANSFERRED '
000637   E3D6C4C1E840C9E2                383           DC  CL45'TODAY IS CANADA DAY '
000664   C3C1D5C1C4C140C4                384           DC  CL45'CANADA DAY IS TRANSFERRED '
000691   E3D6C4C1E840C9E2                385           DC  CL45'TODAY IS INDEPENDENCE DAY '
0006BE   C9D5C4C5D7C5D5C4                386           DC  CL45'INDEPENDENCE DAY IS TRANSFERRED '
0006EB   E3D6C4C1E840C9E2                387           DC  CL45'TODAY IS CIVIC HOLIDAY IN CANADA '
000718   E3D6C4C1E840C9E2                388           DC  CL45'TODAY IS LABOR DAY '
000745   E3D6C4C1E87A40E3                389           DC  CL45'TODAY: THANKSGIVING (CAN), COLUMBUS DAY (US) '
000772   E3D6C4C1E840C9E2                390           DC  CL45'TODAY: IS ELECTION DAY '
00079F   E3D6C4C1E87A40D9                391           DC  CL45'TODAY: REMEMBRANCE (CAN), VETERANS DAY (US) '
0007CC   D9C5D4C5D4C2D9C1                392           DC  CL45'REMEMBRANCE - VETERANS DAY ARE TRANSFERRED '
0007F9   E3D6C4C1E840C9E2                393           DC  CL45'TODAY IS THANKSGIVING DAY '
000826   E3D6C4C1E840C9E2                394           DC  CL45'TODAY IS CHRISTMAS DAY '
000853   C3C8D9C9E2E3D4C1                395           DC  CL45'CHRISTMAS DAY IS TRANSFERRED '
000880   E3D6C4C1E840C9E2                396           DC  CL45'TODAY IS BOXING DAY IN CANADA '
0008AD   C2D6E7C9D5C740C4                397           DC  CL45'BOXING DAY IS TRANSFERRED '
                                         398  *
0008DA   E2E4D5C4C1E84040                399  NAMTAB   DC  CL9'SUNDAY '
0008E3   D4D6D5C4C1E84040                400           DC  CL9'MONDAY '
0008EC   E3E4C5E2C4C1E840                401           DC  CL9'TUESDAY '
0008F5   E6C5C4D5C5E2C4C1                402           DC  CL9'WEDNESDAY'
0008FE   E3C8E4D9E2C4C1E8                403           DC  CL9'THURSDAY '
000907   C6D9C9C4C1E84040                404           DC  CL9'FRIDAY '
000910   E2C1E3E4D9C4C1E8                405           DC  CL9'SATURDAY '
000919   C3C8C540E2E4C2D9                406  TOTAL    DC  C'THE SUBROUTINE WAS EXECUTED       TIMES'
000940   402020202020                    407  MASK     DC  X'402020202020'
000946   00000C                          408  TOT      DC  PL3'0'
000949   E3C5E2E340D6C640                409  HDG      DC  C'TEST OF TIMESUB9 TO DETERMINE HOLIDAY STATUS '
000978   40                              410  SWITCH   DC  X'40'
000980                                   411  FLWD     DS  1D
000988                                   412  SAVE     DS  CL72
                                         413  *
```

**Figure 10.1**  Continued.

```
LOC  OBJECT CODE   ADDR1 ADDR2   STMT   SOURCE STATEMENT                                    DOS/VSE ASSEMBLER 08.14  99-12-31

                                  415  *                                                                              * TS900010
                                  416  *                                                                              * TS900020
                                  417  *                                                                              * TS900030
                                  418  * TTTTTTT  III  MM    MM  EEEEE  SSSS      U    U  BBBBB   999                 * TS900040
                                  419  *    T      I   M M  M M  E      S          U    U  B    B  9   9               * TS900050
                                  420  *    T      I   M  MM  M  EEEE   SSSS      U    U  BBB B   9999                * TS900060
                                  421  *    T      I   M      M  E          S      U    U  B    B      9               * TS900070
                                  422  *    T     III  M      M  EEEEE  SSSS      UUUUU  BBBB     99                  * TS900080
                                  423  *                                                                              * TS900090
                                  424  * **************************************************************               * TS900100
                                  425  * ****  G R E G O R I A N   H O L I D A Y   S U B R O U T I N E  ****         * TS900110
                                  426  * **************************************************************               * TS900120
                                  427  * **************************************************************               * TS900130
                                  428  * **************************************************************               * TS900140
                                  429  * **************************************************************               * TS900150
                                  430  *    THIS SUBROUTINE DETERMINES THE HOLIDAY STATUS OF AN INPUT                * TS900160
                                  431  *        GREGORIAN DATE                                                        * TS900170
                                  432  *                                                                              * TS900180
                                  433  *  1.  VALID INPUT YEARS FOR THIS SUBROUTINE ARE THE YEARS                    * TS900190
                                  434  *        1601 THROUGH 3399 A. D.                                               * TS900200
                                  435  *                                                                              * TS900210
                                  436  *  2.  VALID INPUT MONTH VALUES FOR THIS SUBROUTINE ARE 01                    * TS900220
                                  437  *        THROUGH 12.                                                           * TS900230
                                  438  *                                                                              * TS900240
                                  439  *  3.  VALID INPUT DAY VALUES FOR THIS SUBROUTINE ARE 01                      * TS900250
                                  440  *        THROUGH 31 WITH EXCEPTIONS FOR THE MONTHS LISTED:                    * TS900260
                                  441  *            MONTH          MAXIMUM DAY VALUE                                  * TS900270
                                  442  *             04                30                                            * TS900280
                                  443  *             06                30                                            * TS900290
                                  444  *             09                30                                            * TS900300
                                  445  *             11                30                                            * TS900310
                                  446  *             02                28                                            * TS900320
                                  447  *             02                29 DURING LEAP YEAR                            * TS900330
                                  448  *                                                                              * TS900340
                                  449  *  4.  THE DATE FORMAT MUST BE MMDDYYYY, WHERE MM = THE TWO                   * TS900350
                                  450  *        DIGIT MONTH VALUE, DD = THE TWO DIGIT DAY VALUE AND                  * TS900360
                                  451  *        YYYY = THE FOUR DIGIT YEAR.                                          * TS900370
                                  452  *                                                                              * TS900380
                                  453  *  5.  THE CALLING PROGRAM MUST PLACE THE EIGHT DIGIT DATE,                   * TS900390
                                  454  *        IN ZONED DECIMAL, IN A SUBROUTINE DEFINED EIGHT BYTE                 * TS900400
                                  455  *        FIELD, 'DATEH,' BEFORE EXECUTION OF THE SUBROUTINE.                  * TS900410
                                  456  *        DATEH IS NOT ALTERED BY THE SUBROUTINE.                              * TS900420
                                  457  *                                                                              * TS900430
                                  458  *  6.  A SUBROUTINE DEFINED ONE BYTE FIELD, 'CODE9,' IS RETURNED             * TS900440
                                  459  *        TO THE CALLING PROGRAM AND CONTAINS A PACKED 0 IF THE               * TS900450
                                  460  *        EXECUTION WAS SUCCESSFUL.  NON-ZERO VALUES INDICATE                  * TS900460
                                  461  *        THE FOLLOWING:                                                        * TS900470
                                  462  *                                                                              * TS900480
                                  463  *        A PACKED 2 INDICATES UNSUCCESSFUL EXECUTION: INVALID DATA           * TS900490
                                  464  *        IN DATEH.                                                             * TS900500
                                  465  *                                                                              * TS900510
                                  466  *        INVALID DATA ARE DETERMINED IF THE LOW ORDER BYTE'S ZONE            * TS900520
                                  467  *        CONTAINS AN INVALID SIGN, (AN INVALID SIGN IS OTHER THAN           * TS900530
                                  468  *        X'C', X'A', X'E', OR X'F'), OR IF THE PRECEDING BYTES'             * TS900540
                                  469  *        ZONES ARE OTHER THAN X'F', OR IF ANY BYTE'S LOW ORDER              * TS900550
```

```
LOC   OBJECT CODE   ADDR1 ADDR2   STMT   SOURCE STATEMENT                                      DOS/VSE ASSEMBLER 08.14  99-12-31

                                  470  *   NIBBLE CONTAINS A VALUE GREATER THAN X'9'.                               TS900560
                                  471  *                                                                            TS900570
                                  472  *   A PACKED 4 INDICATES UNSUCCESSFUL EXECUTION: INVALID YEAR                TS900580
                                  473  *   VALUE IN DATEH- A VALUE THAT EXCEEDS THE LIMITS SPECIFIED                TS900590
                                  474  *   IN 1., ABOVE.                                                            TS900600
                                  475  *                                                                            TS900610
                                  476  *   A PACKED 6 INDICATES UNSUCCESSFUL EXECUTION: INVALID                     TS900620
                                  477  *   MONTH VALUE IN DATEH- A VALUE THAT EXCEEDS THE LIMITS                    TS900630
                                  478  *   SPECIFIED IN 2., ABOVE.                                                  TS900640
                                  479  *                                                                            TS900650
                                  480  *   A PACKED 8 INDICATES UNSUCCESSFUL EXECUTION: INVALID DAY                 TS900660
                                  481  *   VALUE IN DATEH- A VALUE THAT EXCEEDS THE LIMITS SPECIFIED                TS900670
                                  482  *   IN 3., ABOVE.                                                            TS900680
                                  483  *                                                                            TS900690
                                  484  *   INSPECTION OF THE RETURN CODE IS IMPORTANT.  THE RETURN                  TS900700
                                  485  *   CODE, CODE9, REFLECTS THE LEVEL OF EDITING.  A RETURN                    TS900710
                                  486  *   CODE OF 2, FOR EXAMPLE, NOT ONLY INDICATES INVALIDITY OF                 TS900720
                                  487  *   DATA, IT ALSO INDICATES THAT NO EDITING HAS BEEN DONE TO                 TS900730
                                  488  *   VALIDATE THE YEAR, MONTH OR DAY VALUES.  A RETURN CODE OF                TS900740
                                  489  *   4 INDICATES THAT THE DATA ARE VALID BUT THAT THE YEAR WAS                TS900750
                                  490  *   FOUND INVALID- THE MONTH AND DAY VALUES HAVE NOT BEEN ED-                TS900760
                                  491  *   ITED.  A RETURN CODE OF 6 INDICATES THAT THE DATA AND                   TS900770
                                  492  *   YEAR ARE VALID BUT THAT THE MONTH IS INVALID- THE DAY                   TS900780
                                  493  *   VALUE HAS NOT BEEN EDITED.  FINALLY, A RETURN CODE OF 8                 TS900790
                                  494  *   INDICATES THAT THE DATA, YEAR AND MONTH ARE VALID BUT                   TS900800
                                  495  *   THAT THE DAY WAS FOUND INVALID FOR THE VALID MONTH GIVEN.               TS900810
                                  496  *   IN SHORT, THE RETURN CODE INDICATES THE LEVEL OF EDITING.               TS900820
                                  497  *   THE EDIT SEQUENCE IS DATA, YEAR, MONTH AND DAY.                         TS900830
                                  498  *                                                                            TS900840
                                  499  *7.                                                                          TS900850
                                  500  *   A SUBROUTINE DEFINED TWO BYTE PACKED FIELD, 'HOLIDA,' IS                 TS900860
                                  501  *   RETURNED TO THE CALLING PROGRAM.  IF THE EXECUTION IS                   TS900870
                                  502  *   SUCCESSFUL THE TWO DIGIT CODE CONTINED IN HOLIDA REPRE-                  TS900880
                                  503  *   SENTS THE HOLIDAY ASSDCIATED WITH THE INPUT DATE.                       TS900890
                                  504  *   HOLIDA WILL CONTAIN NINETY-NINE IF THE DATE IS NOT A                    TS900900
                                  505  *   HOLIDAY OR IF THE EXECUTION HAS NOT BEEN SUCCESSFUL-                    TS900910
                                  506  *   THAT IS, IF THE RETURN CODE, CODE9, CONTAINS A NON-ZERO                 TS900920
                                  507  *   VALUE.  THIS IS PROTECTION AGAINST ILLEGAL USE OF A                     TS900930
                                  508  *   PRIOR EXECUTION'S RESULT.  THE FOLLOWING ARE THE CODES                  TS900940
                                  509  *   ASSOCIATED WITH POPULAR HOLIDAYS OF THE GREGORIAN                       TS900950
                                  510  *   CALENDAR IN NORTH AMERICA:                                              TS900960
                                  511  *                                                                            TS900970
                                  512  *   HOLIDAY NAME                                HOLIDAY CODE                 TS900980
                                  513  *   NEW YEAR'S DAY                                    00                     TS900990
                                  514  *   NEW YEAR TRANSFERRED                              01                     TS901000
                                  515  *   NEW YEAR TRANSFERRED FROM NEXT YEAR              02                     TS901010
                                  516  *   MARTIN LUTHER KING'S BIRTHDAY                     03                     TS901020
                                  517  *   MARTIN LUTHER KING'S BIRTHDAY TRANSFERRED         04                     TS901030
                                  518  *   LINCOLN'S BIRTHDAY                                05                     TS901040
                                  519  *   LINCOLN'S BIRTHDAY TRANSFERRED                    06                     TS901050
                                  520  *   WASHINGTON'S BIRTHDAY                             07                     TS901060
                                  521  *   GOOD FRIDAY                                       08                     TS901070
                                  522  *   EASTER SUNDAY                                     09                     TS901080
                                  523  *   EASTER MONDAY (CAN)                               10                     TS901090
                                  524  *   VICTORIA DAY (CAN)                                11                     TS901100
                                       *   MEMORIAL DAY                                      12
```

**Figure 10.1** *Continued*

```
LOC   OBJECT CODE   ADDR1 ADDR2   STMT   SOURCE STATEMENT                                    DOS/VSE ASSEMBLER 08.14 99-12-31

                                  525  *  ST JOHN THE BAPTIST'S DAY (QUE.-CAN)          13    * TS901110
                                  526  *  ST JOHN THE BAPTIST'S DAY TRANSFERRED         14    * TS901120
                                  527  *  CANADA DAY (CAN)                              15    * TS901130
                                  528  *  CANADA DAY TRANSFERRED                        16    * TS901140
                                  529  *  INDEPENDENCE DAY                              17    * TS901150
                                  530  *  INDEPENDENCE DAY TRANSFERRED                  18    * TS901160
                                  531  *  CIVIC HOLIDAY (CAN)                           19    * TS901170
                                  532  *  LABOR DAY                                     20    * TS901180
                                  533  *  THANKSGIVING (CAN)- COLUMBUS DAY (US)         21    * TS901190
                                  534  *  ELECTION DAY                                  22    * TS901200
                                  535  *  REMEMBRANCE DAY (CAN)- VETERANS' DAY (US)     23    * TS901210
                                  536  *  REMEMBRANCE DAY - VETERANS' DAY TRANSFERRED   24    * TS901220
                                  537  *  THANKSGIVING DAY                              25    * TS901230
                                  538  *  CHRISTMAS DAY                                 26    * TS901240
                                  539  *  CHRISTMAS DAY TRANSFERRED                     27    * TS901250
                                  540  *  BOXING DAY (CAN)                              28    * TS901260
                                  541  *  BOXING DAY TRANSFERRED                        29    * TS901270
                                  542  *  NOT A HOLIDAY- EITHER COUNTRY                 99    * TS901280
                                  543  *                                                     * TS901290
                                  544  *  8. A SUBROUTINE DEFINED ONE BYTE FIELD, 'WEEKDA,' IS   * TS901300
                                  545  *     RETURNED TO THE CALLING PROGRAM. WEEKDA CONTAINS    * TS901310
                                  546  *     A PACKED VALUE LESS THAN 7 IF EXECUTION HAS BEEN SUC- * TS901320
                                  547  *     CESSFUL. IF EXECUTION IS UNSUCCESSFUL, THAT IS, IF CODE9 * TS901330
                                  548  *     CONTAINS A NON-ZERO VALUE, THEN WEEKDA WILL CONTAIN  * TS901340
                                  549  *     A PACKED 9. THIS IS PROTECTION AGAINST ILLEGAL USE OF * TS901350
                                  550  *     A PRIOR EXECUTION'S RESULT.                         * TS901360
                                  551  *                                                     * TS901370
                                  552  *     THE PACKED VALUES CONTAINED IN WEEKDA UPON SUCCESSFUL * TS901380
                                  553  *     EXECUTION CORRESPOND TO NAMES OF DAYS OF THE WEEK ON THE * TS901390
                                  554  *     GREGORIAN CALENDAR. THE CORRESPONDENCES ARE AS FOLLOWS: * TS901400
                                  555  *                                                     * TS901410
                                  556  *          PACKED VALUE        DAY NAME REPRESENTED   * TS901420
                                  557  *               0                SUNDAY               * TS901430
                                  558  *               1                MONDAY               * TS901440
                                  559  *               2                TUESDAY              * TS901450
                                  560  *               3                WEDNESDAY            * TS901460
                                  561  *               4                THURSDAY             * TS901470
                                  562  *               5                FRIDAY               * TS901480
                                  563  *               6                SATURDAY             * TS901490
                                  564  *                                                     * TS901500
                                  565  *  9. ALL OTHER SUBROUTINE DEFINED FIELDS AND LABELS ARE  * TS901510
                                  566  *     TRANSPARENT TO THE CALLING PROGRAM.                 * TS901520
                                  567  *                                                     * TS901530
                                  568  *                                                     * TS901540
                                  569  * 10. THIS SUBROUTINE IS WRITTEN TO BE ASSEMBLED WITH THE * TS901550
                                  570  *     CALLING PROGRAM AND SHOULD BE INSERTED IN THE CALLING * TS901560
                                  571  *     PROGRAM IMMEDIATELY BEFORE THE 'END' OPCODE.        * TS901570
                                  572  *                                                     * TS901580
                                  573  * 11. THIS SUBROUTINE USES REGISTER 6 AS THE LINK REGISTER. * TS901590
                                  574  *     IF REGISTER 6 IS ASSIGNED IN THE CALLING PROGRAM FOR * TS901600
                                  575  *     OTHER USES, IT MUST BE SAVED PRIOR TO EXECUTING THE * TS901610
                                  576  *     'BALR.'                                            * TS901620
                                  577  *                                                     * TS901630
                                  578  *                                                     * TS901640
                                  579  *                                   JEROME T. MURRAY  * TS901650
```

```
LOC     OBJECT CODE       ADDR1  ADDR2  STMT  SOURCE STATEMENT                                    DOS/VSF ASSEMBLER 08.14  99-12-31

                                                                                                    MARILYN J. MURRAY  *      TS901660
                                         580  *                                                                       *      TS901670
                                         581  * GLEN ELLYN, ILLINOIS                                                  *      TS901680
                                         582  *                                                                       *      TS901690
                                         583  * *********************************************************************  *      TS901700
                                         584  * *********************************************************************  *      TS901710
                                         585  * *********************************************************************  *      TS901720
                                         586  *                                                                              TS901730
                                         587  *         +++ SECTION 1- GENERAL HOUSEKEEPING  +++                             TS901740
                                         588  *                                                                              TS901750
                                         589  *               INITIALIZE INDICATIVE AND WORK FIELDS                          TS901760
                                         590  *               CLEAR TRANSFER ENTRIES IN TABLE                               TS901770
                                         591  *                                                                              TS901780
0009D0  F811 9B09 9C66  01BBF  01D1C     592  TIMESUB9 ZAP  HOLIDA,=P'99'                                                    TS901790
0009D6  F800 9B08 9CFC  01BBE  01DB2     593           ZAP  WEEKDA,=P'9'                                                     TS901800
0009DC  F800 9B0B 9CBE  01BC1  01D74     594           ZAP  CODE9,=P'O'                                                      TS901810
0009E2  F810 9B27 9CBE  01BDD  01D74     595           ZAP  #$901,=P'O'                                                      TS901820
0009E8  F810 9B97 9CBE  01C4D  01D74     596           ZAP  #$902,=P'O'                                                      TS901830
0009EE  F810 9B2F 9CBE  01BE5  01D74     597           ZAP  #$904,=P'O'                                                      TS901840
0009F4  F810 9B37 9CBE  01BED  01D74     598           ZAP  #$906,=P'O'                                                      TS901850
0009FA  F810 9B57 9CBE  01C0D  01D74     599           ZAP  #$914,=P'O'                                                      TS901860
000A00  F810 9B5F 9CBE  01C15  01D74     600           ZAP  #$916,=P'O'                                                      TS901870
000A06  F810 9B67 9CBE  01C1D  01D74     601           ZAP  #$918,=P'O'                                                      TS901880
000A0C  F810 9B7F 9CBE  01C35  01D74     602           ZAP  #$924,=P'O'                                                      TS901890
000A12  F810 9B8B 9CBE  01C41  01D74     603           ZAP  #$927,=P'O'                                                      TS901900
000A18  F810 9B93 9CBE  01C49  01D74     604           ZAP  #$929,=P'O'                                                      TS901910
000A1E  D207 9B19 9B0C  01BCF  01BC2     605           MVC  #$9DATEH,DATEH                                                   TS901920
                                         606  *                                                                              TS901930
                                         607  *               SAVE REGISTERS 1 - 7 IN SAVE FIELD                            TS901940
                                         608  *                                                                              TS901950
000A24  9017 9B9E       01C54            609           STM  1,7,#$9RSAVE                                                     TS901960
                                         610  *                                                                              TS901970
                                         611  *         +++ SECTION 2- FIND NAME OF INPUT DAY  +++                          TS901980
                                         612  *                                                                              TS901990
000A28  D207 974E 9B19  01BCF  01B04     613           MVC  INDATE,#$9DATEH                                                 TS902000
000A2E  4160 93F8       014AE            614           LA   6,T6X                                                           TS902010
000A32  0576                             615           BALR 7,6                                                             TS902020
000A34  F800 9B0B 974D  01BC1  01803     616           ZAP  CODE9,CODE6                                                    TS902030
000A3A  F900 9B0B 9CBE  01BC1  01D74     617           CP   CODE9,=P'O'                                                    TS902040
000A40  4720 9BBA       01C70            618           BH   #$9TERM                                                        TS902050
000A44  F800 9B08 9756  01BBE  0180C     619           ZAP  WEEKDA,OUTDAY                                                  TS902060
                                         620  *                                                                              TS902070
                                         621  *         +++ SECTION 3- CALCULATE ORDINAL DAY OF DATEH  +++                 TS902080
                                         622  *                                                                              TS902090
000A4A  D207 9248 9B19  012FE  01BCF     623           MVC  DATEA,#$9DATEH                                                 TS902100
000A50  4160 90A2       01158            624           LA   6,T2X                                                           TS902110
000A54  0576                             625           BALR 7,6                                                             TS902120
000A56  F811 9B14 9245  01BCA  012FB     626           ZAP  #$9ORD,NEDJUL+2(2)                                             TS902130
                                         627  *                                                                              TS902140
                                         628  *               PLUG END OF TABLE WITH ORDINAL DAY                           TS902150
                                         629  *                                                                              TS902160
000A5C  F811 9B9B 9B14  01C51  01BCA     630           ZAP  #$9END,#$9ORD                                                  TS902170
                                         631  *                                                                              TS902180
                                         632  *         +++ SECTION 4- FIND LEAP YEAR STATUS OF DATEH  +++                 TS902190
                                         633  *                                                                              TS902200
000A62  D203 8F76 9B1D  0102C  01BD3     634           MVC  YEAR(4),#$9DATEH+4
```

**Figure 10.1** *Continued*

```
                                                                    DOS/VSE ASSEMBLER  08.14  99-12-31

LOC     OBJECT CODE     ADDR1 ADDR2  STMT  SOURCE STATEMENT

000A68  4160 8EA8             00F5E   635        LA    6,T1X                                              TS902210
000A6C  0576                           636        BALR  7,6                                               TS902220
                                       637  *                                                            TS902230
                                       638  *   +++   SECTION 5- FIND NEW YEAR ASSOCIATED DATES   +++    TS902240
                                       639  *                                                            TS902250
                                       640  *          FIND DAY NAME OF NEW YEAR'S DAY THIS YEAR         TS902260
                                       641  *                                                            TS902270
000A6E  D203 974E 9C16  01804 01CCC   642        MVC   INDATE(4),=C'0101'                                TS902280
000A74  4160 93F8             014AE   643        LA    6,T6X                                             TS902290
000A78  0576                           644        BALR  7,6                                               TS902300
                                       645  *                                                            TS902310
                                       646  *      IF OUTDAY = 0. SUN.. UPDATE #$901 WITH 002            TS902320
                                       647  *                                                            TS902330
000A7A  F900 9756 9CBE  0180C 01D74   648        CP    OUTDAY,=P'0'                                      TS902340
000A80  4770 89D4       00A8A          649        BNE   #$9NEWY                                           TS902350
000A84  F810 9B27 9CBF  01BDD 01D75   650        ZAP   #$901,=P'2'                                       TS902360
                                       651  *                                                            TS902370
                                       652  *        FIND DAY NAME OF NEXT NEW YEAR'S DAY. (Y + 1)       TS902380
                                       653  *                                                            TS902390
000A8A  F223 9B16 8F76  01BCC 01D72   654  #$9NEWY PACK  #$9YR,YEAR                                       TS902400
000A90  FA20 9B16 9CBC  01BCC 01BCC   655        AP    #$9YR,=P'1'                                       TS902410
000A96  F332 9752 9B16  01808 01BCC   656        UNPK  INDATE+4(4),#$9YR                                 TS902420
000A9C  4160 93F8             014AE   657        LA    6,T6X                                             TS902430
000AA0  0576                           658        BALR  7,6                                               TS902440
000AA2  D203 9752 8F76  01808 01D72   659        MVC   INDATE+4(4),YEAR                                  TS902450
                                       660  *                                                            TS902460
                                       661  *    IF OUTDAY = 6. SAT.. UPDATE #$902 WITH 365 + L         TS902470
                                       662  *                                                            TS902480
000AA8  F900 9756 9CC1  0180C 01D77   663        CP    OUTDAY,=P'6'                                      TS902490
000AAE  4770 8A08       00ABE          664        BNE   #$9MLK                                            TS902500
000AB2  F811 9B97 9C68  01C4D 01D1E   665        ZAP   #$902,=P'365'                                     TS902510
000AB8  FA10 9B97 8F74  01C4D 0102A   666        AP    #$902,L                                           TS902520
                                       667  *                                                            TS902530
                                       668  *   +++   SECTION 6- MARTIN LUTHER KING TRANSFERRED   +++    TS902540
                                       669  *                                                            TS902550
000ABE  D203 974E 9C1A  01804 01CD0   670  #$9MLK  MVC   INDATE(4),=C'0115'                              TS902560
000AC4  4160 93F8             014AE   671        LA    6,T6X                                             TS902570
000AC8  0576                           672        BALR  7,6                                               TS902580
                                       673  *                                                            TS902590
                                       674  *      IF OUTDAY = 6. SAT.. UPDATE #$904 WITH 014            TS902600
                                       675  *                                                            TS902610
000ACA  F900 9756 9CC1  0180C 01D77   676        CP    OUTDAY,=P'6'                                      TS902620
000AD0  4770 8A24       00ADA          677        BNE   #$9MLK2                                           TS902630
000AD4  F811 9B2F 9C6A  01BE5 01D20   678        ZAP   #$904,=P'14'                                      TS902640
                                       679  *                                                            TS902650
                                       680  *      IF OUTDAY = 0. SUN.. UPDATE #$904 WITH 016            TS902660
                                       681  *                                                            TS902670
000ADA  F900 9756 9CBE  0180C 01D74   682  #$9MLK2 CP    OUTDAY,=P'0'                                     TS902680
000AE0  4770 8A34       00AEA          683        BNE   #$9LINC                                           TS902690
000AE4  F811 9B2F 9C6C  01BE5 01D22   684        ZAP   #$904,=P'16'                                      TS902700
                                       685  *                                                            TS902710
                                       686  *   +++   SECTION 7- LINCOLN TRANSFERRED   +++               TS902720
                                       687  *                                                            TS902730
000AEA  D203 974E 9C1E  01804 01CD4   688  #$9LINC MVC   INDATE(4),=C'0212'                              TS902740
000AF0  4160 93F8             014AE   689        LA    6,T6X                                             TS902750
```

```
                                        DOS/VSE ASSEMBLER 08.14 99-12-31

LOC    OBJECT CODE     ADDR1 ADDR2  STMT  SOURCE STATEMENT

000AF4 0576                          690          BALR  7,6                                        TS902760
                                     691  *                                                       TS902770
                                     692  *      IF OUTDAY = 6, SAT.. UPDATE #$906 WITH 042        TS902780
                                     693  *                                                       TS902790
000AF6 F900 9756 9CC1 018OC 01D77    694          CP    OUTDAY,=P'6'                               TS902800
000AFC 4770 8A50      00B06          695          BNE   #$9LIN2                                    TS902810
000B00 F811 9B37 9C6E 01BED 01D24    696          ZAP   #$906,=P'42'                              TS902820
                                     697  *                                                       TS902830
                                     698  *      IF OUTDAY = 0, SUN.. UPDATE #$906 WITH 044        TS902840
                                     699  *                                                       TS902850
000B06 F900 9756 9CBE 018OC 01D74    700  #$9LIN2 CP    OUTDAY,=P'0'                               TS902860
000B0C 4770 8A60      00B16          701          BNE   #$9WASH                                    TS902870
000B10 F811 9B37 9C70 01BED 01D26    702          ZAP   #$906,=P'44'                              TS902880
                                     703  *                                                       TS902890
                                     704  *      +++ SECTION 8- WASHINGTON - PRESIDENTS   +++      TS902900
                                     705  *                                                       TS902910
                                     706  *           FIND NAME OF FEBRUARY 1                      TS902920
                                     707  *                                                       TS902930
000B16 D203 974E 9C22 01804 01CD8    708  #$9WASH MVC   INDATE(4),=C'0201'                         TS902940
000B1C 4160 93F8      014AE          709          LA    6,T6X                                      TS902950
000B20 0576                          710          BALR  7,6                                        TS902960
                                     711  *                                                       TS902970
                                     712  *         WASHINGTON IS THIRD MONDAY                     TS902980
                                     713  *         C = 1, N = 3. ORD = E FOR 02/01/Y              TS902990
                                     714  *                                                       TS903000
000B22 F900 9756 9CBC 018OC 01D72    715          CP    OUTDAY,=P'1'                               TS903010
000B28 4740 8A84      00B3A          716          BL    #$9WASH2                                   TS903020
000B2C 4720 8A8E      00B44          717          BH    #$9WASH3                                   TS903030
                                     718  *                                                       TS903040
                                     719  *              OUTDAY = C                                TS903050
                                     720  *              ORD = ORD + 7(N - 1)                      TS903060
                                     721  *                                                       TS903070
000B30 F811 9B3B 9C72 01BF1 01D28    722          ZAP   #$907,=P'46'                              TS903080
000B36 47F0 8A9A      00B50          723          B     #$9EAST                                    TS903090
                                     724  *                                                       TS903100
                                     725  *              OUTDAY < C                                TS903110
                                     726  *              ORD = ORD + 7 - OUTDAY + 7(N - 1)         TS903120
                                     727  *                                                       TS903130
000B3A F811 9B3B 9C74 01BF1 01D2A    728  #$9WASH2 ZAP  #$907,=P'47'                              TS903140
000B40 47F0 8A9A      00B50          729          B     #$9EAST                                    TS903150
                                     730  *                                                       TS903160
                                     731  *              OUTDAY > C                                TS903170
                                     732  *              ORD = ORD + 7 - (OUTDAY - C) + 7(N - 1)   TS903180
                                     733  *                                                       TS903190
000B44 F811 9B3B 9C76 01BF1 01D2C    734  #$9WASH3 ZAP  #$907,=P'54'                              TS903200
000B4A F810 9B3B 9756 01BF1 018OC    735          SP    #$907,OUTDAY                              TS903210
                                     736  *                                                       TS903220
                                     737  *      +++ SECTION 9- COMPUTE EASTER DATES FOR YEAR +++  TS903230
                                     738  *                                                       TS903240
000B50 D203 9AD9 9B1D 01B8F 01BD3    739  #$9EAST MVC   EYEAR(4),#$9DATEH+4                        TS903250
000B56 4160 97A8      0185E          740          LA    6,T8X                                      TS903260
000B5A 0576                          741          BALR  7,6                                        TS903270
                                     742  *                                                       TS903280
                                     743  *           CALCULATE ORDINAL DAY FOR EASTER            TS903290
                                     744  *                                                       TS903300
```

Figure 10.1  *Continued*

```
LOC    OBJECT CODE        ADDR1 ADDR2   STMT   SOURCE STATEMENT

000B5C F374 9248 9AD3     012FE 01889    745          UNPK  DATEA,EASTER          TS903310
000B62 4160 90A2                01158    746          LA    6,T2X                 TS903320
000B66 0576                              747          BALR  7,6                   TS903330
                                         748   *                                 TS903340
                                         749   *        UPDATE GOOD FRIDAY ENTRY, EASTER - 2 DAYS   TS903350
                                         750   *                                 TS903360
000B68 F811 9B3F 9245     01BF5 012FB    751          ZAP   #$908,NEOJUL+2(2)     TS903370
000B6E FB10 9B3F 9CBF     01BF5 01D75    752          SP    #$908,=P'2'           TS903380
                                         753   *                                 TS903390
                                         754   *        UPDATE EASTER SUNDAY ENTRY   TS903400
                                         755   *                                 TS903410
000B74 F811 9B43 9245     01BF9 012FB    756          ZAP   #$909,NEOJUL+2(2)     TS903420
                                         757   *                                 TS903430
                                         758   *        UPDATE EASTER MONDAY ENTRY, EASTER + 1   TS903440
                                         759   *                                 TS903450
000B7A F811 9B47 9B43     01BFD 01BF9    760          ZAP   #$910,#$909           TS903460
000B80 FA10 9B47 9CBC     01BFD 01D72    761          AP    #$910,=P'1'           TS903470
                                         762   *                                 TS903480
                                         763   *        +++ SECTION 10- VICTORIA  +++   TS903490
                                         764   *                                 TS903500
                                         765   *        FIND DAY NAME OF MAY 25   TS903510
                                         766   *                                 TS903520
000B86 D203 974E 9C26     01804 01CDC    767          MVC   INDATE(4),=C'0525'    TS903530
000B8C 4160 93F8                014AE    768          LA    6,T6X                 TS903540
000B90 0576                              769          BALR  7,6                   TS903550
                                         770   *                                 TS903560
                                         771   *        VICTORIA IS PRECEDING MONDAY   TS903570
                                         772   *        C = 1, ORD = E FOR 05/25/Y   TS903580
                                         773   *                                 TS903590
000B92 F900 9756 9CBC     01806 01D72    774          CP    OUTDAY,=P'1'          TS903600
000B98 4740 8AFA                00BB0    775          BL    #$9VLO                TS903610
000B9C 4720 8B0A                00BC0    776          BH    #$9VHI                TS903620
                                         777   *                                 TS903630
                                         778   *        OUTDAY = C                TS903640
                                         779   *        ORD = ORD - 7             TS903650
                                         780   *                                 TS903660
000BA0 F811 9B4B 9C78     01C01 01D2E    781          ZAP   #$911,=P'138'         TS903670
000BA6 FA10 9B4B 8F74     01C01 0102A    782          AP    #$911,L               TS903680
000BAC 47F0 8B22                00BD8    783          B     #$9MEM                TS903690
                                         784   *                                 TS903700
                                         785   *        OUTDAY < C                TS903710
                                         786   *        ORD = ORD - 6             TS903720
                                         787   *                                 TS903730
000BB0 F811 9B4B 9C7A     01C01 01D30    788 #$9VLO    ZAP   #$911,=P'139'         TS903740
000BB6 FA10 9B4B 8F74     01C01 0102A    789          AP    #$911,L               TS903750
000BBC 47F0 8B22                00BD8    790          B     #$9MEM                TS903760
                                         791   *                                 TS903770
                                         792   *        OUTDAY > C                TS903780
                                         793   *        ORD = ORD - (OUTDAY - C)  TS903790
                                         794   *                                 TS903800
000BC0 F811 9B4B 9C7C     01C01 01D32    795 #$9VHI    ZAP   #$911,=P'145'         TS903810
000BC6 FB00 9756 9B4B     01806 01C01    796          SP    OUTDAY,=P'1'          TS903820
000BCC FB10 9B4B 9756     01C01 0180C    797          SP    #$911,OUTDAY          TS903830
000BD2 FA10 9B4B 8F74     01C01 0102A    798          AP    #$911,L               TS903840
                                         799   *                                 TS903850
```

```
LOC     OBJECT CODE        ADDR1 ADDR2  STMT   SOURCE STATEMENT                                      DOS/VSE ASSEMBLER 08.14  99-12-31

                                         800  *         +++   SECTION 11- MEMORIAL   +++                                      TS903860
                                         801  *                                                                              TS903870
                                         802  *               FIND DAY NAME OF MAY 31                                        TS903880
                                         803  *                                                                              TS903890
000BD8  D203 974E 9C2A    01804 01CE0    804  #$MEM    MVC   INDATE(4),=C'0531'                                              TS903900
000BDE  4160 93F8               014AE    805           LA    6,T6X                                                           TS903910
000BE2  0576                             806           BALR  7,6                                                             TS903920
                                         807  *                                                                              TS903930
                                         808  *               MEMORIAL DAY IS LAST MONDAY IN MAY                             TS903940
                                         809  *               C = 1, ORD = E OF 05/31/Y                                      TS903950
                                         810  *                                                                              TS903960
000BE4  F900 9756 9CBC    0180C 01D72    811           CP    OUTDAY,=P'1'                                                    TS903970
000BEA  4740 8B4C               00C02    812           BL    #$9MLO                                                          TS903980
000BEE  4720 8B5C               00C12    813           BH    #$9MHI                                                          TS903990
                                         814  *                                                                              TS904000
                                         815  *                    OUTDAY = C                                                TS904010
                                         816  *                    ORD = E                                                   TS904020
                                         817  *                                                                              TS904030
000BF2  F811 9B4F 9C7E    01C05 01D34    818           ZAP   #$912,=P'151'                                                   TS904040
000BF8  FA10 9B4F 8F74    01C05 0102A    819           AP    #$912,L                                                         TS904050
000BFE  47F0 8B74               00C2A    820           B     #$9STJ                                                          TS904060
                                         821  *                                                                              TS904070
                                         822  *                    OUTDAY < C                                                TS904080
                                         823  *                    ORD = ORD - 6                                             TS904090
                                         824  *                                                                              TS904100
000C02  F811 9B4F 9C7C    01C05 01D32    825  #$9MLO   ZAP   #$912,=P'145'                                                   TS904110
000C08  FA10 9B4F 8F74    01C05 0102A    826           AP    #$912,L                                                         TS904120
000C0E  47F0 8B74               00C2A    827           B     #$9STJ                                                          TS904130
                                         828  *                                                                              TS904140
                                         829  *                    OUTDAY > C                                                TS904150
                                         830  *                    ORD = ORD - (OUTDAY - 1)                                  TS904160
                                         831  *                                                                              TS904170
000C12  F811 9B4F 9C7E    01C05 01D34    832  #$9MHI   ZAP   #$912,=P'151'                                                   TS904180
000C18  FB00 9756 9CBC    0180C 01D72    833           SP    OUTDAY,=P'1'                                                    TS904190
000C1E  FB10 9B4F 8F74    0180C 0102A    834           SP    #$912,OUTDAY                                                    TS904200
000C24  FA10 9B4F 8F74    01C05 0102A    835           AP    #$912,L                                                         TS904210
                                         836  *                                                                              TS904220
                                         837  *         +++   SECTION 12- ST JOHN THE BAPTIST TRANSFERRED   +++              TS904230
                                         838  *                                                                              TS904240
                                         839  *               ADJUST FIXED DATE FOR LEAP YEAR FACTOR                         TS904250
                                         840  *                                                                              TS904260
000C2A  FA10 9B53 8F74    01C09 0102A    841  #$9STJ   AP    #$913,L                                                         TS904270
                                         842  *                                                                              TS904280
                                         843  *               FIND DAY NAME OF ST JOHN'S DAY                                 TS904290
                                         844  *                                                                              TS904300
000C30  D203 974E 9C2E    01804 01CE4    845           MVC   INDATE(4),=C'0624'                                             TS904310
000C36  4160 93F8               014AE    846           LA    6,T6X                                                           TS904320
000C3A  0576                             847           BALR  7,6                                                             TS904330
                                         848  *                                                                              TS904340
                                         849  *               IF OUTDAY = 6, SAT., UPDATE #$914 WITH #$913 - 1              TS904350
                                         850  *                                                                              TS904360
000C3C  F900 9756 9CC1    0180C 01D77    851           CP    OUTDAY,=P'6'                                                    TS904370
000C42  4770 8B9C               00C52    852           BNE   #$9STJ2                                                         TS904380
000C46  F811 9B57 9B53    01C0D 01C09    853           ZAP   #$914,#$913                                                     TS904390
000C4C  FB10 9B57 9CBC    01C0D 01D72    854           SP    #$914,=P'1'                                                     TS904400
```

Figure 10.1  *Continued*

```
LOC    OBJECT CODE       ADDR1 ADDR2  STMT  SOURCE STATEMENT                          DOS/VSE ASSEMBLER 08.14  99-12-31

                                      855 *                                                                             TS904410
                                      856 *            IF OUTDAY = O. SUN.. UPDATE #$913 WITH #$913 + 1                 TS904420
                                      857 *                                                                             TS904430
000C52 F900 9756  9CBE 018OC 01D74    858 #$9STJ2  CP   OUTDAY,=P'O'                                                    TS904440
000C58 4770 8BB2       00C68          859          BNE  #$9CAND                                                         TS904450
000C5C F811 9B57 9B53 01COD 01C09     860          ZAP  #$914,#$913                                                     TS904460
000C62 FA10 9B57       01COD 01D72    861          AP   #$914,=P'1'                                                     TS904470
                                      862 *                                                                             TS904480
                                      863 *            +++  SECTION 13- CANADA TRANSFERRED  +++                         TS904490
                                      864 *                                                                             TS904500
                                      865 *            ADJUST FIXED DATE FOR LEAP YEAR FACTOR                           TS904510
                                      866 *                                                                             TS904520
000C68 FA10 9B5B 8F74 01C11 0102A     867 #$9CAND  AP   #$915.L                                                         TS904530
                                      868 *                                                                             TS904540
                                      869 *            FIND DAY NAME OF CANADA DAY                                       TS904550
                                      870 *                                                                             TS904560
000C6E D203 974E 9C32 01804 01CE8     871          MVC  INDATE(4).=C'0701'                                             TS904570
000C74 4160 93F8       014AE          872          LA   6.T6X                                                           TS904580
000C78 0576                           873          BALR 7,6                                                             TS904590
                                      874 *                                                                             TS904600
                                      875 *            IF OUTDAY = 6.  SAT.. UPDATE #$916 WITH #$915 - 1                TS904610
                                      876 *                                                                             TS904620
000C7A F900 9756 9CC1 018OC 01D77     877          CP   OUTDAY,=P'6'                                                    TS904630
000C80 4770 8BDA       00C90          878          BNE  #$9CAN2                                                         TS904640
000C84 F811 9B5F 9B5B 01C15 01C11     879          ZAP  #$916.#$915                                                     TS904650
000C8A FB10 9B5F 9CBC 01C15 01D72     880          SP   #$916,=P'1'                                                     TS904660
                                      881 *                                                                             TS904670
                                      882 *                                                                             TS904680
                                      883 *                                                                             TS904690
000C90 F900 9756 9CBE 018OC 01D74     884 #$9CAN2  CP   OUTDAY,=P'O'                                                    TS904700
000C96 4770 8BFO       00CA6          885          BNE  #$9INDD                                                         TS904710
000C9A F811 9B5F 9B5B 01C15 01C11     886          ZAP  #$916.#$915                                                     TS904720
000CAO FA10 9B5F 9CBC 01C15 01D72     887          AP   #$916,=P'1'                                                     TS904730
                                      888 *                                                                             TS904740
                                      889 *            +++  SECTION 14- INDEPENDENCE TRANSFERRED  +++                   TS904750
                                      890 *                                                                             TS904760
                                      891 *            ADJUST FIXED DATE FOR LEAP YEAR FACTOR                           TS904770
                                      892 *                                                                             TS904780
000CA6 FA10 9B63 8F74 01C19 0102A     893 #$9INDD  AP   #$917.L                                                         TS904790
                                      894 *                                                                             TS904800
                                      895 *            FIND DAY NAME OF INDEPENDENCE DAY                                 TS904810
                                      896 *                                                                             TS904820
000CAC D203 974E 9C36 01804 01CEC     897          MVC  INDATE(4).=C'0704'                                             TS904830
000CB2 4160 93F8       014AE          898          LA   6.T6X                                                           TS904840
000CB6 0576                           899          BALR 7,6                                                             TS904850
                                      900 *                                                                             TS904860
                                      901 *            IF OUTDAY = 6.  SAT.. UPDATE #$918 WITH #$917 - 1                TS904870
                                      902 *                                                                             TS904880
000CB8 F900 9756 9CC1 018OC 01D77     903          CP   OUTDAY,=P'6'                                                    TS904890
000CBE 4770 8C18       00CCE          904          BNE  #$9IND2                                                         TS904900
000CC2 F811 9B67 9B63 01C1D 01C19     905          ZAP  #$918.#$917                                                     TS904910
000CC8 FB10 9B67 9CBC 01C1D 01D72     906          SP   #$918,=P'1'                                                     TS904920
                                      907 *                                                                             TS904930
                                      908 *                                                                             TS904940
                                      909 *                                                                             TS904950
```

```
                                                                      DOS/VSE ASSEMBLER 08.14  99-12-31

LOC     OBJECT CODE     ADDR1  ADDR2   STMT   SOURCE STATEMENT

000CCE  F900 9756 9CBE  0180C  01D74   910  #$9IND2  CP   OUTDAY,=P'O'                                      TS904960
000CD4  4770 8C2E       00CE4          911           BNE  #$9CIV                                            TS904970
000CD8  F811 9B67 9863  01C1D  01C19   912           ZAP  #$918,#$917                                       TS904980
000CDE  FA10 9B67 9CBC  01C1D  01D72   913           AP   #$918,=P'1'                                       TS904990
                                       914  *                                                               TS905000
                                       915  *       +++  SECTION 15- CIVIC HOLIDAY  +++                     TS905010
                                       916  *                                                               TS905020
                                       917  *             FIND DAY NAME OF AUGUST 1                          TS905030
                                       918  *                                                               TS905040
000CE4  D203 974E 9C3A  01804  01CF0   919  #$9CIV   MVC  INDATE(4),=C'0801'                                TS905050
000CEA  4160 93F8       014AE          920           LA   6,T6X                                             TS905060
000CEE  0576                           921           BALR 7,6                                               TS905070
                                       922  *                                                               TS905080
                                       923  *       CIVIC HOLIDAY IS FIRST MONDAY IN AUGUST                 TS905090
                                       924  *       C = 1, N = 1, ORD = E OF 08/01/Y                        TS905100
                                       925  *                                                               TS905110
000CF0  F900 9756 9CBC  0180C  01D72   926           CP   OUTDAY,=P'1'                                      TS905120
000CF6  4740 8C58       00D0E          927           BL   #$9CLO                                            TS905130
000CFA  4720 8C68       00D1E          928           BH   #$9CHI                                            TS905140
                                       929  *                                                               TS905150
                                       930  *             OUTDAY = C                                        TS905160
                                       931  *             ORD = ORD + 7(N - 1)                              TS905170
                                       932  *                                                               TS905180
000CFE  F811 9B6B 9C80  01C21  01D36   933           ZAP  #$919,=P'213'                                     TS905190
000D04  FA10 9B6B 8F74  01C21  0102A   934           AP   #$919,L                                           TS905200
000D0A  47F0 8C7A       00D30          935           B    #$9LDA                                            TS905210
                                       936  *                                                               TS905220
                                       937  *             OUTDAY < C                                        TS905230
                                       938  *             ORD = ORD +  C - OUTDAY + 7(N - 1)                TS905240
                                       939  *                                                               TS905250
000D0E  F811 9B6B 9C82  01C21  01D38   940  #$9CLO   ZAP  #$919,=P'214'                                     TS905260
000D14  FA10 9B6B 8F74  01C21  0102A   941           AP   #$919,L                                           TS905270
000D1A  47F0 8C7A       00D30          942           B    #$9LDA                                            TS905280
                                       943  *                                                               TS905290
                                       944  *             OUTDAY > C                                         TS905300
                                       945  *             ORD = ORD + 7 - (OUTDAY - C) + 7(N - 1)           TS905310
                                       946  *                                                               TS905320
000D1E  F811 9B6B 9C84  01C21  01D3A   947  #$9CHI   ZAP  #$919,=P'221'                                     TS905330
000D24  FB10 9B6B 9756  01C21  0180C   948           SP   #$919,OUTDAY                                      TS905340
000D2A  FA10 9B6B 8F74  01C21  0102A   949           AP   #$919,L                                           TS905350
                                       950  *       +++  SECTION 16- LABOR  +++                             TS905360
                                       951  *                                                               TS905370
                                       952  *             FIND DAY NAME OF SEPTEMBER 1                      TS905380
                                       953  *                                                               TS905390
                                       954  *                                                               TS905400
000D30  D203 974E 9C3E  01804  01CF4   955  #$9LDA   MVC  INDATE(4),=C'0901'                                TS905410
000D36  4160 93F8       014AE          956           LA   6,T6X                                             TS905420
000D3A  0576                           957           BALR 7,6                                               TS905430
                                       958  *       LABOR DAY IS FIRST MONDAY IN SEPTEMBER                  TS905440
                                       959  *       C = 1, N = 1, ORD = E OF 09/01/Y                        TS905450
                                       960  *                                                               TS905460
                                       961  *                                                               TS905470
000D3C  F900 9756 9CBC  0180C  01D72   962           CP   OUTDAY,=P'1'                                      TS905480
000D42  4740 8CA4       00D5A          963           BL   #$9LLO                                            TS905490
000D46  4720 8CB4       00D6A          964           BH   #$9LHI                                            TS905500
```

**Figure 10.1** *Continued*

```
LOC    OBJECT CODE      ADDR1 ADDR2   STMT   SOURCE STATEMENT                          DOS/VSE ASSEMBLER 08.14 99-12-31

                                      965  *             OUTDAY = C                                           TS905510
                                      966  *             DRD = E                                              TS905520
                                      967  *                                                                  TS905530
                                      968  *                                                                  TS905540
000D4A F811 9B6F 9C86  01C25 01D3C    969        ZAP   #$920,=P'244'                                          TS905550
000D50 FA10 9B6F 8F74  01C25 0102A    970        AP    #$920,L                                                TS905560
000D56 47F0 8CC6       00D7C          971        B     #$9CTC                                                 TS905570
                                      972  *                                                                  TS905580
                                      973  *             OUTDAY < C                                           TS905590
                                      974  *                                                                  TS905600
                                      975  *             ORD = ORD + C - OUTDAY + 7(N - 1)                    TS905610
000D5A F811 9B6F 9C88  01C25 01D3E    976  #$9LLO ZAP   #$920,=P'245'                                         TS905620
000D60 FA10 9B6F 8F74  01C25 0102A    977        AP    #$920,L                                                TS905630
000D66 47F0 8CC6       00D7C          978        B     #$9CTC                                                 TS905640
                                      979  *                                                                  TS905650
                                      980  *             OUTDAY > C                                           TS905660
                                      981  *             ORD = ORD + 7 - (OUTDAY - C) + 7(N - 1)              TS905670
                                      982  *                                                                  TS905680
000D6A F811 9B6F 9C8A  01C25 01D40    983  #$9LHI ZAP   #$920,=P'252'                                         TS905690
000D70 FB10 9B6F 9756  01C25 01D0C    984        SP    #$920,OUTDAY                                           TS905700
000D76 FA10 9B6F 8F74  01C25 0102A    985        AP    #$920,L                                                TS905710
                                      986  *                                                                  TS905720
                                      987  *       +++  SECTION 17- THANKSGIVING (CAN)- COLUMBUS  +++         TS905730
                                      988  *                                                                  TS905740
                                      989  *             FIND DAY NAME OF OCTOBER 1                           TS905750
                                      990  *                                                                  TS905760
000D7C D203 974E 9C42  01804 01CF8    991  #$9CTC MVC   INDATE(4),=C'1001'                                    TS905770
000D82 4160 93F8       014AE          992        LA    6,T6X                                                  TS905780
000D86 0576            0576           993        BALR  7,6                                                    TS905790
                                      994  *                                                                  TS905800
                                      995  *             T-C DAY IS SECOND MONDAY IN OCTOBER                  TS905810
                                      996  *             C = 1, N = 2, ORD = E OF 10/01/Y                     TS905820
                                      997  *                                                                  TS905830
000D88 F900 9756 9CBC  01D0C 01D72    998        CP    OUTDAY,=P'1'                                           TS905840
000D8E 4740 8CF0       00DA6          999        BL    #$9TCLO                                                TS905850
000D92 4720 8D00       00DB6          1000       BH    #$9TCHI                                                TS905860
                                      1001 *                                                                  TS905870
                                      1002 *             OUTDAY = C                                           TS905880
                                      1003 *             ORD = ORD + 7(N - 1)                                 TS905890
                                      1004 *                                                                  TS905900
000D96 F811 9B73 9C8C  01C29 01D42    1005       ZAP   #$921,=P'281'                                          TS905910
000D9C FA10 9B73 8F74  01C29 0102A    1006       AP    #$921,L                                                TS905920
000DA2 47F0 8D12       00DC8          1007       B     #$9ELD                                                 TS905930
                                      1008 *                                                                  TS905940
                                      1009 *             OUTDAY < C                                           TS905950
                                      1010 *             ORD = ORD + C - OUTDAY + 7(N - 1)                    TS905960
                                      1011 *                                                                  TS905970
000DA6 F811 9B73 9C8E  01C29 01D44    1012 #$9TCLO ZAP  #$921,=P'282'                                         TS905980
000DAC FA10 9B73 8F74  01C29 0102A    1013       AP    #$921,L                                                TS905990
000DB2 47F0 8D12       00DC8          1014       B     #$9ELD                                                 TS906000
                                      1015 *                                                                  TS906010
                                      1016 *             OUTDAY > C                                           TS906020
                                      1017 *             ORD = ORD + 7 - (OUTDAY - C) + 7(N - 1)              TS906030
                                      1018 *                                                                  TS906040
000DB6 F811 9B73 9C90  01C29 01D46    1019 #$9TCHI ZAP  #$921,=P'289'                                         TS906050
```

```
                                                      DOS/VSE ASSEMBLER 08.14  99-12-31

LOC    OBJECT CODE      ADDR1 ADDR2  STMT  SOURCE STATEMENT

000DBC FB10 9B73 9756   01C29 0180C  1020         SP    #$921,OUTDAY                                         TS906060
000DC2 FA10 9B73 8F74   01C29 0102A  1021         AP    #$921,L                                              TS906070
                                     1022  *                                                                 TS906080
                                     1023  *            +++  SECTION 18- ELECTION  +++                       TS906090
                                     1024  *                                                                 TS906100
                                     1025  *            FIND DAY NAME OF NOVEMBER 1                           TS906110
                                     1026  *                                                                 TS906120
000DC8 D203 974E 9C46   01804 01CFC  1027  #$9ELD MVC   INDATE(4),=C'1101'                                   TS906130
000DCE 4160 93F8        014AE        1028         LA    6,T6X                                                TS906140
000DD2 0576                          1029         BALR  7,6                                                  TS906150
                                     1030  *                                                                 TS906160
                                     1031  *            ELECTION DAY IS FIRST TUESDAY AFTER FIRST MONDAY      TS906170
                                     1032  *            C = 1, N = 1, ORD = E OF 11/01/Y                      TS906180
                                     1033  *                                                                 TS906190
000DD4 F900 9756 9CBC   0180C 01D72  1034         CP    OUTDAY,=P'1'                                         TS906200
000DDA 4740 8D3C        00DF2        1035         BL    #$9ELO                                               TS906210
000DDE 4720 8D4C        00E02        1036         BH    #$9EHI                                               TS906220
                                     1037  *                                                                 TS906230
                                     1038  *            OUTDAY = C                                            TS906240
                                     1039  *            ORD = ORD + 1                                         TS906250
                                     1040  *                                                                 TS906260
000DE2 F811 9B77 9C92   01C2D 01D48  1041         ZAP   #$922,=P'306'                                        TS906270
000DE8 FA10 9B77 8F74   01C2D 0102A  1042         AP    #$922,L                                              TS906280
000DEE 47F0 8D5E        00E14        1043         B     #$9ARM                                               TS906290
                                     1044  *                                                                 TS906300
                                     1045  *            OUTDAY < C                                            TS906310
                                     1046  *            ORD = ORD + C - OUTDAY + 7(N - 1) + 1                 TS906320
                                     1047  *                                                                 TS906330
000DF2 F811 9B77 9C94   01C2D 01D4A  1048  #$9ELO ZAP   #$922,=P'307'                                        TS906340
000DF8 FA10 9B77 8F74   01C2D 0102A  1049         AP    #$922,L                                              TS906350
000DFE 47F0 8D5E        00E14        1050         B     #$9ARM                                               TS906360
                                     1051  *                                                                 TS906370
                                     1052  *            OUTDAY > C                                            TS906380
                                     1053  *            ORD = ORD + 7 - (OUTDAY - C) + 7(N - 1) + 1           TS906390
                                     1054  *                                                                 TS906400
000E02 F811 9B77 9C96   01C2D 01D4C  1055  #$9EHI ZAP   #$922,=P'314'                                        TS906410
000E08 FB10 9B77 9756   01C2D 0180C  1056         SP    #$922,OUTDAY                                         TS906420
000E0E FA10 9B77 8F74   01C2D 0102A  1057         AP    #$922,L                                              TS906430
                                     1058  *                                                                 TS906440
                                     1059  *            +++  SECTION 19- REMEMBRANCE-VETERANS' TRANSFERRED +++ TS906450
                                     1060  *                                                                 TS906460
                                     1061  *            ADJUST FIXED DATE FOR LEAP YEAR FACTOR               TS906470
                                     1062  *                                                                 TS906480
000E14 FA10 9B7B 8F74   01C31 0102A  1063  #$9ARM AP    #$923,L                                              TS906490
                                     1064  *                                                                 TS906500
                                     1065  *            FIND DAY NAME OF ARMISTICE DAY                        TS906510
                                     1066  *                                                                 TS906520
000E1A D203 974E 9C4A   01804 01D00  1067         MVC   INDATE(4),=C'1111'                                   TS906530
000E20 4160 93F8        014AE        1068         LA    6,T6X                                                TS906540
000E24 0576                          1069         BALR  7,6                                                  TS906550
                                     1070  *                                                                 TS906560
                                     1071  *            IF OUTDAY = 6, SAT., UPDATE #$924 WITH #$923 - 1      TS906570
                                     1072  *                                                                 TS906580
000E26 F900 9756 9CC1   0180C 01D77  1073         CP    OUTDAY,=P'6'                                         TS906590
000E2C 4770 8D86        00E3C        1074         BNE   #$9ARM2                                              TS906600
```

**Figure 10.1** *Continued*

```
LOC    OBJECT CODE        ADDR1 ADDR2  STMT          SOURCE STATEMENT                                DOS/VSE ASSEMBLER 08.14  99-12-31

000E30 F811 9B7F 9B7B    01C35 01C31  1075          ZAP   #$924,#$923                                                       TS906610
000E36 FB10 9B7F 9CBC    01C35 01D72  1076          SP    #$924,=P'1'                                                       TS906620
                                      1077  *                                                                               TS906630
                                      1078  *       IF OUTDAY = O. SUN.. UPDATE #$924 WITH #$923 + 1                        TS906640
                                      1079  *                                                                               TS906650
000E3C F900 9756 9CBE    0180C 01D74  1080  #$9ARM2 CP    OUTDAY,=P'0'                                                      TS906660
000E42 4770 809C               00E52  1081          BNE   #$9TKS                                                            TS906670
000E46 F811 9B7F 9B7B    01C35 01C31  1082          ZAP   #$924,#$923                                                       TS906680
000E4C FA10 9B7F 9CBC    01C35 01D72  1083          AP    #$924,=P'1'                                                       TS906690
                                      1084  *                                                                               TS906700
                                      1085  *       +++ SECTION 20- THANKSGIVING  +++                                       TS906710
                                      1086  *                                                                               TS906720
                                      1087  *       FIND DAY NAME OF NOVEMBER 1                                             TS906730
                                      1088  *                                                                               TS906740
000E52 D203 974E 9C46    01804 01CFC  1089  #$9TKS  MVC   INDATE(4),=C'1101'                                                TS906750
000E58 4160 93F8               014AE  1090          LA    6,T6X                                                             TS906760
000E5C 0576                           1091          BALR  7,6                                                               TS906770
                                      1092  *                                                                               TS906780
                                      1093  *       THANKSGIVING IS FOURTH THURSDAY                                         TS906790
                                      1094  *       C = 4, N = 4, ORD = E OF 11/01/Y                                        TS906800
                                      1095  *                                                                               TS906810
000E5E F900 9756 9CC0    0180C 01D76  1096          CP    OUTDAY,=P'4'                                                      TS906820
000E64 4740 8DC6               00E7C  1097          BL    #$9TLO                                                            TS906830
000E68 4720 8DDC               00E92  1098          BH    #$9THI                                                            TS906840
                                      1099  *                                                                               TS906850
                                      1100  *       OUTDAY = C                                                              TS906860
                                      1101  *       ORD = ORD + 7(N - 1)                                                    TS906870
                                      1102  *                                                                               TS906880
000E6C F811 9B83 9C98    01C39 01D4E  1103          ZAP   #$925,=P'326'                                                     TS906890
000E72 FA10 9B83 8F74    01C39 0102A  1104          AP    #$925,L                                                           TS906900
000E78 47F0 8DEE               00EA4  1105          B     #$9XMS                                                            TS906910
                                      1106  *                                                                               TS906920
                                      1107  *       OUTDAY < C                                                              TS906930
                                      1108  *       ORD = ORD + C - OUTDAY + 7(N - 1)                                       TS906940
                                      1109  *                                                                               TS906950
000E7C F811 9B83 9C9A    01C39 01D50  1110  #$9TLO  ZAP   #$925,=P'330'                                                     TS906960
000E82 FB10 9B83 9756    01C39 0180C  1111          SP    #$925,OUTDAY                                                      TS906970
000E88 FA10 9B83 8F74    01C39 0102A  1112          AP    #$925,L                                                           TS906980
000E8E 47F0 8DEE               00EA4  1113          B     #$9XMS                                                            TS906990
                                      1114  *                                                                               TS907000
                                      1115  *       OUTDAY > C                                                              TS907010
                                      1116  *       ORD = ORD + 7 - (OUTDAY - C) + 7(N - 1)                                 TS907020
                                      1117  *                                                                               TS907030
000E92 F811 9B83 9C9C    01C39 01D52  1118  #$9THI  ZAP   #$925,=P'337'                                                     TS907040
000E98 FB10 9B83 9756    01C39 0180C  1119          SP    #$925,OUTDAY                                                      TS907050
000E9E FA10 9B83 8F74    01C39 0102A  1120          AP    #$925,L                                                           TS907060
                                      1121  *                                                                               TS907070
                                      1122  *       +++ SECTION 21- CHRISTMAS- BOXING TRANSFERRED  +++                      TS907080
                                      1123  *                                                                               TS907090
                                      1124  *       ADJUST FIXED DATES FOR LEAP YEAR FACTOR                                 TS907100
                                      1125  *                                                                               TS907110
000EA4 FA10 9B87 8F74    01C3D 0102A  1126  #$9XMS  AP    #$926,L                                                           TS907120
000EAA FA10 9B8F 8F74    01C45 0102A  1127          AP    #$928,L                                                           TS907130
                                      1128  *                                                                               TS907140
                                      1129  *       FIND DAY NAME OF CHRISTMAS DAY                                          TS907150
```

DOS/VSE ASSEMBLER 08.14 99-12-31

```
LOC      OBJECT CODE     ADDR1 ADDR2  STMT   SOURCE STATEMENT

                                      1130  *                                                                      TS907160
000EB0   D203 974E 9C4E  01804 014AE  1131       MVC   INDATE(4),=C'1225'                                         TS907170
000EB6   4160 93F8              014AE  1132       LA    6,T6X                                                      TS907180
000EBA   0576                          1133       BALR  7,6                                                        TS907190
                                      1134  *                                                                      TS907200
                                      1135  *                                                                      TS907210
                                      1136  *        IF OUTDAY = 5, FRI., UPDATE #$929 WITH #$926 + 3              TS907220
000EBC   F900 9756 9CFD  0180C 01DB3  1137  #$9XMS1  CP    OUTDAY,=P'5'                                            TS907230
000EC2   4770 8E1C        00ED2        1138       BNE   #$9XMS1                                                    TS907240
000EC6   F811 9B93 9B87  01C49 01C3D  1139       ZAP   #$929,#$926                                                TS907250
000ECC   FA10 9B93 9CFE  01C49 01DB4  1140       AP    #$929,=P'3'                                                TS907260
                                      1141  *                                                                      TS907270
                                      1142  *        IF OUTDAY = 6, SAT., UPDATE #$927 WITH #$926 - 1              TS907280
                                      1143  *                             UPDATE #$929 WITH #$926 - 2             TS907290
                                      1144  *                                                                      TS907300
000ED2   F900 9756 9CC1  0180C 01D77  1145  #$9XMS1  CP    OUTDAY,=P'6'                                            TS907310
000ED8   4770 8E3E        00EF4        1146       BNE   #$9XMS2                                                    TS907320
000EDC   F811 9B88 9B87  01C41 01C3D  1147       ZAP   #$927,#$926                                                TS907330
000EE2   FB10 9B88 9CBC  01C41 01D72  1148       SP    #$927,=P'1'                                                TS907340
000EE8   F811 9B93 9B87  01C49 01C3D  1149       ZAP   #$929,#$926                                                TS907350
000EEE   FA10 9B93 9CBF  01C49 01D75  1150       AP    #$929,=P'2'                                                TS907360
                                      1151  *                                                                      TS907370
                                      1152  *        IF OUTDAY = 0, SUN., UPDATE #$927 WITH #$926 + 1              TS907380
                                      1153  *                             UPDATE #$929 WITH #$926 + 2             TS907390
                                      1154  *                                                                      TS907400
000EF4   F900 9756 9CBE  0180C 01D74  1156  #$9XMS2  CP    OUTDAY,=P'0'                                            TS907420
000EFA   4770 8E60        00F16        1157       BNE   #$9LOAD                                                    TS907430
000EFE   F811 9B88 9B87  01C41 01C3D  1158       ZAP   #$927,#$926                                                TS907440
000F04   FA10 9B88 9CBC  01C41 01D72  1159       AP    #$927,=P'1'                                                TS907450
000F0A   F811 9B93 9B87  01C49 01C3D  1160       ZAP   #$929,#$926                                                TS907460
000F10   FA10 9B93 9CBF  01C49 01D75  1161       AP    #$929,=P'2'                                                TS907470
                                      1162  *                                                                      TS907480
                                      1163  *     +++ SECTION 22 - DETERMINE INPUT HOLIDAY STATUS  +++            TS907490
                                      1164  *     A) LOAD ADDRESS OF FIRST DATE IN REGISTER 5                     TS907500
                                      1165  *                                                                      TS907510
000F16   4150 9B23        01BD9        1166  #$9LOAD  LA    5,#$9DATES+2                                           TS907520
                                      1167  *                                                                      TS907530
                                      1168  *     B) COMPARE - IF #$9ORD = ENTRY, EXIT LOOP                       TS907540
                                      1169  *                                                                      TS907550
000F1A   F911 9B14 5000  01BCA 00000  1170  #$9LOOP  CP    #$9ORD,0(2,5)                                          TS907560
000F20   4780 8E76        00F2C        1171       BE    #$9HOLYD                                                  TS907570
                                      1172  *                                                                      TS907580
                                      1173  *     C) ELSE, LOAD ADDRESS OF NEXT TABLE ENTRY                       TS907590
                                      1174  *             INTO REGISTER 5 AND DO LOOP                             TS907600
                                      1175  *                                                                      TS907610
000F24   4155 0004        00F1A 00004 1176       LA    5,4(5)                                                     TS907620
000F28   47F0 8E64        00F1A        1177       B     #$9LOOP                                                   TS907630
                                      1178  *                                                                      TS907640
                                      1179  *     D) ADDRESS INDICATOR PREVIOUS TO DATE                           TS907650
                                      1180  *                                                                      TS907660
000F2C   4B50 9C9E        01D54        1181  #$9HOLYD SH    5,=H'2'                                               TS907670
                                      1182  *                                                                      TS907680
                                      1183  *     E) LOAD INDICATOR TO HOLIDA FIELD FOR OUTPUT                    TS907690
                                      1184  *                                                                      TS907700
```

**Figure 10.1** *Continued*

```
                                                              DOS/VSE ASSEMBLER 08.14 99-12-31

LOC     OBJECT CODE       ADDR1 ADDR2   STMT  SOURCE STATEMENT

000F30  F811 9B09 5000    01BBF 00000   1185        ZAP   HOLIDA,0(2,5)                               TS907710
                                        1186  *                                                       TS907720
                                        1187  *     +++ SECTION 23- SUBTRACT L FROM FIXED DATES +++   TS907730
                                        1188  *                                                       TS907740
000F36  FB10 9B53 8F74    01C09 0102A   1189        SP    #$913.L                                     TS907750
000F3C  FB10 9B5B 8F74    01C11 0102A   1190        SP    #$915.L                                     TS907760
000F42  FB10 9B63 8F74    01C19 0102A   1191        SP    #$917.L                                     TS907770
000F48  FB10 9B7B 8F74    01C31 0102A   1192        SP    #$923.L                                     TS907780
000F4E  FB10 9B87 8F74    01C3D 0102A   1193        SP    #$926.L                                     TS907790
000F54  FB10 9B8F 8F74    01C45 0102A   1194        SP    #$928.L                                     TS907800
000F5A  47F0 9BBA               01C70   1195        B     #$9TERM                                     TS907810
                                        1196  *                                                       TS907820
                                        1197  *     +++ SECTION 24- MACRO SUBROUTINES +++             TS907830
                                        1198  *                                                       TS907840
00F5E                                   1199  T1X   EQU   *                                           TS907850
                                        1200        TIME1                                             TS907860
001156  07F7                            1252        BR    7                                           TS907870
                                        1253  *                                                       TS907880
01158                                   1254  T2X   EQU   *                                           TS907890
                                        1255        TIME2                                             TS907900
0014AC  07F7                            1378        BR    7                                           TS907910
                                        1379  *                                                       TS907920
014AE                                   1380  T6X   EQU   *                                           TS907930
                                        1381        TIME6                                             TS907940
00185C  07F7                            1521        BR    7                                           TS907950
                                        1522  *                                                       TS907960
0185E                                   1523  T8X   EQU   *                                           TS907970
                                        1524        TIME8                                             TS907980
001BBC  07F7                            1642        BR    7                                           TS907990
                                        1643  *                                                       TS908000
                                        1644  *     +++ SECTION 25- DEFINE STORAGE AND CONSTANTS +++  TS908010
                                        1645  *                                                       TS908020
001BBE  9C                              1646  WEEKDA    DC    PL1'9'                                   TS908030
001BBF  099C                            1647  HOLIDA    DC    PL2'99'                                 TS908040
001BC1  4C                              1648  CODE9     DC    PL1'4'                                   TS908050
001BC2  F0F0F0F0F0F0F0C0                1649  DATEH     DC    ZL8'00000000'                           TS908060
001BCA                                  1650  #$9RD     DS    PL2                                     TS908070
001BCC                                  1651  #$9YR     DS    PL3                                     TS908080
001BCF                                  1652  #$9DATEH  DS    CL8                                     TS908090
                                        1653  *                                                       TS908100
                                        1654  *                THIS IS THE HOLIDAY TABLE              TS908110
                                        1655  *                                                       TS908120
001BD7                                  1656  #$9DATES  DS    OCL116                                  TS908130
001BD7  000C                            1657  #$900     DC    PL2'00'                                 TS908140
001BD9  001C                            1658  #$901     DC    PL2'001'  NEW YEAR'S DAY                TS908150
001BDB  001C                            1659            DC    PL2'01'   NEW YEAR'S DAY TRANSFERRED DATE TS908160
001BDD  000C                            1660  #$903     DC    PL2'000'                                TS908170
001BDF  003C                            1661            DC    PL2'03'   MARTIN L. KING'S BIRTHDAY     TS908180
001BE1  015C                            1662  #$904     DC    PL2'015'                                TS908190
001BE3  004C                            1663            DC    PL2'04'   MARTIN L. KING'S BIRTHDAY TRANSFERRED TS908200
001BE5  000C                            1664  #$905     DC    PL2'000'                                TS908210
001BE7  005C                            1665            DC    PL2'05'   LINCOLN'S BIRTHDAY            TS908220
001BE9  043C                            1666  #$906     DC    PL2'043'                                TS908230
001BEB  006C                            1667            DC    PL2'06'   LINCOLN'S BIRTHDAY TRANSFERRED TS908240
001BED  000C                            1668            DC    PL2'000'                                TS908250
```

```
                                                          DOS/VSE ASSEMBLER 08.14  99-12-31
LOC    OBJECT CODE  ADDR1 ADDR2  STMT  SOURCE STATEMENT
```

| LOC | OBJECT CODE | STMT | SOURCE STATEMENT | | | SEQ |
|-----|-------------|------|------------------|---|---|-----|
| 001BEF | 007C | 1669 | #$907 | DC | PL2'07'  WASHINGTON'S BIRTHDAY | TS908260 |
| 001BF1 | 000C | 1670 | | DC | PL2'000' | TS908270 |
| 001BF3 | 008C | 1671 | | DC | PL2'08'  GOOD FRIDAY | TS908280 |
| 001BF5 | 000C | 1672 | #$908 | DC | PL2'000' | TS908290 |
| 001BF7 | 009C | 1673 | | DC | PL2'09'  EASTER SUNDAY | TS908300 |
| 001BF9 | 000C | 1674 | #$909 | DC | PL2'000' | TS908310 |
| 001BFB | 010C | 1675 | | DC | PL2'10'  EASTER MONDAY | TS908320 |
| 001BFD | 000C | 1676 | #$910 | DC | PL2'000' | TS908330 |
| 001BFF | 011C | 1677 | | DC | PL2'11'  VICTORIA DAY | TS908340 |
| 001C01 | 000C | 1678 | #$911 | DC | PL2'000' | TS908350 |
| 001C03 | 012C | 1679 | | DC | PL2'12'  MEMORIAL DAY | TS908360 |
| 001C05 | 000C | 1680 | #$912 | DC | PL2'000' | TS908370 |
| 001C07 | 013C | 1681 | | DC | PL2'13'  ST. JOHN THE BAPTIST'S DAY | TS908380 |
| 001C09 | 175C | 1682 | #$913 | DC | PL2'175'  ST. JOHN THE BAPTIST'S DAY TRANSFERRED | TS908390 |
| 001C0B | 014C | 1683 | | DC | PL2'14'  CANADA DAY | TS908400 |
| 001C0D | 000C | 1684 | #$914 | DC | PL2'000' | TS908410 |
| 001C0F | 015C | 1685 | | DC | PL2'15' | TS908420 |
| 001C11 | 182C | 1686 | #$915 | DC | PL2'182'  CANADA DAY TRANSFERRED | TS908430 |
| 001C13 | 016C | 1687 | | DC | PL2'16'  INDEPENDENCE DAY | TS908440 |
| 001C15 | 000C | 1688 | #$916 | DC | PL2'000' | TS908450 |
| 001C17 | 017C | 1689 | | DC | PL2'17' | TS908460 |
| 001C19 | 185C | 1690 | #$917 | DC | PL2'185'  INDEPENDENCE DAY TRANSFERRED | TS908470 |
| 001C1B | 018C | 1691 | | DC | PL2'18'  CIVIC HOLIDAY | TS908480 |
| 001C1D | 000C | 1692 | #$918 | DC | PL2'000' | TS908490 |
| 001C1F | 019C | 1693 | | DC | PL2'19'  LABOR DAY | TS908500 |
| 001C21 | 020C | 1694 | #$919 | DC | PL2'20' | TS908510 |
| 001C23 | 020C | 1695 | | DC | PL2'000' | TS908520 |
| 001C25 | 000C | 1696 | #$920 | DC | PL2'000' | TS908530 |
| 001C27 | 021C | 1697 | | DC | PL2'21'  CANADIAN THANKSGIVING - COLUMBUS DAY | TS908540 |
| 001C29 | 000C | 1698 | #$921 | DC | PL2'000' | TS908550 |
| 001C2B | 022C | 1699 | | DC | PL2'22'  ELECTION DAY | TS908560 |
| 001C2D | 000C | 1700 | #$922 | DC | PL2'000' | TS908570 |
| 001C2F | 023C | 1701 | | DC | PL2'23'  REMEMBRANCE DAY - VETERANS' DAY | TS908580 |
| 001C31 | 315C | 1702 | #$923 | DC | PL2'315'  REMEMBRANCE - VETERANS' TRANSFERRED | TS908590 |
| 001C33 | 024C | 1703 | | DC | PL2'24'  THANKSGIVING | TS908600 |
| 001C35 | 000C | 1704 | #$924 | DC | PL2'000' | TS908610 |
| 001C37 | 025C | 1705 | | DC | PL2'25'  CHRISTMAS DAY | TS908620 |
| 001C39 | 000C | 1706 | #$925 | DC | PL2'000' | TS908630 |
| 001C3B | 026C | 1707 | | DC | PL2'26' | TS908640 |
| 001C3D | 359C | 1708 | #$926 | DC | PL2'359'  CHRISTMAS DAY TRANSFERRED | TS908650 |
| 001C3F | 027C | 1709 | | DC | PL2'27'  BOXING DAY | TS908660 |
| 001C41 | 028C | 1710 | #$927 | DC | PL2'000' | TS908670 |
| 001C43 | 028C | 1711 | | DC | PL2'28' | TS908680 |
| 001C45 | 360C | 1712 | #$928 | DC | PL2'360'  BOXING DAY TRANSFERRED | TS908690 |
| 001C47 | 029C | 1713 | | DC | PL2'29' | TS908700 |
| 001C49 | 000C | 1714 | #$929 | DC | PL2'000' | TS908710 |
| 001C4B | 002C | 1715 | | DC | PL2'02'  NEW YEAR DAY TRANSFERRED FROM NEXT YEAR | TS908720 |
| 001C4D | 000C | 1716 | #$902 | DC | PL2'000' | TS908730 |
| 001C4F | 099C | 1717 | | DC | PL2'99'  NO HOLIDAY THIS DATE | TS908740 |
| 001C51 | 000C | 1718 | #$END | DC | PL2'000' | TS908750 |
| 001C54 | | 1719 | #$9RSAVE | DS | 7F | TS908760 |
| | | 1720 | * | | | TS908770 |
| | | 1721 | * | | +++ SECTION 26- RESTORE REGISTERS AND EXIT +++ | TS908780 |
| | | 1722 | * | | | TS908790 |
| 001C70 9817 9B9E | | 01C54 | 1723 | #$9TERM | LM | 1,7,#$9RSAVE | TS908800 |

**Figure 10.1** *Continued*

DOS/VSE ASSEMBLER 08.14 99-12-31

TS908810

```
LOC    OBJECT CODE        ADDR1 ADDR2  STMT   SOURCE STATEMENT

001C74 07F6                     000B4  1724       BR
                                       1725       END   BEGIN
                                       1726   =C'$$BOPEN '
001C78 5B5BC2D6D7C5D540           1727   =C'SUBROUTINE ERROR'
001C80 E2E4C2D9D6E4E3C9           1728   =C'$$BCLOSE'
001C90 5B5BC2C3D3D6E2C5           1729   =A(LIST)
001C98 00000080                   1730   =A(REQUEST)
001C9C 00000000                   1731   =C'INVALID DATA'
001CA0 C9D5E5C1D3C9C440           1732   =C'INVALID YEAR'
001CAC C9D5E5C1D3C9C440           1733   =C'AND IS NOT A HOLIDAY'
001CB8 C1D5C44OC9E24OD5           1734   =C'0101'
001CCC F0F1F0F1                   1735   =C'0115'
001CD0 F0F1F1F5                   1736   =C'0212'
001CD4 F0F2F1F2                   1737   =C'0201'
001CD8 F0F2F0F1                   1738   =C'0525'
001CDC F0F5F2F5                   1739   =C'0531'
001CE0 F0F5F3F1                   1740   =C'0624'
001CE4 F0F6F2F4                   1741   =C'0701'
001CE8 F0F7F0F1                   1742   =C'0704'
001CEC F0F7F0F4                   1743   =C'0801'
001CF0 F0F8F0F1                   1744   =C'0901'
001CF4 F0F9F0F1                   1745   =C'1001'
001CF8 F1F0F0F1                   1746   =C'1101'
001CFC F1F1F0F1                   1747   =C'1111'
001D00 F1F1F1F1                   1748   =C'1225'
001D04 F1F2F2F5                   1749   =C'IS A XXXXXXXXX'
001D08 C9E24OC140E7E7E7           1750   =H'9'
001D16 0009                       1751   =P'099'
001D18 099C                       1752   =H'45'
001D1A 002D                       1753   =P'99'
001D1C 099C                       1754   =P'365'
001D1E 365C                       1755   =P'14'
001D20 014C                       1756   =P'16'
001D22 016C                       1757   =P'42'
001D24 042C                       1758   =P'44'
001D26 044C                       1759   =P'46'
001D28 046C                       1760   =P'47'
001D2A 047C                       1761   =P'54'
001D2C 054C                       1762   =P'138'
001D2E 138C                       1763   =P'139'
001D30 139C                       1764   =P'145'
001D32 145C                       1765   =P'151'
001D34 151C                       1766   =P'213'
001D36 213C                       1767   =P'214'
001D38 214C                       1768   =P'221'
001D3A 221C                       1769   =P'244'
001D3C 244C                       1770   =P'245'
001D3E 245C                       1771   =P'252'
001D40 252C                       1772   =P'281'
001D42 281C                       1773   =P'282'
001D44 282C                       1774   =P'289'
001D46 289C                       1775   =P'306'
001D48 306C                       1776   =P'307'
001D4A 307C                       1777   =P'314'
001D4C 314C                       1778   =P'326'
001D4E 326C
```

DOS/VSE ASSEMBLER 08.14 99-12-31

| LOC | OBJECT CODE | ADDR1 | ADDR2 | STMT | SOURCE STATEMENT |
|---|---|---|---|---|---|
| 001D50 | 330C | | | 1779 | =P'330' |
| 001D52 | 337C | | | 1780 | =P'337' |
| 001D54 | 0002 | | | 1781 | =H'2' |
| 001D56 | 100C | | | 1782 | =P'100' |
| 001D58 | 400C | | | 1783 | =P'400' |
| 001D5A | 000C | | | 1784 | =P'00' |
| 001D5C | 019C | | | 1785 | =P'19' |
| 001D5E | 025C | | | 1786 | =P'25' |
| 001D60 | 010C | | | 1787 | =P'10' |
| 001D62 | 011C | | | 1788 | =P'11' |
| 001D64 | 020C | | | 1789 | =P'20' |
| 001D66 | 030C | | | 1790 | =P'30' |
| 001D68 | 024C | | | 1791 | =P'24' |
| 001D6A | 021C | | | 1792 | =P'21' |
| 001D6C | 031C | | | 1793 | =P'31' |
| 001D6E | F0F4 | | | 1794 | =C'04' |
| 001D70 | F0F3 | | | 1795 | =C'03' |
| 001D72 | 1C | | | 1796 | =P'1' |
| 001D73 | 61 | | | 1797 | =C'/' |
| 001D74 | 0C | | | 1798 | =P'0' |
| 001D75 | 2C | | | 1799 | =P'2' |
| 001D76 | 4C | | | 1800 | =P'4' |
| 001D77 | 6C | | | 1801 | =P'6' |
| 001D78 | C9D5E5C1D3C9C440 | | | 1802 | =C'INVALID MONTH' |
| 001D85 | 8C | | | 1803 | =P'8' |
| 001D86 | C9D5E5C1D3C9C440 | | | 1804 | =C'INVALID DAY' |
| 001D91 | C8D6D3C9C4C1E840 | | | 1805 | =C'HOLIDAY STATUS...' |
| 001DA2 | C3D6C4C5F940C3D6 | | | 1806 | =C'CODE9 CONTENTS:' |
| 001DB1 | F0 | | | 1807 | =C'0' |
| 001DB2 | 9C | | | 1808 | =P'9' |
| 001DB3 | 5C | | | 1809 | =P'5' |
| 001DB4 | 3C | | | 1810 | =P'3' |
| 001DB5 | 01600C | | | 1811 | =P'1600' |
| 001DB8 | 03399C | | | 1812 | =P'3399' |
| 001DBB | 01000C | | | 1813 | =P'1000' |
| 001DBE | 01601C | | | 1814 | =P'1601' |
| 001DC1 | 36525C | | | 1815 | =P'36525' |
| 001DC4 | 7C | | | 1816 | =P'7' |
| 001DC5 | F1 | | | 1817 | =C'1' |

**Figure 10.1** *Continued*

RELOCATION DICTIONARY                                                                                99-12-31

| ESDID FOR ADDR CON | ESDID FOR REF SYMBOL | TYPE | LENGTH | ADDRESS |
|---|---|---|---|---|
| 001 | +001 | A | 4 | 000008 |
| 001 | +002 | V | 3 | 000011 |
| 001 | +001 | A | 4 | 000018 |
| 001 | +001 | CCW | 3 | 000029 |
| 001 | +001 | A | 4 | 000060 |
| 001 | +001 | A | 4 | 00007A |
| 001 | +001 | A | 4 | 00008C |
| 001 | +001 | A | 4 | 000098 |
| 001 | +001 | A | 4 | 0000C8 |
| 001 | +001 | A | 4 | 0000CC |
| 001 | +001 | A | 4 | 000270 |
| 001 | +001 | A | 4 | 0002B4 |
| 001 | +001 | A | 4 | 0C0390 |
| 001 | +001 | A | 4 | 001C98 |
| 001 | +001 | A | 4 | 001C9C |

DIAGNOSTICS AND STATISTICS                                                                           99-12-31

NO ERRORS FOUND

THE FOLLOWING MACRO NAMES HAVE BEEN FOUND IN MACRO INSTRUCTIONS

```
DTFPR     PRMOD     ACB       RPL       EXLST     OPEN      GET       CNTRL     PUT       PRTOV     CLOSE     EOJ       TIME1
TIME2     TIME6     TIME8     WAIT      EXCP      IKQERMAC  IKQACB1   ISTACB1   IKQEXL1   ISTEXL1   IKQRPL1   ISTRPL1   BTWAIT
IKQACBG   IKQEXLG   IKQRPLG
```

OPTIONS FOR THIS ASSEMBLY - ALIGN, LIST, NOXREF, LINK, RLD, NODECK, NODECK

THE ASSEMBLER WAS RUN IN 524168 BYTES
END OF ASSEMBLY

```
TEST OF TIMESUB9 TO DETERMINE HOLIDAY STATUS

01/01/1982  IS A FRIDAY     HOLIDAY STATUS... TODAY IS NEW YEAR'S DAY                        CODE9 CONTENTS: 0
01/02/1982  IS A SATURDAY   AND IS NOT A HOLIDAY                                             CODE9 CONTENTS: 0
12/31/1982  IS A FRIDAY     HOLIDAY STATUS... NEXT NEW YEAR IS ON SATURDAY- TRANSFERRED <--  CODE9 CONTENTS: 0
01/01/1982  IS A FRIDAY     HOLIDAY STATUS... TODAY IS NEW YEAR'S DAY                        CODE9 CONTENTS: 0
01/15/1982  IS A FRIDAY     HOLIDAY STATUS... TODAY IS MARTIN LUTHER KING'S BIRTHDAY         CODE9 CONTENTS: 0
01/16/1982  IS A SATURDAY   AND IS NOT A HOLIDAY                                             CODE9 CONTENTS: 0
02/12/1982  IS A FRIDAY     HOLIDAY STATUS... TODAY IS LINCOLN'S BIRTHDAY                    CODE9 CONTENTS: 0
02/13/1982  IS A SATURDAY   AND IS NOT A HOLIDAY                                             CODE9 CONTENTS: 0
02/15/1982  IS A MONDAY     HOLIDAY STATUS... TODAY IS WASHINGTON - PRESIDENTS DAY           CODE9 CONTENTS: 0
02/16/1982  IS A TUESDAY    AND IS NOT A HOLIDAY                                             CODE9 CONTENTS: 0
04/09/1982  IS A FRIDAY     HOLIDAY STATUS... TODAY IS GOOD FRIDAY                           CODE9 CONTENTS: 0
04/10/1982  IS A SATURDAY   AND IS NOT A HOLIDAY                                             CODE9 CONTENTS: 0
04/11/1982  IS A SUNDAY     HOLIDAY STATUS... TODAY IS EASTER SUNDAY                         CODE9 CONTENTS: 0
04/12/1982  IS A MONDAY     HOLIDAY STATUS... TODAY IS EASTER MONDAY IN CANADA               CODE9 CONTENTS: 0
04/13/1982  IS A TUESDAY    AND IS NOT A HOLIDAY                                             CODE9 CONTENTS: 0
05/24/1982  IS A MONDAY     HOLIDAY STATUS... TODAY IS VICTORIA DAY IN CANADA                CODE9 CONTENTS: 0
05/25/1982  IS A TUESDAY    AND IS NOT A HOLIDAY                                             CODE9 CONTENTS: 0
05/31/1982  IS A MONDAY     HOLIDAY STATUS... TODAY IS MEMORIAL DAY                          CODE9 CONTENTS: 0
06/01/1982  IS A TUESDAY    AND IS NOT A HOLIDAY                                             CODE9 CONTENTS: 0
06/24/1982  IS A THURSDAY   HOLIDAY STATUS... TODAY IS ST. JOHN THE BAPTIST DAY IN CANADA    CODE9 CONTENTS: 0
06/25/1982  IS A FRIDAY     AND IS NOT A HOLIDAY                                             CODE9 CONTENTS: 0
07/01/1982  IS A THURSDAY   HOLIDAY STATUS... TODAY IS CANADA DAY                            CODE9 CONTENTS: 0
07/02/1982  IS A FRIDAY     AND IS NOT A HOLIDAY                                             CODE9 CONTENTS: 0
07/04/1982  IS A SUNDAY     HOLIDAY STATUS... TODAY IS INDEPENDENCE DAY                      CODE9 CONTENTS: 0
07/05/1982  IS A MONDAY     HOLIDAY STATUS... INDEPENDENCE DAY IS TRANSFERRED                CODE9 CONTENTS: 0
07/06/1982  IS A TUESDAY    AND IS NOT A HOLIDAY                                             CODE9 CONTENTS: 0
08/02/1982  IS A MONDAY     HOLIDAY STATUS... TODAY IS CIVIC HOLIDAY IN CANADA               CODE9 CONTENTS: 0
08/03/1982  IS A TUESDAY    AND IS NOT A HOLIDAY                                             CODE9 CONTENTS: 0
09/06/1982  IS A MONDAY     HOLIDAY STATUS... TODAY IS LABOR DAY                             CODE9 CONTENTS: 0
09/07/1982  IS A TUESDAY    AND IS NOT A HOLIDAY                                             CODE9 CONTENTS: 0
10/11/1982  IS A MONDAY     HOLIDAY STATUS... TODAY: THANKSGIVING (CAN), COLUMBUS DAY (US)   CODE9 CONTENTS: 0
10/12/1982  IS A TUESDAY    AND IS NOT A HOLIDAY                                             CODE9 CONTENTS: 0
11/02/1982  IS A TUESDAY    HOLIDAY STATUS... TODAY IS ELECTION DAY                          CODE9 CONTENTS: 0
11/03/1982  IS A WEDNESDAY  AND IS NOT A HOLIDAY                                             CODE9 CONTENTS: 0
11/11/1982  IS A THURSDAY   HOLIDAY STATUS... TODAY: REMEMBRANCE (CAN), VETERANS DAY (US)    CODE9 CONTENTS: 0
11/12/1982  IS A FRIDAY     AND IS NOT A HOLIDAY                                             CODE9 CONTENTS: 0
11/25/1982  IS A THURSDAY   HOLIDAY STATUS... TODAY IS THANKSGIVING DAY                      CODE9 CONTENTS: 0
12/24/1982  IS A FRIDAY     HOLIDAY STATUS... CHRISTMAS DAY IS TRANSFERRED                   CODE9 CONTENTS: 0
12/25/1982  IS A SATURDAY   HOLIDAY STATUS... TODAY IS CHRISTMAS DAY                         CODE9 CONTENTS: 0
12/26/1982  IS A SUNDAY     HOLIDAY STATUS... TODAY IS BOXING DAY IN CANADA                  CODE9 CONTENTS: 0
12/27/1982  IS A MONDAY     HOLIDAY STATUS... BOXING DAY IS TRANSFERRED                      CODE9 CONTENTS: 0
12/28/1982  IS A TUESDAY    AND IS NOT A HOLIDAY                                             CODE9 CONTENTS: 0
  /  /      INVALID DATA                                                                     CODE9 CONTENTS: 2
01/01/1983  IS A SATURDAY   HOLIDAY STATUS... TODAY IS NEW YEAR'S DAY                        CODE9 CONTENTS: 0

THE SUBROUTINE WAS EXECUTED   44  TIMES
```

**Figure 10.1** *Continued*

## Applications of TIMESUB Subroutines and Macros

Clearly, using the subroutines presented in this book imposes a minimal restriction on the ALC programmer in that each subroutine or macro presents an important set of reserved words, as follows:

**TIMESUBF MACROF.** DATEF, SIGF, FORMAT, CODEF, TIMEF

**TIMESUBG MACROG.** DATEG, SIGG, FORMT8, CODEG, TIMEG

**TIMESUB1 MACRO1.** YEAR, L, CODE1, TIME1

**TIMESUB2 MACRO2.** DATEA, JULIAN, NEOJUL, CODE2, TIME2

**TIMESUB3 MACRO3.** DATE1, DATE2, DCOUNT, CODE3, TIME3

**TIMESUB4 MACRO4.** DATEX, DATEY, PYEAR, PMONTH, PDAY, CODE4, TIME4

**TIMESUB5 MACRO5.** DATEI, MODIFY, NUDATE, CODE5, TIME5

**TIMESUB6 MACRO6.** INDATE, OUTDAY, CODE6, TIME6

**TIMESUB7 MACRO7.** NEOJIN, EXJULI, CODE7, TIME7

**TIMESUB8 MACRO8.** EYEAR, EASTER, CODE8, TIME8

**TIMESUB9 MACRO9.** DATEH, HOLIDA, WEEKDA, CODE9, T1X, T2X, T6X, T8X, TIME1, TIME2, TIME6, TIME8, TIME9

It's impossible to anticipate the many diverse requirements that might be encountered when analyzing computations of worldwide dates. While we've presented programming tools more than sufficient to build a complete Gregorian calendar for any year from 1601 to 3399, there are certainly problems whose solutions require considerable creative effort. These realities make the following and last chapter of this book perhaps even more important.

# The Conversion Plan

Most data-processing professionals are familiar with conversions that involve migrating to new hardware or new operating systems. User management generally understands the objectives of the change and looks forward to the benefits, fully aware that, based on past experience, the project will probably come in late and over budget.

Typically, a conversion requires changing the source code to accommodate syntax variations, transferring files to managed databases, and concurrently modifying the JCL. None of these processes is simple and none is anticipated with equanimity. However, all such conversions are routine if vendors have a stake in their success and, therefore, have at the very least committed resources to check-pointing the conversion path. To this extent, computer users haven't really been alone in their conversion efforts.

Probably the most extensive conversion efforts to date in the short history of computing are marked by the introduction of System/360 and the much later adoption of client/server architecture. Although these two events are separated by nearly 30 years, some installations are still executing 1400-series programs in emulation and are encumbered with awkwardly designed DASD equivalents of prehistoric tabulating systems—subtle testimony to the fact that IS personnel do not greet conversions with unbridled enthusiasm. It has been humorously claimed that IS managers have but a limited number of conversions in their constitution.

The current crisis requires a different kind of conversion, and doesn't allow for the luxury of flexible scheduling. Worse yet, it's worldwide in scope, mandatory in nature, consuming of resources, and totally without benefit other than saving us from a fate until now we didn't recognize. A successful conversion merely assures that we can continue to transact business beyond December 31, 1999, and for some the deadline is much earlier. User management is clearly not impressed by the return on investment.

There has been much procrastination and denial since we last addressed this problem in *Computers in Crisis: How to Avert the Coming Worldwide Computer Systems Collapse* by Petrocelli Books, Inc., 1984. A most important resource has been wasted in the interim—*time*.

The conversion we're contemplating now, more than 10 years later, must still analyze and alter stored data, re-create source logic, modify input protocols, and forever change programming practices, but all in a much reduced time frame. There are problems associated with client/server networks that will challenge the most creative technicians. Be assured that, due to the sheer force of numbers, we all must act alone. What vendor can muster sufficient resources in the face of such massive need? As was said earlier, "this is a user problem."

All of this explodes in the midst of a world economy totally dependent on computer resources for its survival and demanding of the services of skilled technical personnel whose availability is in dreadfully short supply. Yet we must succeed because there's no time to waste. This is a crisis so much of our own making that to hesitate to act immediately is irresponsible and inimical to national welfare, if not simple economic suicide. Nonetheless, we know there are those who will fail and we might very well be numbered among them; all we need to do is procrastinate.

## Preconversion Objectives: An Overview

Generally, a conversion is an exceptional activity to be completed one way or another and gotten out of the way of the application backlog so the important business can go forward. Consequently, conversion techniques occupy a minor place in computer science and technology. Unfortunately, you'd be hard pressed to find mention of conversion techniques in the literature, other than in project control references— an area not addressed by this book.

Lengthy research uncovers a single book on the topic: *Conversion of Computer Software* by John R. Wolberg of the Technion-Israel Institute of Technology. Turning to a review of IBM resources on this subject, you'll discover GC28-1251-00, *The Year 2000 and 2-Digit Dates: A Guide for Planning and Implementation*. A dearth of material, to be sure, but at least a beginning.

Observing the two offerings, one eminently academic and the other eminently practical, we're brought face to face with the chasm between computer science and data-processing practice. One approach, computer science, is seemingly preoccupied with conceptualizing while the other, data-processing practice, is obviously preoccupied with getting the job done. Our task is clearly one of combining the two.

Conversion is a three-stage effort comprising preconversion activities, implementation, and postconversion activities. The preconversion steps produce parameters that reveal the apparent implementation resource requirements: machine time, staffing needs, and duration. The implementation stage addresses the active application of the solution. The postimplementation stage addresses cleaning up, monitoring, and observing the installed system. Preconversion steps are best kept separate of requested system modifications, enhancements, or addenda. Preconversion activities target date usage and provide the parameters necessary to schedule the conversion's implementation. When later considered in relation to the application backlog, these resulting parameters should aid in identifying backlog projects that will be deferred until the completion of the implementation stage. Undertaking extraneous technical efforts, which only adds to the inventory of problem programs even as we work to solve such problems, doesn't make sense.

The steps that must be taken in the preconversion stage are explicit. They are a product of the available literature, extensive consulting experience, and an intimate awareness of the social and political pressures brought to bear in both large and small computer user environments. Above all, the preconversion stage must produce knowledge, and seeks to answer the following six questions:

- What are IS's technical options?
- How many work-days are implied by the program and database inventory in need of repair?
- What machine resources are required for this conversion?
- Given the required versus the available resources, what's the time requirement to complete the implementation?
- Since continued backlog programming and system development will add to the conversion requirements, can activity be suspended until implementation is completed?
- What's the total cost?

## Technical Options

The preconversion steps depend on assumptions about the status of the system. Of primary importance is the status of the system date. Will the accessible system date be six digits or eight digits? A good deal hinges on the answer to this question. Only one vendor, IBM, has issued a statement of intent to provide eight-digit dating for its software current with the end of 1996. If only a six-digit date is accessible, an early problem develops in that TIMESUB2 creates the Neojulian date from an eight-digit input date.

### The century table

In order to access an eight-digit date when there's only a six-digit date available, it's necessary to invoke a century table, also known as a "sliding-century window." You must decide how many years in the past and how many years into the future the table will function. This is governed by the firm's computing horizon. Generally, the current year minus 35 years and plus 64 years define the century table's architecture, although any contiguous 100-year span is allowable. Thus, assuming a current year of 1995, you're looking at a table whose lowest entry is 1960 and whose highest entry is 2059. Here we define 19 and 20 as the table functions while 60, 61, 62, . . . 00, . . . 59 are the table arguments. The search argument, of course, is the two-digit year component of the six-digit date whose century you're attempting to isolate.

If the table is programmed so that each year it increases all of its components by 1, the century table remains in relative step with the calendar. The benefits of the table are obvious in that a six-digit date can be input, its two-digit year used as a search argument in the century table, and the two-digit century table function returned. Six-digit year-2000 dates merely execute the table lookup with the two-digit year 00. When a match is found for the table argument, 00, the table function is accessed, 20. Thus the four-digit year 2000 is assembled and made available to the program.

All of this works, however, only if no date prior to 1960 enters the system. The century table is an excellent emergency solution for firms operating well within the limits of the table's effectiveness, and with no foreseeable future exposure to merger, expansion, or accelerated growth. Unfortunately, all too often a problem with using the century table is the tendency to standardize it. Advocates' typical claims often sound partisan:

"Now that we can acquire a four-digit year from the century table, we can invoke any of the subroutines we have available to accomplish the program corrections required. Quite simply, it's possible to create a program environment whose logic is internally eight-digit-date-oriented while all of its output is six-digit dates. Thus, we can patch programs without having to update databases. This approach reduces the total workload in that the stored data is untouched. Even more attractive is the fact that individual programs can be updated and returned to service after testing—there's no need to go through the rigors of lengthy planning and subsystem scheduling."

*Beware!* For the effort that's saved versus the risk taken, we advise the more thorough approach. Conversion to an eight-digit-date standard both within programs and within databases staves off ultimate disaster and preserves the investment demanded by the current crisis. While the options must be explained to user management, so must their hazards.

Among the aftershocks of our present crisis will be a clearer view of IS as either a financial asset or a liability. Typically, IS departments are rarely audited prior to a merger or acquisition. After corporations are confronted with multimillion-dollar invoices for their share of the current cleanup effort, however, they'll very likely be extremely circumspect about a possible future liability for what could be called a "less than thorough" date conversion. Future mergers and acquisitions might well hang in the balance.

## IBM offerings

Various vendors offer technical options. IBM has developed a COBOL compiler for MVS and VM. Another compiler, VS COBOL II, is available as an intermediate migration aid for those using the discontinued OS/VS COBOL compiler.

VS COBOL II doesn't provide sliding-century window support or intrinsic functions, although, as we mentioned earlier, IBM has announced its intent that the most recent releases of IBM software products as of year-end 1996 will support dates and date fields for A.D. 2000 and beyond.

COBOL for MVS and VM features ANSI COBOL standard intrinsic functions and a sliding-century window. A multilanguage runtime library and language environment for MVS and VM supports PL/I for MVS and VM, COBOL for MVS and VM, C/C++, Fortran, and MVS/ESA, and also provides additional date manipulation support.

PL/I for MVS and VM, like COBOL for MVS and VM, brings with it four-digit-year support, sliding-century window support, and built-in functions—PL/I's equivalent of the intrinsic functions of COBOL.

The VSE environment offers COBOL for VSE/ESA, a compiler, and language environment for VSE/ESA, the runtime library. ANSI COBOL standard intrinsic functions provide four-digit-year date manipulation capability. Sliding-century window support is also available; it isn't an ANSI facility. Also available to the VSE market are COBOL compilers DOS/VS COBOL and VS COBOL II, neither of which can handle four-digit-year dates. VS COBOL II is recommended as an intermediate compiler to the installation of COBOL for VSE/ESA.

PL/I for VSE/ESA, a compiler, and language environment for VSE/ESA, the runtime library, provide a sliding-century window and built-in functions.

There are three RPG compilers, focused mostly on the AS/400: the Integrated Language Environment (ILE) RPG IV, Original Program Model (OPM) RPG/400, and a System/36-compatible compiler. The first two compilers, ILE and OPM, allow you to retrieve a four-digit-year using *YEAR or *DATE. The two-digit date components or the full six-digit date is subject to retrieval via UDATE, UYEAR, UMONTH, and UDAY—analogs to *DATE, *YEAR, *MO, and *DAY. The System/36-compatible compiler is restricted to the two-digit year of the six-digit-date environment.

## Built-in calendar functions and intrinsic functions

Collectively, additional functions featured in a compiler or language environment (runtime library) provide for the accessibility of a four-digit-year as well as limited date arithmetic. Intrinsic functions return values. In one intrinsic function for VSE COBOL, submitting DAY-OF-INTEGER returns YYYYDDD, the neo-Julian date, while submitting DATE-OF-INTEGER returns YYYYMMDD, the full eight-digit date.

RPG arithmetic facilities for the AS/400, for instance, allow duration calculations; ADDUR (add duration) adds years, months, or days to a given date. Similarly, subtraction can be performed. The results, however, are prone to the same vagaries encountered in extended-interval aging.

We could go on to review the feature offerings of any number of vendors after exhausting IBM's inventory of software for the year 2000. There are a multitude of CASE tools designed to aid re-engineering and tools to unlock the secrets of files. Space and time, however, don't permit an in-depth review.

We earlier urged that this conversion would be well served if other agendas were suppressed. Indeed, this is true. Nonetheless, we see that upgrade software can be purchased in the midst of this, the world's most widespread conversion effort. Computer users must determine for themselves the feasibility of attempting to upgrade to a more contemporary language compiler or operating system while solving the year 2000 date problem. Many installations have become seriously out of date and could have much work to do just to be able to attempt this conversion.

## Sizing the Task

An informed judgment can't be rendered without numbers. The IS quest for knowledge addresses the number of programs in which date calculations are taking place. In stored data (databases), where are dates, date derivatives (date elements used as counters, and so on) or dates used in file identification or indexing? Where are dates entering the system? How are they being used? Are all dates equal in importance?

By isolating an instance of date input, you might be able to see the relative unimportance of some dates. Consider the following electronic data interchange (EDI) scenario:

You receive an EDI purchase order containing a six-digit date that your system ignores in favor of its system date as the order date. Other suppliers receiving this EDI purchase order might use the date as a sort field. Due to this diversity, it's difficult to determine truly important dates. It's incumbent on IS to make its system date proof.

### A case in point

Perhaps the most delicate part of sizing the task is making determinations relative to a given date's true activity. While it's necessary to closely scrutinize each detail, it would be naïve today to think that you could size the conversion task efficiently without the aid of software tools.

Nonetheless, several years ago we undertook the chore of sizing an anonymous client's application program, utility, and database inventory. To determine the degree of difficulty and the probability that the task could be automated, we performed the sizing manually. It required two people working for 96 hours. The findings were as follows: All database records bore dates. Fifty-two percent of application programming was obviously involved in date usage. Sort utilities constituted approximately 15 percent of the involved software.

Reviewing the installation's change management documents permitted us to peek into the productivity of the programming personnel. The programming backlog was reviewed and prioritized, resolving conflicts with the programs in need of date format correction for the year 2000. Invoking the installation's programmer productivity expectations, we concluded that the staff had to be increased by 30 percent in order to complete its task by 1999. This client task was to be handled totally in-house using manual techniques.

Given the time frame, number of programs, databases, utilities, complexity of the task, and lack of telecommunications involvement, early resolution was promising. Today's analytic software tools would reduce the size of the effort considerably, but there will always be the difficulty of determining the importance of some dates. No tool is a panacea.

The end of this chapter has a list of firms that have identified themselves or their products as being useful in one or another area of the conversion effort. We haven't reviewed their products or services due to time constraints, but have listed them for your convenience. Send one or more of the companies a query letter or postcard for product information. We've omitted telephone numbers for the sake of the vendors and potential clients who could end up on hold.

## Machine Resources

Machine time is always in short supply and, as more complexity develops, computer availability becomes a key factor. While the task-sizing effort is going forward, the installation's total application system must be separated into a group of noninterlocking subsystems. The smaller these subsystems can be made, the less complex will be the implementation of the solution plan. In cases where dependencies are permanent, additional ancillary programming must be created to free the subsystems.

The sizing task addresses not only the location, type and, quantity of date usage in programming, databases, utilities, JCL or CL, and screens (CICS, or display files) but added to this are client/server and miscellaneous networks, as well as free-standing PCs. Because the days of single-vendor procurement have disappeared, these devices and their software could pose an enhanced learning curve at the operating system level where dates dwell.

Machine resource requirements can be assessed with software that estimates run times based on subsystem performance. You can also find programmers' machine requirements reflected in the records of the change management logs. In the event that machine availability is extremely tight, the only solution might be to employ an additional computer configuration.

Because the modified subsystems will be tested at the unit level then at the subsystem level, and finally executed in parallel with the production subsystem, an additional computer configuration might be mandatory. It isn't a luxury to parallel both the test system and the production system when modifications are complete; machine time requirements might continue to grow.

If you'll be conducting testing on the installation's production machine, take considerable care to ensure that changes to the system's date are isolated. Several of the vendors listed at the end of this chapter offer date-change software.

This conversion is pervasive. Other conversions have addressed specific differences; this one will take you where you don't want to be. Be aware that your month-end, quarter-end, and year-end closing programming could be affected by date modifications. It might be necessary to execute a system test using month-end, quarter-end, or year-end data from a prior period. And you'll need machine time to test areas that other conversions won't affect.

## The Time Requirement

Your ability to arrive at a total implementation time requirement will be no better than the quality of your installed change management system. Reviewing changes made to the system allows you to become familiar with the installation's level of productivity. Using Wolberg's productivity equations offers some help, but the short time available to solve this problem leads to some more intuitive measures.

The total time requirement consists of estimates. The total number of lines of code requiring modification divided by the installation's programmer productivity level constitutes the rock-bottom work-day estimate. If the decision has been made to use a century table, only this programming can be involved.

If you decide to execute a proper conversion, you must add to the total time the work days required to create the "throw-away" interim programs to isolate the subsystems into separate entities. Presumably, the whereabouts of dates in the databases has already been roughly determined and the requirement to create database updating programs evaluated. You must also add the work days required for these procedures.

At this point, total the work days. It's now time to begin the resources-versus-work-days evaluation. Few organizations carry surplus personnel on their programming staff. The solution to the date problem is, in all likelihood, going to require additional personnel. New personnel result in the expenditure of location and hiring time as well as time for the new employees to become familiar with the installation and its programming practices. This time must also be added to the implementation time total. At long last, total the full time requirement. Few will be happy with the results.

The longer an installation procrastinates, the less likely it will be able to "staff up" with capable personnel. The marketplace will become more and more competitive as the pool of professional personnel dries up. Companies might need to make counter offers to disaffected personnel bent on resigning for opportunities elsewhere. And beyond all of this is the possibility that the implementation stage will overrun the time calculated, placing additional pressure on the IS team.

## Suspend backlog development?

It's important to review backlog tasks, which tend to execute under the status quo, thus adding to the conversion problem. Quite often there's an opportunity to place backlog projects in limbo until the implementation stage has ended. Having presented the implementation time resource requirements, management is often quite receptive to any possible reductions.

The benefits of a backlog furlough are valuable. Personnel not working on backlog tasks are available to participate in conversion implementation, and these work days can be subtracted from the total. Further, fewer active backlog tasks mean less competition for resources.

Clearly, no one benefits from backlog programming that's written one day and discarded the next. Backlog expansion need not be stopped, but programming in this area should be restricted if not put on hold.

## What Does the Conversion Cost?

By no means will the conversion into the land of eight-digit dates be inexpensive. Costs of thousands, tens of thousands, hundreds of thousands, millions, and even tens of millions of dollars are commonplace. Those who have attempted to calculate the cost of solving this problem on a worldwide basis have ended up with estimates of more than 300 billion dollars. As would be expected, the more dependent an organization is on computer support, the more likely its program library and costs will be huge.

Certainly, after executing the preconversion steps, the dollar amounts should be known; they're the product of the work days multiplied by the cost of personnel, plus software tools, plus the cost of lost profit opportunities. Unfortunately, profit opportunities are also lost to more aggressive competitors who have already converted.

If the final dollar count is the determining factor in pursuing a solution to the date problem, you're placing a very low value on your firm's business. We've also possibly missed something in our analysis and presentation.

Consider what will happen if management turns down the project after the preconversion effort. The presence of formal management controls, accountability, and formal reporting often make the difference. A pilot implementation might also aid in tying down elusive times and cost figures.

## Management Protocols

### Step 1

In preparing for the preconversion effort, you should select an in-house consultant from among a technician pool. Once the preconversion phase starts, he or she should report to the IS director and to the chief executive officer jointly. The in-house consultant is charged with the task of answering the six questions outlined earlier in the chapter.

The consultant's responsibility to IS is technical, and his responsibility to the CEO is informative. This triumvirate defines the preconversion management team. If staffing levels are so low that a consultant-caliber technician doesn't exist or can't be spared, or if the fortunes of business preclude the luxury of appointing a consultant, the effort is at mortal risk.

Remember that this crisis will destroy many firms that have waited too long to begin their conversion effort. Yours could be one of these, and you'll know this early on.

### Step 2

Having been assigned this task, the consultant must become familiar with the nature of the problem of date computation by thoroughly reading the contents of this book. Additionally, the consultant should review IBM's earlier-cited GC28-1251-00 and, if possible, Wolberg's work on software conversion.

### Step 3

The consultant, already familiar with the installation's system structure, identifies, in concert with IS, the technical resources required to carry out the steps of the preconversion stage. This step culminates in a joint meeting with the CEO. The meeting's agenda is the first preconversion document. The objective of this meeting is to enumerate and procure the required resources for the successful completion of the preconversion task. The CEO should, in fact, be asked for a permanent, firm commitment of those resources.

Just as there's nothing informal about asking for corporate funds, it's not politically wise to allow room for failure by compromising the task's true requirements. It's important to formally prepare a meeting agenda containing the enumerated resource requirements. It's equally important to prepare a postmeeting memo that recapitulates the meeting's conclusions.

Among the resources often requested are additional personnel to support the preconversion activities, purchase software to reorganize "spaghetti code" COBOL programs, develop program file/record/field usage documents, identify date fields within the database, and so on.

The remaining steps define the work to which those resources must be committed without reservation. The CEO must be apprised of the reason for the request of each resource.

**Step 4**

The targets of the conversion are: application programs, sorts, utilities, JCL, source library inclusion books, card decks in drawers, data entry formats (desktop terminals, key to tape, key to disk, OCR, data communication, punched paper tape, bar code, plastic card, diskette, hand-held terminal, tape cassette, prepunched style tag and POS are but a few), and the database. Consequently, an inventory must be made in preparation for a subsequent meeting with IS and the CEO.

The objective of this inventory is to isolate mutually exclusive, date-dependent subsystems. Mutually exclusive subsystems are discrete groups of programs, sorts, or utilities that involve computation of dates but share no common files or other common data resources. The goal is to create subsystems whose date-related program logic and files can be converted and returned to production to function in an eight-digit date environment independently of other systems. The corresponding data-entry formats are necessary to assure conversion of the input interface. The related JCL is required for subsystem testing and debugging as well as verification of file identification. These objectives must be explained to the CEO.

It's necessary to review the installation's entire application software collection in order to compile this inventory. The person or people conducting this review must scour operations schedules, special request procedures, and library directory listings. Perhaps the most disheartening discovery in this process is uncovering executing phases for which no source books are available or for which the synchronization between source and object no longer exists.

The degree to which an installation is organized will determine the degree of difficulty encountered in compiling an inventory. If no installation-wide program/file cross reference or data dictionary exists, it will be necessary to consult JCL (production cataloged procedures) to identify the data resources. We offer the following guidelines:

- If your installation doesn't now employ a maintenance and change control system, one must be implemented. The spirit of such a system is that no programming or design be undertaken without the receipt of a written assignment from IS management. Thus, a formal backlog is maintained, complete with time estimates. The consequence of change control is that the consultant can be kept continuously aware of the status of the elements he or she is attempting to inventory. This system will be of even greater importance during the implementation stage.

- Compile a list of files containing date fields, parts of dates, or time-related parameters, for example day, month, or year counts. You might want to divide your file collection into categories according to media: cards, diskettes, screen, telecommunication transmission, and so on. The important consideration is that this list must establish a complete enumeration of date-related files. (Of equal importance with permanent files are those intermediate files and work files that have brief lives, often created and destroyed within the same job.)

- Now it's necessary to review the installation's entire programming collection. The objective of this review is to determine the programs, sorts, and utilities that address the data resources that were identified in the previous guideline. A file/program cross reference chart must be created and, if at all possible, segregated into mutually exclusive subsystems.

**Step 5**

The output of Step 4 combined with the peculiarities of your installation's fiscal closing, industry peak periods, and applications development in progress allows you to establish a tentative conversion sequence.

Recognizing that both maintenance and change/enhancement must be frozen for the program components of each subsystem during the conversion, the consultant must consider multiple factors in the final prioritization of components within subsystems. Further, if multiple small subsystems were not developed in Step 4, the conversion implementation team requirements will be greater in order to reduce the duration of these freeze periods. Thus, prioritizing the component programs is to some extent governed by the programs' change and maintenance volatility.

**Step 6**

Now you must detail the conversion methods and procedures and the standards that must be maintained during the implementation. Here we're referring to such things as the form and extent of a century table if this has been chosen as a integral part of the conversion. If routines from this publication are to be used, will they be macros or subroutines? If they're necessary, are the linkage conventions available?

Have subsystem conversion teams been tentatively designated? No programmer must be left to his or her own devices in implementing any date computation solution. The more comprehensive the developed details of the implementation, the more likely management will be inclined to give it the go-ahead.

Finally, there's the cost and necessity of creating documentation that reflects the changes made to the system. This encompasses users' manuals as well as programming documentation and system documents.

**Step 7**

A set of programs and related files must now be chosen for the purpose of executing a pilot conversion. It is from the pilot conversion that specific time utilization parameters are collected for comparison with estimates made earlier. Consequently, the sample must be chosen by the consultant with considerable care, being aware that it will test the recently established procedures and standards as well.

While the inventory was being compiled in Step 4 or while the standards were being created in Step 6, various levels of conversion complexity were recognized for each programming conversion problem. It is important that the pilot conversion sample contain a representative assortment of these complexities.

It should be noted that only the more common problems have been addressed by the subroutines presented in this text. Two-digit year-numbers will be encountered in peripheral storage, allowing their replacement only by binary equivalents of the full four-digit value if the same storage bytes are to be occupied, thus avoiding reformatting. The unexpected becomes the expected given the performance of programmers over the past 50 years.

## Step 8

Having successfully completed the preponderance of the preconversion steps, it is now necessary to create a document that will embody the planning to date. The technical solutions, aids, ancillary programs specified, the anticipated staffing and team structure, as well as the assignment of responsibilities and the schedule for the implementation of the parallel testing must each be clearly stated. This document is the repository of the entire effort to this point. The sequencing of the conversion, the training requirement for the participants, the programming standards, and the testing protocols are all within its content. The benefits are twofold:

- An objective record is created with which the members of the preconversion team may reach agreement.

- A basis is provided for modification and improvement upon the acquisition of practical experience.

Because parameters are to be sought vigorously during the execution of the pilot conversion, it is important to lay out carefully individual work plans that will facilitate the comparison of estimated to actual performance. Among other benefits, the pilot conversion allows the testing of the change/maintenance control system as well as the procedure for logging needed modifications to the procedures themselves as they become apparent. To facilitate all of this, it is important to build a reporting facility into the pilot conversion's work planning.

## Step 9

Execute the pilot conversion. On the assumption that the technical homework has been done well, the emphasis shifts from the technical to the managerial as the preconversion activities become involved with the pilot conversion now underway. The importance of an adequate project control system cannot be overstated at this stage.

It is during this pilot conversion that the team participants will be trained, the ancillary programming tools will be created, the programs in conversion "frozen" with respect to further maintenance or change, and in every respect a mini-implementation executed. While we are interested in comparing actual *versus* estimated parameters for each aspect of the pilot conversion, it is the collection of the actual parameters that must occupy our primary focus.

## A Time for Decision

Having completed the pilot conversion and having acquired the much needed parameters, it is now possible to perform the calculations that will allow human, machine, and time resource requirements to be associated with the entire inventory. If a mathematical result is sought, Wolberg's work contains resource requirement calculation formulae that may be useful. The process of extending the parameters gathered during the pilot conversion is largely based upon common sense and simple arithmetic.

The consultant is now able to answer the six questions initially presented:

- What are IS's technical options?
- How many work days are implied by the program and database inventory in need of repair?
- What machine utilization resources are required for this conversion?
- Given the required versus the available resources, what is the time requirement to complete the implementation?
- Since continued backlog programming and system development will add to the conversion requirements, what are our options in suspending activity until implementation is completed?
- What is the total cost?

A final meeting between the consultant, IS director, and the CEO now permits a complete presentation of the forthcoming conversion plan. The total cost of the date conversion may be calculated and the final implementation and postimplementation activities scheduled.

What of the preconversion stage? Are there alternatives to employing an in-house effort?

We have just reviewed an intuitive, and a more formal approach to an in-house conversion. Most conversions will fall somewhere between these poles. There is the possibility that management may want to outsource its conversion hoping for a fixed dollar cost for the whole effort.

IBM's Information Systems Solution Corporation (ISSC) offers consulting services as well as an "Assessment and Strategy" session that covers an eight- to twelve-week period during which ISSC offers to identify the magnitude of the client's date problem.

ISSC offers to direct this effort to clients executing 5 to 150+ million lines of code in a mixed language environment. The user might view these eight- to twelve-week parameters as minimums given the case that ISSC personnel are specially equipped to perform this service.

The preconversion stage is of paramount importance. It provides the basis for intelligent judgment regarding the installation's future course in the face of the relentless march of time . . . a time for decision.

## Vendor Tools and Service Offerings

ADPAC Corp.
425 Market St.
San Francisco, CA 94105

COGNICASE
425 Viger Ouest
Montreal, Quebec H2Z 1X2
Canada

Computer Software Corp.
19100 Detroit Road
Cleveland, OH 44116

Compuware Corp.
31440 Northwestern Hgwy.
Farmington Hills, MI 48334

EDGE Information Group
2250 East Devon
Des Plaines, IL 60018

Forecross Corporation
90 New Montgomery St.
San Francisco, CA 94105

Global Software, Inc.
P.O. Box 2813, 15 Depot St.
Duxbury, MA 02331

Ironsoft, Inc.
4323 Winnequah Rd.
Monona, WI 53716

ISOGON Corp.
330 Seventh Ave.
New York, NY 10001

Izar Associates, Inc.
4 Emery Ave.
Randolph, NJ 07869

Mainware, Inc.
7176 Pioneer Creek Rd.
Maple Plain, MN 55359

Micro Focus
2465 East Bayshore Rd.
Palo Alto, CA 94303

Quintic Systems, Inc.
3166 Des Plaines Ave.
Des Plaines, IL 60018

Reasoning Systems
3260 Hillview Ave.
Palo Alto, CA 94304

REPPIN Consulting and
   Software Ltd.
P.O. Box 6912, Station J
Ottawa, Ontario K2A 3Z5
Canada

SEEC, Inc.
5001 Baum Blvd.
Pittsburgh, PA 15213

Software Eclectics, Inc.
10955 Jones Bridge Rd.
Alpharetta, GA 30202

TransCentury Data Systems
111 Pine St.
San Francisco, CA 94111

VIASOFT
3033 North 44th St.
Phoenix, AZ 85018

# Epilogue

The underlying technical realities that support the year-2000 computing crisis don't present themselves casually to systems professionals. Maybe a closer inspection will highlight the potential for disaster with which we live daily.

In aging credit purchases, the difference between two dates determines the number of days or years for which interest is calculated. The basic design assumption in this kind of programming is that the date of the purchase is represented by a smaller number than the current date. Otherwise, the purchase is a future intention and not a fact of indebtedness.

Universally, aging programs pay no attention to a negative number, since it's assumed that the date on the purchase transaction is less than the date being used as the standard of comparison—the current date.

When the age of a purchase made during December of 1999 is found for a billing date of January 1, 2000 in a six-digit date environment, the difference between 99 and 00 is what's calculated, and it's –99. If you aren't anticipating a negative number, you'll certainly issue a bill that's more than 99 years delinquent. The interest will be calculated accordingly, with (depending on the editing of the dollar result) the credit or debit representing a magnificent sum. We chose the debit, in the scenario in the Introduction, of $6,243.00 since dollar-amount editing of such interest-due calculations regularly ignores negative sign development. In either case, however, the result contaminates the database. The host company will become overwhelmed by customer complaints, verbal and written. If many companies hosted this disaster, the cash flow and economic repercussions would be devastating.

From what has been illustrated, it's plain that industrial control programming that depends on date calculations will be quite vulnerable in the year 2000. There are two general control methods: parameter-driven and event-driven. The parameter-driven control approach can be successfully used in environments where the process is totally predictable (blend the batch for two days, then move it to the conveyor). The event-driven control approach requires the insertion of sensors that are read by the program, which adjusts its response according to a mathematical formula (when the temperature reading reaches 200 degrees, shut off the heater). Often a combination of the two approaches can be used in industrial control applications.

Any parameter-driven control system depending on a time-related counter will be sent astray by the conditions we've described. Let's calculate the number of days separating two dates, the date the process begins and the current date. When the difference reaches 2, we'll terminate the industrial process. We'll calculate the difference every 15 minutes during the process control period, which begins, say, the morning of 12/31/1999. At midnight, when 12/31/1999 rolls over to become 01/01/00, the calculation will find an absolute difference greater than 36,000 days between the two dates. The program will never find a value of 2 as a difference, so the process will be uncontrolled. The effect of friction heat alone, even in the most predictable process, can have devastating effects if a process is uncontrolled.

Each time an IBM mainframe computer is powered on, its memory is reloaded with the microcode (IML) that gives the machine its individual personality. This must be followed by initial program load (IPL) if the computer is to be used for productive processing. IPL causes the operating system's programs to be loaded into the computer's memory, where they act as resource managers, as indicated earlier.

It's a near certainty that computers with unmodified software will grind to a halt in the year 2000. At IPL time, the computer operator enters the day's date and proceeds to initiate the day's processing. Generally, the start of processing involves producing output either to terminal viewers or to printers. Discrepancies in output might be missed by an inattentive operator, but certainly the end-user departments won't hesitate to call attention to garbled information. If a problem is reported, steps to correct it are usually begun immediately, even though it might seem otherwise to a more distant observer.

Problems caused by miscalculations of dates are extremely serious and will cause processing to be suspended until a solution is determined. The reasons are associated with pure self-interest. Every file in a system can be invalidated by faulty date output and no one but no one in the operations department wants to be involved with the complex and lengthy task of reconstructing the database. Expect widespread suspension of computer processing in the year 2000 and beyond, with many terminal screens as dark as a villain's heart.

Certainly, as we approach the year 2000 more and more systems users will be confronted by this problem in one form or another. The true potential for disaster lies in our tendency to procrastinate, to continue system and software development using inadequate dating data, and the currently inadequate algorithmic support this imposes. Our fault is in our readiness to patch or treat symptoms until it's too late to successfully eradicate the disease.

This is a true computer crisis; it's application- and nationality-independent. It's worldwide. It has but one certain remedy—immediate action to terminate six-digit-date involvement in current system development and scheduling the ultimate conversion of existing systems.

# Converting Subroutines to a Macro

Each of the subroutines, TIMESUBF through TIMESUB9, was converted by a converter program to a macro. Then they were edited and cataloged to a VSE sublibrary. We then wrote a test program, assembled it, and executed it against the same input data used in testing the original subroutine. In each case, the macro produced results identical to those obtained from the corresponding subroutine's test.

The benefits offered by a macro include protection against damage to tested and proven source code and reducing the size of post listings by eliminating redundant code via PRINT NOGEN. As you've seen, the macro can be coded into a subroutine structure and so need not be coded repeatedly inline.

Figures A.1 through A.11 are post listings from the macro edit executions.

```
LOC  OBJECT CODE  ADDR1 ADDR2  STMT  SOURCE STATEMENT                                        DOS/VSE ASSEMBLER 16.31  99-12-31

                                 1          MACRO                                                                          TSF00010
                                 2  *                                                                                    * TSF00020
                                 3  *                                                                                    * TSF00030
                                 4  *  ************************************************************************           * TSF00040
                                 5  *                                                                                    * TSF00050
                                 6  *     TTTTTTT   III   MM    MM   EEEEE   FFFFF                                        * TSF00060
                                 7  *        T       I    M M  M M   E       F                                           * TSF00070
                                 8  *        T       I    M  MM  M   EEEE    FFF                                         * TSF00080
                                 9  *        T       I    M      M   E       F                                           * TSF00090
                                10  *        T      III   M      M   EEEEE   F                                           * TSF00100
                                11  *                                                                                    * TSF00110
                                12  *     D A T E   F O R M A T   C O N V E R S I O N   S U B R O U T I N E              * TSF00120
                                13  *  ************************************************************************           * TSF00130
                                14  *                                                                                    * TSF00140
                                15  *  THIS MACRO CONVERTS SIX DIGIT INPUT DATES WHOSE FORMATS ARE                       * TSF00150
                                16  *                FIPS - COMMERCIAL - EUROPEAN                                         * TSF00160
                                17  *        TO PACKED STANDARD EIGHT DIGIT COMMERCIAL DATES                             * TSF00170
                                18  *                                                                                    * TSF00180
                                19  *                                                                                    * TSF00190
                                20  *    1.  THE DOCUMENTATION FOR THIS MACRO IS IDENTICAL WITH THAT                     * TSF00200
                                21  *        DISPLAYED IN THE SUBROUTINE TIMESUBF.  THE IN-CODE                          * TSF00210
                                22  *        COMMENTS HAVE BEEN REMOVED IN THE INTEREST OF SPACE                         * TSF00220
                                23  *        CONSERVATION.                                                               * TSF00230
                                24  *                                                                                    * TSF00240
                                25  *    2.  THIS MACRO IS WRITTEN TO BE CODED AS 'TIMEF' IN THE                         * TSF00250
                                26  *        USING PROGRAM AND REQUIRES NO OPERANDS UNLESS THE USING                     * TSF00260
                                27  *        PROGRAM MUST SUPPLY ITS OWN DATEF, CODEF, SIGF OR FORMAT                    * TSF00270
                                28  *        FIELDS.  IN THAT EVENT, THE FIELDS, CODEF, SPECIFICATIONS MUST              * TSF00280
                                29  *        BE AS IN TIMESUBF AND THE MACRO STATEMENT MUST SPECIFY                      * TSF00290
                                30  *        THE FIELDNAME(S) AS FOLLOWS:                                                * TSF00300
                                31  *                                                                                    * TSF00310
                                32  *        TIMEF DATEF=FIELDNAME,                                             X         * TSF00320
                                33  *              CODEF=FIELDNAME,                                             X         * TSF00330
                                34  *              SIGF=FIELDNAME,                                              X         * TSF00340
                                35  *              FORMAT=FIELDNAME                                                      * TSF00350
                                36  *                                                                                    * TSF00360
                                37  *                                                                                    * TSF00370
                                38  *  GLEN ELLYN, ILLINOIS                           JEROME T. MURRAY                   * TSF00380
                                39  *                                                 MARILYN J. MURRAY                  * TSF00390
                                40  *                                                                                    * TSF00400
                                41  *  ************************************************************************           * TSF00410
                                42  *                                                                                    * TSF00420
                                43  *                                                                                    * TSF00430
                                44  *              MACRO PROTOTYPE STATEMENT                                             * TSF00440
                                45  *                                                                                    * TSF00450
                                46  *                                                                                    * TSF00460
                                47  .*                                                                                     TSF00470
                                48        TIMEF &DATEF=DATEF,&CODEF=CODEF,&FORMAT=FORMAT,&SIGF=SIGF                        TSF00480
                                49        ZAP   &FORMAT,=P'O'                                                             TSF00490
                                50        ZAP   &CODEF,=P'O'                                                              TSF00500
                                51        STM   1,4,#$FRSAVE                                                              TSF00510
                                52        MVC   #$FTABL+243(7),=X'1C1C1C1C1C1C1C'                                         TSF00520
                                53        TRT   &SIGF(1),#$FTABL                                                         TSF00530
                                54        BC    8,#$FHKEP                                                                TSF00540
                                55        MVC   #$FTABL+243(7),=X'00000000000000'
```

```
LOC  OBJECT CODE  ADDR1  ADDR2  STMT  SOURCE STATEMENT              DOS/VSE ASSEMBLER 16.31 99-12-31

                                 56           ZAP   &CODEF,=P'1'                                TSF00550
                                 57           B     #$FTERM                                     TSF00560
                                 58  #$FHKEP  MVC   #$FTABL+243(7),=X'00000000000000'           TSF00570
                                 59           MVC   #$FWORK6,&DATEF                             TSF00580
                                 60           MVC   #$FSIGN,#$FWORK6+5                          TSF00590
                                 61           MVC   #$FTABL+160(10),#$FZRO                      TSF00600
                                 62           MVC   #$FTABL+192(10),#$FZRO                      TSF00610
                                 63           MVC   #$FTABL+224(10),#$FZRO                      TSF00620
                                 64           TRT   #$FSIGN(1),#$FTABL                          TSF00630
                                 65           BC    8,#$FNUM                                    TSF00640
                                 66           MVC   #$FTABL+1(239),#$FTABL                      TSF00650
                                 67           B     #$FBDATA                                    TSF00660
                                 68  #$FNUM   MVC   #$FTABL+1(239),#$FTABL                      TSF00670
                                 69           TRT   #$FWORK6(5),#$FTABL                         TSF00680
                                 70           BC    8,#$FPACK                                   TSF00690
                                 71  #$FBDATA ZAP   &CODEF,=P'2'                                TSF00700
                                 72           B     #$FTERM                                     TSF00710
                                 73  #$FPACK  CLC   &SIGF,=C'1'                                 TSF00720
                                 74           BE    #$FFC                                       TSF00730
                                 75           BH    #$FEC                                       TSF00740
                                 76           PACK  #$FMO,#$FWORK6(2)                           TSF00750
                                 77           PACK  #$FDA,#$FWORK6+2(2)                         TSF00760
                                 78           PACK  #$FYR,#$FWORK6+4(2)                         TSF00770
                                 79           B     #$FMAT                                      TSF00780
                                 80  #$FEC    PACK  #$FMO,#$FWORK6+2(2)                         TSF00790
                                 81           PACK  #$FDA,#$FWORK6+4(2)                         TSF00800
                                 82           PACK  #$FYR,#$FWORK6(2)                           TSF00810
                                 83           B     #$FMAT                                      TSF00820
                                 84  #$FFC    PACK  #$FMO,#$FWORK6+2(2)                         TSF00830
                                 85           PACK  #$FDA,#$FWORK6+4(2)                         TSF00840
                                 86           PACK  #$FYR,#$FWORK6(2)                           TSF00850
                                 87           AP    #$FYR,#$FCENT                               TSF00860
                                 88  #$FMAT   ZAP   #$FL,=P'0'                                  TSF00870
                                 89  #$FLPYRT ZAP   #$FWORK,#$FYR                               TSF00880
                                 90           DP    #$FWORK,=P'4'                               TSF00890
                                 91           CP    #$FWORK+4(1),=P'0'                          TSF00900
                                 92           BH    #$FMOEDT                                    TSF00910
                                 93           ZAP   #$FWORK,#$FYR                               TSF00920
                                 94           DP    #$FWORK,=P'100'                             TSF00930
                                 95           CP    #$FWORK+3(2),=P'0'                          TSF00940
                                 96           BH    #$FLPYR                                     TSF00950
                                 97           ZAP   #$FWORK,#$FYR                               TSF00960
                                 98           DP    #$FWORK,=P'400'                             TSF00970
                                 99           CP    #$FWORK+3(2),=P'0'                          TSF00980
                                100           BH    #$FMOEDT                                    TSF00990
                                101  #$FLPYR  ZAP   #$FL,=P'1'                                  TSF01000
                                102  #$FMOEDT ZAP   #$FCVB,#$FMO                                TSF01010
                                103           CVB   3,#$FCVB                                    TSF01020
                                104           STC   3,#$FFLD                                    TSF01030
                                105           MVC   #$FTABL+1(12),#$FZRO                        TSF01040
                                106           TRT   #$FFLD(1),#$FTABL                           TSF01050
                                107           BC    8,#$FDAEDT                                  TSF01060
                                108           MVC   #$FTABL+1(12),#$FTABL                       TSF01070
                                109           ZAP   &CODEF,=P'6'                                TSF01080
                                110           B     #$FTERM                                     TSF01090
```

**Figure A.1**  The macro edit post listing for TIMEF, the TIMESUBF macro equivalent.

DOS/VSE ASSEMBLER 16.31 99-12-31

```
LOC  OBJECT CODE  ADDR1 ADDR2  STMT  SOURCE STATEMENT

                                111  #$FDAEDT  MVC   #$FTABL+(12),#$FTABL      TSF01100
                                112            LA    4,#$FDATAB               TSF01110
                                113            CP    #$FL,=P'0'               TSF01120
                                114            BE    #$FNOL                   TSF01130
                                115            LA    4,2(4)                   TSF01140
                                116  #$FNOL    BCTR  3,0                      TSF01150
                                117            SLL   3,2                      TSF01160
                                118            LA    4,0(3,4)                 TSF01170
                                119            ZAP   #$FDA,#$FDA              TSF01180
                                120            CLC   #$FDA,O(4)               TSF01190
                                121            BNH   #$FDALO                  TSF01200
                                122  #$FBADA   ZAP   &CODEF,=P'8'             TSF01210
                                123            B     #$FTERM                  TSF01220
                                124  #$FDALO   CP    #$FDA,=P'00'             TSF01230
                                125            BE    #$FBADA                  TSF01240
                                126            UNPK  #$FWORK8+4(4),#$FYR      TSF01250
                                127            UNPK  #$FWORK8+2(2),#$FDA      TSF01260
                                128            UNPK  #$FWORK8(2),#$FMO        TSF01270
                                129            PACK  &FORMAT,#$FWORK8         TSF01280
                                130            B     #$FTERM                  TSF01290
                                131  FORMAT    DC    PL5'0'                   TSF01300
                                132  CODEF     DC    PL1'2'                   TSF01310
                                133  DATEF     DC    ZL6'000000'              TSF01320
                                134  SIGF      DC    ZL1'0'                   TSF01330
                                135  #$FDATAB  DC    PL2'31',PL2'31'   JAN    TSF01340
                                136            DC    PL2'28',PL2'29'   FEB    TSF01350
                                137            DC    PL2'31',PL2'31'   MAR    TSF01360
                                138            DC    PL2'30',PL2'30'   APR    TSF01370
                                139            DC    PL2'31',PL2'31'   MAY    TSF01380
                                140            DC    PL2'30',PL2'30'   JUN    TSF01390
                                141            DC    PL2'31',PL2'31'   JUL    TSF01400
                                142            DC    PL2'31',PL2'31'   AUG    TSF01410
                                143            DC    PL2'30',PL2'30'   SEP    TSF01420
                                144            DC    PL2'31',PL2'31'   OCT    TSF01430
                                145            DC    PL2'30',PL2'30'   NOV    TSF01440
                                146            DC    PL2'31',PL2'31'   DEC    TSF01450
                                147  #$FTABL   DC    240X'1C'                 TSF01460
                                148            DC    10X'00'                  TSF01470
                                149            DC    6X'1C'                   TSF01480
                                150  #$FZRD    DC    12X'00'                  TSF01490
                                151  #$FCENT   DC    PL3'1900'                TSF01500
                                152  #$FSIGN   DS    ZL1                      TSF01510
                                153  #$FL      DS    PL1                      TSF01520
                                154  #$FWORK8  DS    CL8                      TSF01530
                                155  #$FWORK6  DS    CL8                      TSF01540
                                156  #$FWORK   DS    PL5                      TSF01550
                                157  #$FMO     DS    PL2                      TSF01560
                                158  #$FDA     DS    PL2                      TSF01570
                                159  #$FYR     DS    PL3                      TSF01580
                                160  #$FFLD    DS    CL1                      TSF01590
                                161  #$FRSAVE  DS    4F                       TSF01600
                                162  #$FCVB    DS    1D                       TSF01610
                                163  #$FTERM   LM    1,4,#$FRSAVE             TSF01620
                                164            MEND
                                165            END
```

99-12-31

DIAGNOSTICS AND STATISTICS

NO ERRORS FOUND

EDECK PUNCHED FOR MACRO 'TIMEF', NUMBER OF CARDS IS 72

OPTIONS FOR THIS ASSEMBLY - ALIGN, LIST, NOXREF, NOLINK, RLD, NODECK, EDECK

THE ASSEMBLER WAS RUN IN 98184 BYTES
END OF ASSEMBLY

**Figure A.1** *Continued*

```
LOC  OBJECT CODE   ADDR1 ADDR2   STMT   SOURCE STATEMENT                                    DOS/VSE ASSEMBLER 16.33  99-12-31

                                   1  *        MACRO                                                                          TSG00010
                                   2  *                                                                                       TSG00020
                                   3  *                                                                                       TSG00030
                                   4  *        ***************************************************                           TSG00040
                                   5  *        TTTTTT   III   MM      MM   EEEEE   GGGG                                       TSG00050
                                   6  *          T       I    M M    M M   E       G                                          TSG00060
                                   7  *          T       I    M   M M  M   EEEE    G  GG                                       TSG00070
                                   8  *          T       I    M     M  M   E       G   G                                      TSG00080
                                   9  *          T      III   M     M  M   EEEEE   GGGG                                       TSG00090
                                  10  *                                                                                       TSG00100
                                  11  *        ***************************************************                           TSG00110
                                  12  *  *****  D A T E   F O R M A T   C O N V E R S I O N   M A C R O  *****                TSG00120
                                  13  *        ***************************************************                           TSG00130
                                  14  *        ***************************************************                           TSG00140
                                  15  *        ***************************************************                           TSG00150
                                  16  *                                                                                       TSG00160
                                  17  *        THIS MACRO CONVERTS INPUT DATES FROM ONE FORMAT TO ANOTHER                    TSG00170
                                  18  *                   FIPS   COMMERCIAL   EUROPEAN                                        TSG00180
                                  19  *                                                                                       TSG00190
                                  20  *        1.  THE DOCUMENTATION FOR THIS MACRO IS IDENTICAL WITH THAT                   TSG00200
                                  21  *            DISPLAYED IN THE SUBROUTINE TIMESUBG.  THE IN-CODE                         TSG00210
                                  22  *            COMMENTS HAVE BEEN REMOVED IN THE INTEREST OF SPACE                        TSG00220
                                  23  *            CONSERVATION.                                                             TSG00230
                                  24  *                                                                                       TSG00240
                                  25  *        2.  THIS MACRO IS WRITTEN TO BE CODED AS 'TIMEG' IN THE                       TSG00250
                                  26  *            USING PROGRAM AND REQUIRES NO OPERANDS UNLESS THE USING                    TSG00260
                                  27  *            PROGRAM MUST SUPPLY ITS OWN DATEG, CODEG, FORMT8 AND SIGG                  TSG00270
                                  28  *            FIELDS.  IN THAT EVENT, THE FIELDS' SPECIFICATIONS                        TSG00280
                                  29  *            MUST BE AS IN TIMESUBG AND THE MACRO STATEMENT MUST                        TSG00290
                                  30  *            SPECIFY THE FIELDNAME(S) AS FOLLOWS:                                       TSG00300
                                  31  *                                                                                       TSG00310
                                  32  *            TIME7  DATEG=FIELDNAME,                                 X                  TSG00320
                                  33  *                   CODEG=FIELDNAME,                                 X                  TSG00330
                                  34  *                   SIGG=FIELDNAME,                                  X                  TSG00340
                                  35  *                   FORMT8=FIELDNAME                                                    TSG00350
                                  36  *                                                                                       TSG00360
                                  37  *        ***************************************************                           TSG00370
                                  38  *                                               JEROME T. MURRAY                        TSG00380
                                  39  *        GLEN ELLYN, ILLINOIS                    MARILYN J. MURRAY                      TSG00390
                                  40  *        ***************************************************                           TSG00400
                                  41  *        ***************************************************                           TSG00410
                                  42  *        ***************************************************                           TSG00420
                                  43  *        ***************************************************                           TSG00430
                                  44  *                 MACRO PROTOTYPE STATEMENT                                            TSG00440
                                  45  *        ***************************************************                           TSG00450
                                  46  *        ***************************************************                           TSG00460
                                  47          TIMEG &DATEG=DATEG,&CODEG=CODEG,&FORMT8=FORMT8,&SIGG=SIGG                       TSG00470
                                  48          ZAP    &FORMT8,=P'O'                                                           TSG00480
                                  49          ZAP    &CODEG,=P'O'                                                            TSG00490
                                  50          STM    1,4,#$GRSAVE                                                            TSG00500
                                  51          MVC    #$GTABL+247(3),=X'1C1C1C'                                               TSG00510
                                  52          TRT    &SIGG(1),#$GTABL                                                        TSG00520
                                  53          BC     8,#$GHKEP                                                               TSG00530
                                  54          MVC    #$GTABL+247(3),=X'OOOOOO'                                               TSG00540
                                  55          ZAP    &CODEG,=P'1'
```

```
LOC   OBJECT CODE   ADDR1 ADDR2   STMT   SOURCE STATEMENT              DOS/VSE ASSEMBLER 16.33 99-12-31

                                   56            B     #$GTERM                                        TSGO0550
                                   57    #$GHKEP MVC   #$GTABL+247(3),=X'000000'                       TSGO0560
                                   58            MVC   #$GWORK8,&DATEG                                 TSGO0570
                                   59            MVC   #$GSIGN,#$GWORK8+7                              TSGO0580
                                   60            MVC   #$GTABL+160(10),#$GZRO                          TSGO0590
                                   61            MVC   #$GTABL+192(10),#$GZRO                          TSGO0600
                                   62            MVC   #$GTABL+224(10),#$GZRO                          TSGO0610
                                   63            TRT   #$GSIGN(1),#$GTABL                             TSGO0620
                                   64            BC    8,#$GNUM                                        TSGO0630
                                   65            MVC   8,#$GTABL                                       TSGO0640
                                   66            B     #$GBDATA                                        TSGO0650
                                   67    #$GNUM  MVC   #$GTABL+1(239),#$GTABL                          TSGO0660
                                   68            TRT   #$GWORK8(7),#$GTABL                            TSGO0670
                                   69            BC    8,#$GPACK                                       TSGO0680
                                   70    #$GBDATA ZAP  &CODEG,=P'2'                                    TSGO0690
                                   71            B     #$GTERM                                         TSGO0700
                                   72    #$GPACK CLC   &SIGG,=C'4'                                      TSGO0710
                                   73            BH    #$GFED                                          TSGO0720
                                   74            CLC   &SIGG,=C'2'                                      TSGO0730
                                   75            BH    #$GEUR                                          TSGO0740
                                   76            CLC   &SIGG,=C'0'                                      TSGO0750
                                   77            BH    #$GCOM                                          TSGO0760
                                   78            PACK  &FORMT8,&DATEG                                  TSGO0770
                                   79            B     #$GTERM                                         TSGO0780
                                   80    #$GCOM  PACK  #$GMO,#$GWORK8(2)                              TSGO0790
                                   81            PACK  #$GDA,#$GWORK8+2(2)                            TSGO0800
                                   82            PACK  #$GYR,#$GWORK8+4(4)                            TSGO0810
                                   83            B     #$GYEDT                                         TSGO0820
                                   84    #$GEUR  PACK  #$GDA,#$GWORK8(2)                              TSGO0830
                                   85            PACK  #$GMO,#$GWORK8+2(2)                            TSGO0840
                                   86            PACK  #$GYR,#$GWORK8+4(4)                            TSGO0850
                                   87            B     #$GYEDT                                         TSGO0360
                                   88    #$GFED  PACK  #$GYR,#$GWORK8(4)                              TSGO0870
                                   89            PACK  #$GMO,#$GWORK8+4(2)                            TSGO0880
                                   90            PACK  #$GDA,#$GWORK8+6(2)                            TSGO0890
                                   91    #$GYEDT CP    #$GYR,=P'1600'                                  TSGO0900
                                   92            BH    #$GYRHI                                         TSGO0910
                                   93    #$GBADYR ZAP  &CODEG,=P'4'                                    TSGO0920
                                   94            B     #$GTERM                                         TSGO0930
                                   95    #$GYRHI CP    #$GYR,=P'3399'                                  TSGO0940
                                   96            BH    #$GBADYR                                        TSGO0950
                                   97            ZAP   #$GL,=P'0'                                       TSGO0960
                                   98            ZAP   #$GWORK,#$GYR                                   TSGO0970
                                   99            DP    #$GWORK,=P'4'                                    TSGO0980
                                  100            CP    #$GWORK+4(1),=P'0'                              TSGO0990
                                  101            BH    #$GMOEDT                                        TSGO1000
                                  102            ZAP   #$GWORK,#$GYR                                   TSGO1010
                                  103            DP    #$GWORK,=P'100'                                 TSGO1020
                                  104            CP    #$GWORK+3(2),=P'0'                              TSGO1030
                                  105            BH    #$GLPYR                                         TSGO1040
                                  106            ZAP   #$GWORK,#$GYR                                   TSGO1050
                                  107            DP    #$GWORK,=P'400'                                 TSGO1060
                                  108            CP    #$GWORK+3(2),=P'0'                              TSGO1070
                                  109            BH    #$GMOEDT                                        TSGO1080
                                  110    #$GLPYR ZAP   #$GL,=P'1'                                       TSGO1090
```

**Figure A.2**   The macro edit post listing for TIMEG, the TIMESUBG macro equivalent.

```
LOC   OBJECT CODE   ADDR1 ADDR2   STMT   SOURCE STATEMENT                                DOS/VSE ASSEMBLER 16.33  99-12-31

                                   111 #$GMOEDT ZAP   #$GCVB,#$GMO                                                TSGO1100
                                   112          CVB   3,#$GCVB                                                    TSGO1110
                                   113          STC   3,#$GFLD                                                    TSGO1120
                                   114          MVC   #$GTABL+1(12),#$GZRO                                        TSGO1130
                                   115          TRT   #$GFLD(1),#$GTABL                                           TSGO1140
                                   116          BC    8,#$GDAEDT                                                  TSGO1150
                                   117          MVC   #$GTABL+1(12),#$GTABL                                       TSGO1160
                                   118          ZAP   &CODEG,=P'6'                                                TSGO1170
                                   119          B     #$GTERM                                                     TSGO1180
                                   120 #$GDAEDT MVC   #$GTABL+1(12),#$GTABL                                       TSGO1190
                                   121          LA    4,#$GDATAB                                                  TSGO1200
                                   122          CP    #$GL,=P'O'                                                  TSGO1210
                                   123          BE    #$GNOL                                                      TSGO1220
                                   124          LA    4,2(4)                                                      TSGO1230
                                   125 #$GNOL   BCTR  3,0                                                         TSGO1240
                                   126          SLL   3,2                                                         TSGO1250
                                   127          LA    4,0(3,4)                                                    TSGO1260
                                   128          ZAP   #$GDA,#$GDA                                                 TSGO1270
                                   129          CLC   #$GDA,0(4)                                                  TSGO1280
                                   130          BNH   #$GDALO                                                     TSGO1290
                                   131 #$GBADA  ZAP   &CODEG,=P'8'                                                TSGO1300
                                   132          B     #$GTERM                                                     TSGO1310
                                   133 #$GDALO  CP    #$GDA,=P'OO'                                                TSGO1320
                                   134          BE    #$GBADA                                                     TSGO1330
                                   135          CLC   &SIGG,=C'5'                                                 TSGO1340
                                   136          BH    #$GXE                                                       TSGO1350
                                   137          CLC   &SIGG,=C'4'                                                 TSGO1360
                                   138          BH    #$GXC                                                       TSGO1370
                                   139          CLC   &SIGG,=C'3'                                                 TSGO1380
                                   140          BH    #$GXF                                                       TSGO1390
                                   141          CLC   &SIGG,=C'2'                                                 TSGO1400
                                   142          BH    #$GXC                                                       TSGO1410
                                   143          CLC   &SIGG,=C'1'                                                 TSGO1420
                                   144          BH    #$GXF                                                       TSGO1430
                                   145 #$GXE    UNPK  #$GWRK(2),#$GDA                                             TSGO1440
                                   146          UNPK  #$GWRK+2(2),#$GMO                                           TSGO1450
                                   147          UNPK  #$GWRK+4(4),#$GYR                                           TSGO1460
                                   148          PACK  &FORMT8,#$GWRK                                              TSGO1470
                                   149          B     #$GTERM                                                     TSGO1480
                                   150 #$GXF    UNPK  #$GWRK(4),#$GYR                                             TSGO1490
                                   151          UNPK  #$GWRK+2(2),#$GMO                                           TSGO1500
                                   152          UNPK  #$GWRK+6(2),#$GDA                                           TSGO1510
                                   153          PACK  &FORMT8,#$GWRK                                              TSGO1520
                                   154          B     #$GTERM                                                     TSGO1530
                                   155 #$GXC    UNPK  #$GWRK(2),#$GMO                                             TSGO1540
                                   156          UNPK  #$GWRK+2(2),#$GDA                                           TSGO1550
                                   157          UNPK  #$GWRK+4(4),#$GYR                                           TSGO1560
                                   158          PACK  &FORMT8,#$GWRK                                              TSGO1570
                                   159          B     #$GTERM                                                     TSGO1580
                                   160 FORMT8   DC    PL5'0'                                                      TSGO1590
                                   161 CODEG    DC    PL1'2'                                                      TSGO1600
                                   162 DATEG    DC    ZL8'OOOOOOOO'                                               TSGO1610
                                   163 SIGG     DC    ZL1'O'                                                      TSGO1620
                                   164 #$GDATAB DC    PL2'31',PL2'31'                          JAN                TSGO1630
                                   165          DC    PL2'28',PL2'29'                          FEB                TSGO1640
```

```
LOC   OBJECT CODE   ADDR1 ADDR2   STMT   SOURCE STATEMENT                                    DOS/VSE ASSEMBLER 16.33  99-12-31

                                   166             DC    PL2'31',PL2'31'        MAR           TSG01650
                                   167             DC    PL2'30',PL2'30'        APR           TSG01660
                                   168             DC    PL2'31',PL2'31'        MAY           TSG01670
                                   169             DC    PL2'30',PL2'30'        JUN           TSG01680
                                   170             DC    PL2'31',PL2'31'        JUL           TSG01690
                                   171             DC    PL2'31',PL2'31'        AUG           TSG01700
                                   172             DC    PL2'30',PL2'30'        SEP           TSG01710
                                   173             DC    PL2'31',PL2'31'        OCT           TSG01720
                                   174             DC    PL2'30',PL2'30'        NOV           TSG01730
                                   175             DC    PL2'31',PL2'31'        DEC           TSG01740
                                   176   #$GTABL   DC    240X'1C'                             TSG01750
                                   177             DC    10X'1C'                              TSG01760
                                   178             DC    6X'1C'                               TSG01770
                                   179   #$GZRO    DC    12X'00'                              TSG01780
                                   180   #$GSIGN   DS    ZL1                                  TSG01790
                                   181   #$GL      DS    PL1                                  TSG01800
                                   182   #$GWORK8  DS    CL8                                  TSG01810
                                   183   #$GWORK   DS    PL5                                  TSG01820
                                   184   #$GWRK    DS    CL8                                  TSG01830
                                   185   #$GMO     DS    PL2                                  TSG01840
                                   186   #$GDA     DS    PL2                                  TSG01850
                                   187   #$GYR     DS    PL3                                  TSG01860
                                   188   #$GFLD    DS    CL1                                  TSG01870
                                   189   #$GRSAVE  DS    4F                                   TSG01880
                                   190   #$GCVB    DS    1D                                   TSG01890
                                   191   #$GTERM   LM    1,4,#$GRSAVE                         TSG01900
                                   192             MEND
                                   193             END
```

DIAGNOSTICS AND STATISTICS                                                                    99-12-31

NO ERRORS FOUND

EDECK PUNCHED FOR MACRO 'TIMEG'. NUMBER OF CARDS IS 88

OPTIONS FOR THIS ASSEMBLY - ALIGN, LIST, NOXREF, NOLINK, RLD, NODECK, EDECK

THE ASSEMBLER WAS RUN IN 98184 BYTES
END OF ASSEMBLY

**Figure A.2** *Continued*

```
LOC   OBJECT CODE   ADDR1  ADDR2   STMT   SOURCE STATEMENT                                          DOS/VSE ASSEMBLER 16.35  99-12-31

                                     1           MACRO                                                                          *  TS100010
                                     2    * .*                                                                                  *  TS100020
                                     3    * .*                                                                                  *  TS100030
                                     4    *                                                                                     *  TS100040
                                     5    *      TTTTTT    III        MM      MM    EEEEE                                        *  TS100050
                                     6    *         T       I         M M    M M    E        1                                  *  TS100060
                                     7    *         T       I         M  M  M  M    E        11                                 *  TS100070
                                     8    *         T       I         M   MM   M    EEEEE    1                                  *  TS100080
                                     9    *         T      III        M        M    E        1                                 *  TS100090
                                    10    *         T                 M        M    EEEEE    111                                *  TS100100
                                    11    *                                                                                     *  TS100110
                                    12    ****************  L E A P   Y E A R   M A C R O  *******************                   *  TS100120
                                    13    *                                                                                     *  TS100130
                                    14    *                                                                                     *  TS100140
                                    15    *                                                                                     *  TS100150
                                    16    *                                                                                     *  TS100160
                                    17    *           THIS MACRO IDENTIFIES GREGORIAN LEAP YEARS                                *  TS100170
                                    18    *                                                                                     *  TS100180
                                    19    *      1.   DOCUMENTATION FOR THIS MACRO IS IDENTICAL WITH                            *  TS100190
                                    20    *           THAT DISPLAYED IN THE SUBROUTINE TIMESUB1. THE                            *  TS100200
                                    21    *           IN-CODE COMMENTS HAVE BEEN REMOVED IN THE INTEREST                        *  TS100210
                                    22    *           OF SPACE CONSERVATION.                                                    *  TS100220
                                    23    *                                                                                     *  TS100230
                                    24    *      2.   THIS MACRO IS WRITTEN TO BE CODED AS 'TIME1' IN THE                       *  TS100240
                                    25    *           USING PROGRAM AND REQUIRES NO OPERANDS UNLESS THE USING                   *  TS100250
                                    26    *           PROGRAM MUST SUPPLY ITS OWN YEAR, CODE1 OR L FIELDS.                      *  TS100260
                                    27    *           IN THAT EVENT, THE FIELDS' SPECIFICATIONS MUST BE AS                      *  TS100270
                                    28    *           IN TIMESUB1 AND THE MACRO STATEMENT MUST SPECIFY THE                      *  TS100280
                                    29    *           FIELDNAME(S) AS FOLLOWS:                                                  *  TS100290
                                    30    *                                                                                     *  TS100300
                                    31    *           TIME1 YEAR=FIELDNAME,                              X                      *  TS100310
                                    32    *                 L=FIELDNAME,                                 X                      *  TS100320
                                    33    *                 CODE1=FIELDNAME                                                     *  TS100330
                                    34    *                                                                                     *  TS100340
                                    35    *                                                            JEROME T. MURRAY         *  TS100350
                                    36    *  GLEN ELLYN, ILLINOIS                                       MARILYN J. MURRAY       *  TS100360
                                    37    *                                                                                     *  TS100370
                                    38    ***************************************************************************           *  TS100380
                                    39    *                                                                                     *  TS100390
                                    40    *                                                                                     *  TS100400
                                    41    *                                                                                     *  TS100410
                                    42    *                    MACRO PROTOTYPE STATEMENT                                        *  TS100420
                                    43    *                                                                                        TS100430
                                    44          TIME1 &YEAR=YEAR,&CODE1=CODE1,&L=L                                                 TS100440
                                    45          ZAP   &CODE1,=P'0'                                                                 TS100450
                                    46          ZAP   &L,=P'9'                                                                     TS100460
                                    47          STM   1,2,#$1RSAVE                                                                 TS100470
                                    48          MVC   #$1WORK4,&YEAR                                                               TS100480
                                    49          MVC   #$1SIGN,#$1WORK4+3                                                           TS100490
                                    50          MVC   #$1TABL+160(10),#$1ZRO                                                       TS100500
                                    51          MVC   #$1TABL+192(10),#$1ZRO                                                       TS100510
                                    52          MVC   #$1TABL+224(10),#$1ZRO                                                       TS100520
                                    53          TRT   #$1SIGN(1),#$1TABL                                                           TS100530
                                    54          BC    8,#$1NUM                                                                     TS100540
                                    55          B     #$1BDATA
```

```
LOC   OBJECT CODE   ADDR1  ADDR2   STMT   SOURCE   STATEMENT                              DOS/VSE ASSEMBLER  16.35  99-12-31

                                    56   #$1NUM    MVC   #$1TABL+1(239),#$1TABL           TS100550
                                    57             TRT   #$1WORK4(3),#$1TABL              TS100560
                                    58             BC    8,#$1PACK                        TS100570
                                    59   #$1BDATA  ZAP   &CODE1,=P'2'                     TS100580
                                    60             B     #$1TERM                          TS100590
                                    61   #$1PACK   PACK  #$1YR,&YEAR                      TS100600
                                    62             CP    #$1YR,=P'1600'                   TS100610
                                    63             BH    #$1YRHI                          TS100620
                                    64   #$1BADYR  ZAP   &CODE1,=P'4'                     TS100630
                                    65             B     #$1TERM                          TS100640
                                    66   #$1YRHI   CP    #$1YR,=P'3399'                   TS100650
                                    67             BH    #$1BADYR                         TS100660
                                    68             ZAP   &L,=P'0'                         TS100670
                                    69             ZAP   #$1WORK,#$1YR                    TS100680
                                    70             DP    #$1WORK,=P'4'                    TS100690
                                    71             CP    #$1WORK+4(1),=P'0'               TS100700
                                    72             BH    #$1TERM                          TS100710
                                    73             ZAP   #$1WORK,#$1YR                    TS100720
                                    74             DP    #$1WORK,=P'100'                  TS100730
                                    75             CP    #$1WORK+3(2),=P'0'               TS100740
                                    76             BH    #$1LPYR                          TS100750
                                    77             ZAP   #$1WORK,#$1YR                    TS100760
                                    78             DP    #$1WORK,=P'400'                  TS100770
                                    79             CP    #$1WORK+3(2),=P'0'               TS100780
                                    80             BH    #$1TERM                          TS100790
                                    81   #$1LPYR   ZAP   &L,=P'1'                         TS100800
                                    82             B     #$1TERM                          TS100810
                                    83   L         DC    PL1'9'                           TS100820
                                    84   CODE1     DC    PL1'4'                           TS100830
                                    85   YEAR      DC    ZL4'0'                           TS100840
                                    86   #$1TABL   DC    240X'1C'                         TS100850
                                    87             DC    10X'00'                          TS100860
                                    88             DC    6X'1C'                           TS100870
                                    89   #$1ZRO    DC    10X'00'                          TS100880
                                    90   #$1SIGN   DS    CL1                              TS100890
                                    91   #$1WORK4  DS    ZL4                              TS100900
                                    92   #$1YR     DS    PL3                              TS100910
                                    93   #$1RSAVE  DS    2F                               TS100920
                                    94   #$1WORK   DS    PL5                              TS100930
                                    95   #$1TERM   LM    1,2,#$1RSAVE                     TS100940
                                    96             MEND
                                    97             END
```

**Figure A.3**  The macro edit post listing for TIME1, the TIMESUB1 macro equivalent.

99-12-31

DIAGNOSTICS AND STATISTICS

NO ERRORS FOUND

EDECK PUNCHED FOR MACRO 'TIME1', NUMBER OF CARDS IS 34

OPTIONS FOR THIS ASSEMBLY - ALIGN, LIST, NOXREF, NOLINK, RLD, NODECK, EDECK

THE ASSEMBLER WAS RUN IN 98184 BYTES
END OF ASSEMBLY

**Figure A.3** *Continued*

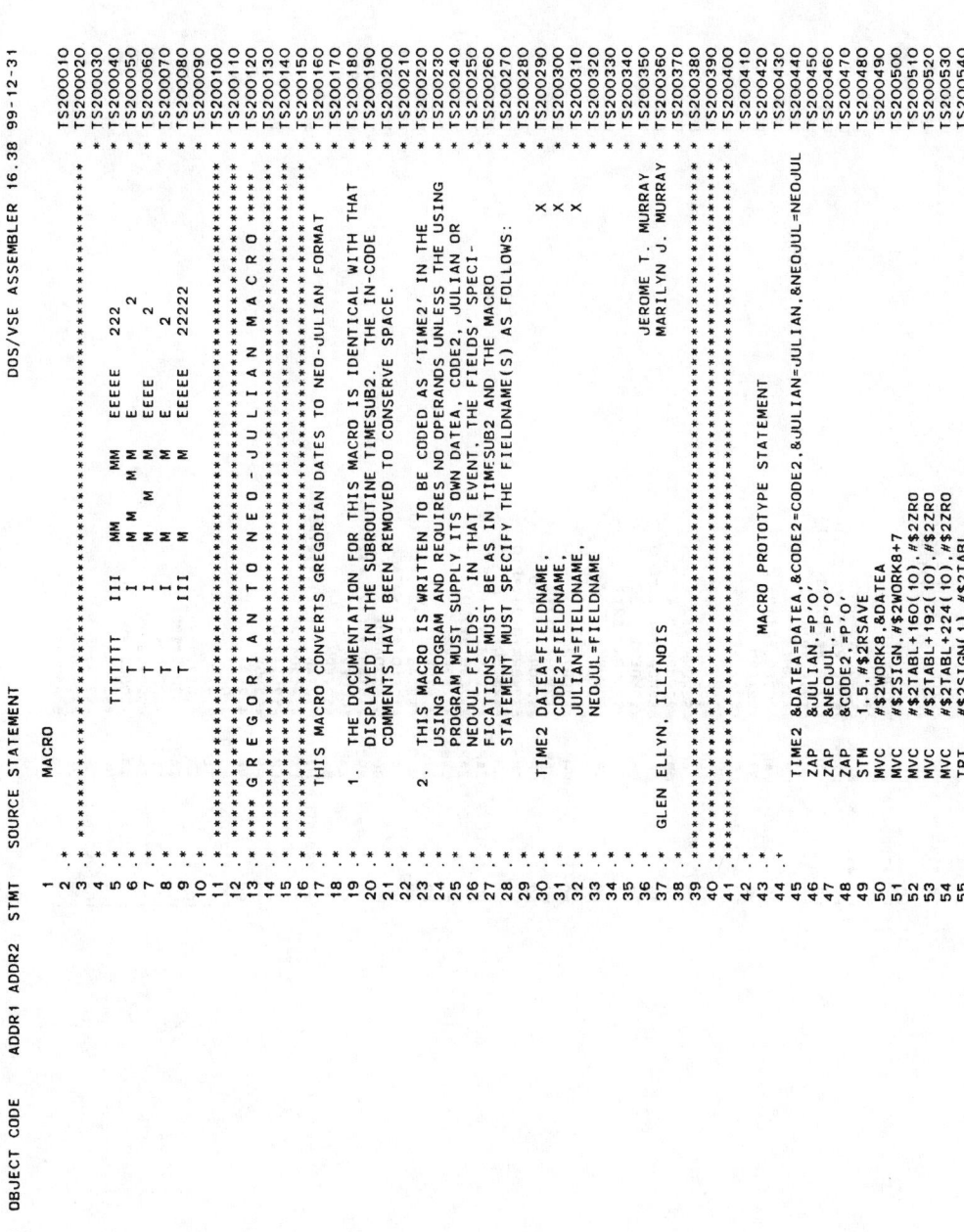

```
LOC   OBJECT CODE   ADDR1   ADDR2   STMT   SOURCE STATEMENT                                    DOS/VSE ASSEMBLER 16.38  99-12-31

                                      1            MACRO                                                                      * TS200010
                                      2   *                                                                                  * TS200020
                                      3   *                                                                                  * TS200030
                                      4   *                                                                                  * TS200040
                                      5   *        TTTTTT   III   MM     MM   EEEEE   222                                     * TS200050
                                      6   *          T       I    M M   M M   EEEE       2                                    * TS200060
                                      7   *          T       I    M  M M  M   E          2                                    * TS200070
                                      8   *          T       I    M   M   M   EEEE      2                                     * TS200080
                                      9   *          T      III   M       M   EEEEE   22222                                   * TS200090
                                     10   *                                                                                  * TS200100
                                     11   *   ****************************************************                           * TS200110
                                     12   ****  G R E G O R I A N  T O  N E O - J U L I A N  M A C R O  *****                 * TS200120
                                     13   *   ****************************************************                           * TS200130
                                     14   *   ****************************************************                           * TS200140
                                     15   *                                                                                  * TS200150
                                     16   *                                                                                  * TS200160
                                     17   *   THIS MACRO CONVERTS GREGORIAN DATES TO NEO-JULIAN FORMAT                       * TS200170
                                     18   *                                                                                  * TS200180
                                     19   *   1.  THE DOCUMENTATION FOR THIS MACRO IS IDENTICAL WITH THAT                    * TS200190
                                     20   *       DISPLAYED IN THE SUBROUTINE TIMESUB2.  THE IN-CODE                         * TS200200
                                     21   *       COMMENTS HAVE BEEN REMOVED TO CONSERVE SPACE.                              * TS200210
                                     22   *                                                                                  * TS200220
                                     23   *   2.  THIS MACRO IS WRITTEN TO BE CODED AS 'TIME2' IN THE                        * TS200230
                                     24   *       USING PROGRAM AND REQUIRES NO OPERANDS UNLESS THE USING                    * TS200240
                                     25   *       PROGRAM MUST SUPPLY ITS OWN DATEA, CODE2, JULIAN OR                        * TS200250
                                     26   *       NEOJUL FIELDS.  IN THAT EVENT, THE FIELDS' SPECI-                          * TS200260
                                     27   *       FICATIONS MUST BE AS IN TIMESUB2 AND THE MACRO                             * TS200270
                                     28   *       STATEMENT MUST SPECIFY THE FIELDNAME(S) AS FOLLOWS:                        * TS200280
                                     29   *                                                                                  * TS200290
                                     30   *       TIME2  DATEA=FIELDNAME,                                         X          * TS200300
                                     31   *              CODE2=FIELDNAME,                                         X          * TS200310
                                     32   *              JULIAN=FIELDNAME,                                        X          * TS200320
                                     33   *              NEOJUL=FIELDNAME                                                    * TS200330
                                     34   *                                                                                  * TS200340
                                     35   *                                                                                  * TS200350
                                     36   *                                              JEROME T. MURRAY                    * TS200360
                                     37   *   GLEN ELLYN, ILLINOIS                        MARILYN J. MURRAY                   * TS200370
                                     38   *                                                                                  * TS200380
                                     39   *   ****************************************************                           * TS200390
                                     40   *   ****************************************************                           * TS200400
                                     41   *                                                                                  * TS200410
                                     42   *          MACRO PROTOTYPE STATEMENT                                               * TS200420
                                     43   *                                                                                  * TS200430
                                     44   +                                                                                  * TS200440
                                     45        TIME2  &DATEA=DATEA,&CODE2=CODE2,&JULIAN=JULIAN,&NEOJUL=NEOJUL                   TS200450
                                     46        ZAP    &JULIAN,=P'0'                                                            TS200460
                                     47        ZAP    &NEOJUL,=P'0'                                                            TS200470
                                     48        ZAP    &CODE2,=P'0'                                                             TS200480
                                     49        STM    1,5,#$2RSAVE                                                            TS200490
                                     50        MVC    #$2WORK8,&DATEA                                                         TS200500
                                     51        MVC    #$2SIGN,#$2WORK8+7                                                      TS200510
                                     52        MVC    #$2TABL+160(10),#$2ZRO                                                  TS200520
                                     53        MVC    #$2TABL+192(10),#$2ZRO                                                  TS200530
                                     54        MVC    #$2TABL+224(10),#$2ZRO                                                  TS200540
                                     55        TRT    #$2SIGN(1),#$2TABL
```

**Figure A.4**  The macro edit post listing for TIME2, the TIMESUB2 macro equivalent.

DOS/VSE ASSEMBLER  16.38  99-12-31

```
LOC   OBJECT CODE   ADDR1 ADDR2   STMT   SOURCE STATEMENT

                                   56            BC    8,#$2NUM              TS200550
                                   57            B     #$2BDATA              TS200560
                                   58   #$2NUM   MVC   #$2TABL+1(239),#$2TABL TS200570
                                   59            TRT   #$2WORK8(7),#$2TABL   TS200580
                                   60            BC    8,#$2PACK             TS200590
                                   61   #$2BDATA ZAP   &CODE2,=P'2'          TS200600
                                   62            B     #$2TERM               TS200610
                                   63   #$2PACK  PACK  #$2MO,#$2WORK8(2)     TS200620
                                   64            PACK  #$2DA,#$2WORK8+2(2)   TS200630
                                   65            PACK  #$2YR,#$2WORK8+4(4)   TS200640
                                   66            CP    #$2YR,=P'1600'        TS200650
                                   67            BH    #$2YRHI               TS200660
                                   68   #$2BADYR ZAP   &CODE2,=P'4'          TS200670
                                   69            B     #$2TERM               TS200680
                                   70   #$2YRHI  CP    #$2YR,=P'3399'        TS200690
                                   71            BH    #$2BADYR              TS200700
                                   72            ZAP   #$2L,=P'0'            TS200710
                                   73            ZAP   #$2WORK,#$2YR         TS200720
                                   74            DP    #$2WORK,=P'4'         TS200730
                                   75            CP    #$2WORK+4(1),=P'0'    TS200740
                                   76            BH    #$2MOEDT              TS200750
                                   77            ZAP   #$2WORK,#$2YR         TS200760
                                   78            DP    #$2WORK,=P'100'       TS200770
                                   79            CP    #$2WORK+3(2),=P'0'    TS200780
                                   80            BH    #$2LPYR               TS200790
                                   81            ZAP   #$2WORK,#$2YR         TS200800
                                   82            DP    #$2WORK,=P'400'       TS200810
                                   83            CP    #$2WORK+3(2),=P'0'    TS200820
                                   84            BH    #$2MOEDT              TS200830
                                   85   #$2LPYR  ZAP   #$2L,=P'1'            TS200840
                                   86   #$2MOEDT ZAP   #$2CVB,#$2MO          TS200850
                                   87            CVB   3,#$2CVB              TS200860
                                   88            STC   3,#$2FLD              TS200870
                                   89            MVC   #$2TABL+1(12),#$2ZRO  TS200880
                                   90            TRT   #$2FLD(1),#$2TABL     TS200890
                                   91            BC    8,#$2DAEDT            TS200900
                                   92            MVC   #$2TABL+1(12),#$2TABL TS200910
                                   93            ZAP   &CODE2,=P'6'          TS200920
                                   94            B     #$2TERM               TS200930
                                   95   #$2DAEDT MVC   #$2TABL+1(12),#$2TABL TS200940
                                   96            LA    4,#$2DATAB            TS200950
                                   97            CP    #$2L,=P'0'            TS200960
                                   98            BE    #$2NOL                TS200970
                                   99            LA    4,2(4)                TS200980
                                  100   #$2NOL   BCTR  3,0                   TS200990
                                  101            SLL   3,2                   TS201000
                                  102            LA    4,0(3,4)              TS201010
                                  103            ZAP   #$2DA,#$2DA           TS201020
                                  104            CLC   #$2DA,0(4)            TS201030
                                  105            BNH   #$2DALO               TS201040
                                  106   #$2BADA  ZAP   &CODE2,=P'8'          TS201050
                                  107            B     #$2TERM               TS201060
                                  108   #$2DALO  CP    #$2DA,=P'00'          TS201070
                                  109            BE    #$2BADA               TS201080
                                  110            LA    5,#$2DAYS             TS201090
```

```
LOC   OBJECT CODE   ADDR1 ADDR2   STMT   SOURCE STATEMENT                          DOS/VSE ASSEMBLER  16.38  99-12-31

                                   111              CP    #$2L,=P'0'                                          TS201100
                                   112              BE    #$2NDLL                                             TS201110
                                   113              LA    5,2(5)                                              TS201120
                                   114   #$2NDLL    LA    5,0(3,5)                                            TS201130
                                   115              ZAP   &JULIAN,0(2,5)                                      TS201140
                                   116              AP    &JULIAN,#$2DA                                       TS201150
                                   117              PACK  #$2WORK,#$2WORK8+6(2)                               TS201160
                                   118              MP    #$2WORK,=P'1000'                                    TS201170
                                   119              AP    &JULIAN,#$2WORK+2(3)                                TS201180
                                   120              PACK  #$2WORK8,#$2WORK+4(4)                               TS201190
                                   121              MP    #$2WORK8,=P'1000'                                   TS201200
                                   122              ZAP   &NEDJUL,#$2WORK8+4(4)                               TS201210
                                   123              AP    &NEDJUL,&JULIAN+1(2)                                TS201220
                                   124              B     #$2TERM                                             TS201230
                                   125   JULIAN     DC    PL3'0'                                              TS201240
                                   126   NEDJUL     DC    PL4'0'                                              TS201250
                                   127   CODE2      DC    PL1'4'                                              TS201260
                                   128   DATEA      DC    ZL8'00000000'                                       TS201270
                                   129   #$2DATAB   DC    PL2'31',PL2'31'      JAN                            TS201280
                                   130              DC    PL2'28',PL2'29'      FEB                            TS201290
                                   131              DC    PL2'31',PL2'31'      MAR                            TS201300
                                   132              DC    PL2'30',PL2'30'      APR                            TS201310
                                   133              DC    PL2'31',PL2'31'      MAY                            TS201320
                                   134              DC    PL2'30',PL2'30'      JUN                            TS201330
                                   135              DC    PL2'31',PL2'31'      JUL                            TS201340
                                   136              DC    PL2'31',PL2'31'      AUG                            TS201350
                                   137              DC    PL2'30',PL2'30'      SEP                            TS201360
                                   138              DC    PL2'31',PL2'31'      OCT                            TS201370
                                   139              DC    PL2'30',PL2'30'      NOV                            TS201380
                                   140              DC    PL2'31',PL2'31'      DEC                            TS201390
                                   141   #$2DAYS    DC    PL2'00',PL2'00'      JAN                            TS201400
                                   142              DC    PL2'31',PL2'31'      FEB                            TS201410
                                   143              DC    PL2'59',PL2'60'      MAR                            TS201420
                                   144              DC    PL2'90',PL2'91'      APR                            TS201430
                                   145              DC    PL2'120',PL2'121'    MAY                            TS201440
                                   146              DC    PL2'151',PL2'152'    JUN                            TS201450
                                   147              DC    PL2'181',PL2'182'    JUL                            TS201460
                                   148              DC    PL2'212',PL2'213'    AUG                            TS201470
                                   149              DC    PL2'243',PL2'244'    SEP                            TS201480
                                   150              DC    PL2'273',PL2'274'    OCT                            TS201490
                                   151              DC    PL2'304',PL2'305'    NOV                            TS201500
                                   152              DC    PL2'334',PL2'335'    DEC                            TS201510
                                   153   #$2TABL    DC    240X'1C'                                            TS201520
                                   154              DC    10X'00'                                             TS201530
                                   155              DC    6X'1C'                                              TS201540
                                   156   #$2ZRD     DC    12X'00'                                             TS201550
                                   157   #$2SIGN    DC    ZL1                                                 TS201560
                                   158   #$2L       DS    PL1                                                 TS201570
                                   159   #$2WORK8   DS    CL8                                                 TS201580
                                   160   #$2MD      DS    PL2                                                 TS201590
                                   161   #$2DA      DS    PL2                                                 TS201600
                                   162   #$2YR      DS    PL3                                                 TS201610
                                   163   #$2WORK    DS    PL5                                                 TS201620
                                   164   #$2FLD     DS    CL1                                                 TS201630
                                   165   #$2RSAVE   DS    5F                                                  TS201640
```

**Figure A.4** *Continued*

```
LOC   OBJECT CODE    ADDR1 ADDR2   STMT   SOURCE STATEMENT                            DOS/VSE ASSEMBLER 16.38  99-12-31

                                   166  #$2CVB   DS    1D                                                        TS201650
                                   167  #$2TERM  LM    1,5,#$2RSAVE                                              TS201660
                                   168           MEND
                                   169           END
```

DIAGNOSTICS AND STATISTICS                                                                     99-12-31

NO ERRORS FOUND

EDECK PUNCHED FOR MACRO 'TIME2', NUMBER OF CARDS IS 76

OPTIONS FOR THIS ASSEMBLY - ALIGN, LIST, NOXREF, NOLINK, RLD, NODECK, EDECK

THE ASSEMBLER WAS RUN IN 98184 BYTES
END OF ASSEMBLY

**Figure A.4** *Continued*

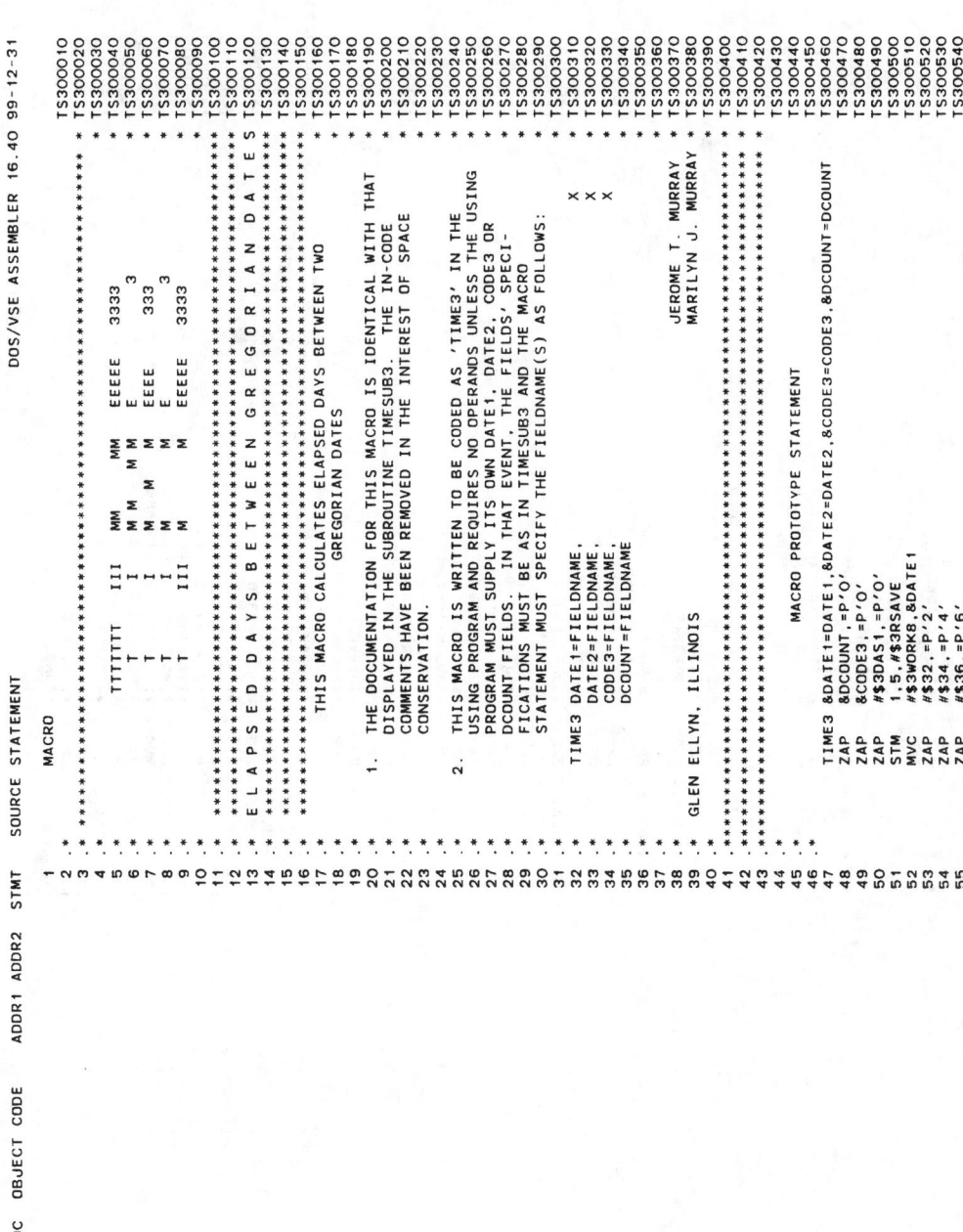

```
LOC  OBJECT CODE  ADDR1 ADDR2  STMT  SOURCE STATEMENT                    DOS/VSE ASSEMBLER 16.40  99-12-31

                                 1         MACRO                                                        TS300010
                                 2   *                                                                  TS300020
                                 3   *                                                                  TS300030
                                 4   * *********************************************************        TS300040
                                 5   *     TTTTTT  III        MM      MM   EEEEE   3333                  TS300050
                                 6   *       T      I         M M    M M   E          333                TS300060
                                 7   *       T      I         M  M  M  M   E            3                TS300070
                                 8   *       T      I         M   MM   M   E          333                TS300080
                                 9   *       T     III        M        M   EEEEE   3333                  TS300090
                                10   *                                                                  TS300100
                                11   * *********************************************************        TS300110
                                12   * E L A P S E D   D A Y S   B E T W E E N   G R E G O R I A N   D A T E S   TS300120
                                13   * *********************************************************        TS300130
                                14   * *********************************************************        TS300140
                                15   *                                                                  TS300150
                                16   *                                                                  TS300160
                                17   *        THIS MACRO CALCULATES ELAPSED DAYS BETWEEN TWO            TS300170
                                18   *             GREGORIAN DATES                                      TS300180
                                19   *                                                                  TS300190
                                20   * 1.  THE DOCUMENTATION FOR THIS MACRO IS IDENTICAL WITH THAT      TS300200
                                21   *     DISPLAYED IN THE SUBROUTINE TIMESUB3.  THE IN-CODE           TS300210
                                22   *     COMMENTS HAVE BEEN REMOVED IN THE INTEREST OF SPACE          TS300220
                                23   *     CONSERVATION.                                                TS300230
                                24   *                                                                  TS300240
                                25   * 2.  THIS MACRO IS WRITTEN TO BE CODED AS 'TIME3' IN THE          TS300250
                                26   *     USING PROGRAM AND REQUIRES NO OPERANDS UNLESS THE USING      TS300260
                                27   *     PROGRAM MUST SUPPLY ITS OWN DATE1, DATE2, CODE3 OR           TS300270
                                28   *     DCOUNT FIELDS.  IN THAT EVENT, THE FIELDS' SPECI-            TS300280
                                29   *     FICATIONS MUST BE AS IN TIMESUB3 AND THE MACRO               TS300290
                                30   *     STATEMENT MUST SPECIFY THE FIELDNAME(S) AS FOLLOWS:          TS300300
                                31   *                                                                  TS300310
                                32   *        TIME3 DATE1=FIELDNAME,                               X    TS300320
                                33   *              DATE2=FIELDNAME,                               X    TS300330
                                34   *              CODE3=FIELDNAME,                               X    TS300340
                                35   *              DCOUNT=FIELDNAME                                     TS300350
                                36   *                                                                  TS300360
                                37   *                                    JEROME T. MURRAY             TS300370
                                38   *                                    MARILYN J. MURRAY            TS300380
                                39   *   GLEN ELLYN, ILLINOIS                                           TS300390
                                40   *                                                                  TS300400
                                41   * *********************************************************        TS300410
                                42   *                                                                  TS300420
                                43   *                                                                  TS300430
                                44   *             MACRO PROTOTYPE STATEMENT                            TS300440
                                45   *                                                                  TS300450
                                46   *                                                                  TS300460
                                47         TIME3 &DATE1=DATE1,&DATE2=DATE2,&CODE3=CODE3,&DCOUNT=DCOUNT  TS300470
                                48         ZAP   &DCOUNT,=P'0'                                          TS300480
                                49         ZAP   &CODE3,=P'0'                                           TS300490
                                50         ZAP   #$3DAS1,=P'0'                                          TS300500
                                51         STM   1,5,#$3RSAVE                                           TS300510
                                52         MVC   #$3WORK8,&DATE1                                        TS300520
                                53         ZAP   #$32,=P'2'                                             TS300530
                                54         ZAP   #$34,=P'4'                                             TS300540
                                55         ZAP   #$36,=P'6'
```

Figure A.5  The macro edit post listing for TIME3, the TIMESUB3 macro equivalent.

```
LOC   OBJECT CODE   ADDR1 ADDR2   STMT   SOURCE STATEMENT                                    DOS/VSE ASSEMBLER 16.40 99-12-31

                                   56              ZAP    #$38.,=P'8'                         TS300550
                                   57              B      #$31DATE                            TS300560
                                   58    #$32DATE  MVC    #$3WORK8,&DATE2                     TS300570
                                   59              ZAP    #$32.,=P'3'                         TS300580
                                   60              ZAP    #$34.,=P'5'                         TS300590
                                   61              ZAP    #$36.,=P'7'                         TS300600
                                   62              ZAP    #$38.,=P'9'                         TS300610
                                   63    #$31DATE  MVC    #$3SIGN,#$3WORK8+7                  TS300620
                                   64              MVC    #$3TABL+160(10),#$3ZRO             TS300630
                                   65              MVC    #$3TABL+192(10),#$3ZRO             TS300640
                                   66              MVC    #$3TABL+224(10),#$3ZRO             TS300650
                                   67              TRT    #$3SIGN(1),#$3TABL                 TS300660
                                   68              BC     8,#$3NUM                            TS300670
                                   69              B      #$3BDATA                            TS300680
                                   70    #$3NUM    MVC    #$3TABL+1(239),#$3TABL             TS300690
                                   71              TRT    #$3WORK8(7),#$3TABL                TS300700
                                   72              BC     8,#$3PACK                           TS300710
                                   73    #$3BDATA  ZAP    &CODE3,#$32                         TS300720
                                   74              B      #$3TERM                             TS300730
                                   75    #$3PACK   PACK   #$3MO,#$3WORK8(2)                  TS300740
                                   76              PACK   #$3DA,#$3WORK8+2(2)                TS300750
                                   77              PACK   #$3YR,#$3WORK8+4(4)                TS300760
                                   78              CP     #$3YR,=P'1600'                      TS300770
                                   79              BH     #$3YRHI                             TS300780
                                   80    #$3BADYR  ZAP    &CODE3,#$34                         TS300790
                                   81              B      #$3TERM                             TS300800
                                   82    #$3YRHI   CP     #$3YR,=P'3399'                      TS300810
                                   83              BH     #$3BADYR                            TS300820
                                   84              ZAP    #$3L,=P'0'                          TS300830
                                   85              ZAP    #$3WORK,#$3YR                       TS300840
                                   86              DP     #$3WORK.,=P'4'                      TS300850
                                   87              CP     #$3WORK+4(1),=P'0'                 TS300860
                                   88              BH     #$3MOEDT                            TS300870
                                   89              ZAP    #$3WORK,#$3YR                       TS300880
                                   90              DP     #$3WORK.,=P'100'                    TS300890
                                   91              CP     #$3WORK+3(2),=P'0'                 TS300900
                                   92              BH     #$3LPYR                             TS300910
                                   93              ZAP    #$3WORK,#$3YR                       TS300920
                                   94              DP     #$3WORK.,=P'400'                    TS300930
                                   95              CP     #$3WORK+3(2),=P'0'                 TS300940
                                   96              BH     #$3MOEDT                            TS300950
                                   97    #$3LPYR   ZAP    #$3L,=P'1'                          TS300960
                                   98    #$3MOEDT  ZAP    #$3CVB,#$3MO                        TS300970
                                   99              CVB    3,#$3CVB                            TS300980
                                  100              STC    3,#$3FLD                            TS300990
                                  101              MVC    #$3TABL+1(12),#$3ZRO              TS301000
                                  102              TRT    #$3FLD(1),#$3TABL                 TS301010
                                  103              BC     8,#$3DAEDT                          TS301020
                                  104              MVC    #$3TABL+1(12),#$3TABL            TS301030
                                  105              ZAP    &CODE3,#$36                         TS301040
                                  106              B      #$3TERM                             TS301050
                                  107    #$3DAEDT  MVC    #$3TABL+1(12),#$3TABL            TS301060
                                  108              LA     4,#$3DATAB                          TS301070
                                  109              CP     #$3L,=P'0'                          TS301080
                                  110              BE     #$3NOL                              TS301090
```

LOC   OBJECT CODE   ADDR1 ADDR2   STMT   SOURCE STATEMENT                                    DOS/VSE ASSEMBLER 16.40 99-12-31

```
                              111              LA    4,2(4)                                  TS301100
                              112  #$3NOL      BCTR  3,0                                     TS301110
                              113              SLL   3,2                                     TS301120
                              114              LA    4,0(3,4)                                TS301130
                              115              ZAP   #$3DA,#$3DA                             TS301140
                              116              CLC   #$3DA,0(4)                              TS301150
                              117              BNH   #$3DALO                                 TS301160
                              118  #$3BADA     ZAP   &CODE3,#$38                             TS301170
                              119              B     #$3TERM                                 TS301180
                              120  #$3DALO     ZAP   #$3DA,=P'00'                            TS301190
                              121              BE    #$3BADA                                 TS301200
                              122              LA    5,#$3DAYS                               TS301210
                              123              CP    #$3L,=P'O'                              TS301220
                              124              BE    #$3NOLL                                 TS301230
                              125              LA    5,2(5)                                  TS301240
                              126  #$3NOLL     LA    5,0(3,5)                                TS301250
                              127              ZAP   #$3JLIAN,0(2,5)                         TS301260
                              128              AP    #$3JLIAN,#$3DA                          TS301270
                              129              ZAP   #$3WORK6,#$3YR                          TS301280
                              130              SP    #$3WORK6,=P'1601'                       TS301290
                              131              MP    #$3WORK6,=P'36525'                      TS301300
                              132              UNPK  #$3WORK9,#$3WORK6+1(5)                  TS301310
                              133              PACK  #$3T1,#$3WORK9(7)                       TS301320
                              134              ZAP   #$3WORK,#$3YR                           TS301330
                              135              SP    #$3WORK,=P'1601'                        TS301340
                              136              DP    #$3WORK,=P'400'                         TS301350
                              137              ZAP   #$3T2,#$3WORK+1(2)                      TS301360
                              138              MP    #$3T2,=P'3'                             TS301370
                              139              ZAP   #$3WORK,#$3WORK+3(2)                    TS301380
                              140              DP    #$3WORK,=P'100'                         TS301390
                              141              ZAP   #$3T3,#$3WORK+2(1)                      TS301400
                              142              AP    #$3JLIAN,#$3T1                          TS301410
                              143              SP    #$3JLIAN,#$3T2                          TS301420
                              144              ZAP   #$3JLIAN,#$3T3                          TS301430
                              145              CP    #$3DAS1,=P'O'                           TS301440
                              146              BH    #$3DAY2                                 TS301450
                              147              ZAP   #$3DAS1,#$3JLIAN                        TS301460
                              148              B     #$32DATE                                TS301470
                              149  #$3DAY2     ZAP   #$3DAS2,#$3JLIAN                        TS301480
                              150              SP    #$3DAS2,#$3DAS1                         TS301490
                              151              MVN   #$3DAS2+4(1),=P'1'                      TS301500
                              152              ZAP   &DCOUNT,#$3DAS2+1(4)                    TS301510
                              153              B     #$3TERM                                 TS301520
                              154  #$3JLIAN    DC    PL5'O'                                  TS301530
                              155  #$3DATAB    DC    PL2'31',PL2'31'         JAN             TS301540
                              156              DC    PL2'28',PL2'29'         FEB             TS301550
                              157              DC    PL2'31',PL2'31'         MAR             TS301560
                              158              DC    PL2'30',PL2'30'         APR             TS301570
                              159              DC    PL2'31',PL2'31'         MAY             TS301580
                              160              DC    PL2'30',PL2'30'         JUN             TS301590
                              161              DC    PL2'31',PL2'31'         JUL             TS301600
                              162              DC    PL2'31',PL2'31'         AUG             TS301610
                              163              DC    PL2'30',PL2'30'         SEP             TS301620
                              164              DC    PL2'31',PL2'31'         OCT             TS301630
                              165              DC    PL2'30',PL2'30'         NOV             TS301640
```

Figure A.5  *Continued*

DOS/VSE ASSEMBLER  16.40  99-12-31

```
LOC   OBJECT CODE   ADDR1 ADDR2   STMT   SOURCE STATEMENT

                                  166              DC    PL2'31',PL2'31'       DEC   TS301650
                                  167   #$3DAYS    DC    PL2'00',PL2'00'       JAN   TS301660
                                  168              DC    PL2'31',PL2'31'       FEB   TS301670
                                  169              DC    PL2'59',PL2'60'       MAR   TS301680
                                  170              DC    PL2'90',PL2'91'       APR   TS301690
                                  171              DC    PL2'120',PL2'121'     MAY   TS301700
                                  172              DC    PL2'151',PL2'152'     JUN   TS301710
                                  173              DC    PL2'181',PL2'182'     JUL   TS301720
                                  174              DC    PL2'212',PL2'213'     AUG   TS301730
                                  175              DC    PL2'243',PL2'244'     SEP   TS301740
                                  176              DC    PL2'273',PL2'274'     OCT   TS301750
                                  177              DC    PL2'304',PL2'305'     NOV   TS301760
                                  178              DC    PL2'334',PL2'335'     DEC   TS301770
                                  179   #$3TABL    DC    240X'1C'                   TS301780
                                  180              DC    10X'00'                    TS301790
                                  181              DC    6X'1C'                     TS301800
                                  182   #$3ZRO     DC    12X'00'                    TS301810
                                  183   DCOUNT     DC    PL4'0'                     TS301820
                                  184   CODE3      DC    PL1'4'                     TS301830
                                  185   DATE1      DC    ZL8'00000000'              TS301840
                                  186   DATE2      DC    ZL8'00000000'              TS301850
                                  187   #$3DAS1    DS    PL5                        TS301860
                                  188   #$3DAS2    DS    PL5                        TS301870
                                  189   #$32       DS    PL1                        TS301880
                                  190   #$34       DS    PL1                        TS301890
                                  191   #$36       DS    PL1                        TS301900
                                  192   #$38       DS    PL1                        TS301910
                                  193   #$3L       DS    PL1                        TS301920
                                  194   #$3SIGN    DS    ZL1                        TS301930
                                  195   #$3WORK6   DS    PL6                        TS301940
                                  196   #$3WORK8   DS    ZL8                        TS301950
                                  197   #$3WORK9   DS    ZL9                        TS301960
                                  198   #$3MO      DS    PL2                        TS301970
                                  199   #$3DA      DS    PL2                        TS301980
                                  200   #$3YR      DS    PL3                        TS301990
                                  201   #$3T1      DS    PL5                        TS302000
                                  202   #$3T2      DS    PL2                        TS302010
                                  203   #$3T3      DS    PL1                        TS302020
                                  204   #$3WORK    DS    PL5                        TS302030
                                  205   #$3FLD     DS    CL1                        TS302040
                                  206   #$3RSAVE   DS    5F                         TS302050
                                  207   #$3CVB     DS    1D                         TS302060
                                  208   #$3TERM    LM    1,5,#$3RSAVE               TS302070
                                  209              MEND
                                  210              END
```

99-12-31

DIAGNOSTICS AND STATISTICS

NO ERRORS FOUND

EDECK PUNCHED FOR MACRO 'TIME3', NUMBER OF CARDS IS 97

OPTIONS FOR THIS ASSEMBLY - ALIGN, LIST, NOXREF, NOLINK, RLD, NODECK, EDECK

THE ASSEMBLER WAS RUN IN 98184 BYTES
END OF ASSEMBLY

**Figure A.5** *Continued*

LOC   OBJECT CODE   ADDR1 ADDR2   STMT   SOURCE STATEMENT                                          DOS/VSE ASSEMBLER 16.42  99-12-31

```
                                  1           MACRO                                                      TS400010
                                  2    *                                                                 TS400020
                                  3    *                                                                 TS400030
                                  4    * *********************************************                   TS400040
                                  5    *   TTTTTT   III    MM     MM   EEEEE    4   4                     TS400050
                                  6    *     T       I     M M   M M   E        4   4                     TS400060
                                  7    *     T       I     M  M M  M   EEEE    444444                     TS400070
                                  8    *     T       I     M   M   M   E           4                     TS400080
                                  9    *     T      III    M       M   EEEEE       4                     TS400090
                                 10    * *********************************************                   TS400100
                                 11    * *********************************************                   TS400110
                                 12    *  E L A P S E D   D A Y S,   M O N T H S,   Y E A R S   B E T W E E N   TS400120
                                 13    *            G R E G O R I A N   D A T E S                         TS400130
                                 14    * *********************************************                   TS400140
                                 15    * *********************************************                   TS400150
                                 16    *                                                                 TS400160
                                 17    *   THIS MACRO CALCULATES ELAPSED DAYS, MONTHS AND YEARS BETWEEN  TS400170
                                 18    *          GREGORIAN DATES                                        TS400180
                                 19    *                                                                 TS400190
                                 20    *                                                                 TS400200
                                 21    *   1.  THE DOCUMENTATION FOR THIS MACRO IS IDENTICAL WITH THAT   TS400210
                                 22    *       DISPLAYED IN THE SUBROUTINE TIMESUB4.  THE IN-CODE        TS400220
                                 23    *       COMMENTS HAVE BEEN REMOVED IN THE INTEREST OF SPACE       TS400230
                                 24    *       CONSERVATION.                                             TS400240
                                 25    *                                                                 TS400250
                                 26    *   2.  THIS MACRO IS WRITTEN TO BE CODED AS 'TIME4' IN THE       TS400260
                                 27    *       USING PROGRAM AND REQUIRES NO OPERANDS UNLESS THE USING   TS400270
                                 28    *       PROGRAM MUST SUPPLY ITS OWN DATEX, DATEY, CODE4 OR        TS400280
                                 29    *       PYEAR, PMONTH AND PDAY FIELDS.  IN THAT EVENT, THE        TS400290
                                 30    *       FIELDS' SPECIFICATIONS MUST BE AS IN TIMESUB4 AND THE     TS400300
                                 31    *       MACRO STATEMENT MUST SPECIFY THE FIELDNAME(S) AS          TS400310
                                 32    *       FOLLOWS:                                                  TS400320
                                 33    *                                                                 TS400330
                                 34    *       TIME4  DATEX=FIELDNAME,                              X    TS400340
                                 35    *              DATEY=FIELDNAME,                              X    TS400350
                                 36    *              CODE4=FIELDNAME,                              X    TS400360
                                 37    *              PYEAR=FIELDNAME,                              X    TS400370
                                 38    *              PMONTH=FIELDNAME,                             X    TS400380
                                 39    *              PDAY=FIELDNAME                                     TS400390
                                 40    *                                                                 TS400400
                                 41    *                                                   JEROME T. MURRAY   TS400410
                                 42    *                                                   MARILYN J. MURRAY  TS400420
                                 43    *   GLEN ELLYN, ILLINOIS                                           TS400430
                                 44    *                                                                 TS400440
                                 45    * *********************************************                   TS400450
                                 46    * *********************************************                   TS400460
                                 47    *                                                                 TS400470
                                 48    *                                                                 TS400480
                                 49    *            MACRO PROTOTYPE STATEMENT                            TS400490
                                 50    *                                                                 TS400500
                                 51           TIME4 &DATEX=DATEX,&DATEY=DATEY,&CODE4=CODE4,&PYEAR=PYEAR, X TS400510
                                              &PMONTH=PMONTH,&PDAY=PDAY                                  TS400510
                                 52           ZAP   &CODE4,=P'0'                                         TS400520
                                 53           ZAP   #$4YRSVX,=P'0'                                       TS400530
                                 54           ZAP   &PDAY,=P'0'                                          TS400540
```

```
LOC   OBJECT CODE   ADDR1 ADDR2   STMT   SOURCE STATEMENT              DOS/VSE ASSEMBLER 16.42 99-12-31

                                   55          ZAP    &PMONTH,=P'0'                                TS400550
                                   56          ZAP    &PYEAR,=P'0'                                 TS400560
                                   57          ZAP    #$4COUNT,=P'0'                               TS400570
                                   58          STM    1,6,#$4RSAVE                                 TS400580
                                   59          MVC    #$4WORK8,&DATEX                              TS400590
                                   60          MVC    #$4WPK8X(4),&DATEX+4                         TS400600
                                   61          MVZ    #$4WRK8X+3(1),=C'0'                          TS400610
                                   62          MVC    #$4WRK8X+4(4),&DATEX                         TS400620
                                   63          ZAP    #$42,=P'2'                                   TS400630
                                   64          ZAP    #$44,=P'4'                                   TS400640
                                   65          ZAP    #$46,=P'6'                                   TS400650
                                   66          ZAP    #$48,=P'8'                                   TS400660
                                   67          B      #$41DATE                                     TS400670
                                   68   #$42DATE MVC   #$4WORK8,&DATEY                             TS400680
                                   69          MVC    #$4WRK8Y(4),&DATEY+4                         TS400690
                                   70          MVZ    #$4WRK8Y+3(1),=C'0'                          TS400700
                                   71          MVC    #$4WRK8Y+4(4),&DATEY                         TS400710
                                   72          ZAP    #$42,=P'3'                                   TS400720
                                   73          ZAP    #$44,=P'5'                                   TS400730
                                   74          ZAP    #$46,=P'7'                                   TS400740
                                   75          ZAP    #$48,=P'9'                                   TS400750
                                   76   #$41DATE MVC   #$4SIGN,#$4WORK8+7                          TS400760
                                   77          MVC    #$4TABL+160(10),#$4ZRO                       TS400770
                                   78          MVC    #$4TABL+192(10),#$4ZRO                       TS400780
                                   79          MVC    #$4TABL+224(10),#$4ZRO                       TS400790
                                   80          TRT    #$4SIGN(1),#$4TABL                           TS400800
                                   81          BC     8.#$4NUM                                     TS400810
                                   82          B      #$4BDATA                                     TS400820
                                   83   #$4NUM   MVI   #$4TABL,X'1C'                               TS400830
                                   84          MVC    #$4TABL+1(239),#$4TABL                       TS400840
                                   85          TRT    #$4WORK8(7),#$4TABL                          TS400850
                                   86          BC     8.#$4PACK                                    TS400860
                                   87   #$4BDATA ZAP   #$4CODE4,#$42                               TS400870
                                   88          B      #$4TERM                                      TS400880
                                   89   #$4PACK  PACK  #$4M,#$4WORK8(2)                            TS400890
                                   90          PACK   #$4D,#$4WORK8+2(2)                           TS400900
                                   91          PACK   #$4Y,#$4WORK8+4(4)                           TS400910
                                   92          CP     #$4YRSVX,=P'0'                               TS400920
                                   93          BH     #$4SECND                                     TS400930
                                   94          ZAP    #$4MOSVX,#$4M                                TS400940
                                   95          ZAP    #$4DASVX,#$4D                                TS400950
                                   96          ZAP    #$4YRSVX,#$4Y                                TS400960
                                   97          B      #$4YRX                                       TS400970
                                   98   #$4SECND ZAP   #$4MOSVY,#$4M                               TS400980
                                   99          ZAP    #$4DASVY,#$4D                                TS400990
                                  100          ZAP    #$4YRSVY,#$4Y                                TS401000
                                  101   #$4YRX   CP    #$4Y,=P'1600'                               TS401010
                                  102          BH     #$4YRHI                                      TS401020
                                  103   #$4BADYR ZAP   #$4CODE4,#$44                               TS401030
                                  104          B      #$4TERM                                      TS401040
                                  105   #$4YRHI  CP    #$4Y,=P'3399'                               TS401050
                                  106          BH     #$4BADYR                                     TS401060
                                  107          LA     5.#$4LEAPY                                   TS401070
                                  108          BALR   6.5                                          TS401080
                                  109          ZAP    #$4CVB,#$4M                                  TS401090
```

**Figure A.6** The macro edit post listing for TIME4, the TIMESUB4 macro equivalent.

```
LOC   OBJECT CODE   ADDR1 ADDR2   STMT            SOURCE STATEMENT                          DOS/VSE ASSEMBLER 16.42  99-12-31

                                  110                     CVB   3,#$4CVB                                              TS401100
                                  111                     STC   3,#$4FLD                                              TS401110
                                  112                     MVC   #$4TABL+1(12),#$4ZRO                                  TS401120
                                  113                     TRT   #$4FLD(1),#$4TABL                                     TS401130
                                  114                     BC    8,#$4DAEDT                                            TS401140
                                  115                     MVC   #$4TABL+1(12),#$4TABL                                 TS401150
                                  116                     ZAP   &CODE4,#$46                                           TS401160
                                  117                     B     #$4TERM                                               TS401170
                                  118   #$4DAEDT          MVC   #$4TABL+1(12),#$4TABL                                 TS401180
                                  119                     LA    5,#$4GETAB                                            TS401190
                                  120                     BALR  6,5                                                   TS401200
                                  121                     ZAP   #$4D,#$4D                                             TS401210
                                  122                     CLC   #$4D,0(4)                                             TS401220
                                  123                     BNH   #$4DALO                                               TS401230
                                  124   #$4BADA           ZAP   &CODE4,#$48                                           TS401240
                                  125                     B     #$4TERM                                               TS401250
                                  126   #$4DALO           CP    #$4D,=P'00'                                           TS401260
                                  127                     BE    #$4BADA                                               TS401270
                                  128                     CP    #$4B,=P'9'                                            TS401280
                                  129                     BNE   #$42DATE                                              TS401290
                                  130                     CLC   #$4WRK8X,#$4WRK8Y                                     TS401300
                                  131                     BH    #$4YR2                                                TS401310
                                  132                     ZAP   #$4Y,#$4YRSVX                                         TS401320
                                  133                     ZAP   #$4TY,#$4YRSVY                                        TS401330
                                  134                     ZAP   #$4M,#$4MOSVX                                         TS401340
                                  135                     ZAP   #$4TM,#$4MOSVY                                        TS401350
                                  136                     ZAP   #$4D,#$4DASVX                                         TS401360
                                  137                     ZAP   #$4TD,#$4DASVY                                        TS401370
                                  138                     B     #$4YRMO                                               TS401380
                                  139   #$4YR2            ZAP   #$4Y,#$4YRSVY                                         TS401390
                                  140                     ZAP   #$4TY,#$4YRSVX                                        TS401400
                                  141                     ZAP   #$4M,#$4MOSVY                                         TS401410
                                  142                     ZAP   #$4TM,#$4MOSVX                                        TS401420
                                  143                     ZAP   #$4D,#$4DASVY                                         TS401430
                                  144   #$4YRMO           ZAP   #$4TD,#$4DASVX                                        TS401440
                                  145                     CP    #$4Y,#$4TY                                            TS401450
                                  146                     BNE   #$4DALIM                                              TS401460
                                  147                     CP    #$4M,#$4TM                                            TS401470
                                  148                     BNE   #$4DALIM                                              TS401480
                                  149                     ZAP   8PDAY,#$4TD                                           TS401490
                                  150                     SP    8PDAY,#$4D                                            TS401500
                                  151                     B     #$4TERM                                               TS401510
                                  152   #$4DALIM          LA    5,#$4LEAPY                                            TS401520
                                  153                     BALR  6,5                                                   TS401530
                                  154                     ZAP   #$4CVB,#$4M                                           TS401540
                                  155                     CVB   3,#$4CVB                                              TS401550
                                  156                     LA    5,#$4GETAB                                            TS401560
                                  157                     BALR  6,5                                                   TS401570
                                  158                     ZAP   #$4IMAX,0(2,4)                                        TS401580
                                  159                     ZAP   #$4ID,#$4D                                            TS401590
                                  160   #$4AGE            CP    #$4Y,#$4TY                                            TS401600
                                  161                     BL    #$4UNDER                                              TS401610
                                  162                     CP    #$4M,#$4TM                                            TS401620
                                  163                     BL    #$4UNDER                                              TS401630
                                  164                     B     #$4EVEN                                               TS401640
```

```
LOC   OBJECT CODE   ADDR1 ADDR2   STMT   SOURCE STATEMENT                          DOS/VSE ASSEMBLER 16.42  99-12-31

                                  165  #$4UNDER  AP   #$4M,=P'1'                    TS401650
                                  166            AP   #$4COUNT,=P'1'                TS401660
                                  167            CP   #$4M,=P'13'                   TS401670
                                  168            BL   #$4AGE                        TS401680
                                  169            SP   #$4M,=P'12'                   TS401690
                                  170            AP   #$4Y,=P'1'                    TS401700
                                  171            B    #$4AGE                        TS401710
                                  172  #$4EVEN   LA   5,#$4LEAPY                    TS401720
                                  173            BALR 6,5                           TS401730
                                  174            ZAP  #$4CVB,#$4M                   TS401740
                                  175            CVB  3,#$4CVB                      TS401750
                                  176            LA   5,#$4GETAB                    TS401760
                                  177            BALR 6,5                           TS401770
                                  178            ZAP  #$4D,0(2,4)                   TS401780
                                  179            ZAP  #$4X,#$4TD                    TS401790
                                  180            SP   #$4X,#$4D                     TS401800
                                  181            CP   #$4X,=P'0'                    TS401810
                                  182            BL   #$4OSHOT                      TS401820
                                  183            ZAP  #$4TD,#$4X                    TS401830
                                  184            AP   #$4TD,#$41MAX                 TS401840
                                  185            SP   #$4TD,#$41D                   TS401850
                                  186            B    #$4PARAM                      TS401860
                                  187  #$4OSHOT  SP   #$4COUNT,=P'1'                TS401870
                                  188            AP   #$4TD,#$41MAX                 TS401880
                                  189            SP   #$4TD,#$41D                   TS401890
                                  190            CP   #$4TD,#$41MAX                 TS401900
                                  191            BL   #$4PARAM                      TS401910
                                  192            CP   #$4ID,=P'29'                  TS401920
                                  193            BNL  #$4PARAM                      TS401930
                                  194            SP   #$4TD,#$41MAX                 TS401940
                                  195            AP   #$4COUNT,=P'1'                TS401950
                                  196  #$4PARAM  ZAP  #$4WORK5,#$4COUNT            TS401960
                                  197            DP   #$4WORK5,=P'12'               TS401970
                                  198            AP   8,PYEAR,#$4WORK5(3)          TS401980
                                  199            AP   8,PMONTH,#$4WORK5+3(2)       TS401990
                                  200            AP   8PDAY,#$4TD                   TS402000
                                  201            B    #$4TERM                       TS402010
                                  202  #$4LEAPY  ZAP  #$4L,=P'0'                    TS402020
                                  203            ZAP  #$4WORK,#$4Y                  TS402030
                                  204            DP   #$4WORK,=P'4'                 TS402040
                                  205            CP   #$4WORK+4(1),=P'0'           TS402050
                                  206            BH   #$4NOLPY                      TS402060
                                  207            ZAP  #$4WORK,#$4Y                  TS402070
                                  208            DP   #$4WORK,=P'100'               TS402080
                                  209            CP   #$4WORK+3(2),=P'0'           TS402090
                                  210            BH   #$4LPYR                       TS402100
                                  211            ZAP  #$4WORK,#$4Y                  TS402110
                                  212            DP   #$4WORK,=P'400'               TS402120
                                  213            CP   #$4WORK+3(2),=P'0'           TS402130
                                  214            BH   #$4NOLPY                      TS402140
                                  215  #$4LPYR   ZAP  #$4L,=P'1'                    TS402150
                                  216  #$4NOLPY  BR   6                             TS402160
                                  217  #$4GETAB  LA   4,#$4DATAB                    TS402170
                                  218            CP   #$4L,=P'0'                    TS402180
                                  219            BE   #$4NOL                        TS402190
```

**Figure A.6** *Continued*

```
LOC   OBJECT CODE   ADDR1 ADDR2   STMT   SOURCE STATEMENT

                                  220              LA    4,2(4)                        TS402200
                                  221   #$4NOL     BCTR  3,0                           TS402210
                                  222              SLL   3,2                           TS402220
                                  223              LA    4,0(3,4)                      TS402230
                                  224              BR    6                             TS402240
                                  225   CODE4      DC    PL1'2'                        TS402250
                                  226   #$4DATAB   DC    PL2'31',PL2'31'      JAN      TS402260
                                  227              DC    PL2'28',PL2'29'      FEB      TS402270
                                  228              DC    PL2'31',PL2'31'      MAR      TS402280
                                  229              DC    PL2'30',PL2'30'      APR      TS402290
                                  230              DC    PL2'31',PL2'31'      MAY      TS402300
                                  231              DC    PL2'30',PL2'30'      JUN      TS402310
                                  232              DC    PL2'31',PL2'31'      JUL      TS402320
                                  233              DC    PL2'31',PL2'31'      AUG      TS402330
                                  234              DC    PL2'30',PL2'30'      SEP      TS402340
                                  235              DC    PL2'31',PL2'31'      OCT      TS402350
                                  236              DC    PL2'30',PL2'30'      NOV      TS402360
                                  237              DC    PL2'31',PL2'31'      DEC      TS402370
                                  238   #$4TABL    DC    240X'1C'                      TS402380
                                  239              DC    10X'00'                       TS402390
                                  240              DC    6X'1C'                        TS402400
                                  241   #$4ZRO     DC    12X'00'                       TS402410
                                  242   DATEX      DC    ZL8'00000000'                 TS402420
                                  243   DATEY      DC    ZL8'00000000'                 TS402430
                                  244   PMONTH     DC    PL2'0'                        TS402440
                                  245   PDAY       DC    PL2'0'                        TS402450
                                  246   PYEAR      DC    PL3'0'                        TS402460
                                  247   #$42       DS    PL1                           TS402470
                                  248   #$44       DS    PL1                           TS402480
                                  249   #$46       DS    PL1                           TS402490
                                  250   #$48       DS    PL1                           TS402500
                                  251   #$4L       DS    PL1                           TS402510
                                  252   #$4SIGN    DS    ZL1                           TS402520
                                  253   #$4WORK5   DS    PL5                           TS402530
                                  254   #$4WORK8   DS    ZL8                           TS402540
                                  255   #$4WRK8X   DS    ZL8                           TS402550
                                  256   #$4WRK8Y   DS    ZL8                           TS402560
                                  257   #$4COUNT   DS    PL3                           TS402570
                                  258   #$4M       DS    PL2                           TS402580
                                  259   #$4MOSVX   DS    PL2                           TS402590
                                  260   #$4MOSVY   DS    PL2                           TS402600
                                  261   #$4D       DS    PL2                           TS402610
                                  262   #$4ID      DS    PL2                           TS402620
                                  263   #$4DASVX   DS    PL2                           TS402630
                                  264   #$4DASVY   DS    PL2                           TS402640
                                  265   #$4TD      DS    PL2                           TS402650
                                  266   #$4X       DS    PL2                           TS402660
                                  267   #$4IMAX    DS    PL2                           TS402670
                                  268   #$4TM      DS    PL2                           TS402680
                                  269   #$4Y       DS    PL3                           TS402690
                                  270   #$4TY      DS    PL3                           TS402700
                                  271   #$4YRSVX   DS    PL3                           TS402710
                                  272   #$4YRSVY   DS    PL3                           TS402720
                                  273   #$4WORK    DS    PL5                           TS402730
                                  274   #$4FLD     DS    CL1                           TS402740
```

```
LOC  OBJECT CODE    ADDR1  ADDR2  STMT   SOURCE STATEMENT                      DOS/VSE ASSEMBLER 16.42 99-12-31

                                  275  #$4RSAVE  DS    6F                                          TS402750
                                  276  #$4CVB    DS    1D                                          TS402760
                                  277  #$4TERM   LM    1,6,#$4RSAVE                                TS402770
                                  278            MEND
                                  279            END
```

DIAGNOSTICS AND STATISTICS

NO ERRORS FOUND                                                                                   99-12-31

EDECK PUNCHED FOR MACRO 'TIME4', NUMBER OF CARDS IS 130

OPTIONS FOR THIS ASSEMBLY - ALIGN, LIST, NOXREF, NOLINK, RLD, NODECK, EDECK

THE ASSEMBLER WAS RUN IN 98184 BYTES
END OF ASSEMBLY

**Figure A.6** *Continued*

```
LOC   OBJECT CODE   ADDR1 ADDR2   STMT   SOURCE STATEMENT                                    DOS/VSE ASSEMBLER 16.44  99-12-31

                                     1           MACRO                                                                  TS500010
                                     2    *                                                                             TS500020
                                     3    *                                                                             TS500030
                                     4    *********************************************************                     TS500040
                                     5    *        TTTTTTT  III    MM   MM   EEEE   55555                                TS500050
                                     6    *           T      I     M M M M   E         5                                TS500060
                                     7    *           T      I     M  M  M   EEEE   5555                                TS500070
                                     8    *           T      I     M     M   E          5                               TS500080
                                     9    *           T     III    M     M   EEEE   5555                                TS500090
                                    10    *                                                                             TS500100
                                    11    *                                                                             TS500110
                                    12    *********************************************************                     TS500120
                                    13    * I N C R E M E N T / D E C R E M E N T - G R E G O R I A N   D A T E         TS500130
                                    14    *********************************************************                     TS500140
                                    15    *                                                                             TS500150
                                    16    *********************************************************                     TS500160
                                    17    *        THIS MACRO INCREMENTS/DECREMENTS A GIVEN                             TS500170
                                    18    *        GREGORIAN DATE                                                       TS500180
                                    19    *                                                                             TS500190
                                    20    *   1.  THE DOCUMENTATION FOR THIS MACRO IS IDENTICAL WITH THAT               TS500200
                                    21    *       DISPLAYED IN THE SUBROUTINE TIMESUB5.  THE IN-CODE                    TS500210
                                    22    *       COMMENTS HAVE BEEN REMOVED IN THE INTEREST OF SPACE                   TS500220
                                    23    *       CONSERVATION.                                                        TS500230
                                    24    *                                                                             TS500240
                                    25    *   2.  THIS MACRO IS WRITTEN TO BE CODED AS 'TIME5' IN THE                   TS500250
                                    26    *       USING PROGRAM AND REQUIRES NO OPERANDS UNLESS THE USING               TS500260
                                    27    *       PROGRAM MUST SUPPLY ITS OWN DATEI, CODE5, MODIFY OR                   TS500270
                                    28    *       NUDATE FIELDS.  IN THAT EVENT, THE FIELDS' SPECIFICATIONS             TS500280
                                    29    *       MUST BE AS IN TIMESUB5 AND THE MACRO STATEMENT MUST                   TS500290
                                    30    *       SPECIFY THE FIELDNAME(S) AS FOLLOWS:                                  TS500300
                                    31    *                                                                             TS500310
                                    32    *       TIME5 DATEI=FIELDNAME,                                                TS500320
                                    33    *             CODE5=FIELDNAME,                          X                     TS500330
                                    34    *             MODIFY=FIELDNAME.                         X                     TS500340
                                    35    *             NUDATE=FIELDNAME                          X                     TS500350
                                    36    *                                                                             TS500360
                                    37    *********************************************************                     TS500370
                                    38    *                                JEROME T. MURRAY                            TS500380
                                    39    *                               MARILYN J. MURRAY                            TS500390
                                    40    *********************************************************                     TS500400
                                    41    *                                                                             TS500410
                                    42    *********************************************************                     TS500420
                                    43    *  GLEN ELLYN, ILLINOIS                                                       TS500430
                                    44    *********************************************************                     TS500440
                                    45    *                                                                             TS500450
                                    46    *        MACRO PROTOTYPE STATEMENT                                            TS500460
                                    47           TIME5 &DATEI=DATEI,&CODE5=CODE5,&MODIFY=MODIFY,&NUDATE=NUDATE          TS500470
                                    48           ZAP  &NUDATE.=P'0'                                                     TS500480
                                    49           ZAP  &CODE5.=P'0'                                                      TS500490
                                    50           ZAP  #$5MOCTR.=P'0'                                                    TS500500
                                    51           STM  1,6,#$5RSAVE                                                      TS500510
                                    52           MVC  #$5SIGN,#$5WORK8+7                                                TS500520
                                    53           MVC  #$5WORK8,&DATEI                                                   TS500530
                                    54           MVC  #$5TABL+160(10),#$5ZRO                                            TS500540
                                    55           MVC  #$5TABL+192(10),#$5ZRO
```

```
LOC   OBJECT CODE   ADDR1  ADDR2   STMT   SOURCE STATEMENT                      DOS/VSE ASSEMBLER  16.44  99-12-31

                                     56            MVC   #$5TABL+224(10),#$5ZR0          TS500550
                                     57            TRT   #$5SIGN(1),#$5TABL              TS500560
                                     58            BC    8,#$5NUM                        TS500570
                                     59            B     #$5BDATA                        TS500580
                                     60   #$5NUM   MVI   #$5TABL,X'1C'                   TS500590
                                     61            MVC   #$5TABL+1(239),#$5TABL          TS500600
                                     62            TRT   #$5WORK8(7),#$5TABL             TS500610
                                     63            BC    8,#$5PACK                       TS500620
                                     64   #$5BDATA ZAP   &CODE5,=P'2'                    TS500630
                                     65            B     #$5TERM                         TS500640
                                     66   #$5PACK  PACK  #$5MO,#$5WORK8(2)               TS500650
                                     67            PACK  #$5DA,#$5WORK8+2(2)             TS500660
                                     68            PACK  #$5YR,#$5WORK8+4(4)             TS500670
                                     69            CP    #$5YR,=P'1600'                  TS500680
                                     70            BH    #$5YRHI                         TS500690
                                     71   #$5BADYR ZAP   &CODE5,=P'4'                    TS500700
                                     72            B     #$5TERM                         TS500710
                                     73   #$5YRHI  CP    #$5YR,=P'3399'                  TS500720
                                     74            BH    #$5BADYR                        TS500730
                                     75            LA    5,#$5LEAPY                      TS500740
                                     76            BALR  6,5                             TS500750
                                     77            ZAP   #$5CVB,#$5MO                    TS500760
                                     78            CVB   3,#$5CVB                        TS500770
                                     79            STC   3,#$5FLD                        TS500780
                                     80            MVC   #$5TABL+1(12),#$5ZR0            TS500790
                                     81            TRT   #$5FLD(1),#$5TABL               TS500800
                                     82            BC    8,#$5DAEDT                      TS500810
                                     83            MVC   #$5TABL+1(12),#$5TABL           TS500820
                                     84            ZAP   &CODE5,=P'6'                    TS500830
                                     85            B     #$5TERM                         TS500840
                                     86   #$5DAEDT MVC   #$5TABL+1(12),#$5TABL           TS500850
                                     87            LA    5,#$5GETAB                      TS500860
                                     88            BALR  6,5                             TS500870
                                     89            ZAP   #$5DA,#$5DA                     TS500880
                                     90            CLC   #$5DA,O(4)                      TS500890
                                     91            BNH   #$5DALO                         TS500900
                                     92   #$5BADA  ZAP   &CODE5,=P'8'                    TS500910
                                     93            B     #$5TERM                         TS500920
                                     94   #$5DALO  CP    #$5DA,=P'OO'                    TS500930
                                     95            BE    #$5BADA                         TS500940
                                     96            MVC   #$5WORKX,&MODIFY                TS500950
                                     97            MVC   #$5SIGN,#$5WORKX+5              TS500960
                                     98            MVC   #$5TABL+160(10),#$5ZR0          TS500970
                                     99            MVC   #$5TABL+176(10),#$5ZR0          TS500980
                                    100            MVC   #$5TABL+192(10),#$5ZR0          TS500990
                                    101            MVC   #$5TABL+208(10),#$5ZR0          TS501000
                                    102            MVC   #$5TABL+224(10),#$5ZR0          TS501010
                                    103            TRT   #$5SIGN(1),#$5TABL              TS501020
                                    104            BC    8,#$5ZONE                       TS501030
                                    105            B     #$5BADMD                        TS501040
                                    106   #$5ZONE  MVI   #$5TABL,X'1C'                   TS501050
                                    107            MVC   #$5TABL+1(239),#$5TABL          TS501060
                                    108            TRT   #$5WORKX(5),#$5TABL             TS501070
                                    109            BC    8,#$5SIZE                       TS501080
                                    110   #$5BADMD ZAP   &CODE5,=P'3'                    TS501090
```

**Figure A.7** The macro edit post listing for TIME5, the TIMESUB5 macro equivalent.

```
LOC   OBJECT CODE   ADDR1 ADDR2  STMT  SOURCE STATEMENT

                                 111           B     #$5TERM                         TS501100
                                 112  #$5SIZE  PACK  #$5MDA,#$5WORKX                  TS501110
                                 113           MVN   #$5MDA+3,=P'1'                   TS501120
                                 114           CP    #$5MDA,=P'0'                     TS501130
                                 115           BNE   #$5LIMIT                         TS501140
                                 116           ZAP   #$5NEWM,#$5MO                    TS501150
                                 117           ZAP   #$5NEWD,#$5DA                    TS501160
                                 118           ZAP   #$5NEWY,#$5YR                    TS501170
                                 119           B     #$5BUILD                         TS501180
                                 120  #$5LIMIT CP    #$5MDA,=P'657070'                TS501190
                                 121           BNH   #$5SGN                           TS501200
                                 122           ZAP   &CODE5,=P'5'                     TS501210
                                 123           B     #$5TERM                          TS501220
                                 124  #$5SGN   PACK  #$5MDA,#$5WORKX                  TS501230
                                 125           LA    5,#$5DAYS                        TS501240
                                 126           CP    #$5L,=P'0'                       TS501250
                                 127           BE    #$5NDLL                          TS501260
                                 128           LA    5,2(5)                           TS501270
                                 129  #$5NDLL  LA    5,O(3,5)                         TS501280
                                 130           ZAP   #$5JLIAN,O(2,5)                  TS501290
                                 131           AP    #$5JLIAN,#$5DA                   TS501300
                                 132           ZAP   #$5WORK6,#$5YR                   TS501310
                                 133           SP    #$5WORK6,=P'1601'                TS501320
                                 134           MP    #$5WORK6,=P'36525'               TS501330
                                 135           UNPK  #$5WORK9,#$5WORK6+1(5)           TS501340
                                 136           PACK  #$5T1,#$5WORK9(7)                TS501350
                                 137           ZAP   #$5WORK,#$5YR                    TS501360
                                 138           SP    #$5WORK,=P'1601'                 TS501370
                                 139           DP    #$5WORK,=P'400'                  TS501380
                                 140           ZAP   #$5T2,#$5WORK+1(2)               TS501390
                                 141           MP    #$5T2,=P'3'                      TS501400
                                 142           ZAP   #$5WORK,#$5WORK+3(2)             TS501410
                                 143           DP    #$5WORK,=P'100'                  TS501420
                                 144           ZAP   #$5T3,#$5WORK+2(1)               TS501430
                                 145           AP    #$5JLIAN,#$5T1                   TS501440
                                 146           SP    #$5JLIAN,#$5T2                   TS501450
                                 147           SP    #$5JLIAN,#$5T3                   TS501460
                                 148           AP    #$5JLIAN,#$5MDA                  TS501470
                                 149           ZAP   #$5WORK,#$5JLIAN                 TS501480
                                 150           DP    #$5WORK,=P'365'                  TS501490
                                 151           ZAP   #$5C,#$5WORK(3)                  TS501500
                                 152           ZAP   #$5R,#$5WORK+3(2)                TS501510
                                 153           ZAP   #$5WORK,#$5C                     TS501520
                                 154           DP    #$5WORK,=P'4'                    TS501530
                                 155           SP    #$5R,#$5WORK+2(2)                TS501540
                                 156           ZAP   #$5WORK,#$5C                     TS501550
                                 157           DP    #$5WORK,=P'400'                  TS501560
                                 158           ZAP   #$5T2,#$5WORK+1(2)               TS501570
                                 159           MP    #$5T2,=P'3'                      TS501580
                                 160           ZAP   #$5WORK,#$5WORK+3(2)             TS501590
                                 161           DP    #$5WORK,=P'100'                  TS501600
                                 162           ZAP   #$5T3,#$5WORK+2(1)               TS501610
                                 163           AP    #$5R,#$5T2                       TS501620
                                 164           AP    #$5R,#$513                       TS501630
                                 165  #$5RETRY CP    #$5R,=P'0'                       TS501640
```

```
LOC  OBJECT CODE  ADDR1 ADDR2  STMT  SOURCE STATEMENT          DOS/VSE ASSEMBLER 16.44 99-12-31

                               166            BH    #$5REMOK                              TS501650
                               167            SP    #$5C,=P'1'                            TS501660
                               168            ZAP   #$5YR,#$5C                            TS501670
                               169            AP    #$5YR,=P'1601'                        TS501680
                               170            LA    5,#$5LEAPY                            TS501690
                               171            BALR  6,5                                   TS501700
                               172            AP    #$5R,=P'365'                          TS501710
                               173            AP    #$5R,#$5L                             TS501720
                               174            B     #$5RETRY                              TS501730
                               175  #$5REMOK  ZAP   #$5NEWY,#$5C                          TS501740
                               176            AP    #$5NEWY,=P'1601'                      TS501750
                               177            CP    #$5NEWY,=P'1600'                      TS501760
                               178            BH    #$53399                               TS501770
                               179  #$5OUT    ZAP   8CODE5,=P'7'                          TS501780
                               180            B     #$5TERM                               TS501790
                               181  #$53399   CP    #$5NEWY,=P'3399'                      TS501800
                               182            BH    #$5OUT                                TS501810
                               183            ZAP   #$5YR,#$5NEWY                         TS501820
                               184            LA    5,#$5LEAPY                            TS501830
                               185            BALR  6,5                                   TS501840
                               186            LA    5,#$5DAYS+4                           TS501850
                               187            CP    #$5L,=P'0'                            TS501860
                               188            BE    #$5COUNT                              TS501870
                               189            LA    5,2(5)                                TS501880
                               190  #$5COUNT  AP    #$5MOCTR,=P'1'                        TS501890
                               191            CP    #$5R,0(2,5)                           TS501900
                               192            BNH   #$5GOTNU                              TS501910
                               193            LA    5,4(5)                                TS501920
                               194            B     #$5COUNT                              TS501930
                               195  #$5GOTNU  ZAP   #$5NEWM,#$5MOCTR                      TS501940
                               196            SH    5,=H'4'                               TS501950
                               197            SP    #$5R,0(2,5)                           TS501960
                               198            ZAP   #$5NEWD,#$5R                          TS501970
                               199  #$5BUILD  UNPK  #$5WORK8,#$5NEWY                      TS501980
                               200            UNPK  #$5WORK8+2(2),#$5NEWD                 TS501990
                               201            UNPK  #$5WORK8(2),#$5NEWM                   TS502000
                               202            PACK  8NUDATE.#$5WORK8                      TS502010
                               203            B     #$5TERM                               TS502020
                               204  #$5LEAPY  ZAP   #$5L,=P'0'                            TS502030
                               205            ZAP   #$5WORK,#$5YR                         TS502040
                               206            DP    #$5WORK,=P'4'                         TS502050
                               207            CP    #$5WORK+4(1),=P'0'                    TS502060
                               208            BH    #$5NOLPY                              TS502070
                               209            ZAP   #$5WORK,#$5YR                         TS502080
                               210            DP    #$5WORK,=P'100'                       TS502090
                               211            CP    #$5WORK+3(2),=P'0'                    TS502100
                               212            BH    #$5LPYR                               TS502110
                               213            ZAP   #$5WORK,#$5YR                         TS502120
                               214            DP    #$5WORK,=P'400'                       TS502130
                               215            CP    #$5WORK+3(2),=P'0'                    TS502140
                               216            BH    #$5NOLPY                              TS502150
                               217  #$5LPYR   ZAP   #$5L,=P'1'                            TS502160
                               218  #$5NOLPY  BR    6                                     TS502170
                               219  #$5GETAB  LA    4,#$5DATAB                            TS502180
                               220            CP    #$5L,=P'0'                            TS502190
```

**Figure A.7** *Continued*

DOS/VSE ASSEMBLER  16.44  99-12-31

```
LOC   OBJECT CODE   ADDR1 ADDR2   STMT   SOURCE STATEMENT

                                  221            BE    #$5NOL                                    TS502200
                                  222            LA    4,2(4)                                    TS502210
                                  223   #$5NOL   BCTR  3,0                                       TS502220
                                  224            SLL   3,2                                       TS502230
                                  225            LA    4,0(3,4)                                  TS502240
                                  226            BR    6                                         TS502250
                                  227   MODIFY   DC    ZL6'000000'                               TS502260
                                  228   NUDATE   DC    PL5'0'                                    TS502270
                                  229   #$5DATAB DC    PL2'31',PL2'31'            JAN            TS502280
                                  230            DC    PL2'28',PL2'29'            FEB            TS502290
                                  231            DC    PL2'31',PL2'31'            MAR            TS502300
                                  232            DC    PL2'30',PL2'30'            APR            TS502310
                                  233            DC    PL2'31',PL2'31'            MAY            TS502320
                                  234            DC    PL2'30',PL2'30'            JUN            TS502330
                                  235            DC    PL2'31',PL2'31'            JUL            TS502340
                                  236            DC    PL2'31',PL2'31'            AUG            TS502350
                                  237            DC    PL2'30',PL2'30'            SEP            TS502360
                                  238            DC    PL2'31',PL2'31'            OCT            TS502370
                                  239            DC    PL2'30',PL2'30'            NOV            TS502380
                                  240            DC    PL2'31',PL2'31'            DEC            TS502390
                                  241   #$5DAYS  DC    PL2'00',PL2'00'            JAN            TS502400
                                  242            DC    PL2'31',PL2'31'            FEB            TS502410
                                  243            DC    PL2'59',PL2'60'            MAR            TS502420
                                  244            DC    PL2'90',PL2'91'            APR            TS502430
                                  245            DC    PL2'120',PL2'121'          MAY            TS502440
                                  246            DC    PL2'151',PL2'152'          JUN            TS502450
                                  247            DC    PL2'181',PL2'182'          JUL            TS502460
                                  248            DC    PL2'212',PL2'213'          AUG            TS502470
                                  249            DC    PL2'243',PL2'244'          SEP            TS502480
                                  250            DC    PL2'273',PL2'274'          OCT            TS502490
                                  251            DC    PL2'304',PL2'305'          NOV            TS502500
                                  252            DC    PL2'334',PL2'335'          DEC            TS502510
                                  253            DC    PL2'999',PL2'999'          END            TS502520
                                  254   #$5TABL  DC    240X'1C'                                  TS502530
                                  255            DC    10X'00'                                   TS502540
                                  256            DC    6X'1C'                                    TS502550
                                  257   #$5ZRO   DC    12X'00'                                   TS502560
                                  258   CODE5    DC    PL1'4'                                    TS502570
                                  259   DATEI    DC    ZL8'00000000'                             TS502580
                                  260   #$5JLIAN DS    PL5                                       TS502590
                                  261   #$5R     DS    PL5                                       TS502600
                                  262   #$5C     DS    PL5                                       TS502610
                                  263   #$5L     DS    PL1                                       TS502620
                                  264   #$5SIGN  DS    ZL1                                       TS502630
                                  265   #$5WORK6 DS    PL6                                       TS502640
                                  266   #$5WORK8 DS    ZL8                                       TS502650
                                  267   #$5WORK9 DS    ZL9                                       TS502660
                                  268   #$5WORKX DS    ZL6                                       TS502670
                                  269   #$5NEWY  DS    PL3                                       TS502680
                                  270   #$5NEWM  DS    PL2                                       TS502690
                                  271   #$5NEWD  DS    PL2                                       TS502700
                                  272   #$5MO    DS    PL2                                       TS502710
                                  273   #$5DA    DS    PL2                                       TS502720
                                  274   #$5YR    DS    PL3                                       TS502730
                                  275   #$5MOCTR DS    PL2                                       TS502740
```

```
LOC   OBJECT CODE   ADDR1 ADDR2   STMT   SOURCE STATEMENT                    DOS/VSE ASSEMBLER 16.44 99-12-31

                                  276  #$5MDA    DS    PL4                                      TS502750
                                  277  #$5T1     DS    PL5                                      TS502760
                                  278  #$5T2     DS    PL2                                      TS502770
                                  279  #$5T3     DS    PL1                                      TS502780
                                  280  #$5WORK   DS    PL5                                      TS502790
                                  281  #$5FLD    DS    CL1                                      TS502800
                                  282  #$5CVB    DS    1D                                       TS502810
                                  283  #$5RSAVE  DS    6F                                       TS502820
                                  284  #$5TERM   LM    1,6,#$5RSAVE                             TS502830
                                  285            MEND
                                  286            END
```

DIAGNOSTICS AND STATISTICS

NO ERRORS FOUND

EDECK PUNCHED FOR MACRO 'TIME5', NUMBER OF CARDS IS 140

OPTIONS FOR THIS ASSEMBLY - ALIGN, LIST, NOXREF, NOLINK, RLD, NODECK, EDECK

THE ASSEMBLER WAS RUN IN 98184 BYTES
END OF ASSEMBLY

99-12-31

**Figure A.7** *Continued*

```
LOC   OBJECT CODE   ADDR1  ADDR2   STMT   SOURCE STATEMENT                              DOS/VSE ASSEMBLER 16.46  99-12-31

                                     1    *                                                                              TS600010
                                     2    *                                                                              TS600020
                                     3    *              MACRO                                                           TS600030
                                     4    *                                                                              TS600040
                                     5    *    TTTTTTT   III   MM     MM   EEEEE   666                                   TS600050
                                     6    *       T       I    M M   M M   E         6                                  TS600060
                                     7    *       T       I    M  M M  M   EEEE    6666                                 TS600070
                                     8    *       T       I    M   M   M   E       6  6                                 TS600080
                                     9    *       T      III   M       M   EEEEE   666                                  TS600090
                                    10    *                                                                              TS600100
                                    11    ********************************************************                       TS600110
                                    12    *  D A Y   N A M E   O F   A   G I V E N   G R E G O R I A N   D A T E  *       TS600120
                                    13    ********************************************************                       TS600130
                                    14    *                                                                              TS600140
                                    15    *                                                                              TS600150
                                    16    *                                                                              TS600160
                                    17    *          THIS MACRO CALCULATES THE DAY NAME OF A GIVEN                       TS600170
                                    18    *          GREGORIAN DATE                                                      TS600180
                                    19    *                                                                              TS600190
                                    20    *    1.    THE DOCUMENTATION FOR THIS MACRO IS IDENTICAL WITH THAT             TS600200
                                    21    *          DISPLAYED IN THE SUBROUTINE TIMESUB6.  THE IN-CODE                  TS600210
                                    22    *          COMMENTS HAVE BEEN REMOVED IN THE INTEREST OF SPACE                 TS600220
                                    23    *          CONSERVATION.                                                       TS600230
                                    24    *                                                                              TS600240
                                    25    *    2.    THIS MACRO IS WRITTEN TO BE CODED AS 'TIME6' IN THE                 TS600250
                                    26    *          USING PROGRAM AND REQUIRES NO OPERANDS UNLESS THE USING             TS600260
                                    27    *          PROGRAM MUST SUPPLY ITS OWN INDATE, CODE6 AND OUTDAY               TS600270
                                    28    *          FIELDS.  IN THAT EVENT, THE FIELDS' SPECIFICATIONS                  TS600280
                                    29    *          MUST BE AS IN TIMESUB6 AND THE MACRO STATEMENT MUST                 TS600290
                                    30    *          SPECIFY THE FIELDNAME(S) AS FOLLOWS:                                TS600300
                                    31    *                                                                              TS600310
                                    32    *          TIME6  INDATE=FIELDNAME.                                            TS600320
                                    33    *                 CODE6=FIELDNAME.                                  X          TS600330
                                    34    *                 OUTDAY=FIELDNAME                                  X          TS600340
                                    35    *                                                                              TS600350
                                    36    *                                                         JEROME T. MURRAY     TS600360
                                    37    *                                                         MARILYN J. MURRAY    TS600370
                                    38    *    GLEN ELLYN, ILLINOIS                                                      TS600380
                                    39    *                                                                              TS600390
                                    40    ********************************************************                       TS600400
                                    41    *                                                                              TS600410
                                    42    *                                                                              TS600420
                                    43    *              MACRO PROTOTYPE STATEMENT                                       TS600430
                                    44    *                                                                              TS600440
                                    45    *                                                                              TS600450
                                    46          TIME6 &INDATE=INDATE,&CODE6=CODE6,&OUTDAY=OUTDAY                          TS600460
                                    47          ZAP   &OUTDAY,=P'9'                                                      TS600470
                                    48          ZAP   &CODE6,=P'0'                                                       TS600480
                                    49          STM   1,5,#$6RSAVE                                                       TS600490
                                    50          MVC   #$6WORK8,&INDATE                                                   TS600500
                                    51          MVC   #$6SIGN,#$6WORK8+7                                                 TS600510
                                    52          MVC   #$6TABL+160(10),#$6ZRO                                             TS600520
                                    53          MVC   #$6TABL+192(10),#$6ZRO                                             TS600530
                                    54          MVC   #$6TABL+224(10),#$6ZRO                                             TS600540
                                    55          TRT   #$6SIGN(1),#$6TABL
```

```
LOC   OBJECT CODE   ADDR1 ADDR2   STMT   SOURCE STATEMENT                    DOS/VSE ASSEMBLER 16.46 99-12-31

                                   56             BC    8,#$6NUM                                    TS600550
                                   57             B     #$6BDATA                                    TS600560
                                   58   #$6NUM    MVI   #$6TABL.X'1C'                               TS600570
                                   59             MVC   #$6TABL+1(239).#$6TABL                      TS600580
                                   60             TRT   #$6WORK8(7).#$6TABL                         TS600590
                                   61             BC    8.#$6PACK                                   TS600600
                                   62   #$6BDATA  ZAP   &CODE6.=P'2'                                TS600610
                                   63             B     #$6TERM                                     TS600620
                                   64   #$6PACK   PACK  #$6MO.#$6WORK8(2)                           TS600630
                                   65             PACK  #$6DA.#$6WORK8+2(2)                         TS600640
                                   66             PACK  #$6YR.#$6WORK8+4(4)                         TS600650
                                   67             CP    #$6YR.=P'1600'                              TS600660
                                   68             BH    #$6YRHI                                     TS600670
                                   69   #$6BADYR  ZAP   &CODE6.=P'4'                                TS600680
                                   70             B     #$6TERM                                     TS600690
                                   71   #$6YRHI   CP    #$6YR.=P'3399'                              TS600700
                                   72             BH    #$6BADYR                                    TS600710
                                   73             ZAP   #$6L.=P'O'                                  TS600720
                                   74             ZAP   #$6WORK.#$6YR                               TS600730
                                   75             DP    #$6WORK.=P'4'                               TS600740
                                   76             CP    #$6WORK+4(1).=P'O'                          TS600750
                                   77             BH    #$6MOEDT                                    TS600760
                                   78             ZAP   #$6WORK.#$6YR                               TS600770
                                   79             DP    #$6WORK.=P'100'                             TS600780
                                   80             CP    #$6WORK+3(2).=P'O'                          TS600790
                                   81             BH    #$6LPYR                                     TS600800
                                   82             ZAP   #$6WORK.#$6YR                               TS600810
                                   83             DP    #$6WORK.=P'400'                             TS600820
                                   84             CP    #$6WORK+3(2).=P'O'                          TS600830
                                   85             BH    #$6MOEDT                                    TS600840
                                   86   #$6LPYR   ZAP   #$6L.=P'1'                                  TS600850
                                   87   #$6MOEDT  ZAP   #$6CVB.$6MO                                 TS600860
                                   88             CVB   3.#$6CVB                                    TS600870
                                   89             STC   3.#$6FLD                                    TS600880
                                   90             MVC   #$6TABL+1(12).#$6ZRO                        TS600890
                                   91             TRT   #$6FLD(1).#$6TABL                           TS600900
                                   92             BC    8.#$6DAEDT                                  TS600910
                                   93             MVC   #$6TABL+1(12).#$6TABL                       TS600920
                                   94             ZAP   &CODE6.=P'6'                                TS600930
                                   95             B     #$6TERM                                     TS600940
                                   96   #$6DAEDT  MVC   #$6TABL+1(12).#$6TABL                       TS600950
                                   97             LA    4.#$6DATAB                                  TS600960
                                   98             CP    #$6L.=P'O'                                  TS600970
                                   99             BE    #$6NOL                                      TS600980
                                  100             LA    4.2(4)                                      TS600990
                                  101   #$6NOL    BCTR  3.0                                         TS601000
                                  102             SLL   3.2                                         TS601010
                                  103             LA    4.O(3.4)                                    TS601020
                                  104             ZAP   #$6DA.#$6DA                                 TS601030
                                  105             CLC   #$6DA.O(4)                                  TS601040
                                  106             BNH   #$6DALO                                     TS601050
                                  107             ZAP   &CODE6.=P'8'                                TS601060
                                  108             B     #$6TERM                                     TS601070
                                  109   #$6DALO   CP    #$6DA.=P'OO'                                TS601080
                                  110             BE    #$6BADA                                     TS601090
```

**Figure A.8**  The macro edit post listing for TIME6, the TIMESUB6 macro equivalent.

```
                                                              DOS/VSE ASSEMBLER  16.46  99-12-31

LOC   OBJECT CODE   ADDR1 ADDR2   STMT   SOURCE STATEMENT

                                  111             LA    5,#$6DAYS                              TS601100
                                  112             CP    #$6L,=P'0'                             TS601110
                                  113             BE    #$6NOLL                                TS601120
                                  114             LA    5,2(5)                                 TS601130
                                  115    #$6NOLL  LA    5,0(3,5)                               TS601140
                                  116             ZAP   #$6JULIAN,0(2,5)                       TS601150
                                  117             AP    #$6JULIAN,#$6DA                        TS601160
                                  118             ZAP   #$6WORK6,#$6YR                         TS601170
                                  119             SP    #$6WORK6,=P'1601'                      TS601180
                                  120             MP    #$6WORK6,=P'36525'                     TS601190
                                  121             UNPK  #$6WORK9,#$6WORK6+1(5)                 TS601200
                                  122             PACK  #$6P1,#$6WORK9(7)                      TS601210
                                  123             ZAP   #$6WORK,#$6YR                          TS601220
                                  124             SP    #$6WORK,=P'1601'                       TS601230
                                  125             ZAP   #$6WORK,=P'400'                        TS601240
                                  126             DP    #$6P2,#$6WORK+1(2)                     TS601250
                                  127             MP    #$6P2,=P'3'                            TS601260
                                  128             ZAP   #$6WORK,#$6WORK+3(2)                   TS601270
                                  129             DP    #$6WORK,=P'100'                        TS601280
                                  130             ZAP   #$6Q1,#$6WORK+2(1)                     TS601290
                                  131             AP    #$6JULIAN,#$6P1                        TS601300
                                  132             SP    #$6JULIAN,#$6P2                        TS601310
                                  133             SP    #$6JULIAN,#$6Q1                        TS601320
                                  134             ZAP   #$6WORK,#$6JULIAN                      TS601330
                                  135             DP    #$6WORK,=P'7'                          TS601340
                                  136             ZAP   &OUTDAY,#$6WORK+4(1)                   TS601350
                                  137             B     #$6TERM                                TS601360
                                  138    #$6JULIAN DC   PL5'0'                                 TS601370
                                  139    #$6DATAB DC    PL2'31',PL2'31'          JAN           TS601380
                                  140             DC    PL2'28',PL2'29'          FEB           TS601390
                                  141             DC    PL2'31',PL2'31'          MAR           TS601400
                                  142             DC    PL2'30',PL2'30'          APR           TS601410
                                  143             DC    PL2'31',PL2'31'          MAY           TS601420
                                  144             DC    PL2'30',PL2'30'          JUN           TS601430
                                  145             DC    PL2'31',PL2'31'          JUL           TS601440
                                  146             DC    PL2'31',PL2'31'          AUG           TS601450
                                  147             DC    PL2'30',PL2'30'          SEP           TS601460
                                  148             DC    PL2'31',PL2'31'          OCT           TS601470
                                  149             DC    PL2'30',PL2'30'          NOV           TS601480
                                  150             DC    PL2'31',PL2'31'          DEC           TS601490
                                  151    #$6DAYS  DC    PL2'00',PL2'00'          JAN           TS601500
                                  152             DC    PL2'31',PL2'31'          FEB           TS601510
                                  153             DC    PL2'59',PL2'60'          MAR           TS601520
                                  154             DC    PL2'90',PL2'91'          APR           TS601530
                                  155             DC    PL2'120',PL2'121'        MAY           TS601540
                                  156             DC    PL2'151',PL2'152'        JUN           TS601550
                                  157             DC    PL2'181',PL2'182'        JUL           TS601560
                                  158             DC    PL2'212',PL2'213'        AUG           TS601570
                                  159             DC    PL2'243',PL2'244'        SEP           TS601580
                                  160             DC    PL2'273',PL2'274'        OCT           TS601590
                                  161             DC    PL2'304',PL2'305'        NOV           TS601600
                                  162             DC    PL2'334',PL2'335'        DEC           TS601610
                                  163    #$6TABL  DC    240X'1C'                               TS601620
                                  164             DC    10X'00'                                TS601630
                                  165             DC    6X'1C'                                 TS601640
```

```
LOC   OBJECT CODE    ADDR1 ADDR2  STMT  SOURCE STATEMENT                    DOS/VSE ASSEMBLER 16.46  99-12-31

                                  166  #$6ZRO     DC    12X'00'                                        TS601650
                                  167  CODE6       DC    PL1'4'                                        TS601660
                                  168  INDATE      DC    ZL8'00000000'                                 TS601670
                                  169  OUTDAY      DC    PL1'9'                                        TS601680
                                  170  #$6L        DS    PL1                                           TS601690
                                  171  #$6SIGN     DS    ZL1                                           TS601700
                                  172  #$6WORK6    DS    PL6                                           TS601710
                                  173  #$6WORK8    DS    ZL8                                           TS601720
                                  174  #$6WORK9    DS    ZL9                                           TS601730
                                  175  #$6MO       DS    PL2                                           TS601740
                                  176  #$6DA       DS    PL2                                           TS601750
                                  177  #$6YR       DS    PL3                                           TS601760
                                  178  #$6P1       DS    PL5                                           TS601770
                                  179  #$6P2       DS    PL2                                           TS601780
                                  180  #$6Q1       DS    PL1                                           TS601790
                                  181  #$6WORK     DS    PL5                                           TS601800
                                  182  #$6FLD      DS    CL1                                           TS601810
                                  183  #$6RSAVE    DS    5F                                            TS601820
                                  184  #$6CVB      DS    1D                                            TS601830
                                  185  #$6TERM     LM    1,5,#$6RSAVE                                  TS601840
                                  186              MEND
                                  187              END
```

DIAGNOSTICS AND STATISTICS                                                                         99-12-31

NO ERRORS FOUND

EDECK PUNCHED FOR MACRO 'TIME6', NUMBER OF CARDS IS 85

OPTIONS FOR THIS ASSEMBLY - ALIGN, LIST, NOXREF, NOLINK, RLD, NODECK, EDECK

THE ASSEMBLER WAS RUN IN 98184 BYTES
END OF ASSEMBLY

**Figure A.8** *Continued*

```
LOC   OBJECT CODE   ADDR1 ADDR2   STMT   SOURCE STATEMENT                          DOS/VSE ASSEMBLER 16.49  99-12-31

                                    1   *                                                               *    TS700010
                                    2   *                                                               *    TS700020
                                    3   *                                                               *    TS700030
                                    4         MACRO                                                          TS700040
                                    5   *                                                               *    TS700050
                                    6   *     TTTTTTT   III     MM    MM    EEEEE   77777               *    TS700060
                                    7   *        T       I     M M   M M    E           7               *    TS700070
                                    8   *        T       I     M  M  M      EEEE        7               *    TS700080
                                    9   *        T       I     M     M      E           7               *    TS700090
                                   10   *        T      III    M     M      EEEEE       7               *    TS700100
                                   11   *                                                               *    TS700110
                                   12   * N E O J U L I A N  T O  G R E G O R I A N  C O N V E R S I O N *    TS700120
                                   13   * ***********************************************************   *    TS700130
                                   14   * ***********************************************************   *    TS700140
                                   15   *                                                               *    TS700150
                                   16   *       THIS MACRO CONVERTS A NEOJULIAN DATE TO                 *    TS700160
                                   17   *                A GREGORIAN DATE                               *    TS700170
                                   18   *                                                               *    TS700180
                                   19   *                                                               *    TS700190
                                   20   *  1.  THE DOCUMENTATION FOR THIS MACRO IS IDENTICAL WITH THAT   *    TS700200
                                   21   *      DISPLAYED IN THE SUBROUTINE TIMESUB7.  THE IN-CODE        *    TS700210
                                   22   *      COMMENTS HAVE BEEN REMOVED IN THE INTEREST OF SPACE       *    TS700220
                                   23   *      CONSERVATION.                                            *    TS700230
                                   24   *                                                               *    TS700240
                                   25   *  2.  THIS MACRO IS WRITTEN TO BE CODED AS 'TIME7' IN THE       *    TS700250
                                   26   *      USING PROGRAM AND REQUIRES NO OPERANDS UNLESS THE USING   *    TS700260
                                   27   *      PROGRAM MUST SUPPLY ITS OWN NEOJIN, CODE7 AND EXJULI      *    TS700270
                                   28   *      FIELDS.  IN THAT EVENT, THE FIELDS' SPECIFICATIONS        *    TS700280
                                   29   *      MUST BE AS IN TIMESUB7 AND THE MACRO STATEMENT MUST       *    TS700290
                                   30   *      SPECIFY THE FIELDNAME(S) AS FOLLOWS:                      *    TS700300
                                   31   *                                                               *    TS700310
                                   32   *      TIME7 NEOJIN=FIELDNAME,                      X            *    TS700320
                                   33   *            CODE7=FIELDNAME,                       X            *    TS700330
                                   34   *            EXJULI=FIELDNAME                                    *    TS700340
                                   35   *                                                               *    TS700350
                                   36   *                                       JEROME T. MURRAY        *    TS700360
                                   37   *                                       MARILYN J. MURRAY       *    TS700370
                                   38   *  GLEN ELLYN, ILLINOIS                                         *    TS700380
                                   39   *                                                               *    TS700390
                                   40   * ***********************************************************   *    TS700400
                                   41   * ***********************************************************   *    TS700410
                                   42   * ***********************************************************   *    TS700420
                                   43   * ***********************************************************   *    TS700430
                                   44   *            MACRO PROTOTYPE STATEMENT                               TS700440
                                   45   *                                                                    TS700450
                                   46   TIME7 &NEOJIN=NEOJIN,&CODE7=CODE7,&EXJULI=EXJULI                     TS700460
                                   47   ZAP   &EXJULI,=P'O'                                                  TS700470
                                   48   ZAP   &CODE7,=P'O'                                                   TS700480
                                   49   ZAP   #$7MOCTR,=P'O'                                                 TS700490
                                   50   STM   1,3,#$7RSAVE                                                   TS700500
                                   51   MVC   #$7WORK7,&NEOJIN                                               TS700510
                                   52   MVC   #$7SIGN,#$7WORK7+6                                             TS700520
                                   53   MVC   #$7TABL+160(10),#$7ZRO                                         TS700530
                                   54   MVC   #$7TABL+192(10),#$7ZRO                                         TS700540
                                   55   MVC   #$7TABL+224(10),#$7ZRO
```

```
LOC   OBJECT CODE   ADDR1 ADDR2   STMT  SOURCE STATEMENT                      DOS/VSE ASSEMBLER 16.49  99-12-31

                                   56            TRT   #$7SIGN(1),#$7TABL            TS700550
                                   57            BC    8,#$7NUM                      TS700560
                                   58            B     #$7BDATA                      TS700570
                                   59  #$7NUM    MVI   #$7TABL,X'1C'                 TS700580
                                   60            MVC   #$7TABL+1(239),#$7TABL        TS700590
                                   61            TRT   #$7WORK7(6),#$7TABL           TS700600
                                   62            BC    8,#$7PACK                     TS700610
                                   63  #$7BDATA  ZAP   &CODE7,=P'2'                  TS700620
                                   64            B     #$7TERM                       TS700630
                                   65  #$7PACK   PACK  #$7YR,#$7WORK7(4)             TS700640
                                   66            PACK  #$7DA,#$7WORK7+4(3)           TS700650
                                   67            CP    #$7YR,=P'1600'                TS700660
                                   68            BH    #$7YRHI                       TS700670
                                   69  #$7BADYR  ZAP   &CODE7,=P'4'                  TS700680
                                   70            B     #$7TERM                       TS700690
                                   71  #$7YRHI   CP    #$7YR,=P'3399'                TS700700
                                   72            BH    #$7BADYR                      TS700710
                                   73            ZAP   #$7L,=P'0'                    TS700720
                                   74            ZAP   #$7WORK,#$7YR                 TS700730
                                   75            DP    #$7WORK,=P'4'                 TS700740
                                   76            CP    #$7WORK+4(1),=P'0'            TS700750
                                   77            BH    #$7DAEDT                      TS700760
                                   78            ZAP   #$7WORK,#$7YR                 TS700770
                                   79            DP    #$7WORK,=P'100'               TS700780
                                   80            CP    #$7WORK+3(2),=P'0'            TS700790
                                   81            BH    #$7LPYR                       TS700800
                                   82            ZAP   #$7WORK,#$7YR                 TS700810
                                   83            DP    #$7WORK,=P'400'               TS700820
                                   84            CP    #$7WORK+3(2),=P'0'            TS700830
                                   85            BH    #$7DAEDT                      TS700840
                                   86  #$7LPYR   ZAP   #$7L,=P'1'                    TS700850
                                   87  #$7DAEDT  CP    #$7DA,=P'000'                 TS700860
                                   88            BH    #$7HIVAL                      TS700870
                                   89  #$7BADA   ZAP   &CODE7,=P'6'                  TS700880
                                   90            B     #$7TERM                       TS700890
                                   91  #$7HIVAL  CP    #$7L,=P'0'                    TS700900
                                   92            BH    #$7DAHI                       TS700910
                                   93            CP    #$7DA,=P'365'                 TS700920
                                   94            BH    #$7BADA                       TS700930
                                   95  #$7DAHI   CP    #$7DA,=P'366'                 TS700940
                                   96            BH    #$7BADA                       TS700950
                                   97            LA    3,#$7DAYS+4                   TS700960
                                   98            CP    #$7L,=P'0'                    TS700970
                                   99            BE    #$7COUNT                      TS700980
                                  100            LA    3,2(3)                        TS700990
                                  101  #$7COUNT  AP    #$7MOCTR,=P'1'                TS701000
                                  102            CP    #$7DA,O(2,3)                  TS701010
                                  103            BNH   #$7GOTNU                      TS701020
                                  104            LA    3,4(3)                        TS701030
                                  105            B     #$7COUNT                      TS701040
                                  106  #$7GOTNU  ZAP   #$7MO,#$7MOCTR                TS701050
                                  107            SH    3,=H'4'                       TS701060
                                  108            SP    #$7DA,O(2,3)                  TS701070
                                  109  #$7BUILD  UNPK  #$7WORK8,#$7YR                TS701080
                                  110            UNPK  #$7WORK8+2(2),#$7DA           TS701090
```

**Figure A.9**  The macro edit post listing for TIME7, the TIMESUB7 macro equivalent.

```
LOC   OBJECT CODE   ADDR1 ADDR2   STMT   SOURCE STATEMENT                              DOS/VSE ASSEMBLER  16.49  99-12-31

                                  111             UNPK  #$7WORK8(2),#$7MO                                  TS701100
                                  112             PACK  &EXJULI,#$7WORK8                                   TS701110
                                  113             B     #$7TERM                                            TS701120
                                  114    EXJULI   DC    PL5'0'                                             TS701130
                                  115    NEOJIN   DC    ZL7'0000000'                                       TS701140
                                  116    CODE7    DC    PL1'2'                                             TS701150
                                  117    #$7DAYS  DC    PL2'00',PL2'00'        JAN                         TS701160
                                  118             DC    PL2'31',PL2'31'        FEB                         TS701170
                                  119             DC    PL2'59',PL2'60'        MAR                         TS701180
                                  120             DC    PL2'90',PL2'91'        APR                         TS701190
                                  121             DC    PL2'120',PL2'121'      MAY                         TS701200
                                  122             DC    PL2'151',PL2'152'      JUN                         TS701210
                                  123             DC    PL2'181',PL2'182'      JUL                         TS701220
                                  124             DC    PL2'212',PL2'213'      AUG                         TS701230
                                  125             DC    PL2'243',PL2'244'      SEP                         TS701240
                                  126             DC    PL2'273',PL2'274'      OCT                         TS701250
                                  127             DC    PL2'304',PL2'305'      NOV                         TS701260
                                  128             DC    PL2'334',PL2'335'      DEC                         TS701270
                                  129             DC    PL2'999',PL2'999'      END                         TS701280
                                  130    #$7TABL  DC    240X'1C'                                           TS701290
                                  131             DC    10X'00'                                            TS701300
                                  132             DC    6X'1C'                                             TS701310
                                  133    #$7ZRO   DC    12X'00'                                            TS701320
                                  134    #$7L     DS    PL1                                                TS701330
                                  135    #$7SIGN  DS    ZL1                                                TS701340
                                  136    #$7WORK8 DS    ZL8                                                TS701350
                                  137    #$7MO    DS    PL2                                                TS701360
                                  138    #$7DA    DS    PL2                                                TS701370
                                  139    #$7YR    DS    PL3                                                TS701380
                                  140    #$7MOCTR DS    PL2                                                TS701390
                                  141    #$7WORK7 DS    PL7                                                TS701400
                                  142    #$7WORK  DS    PL5                                                TS701410
                                  143    #$7RSAVE DS    3F                                                 TS701420
                                  144    #$7TERM  LM    1,3,#$7RSAVE                                       TS701430
                                  145             MEND
                                  146             END
```

99-12-31

DIAGNOSTICS AND STATISTICS

NO ERRORS FOUND

EDECK PUNCHED FOR MACRO 'TIME7', NUMBER OF CARDS IS 61

OPTIONS FOR THIS ASSEMBLY - ALIGN, LIST, NOXREF, NOLINK, RLD, NODECK, EDECK

THE ASSEMBLER WAS RUN IN 98184 BYTES
END OF ASSEMBLY

**Figure A.9** *Continued*

```
LOC  OBJECT CODE  ADDR1 ADDR2  STMT   SOURCE STATEMENT                    DOS/VSE ASSEMBLER 16.51   99-12-31

                                1        MACRO                                                           TS800010
                                2 .*                                                                     TS800020
                                3 .*                                                                     TS800030
                                4 .* **************************************************** *              TS800040
                                5 .*      TTTTTT III     MM    MM  EEEEE   888             *              TS800050
                                6 .*        T     I      M M  M M  E      8   8            *              TS800060
                                7 .*        T     I      M  MM  M  EEEE   888              *              TS800070
                                8 .*        T     I      M      M  E      8   8            *              TS800080
                                9 .*        T    III     M      M  EEEEE   888             *              TS800090
                               10 .*                                                       *              TS800100
                               11 .* **************************************************** *              TS800110
                               12 .* *********** E A S T E R   M A C R O **************** *              TS800120
                               13 .* **************************************************** *              TS800130
                               14 .* **************************************************** *              TS800140
                               15 .*                                                       *              TS800150
                               16 .*         THIS MACRO CALCULATES THE DATE OF EASTER      *              TS800160
                               17 .*                                                       *              TS800170
                               18 .*                                                       *              TS800180
                               19 .* 1.  THE DOCUMENTATION FOR THIS MACRO IS IDENTICAL WITH THAT *        TS800190
                               20 .*         DISPLAYED IN THE SUBROUTINE TIMESUB8.  THE IN-CODE *         TS800200
                               21 .*         COMMENTS HAVE BEEN REMOVED IN THE INTEREST OF SPACE *        TS800210
                               22 .*         CONSERVATION.                                 *              TS800220
                               23 .*                                                       *              TS800230
                               24 .* 2.  THIS MACRO IS WRITTEN TO BE CODED AS 'TIME8' IN THE *            TS800240
                               25 .*         USING PROGRAM AND REQUIRES NO OPERANDS UNLESS THE USING *    TS800250
                               26 .*         PROGRAM MUST SUPPLY ITS OWN EYEAR, CODE8, AND EASTER *       TS800260
                               27 .*         FIELDS.  IN THAT EVENT, THE FIELDS' SPECIFICATIONS *         TS800270
                               28 .*         MUST BE AS IN TIMESUB8 AND THE MACRO STATEMENT MUST *        TS800280
                               29 .*         SPECIFY THE FIELDNAME(S) AS FOLLOWS:          *              TS800290
                               30 .*                                                       *              TS800300
                               31 .*            TIME8 EYEAR=FIELDNAME,                    X *              TS800310
                               32 .*                  CODE8=FIELDNAME,                    X *              TS800320
                               33 .*                  EASTER=FIELDNAME                      *              TS800330
                               34 .*                                                       *              TS800340
                               35 .*                                                       *              TS800350
                               36 .*                               JEROME T. MURRAY        *              TS800360
                               37 .*                               MARILYN J. MURRAY       *              TS800370
                               38 .*  GLEN ELLYN, ILLINOIS                                 *              TS800380
                               39 .* **************************************************** *              TS800390
                               40 .* **************************************************** *              TS800400
                               41 .* **************************************************** *              TS800410
                               42 .*                                                       *              TS800420
                               43 .*            MACRO PROTOTYPE STATEMENT                   *              TS800430
                               44 .*                                                       *              TS800440
                               45        TIME8 &EYEAR=EYEAR,&CODE8=CODE8,&EASTER=EASTER                    TS800450
                               46        ZAP   &CODE8,=P'0'                                                TS800460
                               47        ZAP   &EASTER,=P'0'                                               TS800470
                               48        STM   1,2,#$BRSAVE                                                TS800480
                               49        MVC   #$BWORK4,&EYEAR                                             TS800490
                               50        MVC   #$BSIGN,#$BWORK4+3                                          TS800500
                               51        MVC   #$BTABL+160(10),#$BZRO                                      TS800510
                               52        MVC   #$BTABL+192(10),#$BZRO                                      TS800520
                               53        MVC   #$BTABL+224(10),#$BZRO                                      TS800530
                               54        TRT   #$BSIGN(1),#$BTABL                                          TS800540
                               55        BC    8,#$BNUM
```

```
LOC   OBJECT CODE   ADDR1  ADDR2   STMT   SOURCE STATEMENT                          DOS/VSE ASSEMBLER  16.51  99-12-31

                                    56            B      #$8BDATA                                          TS800550
                                    57   #$8NUM   MVI    #$8TABL,X'1C'                                     TS800560
                                    58            MVC    #$8TABL+1(239),#$8TABL                            TS800570
                                    59            TRT    #$8WORK4(3),#$8TABL                               TS800580
                                    60            BC     8,#$8PACK                                         TS800590
                                    61   #$8BDATA ZAP    &CODE8,=P'2'                                      TS800600
                                    62            B      #$8TERM                                           TS800610
                                    63   #$8PACK  PACK   #$8YR,&EYEAR                                      TS800620
                                    64            CP     #$8YR,=P'1600'                                    TS800630
                                    65            BH     #$8YRHI                                           TS800640
                                    66   #$8BADYR ZAP    &CODE8,=P'4'                                      TS800650
                                    67            B      #$8TERM                                           TS800660
                                    68   #$8YRHI  CP     #$8YR,=P'3399'                                    TS800670
                                    69            BH     #$8BADYR                                          TS800680
                                    70            PACK   #$8CENT,#$8WORK4(2)                               TS800690
                                    71            AP     #$8CENT,=P'1'                                     TS800700
                                    72            ZAP    #$8WORK,#$8YR                                     TS800710
                                    73            SP     #$8WORK,=P'1600'                                  TS800720
                                    74            DP     #$8WORK,=P'400'                                   TS800730
                                    75            ZAP    #$8T2,#$8WORK+1(2)                                TS800740
                                    76            MP     #$8T2,=P'3'                                       TS800750
                                    77            ZAP    #$8WORK,#$8WORK+3(2)                              TS800760
                                    78            DP     #$8WORK,=P'100'                                   TS800770
                                    79            ZAP    #$8T3,#$8WORK+2(1)                                TS800780
                                    80            ZAP    #$8NONL,#$8T2                                     TS800790
                                    81            AP     #$8NONL,#$8T3                                     TS800800
                                    82            ZAP    #$8WORK,#$8YR                                     TS800810
                                    83            DP     #$8WORK,=P'19'                                    TS800820
                                    84            AP     #$8WORK+3(2),=P'1'                                TS800830
                                    85            ZAP    #$8MET,#$8WORK+3(2)                               TS800840
                                    86            ZAP    #$8WORK,#$8CENT                                   TS800850
                                    87            MP     #$8WORK,=P'8'                                     TS800860
                                    88            AP     #$8WORK,=P'5'                                     TS800870
                                    89            DP     #$8WORK,=P'25'                                    TS800880
                                    90            SP     #$8WORK(3),=P'5'                                  TS800890
                                    91            SP     #$8WORK(3),#$8NONL                                TS800900
                                    92            ZAP    #$8METC,#$8WORK+1(2)                              TS800910
                                    93            ZAP    #$8WORK,#$8YR                                     TS800920
                                    94            MP     #$8WORK,=P'5'                                     TS800930
                                    95            DP     #$8WORK,=P'4'                                     TS800940
                                    96            SP     #$8WORK(4),#$8NONL                                TS800950
                                    97            SP     #$8WORK(4),=P'10'                                 TS800960
                                    98            ZAP    #$8DMOD,#$8WORK+1(3)                              TS800970
                                    99            ZAP    #$8WORK,#$8MET                                    TS800980
                                   100            MP     #$8WORK,=P'11'                                    TS800990
                                   101            AP     #$8WORK,=P'20'                                    TS801000
                                   102            AP     #$8WORK,#$8METC                                   TS801010
                                   103            DP     #$8WORK,=P'30'                                    TS801020
                                   104            ZAP    #$8EPACT,#$8WORK+3(2)                             TS801030
                                   105            CP     #$8EPACT,=P'25'                                   TS801040
                                   106            BNE    #$8EADJ                                           TS801050
                                   107            CP     #$8MET,=P'11'                                     TS801060
                                   108            BNH    #$8EADJ                                           TS801070
                                   109            AP     #$8EPACT,=P'1'                                    TS801080
                                   110   #$8EADJ  CP     #$8EPACT,=P'24'                                   TS801090
```

**Figure A.10**  The macro edit post listing for TIME8, the TIMESUB8 macro equivalent.

DOS/VSE ASSEMBLER  16.51  99-12-31

```
LOC   OBJECT CODE   ADDR1 ADDR2   STMT   SOURCE STATEMENT

                             111          BNE   #$8DAYV                              TS801100
                             112          AP    #$8EPACT,=P'1'                       TS801110
                             113 #$8DAYV  ZAP   #$8DAY,=P'44'                        TS801120
                             114          SP    #$8DAY,=P'$8EPACT                    TS801130
                             115          CP    #$8DAY,=P'21'                        TS801140
                             116          BNL   #$8CANDA                             TS801150
                             117          AP    #$8DAY,=P'30'                        TS801160
                             118 #$8CANDA ZAP   #$8WORK4,#$8DAY                      TS801170
                             119          AP    #$8WORK4,=P'7'                       TS801180
                             120          ZAP   #$8WORK,#$8DAY                       TS801190
                             121          AP    #$8WORK,#$8DMOD                      TS801200
                             122          DP    #$8WORK,=P'7'                        TS801210
                             123          SP    #$8WORK4,#$8WORK+4(1)                TS801220
                             124          ZAP   #$8DAY,#$8WORK+4+2(2)                TS801230
                             125          CP    #$8DAY,=P'31'                        TS801240
                             126          BNH   #$8ESTER                             TS801250
                             127          SP    #$8DAY,=P'31'                        TS801260
                             128 #$8ESTER UNPK  #$8WORK,#$8DAY                       TS801270
                             129          MVZ   #$8WORK+4(1),=C'1'                   TS801280
                             130          MVC   #$8ZDATE+4(4),&EYEAR                 TS801290
                             131          MVC   #$8ZDATE+2(2),#$8WORK+3              TS801300
                             132          MVC   #$8ZDATE(2),=C'04'                   TS801310
                             133          B     #$8PK                                TS801320
                             134 #$8ESTER UNPK  #$8WORK,#$8DAY                       TS801330
                             135          MVC   #$8ZDATE+4(4),&EYEAR                 TS801340
                             136          MVC   #$8ZDATE+2(2),#$8WORK+3              TS801350
                             137          MVC   #$8ZDATE(2),=C'03'                   TS801360
                             138 #$8PK    PACK  &EASTER,#$8ZDATE                     TS801370
                             139          B     #$8TERM                              TS801380
                             140 #$8SIGN  DS    CL1                                  TS801390
                             141 #$8WORK4 DS    ZL4                                  TS801400
                             142 #$8YR    DS    PL3                                  TS801410
                             143 #$8WORK  DS    PL5                                  TS801420
                             144 #$8TABL  DC    240X'1C'                             TS801430
                             145          DC    10X'00'                              TS801440
                             146          DC    6X'1C'                               TS801450
                             147 #$8ZRO   DC    10X'00'                              TS801460
                             148 EASTER   DC    PL5'0'                               TS801470
                             149 CODE8    DC    PL1'9'                               TS801480
                             150 EYEAR    DC    ZL4'0'                               TS801490
                             151 #$8T2    DS    PL1                                  TS801500
                             152 #$8T3    DS    PL2                                  TS801510
                             153 #$8CENT  DS    PL2                                  TS801520
                             154 #$8NONL  DS    PL2                                  TS801530
                             155 #$8MET   DS    PL2                                  TS801540
                             156 #$8METC  DS    PL3                                  TS801550
                             157 #$8MOD   DS    PL2                                  TS801560
                             158 #$8EPACT DS    PL2                                  TS801570
                             159 #$8DAY   DS    PL2                                  TS801580
                             160 #$8ZDATE DS    ZL8                                  TS801590
                             161 #$8RSAVE DS    2F                                   TS801600
                             162 #$8TERM  LM    1,2,#$8RSAVE                         TS801610
                             163          MEND
                             164          END
```

99-12-31

DIAGNOSTICS AND STATISTICS

NO ERRORS FOUND

EDECK PUNCHED FOR MACRO 'TIME8', NUMBER OF CARDS IS 72

OPTIONS FOR THIS ASSEMBLY - ALIGN, LIST, NOXREF, NOLINK, RLD, NODECK, EDECK

THE ASSEMBLER WAS RUN IN 98184 BYTES
END OF ASSEMBLY

**Figure A.10** *Continued*

```
LOC   OBJECT CODE   ADDR1 ADDR2   STMT   SOURCE STATEMENT                                          DOS/VSE ASSEMBLER 08.15  99-12-31

                                    1            MACRO                                                                          * TS900010
                                    2     *                                                                                     * TS900020
                                    3     *                                                                                     * TS900030
                                    4     *                                                                                     * TS900040
                                    5     *       TTTTTT  III    MM      MM    EEEEE    999  9                                   * TS900050
                                    6     *         T      I     M M    M M    E          9  9                                   * TS900060
                                    7     *         T      I     M  M  M  M    EEEE    9999                                      * TS900070
                                    8     *         T      I     M   M   M     E          9                                      * TS900080
                                    9     *         T     III    M       M     EEEEE     99                                      * TS900090
                                   10     *                                                                                     * TS900100
                                   11     *************************************************************                         * TS900110
                                   12     *** G R E G O R I A N   H O L I D A Y   S U B R O U T I N E *****                      * TS900120
                                   13     *************************************************************                         * TS900130
                                   14     *************************************************************                         * TS900140
                                   15     *************************************************************                         * TS900150
                                   16     *************************************************************                         * TS900160
                                   17     *    THIS MACRO DETERMINES THE HOLIDAY STATUS OF AN INPUT                             * TS900170
                                   18     *    GREGORIAN DATE                                                                   * TS900180
                                   19     *                                                                                     * TS900190
                                   20     *    1.  THE DOCUMENTATION FOR THIS MACRO IS IDENTICAL WITH THAT                      * TS900200
                                   21     *        DISPLAYED IN THE SUBROUTINE TIMESUB9.  THE IN-CODE                           * TS900210
                                   22     *        COMMENTS HAVE BEEN REMOVED IN THE INTEREST OF SPACE                          * TS900220
                                   23     *        CONSERVATION.                                                               * TS900230
                                   24     *                                                                                     * TS900240
                                   25     *    2.  THIS MACRO IS WRITTEN TO BE CODED AS 'TIME9' IN THE                          * TS900250
                                   26     *        USING PROGRAM AND REQUIRES NO OPERANDS UNLESS THE USING                      * TS900260
                                   27     *        PROGRAM MUST SUPPLY ITS OWN DATEH, CODE9, WEEKDA AND                         * TS900270
                                   28     *        HOLIDA FIELDS.  IN THAT EVENT THE FIELDS' SPECIFICATIONS                     * TS900280
                                   29     *        MUST BE AS IN TIMESUB9 AND THE MACRO STATEMENT MUST                          * TS900290
                                   30     *        SPECIFY THE FIELDNAME(S) AS FOLLOWS:                                         * TS900300
                                   31     *                                                                                     * TS900310
                                   32     *        TIME9 DATEH=FIELDNAME.                                                       * TS900320
                                   33     *              CODE9=FIELDNAME.                                      X                 * TS900330
                                   34     *              HOLIDA=FIELDNAME.                                     X                 * TS900340
                                   35     *              WEEKDA=FIELDNAME                                      X                 * TS900350
                                   36     *                                                                                     * TS900360
                                   37     *                                                   JEROME T. MURRAY                  * TS900370
                                   38     *                                                   MARILYN J. MURRAY                 * TS900380
                                   39     *    GLEN ELLYN, ILLINOIS                                                             * TS900390
                                   40     *                                                                                     * TS900400
                                   41     *************************************************************                         * TS900410
                                   42     *************************************************************                         * TS900420
                                   43     *************************************************************                         * TS900430
                                   44     *                                                                                     * TS900440
                                   45     *                 MACRO PROTOTYPE STATEMENT                                           * TS900450
                                   46     *                                                                                     * TS900460
                                   47     TIME9 &DATEH=DATEH,&CODE9=CODE9,&HOLIDA=HOLIDA,&WEEKDA=WEEKDA                          * TS900470
                                   48           ZAP   &HOLIDA,=P'99'                                                            * TS900480
                                   49           ZAP   &WEEKDA,=P'9'                                                             * TS900490
                                   50           ZAP   &CODE9,=P'0'                                                              * TS900500
                                   51           ZAP   #$901,=P'0'                                                              * TS900510
                                   52           ZAP   #$902,=P'0'                                                              * TS900520
                                   53           ZAP   #$904,=P'0'                                                              * TS900530
                                   54           ZAP   #$906,=P'0'                                                              * TS900540
                                   55           ZAP   #$914,=P'0'
```

```
LOC   OBJECT CODE   ADDR1 ADDR2   STMT   SOURCE STATEMENT                    DOS/VSE ASSEMBLER 08.15  99-12-31

                                    56   ZAP    #$916,=P'0'                                        TS900550
                                    57   ZAP    #$918,=P'0'                                        TS900560
                                    58   ZAP    #$924,=P'0'                                        TS900570
                                    59   ZAP    #$927,=P'0'                                        TS900580
                                    60   ZAP    #$929,=P'0'                                        TS900590
                                    61   MVC    #$9DATEH,&DATEH                                    TS900600
                                    62   STM    1,7,#$9RSAVE                                       TS900610
                                    63   MVC    INDATE,#$9DATEH                                    TS900620
                                    64   LA     6,T6X                                              TS900630
                                    65   BALR   7,6                                                TS900640
                                    66   ZAP    &CODE9,CODE6                                       TS900650
                                    67   CP     &CODE9,=P'0'                                       TS900660
                                    68   BH     #$9TERM                                            TS900670
                                    69   ZAP    &WEEKDA,OUTDAY                                     TS900680
                                    70   MVC    DATEA,#$9DATEH                                     TS900690
                                    71   LA     6,T2X                                              TS900700
                                    72   BALR   7,6                                                TS900710
                                    73   ZAP    #$9DRD,NEOJUL+2(2)                                 TS900720
                                    74   ZAP    #$9END,#$9DRD                                      TS900730
                                    75   MVC    YEAR(4),#$9DATEH+4                                 TS900740
                                    76   LA     6,T1X                                              TS900750
                                    77   BALR   7,6                                                TS900760
                                    78   MVC    INDATE(4),=C'0101'                                 TS900770
                                    79   LA     6,T6X                                              TS900780
                                    80   BALR   7,6                                                TS900790
                                    81   CP     OUTDAY,=P'0'                                       TS900800
                                    82   BNE    #$9NEWY                                            TS900810
                                    83   ZAP    #$901,=P'2'                                        TS900820
                                    84   #$9NEWY PACK #$9YR,YEAR                                   TS900830
                                    85   AP     #$9YR,=P'1'                                        TS900840
                                    86   UNPK   INDATE+4(4),#$9YR                                  TS900850
                                    87   LA     6,T6X                                              TS900860
                                    88   BALR   7,6                                                TS900870
                                    89   MVC    INDATE+4(4),YEAR                                   TS900880
                                    90   CP     OUTDAY,=P'6'                                       TS900890
                                    91   BNE    #$9MLK                                             TS900900
                                    92   ZAP    #$902,=P'365'                                      TS900910
                                    93   AP     #$902,L                                            TS900920
                                    94   #$9MLK  MVC INDATE(4),=C'0115'                            TS900930
                                    95   LA     6,T6X                                              TS900940
                                    96   BALR   7,6                                                TS900950
                                    97   CP     OUTDAY,=P'6'                                       TS900960
                                    98   BNE    #$9MLK2                                            TS900970
                                    99   ZAP    #$904,=P'14'                                       TS900980
                                   100   #$9MLK2 CP OUTDAY,=P'0'                                   TS900990
                                   101   BNE    #$9LINC                                            TS901000
                                   102   ZAP    #$904,=P'16'                                       TS901010
                                   103   #$9LINC MVC INDATE(4),=C'0212'                            TS901020
                                   104   LA     6,T6X                                              TS901030
                                   105   BALR   7,6                                                TS901040
                                   106   CP     OUTDAY,=P'6'                                       TS901050
                                   107   BNE    #$9LIN2                                            TS901060
                                   108   ZAP    #$906,=P'42'                                       TS901070
                                   109   #$9LIN2 CP OUTDAY,=P'0'                                   TS901080
                                   110   BNE    #$9WASH                                            TS901090
```

**Figure A.11**  The macro edit post listing for TIME9, the TIMESUB9 macro equivalent.

DOS/VSE ASSEMBLER 08.15 99-12-31

```
LOC   OBJECT CODE   ADDR1 ADDR2   STMT   SOURCE STATEMENT

                                  111             ZAP   #$906,=P'44'              TS901100
                                  112   #$9WASH   MVC   INDATE(4),=C'0201'        TS901110
                                  113             LA    6,T6X                     TS901120
                                  114             BALR  7,6                       TS901130
                                  115             CP    OUTDAY,=P'1'              TS901140
                                  116             BL    #$9WASH2                  TS901150
                                  117             BH    #$9WASH3                  TS901160
                                  118             ZAP   #$907,=P'46'              TS901170
                                  119             B     #$9EAST                   TS901180
                                  120   #$9WASH2  ZAP   #$907,=P'47'              TS901190
                                  121             B     #$9EAST                   TS901200
                                  122   #$9WASH3  ZAP   #$907,=P'54'              TS901210
                                  123             SP    #$907,OUTDAY             TS901220
                                  124   #$9EAST   MVC   EYEAR(4),#$9DATEH+4       TS901230
                                  125             LA    6,T8X                     TS901240
                                  126             BALR  7,6                       TS901250
                                  127             UNPK  DATEA,EASTER              TS901260
                                  128             LA    6,T2X                     TS901270
                                  129             BALR  7,6                       TS901280
                                  130             ZAP   #$908,NEQJUL+2(2)         TS901290
                                  131             SP    #$908,=P'2'               TS901300
                                  132             ZAP   #$909,NEQJUL+2(2)         TS901310
                                  133             ZAP   #$910,#$909               TS901320
                                  134             AP    #$910,=P'1'               TS901330
                                  135             MVC   INDATE(4),=C'0525'        TS901340
                                  136             LA    6,T6X                     TS901350
                                  137             BALR  7,6                       TS901360
                                  138             CP    OUTDAY,=P'1'              TS901370
                                  139             BL    #$9VLO                    TS901380
                                  140             BH    #$9VHI                    TS901390
                                  141             ZAP   #$911,=P'138'             TS901400
                                  142             AP    #$911,L                   TS901410
                                  143             B     #$9MEM                    TS901420
                                  144   #$9VLO    ZAP   #$911,=P'139'             TS901430
                                  145             AP    #$911,L                   TS901440
                                  146             B     #$9MEM                    TS901450
                                  147   #$9VHI    ZAP   #$911,=P'145'             TS901460
                                  148             SP    OUTDAY,=P'1'              TS901470
                                  149             SP    #$911,OUTDAY             TS901480
                                  150             AP    #$911,L                   TS901490
                                  151   #$9MEM    MVC   INDATE(4),=C'0531'        TS901500
                                  152             LA    6,T6X                     TS901510
                                  153             BALR  7,6                       TS901520
                                  154             CP    OUTDAY,=P'1'              TS901530
                                  155             BL    #$9MLO                    TS901540
                                  156             BH    #$9MHI                    TS901550
                                  157             ZAP   #$912,=P'151'             TS901560
                                  158             AP    #$912,L                   TS901570
                                  159             B     #$9STJ                    TS901580
                                  160   #$9MLO    ZAP   #$912,=P'145'             TS901590
                                  161             AP    #$912,L                   TS901600
                                  162             B     #$9STJ                    TS901610
                                  163   #$9MHI    ZAP   #$912,=P'151'             TS901620
                                  164             SP    OUTDAY,=P'1'              TS901630
                                  165             SP    #$912,OUTDAY             TS901640
```

```
LOC   OBJECT CODE   ADDR1  ADDR2   STMT   SOURCE STATEMENT                        DOS/VSE ASSEMBLER 08.15  99-12-31

                                   166            AP    #$912,L                                          TS901650
                                   167   #$9STJ   AP    #$913,L                                          TS901660
                                   168            MVC   INDATE(4),=C'0624'                               TS901670
                                   169            LA    6,T6X                                            TS901680
                                   170            BALR  7,6                                              TS901690
                                   171            CP    OUTDAY,=P'6'                                     TS901700
                                   172            BNE   #$9STJ2                                          TS901710
                                   173            ZAP   #$914,#$913                                      TS901720
                                   174            SP    #$914,=P'1'                                      TS901730
                                   175   #$9STJ2  CP    OUTDAY,=P'O'                                     TS901740
                                   176            BNE   #$9CAND                                          TS901750
                                   177            ZAP   #$914,#$913                                      TS901760
                                   178            AP    #$914,=P'1'                                      TS901770
                                   179   #$9CAND  AP    #$915,L                                          TS901780
                                   180            MVC   INDATE(4),=C'0701'                               TS901790
                                   181            LA    6,T6X                                            TS901800
                                   182            BALR  7,6                                              TS901810
                                   183            CP    OUTDAY,=P'6'                                     TS901820
                                   184            BNE   #$9CAN2                                          TS901830
                                   185            ZAP   #$916,#$915                                      TS901840
                                   186            SP    #$916,=P'1'                                      TS901850
                                   187   #$9CAN2  CP    OUTDAY,=P'O'                                     TS901860
                                   188            BNE   #$9INDD                                          TS901870
                                   189            ZAP   #$916,#$915                                      TS901880
                                   190            AP    #$916,=P'1'                                      TS901890
                                   191   #$9INDD  AP    #$917,L                                          TS901900
                                   192            MVC   INDATE(4),=C'0704'                               TS901910
                                   193            LA    6,T6X                                            TS901920
                                   194            BALR  7,6                                              TS901930
                                   195            CP    OUTDAY,=P'6'                                     TS901940
                                   196            BNE   #$9IND2                                          TS901950
                                   197            ZAP   #$918,#$917                                      TS901960
                                   198            SP    #$918,=P'1'                                      TS901970
                                   199   #$9IND2  CP    OUTDAY,=P'O'                                     TS901980
                                   200            BNE   #$9CIV                                           TS901990
                                   201            ZAP   #$918,#$917                                      TS902000
                                   202            AP    #$918,=P'1'                                      TS902010
                                   203   #$9CIV   MVC   INDATE(4),=C'0801'                               TS902020
                                   204            LA    6,T6X                                            TS902030
                                   205            BALR  7,6                                              TS902040
                                   206            CP    OUTDAY,=P'1'                                     TS902050
                                   207            BL    #$9CLO                                           TS902060
                                   208            BH    #$9CHI                                           TS902070
                                   209            ZAP   #$919,=P'213'                                    TS902080
                                   210            AP    #$919,L                                          TS902090
                                   211            B     #$9LDA                                           TS902100
                                   212   #$9CLO   ZAP   #$919,=P'214'                                    TS902110
                                   213            AP    #$919,L                                          TS902120
                                   214            B     #$9LDA                                           TS902130
                                   215   #$9CHI   ZAP   #$919,=P'221'                                    TS902140
                                   216            SP    #$919,OUTDAY                                     TS902150
                                   217            AP    #$919,OUTDAY                                     TS902160
                                   218   #$9LDA   MVC   INDATE(4),=C'0901'                               TS902170
                                   219            LA    6,T6X                                            TS902180
                                   220            BALR  7,6                                              TS902190
```

**Figure A.11** *Continued*

```
LOC   OBJECT CODE   ADDR1 ADDR2   STMT   SOURCE STATEMENT                                      DOS/VSE ASSEMBLER 08.15  99-12-31

                                   221           CP    OUTDAY,=P'1'                                                     TS902200
                                   222           BL    #$9LLO                                                           TS902210
                                   223           BH    #$9LHI                                                           TS902220
                                   224           ZAP   #$920,=P'244'                                                    TS902230
                                   225           AP    #$920,L                                                          TS902240
                                   226           B     #$9CTC                                                           TS902250
                                   227   #$9LLO  ZAP   #$920,=P'245'                                                    TS902260
                                   228           AP    #$920,L                                                          TS902270
                                   229           B     #$9CTC                                                           TS902280
                                   230   #$9LHI  ZAP   #$920,=P'252'                                                    TS902290
                                   231           SP    #$920,OUTDAY                                                     TS902300
                                   232           AP    #$920,L                                                          TS902310
                                   233   #$9CTC  MVC   INDATE(4),=C'1001'                                               TS902320
                                   234           LA    6,T6X                                                            TS902330
                                   235           BALR  7,6                                                              TS902340
                                   236           CP    OUTDAY,=P'1'                                                     TS902350
                                   237           BL    #$9TCLO                                                          TS902360
                                   238           BH    #$9TCHI                                                          TS902370
                                   239           ZAP   #$921,=P'281'                                                    TS902380
                                   240           AP    #$921,L                                                          TS902390
                                   241           B     #$9ELD                                                           TS902400
                                   242   #$9TCLO ZAP   #$921,=P'282'                                                    TS902410
                                   243           AP    #$921,L                                                          TS902420
                                   244           B     #$9ELD                                                           TS902430
                                   245   #$9TCHI ZAP   #$921,=P'289'                                                    TS902440
                                   246           SP    #$921,OUTDAY                                                     TS902450
                                   247           AP    #$921,L                                                          TS902460
                                   248   #$9ELD  MVC   INDATE(4),=C'1101'                                               TS902470
                                   249           LA    6,T6X                                                            TS902480
                                   250           BALR  7,6                                                              TS902490
                                   251           CP    OUTDAY,=P'1'                                                     TS902500
                                   252           BL    #$9ELO                                                           TS902510
                                   253           BH    #$9EHI                                                           TS902520
                                   254           ZAP   #$922,=P'306'                                                    TS902530
                                   255           AP    #$922,L                                                          TS902540
                                   256           B     #$9ARM                                                           TS902550
                                   257   #$9ELO  ZAP   #$922,=P'307'                                                    TS902560
                                   258           AP    #$922,L                                                          TS902570
                                   259           B     #$9ARM                                                           TS902580
                                   260   #$9EHI  ZAP   #$922,=P'314'                                                    TS902590
                                   261           SP    #$922,OUTDAY                                                     TS902600
                                   262           AP    #$922,L                                                          TS902610
                                   263   #$9ARM  AP    #$923,L                                                          TS902620
                                   264           MVC   INDATE(4),=C'1111'                                               TS902630
                                   265           LA    6,T6X                                                            TS902640
                                   266           BALR  7,6                                                              TS902650
                                   267           CP    OUTDAY,=P'6'                                                     TS902660
                                   268           BNE   #$9ARM2                                                          TS902670
                                   269           ZAP   #$924,#$923                                                      TS902680
                                   270           SP    #$924,=P'1'                                                      TS902690
                                   271   #$9ARM2 CP    OUTDAY,=P'0'                                                     TS902700
                                   272           BNE   #$9TKS                                                           TS902710
                                   273           ZAP   #$924,#$923                                                      TS902720
                                   274           AP    #$924,=P'1'                                                      TS902730
                                   275   #$9TKS  MVC   INDATE(4),=C'1101'                                               TS902740
```

```
                                           DOS/VSE ASSEMBLER 08.15 99-12-31

LOC   OBJECT CODE   ADDR1 ADDR2   STMT   SOURCE STATEMENT

                                  276             LA    6,T6X                    TS902750
                                  277             BALR  7,6                      TS902760
                                  278             CP    OUTDAY,=P'4'             TS902770
                                  279             BL    #$9TLO                   TS902780
                                  280             BH    #$9THI                   TS902790
                                  281             ZAP   #$925,=P'326'            TS902800
                                  282             AP    #$925,L                  TS902810
                                  283             B     #$9XMS                   TS902820
                                  284   #$9TLO    ZAP   #$925,=P'330'            TS902830
                                  285             SP    #$925,OUTDAY             TS902840
                                  286             AP    #$925,L                  TS902850
                                  287             B     #$9XMS                   TS902860
                                  288   #$9THI    ZAP   #$925,=P'337'            TS902870
                                  289             SP    #$925,OUTDAY             TS902880
                                  290             AP    #$925,L                  TS902890
                                  291   #$9XMS    AP    #$926,L                  TS902900
                                  292             AP    #$928,L                  TS902910
                                  293             MVC   INDATE(4),=C'1225'       TS902920
                                  294             LA    6,T6X                    TS902930
                                  295             BALR  7,6                      TS902940
                                  296             CP    OUTDAY,=P'5'             TS902950
                                  297             BNE   #$9XMS1                  TS902960
                                  298             ZAP   #$929,#$926              TS902970
                                  299             AP    #$929,=P'3'              TS902980
                                  300   #$9XMS1   CP    OUTDAY,=P'6'             TS902990
                                  301             BNE   #$9XMS2                  TS903000
                                  302             ZAP   #$927,#$926              TS903010
                                  303             SP    #$927,=P'1'              TS903020
                                  304             ZAP   #$929,#$926              TS903030
                                  305             AP    #$929,=P'2'              TS903040
                                  306   #$9XMS2   CP    OUTDAY,=P'0'             TS903050
                                  307             BNE   #$9LOAD                  TS903060
                                  308             ZAP   #$927,#$926              TS903070
                                  309             AP    #$927,=P'1'              TS903080
                                  310             ZAP   #$929,#$926              TS903090
                                  311             AP    #$929,=P'2'              TS903100
                                  312   #$9LOAD   LA    5,#$9DATES+2             TS903110
                                  313   #$9LOOP   CP    #$9RD.0(2.5)             TS903120
                                  314             BE    #$9HOLYD                 TS903130
                                  315             LA    5.4(5)                   TS903140
                                  316             B     #$9LOOP                  TS903150
                                  317   #$9HOLYD  SH    5.=H'2'                  TS903160
                                  318             ZAP   8HOLIDA.O(2.5)           TS903170
                                  319             SP    #$913.L                  TS903180
                                  320             SP    #$915.L                  TS903190
                                  321             SP    #$917.L                  TS903200
                                  322             SP    #$923.L                  TS903210
                                  323             SP    #$926.L                  TS903220
                                  324             SP    #$928.L                  TS903230
                                  325             B     #$9TERM                  TS903240
                                  326   T1X       EQU   *                        TS903250
                                  327             TIME1                          TS903260
                                  328             BR    7                        TS903270
                                  329   T2X       EQU   *                        TS903280
                                  330             TIME2                          TS903290
```

**Figure A.11** *Continued*

```
LOC   OBJECT CODE   ADDR1 ADDR2   STMT   SOURCE STATEMENT                      DOS/VSE ASSEMBLER 08.15  99-12-31

                                   331            BR     7                                          TS903300
                                   332    T6X     EQU    *                                          TS903310
                                   333            TIME6  7                                          TS903320
                                   334            BR     7                                          TS903330
                                   335    T8X     EQU    *                                          TS903340
                                   336            TIME8  7                                          TS903350
                                   337            BR     7                                          TS903360
                                   338    WEEKDA  DC     PL1'9'                                      TS903370
                                   339    HOLIDA  DC     PL2'99'                                     TS903380
                                   340    CODE9   DC     PL1'4'                                      TS903390
                                   341    DATEH   DC     ZL8'00000000'                              TS903400
                                   342    #$9ORD  DS     PL2                                         TS903410
                                   343    #$9YR   DS     PL3                                         TS903420
                                   344    #$9DATEH DS    CL8                                         TS903430
                                   345    #$9DATES DS    OCL116                                      TS903440
                                   346            DC     PL2'00'                                     TS903450
                                   347    #$900   DC     PL2'001'                                    TS903460
                                   348            DC     PL2'01'                                     TS903470
                                   349    #$901   DC     PL2'000'                                    TS903480
                                   350            DC     PL2'03'                                     TS903490
                                   351    #$903   DC     PL2'015'                                    TS903500
                                   352            DC     PL2'04'                                     TS903510
                                   353    #$904   DC     PL2'000'                                    TS903520
                                   354            DC     PL2'05'                                     TS903530
                                   355    #$905   DC     PL2'043'                                    TS903540
                                   356            DC     PL2'06'                                     TS903550
                                   357    #$906   DC     PL2'000'                                    TS903560
                                   358            DC     PL2'07'                                     TS903570
                                   359    #$907   DC     PL2'000'                                    TS903580
                                   360            DC     PL2'08'                                     TS903590
                                   361    #$908   DC     PL2'000'                                    TS903600
                                   362            DC     PL2'09'                                     TS903610
                                   363    #$909   DC     PL2'000'                                    TS903620
                                   364            DC     PL2'10'                                     TS903630
                                   365    #$910   DC     PL2'000'                                    TS903640
                                   366            DC     PL2'11'                                     TS903650
                                   367    #$911   DC     PL2'000'                                    TS903660
                                   368            DC     PL2'12'                                     TS903670
                                   369    #$912   DC     PL2'000'                                    TS903680
                                   370            DC     PL2'13'                                     TS903690
                                   371    #$913   DC     PL2'175'                                    TS903700
                                   372            DC     PL2'14'                                     TS903710
                                   373    #$914   DC     PL2'000'                                    TS903720
                                   374            DC     PL2'15'                                     TS903730
                                   375    #$915   DC     PL2'182'                                    TS903740
                                   376            DC     PL2'16'                                     TS903750
                                   377    #$916   DC     PL2'000'                                    TS903760
                                   378            DC     PL2'17'                                     TS903770
                                   379    #$917   DC     PL2'185'                                    TS903780
                                   380            DC     PL2'18'                                     TS903790
                                   381    #$918   DC     PL2'000'                                    TS903800
                                   382            DC     PL2'19'                                     TS903810
                                   383    #$919   DC     PL2'000'                                    TS903820
                                   384            DC     PL2'20'                                     TS903830
                                   385    #$920   DC     PL2'000'                                    TS903840
```

```
                                                                 DOS/VSE ASSEMBLER 08.15 99-12-31

LOC    OBJECT CODE    ADDR1  ADDR2    STMT   SOURCE STATEMENT

                                      386            DC    PL2'21'                                    TS903850
                                      387   #$921    DC    PL2'000'                                   TS903860
                                      388   #$922    DC    PL2'22'                                    TS903870
                                      389   #$922    DC    PL2'000'                                   TS903880
                                      390            DC    PL2'23'                                    TS903890
                                      391   #$923    DC    PL2'315'                                   TS903900
                                      392            DC    PL2'24'                                    TS903910
                                      393   #$924    DC    PL2'000'                                   TS903920
                                      394            DC    PL2'25'                                    TS903930
                                      395   #$925    DC    PL2'000'                                   TS903940
                                      396            DC    PL2'26'                                    TS903950
                                      397   #$926    DC    PL2'359'                                   TS903960
                                      398            DC    PL2'27'                                    TS903970
                                      399   #$927    DC    PL2'000'                                   TS903980
                                      400            DC    PL2'28'                                    TS903990
                                      401   #$928    DC    PL2'360'                                   TS904000
                                      402            DC    PL2'29'                                    TS904010
                                      403   #$929    DC    PL2'000'                                   TS904020
                                      404            DC    PL2'02'                                    TS904030
                                      405   #$902    DC    PL2'000'                                   TS904040
                                      406            DC    PL2'99'                                    TS904050
                                      407   #$9END   DC    PL2'000'                                   TS904060
                                      408   #$9RSAVE DS    7F                                         TS904070
                                      409   #$9TERM  LM    1,7,#$9RSAVE                               TS904080
                                      410            MEND
                                      411            END
```

```
                         DIAGNOSTICS AND STATISTICS


NO ERRORS FOUND

EDECK PUNCHED FOR MACRO 'TIME9', NUMBER OF CARDS IS 192

OPTIONS FOR THIS ASSEMBLY - ALIGN, LIST, NOXREF, NOLINK, RLD, NODECK, EDECK

THE ASSEMBLER WAS RUN IN 98184 BYTES
END OF ASSEMBLY                                                         99-12-31
```

**Figure A.11** *Continued*

# B

# IBM Linkage Conventions

Read the appropriate IBM language manuals to become familiar with the linkage conventions specific to the prevailing operating system and compiler version in your installation.

Two complete linkage examples are presented in this section. The first, shown in Figure B.1, displays the post listing of the assembly for the relocatable module TC1000. The module features the linkage required for an assembly-language subprogram called by COBOL in the VSE environment. The macro TIME1 is featured in the module and, along with PRINT NOGEN, eliminates the reprinting of TIMESUB1 documentation and code. TC1000 was cataloged to a relocatable library.

Figure B.2 shows the complete post listing of CLINK1, the calling COBOL program's compilation. Figure B.3 presents the test results from an execution of CLINK1, the calling COBOL program. The input data set was the same one used to test TIMESUB1. Figure B.4 displays the job stream to produce the assembly, catalog, compilation, linkage, and execution. Note that the relocatable module was "punched" to disk. SYSIPT was then assigned to the disk extent to facilitate cataloging the module to the relocatable library. The second example, Figure B.5, presents the linkage employed when an ALC subprogram is called by RPG II.

RPG is probably the most widely used language in data processing when you consider the vast array of computers executing this language: System/34, System/36, System/3, System/38, the 4300 series, and AS/400. The example presented here applies only in the VSE environment that supports ALC.

Because entirely different coding methods and algorithms lend themselves to non-ALC-supported RPG, refer to the disk accompanying this book. It contains a complete set of RPG subroutines in ready-to-use RPG II source language format.

Figure B.5 shows the post listing of relocatable module TR1000 containing the ALC-RPG linkage, Figure B.6 displays the post listing of RLINK1, the calling RPG program, and Figure B.7 presents the test results obtained from RLINK1's execution.

Finally, Figure B.8 displays the job stream used in assembly, cataloging, compilation, linkage, and execution.

The IBM RPG manuals for VSE distinguish between external subroutines and subprograms: The external subroutine is called by RPG's execution of the EXIT instruction. The RLABL and ULABL codes are associated with external subroutines. The subprogram is called with the CALL instruction. We've ignored this distinction and have referred to the ALC as a subprogram in the documentation of the source code because the distinction doesn't apply to COBOL.

EXTERNAL SYMBOL DICTIONARY

| SYMBOL | TYPE | ID | ADDR | LENGTH | LD-ID |
|--------|------|-----|--------|--------|-------|
| TIMCOB | SD (CSECT) | OO1 | 000000 | 000237 | |
| TC1000 | LD (ENTRY) | | 000000 | | OO1 |

**Figure B.1**  The assembly post listing of the relocatable module TC1000, featuring the linkage required for its incorporation in a calling COBOL program.

```
LOC    OBJECT CODE    ADDR1 ADDR2    STMT    SOURCE STATEMENT                                    DOS/VSE ASSEMBLER  16.55  99-12-31

                                      1             PUNCH  ' CATALR TC1000  '                                          TC100010
                                      2             PRINT  NOGEN                                                       TC100020
000000                                3      TIMCOB START  0                                                           TC100030
                                      4      *                                                                         TC100040
                                      5      *  **************************************************************         TC100050
                                      6      *  *                                                            *         TC100060
                                      7      *  *     TTTTTTT    CCCCC     11          000         000        *         TC100070
                                      8      *  *        T      C          1         0   0       0   0       *         TC100080
                                      9      *  *        T      C          1         0   0       0   0       *         TC100090
                                     10      *  *        T      C          1         0   0       0   0       *         TC100100
                                     11      *  *        T      CCCCC     111          000         000       *         TC100110
                                     12      *  *                                                            *         TC100120
                                     13      *  **************************************************************         TC100130
                                     14      *  *****   L E A P   Y E A R   S U B P R O G R A M   *****       *         TC100140
                                     15      *  **************************************************************         TC100150
                                     16      *                                                                         TC100160
                                     17      *                                                                         TC100170
                                     18      *     THIS SUBPROGRAM IDENTIFIES GREGORIAN LEAP YEARS                     TC100180
                                     19      *                                                                         TC100190
                                     20      *  1. THIS SUBPROGRAM USES THE MACRO EQUIVALENT OF THE TIMESUB1           TC100200
                                     21      *     SUBROUTINE AND IS SEPARATELY ASSEMBLED ALLOWING IT TO BE            TC100210
                                     22      *     CALLED BY A COBOL PROGRAM.  THE NECESSARY LINKAGE IS                TC100220
                                     23      *     DESCRIBED IN THIS DOCUMENTATION SECTION AND HIGHLIGHTED             TC100230
                                     24      *     IN THE ENSUING CODE.                                                TC100240
                                     25      *                                                                         TC100250
                                     26      *  2. THE CALLING PROGRAM MUST DEFINE, AS 77 LEVEL ENTRIES               TC100260
                                     27      *     IN WORKING STORAGE, THE FOLLOWING ITEMS AS SHOWN:                   TC100270
                                     28      *                                                                         TC100280
                                     29      *      77   YEAR        PICTURE X(4) USAGE IS DISPLAY.                     TC100290
                                     30      *      77   CODE1       PICTURE 9 USAGE IS COMPUTATIONAL-3.                TC100300
                                     31      *      77   L           PICTURE 9 USAGE IS COMPUTATIONAL-3.                TC100310
                                     32      *                                                                         TC100320
                                     33      *  3. THE CALLING COBOL PROGRAM MUST CONTAIN THE FOLLOWING                TC100330
                                     34      *     STATEMENT IN ITS PROCEDURE DIVISION IDENTICALLY AS                  TC100340
                                     35      *     SHOWN:  (THE ALC SUBPROGRAM'S MODULE NAME IS 'TC1000')             TC100350
                                     36      *                                                                         TC100360
                                     37      *          CALL 'TC1000' USING YEAR CODE1 L.                             TC100370
                                     38      *                                                                         TC100380
                                     39      *     ADDRESSES OF THE DATA ITEMS, IN THE SEQUENCE OF THEIR              TC100390
                                     40      *     APPEARANCE IN THE CALL STATEMENT, ARE STORED IN A LIST             TC100400
                                     41      *     BY THE CALLING PROGRAM.  THE ADDRESS OF THIS LIST IS, IN           TC100410
                                     42      *     TURN, STORED IN REGISTER 1 BY THE CALLING PROGRAM.                 TC100420
                                     43      *     (THIS IS EXPLAINED FURTHER IN THE NOTE ON REGISTER                 TC100430
                                     44      *     USAGE).                                                            TC100440
                                     45      *                                                                         TC100450
                                     46      *  4. THE CALLING COBOL PROGRAM MUST PLACE A FOUR DIGIT YEAR             TC100460
                                     47      *     IN THE FIELD NAMED YEAR, PRIOR TO ISSUING THE CALL STATE-          TC100470
                                     48      *     MENT.  YEAR IS NOT ALTERED BY THE ALC SUBPROGRAM.  NOTE            TC100480
                                     49      *     THAT YEAR IS DEFINED IN THE COBOL CALLING PROGRAM AS               TC100490
                                     50      *     AN ALPHANUMERIC FIELD.  ZONED DECIMAL IS EXPECTED BY THIS          TC100500
                                     51      *     SUBPROGRAM BUT BLANKS OR OTHER ALPHABETICAL CHARACTERS             TC100510
                                     52      *     WILL NOT CAUSE ABEND DUE TO THE EDITING TECHNIQUES.                TC100520
                                     53      *                                                                         TC100530
                                     54      *  5. CODE1 FUNCTIONS AS A RETURN CODE WHOSE CONTENTS ARE AS
                                     55      *
```

```
LOC     OBJECT CODE   ADDR1 ADDR2  STMT  SOURCE STATEMENT                          DOS/VSE ASSEMBLER 16.55  99-12-31

                                    56  *        DESCRIBED IN THE TIMESUB1 SUBROUTINE DOCUMENTATION.      TC100540
                                    57  *                                                                TC100550
                                    58  * 6.     THE FIELD NAMED L IS THE RESULT FIELD WHOSE CONTENTS ARE TC100560
                                    59  *        AS DESCRIBED IN THE TIMESUB1 SUBROUTINE.                 TC100570
                                    60  *                                                                TC100580
                                    61  * 7. ** NOTE: REGARDING REGISTER USAGE IN LINKAGE CONVENTIONS    TC100590
                                    62  *        OF ALC SUBPROGRAMS CALLED BY COBOL:                     TC100600
                                    63  *                                                                TC100610
                                    64  *        REGISTER 15                                             TC100620
                                    65  *        PRIOR TO GIVING CONTROL TO THE CALLED SUBPROGRAM, COBOL TC100630
                                    66  *        PLACES THE ADDRESS OF THE SUBPROGRAM IN REGISTER 15.    TC100640
                                    67  *                                                                TC100650
                                    68  *        REGISTER 14                                             TC100660
                                    69  *        PRIOR TO GIVING CONTROL TO THE CALLED SUBPROGRAM, COBOL TC100670
                                    70  *        PLACES THE ADDRESS OF THE NEXT SEQUENTIALLY EXECUTABLE  TC100680
                                    71  *        INSTRUCTION FOLLOWING THE EXIT TO THE SUBPROGRAM. IN    TC100690
                                    72  *        REGISTER 14.                                            TC100700
                                    73  *                                                                TC100710
                                    74  *        REGISTER 13                                             TC100720
                                    75  *        PRIOR TO GIVING CONTROL TO THE CALLED SUBPROGRAM, COBOL TC100730
                                    76  *        PLACES THE ADDRESS OF THE SAVE AREA IN REGISTER 13.     TC100740
                                    77  *                                                                TC100750
                                    78  *        REGISTER 1                                              TC100760
                                    79  *        PRIOR TO GIVING CONTROL TO THE CALLED SUBPROGRAM, COBOL TC100770
                                    80  *        PLACES THE ADDRESS OF THE ARGUMENT LIST. THE LIST CON-  TC100780
                                    81  *        TAINING THE ADDRESSES OF THE DATA ITEMS; YEAR, CODE1 AND TC100790
                                    82  *        L, IN REGISTER 1. HENCE, ACCESS TO THESE FIELDS BY THE  TC100800
                                    83  *        CALLED ALC SUBPROGRAM IS MADE POSSIBLE VIA THE LOAD REG-TC100810
                                    84  *        ISTER INSTRUCTIONS NOTED BELOW.                         TC100820
                                    85  *                                                                TC100830
                                    86  *        THE ENTRY LINKAGE CONVENTIONS AS WELL AS THE BRIEF EXIT TC100840
                                    87  *        LINKAGE CONVENTIONS ARE DOCUMENTED IN THE CODE.         TC100850
                                    88  *                                                                TC100860
                                    89  *                                                                TC100870
                                    90  *                                        JEROME T. MURRAY        TC100880
                                    91  *                                        MARILYN J. MURRAY       TC100890
                                    92  *        GLEN ELLYN, ILLINOIS                                    TC100900
                                    93  *                                                                TC100910
                                    94  *********** THIS IS THE ENTRY LINKAGE SECTION ***********        TC100920
                                    95  *                                                                TC100930
                                    96  ************************************************                 TC100940
                                    97  *                                                                TC100950
                                    98  *        THIS SUBPROGRAM'S MODULE NAME IS TC1000. THE SOURCE NAME IS TC100960
                                    99  *        TIMCOB. THE ENTRY POINT IN THIS SUBPROGRAM IS TC1000. REG- TC100970
                                   100  *        ISTER 15 IS ASSIGNED AS THE BASE REGISTER VIA "USING."  TC100980
                                   101  *                                                                TC100990
                                   102          ENTRY TC1000                                            TC101000
                  00000            103          USING *,15                                              TC101010
                                   104  *                                                                TC101020
                                   105  *        REGISTERS 14,15 AND 0 THROUGH 12 ARE SAVED.             TC101030
                                   106  *                                                                TC101040
000000 90EC D00C   0000C           107  TC1000  STM   14,12,12(13)                                      TC101050
                                   108  *                                                                TC101060
                                   109  *        THE ADDRESSES OF YEAR, CODE1 AND L ARE LOADED TO REGISTERS TC101070
                                   110  *        7, 8 AND 9- THE CONTENTS OF REGISTER 1 POINTS TO THE LIST TC101080
```

**Figure B.1** *Continued*

```
LOC    OBJECT CODE   ADDR1 ADDR2   STMT   SOURCE STATEMENT                          DOS/VSE ASSEMBLER 16.55   99-12-31

                                   111   *  CONTAINING THE ADDRESSES OF THE FIELDS BEING PASSED TO THIS       TC101090
                                   112   *  SUBPROGRAM.  THE FIELDS' ADDRESSES ARE STORED IN THE LIST IN      TC101100
                                   113   *  THE SAME SEQUENCE AS THEIR APPEARANCE IN THE CALL STATEMENT.      TC101110
                                   114   *                                                                   TC101120
000004 5870 1000       00000       115         L    7,0(0,1)                                                  TC101130
000008 5880 1004       00004       116         L    8,4(0,1)                                                  TC101140
00000C 5890 1008       00008       117         L    9,8(0,1)                                                  TC101150
                                   118   *                                                                   TC101160
                                   119   ****** END OF THE ENTRY LINKAGE SECTION  ****************            TC101170
                                   120                                                                       TC101180
                                   121                                                                       TC101190
                                   122   *                                                                   TC101200
                                   123   *                                                                   TC101210
                                   124   *        MOVE THE CONTENTS OF THE COBOL FIELD 'YEAR' TO             TC101220
                                   125   *        THE MACRO INPUT FIELD 'YEAR'                                TC101230
                                   126   *                                                                   TC101240
000010 D203 F0E4 7000  000E4 00000 127         MVC  YEAR(4),0(7)                                             TC101250
                                   128   *                                                                   TC101260
                                   129   *        MACRO STATEMENT:                                            TC101270
                                   130   *                                                                   TC101280
                                   131         TIME1                                                         TC101290
                                   183   *                                                                   TC101300
                                   184   *        TRANSFER OUTPUT DATA FROM MACRO FIELDS TO COBOL            TC101310
                                   185   *        FIELDS                                                      TC101320
                                   186   *                                                                   TC101330
                                   187   *                                                                   TC101340
00020E F800 9000 F0E2  00000 000E2 188         ZAP  0(1,9),L                                                 TC101350
000214 F800 8000 F0E3  00000 000E3 189         ZAP  0(1,8),CODE1                                             TC101360
                                   190   *                                                                   TC101370
                                   191   ****** THIS IS THE EXIT LINKAGE SECTION  ****************            TC101380
                                   192   *                                                                   TC101390
                                   193                                                                       TC101400
                                   194   *                                                                   TC101410
                                   195   *        RESTORE REGISTERS THAT WERE SAVED                          TC101420
                                   196   *                                                                   TC101430
00021A 982C D01C       0001C       197         LM   2,12,28(13)                                              TC101440
                                   198   *                                                                   TC101450
                                   199   *        SET THE FLAG IN THE SAVE AREA OF THE COBOL PROGRAM TO INDICATE  TC101460
                                   200   *        THAT CONTROL HAS BEEN RETURN TO COBOL                       TC101470
                                   201   *                                                                   TC101480
00021E 92FF D00C       0000C       202         MVI  12(13),X'FF'                                             TC101490
                                   203   *                                                                   TC101500
                                   204   *        BRANCH TO THE RETURN POINT IN THE COBOL PROGRAM            TC101510
                                   205   *                                                                   TC101520
000222 07FE                        206         BCR  15,14                                                    TC101530
                                   207   *                                                                   TC101540
                                   208   ****** END OF THE EXIT LINKAGE SECTION  *****************            TC101550
                                   209                                                                       TC101560
                                   210   *                                                                   TC101570
                                   211   *                                                                   TC101580
                       00000       212         END  TIMCOB                                                   TC101590
000228 100C            213              =P'100'
00022A 400C            214              =P'400'
00022C 0C              215              =P'0'
00022D 9C              216              =P'9'
```

DOS/VSE ASSEMBLER 16.55 99-12-31

| LOC | OBJECT CODE | ADDR1 | ADDR2 | STMT | SOURCE STATEMENT |
|---|---|---|---|---|---|
| 00022E | 2C | | | 217 | =P'2' |
| 00022F | 01600C | | | 218 | =P'1600' |
| 000232 | 4C | | | 219 | =P'4' |
| 000233 | 03399C | | | 220 | =P'3399' |
| 000236 | 1C | | | 221 | =P'1' |

CROSS-REFERENCE                                          99-12-31

| SYMBOL | LEN | ID | VALUE | DEFN | REFERENCES |
|---|---|---|---|---|---|
| #$1BADYR | 00006 | 001 | 00007C | 00151 | 0154 |
| #$1BDATA | 00006 | 001 | 000062 | 00146 | 0142 |
| #$1LPYR | 00006 | 001 | 0000D8 | 00168 | 0163 |
| #$1NUM | 00006 | 001 | 000052 | 00143 | 0141 |
| #$1PACK | 00006 | 001 | 00006C | 00148 | 0145 |
| #$1RSAVE | 00004 | 001 | 0001FC | 00180 | 0134 0182 |
| #$1SIGN | 00001 | 001 | 0001F2 | 00177 | 0136 0140 |
| #$1TABL | 00001 | 001 | 0000E8 | 00173 | 0138 0139 0140 0143 0143 0144 |
| #$1TERM | 00004 | 001 | 00020A | 00182 | 0152 0157 0159 0167 0169 |
| #$1WORK | 00005 | 001 | 000204 | 00181 | 0147 0156 0158 0160 0161 0162 0164 0165 0166 |
| #$1WORK4 | 00004 | 001 | 0001F3 | 00178 | 0135 0136 0144 |
| #$1YR | 00003 | 001 | 0001F7 | 00179 | 0148 0149 0153 0156 0160 0164 |
| #$1YRHI | 00003 | 001 | 000086 | 00153 | 0150 |
| #$1ZRD | 00001 | 001 | 0001E8 | 00176 | 0137 0138 0139 |
| CODE1 | 00001 | 001 | 0000E3 | 00171 | 0132 0146 0151 0189 |
| L | 00001 | 001 | 0000E2 | 00170 | 0133 0155 0168 0188 |
| TC1000 | 00004 | 001 | 000000 | 00107 | 0102 |
| TIMCOB | 00001 | 001 | 000000 | 00003 | 0212 |
| YEAR | 00004 | 001 | 0000E4 | 00172 | 0127 0135 0148 |
| =P'0' | 00001 | 001 | 00022C | 00215 | 0132 0155 0158 0162 0166 |
| =P'1' | 00001 | 001 | 000236 | 00221 | 0168 |
| =P'100' | 00002 | 001 | 000228 | 00213 | 0161 |
| =P'1600' | 00003 | 001 | 00022F | 00218 | 0149 |
| =P'2' | 00001 | 001 | 00022E | 00217 | 0146 |
| =P'3399' | 00003 | 001 | 000233 | 00220 | 0153 |
| =P'4' | 00001 | 001 | 000232 | 00219 | 0151 0157 |
| =P'400' | 00002 | 001 | 00022A | 00214 | 0165 |
| =P'9' | 00001 | 001 | 00022D | 00216 | 0133 |

**Figure B.1** *Continued*

99-12-31

DIAGNOSTICS AND STATISTICS

NO ERRORS FOUND

THE FOLLOWING MACRO NAMES HAVE BEEN FOUND IN MACRO INSTRUCTIONS
  TIME1

OPTIONS FOR THIS ASSEMBLY - ALIGN, LIST, XREF, NOLINK, RLD, DECK, NOEDECK

THE ASSEMBLER WAS RUN IN 98184 BYTES
END OF ASSEMBLY

**Figure B.1** *Continued*

```
1   IBM DOS VS COBOL                REL 2.5 + PTF53 PP NO. 5746-CB1                16.56.08

CBL SPACE1,SXREF
00001 000010 IDENTIFICATION DIVISION.                                              CLINK1
00002 000020 PROGRAM-ID. CLINK1.                                                   CLINK1
00003 000030 AUTHOR. JEROME T. MURRAY - MARILYN J. MURRAY.                         CLINK1
00004 000040 REMARKS. ILLUSTRATION OF STRUCTURED COBOL PROGRAM LINKAGE.            CLINK1
00005 000050 ENVIRONMENT DIVISION.                                                 CLINK1
00006 000060 CONFIGURATION SECTION.                                                CLINK1
00007 000070 SOURCE-COMPUTER. IBM-4300.                                            CLINK1
00008 000080 OBJECT-COMPUTER. IBM-4300.                                            CLINK1
00009 000090 SPECIAL-NAMES.                                                        CLINK1
00010 000100 C01 IS CHANONE.                                                       CLINK1
00011 000110 INPUT-OUTPUT SECTION.                                                 CLINK1
00012 000120 FILE-CONTROL.                                                         CLINK1
00013 000130 SELECT TESTFIL                                                        CLINK1
00014 000140    ASSIGN TO SYS007-DA-FBA1-AS-TESTFIL                                CLINK1
00015 000150    ORGANIZATION IS SEQUENTIAL                                         CLINK1
00016 000160    ACCESS IS SEQUENTIAL.                                             CLINK1
00017 000170 SELECT LIST                                                           CLINK1
00018 000180    ASSIGN TO SYS010-UR-1403-S-LIST                                    CLINK1
00019 000190    RESERVE NO ALTERNATE AREAS.                                        CLINK1
00020 000200 DATA DIVISION.                                                        CLINK1
00021 000210 FILE SECTION.                                                         CLINK1
00022 000220 FD  TESTFIL                                                           CLINK1
00023 000230    DATA RECORD IS DATE-IN                                             CLINK1
00024 000240    LABEL RECORDS ARE STANDARD.                                        CLINK1
00025 000250 01 DATE-IN.                                                           CLINK1
00026 000260    02 TEST-YEAR       PICTURE X(4).                                   CLINK1
00027 000270    02 FILLER          PICTURE X(76).                                  CLINK1
00028 000280 FD  LIST                                                              CLINK1
00029 000290    RECORDING MODE IS F                                               CLINK1
00030 000300    RECORD CONTAINS 133 CHARACTERS                                     CLINK1
00031 000310    LABEL RECORDS ARE OMITTED                                          CLINK1
00032 000320    DATA RECORD IS LIST-LINE.                                          CLINK1
00033 000330 01 LIST-LINE.                                                         CLINK1
00034 000340    02 SKIP-CTL        PICTURE X.                                      CLINK1
00035 000350    02 PRINT-LINE.                                                     CLINK1
00036 000360       03 YEAR-O          PICTURE 9(4).                                CLINK1
00037 000370       03 FILLER          PICTURE XX.                                  CLINK1
00038 000380       03 COMMENT         PICTURE X(19).                               CLINK1
00039 000390       03 FILLER          PICTURE X.                                   CLINK1
00040 000400       03 L-CONTENT       PICTURE X(12).                              CLINK1
00041 000410       03 L-CONTNT        PICTURE 9.                                   CLINK1
00042 000420       03 PUNCTU          PICTURE XX.                                  CLINK1
00043 000430       03 C-CONTENT       PICTURE X(16).                               CLINK1
00044 000440       03 C-CONTNT        PICTURE 9.                                   CLINK1
00045 000450       03 FILLER          PICTURE X(74).                               CLINK1
00046 000460    02 TOT-LINE REDEFINES PRINT-LINE.                                  CLINK1
00047 000470       03 T-COMMENT       PICTURE X(28).                               CLINK1
00048 000480       03 T-TOT           PICTURE ZZZZ.                                CLINK1
00049 000490       03 W-COMNT         PICTURE X(6).                                CLINK1
00050 000500       03 FILLER          PICTURE X(93).                               CLINK1
00051 000510 WORKING-STORAGE SECTION.                                              CLINK1
00052 000520 77 TOT       PICTURE 9(5) VALUE ZERO.                                 CLINK1
00053 000530 77 HDG       PICTURE X(46) VALUE 'TEST OF TC1000- TO                  CLINK1
00054 000540-     'DETERMINE LEAP YEAR STATUS'.                                    CLINK1
00055 000550 77 TOTAL     PICTURE X(27) VALUE 'THE SUBROUTINE WAS E                CLINK1
00056 000560-     'XECUTED'.                                                       CLINK1
```

**Figure B.2**  The complete compile post listing of CLINK1, the calling COBOL program.

2        CLINK1        16.56.08

```
00057 000570 77  WORD            PICTURE X(6) VALUE ' TIMES'.             CLINK1
00058 000580 77  PUNCT           PICTURE XX VALUE ', '.                   CLINK1
00059 000590 77  BD-DATA         PICTURE X(14) VALUE '* INVALID DATA'.    CLINK1
00060 000600 77  BD-YEAR         PICTURE X(14) VALUE '* INVALID YEAR'.    CLINK1
00061 000610 77  IS-NOT-LEAP     PICTURE X(18) VALUE 'IS NOT A LEAP YEAR' CLINK1
00062 000620 77  IS-LEAP         PICTURE X(14) VALUE 'IS A LEAP YEAR'.    CLINK1
00063 000630 77  L-CONT          PICTURE X(12) VALUE 'L CONTENTS: '.      CLINK1
00064 000640 77  CODE1-CONT      PICTURE X(16) VALUE 'CODE1 CONTENTS: '.  CLINK1
00065 000650 77  SUB-ERROR       PICTURE X(16) VALUE 'SUBROUTINE ERROR'.  CLINK1
00066 000660*                                                            CLINK1
00067 000670*   THE THREE FIELDS BELOW ARE THOSE DEFINED IN THE SUBPROGRAM CLINK1
00068 000680*   THEY MUST APPEAR AS 77 OR 01 LEVEL ENTRIES IN WORKING STOR- CLINK1
00069 000690*   AGE IF THEY ARE TO BE REFERENCED BY THE CALLING PROGRAM.  CLINK1
00070 000700*   NOTE THAT YEAR IS DEFINED AS ALPHANUMERIC- THE SUBPROGRAM CLINK1
00071 000710*   VALIDATES YEAR AS ZONED DECIMAL. HENCE THE CALLING PROGRAM CLINK1
00072 000720*   IS RELEAVED OF THIS REQUIREMENT.                         CLINK1
00073 000730*                                                            CLINK1
00074 000740 77  YEAR            PICTURE X(4) USAGE IS DISPLAY.           CLINK1
00075 000750 77  CODE1           PICTURE 9 USAGE IS COMPUTATIONAL-3.      CLINK1
00076 000760 77  L               PICTURE 9 USAGE IS COMPUTATIONAL-3.      CLINK1
00077 000770*                                                            CLINK1
00078 000780 01  SWITCHES.                                               CLINK1
00079 000790 02  FILE-EOF-SWITCH     PICTURE X    VALUE 'W'.             CLINK1
00080 000800     88 EOF                           VALUE 'E'.             CLINK1
00081 000810 02  HEADING-SWITCH      PICTURE X    VALUE ' '.             CLINK1
00082 000820     88 HEAD-IS-NEEDED                VALUE ' '.             CLINK1
00083 000830 PROCEDURE DIVISION.                                         CLINK1
00084 000840*                                                            CLINK1
00085 000850 000-PRODUCE-LEAP-YEAR-LISTING.                              CLINK1
00086 000860*                                                            CLINK1
00087 000870     OPEN INPUT TESTFIL.                                     CLINK1
00088 000880     OPEN OUTPUT LIST.                                       CLINK1
00089 000890     PERFORM 100-PRODUCE-LEAP-YEAR-LINE UNTIL EOF            CLINK1
00090 000900     CLOSE TESTFIL.                                          CLINK1
00091 000910     CLOSE LIST.                                             CLINK1
00092 000920     STOP RUN.                                               CLINK1
00093 000930*                                                            CLINK1
00094 000940 100-PRODUCE-LEAP-YEAR-LINE.                                 CLINK1
00095 000950*                                                            CLINK1
00096 000960     PERFORM 110-READ-YEAR.                                  CLINK1
00097 000970     PERFORM 120-LEAP-YEAR-ALGORITHM.                        CLINK1
00098 000980     PERFORM 130-PRINT-RESULT.                               CLINK1
00099 000990*                                                            CLINK1
00100 001000 110-READ-YEAR.                                              CLINK1
00101 001010*                                                            CLINK1
00102 001020     READ TESTFIL, AT END MOVE 'E' TO FILE-EOF-SWITCH.       CLINK1
00103 001030*                                                            CLINK1
00104 001040 120-LEAP-YEAR-ALGORITHM.                                    CLINK1
00105 001050*                                                            CLINK1
00106 001060     MOVE TEST-YEAR TO YEAR.                                 CLINK1
00107 001070     ADD 1 TO TOT.                                           CLINK1
00108 001080     CALL 'TC1000' USING YEAR CODE1 L.                       CLINK1
00109 001090*                                                            CLINK1
00110 001100 130-PRINT-RESULT.                                           CLINK1
00111 001110*                                                            CLINK1
00112 001120     IF HEAD-IS-NEEDED, PERFORM 140-HEAD-LINE.               CLINK1
00113 001130     IF CODE1 IS EQUAL TO ZERO. PERFORM 150-LIST-RESULT.     CLINK1
```

```
3           CLINK1           16.56.08

00114   001140        IF CODE1 IS EQUAL TO 2, PERFORM 160-BAD-DATA.          CLINK1
00115   001150        IF CODE1 IS EQUAL TO 4, PERFORM 170-BAD-YEAR.          CLINK1
00116   001160        IF CODE1 IS NOT = 0, AND CODE1 NOT = 2,                CLINK1
00117   001170            AND CODE1 IS NOT = 4, AND NOT EOF,                 CLINK1
00118   001180        PERFORM 180-SUBROUTINE-ERROR.                         CLINK1
00119   001190        IF EOF, PERFORM 190-TOTAL-LINE.                       CLINK1
00120   001200*                                                             CLINK1
00121   001210    140-HEAD-LINE.                                            CLINK1
00122   001220*                                                             CLINK1
00123   001230        MOVE SPACES TO LIST-LINE.                             CLINK1
00124   001240        MOVE HDG TO PRINT-LINE.                               CLINK1
00125   001250        WRITE LIST-LINE AFTER ADVANCING CHANONE.              CLINK1
00126   001260        MOVE 'X' TO HEADING-SWITCH.                           CLINK1
00127   001270*                                                             CLINK1
00128   001280    150-LIST-RESULT.                                          CLINK1
00129   001290*                                                             CLINK1
00130   001300        MOVE SPACES TO LIST-LINE.                             CLINK1
00131   001310        MOVE YEAR TO YEAR-O.                                  CLINK1
00132   001320        IF L IS EQUAL TO 1, MOVE IS-LEAP TO COMMENT,          CLINK1
00133   001330        ELSE MOVE IS-NOT-LEAP TO COMMENT.                     CLINK1
00134   001340        MOVE L-CONT TO L-CONTENT.                             CLINK1
00135   001350        MOVE L TO L-CONTNT.                                   CLINK1
00136   001360        MOVE PUNCT TO PUNCTU.                                 CLINK1
00137   001370        MOVE CODE1-CONT TO C-CONTENT.                         CLINK1
00138   001380        MOVE CODE1 TO C-CONTNT.                               CLINK1
00139   001390        WRITE LIST-LINE AFTER ADVANCING 1 LINES, AT END-OF-PAGE  CLINK1
00140   001400        MOVE SPACES TO LIST-LINE, WRITE LIST-LINE AFTER       CLINK1
00141   001410        ADVANCING CHANONE.                                    CLINK1
00142   001420*                                                             CLINK1
00143   001430    160-BAD-DATA.                                             CLINK1
00144   001440*                                                             CLINK1
00145   001450        MOVE SPACES TO LIST-LINE.                             CLINK1
00146   001460        MOVE YEAR TO YEAR-O.                                  CLINK1
00147   001470        MOVE BD-DATA TO COMMENT.                              CLINK1
00148   001480        MOVE L-CONT TO L-CONTENT.                             CLINK1
00149   001490        MOVE L TO L-CONTNT.                                   CLINK1
00150   001500        MOVE PUNCT TO PUNCTU.                                 CLINK1
00151   001510        MOVE CODE1-CONT TO C-CONTENT.                         CLINK1
00152   001520        MOVE CODE1 TO C-CONTNT.                               CLINK1
00153   001530        WRITE LIST-LINE AFTER ADVANCING 1 LINES, AT END-OF-PAGE  CLINK1
00154   001540        MOVE SPACES TO LIST-LINE, WRITE LIST-LINE AFTER       CLINK1
00155   001550        ADVANCING CHANONE.                                    CLINK1
00156   001560*                                                             CLINK1
00157   001570    170-BAD-YEAR.                                             CLINK1
00158   001580*                                                             CLINK1
00159   001590        MOVE SPACES TO LIST-LINE.                             CLINK1
00160   001600        MOVE YEAR TO YEAR-O.                                  CLINK1
00161   001610        MOVE BD-YEAR TO COMMENT.                              CLINK1
00162   001620        MOVE L-CONT TO L-CONTENT.                             CLINK1
00163   001630        MOVE L TO L-CONTNT.                                   CLINK1
00164   001640        MOVE PUNCT TO PUNCTU.                                 CLINK1
00165   001650        MOVE CODE1-CONT TO C-CONTENT.                         CLINK1
00166   001660        MOVE CODE1 TO C-CONTNT.                               CLINK1
00167   001670        WRITE LIST-LINE AFTER ADVANCING 1 LINES, AT END-OF-PAGE  CLINK1
00168   001680        MOVE SPACES TO LIST-LINE, WRITE LIST-LINE AFTER       CLINK1
00169   001690        ADVANCING CHANONE.                                    CLINK1
00170   001700*                                                             CLINK1
```

**Figure B.2** *Continued*

```
4         CLINK1        16.56.08

00171  001710 180-SUBROUTINE-ERROR.                                          CLINK1
00172  001720*                                                               CLINK1
00173  001730        MOVE SPACES TO LIST-LINE.                               CLINK1
00174  001740        MOVE SUB-ERROR TO LIST-LINE.                            CLINK1
00175  001750        WRITE LIST-LINE AFTER ADVANCING 1 LINES, AT END-OF-PAGE CLINK1
00176  001760        MOVE SPACES TO LIST-LINE. WRITE LIST-LINE AFTER         CLINK1
00177  001770        ADVANCING CHANONE.                                      CLINK1
00178  001780*                                                               CLINK1
00179  001790 190-TOTAL-LINE.                                                CLINK1
00180  001800*                                                               CLINK1
00181  001810        MOVE SPACES TO LIST-LINE.                               CLINK1
00182  001820        MOVE TOTAL TO T-COMMENT.                                CLINK1
00183  001830        MOVE TOT TO T-TOT.                                      CLINK1
00184  001840        MOVE WORD TO W-COMNT.                                   CLINK1
00185  001850        WRITE LIST-LINE AFTER ADVANCING 2 LINES.                CLINK1
```

5        CLINK1        16.56.08

| INTRNL NAME | LVL | SOURCE NAME |
|---|---|---|
| DNM=1-302 | FD | TESTFIL |
| DNM=1-322 | 01 | DATE-IN |
| DNM=1-342 | 02 | TEST-YEAR |
| DNM=1-361 | 02 | FILLER |
| DNM=1-377 | FD | LIST |
| DNM=1-406 | 01 | LIST-LINE |
| DNM=1-428 | 02 | SKIP-CTL |
| DNM=1-446 | 02 | PRINT-LINE |
| DNM=1-472 | 03 | YEAR-O |
| DNM=1-488 | 03 | FILLER |
| DNM=2-000 | 03 | COMMENT |
| DNM=2-020 | 03 | FILLER |
| DNM=2-039 | 03 | L-CONTENT |
| DNM=2-058 | 03 | L-CONTNT |
| DNM=2-076 | 03 | PUNCTU |
| DNM=2-092 | 03 | C-CONTENT |
| DNM=2-111 | 03 | C-CONTNT |
| DNM=2-129 | 03 | FILLER |
| DNM=2-148 | 03 | TOT-LINE |
| DNM=2-169 | 03 | T-COMMENT |
| DNM=2-188 | 03 | T-TOT |
| DNM=2-208 | 03 | W-COMNT |
| DNM=2-225 | 03 | FILLER |
| DNM=2-244 | 03 | TOT |
| DNM=2-257 | 77 | HDG |
| DNM=2-270 | 77 | TOTAL |
| DNM=2-285 | 77 | WORD |
| DNM=2-299 | 77 | PUNCT |
| DNM=2-314 | 77 | BD-DATA |
| DNM=2-334 | 77 | BD-YEAR |
| DNM=2-351 | 77 | IS-NOT-LEAP |
| DNM=2-372 | 77 | IS-LEAP |
| DNM=2-392 | 77 | L-CONT |
| DNM=2-408 | 77 | CODE1-CONT |
| DNM=2-428 | 77 | SUB-ERROR |
| DNM=2-447 | 77 | YEAR |
| DNM=2-461 | 77 | CODE1 |
| DNM=2-476 | 77 | L |
| DNM=2-487 | 01 | SWITCHES |
| DNM=3-000 | 01 | FILE-EOF-SWITCH |
| DNM=3-028 | 88 | EOF |
| DNM=3-042 | 02 | HEADING-SWITCH |
| DNM=3-069 | 88 | HEAD-IS-NEEDED |

| BASE | DISPL | INTRNL NAME | DEFINITION | USAGE | R | O | Q | M |
|---|---|---|---|---|---|---|---|---|
| FIB=01 | 000 | DNM=1-302 | DS 0CL80 | VSAM | | | | |
| BL=1 | 000 | DNM=1-322 | DS 4C | GROUP | | | | |
| BL=1 | 000 | DNM=1-342 | DS 4C | DISP | | | | |
| BL=1 | 004 | DNM=1-361 | DS 76C | DISP | | | | |
| DTF=02 | | DNM=1-377 | | DTFPR | | | | F |
| BL=2 | 000 | DNM=1-406 | DS 0CL133 | GROUP | | | | |
| BL=2 | 000 | DNM=1-428 | DS 1C | DISP | | | | |
| BL=2 | 001 | DNM=1-446 | DS 0CL132 | GROUP | | | | |
| BL=2 | 001 | DNM=1-472 | DS 4C | DISP-NM | | | | |
| BL=2 | 005 | DNM=1-488 | DS 2C | DISP | | | | |
| BL=2 | 007 | DNM=2-000 | DS 19C | DISP | | | | |
| BL=2 | 01A | DNM=2-020 | DS 1C | DISP | | | | |
| BL=2 | 01B | DNM=2-039 | DS 12C | DISP | | | | |
| BL=2 | 027 | DNM=2-058 | DS 1C | DISP-NM | | | | |
| BL=2 | 028 | DNM=2-076 | DS 2C | DISP | | | | |
| BL=2 | 02A | DNM=2-092 | DS 16C | DISP | | | | |
| BL=2 | 03A | DNM=2-111 | DS 1C | DISP-NM | | | | |
| BL=2 | 03B | DNM=2-129 | DS 74C | GROUP | R | | | |
| BL=2 | 001 | DNM=2-148 | DS 0CL132 | DISP | | | | |
| BL=2 | 001 | DNM=2-169 | DS 28C | DISP | | | | |
| BL=2 | 01D | DNM=2-188 | DS 5C | NM-EDIT | | | | |
| BL=2 | 022 | DNM=2-208 | DS 6C | DISP | | | | |
| BL=2 | 028 | DNM=2-225 | DS 93C | DISP-NM | | | | |
| BL=3 | 000 | DNM=2-244 | DS 5C | DISP | | | | |
| BL=3 | 005 | DNM=2-257 | DS 46C | DISP | | | | |
| BL=3 | 033 | DNM=2-270 | DS 27C | DISP | | | | |
| BL=3 | 04E | DNM=2-285 | DS 6C | DISP | | | | |
| BL=3 | 054 | DNM=2-299 | DS 2C | DISP | | | | |
| BL=3 | 056 | DNM=2-314 | DS 14C | DISP | | | | |
| BL=3 | 064 | DNM=2-334 | DS 14C | DISP | | | | |
| BL=3 | 072 | DNM=2-351 | DS 18C | DISP | | | | |
| BL=3 | 084 | DNM=2-372 | DS 14C | DISP | | | | |
| BL=3 | 092 | DNM=2-392 | DS 12C | DISP | | | | |
| BL=3 | 09E | DNM=2-408 | DS 16C | DISP | | | | |
| BL=3 | 0AE | DNM=2-428 | DS 16C | DISP | | | | |
| BL=3 | 0BE | DNM=2-447 | DS 4C | DISP | | | | |
| BL=3 | 0C2 | DNM=2-461 | DS 1P | COMP-3 | | | | |
| BL=3 | 0C3 | DNM=2-476 | DS 1P | COMP-3 | | | | |
| BL=3 | 0C8 | DNM=2-487 | DS 0CL2 | GROUP | | | | |
| BL=3 | 0C8 | DNM=3-000 | DS 1C | DISP | | | | |
| BL=3 | 0C9 | DNM=3-042 | DS 1C | DISP | | | | |
| | | DNM=3-069 | | | | | | |

**Figure B.2** *Continued*

6    CLINK1    16.56.08

MEMORY MAP

| TGT | 00348 |
|---|---|
| SAVE AREA | 00348 |
| SWITCH | 00390 |
| TALLY | 00394 |
| SORT SAVE | 00398 |
| ENTRY-SAVE | 0039C |
| SORT CORE SIZE | 003A0 |
| NSTD-REELS | 003A4 |
| SORT RET | 003A6 |
| WORKING CELLS | 003A8 |
| SORT FILE SIZE | 004D8 |
| SORT MODE SIZE | 004DC |
| PGT-VN TBL | 004E0 |
| TGT-VN TBL | 004E4 |
| SORTAB ADDRESS | 004E8 |
| LENGTH OF VN TBL | 004EC |
| LNGTH OF SORTAB | 004EE |
| PGM ID | 004F0 |
| A(INIT1) | 004F8 |
| UPSI SWITCHES | 004FC |
| DEBUG TABLE PTR | 00504 |
| CURRENT PRIORITY | 00508 |
| TA LENGTH | 00509 |
| PROCEDURE BLOCK1 PTR | 0050C |
| UNUSED | 00510 |
| COUNT TABLE ADDRESS | 00514 |
| VSAM SAVE AREA ADDRESS | 00518 |
| UNUSED | 0051C |
| COUNT CHAIN ADDRESS | 00524 |
| UNUSED | 00528 |
| OVERFLOW CELLS | 0053C |
| BL CELLS | 0053C |
| DTFADR CELLS | 0054C |
| FIB CELLS | 00554 |
| TEMP STORAGE | 00558 |
| TEMP STORAGE-2 | 00560 |
| TEMP STORAGE-3 | 00568 |
| TEMP STORAGE-4 | 00568 |
| BLL CELLS | 00568 |
| VLC CELLS | 0056C |
| SBL CELLS | 0056C |
| INDEX CELLS | 0056C |
| SUBADR CELLS | 0056C |
| ONCTL CELLS | 0056C |
| PFMCTL CELLS | 0056C |
| PFMSAV CELLS | 0056C |
| VN CELLS | 00594 |
| SAVE AREA =2 | 005BC |
| XSASW CELLS | 005BC |
| XSA CELLS | 005BC |
| PARAM CELLS | 005BC |
| RPTSAV AREA | 005C8 |

7       CLINK1           16.56.08

        CHECKPT CTR                      OO5C8
        IOPTR CELLS                      OO5C8

**Figure B.2**  *Continued*

```
B        CLINK1          16.56.08

LITERAL POOL (HEX)

006B8 (LIT+O)   1COF2C4C   OC402020   20202080   0000005B   5BC2D6D7   C5D5405B
006DO (LIT+24)  5BC2C3D3   D6E2C5

                PGT                          005C8

                OVERFLOW CELLS               005C8
                VIRTUAL CELLS                005C8
                PROCEDURE NAME CELLS         005E4
                GENERATED NAME CELLS         00610
                SUBDTF ADDRESS CELLS         00690
                VNI CELLS                    00690
                LITERALS                     006B8
                DISPLAY LITERALS             006D7
                PROCEDURE BLOCK CELLS        006D8

REGISTER ASSIGNMENT

REG 6   BL =3
REG 7   BL =1
REG 8   BL =2
REG 9   BL =4

WORKING-STORAGE STARTS AT LOCATION 00100 FOR A LENGTH OF 000D0.

 0
85
87      0006D8                      START   EQU   *
        0006D8  58 10 D 20C                 L     1,20C(0,13)        FIB=1
        0006DC  50 10 D 274                 ST    1,274(0,13)        PRM=1
        0006E0  D2 03 1 002 C OFB           MVC   002(4,1),OFB(12)                 LIT+11
        0006E6  92 80 D 274                 MVI   274(13),X'80'
        0006EA  41 10 D 274                 LA    1,274(0,13)        PRM=1
        0006EE  58 FO C 004                 L     15,004(0,12)       V(ILBDVOCO)
        0006F2  05 EF                       BALR  14,15
88
        0006F4  58 20 D 1F8                 LA    2,1F8(0,13)        BL =2
        0006F8  41 10 C OFF                 LA    1,OFF(0,12)        LIT+15
        0006FC  58 00 D 208                 LR    0,208(0,13)        DTF=2
        000700  18 40                       LR    4,0
        000702  05 FO                       BALR  15,0
        000704  50 00 F 008                 ST    0,008(0,15)
        000708  45 00 F OOC                 BAL   0,OOC(0,15)
        00070C  00000000                    DC    X'00000000'
        000710  0A 02                       SVC   2
89
        000712  58 00 D 24C                 L     0,24C(0,13)        VN=01
        000716  50 00 D 224                 ST    0,224(0,13)        PSV=1
        00071A  58 00 C 048                 L     0,048(0,12)        GN=01
        00071E  50 00 D 24C                 ST    0,24C(0,13)        VN=01
        000722                      GN=01   EQU   *
        000722  58 20 C 04C                 L     2,04C(0,12)        GN=02
```

```
9     CLINK1              16.56.08

      000726  95 C5 6 0C8            CLI   0C8(6),X'C5'       DNM=3-28
      00072A  07 82                  BCR   8,2
      00072C  58 10 C 01C            L     1,01C(0,12)        PN=01
      000730  07 F1                  BCR   15,1
      000732            GN=02        EQU   *
      000732  58 00 D 224            L     0,224(0,13)        PSV=1
      000736  50 00 D 24C            ST    0,24C(0,13)        VN=01

90    00073A  58 10 D 20C            L     1,20C(0,13)        FIB=1
      00073E  50 10 D 274            ST    1,274(0,13)        PRM=1
      000742  92 00 1 006            MVI   006(1),X'00'
      000746  92 80 D 274            MVI   274(13),X'80'      PRM=1
      00074A  41 10 D 274            LA    1,274(0,13)        PRM=1
      00074E  58 F0 C 008            L     15,008(0,12)       V(ILBDVDC1)
      000752  05 EF                  BALR  14,15

91    000754  58 00 D 208            L     0,208(0,13)        DTF=2
      000758  18 40                  LR    4,0
      00075A  41 10 C 107            LA    1,107(0,12)        LIT+23
      00075E  05 F0                  BALR  15,0
      000760  50 00 F 008            ST    0,008(0,15)
      000764  45 00 F 00C            BAL   0,00C(0,15)
      000768  00000000               DC    X'00000000'
      00076C  0A 02                  SVC   2

92    00076E  1B 11                  SR    1,1
      000770  58 F0 C 00C            L     15,00C(0,12)       V(ILBDTC20)
      000774  05 EF                  BALR  14,15
      000776  0A 0E                  SVC   14

94    000778            PN=01        EQU   *

96    000778  58 00 D 250            L     0,250(0,13)        VN=02
      00077C  50 00 D 228            ST    0,228(0,13)        PSV=2
      000780  58 00 C 050            L     0,050(0,12)        GN=02
      000784  50 00 D 250            ST    0,250(0,13)        VN=02
      000788  58 10 C 020            L     1,020(0,12)        PN=02
      00078C  07 F1                  BCR   15,1
      00078E            GN=03        EQU   *
      00078E  58 00 D 228            L     0,228(0,13)        PSV=2
      000792  50 00 D 250            ST    0,250(0,13)        VN=02

97    000796  58 00 D 254            L     0,254(0,13)        VN=03
      00079A  50 00 D 22C            ST    0,22C(0,13)        PSV=3
      00079E  58 00 C 054            L     0,054(0,12)        GN=04
      0007A2  50 00 D 254            ST    0,254(0,13)        VN=03
      0007A6  58 10 C 024            L     1,024(0,12)        PN=03
      0007AA  07 F1                  BCR   15,1
      0007AC            GN=04        EQU   *
      0007AC  58 00 D 22C            L     0,22C(0,13)        PSV=3
      0007B0  50 00 D 254            ST    0,254(0,13)        VN=03

98    0007B4  58 00 D 258            L     0,258(0,13)        VN=04
      0007B8  50 00 D 230            ST    0,230(0,13)        PSV=4
      0007BC  58 00 C 058            L     0,058(0,12)        GN=05
      0007C0  50 00 D 258            ST    0,258(0,13)        VN=04
      0007C4  58 10 C 028            L     1,028(0,12)        PN=04
```

**Figure B.2** *Continued*

```
10    CLINK1                    16.56.08

0007C8  07 F1                           BCR   15,1
0007CA                    GN=05   EQU   *
0007CA  58 00 D 230               L     0,230(0,13)         PSV=4
0007CE  50 00 D 258               ST    0,258(0,13)         VN=04
0007D2  58 10 D 24C               L     1,24C(0,13)         VN=01
0007D6  07 F1                     BCR   15,1

100
0007D8                    PN=02   EQU   *                   FIB=1

102
0007D8  58 40 D 20C               L     4,20C(0,13)         GN=032
0007DC  58 E0 C 0C4               L     14,0C4(0,12)
0007E0  D2 03 4 020 C 05C         MVC   020(4,4),05C(12)
0007E6  58 F0 4 00C               L     15,00C(0,4)
0007EA  05 1F                     BALR  1,15
0007EC  04C20000                  DC    X'04C20000'         GN=06
0007F0  58 50 C 060       GN=032  L     5,060(0,12)         GN=07
0007F4  07 F5                     BCR   15,5

102
0007F6                    GN=06   EQU   *
0007F6  92 C5 6 0C8               MVI   0C8(6),X'C5'
0007FA                    GN=07   EQU   *
0007FA  58 10 D 250               L     1,250(0,13)         VN=02
0007FE  07 F1                     BCR   15,1

104
000800                    PN=03   EQU   *

106
000800  D2 03 6 0BE 7 000         MVC   0BE(4,6),000(7)     DNM=2-447   DNM=1-342

107
000806  F2 74 D 210 6 000         PACK  210(8,13),000(5,6)  TS=01       DNM=2-447
00080C  FA 30 D 214 C 0F0         AP    214(4,13),0F0(1,12) TS=05       LIT+0
000812  F3 43 6 000 D 214         UNPK  000(5,6),214(4,13)  DNM=2-244   TS=05
000818  96 F0 6 004               OI    004(6),X'F0'        DNM=2-244+4

108
00081C  41 10 6 0BE               LA    1,0BE(0,6)          DNM=2-447
000820  50 10 6 0C2               ST    1,0C2(0,6)          PRM=1
000824  41 10 6 0C2               LA    1,0C2(0,6)          DNM=2-461
000828  50 10 6 0C3               ST    1,0C3(0,6)          PRM=2
00082C  41 10 6 0C3               LA    1,0C3(0,6)          DNM=2-476
000830  50 10 D 27C               ST    1,27C(0,13)         PRM=3
000834  96 80 D 27C               OI    27C(13),X'80'       PRM=3
000838  41 10 D 274               LA    1,274(0,13)         PRM=1
00083C  58 F0 C 010               L     15,010(0,12)        V(TC1000   )
000840  05 EF                     BALR  14,15
000842  58 10 D 254               L     1,254(0,13)         VN=03
000846  07 F1                     BCR   15,1

110
000848                    PN=04   EQU   *

112
000848  58 20 C 064               L     2,064(0,12)         GN=08
00084C  95 40 6 0C9               CLI   0C9(6),X'40'        DNM=3-69
000850  07 72                     BCR   7,2

112
000852  58 00 D 25C               L     0,25C(0,13)         VN=05
000856  50 00 D 234               ST    0,234(0,13)         PSV=5
00085A  58 00 C 068               L     0,068(0,12)         GN=09
00085E  50 00 D 25C               ST    0,25C(0,13)         VN=05
```

```
11      CLINK1              16.56.08

000862  58 10 C 02C           L    1,02C(0,12)           PN=05
000866  07 F1                 BCR  15,1
000868             GN=09      EQU  *
000868  58 00 D 234           L    0,234(0,13)           PSV=5
00086C  50 00 D 25C           ST   0,25C(0,13)           VN=05
                                                         LIT+1
```

```
000870             GN=08      EQU  *                      DNM=2-461
000870  F9 00 6 OC2 C 06C     CP   OC2(1,6),OF1(1,12)     GN=010
000876  58 F0 C 06C           L    15,06C(0,12)
00087A  07 7F                 BCR  7,15
```

```
00087C  58 00 D 260           L    0,260(0,13)            VN=06
000880  50 00 D 238           ST   0,238(0,13)            PSV=6
000884  58 00 C 070           L    0,070(0,12)            GN=011
000888  50 00 D 260           ST   0,260(0,13)            VN=06
00088C  58 10 C 030           L    1,030(0,12)            PN=06
000890  07 F1                 BCR  15,1
000892             GN=011     EQU  *
000892  58 00 D 238           L    0,238(0,13)            PSV=6
000896  50 00 D 260           ST   0,260(0,13)            VN=06
```

```
00089A             GN=010     EQU  *                      DNM=2-461
00089A  F9 00 6 OC2 C 074     CP   OC2(1,6),OF2(1,12)     GN=012
0008A0  58 F0 C 074           L    15,074(0,12)
0008A4  07 7F                 BCR  7,15                    LIT+2
```

```
0008A6  58 00 D 264           L    0,264(0,13)            VN=07
0008AA  50 00 D 23C           ST   0,23C(0,13)            PSV=7
0008AE  58 00 C 078           L    0,078(0,12)            GN=013
0008B2  50 00 D 264           ST   0,264(0,13)            VN=07
0008B6  58 10 C 034           L    1,034(0,12)            PN=07
0008BA  07 F1                 BCR  15,1
0008BC             GN=013     EQU  *
0008BC  58 00 D 23C           L    0,23C(0,13)            PSV=7
0008C0  50 00 D 264           ST   0,264(0,13)            VN=07
```

```
0008C4             GN=012     EQU  *                      DNM=2-461
0008C4  F9 00 6 OC2 C 07C     CP   OC2(1,6),OF3(1,12)     GN=014
0008CA  58 F0 C 07C           L    15,07C(0,12)
0008CE  07 7F                 BCR  7,15                    LIT+3
```

```
0008D0  58 00 D 268           L    0,268(0,13)            VN=08
0008D4  50 00 D 240           ST   0,240(0,13)            PSV=8
0008D8  58 00 C 080           L    0,080(0,12)            GN=015
0008DC  50 00 D 268           ST   0,268(0,13)            VN=08
0008E0  58 10 C 038           L    1,038(0,12)            PN=08
0008E4  07 F1                 BCR  15,1
0008E6             GN=015     EQU  *
0008E6  58 00 D 240           L    0,240(0,13)            PSV=8
0008EA  50 00 D 268           ST   0,268(0,13)            VN=08
```

```
0008EE             GN=014     EQU  *                      DNM=2-461
0008EE  F9 00 6 OC2 C 084     CP   OC2(1,6),OF4(1,12)     GN=016
0008F4  58 F0 C 084           L    15,084(0,12)
0008F8  07 8F                 BCR  8,15                    LIT+4
0008FA  F9 00 6 OC2 C 084     CP   OC2(1,6),OF2(1,12)     DNM=2-461
000900  58 F0 C 084           L    15,084(0,12)            GN=016
                                                          LIT+2
```

**Figure B.2** *Continued*

```
12   CLINK1                    16.56.08

118  000904  07 8F                        BCR   8,15                            LIT+3
     000906  F9 00 6 OC2 C OF3            CP    OC2(1,6),OF3(1,12)    DNM=2-461
     00090C  58 F0 C 084                  L     15,084(0,12)          GN=016
     000910  07 8F                        BCR   8,15
     000912  58 20 C 084                  L     2,084(0,12)           GN=016
     000916  95 C5 6 OC8                  CLI   OC8(6),X'C5'          DNM=3-28
     00091A  07 82                        BCR   8,2

     00091C  58 00 D 26C                  L     0,26C(0,13)           VN=09
     000920  50 00 D 244                  ST    0,244(0,13)           PSV=9
     000924  58 00 D 088                  L     0,088(0,12)           GN=017
     000928  50 00 D 26C                  ST    0,26C(0,13)           VN=09
     00092C  58 10 C 03C                  L     1,03C(0,12)           PN=09
     000930  07 F1                        BCR   15,1
     000932              GN=017           EQU   *
     000932  58 00 D 244                  L     0,244(0,13)           PSV=9
     000936  50 00 D 26C                  ST    0,26C(0,13)           VN=09

119  00093A              GN=016           EQU   *
     00093A  58 20 C 08C                  L     2,08C(0,12)           GN=018
     00093E  95 C5 6 OC8                  CLI   OC8(6),X'C5'          DNM=3-28
     000942  07 72                        BCR   7,2

119  000944  58 00 D 270                  L     0,270(0,13)           VN=010
     000948  50 00 D 248                  ST    0,248(0,13)           PSV=10
     00094C  58 00 C 090                  L     0,090(0,12)           GN=019
     000950  50 00 D 270                  ST    0,270(0,13)           VN=010
     000954  58 10 C 040                  L     1,040(0,12)           PN=010
     000958  07 F1                        BCR   15,1
     00095A              GN=019           EQU   *
     00095A  58 00 D 248                  L     0,248(0,13)           PSV=10
     00095E  50 00 D 270                  ST    0,270(0,13)           VN=010
     000962              GN=018           EQU   *
     000962  58 10 D 258                  L     1,258(0,13)           VN=04
     000966  07 F1                        BCR   15,1

121  000968              PN=05            EQU   *
123  000968  92 40 8 000                  MVI   000(8),X'40'          DNM=1-406
     00096C  D2 83 8 001 8 000            MVC   001(132,8),000(8)     DNM=1-406+1

124  000972  D2 2D 8 001 6 005            MVC   001(46,8),005(6)      DNM=1-446
     000978  92 40 8 02F                  MVI   02F(8),X'40'          DNM=1-446+46
     00097C  D2 54 8 030 8 02F            MVC   030(85,8),02F(8)      DNM=1-446+47

125  000982  58 10 D 208                  L     1,208(0,13)           DTF=2
     000986  92 F1 8 000                  MVI   000(8),X'F1'          DNM=1-406
     00098A  58 F0 1 010                  L     15,010(0,1)
     00098E  45 E0 F 00C                  BAL   14,00C(0,15)

126  000992              GN=020           EQU   *
     000992  92 E7 6 OC9                  MVI   OC9(6),X'E7'          DNM=3-42
     000996  58 10 D 25C                  L     1,25C(0,13)           VN=05
     00099A  07 F1                        BCR   15,1

128
130  00099C              PN=06            EQU   *
```

```
13        CLINK1          16.56.08

131   0009C    92 40 8 000        MVI   000(8),X'40'          DNM=1-406
      0009A0   D2 83 8 001 8 000  MVC   001(132,8),000(8)     DNM=1-406+1

      0009A6   D2 03 8 001 6 0BE  MVC   001(4,8),0BE(6)       DNM=1-472     DNM=2-447
132   0009AC   96 F0 8 004        OI    004(8),X'F0'          DNM=1-472+3

      0009B0   F9 00 6 0C3 C 0F0  CP    0C3(1,6),0F0(1,12)    DNM=2-476     LIT+0
      0009B6   58 F0 C 098        L     15,098(0,12)          GN=021
132   0009BA   07 7F              BCR   7,15

      0009BC   D2 0D 8 007 6 084  MVC   007(14,8),084(6)      DNM=2-0       DNM=2-372
      0009C2   92 40 8 015        MVI   015(8),X'40'          DNM=2-0+14
133   0009C6   D2 03 8 016 8 015  MVC   016(4,8),015(8)       DNM=2-0+15    DNM=2-0+14

      0009CC   58 10 C 09C        L     1,09C(0,12)           GN=022
133   0009D0   07 F1              BCR   15,1

GN=021
      0009D2                      EQU   *
      0009D2   D2 11 8 007 6 072  MVC   007(18,8),072(6)      DNM=2-0       DNM=2-351
134   0009D8   92 40 8 019        MVI   019(8),X'40'          DNM=2-0+18

GN=022
135   0009DC                      EQU   *
      0009DC   D2 0B 8 01B 6 092  MVC   01B(12,8),092(6)      DNM=2-39      DNM=2-392

      0009E2   F3 00 8 027 6 0C3  UNPK  027(1,8),0C3(1,6)     DNM=2-58      DNM=2-476
136   0009E8   96 F0 8 027        OI    027(8),X'F0'          DNM=2-58

137   0009EC   D2 01 8 028 6 054  MVC   028(2,8),054(6)       DNM=2-76      DNM=2-299

138   0009F2   D2 0F 8 02A 6 09E  MVC   02A(16,8),09E(6)      DNM=2-92      DNM=2-408

      0009F8   F3 00 8 03A 6 0C2  UNPK  03A(1,8),0C2(1,6)     DNM=2-111     DNM=2-461
139   0009FE   96 F0 8 03A        OI    03A(8),X'F0'          DNM=2-111

      000A02   58 10 D 208        L     1,208(0,13)           DTF=2
      000A06   96 04 1 002        OI    002(1),X'04'
      000A0A   92 40 8 000        MVI   000(8),X'40'          DNM=1-406
      000A0E   58 F0 1 010        L     15,010(0,1)
      000A12   45 E0 F 00C        BAL   14,00C(0,15)
      000A16   58 F0 C 0A0        L     15,0A0(0,12)          GN=023
      000A1A   94 FB 1 002        NI    002(1),X'FB'
      000A1E   91 01 1 027        TM    027(1),X'01'
140   000A22   07 8F              BCR   8,15

GN=024
      000A24                      EQU   *                     DNM=1-406
      000A24   92 40 8 000        MVI   000(8),X'40'          DNM=1-406
140   000A28   D2 83 8 001 8 000  MVC   001(132,8),000(8)     DNM=1-406+1

      000A2E   58 10 D 208        L     1,208(0,13)           DTF=2
      000A32   92 F1 8 000        MVI   000(8),X'F1'          DNM=1-406
      000A36   58 F0 1 010        L     15,010(0,1)
      000A3A   45 E0 F 00C        BAL   14,00C(0,15)
GN=023
      000A3E                      EQU   *                     VN=06
      000A3E   58 10 D 260        L     1,260(0,13)
143   000A42   07 F1              BCR   15,1

PN=07
      000A44                      EQU   *
```

Figure B.2 *Continued*

14        CLINK1        16.56.08

| Line | Address | Object Code | Label | Op | Operand | Ref 1 | Ref 2 |
|---|---|---|---|---|---|---|---|
| 145 | 000A44 | 92 40 8 000 | | MVI | 000(8),X'40' | DNM=1-406 | |
| | 000A48 | D2 83 8 001 8 000 | | MVC | 001(132,8),000(8) | DNM=1-406+1 | DNM=1-406 |
| 146 | 000A4E | D2 03 8 001 6 0BE | | MVC | 001(4,8),0BE(6) | DNM=1-472 | DNM=2-447 |
| | 000A54 | 96 F0 8 004 | | OI | 004(8),X'F0' | DNM=1-472+3 | |
| 147 | 000A58 | D2 0D 8 007 6 056 | | MVC | 007(14,8),056(6) | DNM=2-0 | DNM=2-314 |
| | 000A5E | 92 40 8 015 | | MVI | 015(8),X'40' | DNM=2-0+14 | DNM=2-0+14 |
| | 000A62 | D2 03 8 016 8 015 | | MVC | 016(4,8),015(8) | DNM=2-0+15 | DNM=2-0+15 |
| 148 | 000A68 | D2 0B 8 01B 6 092 | | MVC | 01B(12,8),092(6) | DNM=2-39 | DNM=2-392 |
| 149 | 000A6E | F3 00 8 027 6 0C3 | | UNPK | 027(1,8),0C3(1,6) | DNM=2-58 | DNM=2-476 |
| | 000A74 | 96 F0 8 027 | | OI | 027(8),X'F0' | DNM=2-58 | |
| 150 | 000A78 | D2 01 8 028 6 054 | | MVC | 028(2,8),054(6) | DNM=2-76 | DNM=2-299 |
| 151 | 000A7E | D2 0F 8 02A 6 09E | | MVC | 02A(16,8),09E(6) | DNM=2-92 | DNM=2-408 |
| 152 | 000A84 | F3 00 8 03A 6 0C2 | | UNPK | 03A(1,8),0C2(1,6) | DNM=2-111 | DNM=2-461 |
| | 000A8A | 96 F0 8 03A | | OI | 03A(8),X'F0' | DNM=2-111 | |
| 153 | 000A8E | 58 10 D 208 | GN=026 | L | 1,208(0,13) | DTF=2 | |
| | 000A92 | 96 04 1 002 | | OI | 002(1),X'04' | | |
| | 000A96 | 92 40 8 000 | | MVI | 000(8),X'40' | DNM=1-406 | |
| | 000A9A | 58 F0 1 010 | | L | 15,010(0,1) | | |
| | 000A9E | 45 E0 F 00C | | BAL | 14,00C(0,15) | | |
| | 000AA2 | 58 F0 C 0A8 | | L | 15,0A8(0,12) | GN=025 | |
| | 000AA6 | 94 FB 1 002 | | NI | 002(1),X'FB' | | |
| | 000AAA | 91 01 1 027 | | TM | 027(1),X'01' | | |
| | 000AAE | 07 8F | | BCR | 8,15 | | |
| 154 | 000AB0 | | GN=026 | EQU | * | | |
| | 000AB0 | 92 40 8 000 | | MVI | 000(8),X'40' | DNM=1-406 | |
| | 000AB4 | D2 83 8 001 8 000 | | MVC | 001(132,8),000(8) | DNM=1-406+1 | DNM=1-406 |
| 154 | 000ABA | 58 10 D 208 | | L | 1,208(0,13) | DTF=2 | |
| | 000ABE | 92 F1 8 000 | | MVI | 000(8),X'F1' | DNM=1-406 | |
| | 000AC2 | 58 F0 1 010 | | L | 15,010(0,1) | | |
| | 000AC6 | 45 E0 F 00C | | BAL | 14,00C(0,15) | | |
| | 000ACA | | GN=025 | EQU | * | | |
| | 000ACA | 58 10 D 264 | | L | 1,264(0,13) | VN=07 | |
| | 000ACE | 07 F1 | | BCR | 15,1 | | |
| 157 | 000AD0 | | PN=08 | EQU | * | | |
| 159 | 000AD0 | 92 40 8 000 | | MVI | 000(8),X'40' | DNM=1-406 | |
| | 000AD4 | D2 83 8 001 8 000 | | MVC | 001(132,8),000(8) | DNM=1-406+1 | DNM=1-406 |
| 160 | 000ADA | D2 03 8 001 6 0BE | | MVC | 001(4,8),0BE(6) | DNM=1-472 | DNM=2-447 |
| | 000AE0 | 96 F0 8 004 | | OI | 004(8),X'F0' | DNM=1-472+3 | |
| 161 | 000AE4 | D2 0D 8 007 6 064 | | MVC | 007(14,8),064(6) | DNM=2-0 | DNM=2-334 |
| | 000AEA | 92 40 8 015 | | MVI | 015(8),X'40' | DNM=2-0+14 | DNM=2-0+14 |
| | 000AEE | D2 03 8 016 8 015 | | MVC | 016(4,8),015(8) | DNM=2-0+15 | DNM=2-0+15 |
| 162 | | | | | | | |

```
15        CLINK1        16.56.08

163   000AF4   D2 0B 8 01B 6 092              MVC    01B(12,8),092(6)       DNM=2-39                      DNM=2-392

164   000AFA   F3 00 8 027 6 0C3              UNPK   027(1,8),0C3(1,6)      DNM=2-58                      DNM=2-476
      000B00   96 F0 8 027                    OI     027(8),X'F0'           DNM=2-58

165   000B04   D2 01 8 028 6 054              MVC    028(2,8),054(6)        DNM=2-76                      DNM=2-299

166   000B0A   D2 0F 8 02A 6 09E              MVC    02A(16,8),09E(6)       DNM=2-92                      DNM=2-408

167   000B10   F3 00 8 03A 6 0C2              UNPK   03A(1,8),0C2(1,6)      DNM=2-111                     DNM=2-461
      000B16   96 F0 8 03A                    OI     03A(8),X'F0'           DNM=2-111

      000B1A   58 10 D 208                    L      1,208(0,13)            DTF=2
      000B1E   96 04 1 002                    OI     002(1),X'04'
      000B22   92 40 8 000                    MVI    000(8),X'40'           DNM=1-406
      000B26   58 F0 1 010                    L      15,010(0,1)
      000B2A   45 E0 F 00C                    BAL    14,00C(0,15)
      000B2E   58 F0 C 0B0                    L      15,0B0(0,12)
      000B32   94 FB 1 002                    NI     002(1),X'FB'
      000B36   91 01 1 027                    TM     027(1),X'01'           GN=027
      000B3A   07 8F                          BCR    8,15

168   000B3C            GN=028               EQU    *
      000B3C   92 40 8 000                    MVI    000(8),X'40'           DNM=1-406
      000B40   D2 83 8 001 8 000              MVC    001(132,8),000(8)      DNM=1-406+1                   DNM=1-406

168   000B46   58 10 D 208                    L      1,208(0,13)            DTF=2
      000B4A   92 F1 8 000                    MVI    000(8),X'F1'           DNM=1-406
      000B4E   58 F0 1 010                    L      15,010(0,1)
      000B52   45 E0 F 00C                    BAL    14,00C(0,15)

      000B56            GN=027               EQU    *
      000B56   58 10 D 268                    L      1,268(0,13)            VN=08
      000B5A   07 F1                          BCR    15,1

171   000B5C            PN=09                EQU    *

173   000B5C   92 40 8 000                    MVI    000(8),X'40'           DNM=1-406
      000B60   D2 83 8 001 8 000              MVC    001(132,8),000(8)      DNM=1-406+1                   DNM=1-406

174   000B66   D2 0F 8 000 6 0AE              MVC    000(16,8),0AE(6)       DNM=1-406                     DNM=2-428
      000B6C   92 40 8 010                    MVI    010(8),X'40'           DNM=1-406+16
      000B70   D2 73 8 011 8 010              MVC    011(116,8),010(8)      DNM=1-406+17                  DNM=1-406+16

175   000B76   58 10 D 208                    L      1,208(0,13)            DTF=2
      000B7A   96 04 1 002                    OI     002(1),X'04'
      000B7E   92 40 8 000                    MVI    000(8),X'40'           DNM=1-406
      000B82   58 F0 1 010                    L      15,010(0,1)
      000B86   45 E0 F 00C                    BAL    14,00C(0,15)
      000B8A   58 F0 C 0B8                    L      15,0B8(0,12)
      000B8E   94 FB 1 002                    NI     002(1),X'FB'
      000B92   91 01 1 027                    TM     027(1),X'01'           GN=029
      000B96   07 8F                          BCR    8,15

176   000B98            GN=030               EQU    *
      000B98   92 40 8 000                    MVI    000(8),X'40'           DNM=1-406
176   000B9C   D2 83 8 001 8 000              MVC    001(132,8),000(8)      DNM=1-406+1                   DNM=1-406
```

**Figure B.2** *Continued*

```
16      CLINK1                    16.56.08

        000BA2  58 10 D 208                L     1,208(0,13)          DTF=2
        000BA6  92 F1 8 000                MVI   000(8),X'F1'         DNM=1-406
        000BAA  58 F0 1 010                L     15,010(0,1)
        000BAE  45 E0 F 00C                BAL   14,00C(0,15)
                            GN=029         EQU   *
 179    000BB2  58 10 D 26C                L     1,26C(0,13)          VN=09
        000BB6  07 F1                      BCR   15,1

 181             000BB8     PN=010         EQU   *
        000BB8  92 40 8 000                MVI   000(8),X'40'         DNM=1-406
        000BBC  D2 83 8 001 8 000          MVC   001(132,8),000(8)    DNM=1-406+1
 182    000BC2  D2 1A 8 001 6 033          MVC   001(27,8),033(6)     DNM=2-169
        000BC8  92 40 8 01C                MVI   01C(8),X'40'         DNM=2-169+27
 183    000BCC  F2 74 D 210 6 000          PACK  210(8,13),000(5,6)   DNM=2-244
        000BD2  D2 05 D 218 C 0F5          MVC   218(6,13),0F5(12)    LIT+5
        000BD8  DE 05 D 218 D 215          ED    218(6,13),215(13)    TS=06
        000BDE  05 30                      BALR  3,0
        000BE0  47 70 3 00E                BC    7,00E(0,3)
        000BE4  92 40 D 219                MVI   219(13),X'40'        TS2=2
        000BE8  D2 03 D 21A D 219          MVC   21A(4,13),219(13)    TS2=2
        000BEE  D2 04 8 01D D 219          MVC   01D(5,8),219(13)     DNM=2-188
 184    000BF4  D2 05 8 022 6 04E          MVC   022(6,8),04E(6)      DNM=2-285
 185    000BFA  58 10 D 208                L     1,208(0,13)          DTF=2
        000BFE  92 F0 8 000                MVI   000(8),X'F0'         DNM=1-406
        000C02  58 F0 1 010                L     15,010(0,1)
        000C06  45 E0 F 00C                BAL   14,00C(0,15)
                            GN=031         EQU   *
        000C0A  58 10 D 270                L     1,270(0,13)          VN=010
        000C0E  07 F1                      BCR   15,1

                 000C10     PN=011         EQU   *
        000C10  0A 0E                      SVC   14
        000C12  50 D0 5 008         INIT2  ST    13,008(0,5)
        000C16  50 50 D 004                ST    5,004(0,13)
        000C1A  58 20 C 000                L     2,000(0,12)          VIR=1
        000C1E  95 00 2 000                CLI   000(2),X'00'
        000C22  07 79                      BCR   7,9
        000C24  92 FF 2 000                MVI   000(2),X'FF'
        000C28  96 10 D 048                OI    048(13),X'10'        SWT+0
        000C2C  50 E0 D 054                ST    14,054(0,13)
        000C30  05 F0                      BALR  15,0
        000C32  91 20 D 048         INIT3  TM    048(13),X'20'        SWT+0
        000C36  47 E0 F 016                BC    14,016(0,15)
        000C3A  58 00 B 048                L     0,048(0,11)
        000C3E  98 2D B 050                LM    2,13,050(11)
        000C46  07 FE                      BCR   15,14
        000C48  96 20 D 048                OI    048(13),X'20'        SWT+0
        000C4C  41 60 0 004                LA    6,004(0,0)           PN=01
        000C50  41 10 C 01C                LA    1,01C(0,12)          LIT+0
        000C54  41 70 C 0F0                LA    7,0F0(0,12)
        000C58  06 70                      BCTR  7,0
        000C5A  05 50                      BALR  5,0
```

```
17    CLINK1              16.56.08

000C5C  58 40  1 000           L     4,000(0,1)
000C60  1E 4B                  ALR   4,11
000C62  50 40  1 000           ST    4,000(0,1)
000C66  87 16  5 000           BXLE  1,6,000(5)            OVF=1
000C6A  41 80  D 1F4           LA    8,1F4(0,13)           TS=01-1
000C6E  41 70  D 20F           LA    7,20F(0,13)
000C72  05 10                  BALR  1,0
000C74  58 00  8 000           L     0,000(0,8)
000C78  1E 0B                  ALR   0,11
000C7A  50 00  8 000           ST    0,000(0,8)
000C7E  87 86  1 000           BXLE  8,6,000(1)
000C82  D2 27  D 24C  C OC8    MVC   24C(40,13),OC8(12)    VNI=1
000C88  58 60  D 1FC           L     6,1FC(0,13)           VN=01
000C8C  58 70  D 1F4           L     7,1F4(0,13)           BL =3
000C90  58 80  D 1F8           L     8,1F8(0,13)           BL =1
000C94  58 90  D 200           L     9,200(0,13)           BL =2
000C98  58 10  C 018           L     1,018(0,12)           BL =4
000C9C  58 F0  C 014           L     15,014(0,12)          VIR=7
000CA0  05 EF                  BALR  14,15                 VIR=6
000CA2  02OC                   DC    X'020C'
000CA4  0001                   DC    X'0001'
000CA6  58 E0  D 1B0           L     14,1B0(0,13)
000CAA  90 6D  E 060           STM   6,13,060(14)
000CAE  58 E0  D 054           L     14,054(0,13)
000CB2  07 FE                  BCR   15,14
000D00  05 F0          INIT1   BALR  15,0
000D02  07 00                  BCR   0,0
000D04  90 0E  F 00A           STM   0,14,00A(15)          VIR=1
000D08  47 F0  F 082           BC    15,082(0,15)
000D0C  00000000               DC    30F'0'
000D84  58 C0  F 0C6           L     12,0C6(0,15)
000D88  58 E0  C 000           L     14,000(0,12)
000D8C  58 D0  F 0CA           L     13,0CA(0,15)
000D90  95 00  E 000           CLI   000(14),X'00'
000D94  47 70  F 0A2           BC    7,0A2(0,15)
000D98  96 10  D 048           OI    048(13),X'10'         SWT=0
000D9C  92 FF  E 000           MVI   000(14),X'FF'
000DA0  47 F0  F 0AC           BC    15,0AC(0,15)
000DA4  98 CE  F 03A           LM    12,14,03A(15)
000DA8  90 EC  D 00C           STM   14,12,00C(13)
000DAC  18 5D                  LR    5,13
000DAE  98 9F  F 0BA           LM    9,15,0BA(15)
000DB2  91 10  D 048           TM    048(13),X'10'         SWT=0
000DB6  07 19                  BCR   1,9
000DB8  07 FF                  BCR   15,15
000DBA  07 00                  BCR   0,0
000DBC  00000C2C               ADCON L4(INIT3)
000DC0  00000000               ADCON L4(INIT1)
000DC4  00000000               ADCON L4(INIT1)
000DC8  000005C8               ADCON L4(PGT)
000DCC  00000348               ADCON L4(TGT)
000DD0  000006D8               ADCON L4(START)
000DD4  00000C12               ADCON L4(INIT2)
000DD8  C3D6C2C6F2F5F5F3       DC    X'C3D6C2C6F2F5F5F3'
000DE0  C3D3C9D5D2F14040       DC    X'C3D3C9D5D2F14040'
000DE8  00000000               DC    X'00000000'
000DEC  F0F461F2F361F8F3       DC    X'F0F461F2F361F8F3'
```

Figure B.2  *Continued*

```
 18       CLINK1        16.56.08


OOOOF4  F1F64BF5F64BFOF8          DC    X'F1F64BF5F64BFOF8'


*STATISTICS*          SOURCE RECORDS =  185      DATA ITEMS =  43      PROC DIV SZ =   87
*STATISTICS*          PARTITION SIZE = 524168    LINE COUNT =  60      BUFFER SIZE =  512
*OPTIONS IN EFFECT*   PMAP RELOC ADR = NONE      SPACING    =          FLOW          NONE
*OPTIONS IN EFFECT*   LISTX     APOST            SYM   NOCATALR   LIST     LINK   NDSTXIT   NOLIB
*OPTIONS IN EFFECT*   NOCLIST   FLAGW            ZWB   NOSUPMAP   NOXREF   ERRS   SXREF     NOOPT
*OPTIONS IN EFFECT*   NOSTATE   TRUNC            SEQ   NOSYMDMP   NODECK   NOVERB  NDSYNTAX  NOLVL
*OPTIONS IN EFFECT*   NOCOUNT                          NOVERBSUM  NOVERBREF
*LISTER OPTIONS*      NONE
```

19   CLINK1   16.56.08

## CROSS-REFERENCE DICTIONARY

| DATA NAMES | DEFN | REFERENCE |
|---|---|---|
| BD-DATA | 000059 | 000147 |
| BD-YEAR | 000060 | 000161 |
| C-CONTENT | 000043 | 000137 000151 000165 |
| C-CONTNT | 000044 | 000138 000152 000166 |
| CODE1 | 000075 | 000108 000113 000114 000115 000116 000138 000152 000166 |
| CODE1-CONT | 000064 | 000137 000151 000165 |
| COMMENT | 000038 | 000132 000133 000147 000161 |
| DATE-IN | 000025 | |
| EOF | 000080 | 000089 000116 000119 |
| FILE-EOF-SWITCH | 000079 | 000102 |
| HDG | 000053 | 000124 |
| HEAD-IS-NEEDED | 000082 | 000112 |
| HEADING-SWITCH | 000081 | 000126 |
| IS-LEAP | 000062 | 000132 |
| IS-NOT-LEAP | 000061 | 000133 |
| L | 000076 | 000108 000132 000135 000149 000163 |
| L-CONT | 000063 | 000134 000148 000162 |
| L-CONTENT | 000040 | 000134 000148 000162 |
| L-CONTNT | 000041 | 000135 000149 000163 |
| LIST | 000017 | 000088 000091 000125 000176 000185 |
| LIST-LINE | 000033 | 000123 000125 000130 000139 000140 000145 000153 000154 000159 000167 000168 000173 000174 000175 000176 000181 000185 |
| PRINT-LINE | 000035 | 000124 |
| PUNCT | 000058 | 000136 000150 000164 |
| PUNCTU | 000042 | 000136 000150 000164 |
| SKIP-CTL | 000034 | |
| SUB-ERROR | 000065 | 000174 |
| SWITCHES | 000078 | |
| T-COMMENT | 000047 | 000182 |
| T-TOT | 000048 | 000183 |
| TEST-YEAR | 000026 | 000106 |
| TESTFIL | 000013 | 000087 000090 000102 |
| TOT | 000052 | 000107 000183 |
| TOT-LINE | 000046 | 000182 |
| TOTAL | 000055 | 000184 |
| W-COMNT | 000049 | 000184 |
| WORD | 000057 | 000106 000108 000131 000146 000160 |
| YEAR | 000074 | 000131 000146 000160 |
| YEAR-0 | 000036 | 000131 000160 |

**Figure B.2** *Continued*

```
20        CLINK1           16.56.08

PROCEDURE NAMES                        DEFN      REFERENCE

000-PRODUCE-LEAP-YEAR-LISTING          000085
100-PRODUCE-LEAP-YEAR-LINE             000094    000089
110-READ-YEAR                          000100    000096
120-LEAP-YEAR-ALGORITHM                000104    000097
130-PRINT-RESULT                       000110    000098
140-HEAD-LINE                          000121    000112
150-LIST-RESULT                        000128    000113
160-BAD-DATA                           000143    000114
170-BAD-YEAR                           000157    000115
180-SUBROUTINE-ERROR                   000171    000118
190-TOTAL-LINE                         000179    000119


21        CLINK1           16.56.08

CARD    ERROR MESSAGE

00102   ILA4072I-W    EXIT FROM PERFORMED PROCEDURE ASSUMED BEFORE PROCEDURE-NAME .
00119   ILA4072I-W    EXIT FROM PERFORMED PROCEDURE ASSUMED BEFORE PROCEDURE-NAME .
00140   ILA4072I-W    EXIT FROM PERFORMED PROCEDURE ASSUMED BEFORE PROCEDURE-NAME .
00154   ILA4072I-W    EXIT FROM PERFORMED PROCEDURE ASSUMED BEFORE PROCEDURE-NAME .
00168   ILA4072I-W    EXIT FROM PERFORMED PROCEDURE ASSUMED BEFORE PROCEDURE-NAME .
00176   ILA4072I-W    EXIT FROM PERFORMED PROCEDURE ASSUMED BEFORE PROCEDURE-NAME .


END OF COMPILATION
```

Figure B.2 *Continued*

```
TEST OF TC1000-  TO DETERMINE LEAP YEAR STATUS
1700  IS NOT A LEAP YEAR  L CONTENTS: 0.  CODE1  CONTENTS: 0
1800  IS NOT A LEAP YEAR  L CONTENTS: 0.  CODE1  CONTENTS: 0
1900  IS NOT A LEAP YEAR  L CONTENTS: 0.  CODE1  CONTENTS: 0
2000  IS A LEAP YEAR      L CONTENTS: 1.  CODE1  CONTENTS: 0
2100  IS NOT A LEAP YEAR  L CONTENTS: 0.  CODE1  CONTENTS: 0
2200  IS NOT A LEAP YEAR  L CONTENTS: 0.  CODE1  CONTENTS: 0
2300  IS NOT A LEAP YEAR  L CONTENTS: 0.  CODE1  CONTENTS: 0
2400  IS A LEAP YEAR      L CONTENTS: 1.  CODE1  CONTENTS: 0
2500  IS NOT A LEAP YEAR  L CONTENTS: 0.  CODE1  CONTENTS: 0
2600  IS NOT A LEAP YEAR  L CONTENTS: 0.  CODE1  CONTENTS: 0
2700  IS NOT A LEAP YEAR  L CONTENTS: 0.  CODE1  CONTENTS: 0
2800  IS A LEAP YEAR      L CONTENTS: 1.  CODE1  CONTENTS: 0
2900  IS NOT A LEAP YEAR  L CONTENTS: 0.  CODE1  CONTENTS: 0
3000  IS NOT A LEAP YEAR  L CONTENTS: 0.  CODE1  CONTENTS: 0
3100  IS NOT A LEAP YEAR  L CONTENTS: 0.  CODE1  CONTENTS: 0
3200  IS A LEAP YEAR      L CONTENTS: 1.  CODE1  CONTENTS: 0
3300  IS NOT A LEAP YEAR  L CONTENTS: 0.  CODE1  CONTENTS: 0
3399  IS NOT A LEAP YEAR  L CONTENTS: 0.  CODE1  CONTENTS: 0
1601  IS NOT A LEAP YEAR  L CONTENTS: 0.  CODE1  CONTENTS: 0
1602  IS NOT A LEAP YEAR  L CONTENTS: 0.  CODE1  CONTENTS: 0
1603  IS NOT A LEAP YEAR  L CONTENTS: 0.  CODE1  CONTENTS: 0
1604  IS A LEAP YEAR      L CONTENTS: 1.  CODE1  CONTENTS: 0
1605  IS NOT A LEAP YEAR  L CONTENTS: 0.  CODE1  CONTENTS: 0
1606  IS NOT A LEAP YEAR  L CONTENTS: 0.  CODE1  CONTENTS: 0
1607  IS NOT A LEAP YEAR  L CONTENTS: 0.  CODE1  CONTENTS: 0
1608  IS A LEAP YEAR      L CONTENTS: 1.  CODE1  CONTENTS: 0
1801  IS NOT A LEAP YEAR  L CONTENTS: 0.  CODE1  CONTENTS: 0
1702  IS NOT A LEAP YEAR  L CONTENTS: 0.  CODE1  CONTENTS: 0
1603  IS NOT A LEAP YEAR  L CONTENTS: 0.  CODE1  CONTENTS: 0
1904  IS A LEAP YEAR      L CONTENTS: 1.  CODE1  CONTENTS: 0
2105  IS NOT A LEAP YEAR  L CONTENTS: 0.  CODE1  CONTENTS: 0
2706  IS NOT A LEAP YEAR  L CONTENTS: 0.  CODE1  CONTENTS: 0
3117  IS NOT A LEAP YEAR  L CONTENTS: 0.  CODE1  CONTENTS: 0
3308  IS A LEAP YEAR      L CONTENTS: 1.  CODE1  CONTENTS: 0
1644  IS A LEAP YEAR      L CONTENTS: 1.  CODE1  CONTENTS: 0
1789  IS NOT A LEAP YEAR  L CONTENTS: 0.  CODE1  CONTENTS: 0
1984  IS A LEAP YEAR      L CONTENTS: 1.  CODE1  CONTENTS: 0
2201  IS NOT A LEAP YEAR  L CONTENTS: 0.  CODE1  CONTENTS: 0
2034  IS NOT A LEAP YEAR  L CONTENTS: 0.  CODE1  CONTENTS: 0
1600  * INVALID YEAR      L CONTENTS: 9.  CODE1  CONTENTS: 4
3400  * INVALID YEAR      L CONTENTS: 9.  CODE1  CONTENTS: 4
   0  * INVALID YEAR      L CONTENTS: 9.  CODE1  CONTENTS: 2
 19  0  * INVALID DATA     L CONTENTS: 9.  CODE1  CONTENTS: 2
 950  * INVALID DATA      L CONTENTS: 9.  CODE1  CONTENTS: 2
 950  * INVALID DATA      L CONTENTS: 9.  CODE1  CONTENTS: 2

THE SUBROUTINE WAS EXECUTED    45 TIMES
```

**Figure B.3**  Test results from the execution of CLINK1.

```
// JOB ASSEM
OPTION DECK,XREF
// DLBL IJSYSPH,'IN',0
// EXTENT SYSPH,(VOL),1,0,(BEG.BLOCK),(NO.BLOCKS)
ASSGN SYSPCH,FBA,VOL=(VOL),SHR
// EXEC ASSEMBLY,SIZE=96K
PUNCH ' CATALR TC1000    ,

*****    SOURCE ALC STATEMENTS FOR THE COBOL LINKAGE  GO HERE    *******
*  /*

CLOSE SYSPCH,X'(POWERDEVICECUU)'
// DLBL IJSYSIN,'IN',0
// EXTENT SYSIPT,(VOL),1,0,(BEG.BLOCK),(NO.BLOCKS)
ASSGN SYSIPT,FBA,VOL=(VOL),SHR
// DLBL (RELOLIBNAME),'(RELO.LIB.LABEL)'
// EXTENT ,(VOL),1,0
// LIBDEF RL,TO=(RELOLIBNAME)
// EXEC MAINT
*  /*
CLOSE SYSIPT,X'(POWERDUMMYDEVICECUU)'
*  /&
// JOB COBOL
DLBL (CORELIBNAME),'(CORE.LIB.LABEL)'
// EXTENT ,(VOL),1,0
// LIBDEF CL,TO=(CORELIBNAME)
OPTION NOLOG,XREF,CATAL,LISTX,NODECK
PHASE CLINK1,S
// EXEC FCOBOL,SIZE=512K

****  SOURCE COBOL STATEMENTS FOR THE CALLING PROGRAM GO HERE ****
*  /*

// EXEC LNKEDT
ASSGN SYSO10,SYSLST
ASSGN SYSO07,CUU   (OF DISK FILE)
DLBL (CORELIBNAME),'(CORE.LIB.LABEL)'
// EXTENT ,(VOL),1,0
// LIBDEF CL,FROM=(CORELIBNAME)
// DLBL IJSYSUC,'(JOB.CAT.LABEL)',,VSAM
// EXTENT SYSO07,(VOL),1,0,(BEG.BLOCK),(NO.BLOCKS)
// DLBL TESTFIL,'(FILE.LABEL)',,VSAM
// EXTENT SYSO07,(VOL)
// EXEC CLINK1,SIZE=AUTO
*  /&
```

**Figure B.4** A job stream used to assemble and catalog TC1000, and subsequently compile, link-edit, and execute CLINK1.

```
                    EXTERNAL SYMBOL DICTIONARY


SYMBOL    TYPE          ID  ADDR    LENGTH  LD-ID

TR1000    SD (CSECT)    001 000000  00026F
L         LD (ENTRY)        0000DE          001
CODE1     LD (ENTRY)        0000DF          001
YEAR      LD (ENTRY)        0000E0          001
```

**Figure B.5** The assembly post listing of the relocatable module TR1000, featuring the linkage required for its incorporation in a calling RPG program.

DOS/VSE ASSEMBLER 16.57    99-12-31

```
LOC     OBJECT CODE   ADDR1 ADDR2   STMT   SOURCE STATEMENT

                                       1            PUNCH ' CATALR TR1000 '                                    TR100010
                                       2            PRINT NOGEN                                                TR100020
000000                                 3    TR1000  CSECT                                                     TR100030
                                       4    *                                                                 TR100040
                                       5    * *******************************************************         TR100050
                                       6    *                                                                 TR100060
                                       7    *   TTTTTTT    RRRR      11                                        TR100070
                                       8    *      T      R    R      1                                        TR100080
                                       9    *      T      RRRR        1                                        TR100090
                                      10    *      T      R   R       1                                        TR100100
                                      11    *      T      R    R     111                                       TR100110
                                      12    *                                                                 TR100120
                                      13    * *******************************************************         TR100130
                                      14    * ********   L E A P   Y E A R   S U B P R O G R A M   ********    TR100140
                                      15    * *******************************************************         TR100150
                                      16    *                                                                 TR100160
                                      17    *                                                                 TR100170
                                      18    *       THIS SUBPROGRAM IDENTIFIES GREGORIAN LEAP YEARS           TR100180
                                      19    *                                                                 TR100190
                                      20    *                                                                 TR100200
                                      21    *  1.  THIS SUBPROGRAM USES THE MACRO EQUIVALENT OF THE TIMESUB1  TR100210
                                      22    *      SUBROUTINE AND IS SEPARATELY ASSEMBLED ALLOWING IT TO BE   TR100220
                                      23    *      CALLED BY AN RPG PROGRAM.  THE NECESSARY LINKAGE IS        TR100230
                                      24    *      DESCRIBED IN THIS DOCUMENTATION SECTION AND HIGHLIGHTED    TR100240
                                      25    *      IN THE ENSUING CODE.                                       TR100250
                                      26    *                                                                 TR100260
                                      27    *  2.  THE CALLING RPG PROGRAM MUST PLACE A FOUR DIGIT YEAR       TR100270
                                      28    *      IN A FOUR BYTE ALPHAMERIC FIELD 'YEAR.' YEAR IS DEFINED    TR100280
                                      29    *      BY THE SUBPROGRAM BUT ALSO MUST APPEAR AS THE OPERAND OF   TR100290
                                      30    *      THE RPG 'ULABL' OPERATION CODE IN THE CALLING PROGRAM.     TR100300
                                      31    *                                                                 TR100310
                                      32    *  3.  THE CALLING RPG PROGRAM MUST CONTAIN THE FIELD 'CODE1'     TR100320
                                      33    *      AS THE OPERAND OF THE RPG 'ULABL' OPERATION CODE. CODE1    TR100330
                                      34    *      IS A ONE BYTE PACKED NUMERIC FIELD ALSO IN THE SUB-        TR100340
                                      35    *      PROGRAM.  CODE1 FUNCTIONS AS A RETURN CODE WHOSE CONTENTS  TR100350
                                      36    *      ARE DESCRIBED IN THE TIMESUB1 SUBROUTINE'S DOCUMENTATION.  TR100360
                                      37    *                                                                 TR100370
                                      38    *  5.  THE CALLING RPG PROGRAM MUST CONTAIN THE FIELD 'L' AS      TR100380
                                      39    *      THE OPERAND OF THE RPG 'ULABL' OPERATION CODE. L IS A      TR100390
                                      40    *      ONE BYTE PACKED NUMERIC FIELD ALSO IN THE SUBPROGRAM.      TR100400
                                      41    *      THE CONTENTS OF THIS FIELD ARE DESCRIBED IN THE TIMESUB1   TR100410
                                      42    *      DOCUMENTATION.                                             TR100420
                                      43    *                                                                 TR100430
                                      44    *  7.  ** NOTE: REGARDING LINKAGE CONVENTIONS:                    TR100440
                                      45    *                                                                 TR100450
                                      46    *      REGISTER 13                                                TR100460
                                      47    *      PRIOR TO BRANCHING TO A CALLED SUBPROGRAM, RPG II LOADS    TR100470
                                      48    *      REGISTER 13 WITH THE ADDRESS OF A REGISTER SAVE AREA       TR100480
                                      49    *      GENERATED BY THE RPG COMPILER. THIS REGISTER SAVE AREA     TR100490
                                      50    *      IS AVAILABLE FOR USE BY THE CALLED SUBPROGRAM VIA THE      TR100500
                                      51    *      ADDRESS MADE AVAILABLE IN REGISTER 13.                     TR100510
                                      52    *                                                                 TR100520
                                      53    *      REGISTER 14                                                TR100530
                                      54    *      PRIOR TO BRANCHING TO A CALLED SUBPROGRAM, RPG II LOADS
                                      55    *      REGISTER 14 WITH THE ADDRESS OF THE NEXT SEQUENTIALLY
```

```
LOC    OBJECT CODE   ADDR1 ADDR2  STMT   SOURCE STATEMENT                                    DOS/VSE ASSEMBLER 16.57  99-12-31

                                   56 *   EXECUTABLE INSTRUCTION FOLLOWING THE EXIT TO THE SUB-        TR100540
                                   57 *   PROGRAM.                                                     TR100550
                                   58 *                                                                TR100560
                                   59 *   REGISTER 15                                                  TR100570
                                   60 *   PRIOR TO BRANCHING TO A CALLED SUBPROGRAM, RPG II LOADS      TR100580
                                   61 *   REGISTER 15 WITH THE ADDRESS OF THE ENTRY POINT OF THE       TR100590
                                   62 *   CALLED SUBPROGRAM.  REGISTER 15 THEN BECOMES AN OPERAND      TR100600
                                   63 *   OF THE BALR INSTRUCTION THAT INITIATES THE TRANSFER OF       TR100610
                                   64 *   CONTROL TO THE SUBPROGRAM.                                   TR100620
                                   65 *                                                                TR100630
                                   66 *   THE ENTRY LINKAGE CONVENTIONS AS WELL AS THE BRIEF EXIT      TR100640
                                   67 *   LINKAGE CONVENTIONS ARE DOCUMENTED IN THE CODE BELOW.        TR100650
                                   68 *                                                                TR100660
                                   69 *                                        JEROME T. MURRAY        TR100670
                                   70 *                                        MARILYN J. MURRAY       TR100680
                                   71 *   GLEN ELLYN, ILLINOIS                                         TR100690
                                   72 *                                                                TR100700
                                   73 *   ***********************  THIS IS THE ENTRY LINKAGE SECTION  ***********************  TR100710
                                   74 *   ***************************************************************                     TR100720
                                   75                                                                  TR100730
                                   76                                                                  TR100740
                                   77                                                                  TR100750
                                   78 *   THE SUBPRGRAM'S ID, TR1000, APPEARS AT THE TOP OF THE        TR100760
                                   79 *   DOCUMENTATION WHERE IT FUNCTIONS AS A CONTROL SECTION        TR100770
                                   80 *   LABEL.                                                       TR100780
                                   81 *   REGISTER 15 IS ASSIGNED AS A BASE REGISTER VIA 'USING':      TR100790
                                   82 *                                                                TR100800
00000                              84       USING  *,15                                               TR100810
                                   85 *                                                                TR100820
                                   86 *   THE REGISTER INFORMATION FROM THE RPG PROGRAM IS NOW SAVED   TR100830
                                   87 *   AS NOTED BELOW:                                              TR100840
                                   88 *                                                                TR100850
                                   89 *                                                                TR100860
                                   90 *                                                                TR100870
                                   91       SAVE  (14,12)     RPG REGISTERS  14, 15, AND 0, 1,....12,  TR100880
                                   94 *                       ARE STORED IN THE SAVE AREA DEFINED      TR100890
                                   95 *                       BY THE RPG II COMPILER.  THE ADDRESS     TR100900
                                   96 *                       OF THE RPG DEFINED SAVE AREA IS PASSED   TR100910
                                   97 *                       TO THE SUBPROGRAM IN REGISTER 13 WHICH   TR100920
                                   98 *                       IS USED BY THE SAVE MACRO IN ADDRESS-    TR100930
                                   99 *                       ING THE SAVE AREA WHEN STORING THE       TR100940
                                  100 *                       REGISTERS.                               TR100950
                                  101 *                                                                TR100960
000004 5000 F21C        0021C     102       ST   13,#$1REGS+4  THE ADDRESS OF THE RPG GENERATED SAVE  TR100970
                                  103 *                       AREA MUST NOW BE SAVED BY THE SUB-       TR100980
                                  104 *                       PROGRAM IN ITS REGISTER SAVE AREA.       TR100990
                                  105 *                                                                TR101000
000008 18CD                       106       LR   12,13        LOAD THE ADDRESS OF THE RPG GENERATED   TR101010
                                  107 *                       SAVE AREA FROM REGISTER 13 TO REGISTER   TR101020
                                  108 *                       12 FOR LATER USE IN STORING THE ADD-     TR101030
                                  109 *                       RESS OF THE SUBPROGRAM DEFINED SAVE      TR101040
                                  110 *                       AREA IN THE RPG GENERATED SAVE AREA.     TR101050
                                  111 *                       THUS, THE SUBPROGRAM AND CALLING         TR101060
                                  112 *                       PROGRAM WILL HAVE MUTUAL ACCESS.         TR101070
                                                                                                       TR101080
```

**Figure B.5** *Continued*

```
                                                        DOS/VSE ASSEMBLER  16.57  99-12-31

LOC     OBJECT CODE   ADDR1 ADDR2  STMT   SOURCE STATEMENT

                                    113  *                                                                   TR101090
00000A  41D0 F218           00218   114        LA    13,#$1REGS    THE ADDRESS OF THE SUBPROGRAM DEFINED  *  TR101100
                                    115  *                         SAVE AREA IS LOADED TO REGISTER 13.    *  TR101110
                                    116  *                                                                *  TR101120
00000E  50DC 0008           00008   117        ST    13,8(12)      NOW REGISTER 12 IS USED TO STORE THE   *  TR101130
                                    118  *                         ADDRESS OF THE SUBPROGRAM DEFINED      *  TR101140
                                    119  *                         SAVE AREA IN THE RPG GENERATED SAVE    *  TR101150
                                    120  *                         AREA.                                  *  TR101160
                                    121  *                                                                *  TR101170
                                    122        ENTRY YEAR          THIS ENTRY ALLOWS YEAR TO BE ADDRESSED *  TR101180
                                    123  *                         SYMBOLICALLY IN THE SUBPROGRAM.        *  TR101190
                                    124  *                                                                *  TR101200
                                    125        ENTRY CODE1         THIS ENTRY ALLOWS CODE1 TO BE ADDRESSED*  TR101210
                                    126  *                         SYMBOLICALLY IN THE SUBPROGRAM.        *  TR101220
                                    127  *                                                                *  TR101230
                                    128        ENTRY L             THIS ENTRY ALLOWS L TO BE ADDRESSED    *  TR101240
                                    129  *                         SYMBOLICALLY IN THE SUBPROGRAM.        *  TR101250
                                    130  *                                                                *  TR101260
                                    131  *                                                                *  TR101270
                                    132  ****************************************************************  *  TR101280
                                    133  *****    END OF THE ENTRY LINKAGE SECTION    *****               *  TR101290
                                    134  ****************************************************************  *  TR101300
                                    135  *                                                                *  TR101310
                                    136  *                                                                *  TR101320
                                    137  *              MACRO STATEMENT:                                  *  TR101330
                                    138  *                                                                *  TR101340
                                    139        TIME1                                                         TR101350
                                    191  *                                                                *  TR101360
                                    192  ****************************************************************  *  TR101370
                                    193  *********  THIS IS THE EXIT LINKAGE SECTION  *****************   *  TR101380
                                    194  ****************************************************************  *  TR101390
                                    195  *                                                                *  TR101400
0002OA  58D0 F21C           0021C   196        L     13,#$1REGS+4  THE ADDRESS OF THE RPG CALLING PROGRAM'S SAVE AREA IS LOADED  TR101410
                                    197  *                         TO REGISTER 13                            TR101420
                                    198  *                                                                *  TR101430
                                    199        RETURN (14,12)      RETURN RESTORES THE REGISTERS AND RETURNS CONTROL TO THE  TR101440
                                    200  *                         CALLING PROGRAM                           TR101450
                                    201  *                                                                *  TR101460
                                    202  *                                                                   TR101470
                                    203  *                                                                   TR101480
                                    204        RETURN (14,12)                                                 TR101490
                                    208  *                         HERE THE REGISTER SAVE AREA STORAGE IS DEFINED  TR101500
                                    209  *                         FOR THE REQUIRED 18 FULL WORDS (72 BYTES)      TR101510
                                    210  *                                                                   TR101520
                                    211  *                                                                   TR101530
000218                              212  #$1REGS DS   0D                                                      TR101540
000218                              213        DS    18F                                                      TR101550
                                    214  *                                                                *  TR101560
                                    215  ****************************************************************  *  TR101570
                                    216  *****    END OF THE EXIT LINKAGE SECTION    *****                *  TR101580
                                    217  ****************************************************************  *  TR101590
                                    218  *                                                                *  TR101600
00000                               219        END   TR1000                                                   TR101610
000260  100C                        220              =P'100'
000262  400C                        221              =P'400'
```

DOS/VSE ASSEMBLER 16.57 99-12-31

```
LOC    OBJECT CODE   ADDR1 ADDR2   STMT   SOURCE STATEMENT

000264 0C                            222              =P'0'
000265 9C                            223              =P'9'
000266 2C                            224              =P'2'
000267 01600C                        225              =P'1600'
00026A 4C                            226              =P'4'
00026B 03399C                        227              =P'3399'
00026E 1C                            228              =P'1'
```

99-12-31

CROSS-REFERENCE

| SYMBOL   | LEN   | ID  | VALUE  | DEFN  | REFERENCES |
|----------|-------|-----|--------|-------|------------|
| #$1BADYR | 00006 | 001 | 000078 | 00159 | 0162 |
| #$1BDATA | 00006 | 001 | 00005E | 00154 | 0150 |
| #$1LPYR  | 00006 | 001 | 0000D4 | 00176 | 0171 |
| #$1NUM   | 00006 | 001 | 00004E | 00151 | 0149 |
| #$1PACK  | 00006 | 001 | 000068 | 00156 | 0153 |
| #$1REGS  | 00004 | 001 | 000218 | 00213 | 0102 0114 0199 |
| #$1RSAVE | 00004 | 001 | 0001F8 | 00188 | 0142 0190 |
| #$1SIGN  | 00001 | 001 | 0001EE | 00185 | 0148 |
| #$1TABL  | 00001 | 001 | 0000E4 | 00181 | 0145 0146 0147 0148 0151 0151 0152 |
| #$1TERM  | 00004 | 001 | 000206 | 00190 | 0155 0160 0167 0175 0177 |
| #$1WORK  | 00005 | 001 | 000200 | 00189 | 0164 0165 0166 0168 0169 0170 0172 0173 0174 |
| #$1WORK4 | 00004 | 001 | 0001EF | 00186 | 0143 0144 0152 0161 0164 0168 0172 |
| #$1YR    | 00003 | 001 | 0001F3 | 00187 | 0156 0157 |
| #$1YRHI  | 00006 | 001 | 000082 | 00161 | 0158 |
| #$1ZRO   | 00001 | 001 | 0001E4 | 00184 | 0145 0146 0147 0154 0159 |
| CODE1    | 00001 | 001 | 0000DF | 00179 | 0125 0140 0154 0163 0176 |
| L        | 00001 | 001 | 0000DE | 00178 | 0128 0141 0163 |
| TR1000   | 00001 | 001 | 000000 | 00003 | 0219 |
| YEAR     | 00004 | 001 | 0000E0 | 00180 | 0122 0143 0156 |
| =P'0'    | 00001 | 001 | 000264 | 00222 | 0140 0163 0166 0170 0174 |
| =P'1'    | 00001 | 001 | 00026E | 00228 | 0176 |
| =P'100'  | 00002 | 001 | 000260 | 00220 | 0169 |
| =P'1600' | 00003 | 001 | 000267 | 00225 | 0157 |
| =P'2'    | 00001 | 001 | 000266 | 00224 | 0154 |
| =P'3399' | 00003 | 001 | 00026B | 00227 | 0161 |
| =P'4'    | 00001 | 001 | 00026A | 00226 | 0159 0165 |
| =P'400'  | 00002 | 001 | 000262 | 00221 | 0173 |
| =P'9'    | 00001 | 001 | 000265 | 00223 | 0141 |

**Figure B.5** *Continued*

99-12-31

DIAGNOSTICS AND STATISTICS

NO ERRORS FOUND

THE FOLLOWING MACRO NAMES HAVE BEEN FOUND IN MACRO INSTRUCTIONS
     SAVE    TIME1    RETURN

OPTIONS FOR THIS ASSEMBLY - ALIGN, LIST, XREF, NOLINK, RLD, DECK, NOEDECK

THE ASSEMBLER WAS RUN IN 98184 BYTES
END OF ASSEMBLY

**Figure B.5** *Continued*

DOS/VS RPGII          JOB - COMPC                                    CL 3-0  + PTF302

     OO-O1O  H                                                     RLINK1

RPG HEADER OPTIONS

     POSITION     FUNCTION                     OPTION          ENTRY

        15        DEBUG                        NO

        21        INVERTED PRINT               STD

        26        ALTERNATE COLLATING SEQ.     NONE

        40        FORCE SIGN                   BOTH

        41        1P FORM ALIGNMENT            NO

        42        INDICATOR SETTING            NO

        43        FILE TRANSLATION             NO

        50        FORMAT DUMP                  YES

        51        CONVERSION NOTES             NO

        55        MAIN/SUB PROGRAM             MAIN

      75 - 80     PROGRAM NAME                 RLINK1

     COMPILER OPTIONS ARE - LIST, NODECK,  LINK,   ERRS. NOTERM - PARTITION SIZE IS  OOO96K      DISK

**Figure B.6**  The complete compile post listing of RLINK1, the calling RPG program.

```
DOS/VS RPGII            JOB - COMPC                          PROGRAM - RLINK1

0001  00-020  F* *********************************************************    RLINK1
0002  00-030  F*                                                         *    RLINK1
0003  00-040  F*                       RLINK1                            *    RLINK1
0004  00-050  F*    THIS RPG PROGRAM AND ITS ACCOMPANYING ALC SUBPROGRAM *    RLINK1
0005  00-060  F*    DEMONSTRATE THE DOS LINKAGE CONVENTIONS FOR AN ALC SUB-    RLINK1
0006  00-070  F*    PROGRAM CALLED BY AN RPG II PROGRAM.                 *    RLINK1
0007  00-080  F*                                                         *    RLINK1
0008  00-090  F*    THE ALC SUBPROGRAM IS SEPARATELY ASSEMBLED AND CATALOGED  RLINK1
0009  00-100  F*    TO THE APPROPRIATE RELOCATABLE LIBRARY. (RPG IS GENERALLY RLINK1
0010  00-110  F*    CONFINED TO DOS SUPPORTED SYSTEMS. HENCE, THE RELO LIB.)  RLINK1
0011  00-120  F*                                                         *    RLINK1
0012  00-130  F*    THIS RPG PROGRAM EMPLOYS THE 'EXIT,' AND 'ULABL' OPERATION RLINK1
0013  00-140  F*    CODES OF RPG II TO TRANSFER CONTROL TO THE ALC SUBPROGRAM  RLINK1
0014  00-150  F*    AND TO MAKE SPECIFIC FIELDS AVAILABLE TO BOTH THE SUB-     RLINK1
0015  00-160  F*    PROGRAM AND THE CALLING PROGRAM.                     *    RLINK1
0016  00-170  F*                                                         *    RLINK1
0017  00-180  F*    THE ALC SUBPROGRAM EXECUTES THE LINKAGE REQUIREMENTS TO    RLINK1
0018  00-190  F*    ASSURE REGISTER CONTENTS AND RETURN OF CONTROL TO THE RPG  RLINK1
0019  00-200  F*    PROGRAM UPON COMPLETION OF THE ALC PROCESSING.       *    RLINK1
0020  00-210  F*                                                         *    RLINK1
0021  00-220  F* *********************************************************    RLINK1
      00-230  F*                                                              RLINK1
0002  00-240  FTESTFIL IPE  F   80           OF      ESDS                     RLINK1
0003  00-250  FLIST    O    F  132           OF      PRINTERSYSLST            RLINK1
0004  00-260  ITESTFIL NS   01                                               RLINK1
0005  00-270  I                                        1   4 TSTYR           RLINK1
0006  00-280  C                    SETOF                      020304         RLINK1
0007  00-290  C   01       TOT     SETOF                      0506           RLINK1
0008  00-300  C   01               ADD  1     TOT          50                RLINK1
0009  00-310  C                    MOVE TSTYR  YEAR                          RLINK1
0010  00-320  C                    EXIT TR1000                               RLINK1
0011  00-330  C                    ULABL       YEAR     4                    RLINK1
0012  00-340  C                    ULABL       CODE1   10                    RLINK1
0013  00-350  C   01       CODE1   COMP 2                 L    02            RLINK1
0014  00-360  C   NO2      CODE1   COMP 4                      03            RLINK1
0015  00-370  C   NO2NO3   CODE1   COMP 0                      04            RLINK1
0016  00-380  C   04       L       COMP 0                      05            RLINK1
0017  00-390  C   04NO5  L L       COMP 1                      06            RLINK1
0018  00-400  OLIST   H 3101            1P                                   RLINK1
0019  00-420  O                              24 'TEST OF TR1000- TO DETE'    RLINK1
0020  00-430  O                              46 'RMINE LEAP YEAR STATUS'     RLINK1
0021  00-440  O       H 3101       OF                                        RLINK1
0022  00-450  O                              04 ' '                          RLINK1
0023  00-460  O       D 01                                                   RLINK1
0024  00-470  O                    YEAR                                      RLINK1
0025  00-480  O                              04 '* INVALID DATA'             RLINK1
0026  00-490  O                              19 '* INVALID YEAR'             RLINK1
0027  00-500  O                              23 'IS NOT A LEAP YEAR'         RLINK1
0028  00-510  O                              19 'IS A LEAP YEAR'             RLINK1
0029  00-520  O                              41 'CODE1 CONTENTS'             RLINK1
0030  00-530  O               CODE1 X        44                             RLINK1
0031  00-540  O                              58 'L CONTENTS'                 RLINK1
0032  00-550  O               L     X        60                             RLINK1
0033  00-560  O       T 11                   24 'THE SUBPROGRAM WAS EXECU'   RLINK1
0034  00-570  O                              39 'TED              TIMES'     RLINK1
0035  00-580  O                                                             RLINK1
```

```
DOS/VS RPGII          JOB - COMPC              PROGRAM - RLINK1

0036                              TOT   1   33

         00-590  O                                                          RLINK1
         00-600  O*                                                         RLINK1
         00-610  O************************************************          RLINK1
         00-620  O*                                                         RLINK1
         00-630  O*                           JEROME T. MURRAY  *           RLINK1
         00-640  O*                           MARILYN J. MURRAY *           RLINK1
         00-650  O*        GLEN ELLYN, ILLINOIS                             RLINK1
         00-660  O************************************************          RLINK1
         00-670  O*                                                         RLINK1
```

E N D   O F   S O U R C E


```
DOS/VS RPGII          JOB - COMPC              PROGRAM - RLINK1
```

T A B L E S   A N D   M A P S

RESULTING INDICATOR TABLE

| OFFSET | RI | OFFSET | RI | OFFSET | RI | OFFSET | RI | OFFSET | RI | OFFSET | RI | OFFSET | RI |
|--------|----|--------|----|--------|----|--------|----|--------|----|--------|----|--------|----|
| 0508 | OF | 0525 | LR | 0526 | HO | 0531 | 1P | 0534 | 01 | 0535 | 02 | 0536 | 03 |
| 0537 | 04 | 0538 | 05 | 0539 | 06 | | | | | | | | |

OFFSETS OF VARIABLE NAMES AND CONSTANT NAMES

| OFFSET | NAME | OFFSET | NAME | OFFSET | NAME | OFFSET | NAME | OFFSET | NAME |
|--------|------|--------|------|--------|------|--------|------|--------|------|
| 063C | YEAR | 0644 | CODE1 | 064C | L | 03C9 | *ERROR | 0654 | TSTYR |
| 0658 | TOT | 065C | TR1000 | | | | | | |

**Figure B.6**  *Continued*

```
DOS/VS RPGII          JOB - COMPC                    PROGRAM - RLINK1

ADDRESS LIST

     BEGINNING OF LITERALS/EDITS        000660
     DETERMINE RECORD TYPE              000738
     INPUT FIELD EXTRACTION             000760
     BUILD OUTPUT FIELDS                000768
     DETAIL LINES                       000824
     TOTAL LINES                        00089C
     TOTAL LINE EPILOG                  0008D0
     OVERFLOW LINES                     000912
     POINTER TO FIB LIST                000958
     DETAIL CALCS                       000C38
     TOTAL CALCS                        000D0C
     DETERMINE FILE TO PROCESS          000D14
     VSAM GENCB PARAMETER LISTS         000B64
     EXLST                              000B64


NO ERROR(S) IN PROGRAM

END OF COMPILATION  -  PROGRAM LENGTH  HEX - 000DD8     DEC - 003544
```

| PHASE | XFR-AD | LOCORE | HICORE | DSK-AD |
|---|---|---|---|---|
| RLINK1 | 037C88 | 037878 | 03A5CE | 00024411 |

| LABEL | LOADED | REL-FR | OFFSET | INPUT | |
|---|---|---|---|---|---|
| RLINK1O | 037878 | 037878 | 000000 | SYSLNK | RELOCATABLE |
| *RLINK1 | 037C88 | | | | |
| IJDFYPIZ | 038650 | 038650 | 000DD8 | IJDFYPIZ | |
| *IJDFY2IZ | 038650 | | | | |
| ILNCNBLK | 0386E8 | 0386E8 | 000E70 | ILNCNBLK | |
| | 038758 | 0386E8 | 000EE0 | ILNCNBLK | |
| ILNDVSQI | 038E60 | 038E60 | 0015E8 | ILNDVSQI | |
| | 038ED0 | 038E60 | 001658 | ILNDVSQI | |
| ILNSGIR | 039238 | 039238 | 0019C0 | ILNSGIR | |
| | 0392A8 | 039238 | 001A30 | ILNSGIR | |
| ILNSINIT | 039448 | 039448 | 001BD0 | ILNSINIT | |
| | 0394B8 | 039448 | 001C40 | ILNSINIT | |
| ILNSPROL | 039638 | 039638 | 001DC0 | ILNSPROL | |
| *ILNSAD | 039A54 | 039638 | 001E30 | ILNSPROL | |
| ILNSTERM | 039AD8 | 039AD8 | 002260 | ILNSTERM | |
| IJJFCBZD | 039B48 | 039AD8 | 0022D0 | ILNSTERM | |
| *IJJFCIZD | 039FC8 | 039FC8 | 002750 | IJJFCBZD | |
| TR1000 | 03A360 | 03A360 | 002AE8 | TR1000 | |
| +YEAR | 03A440 | | | | |
| +CODE1 | 03A43F | | | | |
| +L | 03A43E | | | | |

**Figure B.6**  *Continued*

```
TEST OF TR1000-  TO DETERMINE LEAP YEAR STATUS
1700 IS NOT A LEAP YEAR    CODE1 CONTENTS 0    L CONTENTS 0
1800 IS NOT A LEAP YEAR    CODE1 CONTENTS 0    L CONTENTS 0
1900 IS NOT A LEAP YEAR    CODE1 CONTENTS 0    L CONTENTS 0
2000 IS A LEAP YEAR        CODE1 CONTENTS 0    L CONTENTS 1
2100 IS NOT A LEAP YEAR    CODE1 CONTENTS 0    L CONTENTS 0
2200 IS NOT A LEAP YEAR    CODE1 CONTENTS 0    L CONTENTS 0
2300 IS NOT A LEAP YEAR    CODE1 CONTENTS 0    L CONTENTS 0
2400 IS A LEAP YEAR        CODE1 CONTENTS 0    L CONTENTS 1
2500 IS NOT A LEAP YEAR    CODE1 CONTENTS 0    L CONTENTS 0
2600 IS NOT A LEAP YEAR    CODE1 CONTENTS 0    L CONTENTS 0
2700 IS NOT A LEAP YEAR    CODE1 CONTENTS 0    L CONTENTS 0
2800 IS A LEAP YEAR        CODE1 CONTENTS 0    L CONTENTS 1
2900 IS NOT A LEAP YEAR    CODE1 CONTENTS 0    L CONTENTS 0
3000 IS NOT A LEAP YEAR    CODE1 CONTENTS 0    L CONTENTS 0
3100 IS NOT A LEAP YEAR    CODE1 CONTENTS 0    L CONTENTS 0
3200 IS A LEAP YEAR        CODE1 CONTENTS 0    L CONTENTS 1
3300 IS NOT A LEAP YEAR    CODE1 CONTENTS 0    L CONTENTS 0
3399 IS NOT A LEAP YEAR    CODE1 CONTENTS 0    L CONTENTS 0
1601 IS NOT A LEAP YEAR    CODE1 CONTENTS 0    L CONTENTS 0
1602 IS NOT A LEAP YEAR    CODE1 CONTENTS 0    L CONTENTS 0
1603 IS NOT A LEAP YEAR    CODE1 CONTENTS 0    L CONTENTS 0
1604 IS A LEAP YEAR        CODE1 CONTENTS 0    L CONTENTS 1
1605 IS NOT A LEAP YEAR    CODE1 CONTENTS 0    L CONTENTS 0
1606 IS NOT A LEAP YEAR    CODE1 CONTENTS 0    L CONTENTS 0
1607 IS NOT A LEAP YEAR    CODE1 CONTENTS 0    L CONTENTS 0
1608 IS A LEAP YEAR        CODE1 CONTENTS 0    L CONTENTS 1
1801 IS NOT A LEAP YEAR    CODE1 CONTENTS 0    L CONTENTS 0
1702 IS NOT A LEAP YEAR    CODE1 CONTENTS 0    L CONTENTS 0
1603 IS NOT A LEAP YEAR    CODE1 CONTENTS 0    L CONTENTS 0
1904 IS A LEAP YEAR        CODE1 CONTENTS 0    L CONTENTS 1
2105 IS NOT A LEAP YEAR    CODE1 CONTENTS 0    L CONTENTS 0
2706 IS NOT A LEAP YEAR    CODE1 CONTENTS 0    L CONTENTS 0
3117 IS NOT A LEAP YEAR    CODE1 CONTENTS 0    L CONTENTS 0
3308 IS A LEAP YEAR        CODE1 CONTENTS 0    L CONTENTS 1
1644 IS A LEAP YEAR        CODE1 CONTENTS 0    L CONTENTS 1
1789 IS NOT A LEAP YEAR    CODE1 CONTENTS 0    L CONTENTS 0
1984 IS A LEAP YEAR        CODE1 CONTENTS 0    L CONTENTS 1
2201 IS NOT A LEAP YEAR    CODE1 CONTENTS 0    L CONTENTS 0
2034 IS NOT A LEAP YEAR    CODE1 CONTENTS 0    L CONTENTS 0
1600 * INVALID YEAR        CODE1 CONTENTS 4    L CONTENTS 9
3400 * INVALID YEAR        CODE1 CONTENTS 4    L CONTENTS 9
  19 * INVALID DATA        CODE1 CONTENTS 2    L CONTENTS 9
  95 * INVALID DATA        CODE1 CONTENTS 2    L CONTENTS 9

THE SUBPROGRAM WAS EXECUTED    44 TIMES
```

**Figure B.7** Test results from the execution of RLINK1.

```
// JOB ASSEM
// OPTION DECK,XREF
// DLBL IJSYSPH,'IN',O
// EXTENT SYSPCH,(VOL),1,O,(BEG.BLOCK),(NO.BLOCKS)
ASSGN SYSPCH,FBA,VOL=(VOL),SHR
// EXEC ASSEMBLY,SIZE=96K
   PUNCH ' CATALR TR1000 ,

*****     SOURCE ALC STATEMENTS FOR THE RPG II LINKAGE GO HERE     *******
* /*

CLOSE SYSPCH,X'(POWERDEVICECUU)'
// DLBL IJSYSIN,'IN',O
// EXTENT SYSIPT,(VOL),1,O,(BEG.BLOCK),(NO.BLOCKS)
ASSGN SYSIPT,FBA,VOL=(VOL),SHR
// DLBL (RELOLIBNAME),'(RELO.LIB.LABEL)'
// EXTENT .(VOL),1,O
// LIBDEF RL,TO=(RELOLIBNAME)
// EXEC MAINT
* /*
CLOSE SYSIPT,X'(POWERDUMMYDEVICECUU)'
* /&
// JOB RPGII
// DLBL (CORELIBNAME),'(CORE.LIB.LABEL)'
// EXTENT .(VOL),1,O
// LIBDEF CL,TO=(CORELIBNAME)
// OPTION NODECK,LIST,CATAL
PHASE RLINK1,S
// EXEC RPGII,SIZE=64K

**** SOURCE RPGII STATEMENTS FOR THE CALLING PROGRAM GO HERE ****
* /*

// EXEC LNKEDT
// ASSGN SYSO1O,SYSLST
// ASSGN SYSOO7,CUU  (OF DISK FILE)
// DLBL (CORELIBNAME),'(CORE.LIB.LABEL)'
// EXTENT .(VOL),1,O
// LIBDEF CL,FROM=(CORELIBNAME)
// DLBL IJSYSUC,'(JOB.CAT.LABEL),.VSAM
// EXTENT SYSOO7,(VOL),1,O,(BEG.BLOCK),(NO.BLOCKS)
// DLBL TESTFIL,'(FILE.LABEL)',.VSAM
// EXTENT SYSOO7,(VOL)
// EXEC RLINK1,SIZE=AUTO
* /&
```

**Figure B.8** A job stream used to assemble and catalog TR1000, and subsequently compile, link-edit, and execute RLINK1.

# C

# Subroutines in Software Vendor Offerings

Software vendor offerings generally provide for user exits to ALC. Consequently, you can use the subroutines and macros presented here simply by becoming familiar with the specific linkage requirements. Unfortunately, the software vendor's involvement doesn't end here in all too many cases.

It's impossible to estimate the number and variety of software packages being used worldwide. In some cases, the vendors have ceased to exist, user modifications have violated warranty and support agreements, or the software is a discontinued item. Yet the code continues to execute, serving the purposes of its users. Certainly, the prospects for conversion of these applications are dim at best.

Another category of vendor-provided software is custom-made or vendor-customized. These programs might not be accompanied by the source code and, consequently, the user could be faced with a massive redevelopment task in order to convert to eight-digit date computation.

Don't lose any time in contacting your software vendor and securing a commitment for any necessary conversion aid. If you have any sourceless orphans, replacement is your only alternative.

# References

Dunnington, G. W. 1955. *Karl Friedrich Gauss: Titan of Science*. Smithtown: Exposition Press.

Fliegel, H. G. and Van Flandern, T. C. 1968. Letter to editor. *Communications of the ACM*. 2 (no. 10): 657.

Knuth, D. E. 1968. *The Art of Computer Programming*. Vol. 1, *Fundamental Algorithms*. Reading: Addison-Wesley.

Lyons, M. J. 1981. Salvaging your software asset (tools based maintenance). *AFIPS Conference Proceedings*. Vol. 50, 1981 National Computer Conference. Arlington: AFIPS Press.

Moyer, G. 1982. "The Gregorian Calendar." *Scientific American*. 246 (no. 5): 144–152.

"Nobody Has Any Guts in Washington." *U. S. News & World Report*. 95 (no. 4): 53.

Yourdon, Edward. 1975. *Techniques of Program Structure and Design*. Englewood Cliffs: Prentice-Hall.

# Index

## ABOUT THE AUTHORS

Jerome T. Murray (Tuscon, Arizona) is director of research for Authors in Computer Science, a Tuscon-based group. He is a former director of Roosevelt University Computer Center and the Honeywell Institute of Information Science, both in Chicago.

Marilyn J. Murray (Tuscon, Arizona), staff writer for Authors in Computer Science, is most recently a former vice president of North American Company for Life and Health Insurance, where she previously served as project leader in the installation of insurance-industry software.

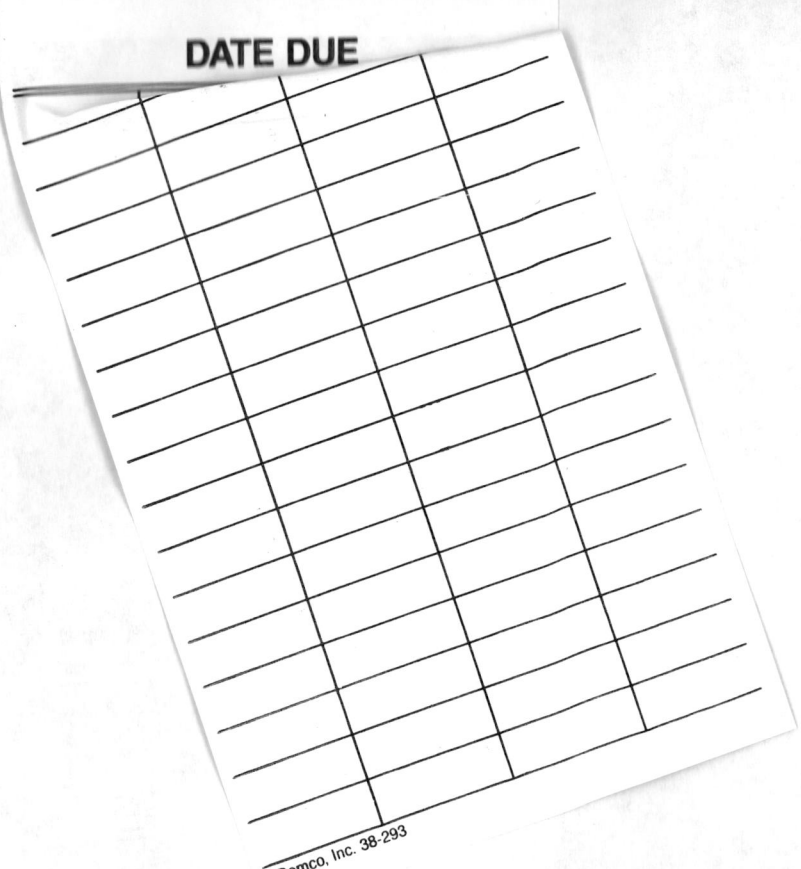

**DATE DUE**

Demco, Inc. 38-293

### About the enclosed diskette . . .

This 3.5-inch, high-density diskette contains three subdirectories. One contains the book's ALC (BAL) source language, a second contains RPG subroutine source language, and a third contains COBOL source code. This diskette's root directory contains a tour of the RPG subroutines that you can activate by making your 3.5-inch drive the default drive, inserting the diskette, typing 2000, and pressing Enter. The tour, however, will be meaningful only after you're familiar with the book and its algorithms.

### IMPORTANT

Read the Disk Warranty terms on the following page before opening the disk envelope. Opening the envelope constitutes acceptance of these terms and renders this entire book-disk package unreturnable except for material defect.

See preceding page for disk instructions.

# DISK WARRANTY

This software is protected by both United States copyright law and international copyright treaty provision. You must treat this software just like a book, except that you may copy it into a computer in order to be used and you may make archival copies of the software for the sole purpose of backing up our software and protecting your investment from loss.

By saying "just like a book," McGraw-Hill means, for example, that this software may be used by any number of people and may be freely moved from one computer location to another, so long as there is no possibility of its being used at one location or on one computer while it also is being used at another. Just as a book cannot be read by two different people in two different places at the same time, neither can the software be used by two different people in two different places at the same time (unless, of course, McGraw-Hill's copyright is being violated).

## LIMITED WARRANTY

McGraw-Hill takes great care to provide you with top-quality software, thoroughly checked to prevent virus infections. McGraw-Hill warrants the physical diskette(s) contained herein to be free of defects in materials and workmanship for a period of sixty days from the purchase date. If McGraw-Hill receives written notification within the warranty period of defects in materials or workmanship, and such notification is determined by McGraw-Hill to be correct, McGraw-Hill will replace the defective diskette(s). Send requests to:

> McGraw-Hill
> Customer Services
> P.O. Box 545
> Blacklick, OH 43004-0545

The entire and exclusive liability and remedy for breach of this Limited Warranty shall be limited to replacement of defective diskette(s) and shall not include or extend to any claim for or right to cover any other damages, including but not limited to, loss of profit, data, or use of the software, or special, incidental, or consequential damages or other similar claims, even if McGraw-Hill has been specifically advised of the possibility of such damages. In no event will McGraw-Hill's liability for any damages to you or any other person ever exceed the lower of suggested list price or actual price paid for the license to use the software, regardless of any form of the claim.

McGRAW-HILL SPECIFICALLY DISCLAIMS ALL OTHER WARRANTIES, EXPRESS OR IMPLIED, INCLUDING, BUT NOT LIMITED TO, ANY IMPLIED WARRANTY OF MERCHANTABILITY OR FITNESS FOR A PARTICULAR PURPOSE.

Specifically, McGraw-Hill makes no representation or warranty that the software is fit for any particular purpose and any implied warranty of merchantability is limited to the sixty-day duration of the Limited Warranty covering the physical diskette(s) only (and not the software) and is otherwise expressly and specifically disclaimed.

This limited warranty gives you specific legal rights; you may have others which may vary from state to state. Some states do not allow the exclusion of incidental or consequential damages, or the limitation on how long an implied warranty lasts, so some of the above may not apply to you.